UNDERSTANDING
CHILDREN

UNDERSTANDING
CHILDREN

JUDITH A. SCHICKEDANZ

Boston University

KAREN HANSEN

Bethesda, Maryland

PEGGY D. FORSYTH

The Pennsylvania State University, Harrisburg

MAYFIELD PUBLISHING COMPANY

Mountain View, California

London • Toronto

Library of Congress Cataloging-in-Publication Data

Schickedanz, Judith A., 1944–
    Understanding children / Judith A. Schickedanz, Karen Hansen,
Peggy D. Forsyth.
            p.   cm.
    Includes bibliographical references (p.   ).
    ISBN 0-87484-802-4
    1. Child development.   2. Child psychology.   3.
Adolescence.
    I. Hansen, Karen,   – . II. Forsyth, Peggy D. III.
Title.
    HQ767.9.S35   1990
    305.23' 1—dc20   89-28623
                                                      CIP

Manufactured in the United States of America
10   9   8   7   6   5   4   3

Mayfield Publishing Company
1240 Villa Street
Mountain View, California 94041

Sponsoring editor, Franklin C. Graham; developmental editor, Kathleen Engelberg;
managing editor, Linda Toy; manuscript editor, Helene Harrington; text and cover
designer, Anna George; cover art, Pablo Picasso, "Claude Drawing," Copyright 1989
ARS N.Y./SPADEM; illustrators, Robin Mouat, Natalie Hill, GTS; photo researcher,
Monica Suder and Associates. The text was set in 10/12 Palatino by Graphic Typesetting
Service and printed on 50# Somerset Matte by R. R. Donnelley & Sons.

Text and photo credits appear on a continuation of the copyright page, p. 680.

BRIEF CONTENTS

CONTENTS

p a r t   t h r e e   **PRESCHOOL CHILDREN**   **295**

PREFACE

Like many other authors, I undertook the job of writing a textbook because I couldn't find a book that satisfied all my teaching needs. In some child development books, the organization or selection of topics didn't match my approach. In others, the writing wasn't as clear or interesting as I thought it should be. In still others, the view of children seemed too fragmented and remote, making it difficult for the student to see children as whole human beings. To make these books work for me and my students, I had to modify the organization or coverage to achieve the necessary coherence, or provide additional illustrations and examples to make the material come to life, or compensate for the fragmented impression the book conveyed. At last I resolved to write a book myself, one that would solve the teaching problems I had encountered over the years. Now that the project is complete, my hope is that others will find the book effective in meeting their teaching needs as well.

AIMS

One of my primary aims in writing this book was to present a balance of research findings, theory, and applications and to integrate these aspects of the study of child development. *Understanding Children* is designed primarily for students who will be living and working with children as teachers, parents, child care providers, nurses, counselors, administrators of children's programs, and practitioners in a variety of other settings. These students need to have comprehensive, accurate, up-to-date information about child development, but they also need to know the uses and implications of this information. Thus, the emphasis throughout is on the working applications of expert knowledge.

I also wanted to present information in an accessible, appealing way, so I've written *Understanding Children* in a personal style that invites students to read, learn, and remember. To that same end, I introduce each chapter and most major topics with a vignette in which the essence of the information or issue about to be presented is captured in a real-life situation involving children and adults. Additionally, each of the first two chapters—Chapter 1, Methods of Studying Children, and Chapter 2, Theories of Child Development—is organized around a specific, practical problem that gives the material immediacy and relevance.

Perhaps my most important goal in this book is the most intangible one— to convey the unique world view of children. I've tried to make clear that children are not miniature adults but individuals with their own ways of thinking and of seeing the world. Only with knowledge, understanding, and respect can students learn how to provide the intelligent, responsible care that children deserve. This important premise is emphasized in the introduction to the book, entitled Prologue: Why Study Children? I hope instructors will encourage students to read this introduction to gain a preliminary orientation to the book.

ORGANIZATION AND CONTENT

Students should be able to see children not as fragmented objects of scientific study but as whole human beings. The best way to convey this sense of wholeness, in my experience, is to present information about all aspects of development in each successive stage of childhood. *Understanding Children* is therefore organized chronologically, introducing students to children as they grow, learn, and change, from earliest infancy to the threshold of adulthood. The book begins with the foundations for the study of child development (Part One)—research methods, theories of child development, and the biology of genetics, prenatal development, and birth. The remaining parts of the book cover four chronological age-stages. Part Two addresses the development of the child between birth and age 3—infancy and toddlerhood. Parts Three, Four, and Five cover the development of the preschool child (aged 3 to 6), the school-age child (aged 6 to 12), and the adolescent (aged 13 to 19), respectively.

Within this chronological framework, material on the different domains of development is presented topically. Parts Two through Five contain four chapters each, covering physical development, cognitive development, language development, and social and emotional development. Each part ends with an applications section called Knowledge in Action, a feature unique to this book. This format—four chapters plus Knowledge in Action—provides a clear and consistent organizational scheme for each part.

Understanding Children provides comprehensive, in-depth coverage of a range of topics and issues, from classic to contemporary, always with an emphasis on the practical uses of knowledge. A sampling of topics will give a sense of the scope and timeliness of coverage:

- the role of values in the study of children (Chapter 2)
- the effects of prenatal exposure to alcohol, cocaine, and other teratogens on the developing fetus (Chapter 3)
- advances in prenatal assessment tools, including chorionic villus sampling, and the latest treatments for infertility (Chapter 3)
- pretend play in infants and toddlers (Chapter 6)
- theories of infant and maternal attachment, with an emphasis on the ethological theory (Chapter 8)
- sex-typing in infancy (Chapter 8)
- children's "theory of mind" (Chapter 10)
- the learning of prosocial behavior (Chapter 12)
- the development of metacognition (Chapter 14) and the emergence of social role-taking ability in school-age children (Chapter 16)
- effects of early and late maturing on adolescent boys and girls (Chapter 17)
- effects of divorce on children (Chapter 20)

SPECIAL FEATURES

Several features distinguish *Understanding Children* from other textbooks. Although all the chapters integrate theory and practice, special Knowledge in Action sections at the end of parts Two through Five focus exclusively on applications. These unnumbered sections put very practical material relating to the care and education of children at the disposal of instructors, but without the suggestion that they *must* use it. Knowledge in Action sections provide information on such topics as the varieties of preschool, after-school, and day care programs; methods of assessing children; ways to ensure children's health and safety; and the kinds of activities and playthings that are appropriate for children of different ages.

Separate chapters on language development in every age-stage (Parts Two through Five) highlight this important area in child development. Typically, child development books include language development in their chapters on cognitive development, or, if they do treat language separately, they treat only the acquisition of language in early childhood. *Understanding Children* provides separate chapters on language right through adolescence, allowing expanded coverage of such topics as toddlers' strategies for opening conversations; emergent literacy in preschoolers and ways to support it; teaching reading through the whole language approach; current thinking on dyslexia; the growing importance of visual literacy in our society; and communication with adolescents.

A separate chapter on the neonate at the beginning of Part Two reflects the wealth of information and current research findings available on this earliest period of adjustment in the child's life. Included are discussions of the effects of obstetrical drugs on newborns, learning in young infants, methods of soothing babies, and learning to live with the newborn.

Focus boxes throughout the text highlight current topics and issues in five different areas—research, health, safety, public policy, and special education—and add depth to discussions without interrupting the ongoing narrative. A few titles will suggest the range of topics covered: The Increase in Cesarean

Births; Social Referencing in Infants; How Does Day Care Affect Parent-Child Attachment?; Making Playgrounds Safe; Stages of Storybook Reading; Young Gifted Children; Coaching Children in Social Skills; Does Early Antisocial Behavior Fade Away?; Children and AIDS; Dangers of Anabolic Steroids; Consequences of Teenage Pregnancy.

A one-page chart of developmental milestones rounds out each age-stage part and functions as a brief summary of the highlights of development for that period.

LEARNING AIDS

A number of learning aids are incorporated in *Understanding Children* to help students understand, organize, and remember the material.

- Each chapter begins with a vignette that shows how a principle or issue discussed in the chapter translates into children's words, actions, or beliefs. The vignette is followed by a brief introduction outlining the topics covered in the chapter.
- Key terms appear in boldface type throughout each chapter and are carefully defined in context. The terms are listed at the end of the chapter for review and are included along with their definitions in a comprehensive glossary at the end of the book.
- Two different kinds of summaries appear at the end of each chapter. One is a brief overview of the chapter, drawn in broad strokes and making connections backward and forward in the child's life. The other is a longer chapter review, outlining the main points of the chapter.
- Annotated Suggestions for Further Reading also appear at the end of every chapter, extending the boundaries of the material for the student.
- Each part opens with an overview and ends with a chart of developmental milestones for that age-stage.
- Numerous tables, charts, drawings, and photographs—many in full color— provide graphic illustration of text material. The captions inform and teach rather than simply label or identify.

ANCILLARY PACKAGE

Available with this book is a complete package of supplemental materials to enhance both teaching and learning and to facilitate the application of knowledge to practical situations. The Instructor's Manual includes learning objectives, chapter summaries, key terms, lecture and demonstration topics, and suggested student projects. It also lists sources for free or inexpensive materials and describes reference materials and audio-visual aids. Finally, it includes, in printed form, an extensive testbank of questions keyed to textbook pages and designed to test for different kinds of thinking.

Many instructors may wish to have their students use the *Study Guide to Accompany Understanding Children*. It includes learning objectives, chapter outlines, and chapter summaries as well as student projects and practice tests with several different kinds of questions. Many chapters also have crossword puzzles and word scrambles that enhance the student's interest in self-testing.

The powerful, easy-to-use Brownstone test generation system provides all test items on computer disk for IBM-compatible and Apple computers. Instructors can select, add, or edit questions, randomize them, and print tests appropriate for their individual classes. The system also includes a convenient "gradebook" that enables the instructor to keep detailed performance records for individual students and for the entire class; maintain student averages; graph each student's progress; and set the desired grade distribution, maximum score, and weight for every test.

A set of 48 overhead transparencies provides supplementary information that is not found in the text or that has been reinterpreted and modified for lecture and discussion purposes.

Also available with *Understanding Children* is an exciting set of videotapes produced for the Annenberg/CPB series entitled *Discovering Psychology*. Narrated by Philip Zimbardo, these six video segments, each about 30 minutes long, have been selected to illustrate important concepts and issues in child development and to explain the latest thinking and research findings on them. Keyed to the text, the segments are entitled *The Developing Child* (covering the effects and interaction of biology and culture on the development of the child); *Language Development* (including an explanation of Chomsky's theories); *Learning* (exploring the behavioral approach to learning and including original film footage of Pavlov's and Watson's experiments); *Testing and Intelligence* (covering models of intelligence and issues in testing); *Sex and Gender* (exploring the roots of gender identity and sex-role behavior); and *The Self* (describing theories of personality, self-concept, and identity).

ACKNOWLEDGMENTS

Many people have contributed to the development of *Understanding Children*. Foremost among these are my two coauthors. Peggy Forsyth wrote the first drafts of various sections of the book and prepared much of the ancillary package. Karen Hansen wrote many of the focus boxes and chapter summaries as well as the first drafts of some sections of the book.

I'm very grateful to the child development experts who gave such detailed critiques and offered so many useful suggestions in their reviews of the manuscript. The names of these academic reviewers are listed separately following this preface. The entire project has been greatly enriched by their suggestions, although any flaws or errors in the book are the responsibility of the authors alone.

Special thanks are due to the staff of Mayfield Publishing Company. Frank Graham, the sponsoring editor, showed a great deal of patience throughout the project and was willing to entertain new ideas and to find ways to make them work. His interest in the project kept it alive during its early, formative stages and supported it whenever spirits began to flag. Kate Engelberg, the developmental editor at Mayfield, also deserves special, special thanks. She is an expert writer whose suggestions for rewrites elevated the quality of the text to a height I could never have achieved alone. Linda Toy, managing editor at Mayfield, saw the book through the various stages of production. Her expert managerial skills kept everything on schedule, no small feat given the very tight time frame.

Finally, I owe a very big debt of gratitude to my family, which includes David, my husband, and Adam, my son. I look forward to spending less time in the "back room" with my computer and more time with them, now that the book I began to imagine so long ago is finally finished.

Judy Schickedanz

REVIEWERS OF *UNDERSTANDING CHILDREN*

The following academic reviewers made an invaluable contribution to this project with their insightful critiques of the manuscript. I'm deeply grateful for their help.

Nancy Hamblen Acuff
Human Development and Learning
East Tennessee State University

Linda Annis
Educational Psychology
Ball State University

Barry Arbuckle
Child Development and Family Studies
University of North Carolina at Greensboro

Patricia Barker
Humanities and Social Sciences
Schenectady County Community College

Fredalene Bowers
Home Economics/Education
Indiana University of Pennsylvania

Sandy Bucknell
Child Development
Modesto Community College

Annette Chavez
Education
Northern Kentucky University

Nancy Cobb
Psychology
California State University at Los Angeles

Janet Gonzalez-Mena
Early Childhood Education
Napa Valley College

Bernard S. Gorman
Psychology
Nassau Community College

Gloria Guzman
Child Development
Rancho Santiago College

Elizabeth A. Hasson
Childhood Studies
West Chester University of Pennsylvania

Eileen Gallagher Haugh
Education
St. Mary's College

Donald Holmlund
Psychology
Marin College

Sheila Jeyfous
Psychology
Indiana University

Betty Johnson
Education
Shelby State Community College

Elaine M. Justice
Psychology
Old Dominion University

Daniel Kee
Psychology
California State University at Fullerton

Dwayne Keller
Family Studies
University of Connecticut

Murray Krantz
Home and Family Life
Florida State University

Eugene W. Krebs
Family Studies and Home Economics
California State University at Fresno

Marylin Lisowski
Education and Junior High Education
Eastern Illinois University

Gloria G. Lyon
Child Development
San Diego City College

Barbara Macci
Early Childhood Education
Imperial Valley College

Patricia Major
Teacher Education
St. Thomas Aquinas College

Mary Ann McLaughlin
Education
Clarion University of Pennsylvania

Thomas Moeschl
Behavioral Sciences
Broward Community College

Philip J. Mohan
Psychology
University of Idaho

Annabelle Nelson-Burford
Human Development
Prescott College

Delores Nieratka
Psychology
Mercy College of Detroit

Grace Nunn
Elementary and Junior High Education
Eastern Illinois University

Cheryl Roberts
Early Childhood Education
Riverside City College

Helen Ross
Family Studies
San Diego State University

Bruce Stam
Early Childhood Education
Chemeketa Community College

Margaret Thornburg
Psychology
Henry Ford Community College

Mark Whitney
Family Studies
San Diego State University

Patricia Worden
Psychology
California State University at Fullerton

UNDERSTANDING
CHILDREN

PROLOGUE:
WHY STUDY CHILDREN?

As you read about children in the pages that follow, you may think of a child you know—a niece or nephew, a young cousin, even your own child if you're already a parent. Or you may think of yourself when you were a child, calling on your memories and the stories your parents have told you. You may know this child—even the child you once were—quite well or not so well. You may have daily contact with children or never see them at all.

No matter what your experience with children, you have one thing in common with all other adults: you will never again directly experience the "magic time" of childhood. Once we become adults, we can no longer see the world through children's eyes. We trade that vision for a more rational understanding of how things work, an understanding that allows us to function competently in the world.

When we were children, we were guided and cared for by our families and teachers. Now the responsibility for guiding the next generation of children to healthy adulthood passes into our hands. And even though we were once children ourselves, we don't understand many of the things children say and do. They charm us—and bewilder us. They seem to live in a world apart, a world different from the one we experience. Their minds don't work the same way ours do. Even when we think we've explained things to them, we discover they have their own beliefs . . .

> . . . that after people die, they can "get alive" again

> . . . that when you get tired of having baby brothers around, you can return them to the hospital where they were "boughted"

> . . . that blankets and stuffed bears can have their own thoughts and feelings

FIGURE 1
Although they're tiny and seemingly helpless, babies are born with many traits and preferences that increase their chances for survival. This premature baby's steady gaze and attraction to the human face and voice help him establish eye contact with adults and engage their attention, subtly enhancing their inclination to love and protect him. Over the years, responsibility for this child's care will be shared by many people, including his parents, relatives, and teachers. A working knowledge of child development principles will help them provide the best conditions for his growth.

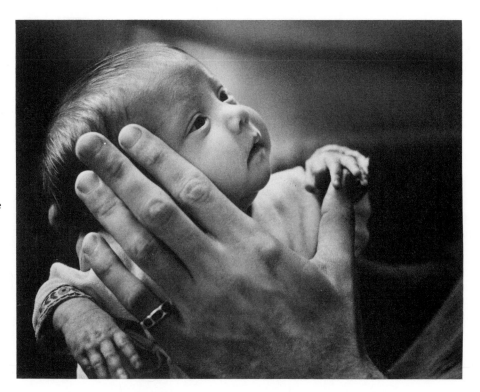

. . . that dreams are "made by the night" when the lights go out

. . . that children can be the secret but true reason for their parents' divorce

When we hear ideas like these, we realize how profoundly different children's experience of the world is from ours. We also realize that before we can take responsibility for them or provide the best conditions for their growth, we have to have some understanding of them. Our actions on their behalf have to be based on knowledge. Knowledge and understanding of children are what this book is designed to provide.

HOW WE APPROACH THE STUDY OF CHILDREN

Of course, children aren't like cars on an assembly line to be analyzed and put together piece by piece. They're whole people, living in the world, bringing themselves completely to their experiences. But this very complexity makes it difficult, at first, for the student to understand children in a whole way.

We have to begin the study of child development by considering its different aspects separately. In this book the study of children is divided into various domains—physical, cognitive, language, social-emotional. It's convenient to treat the various aspects of development this way, but we should never lose sight of the fact that children function as whole people.

We also approach the study of children from the point of view of chronological development, and we organize our material in "age-stages," from infancy

FIGURE 2
Children come into the world with many characteristics determined, but they're also shaped in powerful ways by their environment—the many contexts in which they live. These children are growing up in an affectionate two-parent family on a farm in the American West. How different would they be if they lived in Burlington, Vermont, or Mexico City, or if they were brought up by an exuberant extended family, a harried single mother, or an emotionally unexpressive grandparent? Child development experts once thought they could answer the question, What qualities are children born with and what do they acquire through their interactions with the environment? Now it seems that development is so complex that no simple answer to this question is possible.

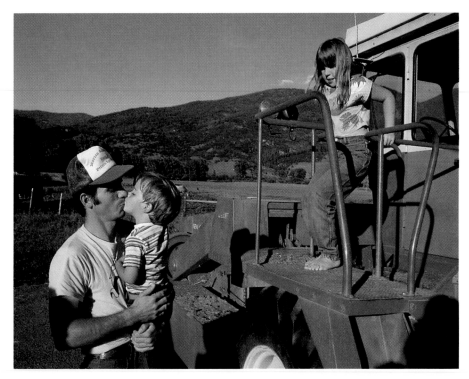

to adolescence. Because we can see changes that set children apart at any point in time from their earlier and later selves, we can talk about how children at one age-stage differ from children at another age-stage. But we also stress continuity in development, the accumulation of experiences that makes a child what she is today and what she will be tomorrow. We look at any single behavior or characteristic as both a result of previous developments and a predictor of subsequent developments.

In addition, we look at the many factors that interact to make children what they are, not the least of which are the unique characteristics that each one brings into the world. But a child's uniqueness is shaped by the many contexts in which the child lives—family, school, community, country, world. Each context leaves its mark and must be taken into account. The threads of a child's life are woven from all these elements into a fabric not easily—or even appropriately—taken apart for closer analysis.

This complexity in human development means that there are limits to our knowledge. Although we have theories, research studies, and a vast amount of information about child development, some questions haven't been answered definitively in ways that help us know how to act. There are many questions that can't even be studied experimentally.

For example, children who watch a great deal of television tend to be poor readers. Does heavy television viewing cause low reading achievement? We can't be sure. To find out, we would have to enlist large numbers of children and ask them to watch many hours of television every day for a fairly long period of time—perhaps five hours a day for a year. Very few parents would

FIGURE 3
This woman probably knows that young children thrive when they have a stimulating environment, toys that provide a moderate challenge to their physical and cognitive abilities, and the close attention of a responsive adult. She may also know that if she's friendly and nurturant, they're more likely to help and nurture each other; that if she points to the words when she reads them books, it will help them learn to read later; and that if she wants to teach them something, she has to provide them with hands-on experiences. This kind of information, used extensively in designing child care and nursery school programs, comes from research findings in child development.

allow their children to participate in such a study, and researchers who propose such an experiment believing that the experience would have a harmful effect would be acting unethically. Left with naturally occurring groups of children in real situations, we don't know if low reading achievement is caused by the television viewing or if some third factor causes both the low achievement and the heavy TV use. And we don't know if turning off the television would improve reading achievement or have no effect. Our knowledge is incomplete.

MAKING CONNECTIONS: THE PRACTICAL ASPECTS OF UNDERSTANDING CHILDREN

Even when research has provided clear-cut information about issues in child development, there's sometimes a gap between the research and the everyday world of parents and teachers. Some of our daily interactions with children raise questions that either haven't been investigated by researchers or haven't been answered in ways that are useful. The connection between scientific information and the everyday situation seems to be missing.

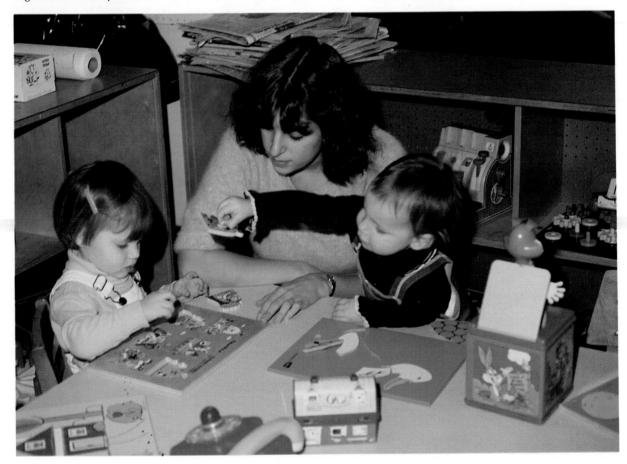

Understanding Children helps to make these connections. From the huge body of information about children—all important and relevant in one way or another—we have selected material that we judged to be particularly relevant to the practitioner, the person who actually cares for or teaches children. We have then explicitly discussed the implications of this knowledge, the way it relates to interaction with real children. Vignettes involving individual children—both real children and composites of children we have known—illustrate and bring to life the principles of development discussed in each chapter.

Our focus throughout is on this practical side of information, but because of the need for a firm theoretical and research base in the chapters on physical, cognitive, language, and social-emotional development, coverage of applications and implications is limited in those chapters. To provide a balance, we include for each age-stage a section called Knowledge in Action. These sections provide practical information on such topics as living with children of different ages, ensuring their health and safety, and providing them with the most appropriate toys and playthings.

WHY WE CAN'T ACCOUNT FOR EVERYTHING: THE ROLE OF VALUES

When we study children, we begin by watching them. We notice how they look, what they do and say, how they respond to what we do and say. We wonder what makes them the way they are. We find ourselves worrying, too, about whether they're the way they "should" be. And sometimes we ask how this "should" is defined and who has established it as the right way. When we ask these questions, we're no longer talking about research alone—we're talking about values.

Whether they're explicitly stated or subtly implied, values are an ever-present element in the study of child development. All research reported, all topics covered, all actions recommended are based on values—ideas and beliefs about what constitutes the "good" parent or teacher, the "good" society, the "best" child. Sometimes we don't agree with the values implied in research studies. We find ourselves making decisions about children that don't seem to follow from findings about child development. Our choices reflect our own histories and ideals as well as the information and theories we've learned. When we live and work with children, we have to take into account these personal factors too.

ABOUT UNDERSTANDING CHILDREN

In *Understanding Children* we begin our study of child development with the "foundations" that provide a perspective for the rest of the study. Part One contains chapters on research methods, theories of child development and the values associated with them, and the biology of genetics, prenatal development, and birth.

Part Two covers the child between birth and age 3—infancy and toddlerhood. It begins with a separate chapter on the newborn, or neonate, who is

FIGURE 4
Many factors have contributed to making these girls the bright, friendly people they are—their genetic make-up, their socioeconomic backgrounds, their experiences in school, their community environment. Another, less obvious factor in their make-up is their parents' values. Were they brought up to believe that it's more important to excel academically or to be well liked? To compete aggressively or to share and cooperate? To express their emotions openly or to conceal what they really feel? To think for themselves or go along with the crowd? To pursue a career or get married and have babies—or both? When we're considering what makes people behave the way they do, we can never overlook the powerful role played by their values.

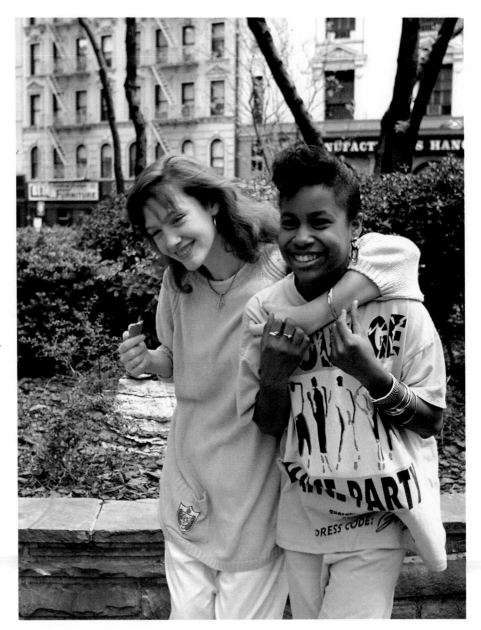

very different from the older infant. The chapters that follow address the various functional domains of the infant and the toddler—physical development, cognitive development, language development, and social-emotional development. Part Two closes with Infant and Toddler Knowledge in Action, focusing on matters of daily concern.

The same format is followed in Parts Three, Four, and Five, covering the development of the preschool child (aged 3 to 6), the school-age child (aged 6 to 12), and the adolescent (aged 13 to 19). Summaries showing the highlights of development are provided at the end of each part to help you make sense of the information and get an overview of the process of development.

FIGURE 5
Caught in the spell of a master storyteller, a young girl momentarily reveals the quality of wonder that children bring to their experience of the world. Perhaps our ultimate goal in dealing with children should be to inspire more moments like this.

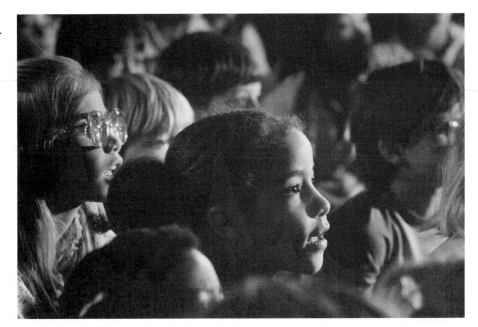

Despite limitations on our knowledge, the study of child development provides information of enormous importance to everyone who lives or works with children. It gives us a framework, a road map, with which to understand, guide, and support children on their journey through childhood—a journey on which it is our privilege and pleasure to assist them.

We wish you well in your study of this important topic and in your use of *Understanding Children*. We know that this book will help you understand children, and we suspect that it may increase your interest in children. We also hope that it will make your life and work with children filled with more wonder and less worry than they might have been had we never had a chance to meet across the pages that follow.

part one

RESEARCH, THEORY, AND BIOLOGY

The study of child development begins not with the moment the child is born nor even with the moment the child is conceived. A solid grounding in child development begins with the basics of how we get our knowledge and information about children—how research on children's behavior is conducted. It also begins with the ideas and principles—the theories— that we use to explain children's behavior and structure our information about them. Finally, it includes an understanding of all the things children bring into the world with them—their genetic inheritance and their formative experiences before birth. Only with these foundations in place does the study of children really make sense.

METHODS OF STUDYING CHILDREN

What would you think if you opened the newspaper one day and read about a research study claiming that differences in IQ between black children and white children had a genetic basis? Would you accept it at face value? Or would you wonder what kind of research could lead to such a conclusion? Would you read the article carefully to see if you could evaluate the research methods used? Would you think about the implications of a study like this for schools, families, and communities?

Such a study *did* appear not too many years ago. A research psychologist reported that the IQs of black children from poverty backgrounds declined as the children progressed through elementary school. He claimed that this "cumulative deficit in intelligence," which wasn't apparent in white children, was due to genetic differences between blacks and whites. When other researchers looked at his study, they found that his data were accurately reported but that his conclusions weren't warranted. He had used a research design that didn't support this interpretation.

Later in this chapter we look more closely at exactly why the conclusions from this study were flawed. Here, we wish to emphasize how vitally important accurate research methods are to our knowledge about children. If this study hadn't been critically examined, some inappropriate, and even damaging, actions might have been taken, based on its conclusions.

Rigorous research thinking provides the foundation for the study of child development. As pointed out in the Prologue, we must have some understanding of children before we can be responsible for them or take action on their behalf. Part of our understanding can come from personal experience or common sense, but this knowledge must be combined with knowledge from research. As a parent, teacher, or caregiver—and as an informed citizen—you will find it important to be able to understand, interpret, and evaluate studies that report research concerning children.

What is research in child development? The term *research* may evoke images of laboratories where children are treated in special ways or asked to do certain things while researchers watch and record what they do. Or maybe it makes you think of statistical data displayed in tables and charts. Although these images do capture some aspects of research in child development, they aren't the whole picture. More than anything else, doing research means *thinking in critical ways*. No matter what methods or settings or experimental designs they use, researchers must be extremely careful about how they arrive at their conclusions if their work is to benefit children rather than harm them.

In this chapter various research procedures are discussed, and both their advantages and disadvantages are considered. The difficulties that researchers inevitably encounter in their work are also discussed. Finally, the ethical obligations researchers must assume, especially when their research involves children, are explored. But before addressing these topics, let's consider a fairly typical situation in which information is being provided to the public. In this story, we see how research methods come into play in our everyday life.

THINKING LIKE A RESEARCHER: A KINDERGARTEN LITERACY PROGRAM

An evening meeting has been arranged by a school district to introduce parents to a new instructional program. The district had undertaken a study, although professional researchers weren't in charge of it, and now was recommending that certain actions be taken, based on the results. In response, parents were doing some research-like thinking. Let's listen in.

SCHOOL DISTRICT SUPERINTENDENT: *We're here tonight to tell you about a new program that will affect your children in next year's kindergarten classes. This program has been developed and pilot-tested by Catherine Pierce in her kindergarten classroom during the past year. We've just completed testing the children in her classroom, and they've done extremely well. In fact, the scores for this group of end-of-the-year kindergartners are similar to what children usually attain only after three-quarters of first grade. We think the program Mrs. Pierce has developed is very good, and we're ready to introduce it into other kindergartens in the school district.*

Let me tell you just a little about the program, and then I'll be happy to answer your questions.

The program involves the use of "big-print books" for story reading. The teacher reads a big-print book to the children each day. The format of these books is very large, as you can see from the one I have here to show you. The print is large too, so that all the children in the group can see the print when the teacher holds it up. The teacher reads the story the first time through, and then she encourages the children to read along with her as she reads it again. Often she reads it even a third time, or she asks the children to find certain words that appear in the text.

We have about 25 different Big Books. The stories have a lot of rhymes and repetition, which makes them easy for children to learn and remember. The teacher points to

FIGURE 1-1
In one approach to reading, the emphasis is on surrounding children with books and writing materials and showing them what spoken words look like on the printed page. In another approach, the emphasis is on teaching children such phonics skills as recognizing the letters of the alphabet and learning the sounds typically associated with the letters. Which is the more effective way to teach reading? An accurate answer to this question depends on carefully thought-out research studies.

the print while she's reading, which helps children know where each word appears. The books are left out in the classroom during activity times so children can read them themselves if they want to.

The program encourages children to read books and to think of themselves as readers. It also teaches them to integrate different cues when they read—the words, the pictures, the sense of the story. When children learn to read by focusing on isolated phonics skills, which was our old system, they can get the idea that reading is a matter of "looking, sounding, and saying." We want them to get the idea that reading involves thinking, *looking, sounding, and saying. Of course, children do need to have the phonics skills, such as knowing which sounds specific letters of the alphabet typically represent, but we know now that reading involves much more than phonics.*

Besides the Big Books, we immerse the children in what we call functional environmental print. This means that they see print and use it in meaningful ways every day in the classroom. Their names appear on their artwork, on job charts, and on attendance sheets. Opportunities for practice in reading and writing are integrated into the daily program, replacing the workbook and phonics drill periods. In sum, the program helps kindergartners think of reading and writing as a normal part of their everyday lives. We think it's a better approach to reading, and the test results from Mrs. Pierce's class bear us out.

Well, I've talked long enough. Since this program will affect your children next year, I'm sure you have some questions.

MR. TAYLOR: *You said you did some testing. What kind of tests did you use?*

SUPERINTENDENT: *We used several different tests to see if the children were acquiring the skills good readers are known to use. One test involves reading a child a short story with every fifth word deleted. The child fills in the word as the teacher pauses. This tells us if the child is thinking about the story and using clues from the context to decide what word would fit.*

Another test involves asking a child to read back a simple story the teacher has just read and to point to the words while reading. This test tells us if children know that print is read from left to right and from top to bottom and if they know that one printed word represents one spoken word. We also did some phonics tests, such as letter recognition, because those are important skills too. We used a balanced set of tests because there are quite a few different understandings involved in reading.

MRS. SMITH: *Who did the testing? Did the school psychologist or the reading specialist test the children?*

SUPERINTENDENT: *No, Mrs. Pierce did all the testing. It would have been too time consuming for the psychologist or reading specialist. It would have been harder for the children, too, since they don't know them. Mrs. Pierce tested a few children a day over the course of a month.*

MRS. SMITH: *Did anyone observe Mrs. Pierce do the testing?*

SUPERINTENDENT: *Not that I know of. Of course, her teaching aide was in the classroom, but I don't believe anyone actually observed the testing.*

MR. TAYLOR: *Were children in other kindergartens also tested, to see what they knew?*

SUPERINTENDENT: *No, they weren't. We usually test children after the first three months of first grade, not in kindergarten.*

MR. TAYLOR: *So you really don't know how well they might have done on the same tests, even if they didn't have this new program?*

SUPERINTENDENT: *That's right.*

MRS. PALMER: *Isn't the school where Mrs. Pierce teaches located in a very affluent area of the school district, where the educational level of the parents is quite high?*

SUPERINTENDENT: *Yes, I think that's an accurate statement.*

MRS. PALMER: *Well, wouldn't these children be expected to do better on tests anyway, regardless of their kindergarten program? Maybe these children would score as well as first graders no matter what program they had.*

SUPERINTENDENT: *Yes, but Mrs. Pierce feels that this group of children made more progress than previous groups that she's had from the same neighborhood. She thinks the program made the difference.*

MRS. WINTER: *Well, even if the program was effective with this group, and even if it was the program that made the difference, how do you know it will work with other children? Maybe other children need a different kind of program, something more structured, one that really teaches the alphabet and phonics skills.*

SUPERINTENDENT: *We don't think so. We think this program provides a better, broader foundation for reading, no matter who the children are.*

MRS. WINTER: *Well, I don't think you can assume that just because the program worked with some children, it will work with all children. If you use the program throughout the whole school district, you'll need to keep a close check on children's progress.*

Also, I wonder about the testing conditions. I wonder if Mrs. Pierce coaxed the children at all as she tested them. Although I'm sure her character is wonderful, I do know, because I used to be a teacher, how difficult it is to resist helping children out. Teachers become used to teaching. If a child makes a mistake, it's very easy to say, "Are you sure? Why don't you think about that a little more?" Then, when the child gives the right answer, you think, "Oh, she knew that all along. I'll just ignore the first answer, which was wrong."

SUPERINTENDENT: *Well, you certainly are asking all the right questions, and you've made some good points. Of course, to be able to answer your questions completely, it would have been necessary to run a pilot program in several classrooms and to have included a control classroom that didn't use the program. We would also have had to hire outside testers. All this would have cost money, and I'm not sure it would have been allocated. So we did the best we could.*

We had formed a group two years ago to evaluate language arts instruction in kindergarten, and this was what they recommended. Mrs. Pierce volunteered to implement the recommendations in her classroom and work out the program. We have every reason to believe the new program is better than the old one, and we would like your support in implementing it.

MRS. COHEN: *You know, I'm sitting here listening to all this talk about teaching reading in kindergarten, and I'm wondering what ever happened to finger painting, nature walks, building with blocks, and all the other activities I thought kindergarten was for. Why not let the first grade teacher worry about teaching reading? Kindergartners should just be playing and learning how to get along with other children.*

SUPERINTENDENT: *I understand your concern, and I'm glad you brought up this point. I want to emphasize that the Big Books program does not take up the whole day, and in fact the teacher actually has more time for other activities when she's using this program. In the old program, the teacher felt she had to set aside a fairly large part of the day for instruction in the so-called reading readiness skills. In the new program, she still reads story books, but other reading and writing practice is integrated into ongoing activities. Children have more time to spend on play activities, but playing includes chances to read and write. So we're actually headed more in the direction you describe than we were before.*

ANALYZING THE STUDY: THE MAJOR RESEARCH ISSUES

In this school meeting we can see some of the major issues all researchers have to face—issues of sampling and generalizability, correlation versus causation, and researcher bias. Let's look at these and other issues in turn.

Sampling and Generalizing

In an ideal world, researchers would study each and every person of interest to determine the effect of a particular program or treatment. Of course, in the real world, it's impossible for researchers to do this. Instead, they study a few people and then apply what they learn to larger populations. But they have to be sure that what they learn from a study of one group can be generalized to other groups. This question of generalizability—referred to as **external validity**—is one of the overriding issues researchers face.

To make certain that their study fulfills the requirements of external validity, researchers have to meet certain conditions. First, they have to be careful to obtain a **representative sample.** If they studied only rural children, for example, they wouldn't be justified in generalizing their findings to urban and suburban children. If they studied only boys, they couldn't apply their findings equally to girls. Although all children are alike in many ways, they also

FIGURE 1-2
Researchers studying children could obtain some interesting information by observing or testing these four 5-year-old boys, but they couldn't apply their findings to 5-year-old girls or to 10-year-old boys. The sample in such a study wouldn't be representative of the general population of children.

differ depending on their age, where they live, what their parents do for a living, and so on.

In the school example, Mrs. Palmer raised a good point: The children in the pilot kindergarten program apparently differed from other children in the school district in terms of their families' socioeconomic status. The school superintendent didn't mention this difference when he proposed that the program be implemented throughout the district on the basis of the good test results in Mrs. Pierce's kindergarten. Perhaps he didn't think about it, or perhaps he was anxious to get the program into all the classrooms.

Whatever his thinking was on this issue, the superintendent would have been on firmer ground if he had implemented the program in two pilot classrooms, located in different parts of the district. He would also have had more credibility at the parent meeting if he had stated these limitations at the outset and explained why he thought the program should be implemented despite the problems of generalizability.

The parents might have made another point about sampling and generalizability. Mrs. Pierce is an experienced teacher who volunteered to pilot the new program. She may not be representative of all the teachers in the district. Maybe she's an exceptional teacher—brighter, more experienced and energetic, more inclined to take risks. Maybe her children's good test scores resulted as much from her own characteristics as a teacher as they did from characteristics of the program. If this is the case, children taught by other teachers wouldn't do as well, regardless of the program. The study would have been better if several teachers tried the new program and if they were selected at random. Then we could be sure they were representative of all the teachers in the district.

However, it's often difficult or impossible to select people randomly in situations like this. In some school districts, for example, teachers' contracts prevent administrators from dictating unilaterally what they must teach. Without the consent of all the teachers, the superintendent couldn't assign them to the new reading program for the sake of a research study.

Correlational versus Experimental Studies

Mrs. Palmer put her finger on another problem when she suggested that the children in Mrs. Pierce's class might have done well with any program. She implied that some factor other than the program—perhaps home environment or native intelligence—was responsible for their good test results. In any study, researchers have to make sure they've eliminated other possible explanations or causes for the behavior they're studying before they can claim to have established a cause-effect relationship. This question of the soundness of the research design—referred to as **internal validity**—is another critical issue researchers have to face.

Mrs. Palmer may have wondered if the new program really had very much to do with the children's test performance. Maybe they already knew most of the content of the program before they entered kindergarten. The superintendent didn't mention any **pretesting**—testing done before the program started—that would have indicated what prior knowledge the children had. Without **baseline data**—information about what people in a study know or can do before a program or treatment is introduced—we can't be sure the children's good test scores actually resulted from the program.

No pretesting would have been necessary if there had been a **control group**— a group of children who are the same in every way as the children in the treatment or experimental group except for the variable of interest, which in this case is the new reading program. If we start with two groups who are alike in every way, then any differences found after the program or treatment can be attributed to the program itself. It wouldn't be due to any prior differences between the groups.

Randomly assigning children is the best way to get two comparable groups— putting their names in a hat, mixing them up, drawing them out, and placing the children alternately in one group or the other. When we do this before beginning a program, we create the conditions for an **experimental study**. But when we take naturally occurring groups that might differ initially in some ways, we have conditions only for a **correlational study**. In an experimental study, we can attribute results to the effects of the treatment or program. But in a correlational study, we can't be sure that any differences existing at the end of a program are due to the program. The differences, or the conditions causing the differences, might have been there from the start.

Mr. Taylor brought up this issue when he asked if children in any other kindergartens had been tested. He was looking for some kind of control or comparison group. Of course, if the children weren't randomly assigned to the kindergarten classes to begin with, we still couldn't be sure that any differences at the end were due to the program.

There's another reason for having both a control group and an experimental group in a study like this one. It may be that some event outside the school had affected the children's reading ability. Perhaps the local library had begun a reading contest and was awarding prizes to children for every book they'd read or had read to them. Or maybe a new educational television program had started, or a series of articles for parents had been appearing in the local newspaper. Any of these events might cause children's reading scores to be higher than expected at the end of the year. But in these cases, we would see improvement in both the control group and the experimental group. We would know that something other than the reading program was causing *all* the children's test scores to go up.

Researcher Bias, Reliability, and Fair Testing

Researchers typically have a vested interest in what they're testing. Perhaps, as in Mrs. Pierce's case, they develop a program or a treatment, and of course they hope it will be effective. When the results of a program or treatment are measured, it's a good idea to have an objective third party collect the data. It's even a good idea for this person to be kept "**blind**," or totally ignorant about which children were in the control group and which were in the experimental group. This helps eliminate the possibility of **researcher bias**—the tendency to want the results to turn out a certain way.

It's also important that different groups be tested under the same conditions. The kindergarten children had very comfortable conditions. They were tested in a familiar setting by someone who knew them very well and who hoped they would succeed. The test scores obtained by Mrs. Pierce may not have been very **reliable**—that is, a different tester might not have been able to obtain the same results.

The first graders with whom the kindergartners were compared, on the other hand, may have been tested under less ideal circumstances. They may have been tested in an unfamiliar room by a tester who didn't care whether they did well or poorly. Adverse circumstances can mask children's actual knowledge to some extent. The first graders' scores might have been much higher if their testing conditions had matched those of the kindergartners.

If we want to compare something like test scores, we have to follow standardized procedures. These can be thought of as "the rules of the testing

FIGURE 1-3
When children are tested under standardized conditions, we know that test results haven't been affected by researcher bias or unfair testing procedures. These children's scores are probably a reliable reflection of how much they know in comparison with each other and with children tested under similar conditions.

game." They make the situation fair for everyone. Just as it isn't fair to compare the free-throw percentages of two basketball players shooting from two different distances, it isn't fair to compare the test scores of children tested under different conditions. Perhaps we should say that it's meaningless rather than unfair—we don't know if we're talking about real knowledge differences or about differences in performance that are related to testing conditions.

Selecting Variables

When Mrs. Pierce wanted to evaluate the kindergartners' reading skills, she couldn't test them on their ability to read in a mature, conventional way. Most of them simply couldn't do that. So she tested them on skills that are thought to be related to later conventional reading ability, such as alphabet recognition and understanding of print conventions. Researchers working with children often have to measure variables that predict or are related to the behavior they really want to study. When predictor variables are measured instead of the final behavior, researchers must be sure that a connection between the two has been demonstrated.

There are many cases in which little or no relationship has been found between predictor variables and final behavior. For example, for many years people thought that reading ability was related to physical and visual-motor skills, such as the abilities to balance on a balance beam and to copy shapes. Many kindergarten programs incorporated activities that would give children practice in these skills. The children did improve their physical and visual-motor skills, but it turned out that these skills are unrelated to reading ability (Vellutino, 1987). Reading ability appears to be related to other skills—skills related to experience with oral and written language.

The school superintendent said that good readers use the skills on which the kindergarten children were tested. If this is so, then there is some **validity** to the tests that the school used. The tests were measuring skills that have been shown to be related to reading ability. When we use a valid measure, we know we're measuring the skill we're interested in, not some other, unrelated skill.

We also have to avoid being too narrow in our thinking when we select variables to test. A process as complicated as reading, for example, is likely to depend on the integrated use of many skills. We would probably feel uncomfortable if the superintendent had said that the school tested children only for alphabet recognition. "Is that all there is to learning to read?" we might ask.

Even if we show that one variable is causally related to a certain behavior, we can't stop there. Any complex phenomenon probably has many causes. **Multifactorial causation**, as this is called, can be illustrated by a look at the "risk factors" for heart disease. Some people are prone to heart disease and develop it at a relatively young age; others seem to have some resistance and live to a fairly ripe old age without developing any signs of it. Why does this difference exist? The **variance,** or difference, between the two groups can be accounted for by a number of factors. Genetic make-up may account for 25 percent of the variance, blood pressure may account for 20 percent, diet for 20 percent, stress for 15 percent, and unknown factors for 20 percent. All these factors have been shown to be causally related to heart disease.

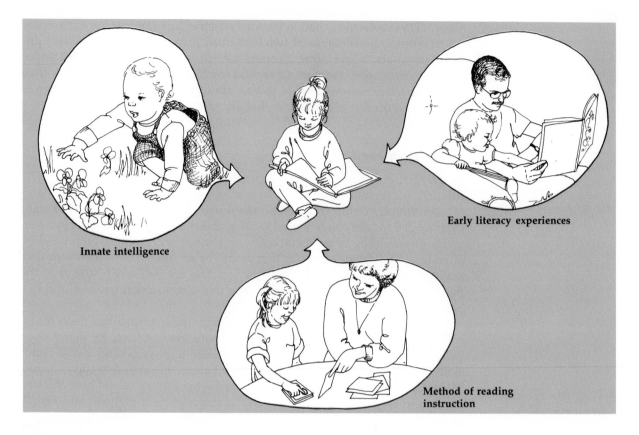

Innate intelligence

Early literacy experiences

Method of reading instruction

FIGURE 1-4
Multifactorial causation is involved in many complex phenomena, including the process of learning to read. Factors that contribute to a 7-year-old's ability to read may include her native intelligence, her early experiences with books, *and* the approach that was used in teaching her to read. For example, a 7-year-old who can't read might be mildly retarded, have an emotional problem that interferes with her ability to learn, *and* lack preschool experience with books and writing materials.

In the same way, a number of different factors are involved in learning to read. Since the school used several different tests to measure different kinds of understandings, they were covering many, although probably not all, of the important variables involved in reading.

It's Easier to Think Than to Do

We can certainly understand why a school district might not be able to undertake an elegant research study. Limited resources—time, money, and people—make it difficult for many schools to do more than what's required. Almost every study has some limitations. But even when a study has limitations, people can still think like researchers. They can examine results critically and draw conclusions with caution. This is what the parents at the school meeting were doing so well. When people understand what's involved in a particular situation, they can make more informed decisions.

THE MAJOR RESEARCH METHODS

Now that we've seen how research-like thinking might work in real life, let's take a more systematic look at the major research methods and their advantages and disadvantages.

Correlational Studies

In correlational studies, two or more variables are measured. A **variable**, as previously mentioned, is something that can change in value or form. A variable is often manipulated in research so that its effects on behavior can be observed. The variable that the researcher manipulates—changes or varies in the course of the study—is called the **independent variable**. The behavior that the researcher observes to see if it changes when the independent variable is changed is called the **dependent variable**.

If changes in one variable are associated with changes in the other variable, we say that the two variables are correlated. For example, one variable might increase in value as a second variable increases in value. Or one variable might decrease in value as a second variable decreases in value. Variables that change in the same direction are said to be **positively correlated**. Variables that change in opposite directions are **negatively correlated**—one variable increases in value while the second variable decreases in value. Variables are uncorrelated when one variable does not change systematically with changes in the other variable.

Even when variables are correlated, however, we can't assume that one causes the other. Height and weight are positively correlated, but we can't say that an increase in height causes an increase in weight. A third variable—growth hormone—causes increases both in height and weight.

A correlational study can tell us whether or not changes in one variable are related to changes in another, but it can't tell us *why* the changes are related. In our kindergarten example, we really didn't know if the achievement of the kindergarten children was due to the new program or if it was due to something else—something about the children, the teacher, or the community. The danger of correlational studies is that they may be interpreted to mean that causation exists when it doesn't.

Studies involving naturally occurring groups, rather than specially constituted ones, are correlational studies. For example, if aggressive behavior is measured in groups of children who watch more or less violent television at home, we can't assume a causal relationship between the two factors. If it turns out that children who watch violent TV shows are more aggressive, we wouldn't be justified in saying that the TV viewing caused the aggressive behavior. Perhaps children who are already aggressive like to watch televised violence more than children who aren't aggressive. Or perhaps the parents of aggressive children allow them to watch more violent shows and also spank or punish their children more than do parents of less aggressive children. It could be that different parental behavior in general rather than television viewing in particular accounts for the difference in aggressive behavior.

Similarly, if we take some action with naturally occurring groups, we can't be sure that any differences found between the groups afterward were caused by our action. If we show a violent cartoon to children from one community and a prosocial program—one that demonstrates caring, sharing, and cooperative behavior—to children from another community, we might find differences afterward in their aggressive behavior. But we wouldn't know if these differences were due to the films or if they existed before we ever undertook the study.

FIGURE 1-5
Does watching violent TV shows make children more aggressive, or do aggressive children choose more violent TV shows, or do parents who buy their children toy guns and let them watch violent TV shows cause them to be more aggressive? Correlations have been established between aggression in children and the viewing of television violence, but a causal relationship is much more difficult to prove.

The advantage of correlational studies is that we're saved the time and effort of administering a treatment to specially constituted groups when no prior relationship between two variables has ever been observed. If we can show that two variables are correlated, then it makes sense to pursue the possibility that they're causally related. If no correlation has ever been demonstrated, it's often a waste of time and money to do experimental studies, which are more complicated and costly.

Correlational studies are appropriate in another situation as well. Sometimes a treatment may actually be harmful, and we can't knowingly inflict it on subjects in an experiment. But if we consider an adverse condition that occurs naturally, we can ethically study it to see what its effects may be or what other conditions may be associated with it.

Experimental Studies

When we want to pinpoint the exact nature of the relationship between two variables, we conduct an **experimental study**. Experimental studies have two major characteristics: (1) a variable of interest is always manipulated, so that one group receives more of it and another group receives less; and (2) groups receiving the different levels or amounts of the variable are always comparable before the study starts.

The best way to ensure that the groups are comparable is to assign large numbers of individuals randomly to different groups. In an experimental study with children, for example, we might put all the names in a hat, shake it up, and draw out one name at a time. The first name would be placed in group 1, the second in group 2, the third in group 3, the fourth in group 1, the fifth in group 2, and so on. We could be fairly certain that children who had similar backgrounds or characteristics would be distributed among the three groups, not bunched up in one group or another. Then we would know that differences found between groups after the study were the result of what was done in the study itself.

Most experimental studies are conducted in a laboratory setting. For example, in a study of the effects of viewing violent TV cartoons on children's behavior, groups of children might be brought into a special room to view films. One group might be shown a violent cartoon, a second might be shown a prosocial film, and a third might be shown a neutral film. Filmed violence is the independent variable that's being manipulated—a high level of violence is shown to one group, a low level to another.

The children's aggressive behavior after watching the various films is the dependent variable. If children who saw violent cartoons are observed to play more aggressively in the lab than children who watched some other kind of film, then we can assume a causal link between watching filmed aggression and aggressive behavior.

Not all experimental studies are conducted solely in the laboratory. The children who saw the different films in the lab could also be observed later in the classroom or playground. Although the dependent variable is now being measured in a naturalistic setting, the study is still experimental. A variable has been manipulated, and the groups were comparable at the beginning of the study, due to random assignment. These are the crucial characteristics of an experimental study that allow us to make statements about causation.

The disadvantage of the experimental method is that it's not always practical or ethical. Then we fall back on correlational methods. Sometimes, too, experimental studies distort events, so that we see a causal relationship in the lab that wouldn't hold true in real-life situations, when other factors are involved. We can overcome this drawback by observing the behavior in both lab and naturalistic settings.

We don't use the experimental method when we don't have much information about variables that might be affecting a behavior we're interested in.

FIGURE 1-6
Experimental studies often are conducted under carefully controlled conditions in a laboratory setting. If a researcher randomly assigns children to two groups, gives practice on specific types of tasks to one group but not to the other, and then finds that the treatment group (practice group) completes a test task in half the time that it takes the control group, the researcher can be fairly certain that the training caused the treatment group's performance to improve.

In these situations, it makes more sense first to ferret out some possible causes using correlational methods and then to conduct follow-up studies using experimental methods.

Descriptive Studies

Sometimes researchers aren't interested in cause-and-effect relationships so much as they just want to gather information about children by describing how they act. For these purposes, descriptive studies are appropriate. No variables are manipulated in descriptive studies, no treatments are applied, and no questions are asked about what causes children to act the way they do.

Descriptive studies can involve large or small numbers of children, many or few observers collecting data, natural or contrived situations, and narrowly or loosely defined categories of behavior. All of these variations determine how much the results can be generalized to other children and how objective and reliable the data are. As explained earlier, reliability refers to the extent to which one researcher's observations match another's or can be duplicated by another. If researchers carefully define what they're observing, their data will be more reliable.

There are three commonly used kinds of descriptive studies—specimen records, behavior checklists, and event and time sampling. Let's briefly examine each one.

SPECIMEN RECORDS. Sometimes, observers try to record everything a child does in a short period of time. The result is called a specimen record. This technique was extremely difficult before audio and video technology gave the researcher the tools with which to observe a moment in a child's life over and over again. The specimen record is used mainly to get a detailed picture of some aspect of a child's everyday behavior.

BEHAVIOR CHECKLISTS. Sometimes observers start out with a list of carefully defined behaviors that they're going to watch for and count. The behavior checklist is a more **closed method** of observation than the specimen record, which we call an **open method** (Wright, 1960). It also doesn't provide the rich detail that specimen records do. On the other hand, the behavior checklist makes it easier to observe children accurately, and the resulting data are more precise and reliable. Behavior checklists are used for keeping track of all types of specific behavior, such as aggression, friendliness, or attention seeking. In research studies, baseline data on a dependent variable of interest can be obtained using a checklist. Then, following the treatment, comparative data can be obtained using the same checklist.

EVENT AND TIME SAMPLING. Event sampling is a descriptive technique in which an observer notes only one, well-defined type of behavior. Narrowing the range of behaviors to be observed means that very precise, accurate recording can be done. One researcher used this method to study children's quarrels (Dawe, 1934). He observed children during free-play in a nursery school, watching for quarrels to occur. When they did, he moved closer to note the details. Because he carefully defined what he meant by a quarrel, other

FIGURE 1-7
This young woman is observing children's behavior in a natural environment for a descriptive study. She may be using the technique called event sampling to note every incident of a particular behavior—sharing, for example—that occurs between the boys. Or she might be using a behavior checklist to record incidences of sharing, helping, verbal communication, aggression, and any number of other behaviors that she sees.

researchers could collect data at other nursery schools and compare them in a meaningful way to his data.

Time sampling is a technique in which regular observations are made on a specific schedule. Observations may be made over a fairly long period of time to ensure that a child's full range of behavior is seen, or observations of individual children may be made for specific lengths of time within one observation period. A researcher may observe one child for five minutes, then another for five minutes, and so on. In this way, the researcher observes each child in a variety of settings, rather than one child on the playground and another during snack, which would make it difficult to compare their behavior.

One researcher used time sampling to see what kinds of play children were involved in (Parten, 1932). She defined four categories of play: (1) solitary play—children played alone; (2) parallel play—children played alongside other children; (3) associative play—children played with other children but without subordinating their own interests to the group; and (4) cooperative play—children played as a group. She set up a schedule allowing for one-minute observations of each child every day for several days, and she varied the schedule systematically so that each child was observed at a different time during the free-play period on different days. The results of a careful data-collection strategy like this one are likely to be very reliable.

In all these types of descriptive studies, it's important that the observer record details of what actually happens rather than opinions, conclusions, or judgments about behavior. Observers should provide "raw data" only, without trying to explain the meaning of a child's behavior. Examples of observations

BOX 1-1
An Observation with
Conclusions

> S arrives at school. He is glad to be at school. He doesn't miss his mother. He seems tired at the beginning of the day. After a while, he decides to play with blocks. He seems not to care about building something with blocks with a girl who is playing there, and he builds a road alone. But he seems to want to build with a boy, and when a boy comes close to the area, he invites him to play. S is very possessive of his road and the toy vehicles used with it. (record continues)

recorded with conclusions are given in Box 1-1. We read phrases like "seems tired," "doesn't seem to care," and "is very possessive." Yet we can't tell how these conclusions were reached because we aren't given any details of behavior.

In the example without conclusions, shown in Box 1-2, we see exactly what went on. Times are carefully recorded, and conclusions are not mixed with observations. Possible conclusions are listed separately. (See Box 1-3)

CONTRIVING SITUATIONS FOR OBSERVATION. Many descriptive studies are carried out in the child's natural environment—home, school, or play area. But sometimes investigators design environments to elicit the kind of behavior they want to observe. One psychologist who was interested in peer interaction among very young children set up a playroom and invited mothers and their children to visit periodically (Bronson, 1981). In this way she ensured herself opportunities to study the situation she wanted to observe. When the researcher contrives a situation for observation, the study is still considered descriptive. The purpose of the study is still to observe what "is."

Descriptive studies give us a broad, rich picture of how children act. Because there's no intervention by the researcher, and often no direct contact at all, ethical issues—concerns about the effect of the study on the child—are kept to a minimum. On the other hand, descriptive studies do not allow us to draw conclusions about the causes of children's behavior.

BOX 1-2
An Observation without
Conclusions

9:10 S arrived at school at 9:05. S's mother came with him into the classroom. S went to his cubby, took off coat, hung it up on hook. Smiled and waved goodbye to mother, who said "Have a good day."

9:15 Stood with back toward cubby. Rubbed eyes with right fist. Looked out into room—first in one direction, then in another. Yawned. Walked over to block area where girl was already playing. S entered area. Began taking a block from the top shelf. "You can't take my blocks," the girl said. "I won't," responded S. "I can use these." (gestured toward shelf).

9:20 S placed a long block on the floor away from the girl's building. S obtained another block, same as the first one, bent over, and placed one end of it next to the end of the first block. "I'm making a road," he said as he looked at the girl and then glanced at her building. "Don't make it go this way," she said (points toward her blocks). "I won't," S said. "It's going to be a long road that way." (points in direction away from girl's blocks)

9:25 A boy entered the block area. "Hi M____," said S. "Want to help me build this road? Then we'll drive on it." "Yeah," the boy said. He began to take blocks from the shelf and place them end to end with S's road. After adding five blocks, he took a truck off the shelf and began to push it along the top of the block road.

9:30 "Hey," said S. "I wanted the truck. You have to use the car. This is my road!" (record continues)

BOX 1-3
Possible Conclusions About a
Child's Behavior

1. The child does not select play areas based on sex of other children playing in the area.
2. The child initiates contacts with other children.
3. The child readily plays with other children.
4. The child shares materials with other children although he protects what is his.
5. The child uses words to communicate wishes to other children.
6. The child offers suggestions for solving problems.

The Case Study

The case study is a special type of method that can be combined with any of the methods we have decribed above. What makes a study a case study is that only one of something—a child, a teacher, a school—is studied. The kindergarten program described at the beginning of the chapter is a good example of a case study. As we saw with the kindergarten program, the limitation of the case study is that its results can't be generalized to other situations. The information it provides is about one case and one case only.

Of course, researchers wouldn't use a method at all if it wasn't helpful in some way, and the case study has some outstanding advantages. Probably the most important one is that it allows us to study something in great detail.

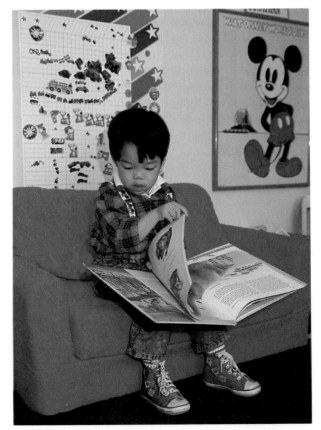

FIGURE 1-8
Parents are in a good position to conduct case studies of their own children. This boy's parents might be interested in studying his fine motor skills as they developed over the course of a year or so, or changes in his literary tastes as he matured, or the effectiveness of the kind of "star chart" we see on the wall behind him.

When we study one child we can collect much more data, given the same amount of time, money, and human resources, than when we study 100 children.

One researcher used the case study method to study the development of literacy in her son between his second and third birthdays (Granucci, 1986). She taped nightly bedtime storytelling sessions. She kept track of the books he owned and the books he chose to have read to him. She kept a log noting the toys he had and what he played with. She wrote down the questions he asked about print, and she kept all his scribblings. She did this day in, day out, for one year, and by his third birthday she had many file boxes full of data. With this information, she was able to put together a complete picture of one 2-year-old's literacy development during this span of time.

This researcher obviously couldn't have studied a large number of children in this detail. A team of researchers might be able to, but it would be very costly. When we study more children, we usually settle for more superficial information.

The other limitation of the case study method, besides the lack of generalizability, is the possibility of researcher bias. We saw this issue raised about the kindergarten program by the parent who questioned whether Mrs. Pierce should have been the one to test the children. She knew that testers or observers with an interest in a child sometimes see and hear things differently than an objective observer would. When a parent studies his or her own child, we have to acknowledge the likelihood of some bias. Of course, when parents are the researchers, we also get information about children that we would probably never have access to under other circumstances.

Despite their limitations, then, case studies provide detailed information about children's behavior in the context of the child's natural environment. This rich detail helps us understand how complex and multifaceted human behavior is. Case studies often give us ideas about the developmental sequence of many abilities and behaviors—how one ability emerges after another in the growing child—although they don't tell us if what we've learned about this one situation is characteristic of any others.

THE MAJOR RESEARCH DESIGNS: CROSS-SECTIONAL AND LONGITUDINAL

Regardless of the research *method*—correlational, experimental, or descriptive—chosen for a study, researchers interested in developmental issues may also choose one of two basic research *designs*. The **cross-sectional design** uses groups of children of different ages—perhaps groups of 2-year-olds, 6-year-olds, and 10-year-olds. The **longitudinal design**, on the other hand, starts with a group of children of a specific age—perhaps 2-year-olds—and then follows them across the age-span of interest—perhaps until they're 10 years old (Figure 1-9). Each design has its advantages and its disadvantages, and we'll consider both below.

Advantages of the Cross-Sectional Design over the Longitudinal Design

The cross-sectional design allows studies to be completed more quickly than the longitudinal design does, because we don't have to wait for the children to reach the upper age of interest. When we use a cross-sectional design, we

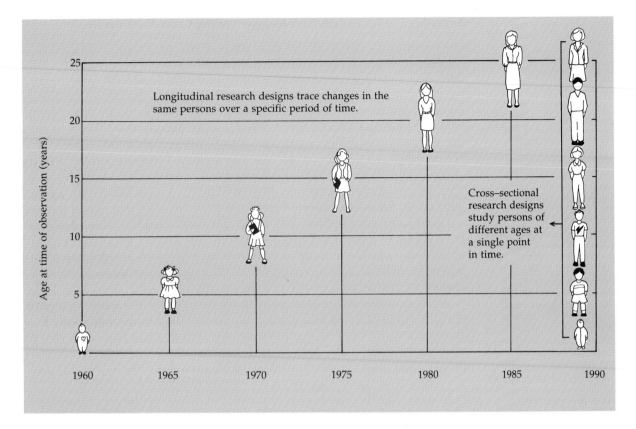

Longitudinal research designs trace changes in the same persons over a specific period of time.

Cross–sectional research designs study persons of different ages at a single point in time.

Age at time of observation (years)

1960   1965   1970   1975   1980   1985   1990

FIGURE 1-9

In experiments with longitudinal designs, the same subjects are followed over a number of years, allowing researchers to focus carefully on the process of development. In experiments with cross-sectional designs, subjects of different ages are studied at the same time, allowing researchers to work more efficiently and reducing the likelihood of certain kinds of research errors. A third type of research design, the cross-sectional/short-term longitudinal, combines the advantages of the two.

simply study children of different ages at the same time. The cross-sectional design also lessens the possibility of biased sampling, which is a problem in the longitudinal design. **Biased sampling** means that children in the study are not representative of the population to which the researcher hopes to generalize the study's results. Biased sampling can occur when certain types of parents refuse to be included in longitudinal studies. This is because parents who allow their children to participate in longitudinal studies may be different from parents who refuse to participate. They have to make a long-term commitment to the research and agree to many observations of their children over a long period of time. They may be better educated, more interested in having their children participate in research, or more socially active. If so, their children wouldn't be typical, and the research results couldn't be generalized to other children.

Another factor that may make longitudinal samples nonrepresentative is the likelihood that some children will withdraw over the course of the study. Their families might move, or their circumstances might change in some way that prevents them from continuing. This means that the group under study is no longer the same as it was in the beginning. Therefore, if the group of children in the study shows a difference in behavior between, say, age 6 and age 8, we can't know if this is an age difference—a difference due to development—or if this is a difference due to the different composition of the groups of children who were included in the study at ages 6 and 8. We don't run into this kind of problem with the cross-sectional design.

Advantages of the Longitudinal Design over the Cross-Sectional Design

The longitudinal design allows us to observe changes in one child's behavior over time, which the cross-sectional design does not. The advantage of the longitudinal design can be seen in studies of the preadolescent growth spurt. Growth at this time is typically very fast, truly a spurt. However, if measurements from a cross-sectional study were plotted on a graph, the growth spurt would appear as a smooth curve rather than an abrupt peak. This is because the timing of the growth spurt varies from individual to individual—some experience it at 11, others at 14. There is a gradual increase in height in the general population of children spanning the entire period from 10½ to 15. This smooth curve tells us how 11-year-olds as a group differ from 14-year-olds, but it doesn't describe the growth experience of an individual.

Group averages like these may be all that are needed by clothes designers, but a parent or a physician also needs to know if an individual child's growth spurt is normal. The smooth curve may seem to suggest that children should experience gradual, continuous growth. Only longitudinal data show that actual abrupt, individual changes are normal for this age.

Another disadvantage of cross-sectional designs is that sometimes we can't tell whether differences between age groups are the results of developmental changes or of the different experiences the groups have had. This was the problem with the study that reported the "cumulative deficit in intelligence" among black children, mentioned at the beginning of this chapter. Psycholo-

FIGURE 1-10
The cohort of young adults who attended natural childbirth classes (and reunions) in the 1980's has a unique set of experiences and values in common that distinguishes them from other cohorts. Their parents' cohort, for example, probably had a very different experience of childbirth in the 1950s. Their children—these babies—form another cohort, one that will come of age in the twenty-first century. We can only guess what experiences will shape their lives.

gist Arthur Jensen reported that the IQs of black children got lower as they progressed through elementary school (1974, 1977). Because he didn't find the same kind of decline among white children, he attributed this decline to genetic differences in mental development curves between blacks and whites. However, his studies were flawed. He interpreted his data as if they were obtained from the same subjects studied over a long period of time rather than from different subjects studied at the same time.

It might be, for example, that the 6-year-olds in the study were in better educational programs than the 12-year-olds had been in when they were 6. Perhaps educational TV or Project Head Start had given the 6-year-olds an advantage the 12-year-olds hadn't had. If so, the older children's IQs at 6 might not have tested as high as those of the 6-year-olds in the study. If we assume that educational opportunity is gradually improving, then we might expect that IQ would appear to decline with age: the older the children, the poorer their early opportunities. One researcher suggests that what seems to be a change related to age may really be a change related to personal history or conditions (Kamin, 1978).

A generation or a group of the same age (like the 12-year-olds in Jensen's study) is called a **cohort**. When differences among cohorts are a result of the common history and experiences unique to each age group, these differences are known as **cohort effects** (Schaie, 1965). The main problem with the cross-sectional design is that it confounds (confuses) age effects with cohort effects. We don't know whether differences we've measured are due to developmental changes from one age to another or to the unique experiences of the different age groups. In his study, Jensen is said to have confounded age with educational history.

Combining the Two Designs

We've seen that both the cross-sectional and the longitudinal designs have their advantages and their limitations. Sometimes researchers combine the best features of each in what we call a **cross-sectional/short-term longitudinal design**. Using this design they can study change in physical aggression, for example, between, say, 8 and 16, and also follow individuals for a fairly long period of time. They would test groups of 8-year-olds, 10-year-olds, 12-year-olds, and 14-year-olds (cross-sectional design feature) and then test them again two years later when they were 10, 12, 14, and 16 years, respectively (longitudinal design feature). This design yields data about development during a span of eight years, yet it only takes two years to complete. It provides information about changes in individual children from one age to the next and also controls somewhat for cohort or history effects.

SELECTING A SUITABLE RESEARCH METHOD

We've looked at a number of research methods and designs, and we've seen that no single one is clearly superior to the others under all circumstances. When people are doing research in child development, how do they decide which method is best for their purposes? The answer depends on three fac-

BOX 1-4
Examples of Descriptive, Cor-relational, and Causal Statements

Which of the following statements do you think are descriptive? correlational? causal?

1. On the average, babies weigh about 7 pounds at birth.
2. The incidence of Down's syndrome in children increases as maternal age increases.
3. Older children tend to have more diseases than infants.
4. When the drug thalidomide is given to pregnant women early in pregnancy, it prevents the formation of arms and legs in the fetus.
5. Girls mature physically faster than boys.
6. Boy toddlers own more vehicle toys than do girl toddlers.
7. Prematurity is a risk factor for problems in attachment.
8. Aggressive behavior can be reduced if children watch prosocial TV programs rather than violent ones.

Descriptive: 1
Correlational: 2, 3, 5, 6, 7
Causal: 4, 8

tors—the research question, the ethical considerations associated with the study, and the circumstances of the person doing the investigating.

THE RESEARCH QUESTION. What kind of questions do we want to answer about children? Do we want to know what children are like or what they do? We could get this information from a descriptive study. Do we want to know what behaviors are likely to be associated with each other? We could find out from a correlational study. Or do we want to know what causes a specific behavior? Then we would have to conduct an experimental study.

These different methods allow us to make different kinds of statements about children—descriptive, correlational, or causal—after we've collected and analyzed data in a research study. We always have to be careful to make only the kind of statement allowed by our research method. (Examples of each kind of statement are given in Box 1-4.)

ETHICAL CONSIDERATIONS. Some questions can't be investigated in the manner that would yield the most conclusive results because doing so might harm the research subjects. We couldn't study the effect of protein in infants' diet on their growth by depriving a group of infants of protein, for example. Instead, we could compare the growth of infants in naturally occurring groups that have more or less protein in their diets. Our results in this case would only be correlational. If we did find a relationship between growth and protein, we couldn't be sure it was a causal relationship. We wouldn't know whether differences in growth were due to differences in protein or to some other differences in the naturally occurring groups. But these are the limits imposed on research by ethical considerations.

The ethics of research, especially research involving children, has been a concern to many groups over the years, including the American Psychological Association, U.S. governmental agencies, and the Society for Research in Child Development. These groups have developed a code of ethics for research with children, which includes the following guidelines:

1. Investigators may not use any research operations that may harm a child physically or psychologically.

FIGURE 1-11
Ethical considerations are the primary consideration in research with children. In this study of infant language development, the baby was held by an adult during the experimental treatment. If the child had cried or become frightened, the experiment would have been interrupted or terminated.

2. Investigators must obtain **informed consent** from the parent or legal guardian of the child before the child can be a subject in a study. This means that the study must be explained completely and accurately to the parent in language he or she can understand.
3. Investigators cannot obtain consent by promising that the research will benefit the child.
4. Investigators may not force an unwilling child to participate in a study.

These guidelines are relevant mainly to research that involves some kind of treatment, interaction, intervention, or manipulation of variables—the kind of action typical in experimental studies. Correlational and descriptive studies, which tend to involve the observation of children in natural settings, are much less likely to run into ethical problems or to meet resistance from parents. Regardless of the research question we're asking or the kind of results we would like to get, ethical considerations have top priority when we're choosing a research method.

THE INVESTIGATOR'S CIRCUMSTANCES. The third factor involved in choosing a research method is the circumstances of the investigator and his or her role in the child's life. A teacher, for example, is in an excellent position to observe children in their natural setting, so if a teacher were going to do a research study, he or she might use descriptive methods or do a case study. On the other hand, teachers are not in a very good position to use the experimental method. They would probably find it difficult to set up experimental and control groups in the classroom and to manipulate variables in a careful, rigorous way.

Let's consider the case of a teacher who notices that her students aren't reading as well as she thinks they should be. She might think of several possible reasons for this problem: (1) the reading books might be uninteresting or unattractive to the children; (2) the children might find reading irrelevant or meaningless because it's not tied to their daily lives; (3) the children might be tired during reading time because it comes right after physical education. To test the three hypotheses in an experimental study, the teacher would first have to divide the class into two groups, a control group and an experimental group. Then she would have to vary each of the three conditions systematically to see if a change in any of them caused a change in reading achievement.

Conducting such a study would be a long and tedious process. How long would the teacher have to use books she judges "very interesting" before she could legitimately expect to see an improvement in reading ability? How would she judge the interest level in the first place? Where would the more interesting books come from if the school budget for books has been spent on the books the class already has? How could the teacher prevent a child in the experimental group from letting a friend in the control group read the more interesting book at home? How would the teacher explain to parents that the books couldn't be changed for six months because of the research study no matter how poorly some children were doing?

Obviously, the teacher is in no position to conduct such a study. If she thinks some change will improve her classroom, she is obligated to make that change as soon as possible and then observe the results as best she can. She might try having reading time first thing in the morning when the children are fresh, or she might try letting the children pick their own books from the school library, or she might explore ways to integrate reading and journal writing. When she finds that the children's reading ability has improved, she won't be able to say that the change she made caused the improvement. Only an experimental study would allow her to make that claim. But because she looked at the problem in a critical way, made careful observations, came up with reasonable hypotheses, and tested her hypotheses in a systematic way, she used what she could of the scientific research method. And probably she's found a practical solution to her problem.

TYING THINGS TOGETHER

Now that you have some idea of what's involved in research, you probably understand why it's so difficult to conduct flawless research with children. You probably also understand why, despite the vast number of studies that have been done on various aspects of child development, our knowledge is still limited. You can see why, for example, after numerous studies, debate continues over the effects of a mother's smoking on her unborn child. Most of these studies have been correlational, not experimental. No matter how brilliantly conceived the hypothesis or how carefully executed the research, every study has limitations imposed by financial constraints or the reality of dealing with human subjects.

FIGURE 1-12
Breastfeeding is currently considered preferable to bottle feeding because breast milk contains important antibodies and is perfectly suited to the baby's nutritional needs and digestive capacities. Despite the prevailing medical advice, some women choose bottle feeding because of personal or cultural values. As these two women demonstrate, both feeding methods are compatible with a loving mother-child relationship.

Even when knowledge is extensive and data about a particular behavior are conclusive, our ability to take action or make changes has limitations as well. Because people have different values, they have different ideas about the way children ought to be. We know, for example, that the amount and quality of parental talk to babies is related to the babies' language development. But it would be pointless to try to persuade a parent to talk more to a baby if the parent thought a quiet child was an ideal child. We know there's an association between watching violent TV shows and behaving aggressively, but that's not going to make parents who value rough-and-tough behavior in their child start to monitor TV viewing. Values are a product of one's philosophy, religion, culture, and personal experience; value questions can't be addressed by research studies alone.

Despite these limitations, research is invaluable as a source of knowledge and information about children. And an understanding of research methods is essential to anyone with a critical interest in the study of child development. Without that understanding, you wouldn't know what was wrong with the study of black and white children's IQs. You wouldn't know how valid the study of the kindergarten reading program was. You wouldn't be as knowledgeable and thoughtful as you could be when observing your own child or classroom group.

When you read about the many different aspects of child development in the chapters ahead, you'll often refer mentally to the material discussed in this chapter. Research methods, designs, and issues are the underlying foundation for the study of child development.

OVERVIEW

Our knowledge of children is based on research, but people who live and work with children will find the research useless unless they're able to understand, interpret, and evaluate the studies. Teachers, parents, and caregivers have to know what research issues might be involved, what kinds of studies might be conducted under different circumstances, and how the results of different studies can be interpreted. They also have to understand why, despite innumerable studies, our knowledge about children is still limited. Perhaps most importantly, they have to be willing to think in critical ways when they encounter research findings in child development. Just as researchers have to be careful about how they design their studies, practitioners have to be careful about how they interpret and apply research conclusions to the children in their care.

CHAPTER REVIEW

THE MAJOR RESEARCH ISSUES

- Researchers have to make sure that the results they obtain from studying a few people can be generalized to other groups of people. They can ensure their study's external validity—its generalizability—by beginning with a representative sample of the population in question.
- Researchers have to make sure they eliminate other possible causes of the behavior they're studying before they claim to have established a cause-effect relationship. They can ensure their study's internal validity—its soundness—by doing pretesting to gather baseline data before they begin their study or by establishing randomly selected experimental and control groups for the study.
- If these conditions are met, researchers can conduct an experimental study, whose results can indicate a cause-effect relationship. If they work with naturally occurring groups, they can conduct a correlational study, whose results don't indicate causality.
- Researchers should have testing or measuring conducted by objective third parties who are "blind," or totally ignorant about which children have received which treatment, in order to obtain reliable results—results that can be duplicated by others. Testing should also be conducted under standardized procedures to ensure fairness.
- Researchers have to make sure they've selected variables to test that have been shown to be related to the final behavior they're studying. They also have to consider the likelihood of multifactorial causation—the causation of the final behavior by many factors.

THE MAJOR RESEARCH METHODS

The three major research methods are the correlational, the experimental, and the descriptive. A special research method is the case study.

- In correlational studies, the researcher manipulates one variable (the independent variable) and observes whether changes then occur in another variable (the dependent variable). If the variables change in the same direction, they're said to be positively correlated; if they change in opposite directions, they're said to be negatively correlated. Correlational studies do not establish cause-effect relationships.
- In experimental studies, the researcher manipulates a variable by applying more of a treatment to one group and less of it to another, comparable group. Experimental studies allow researchers to make statements about causation.
- Descriptive studies provide information about how people act. The three most commonly used descriptive studies are specimen records, behavior checklists, and event and time samples. This kind of method gives a broad, rich picture of children's behavior without establishing causation or suggesting associations.
- The case study is a special research method that can be combined with other methods. In this method, only one person or situation is studied, but in great detail. Limitations of the case study include lack of generalizability and the possibility of researcher bias.

THE MAJOR RESEARCH DESIGNS

- The two basic research designs are the cross-sectional and the longitudinal. In the cross-sectional design, groups of children of different ages are studied at the same point in time. In the longitudinal design, the same group of children is followed over a certain period of time.
- Cross-sectional studies can be completed more quickly than longitudinal studies. They are also less likely to be affected by biased sampling, which occurs when groups that were originally comparable change over time.

- Longitudinal studies allow researchers to observe changes in one child over a fairly long period of time. They also eliminate the possibility that cohort effects will be confounded with age effects—that is, that differences between groups will be attributed to developmental changes when they're really the result of different experiences.
- The cross-sectional/short-term longitudinal design combines the best features of the two designs, yielding data about a long span of development in a relatively short period of time.

SELECTING A SUITABLE RESEARCH METHOD

- Researchers decide on a research method by considering three factors—the research question, the ethical considerations, and the circumstances of the researcher.
- Experimental studies are suitable if researchers want to discover causes of behavior. Correlational studies are suitable if they want to know what behaviors are associated with other behaviors. And descriptive studies are appropriate if they want to know what children do.
- Ethical considerations have highest priority when a research method is being chosen. Experimental studies are much more likely to raise ethical problems than

correlational or descriptive studies, because they usually involve some intervention in the child's life.
- In choosing a research method, researchers also have to take into consideration their own role in the lives of the children they wish to study.
- Our knowledge about children is incomplete, but even when we have indisputable data, people's values play a part in what they do with research results. Despite these limitations, research is an invaluable source of information and knowledge about children; it provides the foundation for the study of child development.

KEY TERMS

external validity	correlational study	variable	cross-sectional design
representative sample	blind study	independent variable	longitudinal design
internal validity	researcher bias	dependent variable	biased sampling
pretesting	reliability	positively correlated	cohort/cohort effects
baseline data	validity	negatively correlated	cross-sectional/short-term
control group	multifactorial causation	closed method	longitudinal design
experimental study	variance	open method	informed consent

SUGGESTIONS FOR FURTHER READING

Beatty, J. J. (1986). *Observing development of the young child.* Columbus, OH: Charles E. Merrill.
Provides checklists for use in observing many aspects of a young child's development, including social play, prosocial behavior, large and small motor development, and language. Very useful for the preschool teacher.

Bissex, G. L. (1980). *GNYS at work: A child learns to write and read.* Cambridge, MA: Harvard University Press.
A good example of a case study, written by a parent. Provides a portrait of the child's literacy development from age 5 to 9.

Cozby, P. C., Worden, P. E., and Kee, D. W. (1989). *Research Methods in Human Development.* Mountain View, CA: Mayfield.
An overview of research techniques for the undergraduate who wants to use research wisely. Written especially for those in applied fields, such as teaching, social work, or counseling.

Vasta, R. (1979). *Studying children: An introduction to research methods.* San Francisco: W. H. Freeman.
A very informative little paperback. Not too technical, but very meaty. Excellent examples and illustrations.

chapter 2

THEORIES OF CHILD DEVELOPMENT

"That's just theoretical," we sometimes hear people say. They usually mean that something can't be proven, or that it doesn't apply in everyday life, or that they simply don't believe it. It's true that theories often don't hold up when tested. But that doesn't mean we shouldn't try to formulate them. In fact, it's difficult to imagine facing the world without theories of one kind or another.

Theories are sets of assumptions about why something happens or works the way it does. All of us, whether we consider ourselves scientists or not, approach the world with some basic assumptions about the causes of events around us. It's one of the ways we organize and make sense of the world.

Theories of child development are sets of assumptions about why children act the way they do. In this chapter we discuss the four major child development theories—the maturational, the psychoanalytical, the behavioral, and the cognitive-interactionist. But before we look at the ideas embodied in these theories, let's consider the experience of a parent seeking advice about her child. In her story, we'll see how theories organize the way people think about the world and how they guide their actions. We'll also get a sense of how the major child development theories translate into advice about real children.

THEORIES IN PRACTICE: ONE PARENT'S EXPERIENCE

Justin's mom, Peggy, was at her wits' end. Justin had become toilet trained during the day when he was 3, but now, a full year later, he still wasn't dry through the night. Peggy waited patiently for his diapers to be dry in the morning—a signal that he didn't need to wear them to bed—but they never were. In fact, things seemed to be getting worse. Some mornings, his pajamas and sheets were even soaked.

Then Peggy noticed that the largest size disposable diaper was starting to be tight on him. She began to worry—not just that she wouldn't be able to find big enough diapers for him but that he wasn't developing normally. If diapers weren't even made for 4-year-olds, why did her son still need them at night?

Finally, Peggy decided to get some advice. She made an appointment with her regular pediatrician, Dr. Blair, a doctor she considered very competent. Dr. Blair listened to Peggy's story and then advised her that Justin just wasn't ready for nighttime dryness. When Justin's body and brain were mature enough, Dr. Blair said, the problem would probably "take care of itself." He explained that Justin's ability to be dry was biologically determined by his genetic timetable and that different children could be expected to mature at different rates.

Dr. Blair even took a detailed history of Peggy and John, Justin's dad, to find out when they, as children, had been able to stay dry at night. Neither Peggy nor John could remember any particular problems with bed-wetting, although they couldn't say for sure what their early history had been. "These things sometimes run in families," said Dr. Blair. "You know, 'like father, like son.' " He told Peggy and John to "give it another six months" and then make another appointment if there had been no improvement.

Peggy didn't really want to wait six months. She was tired of the wet beds and not convinced Justin would become dry by himself. She called a local clinic for a referral and got the name of another pediatrician, Dr. Frazer. When she told Dr. Frazer about Justin's problem and expressed her frustration, he assured her that Justin probably wasn't wetting

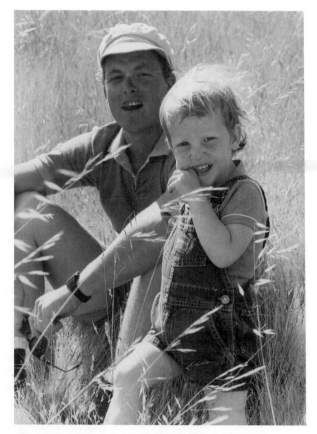

FIGURE 2-1
"Like father, like son." Besides his complexion and facial characteristics, what else has this little boy inherited from his father? Some child development theorists would answer, A great deal of what he is and will become.

his bed on purpose. He asked if there had been any unusual events in the household within the last year, or if anything else could be upsetting Justin.

Peggy explained that Justin's grandmother, who had spent a lot of time at their house, moved out of state about six months earlier to live in a retirement village. Justin hadn't seemed to miss her very much, Peggy told Dr. Frazer. "He goes to nursery school now," she said. "I think he's been too busy to miss her. It's his 20-month-old sister who seems to miss her the most. She stands by the telephone and says 'G'ma, G'ma'—I think because we used to call their grandma quite often to invite her over to our house."

Dr. Frazer noted that there had been three significant events in Justin's life within the fairly recent past—the birth of a baby sister, the start of nursery school, and his grandmother's move out of state. "The bed-wetting could be a symptom of any of these changes," Dr. Frazer explained. "Try talking with him about these events to see if one of them is troubling him. In the meantime, don't press him too hard about the toilet training. He might develop guilty or shameful feelings if you do. This might lead to 'fixation' in this stage of development and possibly to compulsive behavior later in life, such as not being able to go to sleep at night without three or four trips to the bathroom." Dr. Frazer suggested that Peggy give the problem another four to six months. If it hadn't improved by then, they might want to consider some sessions of play therapy.

Peggy was disturbed by Dr. Frazer's advice. She certainly didn't want to make toilet training traumatic for Justin or create any emotional problems that he would have to deal with later in life. She decided to stop trying to do anything about it for the time being. She resolved to stop worrying, too. But then her sister came to visit with her two children, and Peggy found out that her nieces had both been dry at night soon after the age of 3. Peggy's sister advised her to resolve the problem before it became "chronic." She knew of a doctor in Peggy's area who had been quite successful at treating bed-wetting, and Peggy made an appointment with her.

Dr. Rizzoli talked very confidently about her experience with night training. She was most enthusiastic about what she called a "Pavlov pad." This was a device that went on the child's bed at night. When the child urinated and wet the pad, an electric circuit closed. This caused a bell to ring, and the bell woke the child. After a few nights, the sensation of bladder fullness alone would awaken the child, who would then be able to go to the bathroom before wetting the bed.

Dr. Rizzoli also told Peggy how to begin what she called a behavior modification program. This was a systematic plan for changing behavior through rewards. She suggested that Justin be given a small treat or surprise each morning that he had a dry bed. To help "shape" this behavior, Dr. Rizzoli went on, Peggy and John could train Justin to hold his urine for longer and longer periods. They could wake him up to go to the bathroom at midnight for a few nights, then at 1 A.M., then at 2, and so on, until he could go through the whole night.

Peggy was glad to get some concrete advice at last. Yet she hesitated—she'd never heard of any of the things Dr. Rizzoli talked about, and no one she knew had ever had to go to such lengths to toilet train their children. She knew that John, who always seemed to believe that things would work out by themselves, would never go along with anything as elaborate as the Pavlov pad. When she heard another mother talking in the park about what she had done about bed-wetting, she couldn't help but join in the conversation. This mother said that her son had wet his bed until he was 8, and a wonderful doctor had helped them understand why. Naturally, Peggy got the doctor's name.

Dr. Graham stressed the importance of Justin's ability to understand what was involved in being dry at night and his interest in trying to change his behavior. She asked Peggy about Justin's language development and his understanding of some basic concepts,

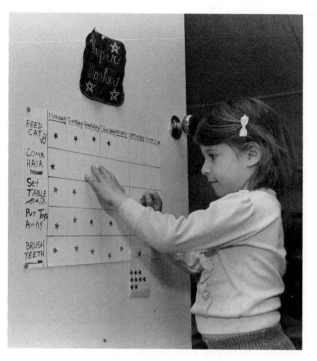

FIGURE 2-2
Behavior modification programs are based on the premise that rewards (such as gold stars) can be used to increase the occurrence of desirable behaviors. The premise seems to be effective for this "Super Worker" except when it comes to combing her hair.

such as why clouds move and where dreams come from. She asked Peggy if she thought Justin understood the whole toilet-training process and the extra work created when sheets and pajamas had to be washed each day. Dr. Graham suggested that Peggy and John have Justin tested with a developmental scale of some sort to determine how egocentric he was in his thinking about the social world. Peggy said she'd call Dr. Graham if she decided to make an appointment for the test.

Peggy went home and thought about everything she'd been told. She had taken notes on what each doctor said, and as she reviewed them she was struck by how differently each doctor approached the problem. For something as common as bed-wetting, she mused, you'd think all these professionals would know what to do. You'd think there would be one tried-and-true solution. Why does what one doctor said contradict what another one said? And what should I do with all this advice? It looks like John and I will have to put our heads together and sort out what seems appropriate for Justin by ourselves.

Peggy may have received contradictory advice, but the pediatricians she saw weren't trying to make her life difficult. The advice each one gave her was, no doubt, good advice, from that doctor's point of view. What none of them told her was that their advice was based on a *specific* point of view. Surely all the doctors knew about the Pavlov pad, yet only one recommended it. And all of them knew that bed-wetting correlates negatively with age—that is, bed-wetting decreases as age increases. Yet only one advised Peggy to wait for the problem to take care of itself as Justin got older.

The way that these doctors sift, sort, pay attention to, and select information is guided by their theoretical orientations, the way they think about the causes of behavior. As we explain the four major child development theories in the discussion that follows, you will be able to see the theoretical "camp" of each of the pediatricians Peggy consulted.

MATURATIONAL THEORY

Peggy's regular pediatrician, Dr. Blair, suggested that individual variations in behavior, like the age at which a child becomes dry at night, are the result of an inherited genetic timetable. This is why he tried to determine if Justin's parents had had bed-wetting problems as children and why he recommended that they just give Justin time. Dr. Blair believes in the maturational theory of child development.

Origins of Maturational Theory

Maturational theory was born in the late nineteenth century. It grew out of the work of Charles Darwin on evolution (1859) and the work of his cousin, Francis Galton. Galton was a British investigator who found that people who are genetically similar have comparable abilities. If one member of a family was intelligent, other members tended to be intelligent too. If one member was slow-witted, others were likely to be slow-witted. Galton concluded from his studies that intellectual abilities are inherited and fixed at birth.

Galton's conclusion, of course, was based on correlational data, and, as we saw in Chapter 1, correlational data can't be used to demonstrate cause-and-effect relationships. Members of the same family aren't just related genetically; they're also usually raised the same way. Family members may have intellectual similarities not because of similar genes but because of a similar environment. Galton's work didn't eliminate the possibility that this might be the case. Still, his discoveries spurred interest in the biological or genetic basis of behavior, the underlying idea of maturational theory.

According to this theory, heredity may influence the individual in two ways: (1) Some characteristics believed to be fixed by genes are present at birth—for example, eye color. (2) Other characteristics aren't present at birth but are believed to be fixed by genes anyway. They unfold according to an inherited timetable that regulates developmental processes. One example of this kind of characteristic is the age at which puberty begins. Another is final adult height. Another, according to Justin's pediatrician, Dr. Blair, is the age at which the bladder can be controlled during the night.

Maturation is the process of biological change and development during which new behaviors steadily emerge one after another. Maturational theory suggests that, within a broad range of normal conditions, the appearance of a particular behavior depends on time, not on experience or environment.

Maturational Theory in the Twentieth Century

The most prominent American advocate of maturational theory in the late nineteenth and early twentieth centuries was psychologist G. Stanley Hall (1844–1924). As the first president of the American Psychological Association and the founder of the first scientific psychological journal, *The Journal of*

FIGURE 2-3
G. Stanley Hall (seated, center) established the first formal laboratory of experimental psychology in the United States, but he was also interested in more introspective approaches to psychology, including the work of Sigmund Freud (seated, left). In 1909 he invited Freud to come to Clark University to give a series of lectures on psychoanalysis. Hall apparently found no contradiction between maturational and psychoanalytical theory, since he claimed that Freud's work was his chief inspiration for the next fifteen years.

FIGURE 2-4
Arnold Gesell devoted his career to studying the orderly emergence of behavior patterns in infants and children, such as the locomotor progression of rolling over, sitting up, crawling, pulling up, walking with support, standing alone, and walking alone. The founder of the Gesell Institute of Child Development at Yale University, he popularized the idea that children can't learn or develop new behaviors until they reach the appropriate level of physical and neurological readiness.

Genetic Psychology, Hall was a tremendously influential person. He expounded a biological view of human behavior with an emphasis on stages of development unfolding in a predetermined way.

One of Hall's most famous students was Arnold Gesell, a physician whose work was influential in the 1920s and 1930s. Gesell observed and described the ages at which different behaviors emerged, such as walking and talking. Like other maturational theorists, he believed that these skills developed in accordance with the individual child's inner timetable, regardless of learning or experience. Learning could occur only after the individual was biologically ready.

Readiness, also called **neurological ripening,** was a major idea put forth by Gesell. Until the nervous system was mature enough for a particular skill or behavior, the child was not considered ready for it. In the 1930s, for example, it was suggested that children not be exposed to any type of reading instruction until they had reached a mental age of 6.5 years, as measured by intelligence tests (Morphett & Washburne, 1931). This landmark, 6.5 years, was thought to be determined by the biological maturation of the nervous system. No one seriously considered the idea that we believe to be true today—that *both* readiness for reading *and* intelligence as measured by intelligence tests might be influenced by other, nonbiological factors, such as a child's experience with language.

Another well-known student of Hall's was Stanford University professor Lewis Terman. Terman's primary interest was intelligence testing, and he wrote an English translation of the test constructed by the Frenchmen, Binet and Simon (1905). This test became known as the Stanford-Binet Intelligence Test (Terman, 1916). It measured a person's intelligence, which was reported as an "intelligence quotient," or IQ. Terman believed that intelligence was basically a genetically fixed characteristic. Although children learned more the older they became, Terman thought their ability to learn—their IQ—was stable. We see later in this book that this assumption is open to question.

Several observers have remarked that child psychology in the first half of the twentieth century consisted merely of gathering data to establish **norms**—

BOX 2-1
Common Statements Based on a Maturational View of Child Development

- "We don't accept children for kindergarten until they're at least 5 years old."
- "Children aren't ready for reading until at least first grade."
- "Don't worry if your 2-year-old isn't toilet trained yet. When he's ready, he'll practically train himself."
- "Oh, she'll grow out of it. Just leave her alone."
- "Girls will be girls and boys will be boys."

age-related standards or patterns of behavior that applied to large groups—without the guidance of a theory. However, to a maturational theorist, establishing norms *is* part of a developmental theory, one in which maturation determines when behaviors will occur. Gathering data about the emergence of intellectual abilities, for example, was viewed as gathering data about the maturation of the nervous system. And maturation was the undisputed explanation of the times for the development of intellectual abilities. Intellectual and physical development were the main interests of maturational theorists.

Today, few psychologists believe that abilities are fixed by genes for life without any influence from the environment. But some people, including some psychologists, parents, teachers, and pediatricians, have ideas that lean in this direction. They believe that inherited characteristics and maturation play a critical role in development and that learning and external conditions aren't very important. Dr. Blair, Justin's pediatrician, holds this point of view about bed-wetting. In fact, we hear statements every day about child development that have a maturational basis—see Box 2-1 for some examples.

PSYCHOANALYTICAL THEORY

The second pediatrician Peggy visited, Dr. Frazer, was concerned about the emotional and social aspects of toilet training. He warned Peggy not to push Justin too much because a traumatic experience could leave him with emotional scars. Dr. Frazer's advice was molded by psychoanalytical theory, a view that originated with Sigmund Freud. We discuss Freud's work below, and then we discuss the work of Erik Erikson, who developed his own theory based on psychoanalytical ideas.

Sigmund Freud

In the early part of the twentieth century, while maturational theorists were looking at intellectual and physical development, Austrian physician Sigmund Freud (1856–1939) was studying social and personality development. Like the maturationists, Freud recognized the importance of biology, but he also stressed the interaction of biology with the environment. Freud was interested in neurology and in nervous disorders such as tics and various types of hysteria. He was advised by another Viennese doctor that patients' nervous symptoms improved when the patients were encouraged to talk about them (Hall & Lindzey, 1970). Freud tried this technique and had some success with it. This was the beginning of psychoanalysis, the therapy Freud sometimes referred to as "the talking cure."

FIGURE 2-5
Sigmund Freud found his heir in his youngest daughter, Anna, shown here in 1913 when she was 18 and he was 57. The only one of his six children to follow in his footsteps, Anna Freud went on to become a noted child psychotherapist in London.

FREUD'S NOTION OF INSTINCT. In his work Freud focused on the biological component of the personality, which he called instinct. Freud used this term differently than other theorists, who use it to refer to an innate behavior in animals. Freud defined instinct as a mental representation of a body state or need, such as hunger or sexual arousal (Freud, 1925). An understanding of Freud's idea of instinct is the key to his entire theory.

According to Freud, all actions are motivated by the desire to maximize instinctual gratification while minimizing punishment, guilt, and anxiety (Maddi, 1976). These motivations are what drive behavior. Because these needs are basically biological or physical, Freud's theory is a biological theory first of all. But environment is important too, because personality development depends on how the biologically based needs are met.

THE PARTS OF THE PERSONALITY. Freud suggested that the psyche or personality has three parts, the id, the ego, and the superego. The **id** is the inherited and unconscious source of instincts. It constantly propels the individual to relieve tension or excitation in the body—that is, to satisfy needs. The life of the young child is dominated by the id and characterized by the tendency to gratify selfish instincts.

TABLE 2-1   Freudian Defense Mechanisms

Defense	Definition	Example
Projection	Attributing an unacceptable thought or feeling to someone else; externalizing an internal experience	A child who dislikes a teacher feels that the teacher dislikes him.
Reaction formation	Doing the opposite of what one feels like doing to avoid experiencing an unacceptable impulse or feeling	A child who feels unsure of himself bullies other children and bosses them around.
Displacement	Transferring feelings from one event or person to a less threatening one	A child who is angry at her parents scolds her doll.
Acting out	Expressing an unconscious impulse directly rather than experiencing the emotion that accompanies it	A child sees her best friend playing with someone else and knocks down their block construction to avoid feeling jealous.
Repression	Blocking out an unacceptable thought or feeling	A child feels he would like to get rid of his father so he can have his mother all to himself, but he keeps the thought from reaching his conscious mind.
Sublimation	Redirecting energy associated with an unacceptable feeling into a socially acceptable activity	A teenager feeling strong sexual urges focuses intensely on practicing the piano.

However, the **ego**—the reality-oriented part of the personality—tries to direct the id to find satisfaction in appropriate ways, ways that won't be punished. The rules for appropriate behavior in a particular society are taught to the child by his or her parents, and these rules become part of the personality too. They make up the part called the superego. The **superego** guides the ego as it directs the id in finding acceptable gratifications, but often the superego blocks gratification altogether (Hall and Lindzey, 1970).

The ego keeps the id in check by means of ego defense mechanisms, such as repression and sublimation. (The Freudian defenses are listed and explained in Table 2-1.) In repression, the mind blocks out a thought that leads to anxiety, such as the thought of hurting another child. In sublimation, the energy associated with the unacceptable thought is displaced into some other, acceptable activity, such as pounding a lump of clay.

Let's consider an illustration to see how this works. Suppose a 2-year-old is still hungry after eating his lunch, and he starts eyeing his older sister's cupcake. In Freudian terms, we would say his id (his unconscious source of instincts) tells his ego (his conscious, reality-oriented mind) to eat the cupcake to relieve a bodily tension (hunger). As he reaches out for the cupcake, his sister may slap him to prevent him from taking her food, which her id is telling her she wants. Now he experiences a new bodily tension—pain—that outweighs the tension of the hunger and prevents him from trying to take the cupcake again.

After a number of encounters like this with the world outside himself, the boy develops a superego (a set of rules that he must obey if he's to avoid punishment or guilt) that guides his ego in choosing actions. In Freudian

When caught in an inner struggle between a strong desire and an equally stong fear of the consequences of disobeying, the child hesitates before choosing a course of action. A Freudian would say his budding ego is formulating ways to balance the demands of his id and his superego.

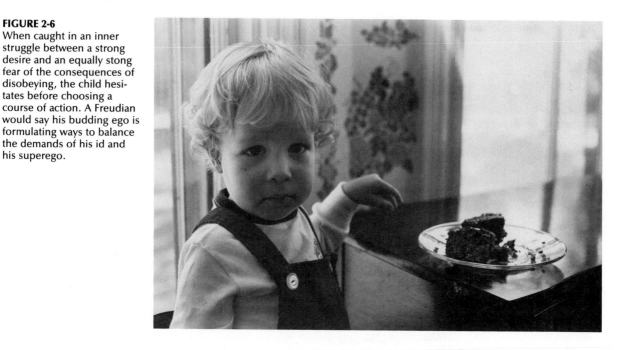

psychology, all behavior is a function of the id, the ego, and the superego, with the ego mediating between the other two. The ego tries to find ways to satisfy the demands of the id without violating the rules of the superego.

STAGES OF DEVELOPMENT IN FREUDIAN THEORY. The instincts responsible for the child's conflicts with the punishing world change "location" as the child moves from one stage of development to the next. Freud identified these stages as oral, anal, phallic, latency, and genital. Each one is associated with the particular zone of the body Freud thought was the source of troublesome instinctual energy for that period of life; that is, as the child matures physically, the instincts that are most likely to get the child into trouble change.

In the oral stage, lasting from birth to about 1 year of age, the mouth is the center of activity, the location of most satisfying (or frustrating) experiences. In the anal stage, which lasts from about the end of the first year to the end of the third, the anal region is the center of instinctual activity that comes in conflict with parental values. During this period, the child's developing sphincter control encourages the parents to attempt toilet training. The child, however, has an urge for immediate gratification of the instincts associated with defecation, so there is a conflict between child and parents. In the phallic stage, which lasts until about age 5, the genitals are the new source of prohibited instinctual activity. These early stages were considered by Freud to be especially important for personality development.

The latency stage lasts from age 5 or 6 until adolescence. During this stage, no new instincts or activities emerge to create problems. In adolescence, the genital stage begins, and mature love of others and socialized adult behavior become possible. Desires may still conflict with social rules, but the ego and superego keep the id in check.

FIGURE 2-7
Stages of development in Freudian theory. Early psychoanalysts believed that if instinctual energy became blocked in any one stage, characteristics of that stage would become embedded in the individual's personality. For example, someone who was fixated at the anal stage, when toilet training is an important issue, might be stingy, compulsive, punctual, and unable to let go of possessions or relationships.

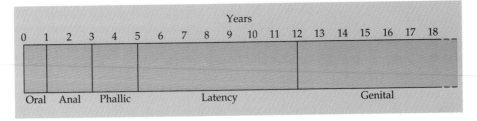

If instincts are not overgratified or undergratified by the parents, the child progresses naturally from one stage to the next, acquiring the defense mechanisms associated with each stage for keeping the id under control. These defense mechanisms largely determine the behavior we see. If the instincts are overgratified or undergratified at any point, however, the individual can become fixated at that stage. Some instinctual energy remains blocked in a previous zone rather than moving on to the next. As an adult, the individual continues to exhibit needs, defenses, and behavior more typical of individuals at an earlier stage. For example, an adult who overeats may be fixated at the oral stage. In our earlier illustration, Dr. Frazer, the second pediatrician Peggy consulted, was concerned that Justin might become fixated at the anal stage if his instinctual needs were undergratified at this point.

THE MEANING OF FREUDIAN THEORY FOR CHILD-REARING PRACTICES. Although Freud's theory asserted that fixation could result from either overgratification or undergratification, Freud lived in a formalized, repressive society with rigid rules about child rearing. It was much more likely in this setting that instincts would be undergratified than overgratified. Application of his theory, therefore, usually meant a loosening of rules to prevent fixation at any one stage. Although there has been very little research that clearly supports Freud's ideas, Freudian theory has been a tremendously influential force in twentieth-century thought. We often hear teachers and parents make statements that show they accept Freud's ideas (see Box 2-2).

Erik Erikson

Active in the 1940s, 1950s, and 1960s, Erik Erikson subscribed to a psychoanalytic view of personality development, but his focus was different from Freud's. Freud focused on the instincts, especially sex, as the driving force behind

BOX 2-2
Common Statements Based on a Psychoanalytic View of Child Development

- "It's better to feed a baby on demand than on a rigid schedule."
- "Children who suck their thumbs weren't allowed to suck the bottle or breast long enough when they were babies."
- "Nursery schools should have a punching bag so that children who tend to quarrel with other children can release their emotions in a constructive way."
- "Don't interfere with children's dramatic play; it's important that they work out their emotional conflicts."

FIGURE 2-8
Erik Erikson proposed that development proceeds through a series of stages, each with a crisis to be overcome, before identity is finally achieved. Many people in early childhood care and education programs find Erikson's theory particularly relevant to their work.

FIGURE 2-9
According to Erikson, a toddler who is allowed to explore without unnecessary restrictions will develop a sense of herself as a separate, autonomous being. Parents and caregivers can help by structuring the environment so it's safe to explore. Similarly, older children who succeed in school will develop feelings of competence and achievement. Teachers can help by individualizing learning experiences so that students at every level of ability experience success.

actions; Erikson focused more on how society affects the ego (in which he included the unconscious defense mechanisms as well as conscious thinking). Freud's emphasis was on the unconscious; Erikson's was more on the conscious and how it interacts with the outside world.

ERIKSON'S PSYCHOSOCIAL THEORY OF DEVELOPMENT. Erikson proposed that the major crisis at each developmental stage originates in the demands of society on the individual, rather than simply in bodily states, as Freud believed. He came to this idea because he recognized that healthy adaptation to reality differs from one society to another, something that wouldn't be true if human biology was the only determining factor in personality formation. He also saw that society's demands on a person change as the person changes and grows and that these demands can influence the course of development and growth. Erikson's theory has been called a psycho*social* theory of development to reflect Erikson's emphasis on the individual's adaptation to social situations and demands in contrast to Freud's psycho*sexual* view.

ERIKSON'S STAGES OF DEVELOPMENT. In Erikson's theory there are eight stages of development. Each stage is characterized by a major crisis or turning point, a time of increased vulnerability as well as increased potential for psychological growth. In Stage 1, which lasts from birth to about 18 months, the psychosocial conflict or crisis is between trust and mistrust. Depending on how the parent responds to the baby's needs, such as hunger, the baby will decide that he or she is either "all right" or "not all right." The appropriate resolution of this stage is the development of trust, but not complete trust, because that would lead to behavior that wasn't truly adaptive. This kind of appropriate resolution applies to each stage.

In Stage 2, which lasts from about 18 months to about 3½ years of age, the conflict is between autonomy on the one hand and shame and doubt on the other. If the child is allowed to move around, touch objects, and explore, and if toilet training is not severe, the child develops a sense of being a separate person, able to make choices and capable of some control over the world. In our illustration, Dr. Frazer considered Justin to be in this stage. He implied that Justin needed to develop a sense of autonomy by learning to stay dry without experiencing shame or doubt.

TABLE 2-2 Erikson's Eight Stages of Development

Psychosocial Conflict (Crisis)	Pivotal Events	Age	What a Person Learns When Development Proceeds Successfully
Trust vs. mistrust	Caregiver response to physical needs of infant, especially in feeding	Birth to 18 months	I am all right.
Autonomy vs. shame or doubt	Toilet-training, locomotion, exploration and touching of objects in environment	18 months to 3½ years	I can make choices.
Initiative vs. guilt	Curiosity resulting from increased language, motor, and cognitive skills	3½ to 6 years	I can do and I can make.
Industry vs. inferiority	School tasks such as learning to read	6 to 12 years	I can join with others in doing and making things.
Identity vs. identity confusion or diffusion	Learning one's vocational and professional orientation	Adolescence	I can be to others what I am to myself.
Intimacy vs. isolation	Love relationship	Young adult	I can risk offering myself to another.
Generativity vs. stagnation	Parenting, nurturing others, civic responsibility	Mature adult	I am concerned for others.
Integrity vs. despair	Reflection on one's life	Older adult	I can accept my life.

SOURCE: *Adapted from material in Erikson, E. H., Identity, youth and crisis.* New York: W. W. Norton, 1968.

Erikson's other stages are summarized in Table 2-2. Unlike Freud's stages, which continue only until the person reaches adulthood, Erikson's stages continue through the entire life span.

BEHAVIORAL THEORY

The third pediatrican Peggy saw, Dr. Rizzoli, didn't talk about Justin's emotional or intellectual development. Instead, she gave Peggy very concrete advice about what she could do to change Justin's bed-wetting behavior. Her emphasis was completely on the external or environmental aspects of the situation. She indicated that behavior is learned, especially through praise and reward. Dr. Rizzoli's advice reflects a behavioral point of view.

In contrast to psychoanalytic theorists, who focus on inner personality developments over time, behavioral theorists pay little attention to inner changes. They focus instead on observable, external behavior and how specific environments affect it. Psychoanalytic theory proposes that biologically based events set personality development in motion. Behavioral theory, on the other hand, recognizes no biological base for development (except, of course, that the individual be physically intact in a normal way).

Origins of Behavioral Theory

Behavioral theory originated in studies with animals, and it has been known by various names over the years, including learning theory, S-R theory, and behaviorism. The name "learning theory," as we saw above, refers to the focus on how a new behavior can be acquired. (In Justin's case, the new, learned behavior would be having a dry bed.) The name "S-R theory" refers to the connection between a stimulus ("S") in the environment and a response ("R") on the part of the organism. The name "behaviorism" reflects the belief that psychological theories should be based only on observable behavior and should not include references to inner states, such as thoughts, feelings, desires, anxieties, and so on. We explain these various aspects of behavioral theory as we summarize the history of its development.

CLASSICAL CONDITIONING. The roots of behavioral theory can be found in the work of the Russian physiologist Ivan Pavlov (1849–1936). Pavlov showed that under certain circumstances an animal can learn a new physiological response to a stimulus in the environment. These circumstances involve the pairing of the stimulus with another stimulus that produces a particular response naturally. After repeated pairings, the new stimulus produces the same response as the original stimulus. The response to the new stimulus is "conditional" on the previous pairing of the two stimuli. This type of learning is known as **classical conditioning.** Pavlov called the stimulus that produces the response naturally the **unconditioned stimulus** (often abbreviated UCS) and the new stimulus that is paired with it, or presented slightly before it, the **conditioned stimulus** (CS).

Pavlov's most famous illustration of classical conditioning involved teaching a dog to salivate at the sound of a bell. He rang a bell (the conditioned stimulus) at the same time that he gave the dog some food (the unconditioned stimulus), which naturally caused the dog to salivate (the **unconditioned response,** or UCR). After several of these learning situations, the sound of the bell alone caused the dog to salivate (the **conditioned response,** or CR).

The Pavlov pad recommended by Dr. Rizzoli is based on the principles of classical conditioning. In this case, the bell is the unconditioned stimulus that leads naturally to waking up, which is the unconditioned response. When the sensation of bladder fullness, the conditioned stimulus, is repeatedly paired with the bell, eventually the sensation alone leads to waking up. Waking up

FIGURE 2-10
In Ivan Pavlov's famous experiment, a minor operation is performed on a dog that exposes part of the salivary gland, and the flow of saliva is measured by a device attached to the dog's cheek. Pavlov conditioned dogs to salivate to a variety of signals, including a bell, a metronome, a light, and a rotating disk. Classical conditioning is a very simple form of learning that occurs only when a response is already one of the subject's naturally appearing behaviors.

now becomes a conditioned response. In diagram form, it would look like this:

Bell ringing (UCS)	leads to........	Waking up (UCR)
paired with		
Bladder fullness (CS)...	leads to.....	Waking up (CR)

We often see apparent examples of classical conditioning in child development. Placing a nipple in a baby's mouth naturally elicits sucking. After the baby repeatedly sees the nipple just before it's placed in her mouth, the sight of the nipple alone may cause her to start sucking. In this case, the sensation of the nipple in the mouth is the unconditioned stimulus that elicits sucking, the unconditioned response. The sight of the nipple is the conditioned stimulus that also comes to elicit sucking, which in this situation is a conditioned response.

One important aspect of classical conditioning is that after the initial conditioning, the unconditioned stimulus must be paired at least occasionally with the conditioned stimulus to "reinforce" the conditioned response. In other words, if the baby continued to see the nipple but didn't experience its being placed in her mouth, she would gradually stop sucking at the sight of the nipple. Another phenomenon associated with classical conditioning is that responses to conditioned stimuli may generalize to other, similar stimuli. In this example, the baby might start sucking at the sight of a pacifier or a nipple-shaped toy.

Another idea related to classical conditioning is that of secondary versus primary rewards. **Primary rewards** reduce the physiological tensions of hunger, thirst, sex, and pain. **Secondary rewards** come to have rewarding qualities by being associated with primary rewards. For example, a mother's smile may become a reward after being paired with food and other primary rewards. Although early behaviorists used terminology like "physiological needs" and "needs reduction," these biological states were never viewed as all-important for personality development in the way they were viewed by Freud.

INSTRUMENTAL CONDITIONING. Pavlov studied how behavior was influenced by stimuli that occurred *before* the behavior. An American psychologist, Edward Thorndike (1874–1949), was interested in how behavior was affected by events that occurred *after* the behavior. He showed that he could increase or decrease the frequency of a voluntary behavior if he followed it consistently with a reward or a punishment. This type of conditioning is known as **instrumental conditioning**, and it provides the basis for **behavior modification** programs. When Dr. Rizzoli advised Peggy to reward Justin each morning he had a dry bed, she was assuming that the frequency of this desired behavior would be affected by rewards contingent on the behavior. This means that the reward would follow only when the behavior, or a close approximation of it, actually occurred. If Peggy gave Justin the reward when he didn't have a dry bed—if she felt he was trying or if he was doing well for a few nights and then had an accident—she would defeat the purpose of the program.

THE SCIENCE OF BEHAVIOR. Another American psychologist, John B. Watson (1878–1958), was sharply critical of the introspective methods of studying human behavior used by other psychologists. He thought there were bound to be inaccuracies in people's own reports of their reactions to various stimuli, and these procedures couldn't be used with children or animals, the subjects in whom he was most interested. Above all, Watson wanted psychology to be a science of behavior, which he called **behaviorism.** He believed that valid data could be obtained only from the observation of behavior, those things that people actually say or do. For his revolutionary work Watson is known as the "father of behaviorism."

B. F. Skinner

The most influential, and probably the most radical, contemporary behaviorist is B. F. Skinner (b. 1904). Skinner's brand of behaviorism completely rejects such concepts as drives that are in some sense inside the organism and therefore unobservable. Instead, it attempts to explain behavior only in terms of what can be observed.

Skinner replaces the concept of reward with the concept of **reinforcement.** A reinforcer is defined as any observable stimulus that increases the frequency of a response when it's presented contingent on the response—that is, when it follows the response. Skinner called this process of increasing the frequency of a behavior by adding a reinforcing stimulus **operant conditioning**. (Thorndike had referred to the same type of learning as instrumental conditioning.)

Some reinforcers are **positive**—they consist of something added to the environment following a response. If a child asks politely for a cookie, for example,

FIGURE 2-11
One of the learning processes demonstrated by B. F. Skinner in experiments with animals was shaping, which he believed accounted for the learning of new behaviors. If he wanted a pigeon to walk with its head held very high, for example, he gave it grain first when it held its head slightly higher than average, then considerably above average, then stretched very high. Eventually the pigeon carried its head high most or all of the time. Skinner suggested that children learn language (among other things) by the process of shaping, increasing the sounds their parents reinforce and dropping those their parents fail to reinforce.

and her parent gives her one, the child is positively reinforced for being polite. If the child begs and whines for the cookie and gets one, she's positively reinforced for begging and whining. The cookie is the positive reinforcer that increases the likelihood that the behavior—whether polite or whiny—will occur again.

Other reinforcers are **negative**—they consist of removing something from the environment following a response. Let's consider the case of the child and the cookie again but from the parent's point of view. If the child is whining and the parent gives her a cookie, the whining stops. Something offensive has been removed from the parent's environment. If the parent then gives cookies more frequently to stop the whining, we say that the parent's cookie-giving behavior has been negatively reinforced. Both positive and negative reinforcers increase the likelihood that certain responses will occur again, the former by adding something, the latter by removing something.

One of Skinner's interests was how new behaviors are acquired. He and his followers became well known for teaching a new behavior by taking an existing, similar behavior and reinforcing it to bring it closer and closer to the desired behavior. This process of reinforcing successive approximations until the desired behavior appears is known as **shaping.**

In our illustration, Dr. Rizzoli suggested that Justin's parents wake him up during the night to have him go to the bathroom and that they wake him up later and later as time went on. Thus, they could reinforce Justin for morning dryness from the beginning, even though his initial behavior only approximated complete nighttime dryness.

Social Learning Theory

Recently, some behavioral theorists, notably Julian Rotter and Albert Bandura, have been much more willing to discuss thinking, reasoning, and other conscious mental processes than earlier behaviorists were (Rotter, Liverant, & Crowne, 1961; Bandura, 1973, 1977). Their ideas have been labeled **social learning theory.** Bandura has pointed out that many behaviors are learned not gradually through shaping but quickly through observation and imitation. It's unlikely, for example, that many of us could learn to drive a car through shaping, which depends so heavily on trial and error. We might not live through the first lesson. Instead, we learn through the cognitive processes of verbal instruction and imitation.

One social learning theorist, Walter Mischell, suggests that an individual's behavior in a particular situation is determined not by the situation alone but by a whole complex of inner qualities that the individual brings to the situation (Mischell, 1976). These might include abilities, values, expectations, interpretations, plans, and so on. These qualities are not observable and are essentially cognitive (that is, they involve knowledge). Mischell noted that the same stimulus or situation—for example, a classroom test—elicits different responses from different individuals, depending on what qualities and interpretations they apply to it. Thus, whereas the radical behaviorist would assert that the stimulus controls the response in a strict way, the social learning theorist allows room for individual variation in the stimulus-response pattern.

Examples of common statements based on behavioral or learning theory are given in Box 2-3.

FIGURE 2-12
Social learning theorists point out that human beings learn many behaviors through verbal instruction, observation, and imitation. This toddler already knows how to sit and look at the pages of a magazine just like his grandpa. He probably also knows that people get important and interesting information by engaging in this behavior.

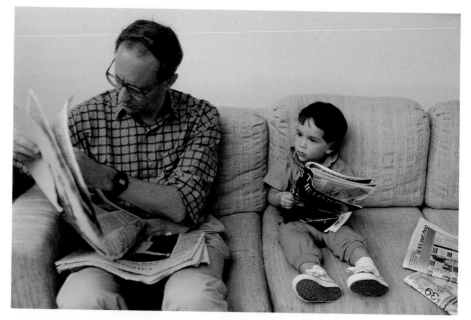

COGNITIVE-INTERACTIONIST THEORY: JEAN PIAGET

The last pediatrician Peggy saw, Dr. Graham, asked if Justin understood what was expected of him and if he seemed to be interested in changing his behavior. This doctor probed Justin's general knowledge and understanding of the world. She wanted to evaluate his level of cognitive development, apparently to determine if he was capable of understanding his behavior and how it affected others. If he didn't have these understandings, a method like rewarding his behavior would be of little use or might even have a negative impact, according to Dr. Graham. If he did have these understandings, then his mother could make use of them to help him become dry at night.

Interest in cognition as a factor in determining behavior grew rapidly in the 1950s. Theorists and researchers began to note that learning often occurred in situations that didn't seem to involve the satisfaction of needs and drives.

BOX 2-3
Common Statements Based on a Behavioral View of Child Development

- "You may watch television after you finish your homework."
- "In our math program children learn just one small step at a time. Success is guaranteed and children want to keep working with the materials."
- "When you finish your reading and math assignments, you may paint, play with blocks, or choose a learning game."
- "Ignore children when they're behaving badly; praise them when they're behaving well."
- "You'll spoil the baby if you pick him up when he cries."
- "Children who answer correctly will receive a gold star on their papers."
- "The baby stops crying as soon as she hears my footsteps. I guess she knows that she'll be fed soon."
- "If children see you hitting, they learn to hit."

One researcher found that monkeys would learn a task when it was followed by an opportunity to look at something outside their cages (Butler, 1953). An earlier researcher had found similar behavior in rats who would cross an electrified grid to get to a maze filled with new objects (Nissen, 1930). Some theorists suggested that there might be a drive to explore or to manipulate (White, 1959), but others looked for a different explanation. The study of cognition seemed to be a fruitful area for investigation.

Since the 1930s, Swiss psychologist and biologist Jean Piaget (1896–1980) had been studying the development of cognition. His work proved to be very important for the insight it provided into children's behavior. Piaget wanted to understand what knowledge is and how people acquire it, and he approached the question of adult knowledge by investigating children's knowledge. He asked two basic questions: Why do children and adults think differently in similar situations? What causes human knowledge to change over time?

In his studies Piaget found that children have different levels of understanding at different ages. Their responses to a situation are determined not just by the situation alone but by how they understand the situation. This is the crux of the cognitive-interactionist theory.

Piaget's Explanation of Knowledge Acquisition

Piaget's explanation for the changes in a person's knowledge over time is quite complex. He sees knowledge as constructed or created gradually as people interact with their environment. Children are thus seen as being active in their own development. In maturational theory, you will recall, the child is at the mercy of the genes that determine the rate of maturation. When the child is physically ready for learning—when neural ripening has occurred for a certain area of development—the child can acquire knowledge quite easily from the environment.

Behavioral theorists also believe that knowledge is external, but they think it can be acquired through experience and reinforcement. Piaget, on the other hand, does not think of knowledge as something that exists independently in

FIGURE 2-13
Jean Piaget devoted his life to the study of children's intellectual development. He was interested in their ideas on every subject, from the rules of games as an index of their moral development to the origin of dreams as a clue to their understanding of thinking.

the external world and that a person can simply acquire. Knowledge is a creation resulting from the interaction of the person and the environment.

PROCESSES BY WHICH KNOWLEDGE IS ACQUIRED. Piaget proposed two processes to explain how knowledge is created and changed over time. **Assimilation** is the process of taking in information about the environment and incorporating it into an existing knowledge structure, or, as Piaget calls it, a **scheme**. A 2-year-old who is familiar with dogs, for example, can be said to have a dog scheme, which may cover medium-sized, four-legged animals found in people's houses. The first time the child sees a cat, she may call it a dog, because that's the most appropriate scheme she has. Gradually, as she sees more cats and notices how they're different from dogs, she develops two schemes, one for cats and one for dogs. This process of changing knowledge structures is known as **accommodation**.

Our schemes are always inadequate to handle all our experiences (Piaget, 1963), so assimilation tends to distort information from the environment to make it fit available schemes. Eventually, these distortions are corrected as we change schemes to accommodate the new information. In this way our schemes come to conform more closely to the world around us. The 2-year-old changes her dog scheme to exclude animals that meow and climb trees, and she develops a cat scheme that includes these characteristics. Eventually her schemes will accurately reflect all the characteristics of both types of animal.

Piaget uses the term **equilibration** to refer to the process by which assimilation and accommodation attempt to balance each other. When children first start to learn about the world, it takes a long time for assimilated information to be accommodated. But as thinking becomes more complex, and as the person develops more and more schemes, accommodation occurs more quickly.

PIAGET'S STAGES OF DEVELOPMENT. Assimilation and accommodation lead not just to more knowledge but to reorganizations of knowledge, to different ways of thinking. The points at which reorganization takes place mark the beginnings of different stages. Each stage is characterized by a unique way of thinking. The four stages proposed by Piaget are summarized in Table 2-3, and we discuss each stage in considerable detail in later chapters.

TABLE 2-3
Piaget's Stages of Cognitive Development

Stage	Description
Sensorimotor (0–18 months)	Knowledge is acquired and structured through sensory perception and motor activity. Schemes involve action rather than symbols.
Preoperational (2–6 years)	Knowledge is acquired and structured through symbols, such as words, but schemes are intuitive rather than logical.
Concrete operational (7–12 years)	Knowledge is acquired and structured symbolically and logically, but schemes are limited to concrete and present objects and events.
Formal operational (12 years and older)	Knowledge is acquired and structured symbolically and logically, and hypothetical/deductive ("if-then") thinking can be used to generate all the possibilities in a particular situation.

BOX 2-4
Common Statements Based on
a Cognitive-Interactionist
View of Child Development

- "Children learn best when they're interested in what they're doing."
- "Children are active learners."
- "When children answer questions incorrectly, ask them why they answered as they did before deciding how to help them arrive at the correct answer."
- "Children seek stimulation."
- "Don't put all of the new toys out in the classroom at once; add new ones gradually to renew interest."

Piaget's Influence

Piaget's theories have been enormously influential in many areas of child development. One implication of his ideas is that children will prefer moderately novel events because these are the events that are most likely to be accommodated (Hunt, 1965). Completely familiar events may be uninteresting to the child because they require no change in scheme. But completely unfamiliar events may be incomprehensible to the child because the child has no scheme into which to assimilate them.

Piaget's ideas provide a theoretical basis for the notion of **intrinsic motivation**, or motivation that comes from cognitive processes (Hunt, 1965). In other words, a child may initiate actions without being motivated by hunger, thirst, sex, or pain and without being rewarded or punished. Children will act simply to understand. When they're interested in something, they're indicating both that they understand it in some sense and that they're trying to understand it in a better way. Because children's schemes differ from adults', children's interests also differ from adults'.

The cognitive-interactionist theory is evident in many child-rearing and educational practices and beliefs, and some examples are listed in Box 2-4.

THEORY, RESEARCH, AND VALUES: WHY THE CONTRADICTIONS EXIST

Each of the four major theories described above has its avid proponents, and each has a body of research that supports it. Each one proposes a different way of approaching child development, and each one structures information about the world in a particular way. In addition, the different theories often focus on different aspects of development. Maturational theory focuses mainly on physical and intellectual development. Psychoanalytic theory focuses on personality development. Cognitive theory deals with intellectual growth. And behavioral theory concerns itself with intellectual and personality development.

Theoretical orientation affects the kind of questions that researchers ask and the kind of research that might be done to answer the questions. A researcher with a maturational orientation might collect data about the average age at which a particular behavior appears. A researcher with a psychoanalytic orientation might collect information about significant experiences occurring during childhood and then see if a relationship to problems during adulthood could be established. A researcher with a behavioral orientation might keep

FIGURE 2-14
When we observe and study children, what questions will we ask? What answers do we hope to find? The way we organize our ideas and perceptions about the world will strongly influence the conclusions we reach.

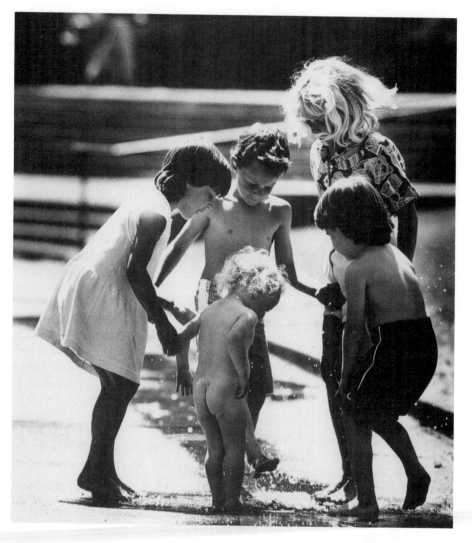

track of the kinds of responses that parents make toward their child's misbehavior. A cognitively oriented researcher might record children's answers to questions about the way things work. Of course, data collected can be explained in different ways, and theoretical orientation guides what a researcher makes of the data.

Some professionals—doctors, teachers, social workers, and so on—will take the time to be well-informed about research that spans a number of theoretical positions and to explain the evidence for each view to parents. But because this does take time, professionals often present the point of view they believe to be most credible without even mentioning the others. Parents often have to visit different doctors, schools, or agencies to get the different "pictures" of the problem. We saw that this was what Peggy had to do.

Why is it that one person will view behaviors as basically driven by internal factors and another will see them as driven by external factors? Why is one person interested in the long-term emotional effects of a treatment and another interested only in how successfully it changes behavior? Theoretical orientations are shaped by several factors, including prevailing social and cultural ideas, the influence of respected teachers and authority figures, religious and philosophical beliefs, and personal inclinations and experience.

We expect scientists to base their theoretical views on objective analysis of evidence rather than on subjective beliefs, but it may not be possible for any human being to do this. There probably is no such thing as a purely "objective" analysis, given that all analyses are undertaken from some theoretical point of view. "We see what we know"—what we think we see is shaped by what we know or expect to be there. (See Wittgenstein, 1963, for a discussion of this intriguing idea.)

In a wonderful contemporary book about the solar system, *Coming of Age in the Milky Way,* Timothy Ferris describes the work of early philosophers and scientists attempting to explain celestial events. Many of them fit "facts" about the planets and stars to their ideas or models of the solar system, rather than allowing the "facts" to shape their models. It took a revolutionary thinker like Copernicus to get the "facts" straight, even though others had observed the same data for many, many years. Theories shaped the heavens in powerful ways for the people of an earlier age, just as theories shape the world for us today.

OVERVIEW

Data and theories interact in complex and subtle ways. We need theories to organize and make sense of the world, but how we perceive the world is influenced by our theories. Theories of child development provide a framework for the infinite variety of interpretations we can make of a child's behavior. Without them, we would lack the signposts and guiding principles that broaden our understanding and give meaning to our observations. At the same time, by their very nature, theories limit the aspects of children's behavior that we see or pay attention to; a single theory is always only one way of viewing a child's experience. When we understand this limitation, we can use the theories of child development in ways that increase our understanding without narrowing our perspectives.

CHAPTER REVIEW

- Theories of child development are sets of assumptions about why children act the way they do. The four major child development theories are the matura-tional, the psychoanalytical, the behavioral, and the cognitive-interactionist. Theoretical orientation strongly influences how experts see children.

MATURATIONAL THEORY

- Maturational theorists believe that particular behaviors emerge at predetermined times, depending on the individual's inherited biological timetable, and that the timing is unaffected by environment or experience.
- Based on the work of Darwin and Galton, maturational theory dates from the nineteenth century and was expounded in the United States in the early twentieth century by G. Stanley Hall.
- Working in the 1920s and 1930s, maturational theorist Arnold Gesell described the regular emergence of dif-ferent behaviors in children and explained them in terms of readiness, or neurological ripening, regardless of experience.
- Lewis Terman was responsible for the Stanford-Binet intelligence test, which measured a person's intelligence quotient, or IQ. Maturationists believe that IQ is fixed at birth.
- Maturational theorists gather data to establish norms. The main focuses of their research are physical and intellectual development.

PSYCHOANALYTICAL THEORY

- Developed by Sigmund Freud in the late nineteenth and early twentieth centuries, psychoanalytical theory is concerned mainly with personality development.
- Freud focused on the biological aspect of the personality, which he called instinct. He believed the body was driven by desires, particularly sexual desires, which were represented by mental images. The way people behaved was a result of their attempts to gratify these desires.
- Behavior is shaped, according to psychoanalytical theory, by the interactions of the id, seeking gratification; the superego, setting limits; and the ego, directing the id to find satisfaction in acceptable ways. The ego keeps the id in check by means of defense mechanisms, such as repression and sublimation.
- The instincts that drive the child change from one period of life to the next. Freud identified five stages of development—oral, anal, phallic, latency, and genital. Children progress smoothly from one stage to another provided they don't become fixated, or stuck, in one stage by over- or undergratification.
- Erik Erikson focused not on instinct as the driving force behind actions but on the interaction of the ego and society. He suggested that conflicts arise at different stages of development because of societal demands on the individual.
- Erikson proposed eight stages of development, spanning not just childhood but the entire lifetime. Each stage is marked by a major crisis, the resolution to which either hampers the individual's growth or allows the person to move on psychologically to the next stage.

BEHAVIORAL THEORY

- Behaviorists focus on observable behavior and how it is affected by the environment. Behavioral theory is also known as learning theory, S-R theory, and behaviorism.
- Russian physiologist Ivan Pavlov demonstrated that animals can learn a new physical response to an environmental stimulus through a process known as classical conditioning. His most famous experiment involved conditioning a dog to salivate at the sound of a bell.
- American psychologist Edward Thorndike showed that he could increase or decrease the number of times a response occurred if he followed it with a reward or a punishment. This type of learning, known as instrumental conditioning, provides the basis for behavior modification programs.
- The best-known contemporary exponent of behaviorism, B. F. Skinner, redefined rewards as reinforcers and instrumental conditioning as operant conditioning. Skinner demonstrated that new behaviors could be taught by reinforcing closer and closer approximations of a desired behavior until the behavior itself appears, a process known as shaping.
- John B. Watson is known as the "father of behaviorism" because he argued that objective observation should replace self-report as the method of studying the effects of stimuli.
- Social learning theorists are more willing to discuss conscious mental processes and inner experiences than strict behaviorists like Skinner. They also pointed out that people learn things through observation and imitation as well as through reinforcement and shaping.

COGNITIVE-INTERACTIONIST THEORY: JEAN PIAGET

- The idea that behavior and learning could be explained by something other than the satisfaction of drives or the reinforcement of responses to stimuli led theorists to begin investigating cognitive factors. The work of Jean Piaget tied in with these interests.
- Piaget discovered that children have different levels of understanding at different ages, which accounts for the fact that they don't think the same way adults do. He also found that responses to the environment depend not just on the situation but on how the individual understands the situation.
- According to Piaget, knowledge is constructed gradually through interactions with the environment. The child takes in information from the environment and incorporates it into an existing knowledge structure, or scheme. This process is known as assimilation. Since schemes are inadequate to handle all new information, the child gradually adjusts the schemes to make better sense of the information. This process is known as accommodation. Equilibration is the process by which assimilation and accommodation are kept in balance.
- Piaget proposed four stages of cognitive development, each characterized by a different, unique way of thinking: sensorimotor, preoperational, concrete operational, and formal operational.
- Piaget's findings suggest that children learn best when confronted with moderately novel events and that the desire to understand is a powerful motivating force behind children's behavior.

THEORY, RESEARCH, AND VALUES

- Theories of child development differ in their focus and in the way they structure information about the world. Maturational theory is concerned mainly with physical and intellectual development, psychoanalytical theory with personality development, behavioral theory with intellectual and personality development, and cognitive-interactionist theory with intellectual development.

- Given the complexity of both the world and the ways we can understand it, it's probably impossible to form a purely "objective" opinion about the causes of human behavior.

KEY TERMS

theories	superego	instrumental conditioning	shaping
maturation	classical conditioning	behavior modification	social learning theory
readiness	unconditioned stimulus	behaviorism	assimilation
neurological ripening	conditioned stimulus	reinforcement	scheme
norms	unconditioned response	operant conditioning	accommodation
instinct	conditioned response	positive reinforcement	equilibration
id	primary rewards	negative reinforcement	intrinsic motivation
ego	secondary rewards		

SUGGESTIONS FOR FURTHER READING

Baroody, A. (1987). *Children's mathematical thinking.* New York: Teachers College Press.

This book opens with a discussion of two views of learning, the cognitive view and the behavioral view. Other chapters highlight corresponding differences in approaches to curriculum and to evaluation and remediation of children's difficulties in learning mathematics. The book provides a concrete example of how different theories lead to different observations and actions.

Ferris, T. (1988). *Coming of age in the Milky Way.* New York: William Morrow.

This book tells the story of how human beings have come to their current understanding of the universe. Throughout history, human models have often matched theories more closely than they matched data. From ancient astronomers to present day astrophysicists, scientists "see what they know." This book provides interesting reading for the lay astronomer or philosopher of science.

Goodfield, J. (1981). *An imagined world.* New York: Harper & Row.

This story of a medical scientist investigating lymphocytes beautifully illustrates how we see what our theory leads us to expect. This scientist saw things differently from other researchers because she went to her microscope with a different theory about lymphocytes. Well-written and engrossing.

Maier, H. (1978). *Three theories of child development.* (3rd ed.). New York: Harper & Row.

This book discusses and compares three theories: the cognitive theory of Piaget, the behavioral theory of Sears, and the psychoanalytic theory of Erikson. It also discusses application of the theories to the helping process.

Nuland, S. B. (1988). *Doctors: The biography of medicine.* New York: Knopf.

This history of medicine and physicians provides many examples of how people's views—their theories—shape what they see and do. Readable and fascinating.

chapter 3

GENETICS, PRENATAL DEVELOPMENT, AND BIRTH

Lindsay woke from an afternoon nap with a start. The phone was ringing, but she couldn't bring herself to answer it. It was four and a half weeks since her amniocentesis, and any phone call could be the one from her obstetrician with the results. She let the answering machine take the call. Then, her heart pounding, she listened to the tape. She recognized her doctor's voice at once.

"Hello, Lindsay," he said. "This is Dr. Cortez. I know you're eager to hear the results of your amniocentesis, so I'll leave a message for you on your machine. Everything appears to be fine this time. And—it's a boy. Congratulations! I'll see you next week for your regular check-up."

Lindsay let out a shout of joy. Five years earlier, she had had a baby who was not fine. Samuel had seemed all right at birth, but when he was 8 months old, she noticed some worrisome changes. Instead of getting stronger and more mobile, he seemed to be getting floppier and weaker. He couldn't sit up as well as he could a month earlier, and he no longer seemed to be able to hold on to his toys. He stopped trying to crawl and pull himself up in his crib. Tests revealed that he was a victim of Tay-Sachs disease, a degenerative disorder of the nervous system. He went through a harrowing deterioration and died at the age of 22 months.

Lindsay's genetic counselor told her that although she and her husband were healthy, they were both carriers of Tay-Sachs disease. Any child they conceived would have a one in four chance of having the disease. For a long time they debated whether they should try to have any more children of their own. At last they decided to try again, this time making sure they had an amniocentesis to determine if the baby was healthy. They hadn't really thought beyond the amniocentesis, but they did know they wanted that information as soon as possible. After that, they'd consider their options.

Lindsay felt euphoric as she dialed her husband to tell him the good news. At last she could allow herself to think about this baby. For the first time in months she would be able to relax.

FIGURE 3-1
Natural childbirth classes help prepare a woman for a birth experience she can manage without excessive use of pain-relieving drugs. In this class, the women's partners are helping them learn relaxation techniques they'll be able to use during labor.

Lindsay's story isn't unusual today, but 25 years ago it would have been unthinkable. Advances in technology and knowledge have revolutionized pregnancy and birth for countless couples. Consider these new practices and trends:

- Couples thinking of starting a family can consult a genetic counselor to find out if they're likely to transmit a hereditary disease or abnormality to their child.
- Couples can choose when and if to have a child by using any of a number of birth control methods, rather than leaving the size of their family up to chance.
- Infertile couples can try a variety of conception methods, including artificial insemination and in vitro fertilization.
- Women can determine whether they're pregnant within 20 to 30 days of conception by using a urine test.
- Pregnant women can find out the sex of their baby and whether certain physical problems or genetic abnormalities are present through the use of ultrasound and amniocentesis.
- Pregnant women are advised to eat well, get adequate exercise and rest, abstain from alcohol, drugs, and cigarettes, and reduce the amount of stress in their lives.

- Women who attend prepared childbirth classes can actively participate in the birth process with reduced use of pain-relieving drugs.
- A majority of women are breastfeeding their babies.
- Fathers can be present at births, even when cesarean sections are performed.
- The emotional aspects of childbirth are being taken seriously by health care professionals. Some women are having their babies in alternative birth centers or at home. Challenged by prospective parents, hospitals are changing many of their traditional practices to promote the emotional well-being of mothers and babies alike.

In this chapter we discuss genetics, prenatal development, and birth. Each of these areas has a direct impact on what kind of child a baby will eventually become. Each of these areas, too, has undergone profound changes in recent years, as a result of research discoveries, new technologies, and changing attitudes and social policies. Now more than ever we have a greater opportunity—and a greater responsibility—to see that all children get as fair a chance as possible, right from the start.

GENETICS: THE BASIS OF BIOLOGICAL INHERITANCE

You don't have to look very far to see the incredible variation that exists within our human species. People come in a vast array of sizes, shapes, and colors, to name just a few of the variables we might observe. Hair, for example, can be thick or thin; coarse or fine; curly, wavy, or straight; and red, brown, black, blond, gray, or white, with many shadings in between. Within the organism, beyond our observing eye, are other variations—blood type, heart rate, hormone levels, intelligence, musical or artistic talent, predisposition to die young or live to a ripe old age.

What accounts for all these differences? What makes every human being a unique individual, unlike any other person who has ever lived or will ever live on the planet? The answer to these questions, or at least a large part of it, is genetic inheritance. Genetic inheritance doesn't *determine* everything a person is and becomes, but it does *influence* everything a person is and becomes. How much the person is affected by genetic inheritance—as opposed to environmental influences—is a long-standing question in the study of child development. We sometimes refer to this so-called **nature-nurture controversy** in subsequent chapters when we discuss the effects of genetic inheritance on various aspects of development. To appreciate the controversy, and to understand an important part of development, you must know the basics of genetics.

Genes and Chromosomes

Genetics is the study of how biological traits are transmitted from one generation to the next. All of these traits are encoded in **genes**, whether we're talking about sex, eye color, final adult height, left- or right-handedness, or any of thousands of characteristics. Every gene is a sequence of nucleic acids (DNA), which encodes the information needed to produce a protein, the basic building block of the cell. Genes are contained on **chromosomes**, extremely

FIGURE 3-2
Scientists learned what substance was responsible for genetic inheritance when they unraveled the structure of deoxyribonucleic acid (DNA). The DNA molecule consists of two strands connected in a twisting, ladder-like spiral known as a double helix. When the DNA molecule replicates, the two complementary sides of the double helix separate, and each strand makes an exact copy of its complement, resulting in two identical molecules. The double helix structure is clear in this photomicrograph of DNA.

FIGURE 3-3
Chromosomes are contained in the nucleus of the cell, which appears as a dark mass in this illustration of a human cell (top). The two twisting strands and the ladderlike bars connecting them are shown in the artist's model of part of a DNA molecule, shown at the bottom.

long strands of DNA coiled up in the nucleus of each cell. Chromosomes are long enough to be visible when we view a dyed cell under a powerful microscope.

Chromosomes occur in pairs, and every normal human body cell contains 23 of these pairs. The genes on one chromosome have counterparts on the other chromosome in the pair. The pairs of genes interact to determine which characteristics a person will inherit. Some genes are **recessive**—the information they carry won't be translated into a particular biological trait unless they're paired with another recessive gene. Blue eye color is an example of a recessive trait. To have blue eyes, a person has to have inherited a recessive gene for eye color from each parent.

Other genes are **dominant**—they override their gene partner so that their characteristic is always expressed. Brown eye color is dominant. A person with brown eyes may have inherited the recessive gene for blue eyes from one parent, but the dominant gene inherited from the other parent overrode that recessive gene. Some characteristics, such as hair color, are controlled by a single gene pair. Many others, such as intelligence, seem to be influenced by the actions of many pairs of genes.

Cell Division and Conception

Each of us has thousands of genes, and each of us has, in every cell, a unique set of genes that makes us distinct individuals. This unique set is produced at the moment of conception from the combining of two cells, an egg contributed by the mother and a sperm contributed by the father. Eggs, or ova (singular, ovum), and sperm—known as **germ cells** because they're involved in reproduction—are different from all other cells in the body, which are known as **somatic cells.**

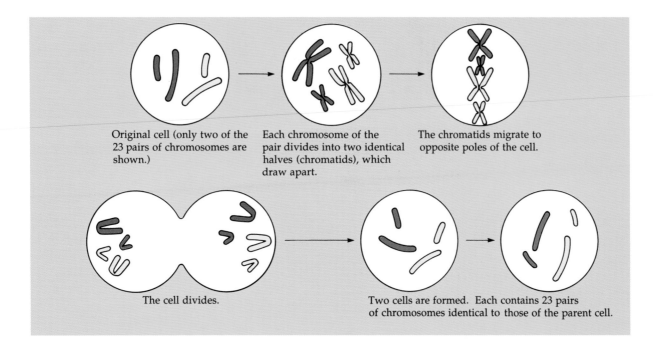

Original cell (only two of the 23 pairs of chromosomes are shown.)

Each chromosome of the pair divides into two identical halves (chromatids), which draw apart.

The chromatids migrate to opposite poles of the cell.

The cell divides.

Two cells are formed. Each contains 23 pairs of chromosomes identical to those of the parent cell.

FIGURE 3-4
Body cells replicate by mitosis. One cell divides, producing two new cells that are genetically identical to the original cell. This is the process by which bone, muscle, skin, and other cells of the body grow and repair themselves.

Germ cells differ from body cells in the way they divide. For example, when we grow new skin cells or hair cells, a parent cell (or original cell) divides to produce two new cells, each containing the same 23 pairs of chromosomes as the parent. Each new cell, with its 46 chromosomes, is identical to the parent cell. This type of cell division, in which the original cell is exactly duplicated, is called **mitosis** (Figure 3-4).

Germ cells, however, are designed to combine with other germ cells to produce an altogether new cell. If each germ cell brought 46 chromosomes to conception, the resulting organism would have 92 chromosomes. Obviously, this isn't what happens. Germ cells are prepared for conception by a different kind of cell division, called **meiosis**. In this kind of cell division, the number of chromosomes in the cell is reduced by half (Figure 3-5).

Meiosis provides the biological mechanism for the mixing and combining of characteristics that make every individual unique. During the crossing-over step shown in Figure 3-5, chromosome pairs in the parent cell wrap around each other and exchange genetic material. When they unwrap and the cell divides, the new cells contain genes that make them different from the parent cell and from each other. This accounts for the differences we see between parents and children and between siblings. Crossing over makes the possibilities for unique combinations virtually limitless (Pai, 1974).

Determination of Sex

One of the 23 pairs of chromosomes determines whether a fetus will be female or male. Females have a matching set of sex chromosomes, called XX (from the way they look under an electron microscope). Males have one X chro-

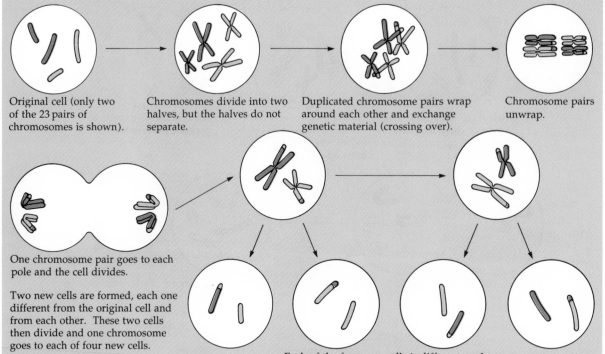

Original cell (only two of the 23 pairs of chromosomes is shown).

Chromosomes divide into two halves, but the halves do not separate.

Duplicated chromosome pairs wrap around each other and exchange genetic material (crossing over).

Chromosome pairs unwrap.

One chromosome pair goes to each pole and the cell divides.

Two new cells are formed, each one different from the original cell and from each other. These two cells then divide and one chromosome goes to each of four new cells.

Each of the four new cells is different, and each contains a total of 23 *single* chromosomes.

FIGURE 3-5
Germ cells replicate by meiosis, a process that results in cells with two important features: They contain 23 single chromosomes rather than 23 pairs of chromosomes, and they're genetically different from the original cell rather than identical to it. With these characteristics, eggs and sperm can combine to create a genetically new human being.

FIGURE 3-6
The wonders of human genetics are responsible for families in which each person resembles everyone else and yet remains a unique individual. The two genetically unrelated sons-in-law in this family are clearly identifiable standing in the back.

FIGURE 3-7
Sex determination. The process of meiosis produces germ cells (eggs and sperm) with just one sex chromosome. If a sperm with an X chromosome fertilizes the egg, the child will be a girl. If a sperm with a Y chromosome fertilizes the egg, the child will be a boy.

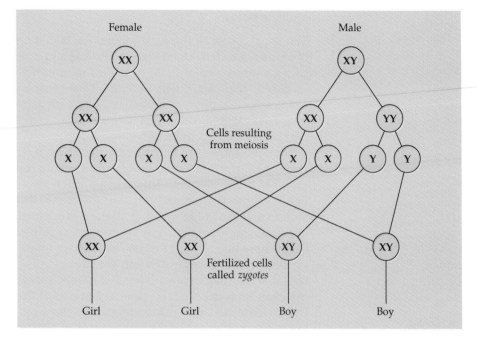

mosome and one Y chromosome. After meiosis, eggs always contain an X chromosome; sperm may contain an X or a Y chromosome. If the sperm contributes an X chromosome to the new organism at conception, the baby will be a girl. If it contributes a Y chromosome, the baby will be a boy (Figure 3-7). The sex of the child, then, is always determined by the father.

You might expect that exactly half the babies conceived would be females and half would be males, but this isn't the case. Actually, about 120 males are conceived for every 100 females. By birth, the ratio has dropped to 105 males for every 100 females. The reason for this is that the sex chromosomes carry many genes other than the ones that determine sex. If one of these genes is defective on an X chromosome in a female, a corresponding healthy gene on the other X chromosome can often compensate for it. A female would have to inherit two defective chromosomes to express the defect and suffer adverse effects from it.

If a male has a defective gene on the X chromosome, on the other hand, there may not be a corresponding healthy gene on the Y chromosome, which is smaller and is thought to carry fewer genes. The male would be more likely to express an abnormality encoded on the X chromosome. As a result, a higher mortality rate exists for male organisms, and more of them have to be conceived if a roughly equal number are to be born.

Characteristics encoded by genes that are carried on the sex chromosomes are known as **sex-linked characteristics.** Many of these characteristics are encoded by recessive genes carried on the X chromosome. They can be expressed in males because males don't have a second X chromosome with a matching dominant gene to override them. Hemophilia and some forms of color-blindness are examples of sex-linked traits that normally occur only in males.

Multiple Births

The usual course of events at conception is that one egg and one sperm unite to produce one fertilized ovum, known as a **zygote**. But sometimes a woman's ovary releases two or more eggs during monthly ovulation. If both eggs are fertilized, two babies will develop. These twins will be no more alike than siblings born at different times, because each came from a different fertilized egg. Twins who develop this way are called **fraternal,** and may be two girls, two boys, or a boy and a girl.

Multiple births are sometimes caused by fertility drugs. Women whose body chemistry prevents them from ovulating (releasing an egg during each monthly cycle) may take these drugs when they want to become pregnant. Fertility drugs trigger ovulation, but sometimes they overstimulate the ovaries, and several ova are released. If all the ova are fertilized, the woman may find she's carrying twins, triplets, or even more fetuses. As many as six or seven babies have been born to women who have taken fertility drugs.

Twins can also originate from the division of a zygote by mitosis into two cells that then separate and develop independently. Because mitosis involves the exact replication of the genetic material in the original cell, these babies will be **identical** twins. These twins are alike in every way and are, naturally, the same sex (Figure 3-8). Identical triplets can develop if the original zygote separates by mitosis twice in a row (producing four identical cells), and then one cell dies.

Twins are born about once in every 89 births, and of these, about one-third are identical twins. Triple births occur about once in every 7,000 births. Quadruplets are very rare, occurring only once in about 400,000 births (Gedda, 1961). The incidence of multiple births varies among different population groups. For example, they are more frequent among Nigerians and quite rare in Chinese

FIGURE 3-8
Identical twins are produced when a fertilized egg divides and forms two cells, each containing the same genetic material. Fraternal twins result when two different eggs are fertilized at the same time and develop side by side in the womb. Their genetic material is as different as that of any two siblings born at different times.

Identical (monozygotic) twins   Egg   Egg   Fraternal (dizygotic) twins

One ovum is available for fertilization.   Sperm   Sperm   Two ova are available for fertilization.

It yields one zygote.   They yield two zygotes.

The zygote divides, and the two new cells separate.

Two genetically identical embryos develop.   Two genetically different embryos develop.

FIGURE 3-9
Fraternal twins, like these baby boys sitting on their young grandmother's lap, can easily be told apart even though they're dressed alike. Identical twins, like the girls posing in matching aprons, are nearly impossible for their friends and parents to distinguish, even if they deliberately wear their hair in different styles.

and Japanese populations (Stern, 1973). Multiple births are also positively correlated with maternal age: as the mother's age increases, so does the probability of a multiple birth.

PRENATAL DEVELOPMENT: LIFE IN THE WOMB

We think of birth as the beginning of a person's life, but a great deal has already happened to that person by the time birth occurs. The basic biological blueprint was laid down at conception, when the ovum was fertilized by a sperm. As we've just seen, the individual's unique genetic make-up was established at that moment. Now the individual begins the 9-month-long period of growth and unfolding that we refer to as **prenatal development**. During this period, development proceeds in a genetically determined pattern common to all human beings, but it is critically influenced by interactions with the mother's body. Human evolution, current social practices, and the parents' personal histories and choices all work together to form this new human being. The baby we see for the first time at birth is the end product of this long process.

The last 25 years have seen an explosion of knowledge about prenatal development. Embryologists can now tell us exactly when the heart, lungs, and other organs are formed, when the eyes open, when the fetus can cry and suck its thumb in the womb. Research scientists can tell us how the fetus is affected by environmental factors, such as alcohol, cigarettes, and drugs, including such diverse substances as tetracycline, Valium, retin-A, and cocaine. Epidemiologists understand a wide range of genetic and developmental problems, and genetic counselors provide information and advice to parents whose babies may have genetic disorders.

Early Ideas about Prenatal Development

Although our knowledge about prenatal development is far from complete, we do have answers to some questions that have intrigued and puzzled people for thousands of years. Aristotle, for example, wrote that the male semen provided the "form" of the embryo and the female provided the material to which form is given. This stood to reason, he wrote, because the male is active and the female is passive (Needham, 1959).

Aristotle wasn't the first to express this idea. Earlier, a Greek dramatist had written that the woman contributes nothing to the child; the child is merely "sown" in her by the male, who is the child's only parent (Needham, 1959). These views reflected the prejudices of Greek society about the comparative value of males and females, views that have had long-range repercussions for women in Western society. Modern genetics informs us, of course, that both parents contribute equally to the genetic make-up—the "form"—of the child.

Aristotle also raised a question that was fiercely debated for centuries: Does the embryo exist preformed from the beginning, perfect in every feature, and merely increase in size during the prenatal period? Or does it develop in successive stages? Aristotle favored the developmental, or **epigenic,** theory, but some scientists claimed they could actually see tiny, preformed embryos in the sperm or egg (Figure 3-10), and they argued against the epigenic view. It wasn't until the late 1700s and early 1800s that preformationism was finally laid to rest. Research on the chick embryo revealed easily observable stages of development, thus confirming the epigenic view.

Periods of Prenatal Development

How, then, does prenatal development proceed? Prior to conception, of course, certain physiological events occur that set the stage. Every month an egg is prepared in one of the woman's ovaries and released sometime between the ninth and sixteenth days of her menstrual cycle. The egg is drawn into the open end of the **fallopian tube** and moved down the tube to the uterus. If it doesn't encounter a sperm, or if fertilization doesn't occur despite the presence of sperm, the egg is flushed out of the body at the end of the monthly cycle, which is usually about 28 days long.

The sperm, of course, have been produced in the man's testes and ejaculated from his penis into the woman's vagina during sexual intercourse. Millions of sperm begin the long journey through the uterus and up the fallopian tubes, but only a few make it to the end, only one of which will be allowed to penetrate the surface of the egg. (Many conditions can prevent fertilization from taking place; see Research Focus—Infertility for a discussion of causes and treatments of infertility.) If the egg is fertilized, prenatal development

FIGURE 3-10
Early microscopes allowed scientists to view individual sperm cells for the first time, and some people proposed that a completely formed human being was curled up inside each sperm. This seventeenth-century drawing shows such a creature, known as a homunculus, or "little man." Others thought the homunculus was contained in the egg. According to these views, the child was really created by only one parent; the role of the other parent was simply to provide the environment for growth or to stimulate growth.

begins, lasting 38 weeks for the full-term infant. We usually divide prenatal development, also known as **gestation,** into three periods, each of which has a different focus of activity.

THE PERIOD OF THE OVUM: CONCEPTION TO WEEK 2. The first period of prenatal development, called the **period of the ovum,** begins in one of the fallopian tubes (see Figure 3-11). It is here that fertilization occurs, when a sperm penetrates the egg. The fertilized cell, or zygote, begins to undergo cell division as it continues moving toward the uterus. In about three days, the cluster of 20 to 30 cells enters the uterine cavity, where it organizes itself into a hollow ball. In one area of this single layer of cells is a group of larger cells, called the **embryoblast,** which will develop into the embryo itself. The rest of the layer, the **trophoblast,** will develop into structures such as the placenta and chorion, which nourish and support the developing embryo. About six or seven days after fertilization, the embryo attaches itself to the uterine wall, and four or five days after that, it becomes embedded there.

Sometimes the developing embryo attaches itself to the wall of the fallopian tube instead of making its way to the uterus. Pregnancies that develop in a

FIGURE 3-11
The complex processes of ovulation, fertilization, cell division in the fallopian tube, and implantation of the embryo in the wall of the uterus take less than two weeks. When a woman becomes pregnant, the first sign is usually the missed menstrual period at the end of her monthly cycle, two weeks after ovulation.

Muscular outer wall of uterus

Glandular inner wall of uterus with many blood vessels

Oviduct (fallopian tube) leading to uterus

Ovary

Cavity of uterus (womb)

1. Glandular cells in site of previousy extruded egg
2. Days 9–16 of menstrual cycle: single egg cell matures and is released from ovary; flagellae at opening of fallopian tube draw it into end of tube
3. 12–24 hours after leaving ovary one sperm enters egg (fertilization)
4. 24–30 hours after fertilization male and female chromosomal material unite
5. Spindle for first egg cell division
6. 36 hours: two cells
7. 48 hours: four cells
8. 3 days: embryo is a small compact ball of 16–32 cells
9. 4 days: embryo is a hollow ball of 64–128 cells
10. 4.5 days: embryo develops an inner cell mass and is still free in the uterus
11. 6–7 days: embryo is attaching to wall of uterus
12. 11–12 days: embryo invades the uterine wall and becomes embedded in it

RESEARCH FOCUS

Infertility

There have always been couples who wanted to have children but couldn't. And there have always been ways of trying to bring about conception, ranging from herbal remedies to ritual practices to ingenious sexual positions. Today, we approach the problem of infertility—the inability to conceive a baby—more scientifically but with no less compelling interest. Infertility is a major trauma for the many people—20 percent of all couples in the United States—who are unable to have the children they want. Women have a higher risk of infertility after the age of 30; perhaps 15 percent of women between 30 and 35 may not be able to bear a child.

Treatment for infertility enables about half of the couples who seek help to have a child. But in many other cases, there isn't anything physicians can do; sometimes they can't even pinpoint the problem. In these cases, all our scientific knowledge and modern medical technology are no more useful than the folk medicine of a previous era.

IDENTIFYING THE CAUSE OF INFERTILITY

After a couple has been trying to conceive for a year, they may turn to an infertility specialist. An initial physical exam and a battery of lab tests may reveal a problem that can be corrected. A variety of conditions can cause infertility. In women these conditions include a failure to ovulate, endometriosis (a condition in which abnormal tissue in the pelvic cavity prevents conception), endocrine imbalances, and scarred fallopian tubes. Some women have physical abnormalities, such as an oddly shaped uterus, that make it more difficult for them to carry a pregnancy to term. In men infertility can be caused by too few sperm or sperm that don't swim properly. These problems are often traced to a case of mumps in early adulthood, untreated gonorrhea, or endocrine imbalances.

About 15 to 20 percent of all pregnancies end in miscarriage, and repeated miscarriage is another form of infertility. Miscarriage often occurs in the first days or weeks of pregnancy because of a serious fetal abnormality, sometimes without the woman ever knowing she was pregnant. Many women have miscarriages of this type and later experience successful pregnancies. But occasionally, one parent will have a chromosomal abnormality that causes repeated miscarriages. Hormone imbalances also may be linked to repeated miscarriages.

Miscarriage in the fifth or six month of pregnancy may be due to abnormalities in the cervix, a condition known as cervical incompetence, or in the uterus. Recent evidence has linked late miscarriages with certain kinds of infections; many women who have these infections are subsequently treated with antibiotics and go on to have successful pregnancies.

TREATMENT OF INFERTILITY

Some kinds of infertility can be treated; others cannot. Surgery can sometimes repair fallopian tubes, clear up endometriosis, and correct problems in anatomy. Fertility drugs can help a woman ovulate, although they carry the risk of causing multiple births. Male infertility can be treated by collecting the father's sperm, concentrating it, and artificially inseminating the mother.

More advanced treatment techniques include in vitro fertilization, the use of frozen embryos, and laser surgery, which can sometimes be used in men to reverse a vasectomy (a sterilization method in which the small ducts that carry semen from the testes are severed) or in women to repair fallopian tubes. Infertility is an area of great interest right now, so new treatments are rapidly emerging. But, as with so many forms of modern technology, new problems arise at

---

fallopian tube are called **ectopic pregnancies**. These pregnancies are dangerous because an embryo developing here can only grow so far before the fallopian tube bursts. If the embryo isn't removed surgically, the mother can die from internal bleeding. In fact, ectopic pregnancies are the leading cause of maternal death in the United States (Dorfman, 1983). An early prenatal exam can reveal whether the embryo is growing properly in the uterus.

Under normal circumstances, the embryo is firmly implanted in the uterine wall by the end of the second week. It's only about the size of the period at the end of this sentence, but it's already begun to form the remarkable system by which it will draw nourishment and oxygen from the mother for the next 36 weeks. The course of prenatal development is shown in Figure 3-15.

THE PERIOD OF THE EMBRYO: WEEK 2 TO WEEK 8. The second period of prenatal development, called the **period of the embryo**, lasts from the second week to the same time that old problems are solved. Two of the more controversial techniques are in vitro fertilization and surrogate motherhood.

In Vitro Fertilization

In this procedure, eggs are extracted from the mother and mixed with the father's sperm in the laboratory. (Babies born this way are commonly called "test tube babies.") One or more of the embryos that result are then implanted in the mother's uterus.

Although this procedure is often successful, it is very tedious and expensive. Not all embryos grow and thrive in the lab, and not all implantations become successful pregnancies. Any unused embryos that do thrive are often frozen and stored for the couple to use later. This aspect of in vitro fertilization has created some vigorous moral and legal debates. For example, a recent court case in Australia involved the legal status of frozen embryos as heirs to the estate of their parents, who were killed in a plane crash before the embryos could be implanted. Another debate has focused on the moral implications of allowing research to be conducted on frozen embryos.

Surrogate Motherhood

The practice of surrogate motherhood is the most controversial of all approaches to infertility. It involves a contract between a fertile woman who agrees to carry a fetus and an infertile woman whose husband provides the sperm. The surrogate mother is impregnated by the father's sperm through artificial insemination, agrees to carry the child for the couple, and names the couple as legal guardians of the child who will be born. In return, she's paid for her services.

Some people question the morality of paying a woman to carry a baby. They see surrogate motherhood as an arrangement essentially to "sell" a baby, and they fear the psychological consequences for chil-dren who learn their biological mothers "sold" them. They also point to the possibility that a woman will change her mind after she has the baby and be unwilling to fulfill the contract she's signed.

In 1986 the public witnessed the very difficult dilemma created by surrogate motherhood, when Mary Beth Whitehead of New Jersey refused to give up a baby to the couple who had contracted with her for the child. She said that she hadn't realized how she would feel about giving the baby up, and she argued that she had the right to keep the baby because she was the real mother. She also tried to return the couple's money to them, but they refused to accept it. After a lengthy battle, the court awarded the baby to the couple and granted the surrogate mother limited visitation rights. Ms. Whitehead appealed the decision, and it may be that a ruling about the legality of surrogate motherhood will eventually come out of this case. It remains to be seen what, if any, psychological consequences there will be for the baby.

THE TRAUMA OF INFERTILITY

Infertility is a painful experience, and treatment for infertility can be a nightmare. Ovulation is monitored, sperm samples are collected and analyzed, intercourse practices are studied, and surgery may be performed. A couple may feel vulnerable and out of control; their sex life may become an unpleasant routine of more interest to their physician than to themselves; and they may lose perspective on the rest of their lives. Solutions that seem radical to outsiders, such as in vitro fertilization or surrogate motherhood, become acceptable options, if the couple can afford them. Many others remain childless or turn to adoption. Support groups for infertile couples can provide help in this difficult situation. Although many advances have been made, there are still very few easy answers to infertility.

the end of the eighth week. This period is a time of extremely rapid differentiation and change. All the major body structures are formed during this time, including the heart, the brain, the liver, the lungs, and the ovaries and testes. Some organs begin to function—the heart starts to beat, the liver begins to make blood cells, and the testes produce sex hormones. The eyes, nose, ears, tooth buds, and jaw form; arms and legs appear; and eyelids seal the eyes shut.

Because body structures are forming during this period, the developing organism is most vulnerable to damage from environmental influences such as drugs, infections, and irradiation. (Later in this chapter we discuss the outside agents that can damage the embryo, along with their effects.) Despite the critically important developments that occur during this second period, the embryo at the end of the eighth week is only about $1\frac{1}{2}$ inches long and weighs less than $\frac{1}{10}$ of an ounce.

FIGURE 3-12
Chronology of Milestones in Prenatal Development. The baby's anatomy is almost completely formed during the first three months of prenatal life, although the fetus is only a few inches long at the end of the first trimester. During the second trimester, the fetal heartbeat can be heard with a stethoscope, and the mother feels vigorous kicking and turning in her abdomen. The largest weight gain occurs during the last few months of prenatal development.

FIGURE 3-13
Scenes from prenatal life. By the sixth week (top left), the embryo is about an inch long. It has simple internal organs, including a heart that's pumping blood through the body. The arms and legs have formed, and the eyes have just appeared. By the fourth month (top right), the fetus is growing rapidly and obtains large amounts of food and oxygen from the placenta. About 10 inches long and weighing about 6 ounces, it can kick, turn its head, frown, and suck. By the seventh month (right), the fetus weighs about 3 pounds and has grown to about 15 inches. Although its lungs aren't completely developed and it still needs to acquire a layer of fat, the fetus can now survive if born prematurely.

THE PERIOD OF THE FETUS: WEEK 9 TO BIRTH. The third and final period of prenatal development, called the **period of the fetus,** lasts from the ninth week until birth. During this period, structural development continues to completion. Hands, fingers, feet, and toes are formed; bones develop; neural cells multiply; and hair and nails appear. All body systems begin to function; even the lungs make breathing movements, moving fluids in and out. Most of the fetus's growth—its increase in weight and length—takes place during this period, especially in the ninth month. By the end of the thirty-eighth week, the average baby weighs a little over 7 pounds and is about 20 inches long.

During this third period, the external male and female genitalia begin to develop. Although the genes inherited at conception determine whether the baby will be a boy or a girl, both sexes initially develop as females. In the sixth week after conception, the male embryo releases male hormones known as androgens, which trigger the development of the male genitalia. On rare occasions, this hormone isn't released, and the child who develops is physically a female but genetically a male.

Beginning in the fifth month, the expectant mother can feel the baby's movements. When the fetus is still very small, it's continually moving—rolling, twisting, stretching, turning over. Later, when its body starts to fill the uterine cavity, it kicks and punches with its feet and arms. The movements become stronger and stronger as the pregnancy progresses, eventually becoming strong enough to keep the mother awake at night. Babies can apparently hear sounds from the outside world, and they often jump or kick in response to a loud noise.

Various parts of the body grow at different rates during prenatal development. At first, the head region grows very quickly compared to the trunk and legs. Later, the lower parts of the body grow faster and begin to catch up. For example, at 2 weeks, 65 percent of the embryo's total body length is head, and 35 percent is trunk. At 8 weeks, 44 percent is head, 36 percent is trunk, and 20 percent is legs. At birth, 25 percent of body length is accounted for by the head, with the trunk accounting for 42 percent and the legs for 33 percent. The head remains more fully developed than the other parts of the body throughout the entire prenatal period. Babies and young children appear "top-heavy" compared to older children and adults, whose heads account for only about 10 percent of their total height. This head-first pattern of development continues after birth, and is discussed further in Chapter 4 on the neonate (newborn).

Prematurity

The normal gestation period is 38 weeks, but premature babies born as early as 24 to 25 weeks have survived, although this is rare. The earlier they're born, the more medical problems they're likely to have. Premature babies are typically thin and scrawny, because fat tissue isn't developed under the skin until the thirtieth to thirty-fourth week. Their low body weight makes them more sensitive to cold and more susceptible to dehydration than full-term babies.

More critical to their survival is the unfinished state of their lungs. The terminal air sacs in the lungs, called alveoli, don't develop until about week 32, and surfactant, a substance in the lungs necessary for gas exchange, isn't present until after week 34. Babies born before this period of gestation aren't equipped to breathe properly. Despite formidable problems, premature babies are being saved at earlier and earlier dates as a result of modern medical technology and advanced neonatal care. The problems and treatments of premature babies are discussed further in Chapter 4.

The process of prenatal development culminates in the birth of the baby, usually full-term and perfectly healthy. Birth—the beginning moment of a person's life—is also the climax for which the baby has been prepared during the nine long months in the womb.

BIRTH: TRANSITION TO LIFE IN THE OUTER WORLD

The journey down the birth canal out of the mother's body is the biggest transition any of us ever makes. It marks the end of life in physical union with the mother—a state in which food, oxygen, and hormones are obtained from her body—and the beginning of life as a separate individual. As you might expect, birth is a complex process, during which many remarkable changes occur that enable the baby to take up this new, physiologically independent existence.

The Physical Process of Birth

The birth process occurs in three stages (see Figure 3-14). Labor starts when hormonal changes in both the baby and the mother cause strong, rhythmic uterine contractions to begin. These contractions exert pressure on the cervix, the neck of the uterus, causing it gradually to pull back and open, or dilate. They also put pressure on the baby so that it descends into the mother's pelvis (in first babies, this descent usually occurs well before labor even begins). This first stage is the longest part of the birth process.

When the cervix is completely dilated, the second stage of birth, referred to as expulsion, begins. The baby slowly moves down, through the bones of the pelvic ring, past the tight, muscular cervix, and into the vagina, which stretches open from the pressure. The baby's back bends, the head turns to fit through the narrowest parts of the passageway, and the soft bones of the baby's skull actually move together and overlap as it's squeezed through the pelvis. The baby's head finally emerges from the vagina, followed quickly by the rest of the body. A new human being appears in the world!

When the cervix is opening during the first stage, the woman having an unmedicated birth is encouraged to relax as much as possible, despite the contractions, and allow labor to proceed without tensing up her muscles. When the baby is being expelled during the second stage, the woman can "bear down" with the contractions to help push the baby out. When the top of the baby's head appears at the vaginal opening, the baby is said to be **crowning.** Since the head is the largest part of the baby's body and wider than the shoulders, the body usually just slips out after the head emerges.

The third stage of birth, known as afterbirth, is the delivery of the placenta. This usually occurs within 10 to 20 minutes of the baby's birth and is accomplished with a few strong uterine contractions. The whole birth process for

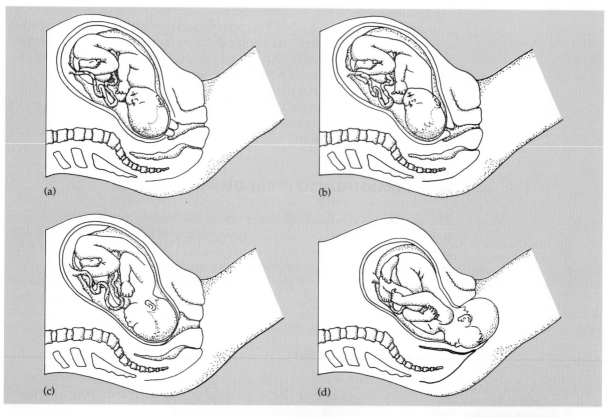

(a)   (b)

(c)   (d)

FIGURE 3-14
The birth process. Before labor begins, the full-term fetus rests comfortably in the uterus, typically in a head-down position (a). In the first stage of labor, uterine contractions pull the cervix open and push the baby downward (b). In the second stage of labor, the baby is pushed further down (c) and out of the mother's body (d). The baby's head turns toward the mother's back during the birth process and is completely turned as it emerges, or crowns.

FIGURE 3-15
Her long labor ends; the baby's life begins.

HEALTH FOCUS

The Increase in Cesarean Births

Cesarean sections have been performed for thousands of years—the procedure is named after Julius Caesar (100 BC–44 BC), who was delivered through an incision in his mother's abdomen—but they were usually performed at the cost of the mother's life. Unsanitary conditions meant the mother was doomed to massive infection, if she didn't bleed to death first. Cesarean sections became a true alternative birth method after antiseptic procedures were developed late in the nineteenth century.

WHY PERFORM A CESAREAN?

Cesarean sections are performed when a baby can't be delivered vaginally. Sometimes a mother's pelvis isn't big enough for the baby's head to pass through during birth. Sometimes the baby is in a feet-down or buttocks-down position in the uterus rather than in the usual head-down position, or even lying sideways across the uterus, all of which make vaginal birth difficult. In some cases the placenta is over the cervix rather than higher in the uterus (Guttmacher, 1973), and vaginal delivery would damage the baby's support system before birth. Mothers with diabetes, high blood pressure, kidney or heart disease, or toxemia (toxins in the blood, a condition that sometimes occurs late in pregnancy) often deliver their babies by cesarean section to reduce the stress on their bodies.

Sometimes a woman is unable to sustain labor. Contractions slow down or stop, and the cervix shows no progressing dilation. After 24 hours, physicians usually perform a cesarean section. This reduces the risk of infection to the newborn, which can be high once the protective membranes have ruptured at the beginning of labor. In the past, cesareans were also performed when women had previously had cesarean births. Physicians believed that the pressure of labor and vaginal delivery on the uterine wall would rupture the old incision. This has not proven to be true, and many women now have vaginal births after cesarean births.

Cesarean sections are major surgery and carry some risk themselves, although much less than 15 or 20 years ago. Better antibiotics and refined understanding and use of anesthesia make the procedure relatively safe. Women now are often given a local anesthetic and remain conscious during the whole operation. The father can be in the operating room if the mother is given a local anesthetic.

WHY HAS THE NUMBER OF CESAREANS INCREASED?

Between 1965 and 1980 cesarean deliveries increased from 5 percent to 15 percent of all births in the United States (O'Driscoll & Foley, 1983). By 1987 the nationwide cesarean rate was reported to be 24 percent, with even higher rates in some states ("Caesareans Up," 1987). The hospitals with very high cesarean rates are usually university hospitals, where many more high-risk pregnancies are handled than in the average community hospital.

One reason for higher cesarean rates is that hospitals now have more sophisticated techniques for detecting fetal distress. Fetal monitoring, for example, can reveal a slowed fetal heart rate due to inadequate oxygen during labor, possibly leading to a decision for cesarean section. Advocates of increased reliance on cesareans claim that the procedure makes birth safer for mothers and babies in a situation where prolonged, stressful labor is the alternative. They point to reduced maternal and neonatal mortality rates and the better health of newborns (fewer babies are born with brain damage from labor and delivery trauma) (Bodner et al., 1986).

Critics of the increased reliance on cesarean deliveries, including many physicians and surgeons, believe that cesareans are often performed unnecessarily and that labor isn't well managed by medical personnel in this country. They claim that not all relevant staff members, for example, can accurately interpret signs of fetal distress. They suggest that cesarean sections are frequently performed more for the convenience of the physician than for the mother's or baby's health. Until physicians can document the need for a cesarean in each and every case, and until the public becomes more aware of the benefits of this procedure for some mothers and babies, this debate is likely to continue.

first babies takes about 12 hours, on the average, and for subsequent babies the process takes about 7 hours. Averages can be misleading, of course. The first stage alone can take anywhere from 8 to 20 hours for a first baby and 3 to 8 hours for a second baby (Ingalls & Salerno, 1975). A variety of conditions can result in birth by cesarean section, the delivery of the baby through an incision in the mother's abdominal wall. This procedure is explained and discussed in Health Focus—The Increase in Cesarean Births.

Important physiological changes occur when the baby is born. As the infant is squeezed through the pelvis, cervix, and vagina, the fluid in the lungs is forced out by the pressure on the baby's chest. Once this pressure is released as the baby emerges from the vagina, the chest expands and the lungs fill with air for the first time. This process ensures that the baby starts breathing immediately after birth.

Other physiological changes occur at birth as well. Special blood vessels that were used during the prenatal period close off, no longer needed now that the lungs are part of the circulatory system; the umbilical cord seals off, even if it's not tied or cut; and changes in the composition of the baby's blood make the baby more suited for life outside the womb.

Emotional Aspects of Birth

The emotional impact of a baby's birth is almost unequalled in the human experience. Confronted with the mystery of the creation of life, moved by profound feelings for the tiny, helpless, but perfect new being, most adults are awed and elated by the birth of a baby. The baby, of course, has had a tumultuous experience too. It seems natural to take the emotional side of childbirth as seriously as the physiological one, but this view hasn't always been acceptable.

THE EVOLUTION OF HOSPITAL CHILDBIRTH PRACTICES. Until about a hundred years ago, birth was treated as a natural event in a woman's life, usually experienced at home with the help of a midwife and some other attendants. Mortality for both infants and mothers was high. As progress was made in medical knowledge and techniques, physicians attempted to lower this mortality rate by increasing medical intervention in the birth process. The use of drugs, forceps, and surgical techniques removed birth from the realm of natural events and placed it in the hands of specialists.

By the 1940s, birth was treated as a medical emergency requiring lengthy hospitalization. In earlier practices, the emotional aspects of birth were simply an integral part of the whole experience; they weren't considered separable from it. Now, the emotional aspects of the experience were ignored as hospitals zealously pursued efficient, safe births. Women were routinely separated from their husbands during labor and birth, given no information about what was happening to them, and sedated during delivery. Immediately after birth, the mother was sent to her room and the baby was whisked away to the nursery. The father had no direct contact with his baby during the hospital stay—he could only look at the baby through the nursery window. The mother had no contact with her other children, who weren't allowed in her room. The baby was brought to the mother at scheduled feeding times and then returned to the nursery, where the hospital staff cared for all the newborns together. After two weeks in the hospital, the mother was sent home with a baby she hardly knew. Here is one woman's reaction to these practices (Bell et al., 1973, p. 204):

> I remember feeling very strange, to have experienced the most remarkable of all things, the birth of my first child, and then to be left all alone. First they took the baby into the nursery. Then I was wheeled into my room, where my huband was able to stay and chat for a while. But he had to work the next day, so he needed some sleep. I was tired, but too excited to sleep. So there I was, alone, remembering the experience full of wonder and amazement that we had all shared. But for the next few hours we were not sharing. The hospital had separated us.

FIGURE 3-16
These seventeenth-century woodcuts show a variety of positions in which babies may present themselves at birth. They were probably based on midwives' experiences and used to teach new midwives what to expect. Today, many of these presentations would lead quickly to a decision to perform a cesarean section.

RESISTANCE TO HOSPITAL PRACTICES. In the early 1970s, many people began to question and resist this approach to birth. Parents were becoming aware of birth practices in other countries and making their dissatisfaction known to physicians and hospitals. In addition, medical research was beginning to show that routine heavy sedation during birth might be harmful to the baby, the mother, or both. Some researchers found that the presence of fathers greatly improved the comfort and emotional well-being of mothers in labor. Other studies suggested that early separation might interfere with later social interaction between mothers and babies.

Social practices changed too. Breastfeeding became the preferred feeding method, and hospitals had to allow more mother-infant contact to accommodate the demand feeding schedule required by nursing infants. It became apparent that older siblings adjusted better to a new brother or sister if they were prepared for the baby's arrival and if they could see their mother while she was in the hospital. And skyrocketing hospital costs made long stays prohibitively expensive for routine births. All these findings and social trends contributed to the changes in childbirth practices that have occurred since the early 1970s.

Current Childbirth Practices

Almost all the hospital childbirth practices just detailed have been modified in the last 20 years. Let's look more closely at what the typical childbirth experience is like today.

PREPARED CHILDBIRTH. Women are no longer routinely sedated during childbirth. The current view is that the less medication used, the better. General anesthesia isn't administered, usually even for cesarean sections. Instead of relying on drugs, many women learn techniques in childbirth preparation classes that help them deal with the discomfort and rigors of labor and delivery.

One method of prepared childbirth was developed by Dr. Grantly Dick-Read. Dick-Read believed that the pain experienced by women during birth was the result of learned fears and anxieties that interfered, through tension, with the naturally painless process of birth. To dispel these fears, childbirth educators teach parents the details of the birth process as well as physical and respiratory relaxation techniques. Dick-Read's method strongly discourages the use of pain-relieving drugs.

Another popular approach to prepared childbirth was developed by Dr. Ferdinand Lamaze. Unlike Dick-Read, Lamaze acknowledged that childbirth involves some inherent pain. But if a woman is concentrating on other activities, such as breathing, her brain will be unreceptive to the pain signals sent out by the uterus (Miller and Brooten, 1977). The Lamaze method teaches breathing techniques designed to occupy the brain and prevent pain messages from getting through to it. Like the Dick-Read method, it also teaches parents about the birth process, on the assumption that ignorance breeds fear and knowledge dispels it.

The Lamaze method advocates minimal use of pain-relieving drugs. This policy ensures that both mother and baby are alert during the birth, and it reduces the risk to the baby. However, the limited use of drugs isn't discouraged, because the mother's comfort is an important part of prepared childbirth.

A third method of childbirth preparation is known as the Bradley Method (Barnes & Hassid, 1985). In this method, relaxation is stressed, but no specific method of relaxation is taught. Instead, women are taught several techniques, including massage, relaxation exercises, and breathing control, so that they will be able to choose what works best for them. Women are encouraged to practice all of the techniques they learn in childbirth classes, which meet in small groups for 10 to 12 sessions.

Most hospitals tend to instruct parents in a combination of Lamaze and other relaxation techniques. Childbirth classes are almost a routine part of the prenatal experience for both mothers and fathers these days. The father typically acts as a coach, supporting the mother emotionally and helping her with her breathing. He might also be ready with various comforts, such as wet washcloths or ice chips to suck on. He remains with the mother throughout labor and delivery, even when a cesarean section is performed. A labor nurse or midwife attends the labor as well. The physician may be present during labor or may arrive just in time for the delivery.

Many hospitals have birthing rooms they can use as alternatives to traditional delivery rooms for births. These are special rooms, often designed to provide the comforts of a bedroom, where the mother can stay for the entire birth process. Traditionally, women went through labor in a "labor room" and then were moved to the more sterile delivery room when they were ready to give birth. But being moved at that critical moment in the birth process is extremely disruptive when a woman is trying to concentrate on staying relaxed and in control of her breathing. In a birthing room, no interruption is necessary.

CONTACT BETWEEN MOTHER AND BABY. One of the most dramatic changes in childbirth practices is in the amount of time hospitals allow babies to stay with their parents. Babies are no longer rushed off to the nursery right after they're born. They spend time with the mother and usually the father immediately following birth. They're taken to the nursery to be weighed and examined, and then they're often returned to the mother for rooming-in. **Rooming-in** is the practice of leaving the baby with the mother in her room for as much or as little time as she desires.

Fathers are encouraged to hold and care for the newborn. Many hospitals offer classes on infant care and fathering to new parents during the mother's hospital stay. Fathers can usually visit at any time. Siblings can visit too but usually only during regular visiting hours. Some hospitals allow the newborn to remain in the room when brothers or sisters are visiting. The older children get a chance to meet the new member of the family, but more important is the chance to see and talk to mom.

Even if they haven't had rooming in, mothers have more contact with their babies than they used to simply because they don't stay in the hospital very long. A two- or three-day stay is typical following a vaginal delivery. Some hospitals release mothers within a few hours of the birth if all is going well. For a cesarean section, a hospital stay of five to seven days is now considered normal, as opposed to the traditional two weeks.

HOME BIRTHS AND OTHER ALTERNATIVES. Despite the dramatic changes hospitals have made in their childbirth practices, some parents have opted to have their babies at home or in alternative birth centers, attended by a midwife or a physician. Here, the surroundings are comfortable, the atmosphere is casual, and the company is familiar. Friends, family members, and children can be present at the birth if the parents wish.

Physicians, midwives, and other personnel who participate in alternative births usually have some medical back-up planned in case of emergency. For example, birth centers may have a car available at all times for immediate

FIGURE 3-17
Current childbirth practices provide benefits to babies, mothers, and families. Attachment between mother and child begins immediately after birth as the baby is placed on the mother's body; she gets her first good look at him and soothes him with her touch (top left). Newborns stay with their mothers after birth and room in with them during their hospital stay; they can begin to nurse right away (bottom left). Fathers are involved in the birth and in the care of the newborn, beginning a relationship with the newest family member (top right). Brothers and sisters can meet the baby in the hospital, see their mom, and be reassured about what this new experience is going to mean for them (bottom right).

FIGURE 3-18
When babies are born at home, women have their childbirth experience in a comfortable setting surrounded by people of their own choosing. This woman wanted her older child with her when she had the baby. They both watched in a hand-held mirror as the baby crowned, and they witnessed the moment of birth together. Later, they contemplated the new person who had joined their lives.

transport to the nearest hospital. They also carefully screen out high-risk cases to ensure that mothers and babies who are likely to have problems go through labor and delivery where they'll have the medical resources they may need. Despite precautions, births that take place at home and in other alternative settings outside hospitals are not without risk, as some advocates have implied.

Benefits of New Childbirth Practices

There is some debate about the actual advantages of these changes in childbirth practices. No one questions the benefits of reducing medication during birth, which allows mothers to play an active role in birth and both mothers and babies to be more alert. The involvement of fathers in labor and delivery is also considered an improvement, with psychological and emotional benefits for both parents. There are also definite financial advantages to shorter hospital stays.

But there are some misgivings over the increase in home births, which tend to be less safe than hospital births. Some people have questioned the importance given to early contact between mothers and babies. During the 1970s and 1980s, a tremendous emphasis was placed on uninterrupted contact as a requirement for attachment and "bonding," as the formation of an early emotional tie between mother and child is called. Research suggested that bonding had to occur immediately after birth or the baby might never form a proper attachment, and this idea was embraced by almost everyone involved in childbirth.

More recent research has contradicted these findings. We now know that bonding can occur even if mother and baby are separated after birth. Premature babies and babies with physical problems at birth are usually placed in neonatal care units, and women who have had general anesthesia are unable to interact with their babies immediately after birth. Attachment still forms between these mothers and babies, and early separation seems to have no permanent detrimental effects. There is no research evidence confirming fears that attachment will be disrupted by early separation (Goldberg, 1983). (We discuss attachment and bonding at length in Chapter 8 on the social and emotional development of infants and toddlers.)

Another problem arises when people adhere slavishly to new ideas and practices without allowing for unexpected complications or expressing their own personal preferences. Parents have sometimes been led to believe that their relationship with their child will be permanently impaired if they're separated following birth. Women have described feelings of failure and guilt for taking pain-relieving drugs during birth or for delivering the baby by cesarean section. The idea that there's only one "right" way to have a baby sets parents up for a disappointment that can be devastating. Actually, a variety of birth situations can have positive physical and psychological outcomes, especially if parents are encouraged to choose what feels comfortable to them.

The positive side of the new childbirth practices is that parents now have more choices. Mothers who choose rooming-in can have their babies with them virtually every minute of their hospital stay. But some mothers may not choose rooming in, and this is acceptable too. They may have older children and many responsibilities to face at home. They need to use the hospital stay to rest and regain their strength. Still others may want to have their babies with them for short periods of time until they become confident that they can care for them. In most hospitals today, parents can decide for themselves what kind of childbirth experience they want to have, and this is an improvement no one disputes.

PROBLEMS IN EARLY DEVELOPMENT: WHEN THINGS GO WRONG

The end result of the long period of prenatal development and the transition period of birth usually is a full-term, healthy baby. Unfortunately, a few babies aren't so lucky at the start. Problems of newborns may be **prenatal** in origin—meaning they originated before the seventh prenatal month—or **perinatal** in origin—meaning they originated between the seventh month and a few minutes after birth (Kopp & Krakow, 1983).

FIGURE 3-19
The probability of inheriting a disease carried by recessive genes depends on whether one or both parents is a carrier.

CASE 1		CASE 2	
Parent 1 (carrier)	Parent 2 (completely normal)	Parent 1 (carrier)	Parent 2 (carrier)
Ss	SS	Ss	Ss

Ss	SS	SS	Ss	SS	Ss	Ss	ss
Carrier	Normal	Normal	Carrier	Normal	Carrier	Carrier	Diseased

Offspring

Offspring

If one parent is a carrier for the disease and the other parent neither has the disease nor carries it, there is a 50% chance that the child will be completely normal. No children will have the disease.

If both parents are carriers for the disease, there is a 25% chance that a child will be normal, a 50% chance that the child will be a carrier, and a 25% chance that the child will have the disease.

Uppercase S indicates a dominant gene. Lowercase s indicates a recessive gene.

FIGURE 3-20
A normal red blood cell looks like a doughnut—round and puffed up (top photo). A sickled red blood cell is elongated, flat, and curved (bottom photo). Sickled cells carry less oxygen and tend to clump together in blood vessels, clogging passageways. Children with this life-threatening genetic disorder tend to tire easily and have difficulty breathing because of insufficient oxygen.

Prenatal Problems

We saw at the beginning of this chapter how one family was affected by a problem in the prenatal development of their baby. Not all prenatal problems are as devastating as Tay-Sachs disease, but almost all create difficulties that the child, her family, and her community will have to deal with for her entire lifetime. Some of these problems result from genetic abnormalities, others from chromosomal errors, and still others from environmental factors. No matter what their origin, and no matter how they show up later in life, prenatal problems can never be erased from the child's make-up.

GENETIC PROBLEMS. As the name implies, genetic problems result from the inheritance of particular genes from the parents. Most common genetic problems are due to the inheritance of a pair of abnormal recessive genes. If you recall, it's only when two recessive genes are passed on that the characteristic they carry is expressed. The probability of inheriting a disease carried by two recessive genes is diagrammed in Figure 3-19.

Four of the most common genetic diseases are sickle-cell anemia, cystic fibrosis, phenylketonuria, and Tay-Sachs disease. Some genetic disorders occur disproportionately among certain groups, because recessive genes develop within a particular gene pool and tend to remain in it. For example, sickle-cell anemia, a disease of the red blood cells, occurs mainly in people of black African ancestry. Tay-Sachs disease, a fatal disorder of the central nervous system, primarily afflicts people of Eastern European Jewish ancestry. The probability of a child inheriting any of these four genetic diseases from carrier (outwardly healthy) parents is 25 percent. Descriptions of these diseases, along with the prognosis for childen born with them, are given in Table 3-1.

Rh disease is a genetically related disorder, but it's not caused by abnormal recessive genes. The Rh factor is a particular protein found in the blood. If an Rh-positive father and an Rh-negative mother conceive an Rh-positive baby, the baby's blood will be incompatible with the mother's. If some of the baby's blood enters the mother's bloodstream during delivery, she will develop antibodies to it just as she would toward a virus. The first baby isn't affected, because at that time the antibodies aren't yet in the mother's bloodstream. But

TABLE 3-1 Diseases Caused by the Inheritance of Two Abnormal Recessive Genes

Disease	Incidence	Description of the Disease and Consequences	Prognosis for Children Who Are Afflicted	Population at Risk
Sickle-cell anemia	1 in 625 live births among blacks in the U.S. (Muir, 1983)	The abnormal hemoglobin in red blood cells sickles (changes shape) during periods of stress caused by such factors as infections or low oxygen. Sickled cells stick together and impair blood flow to organs. Children may be irritable, have swollen abdomens and a yellowish cast to their eyes.	Many children who are victims of this disease do not survive into adulthood.	The recessive gene is carried by a disproportionate number of people with African ancestry.
Cystic fibrosis	1 in every 2,000 live births, 1,500–2,000 per year	Essential enzymes of the pancreas are deficient. Thick mucus develops in the lungs and intestinal tract. Sweat contains a higher than normal concentration of sodium and chloride. Absorption of food is impaired. Susceptibility to respiratory infections is greatly increased, because salt and water are removed from lungs too fast (Clark, Hager, and Gosnell, 1986).	Many victims die in early childhood, although antibiotic and enzyme therapy are effective in prolonging life into adolescence and early adulthood. Some cases remain relatively asymptomatic until early adulthood.	The disease is the most common of the serious recessive diseases afflicting Caucasians.
Phenylketonuria (PKU)	1 in 11,000–14,000 live births in U.S. (Muir, 1983; Cohen et al., 1978)	The enzyme needed to metabolize an amino acid (phenylalanine) into another (tryosine) is absent. Toxins accumulate in nerve tissue and destroy it. Mental retardation can result.	PKU can be detected early in infancy with a urine test. (All newborns are routinely screened in most states.) Foods high in phenylalanine are restricted so that toxins are not formed.	
Tay-Sachs	1 in 1,000 live births for Ashkenazi Jews (National March of Dimes, 1973)	Victims cannot metabolize fat properly. The brain and other nerve tissue deteriorates as a result. Children have motor weakness initially, followed by blindness, seizures, and death.	The condition is lethal. Death usually occurs by age 3 or 4.	The recessive genes causing this disease are carried primarily by Jews with Eastern European ancestry.

subsequent Rh-positive babies will suffer. The antibodies in the mother's blood, passing through the placenta, will destroy the fetus's red blood cells, which carry oxygen throughout the fetus's body. Jaundice, anemia, and other problems, sometimes leading to mental retardation or death, can result (Snyder, Schonfeld, & Offerman, 1945).

Fortunately, a serum now exists, called Rh immune globulin, that destroys Rh-positive cells as they enter the mother's body. It prevents the development of antibodies if it's administered to an Rh-negative mother within a few hours after she's given birth to an Rh-positive baby (Clarke, 1968; Zimmerman, 1973). Before this vaccine was developed in the 1960s, about 40,000 babies were affected each year by complications due to Rh incompatibility. Today, the condition is almost nonexistent.

CHROMOSOMAL PROBLEMS. Other prenatal problems occur when errors are made in the egg or sperm cell during meiosis. Sometimes, complete chromosomes don't separate and go to different cells as intended. Other times, pieces of chromosomes break off, leaving extra genetic material in one cell and a shortage in another. Obviously, children with errors in their chromosomes will have serious problems.

The most common chromosomally related abnormality is **Down's syndrome**, which occurs about once in every 600 births. Individuals with Down's syndrome have three number 21 chromosomes instead of the normal two (Lilienfield, 1969; Kerkay, Zsako, & Kaplan, 1971). Two of those chromosomes came from a defective ovum with an extra chromosome and one came from a normal sperm. Children with Down's syndrome are mentally retarded and have a characteristic physical appearance.

Down's syndrome occurs more frequently in mothers who are either under 20 or over 35. The risk of having a Down's syndrome baby increases from 1 in 885 at age 30 to 1 in 50 at age 40 (Pai, 1974). Why this is so is not entirely clear, but hormonal regulation may be more erratic at the lower and upper ranges of the female reproductive lifetime.

Other chromosomal abnormalities create developmental problems. Klinefelter's syndrome is a disorder that results when a male receives an extra X chromosome. Males with this chromosomal error are mentally retarded and develop some female characteristics at puberty (Johnson et al., 1970). Girls with an extra X chromosome have problems with verbal skills and short-term memory (Rovet & Netley, 1983). In another syndrome in which the short arm of the number 10 chromosome is partially deleted, the child has unusual facial features, a very short neck, and psychomotor delays (Elstner et al., 1984).

PROBLEMS DUE TO ENVIRONMENTAL FACTORS. In 1964–1965 an epidemic of rubella (German measles) swept through the United States, and nearly 50,000 children died in utero or were born with birth defects as a result. A few years earlier, hundreds of European mothers who had taken the tranquilizer thalidomide gave birth to babies without arms or legs (Lenz, 1966). These are just two of the many environmental factors that can adversely affect prenatal development. As mentioned earlier, **teratogens** (agents that cause birth defects) inflict the most damage early in pregnancy, when basic body structures are rapidly forming.

FIGURE 3-21
This little boy with Down's syndrome has a characteristic facial appearance and is mentally retarded. Down's syndrome originates with the fertilization of an egg with two number-21 chromosomes rather than the normal one. Because the additional chromosome gives the child hundreds of extra genes, many areas can be affected, including appearance, physical size, eyesight, heart formation, and mental functioning.

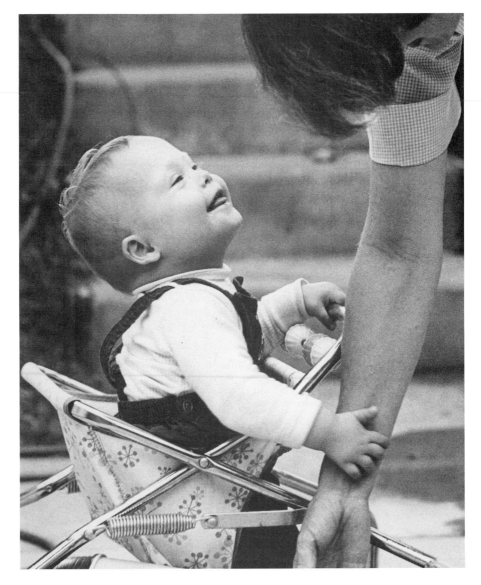

Because of the increase in drug abuse in recent years, researchers have been focusing more intensively on the teratogenic effects of narcotics and other drugs, including cocaine. Currently, there is an alarming increase in the number of babies born who were exposed to cocaine during the prenatal period. These babies are more likely to be born prematurely, to be stillborn (born dead), and to have malformed hearts and skulls (Little et al., 1989). They're extremely irritable and tend to be ultrasensitive to noise and touch. They don't seem to be able to respond or relate to people the way normal babies do, and they're very difficult to comfort or console. These characteristics affect their social and emotional development, because it's difficult for parents to interact with them. As we see in later chapters, positive social interaction is crucial for appropriate language and cognitive development, so many areas of functioning are ultimately affected.

FIGURE 3-22
This premature, cocaine-affected baby is off to a poor start in life. He's likely to be an unresponsive, extremely irritable baby, and when he's strong enough to leave the hospital, he may go home to a drug-addicted mother. The long-term outcome for cocaine-affected babies is something we won't know for years to come.

Other problems have been observed in cocaine-exposed children as well, but so many other factors are usually involved that it's difficult, if not impossible, to sort out cause-and-effect relationships. For example, these children may have been exposed prenatally not just to cocaine but to alcohol, tobacco, and other drugs. Their mothers may have had little or no prenatal care. They may be raised by abusive or neglectful parents in impoverished or dangerous environments. Any of these factors alone or in combination can cause serious problems in a child's development.

Although cocaine is currently in the spotlight as a teratogen, more babies are probably born every year who have been affected prenatally by a legal substance—alcohol. High levels of alcohol consumption during pregnancy are consistently associated not only with spontaneous abortions and stillbirths but also, in live babies, with mental retardation, lower-than-average birth weight, microcephaly (abnormal smallness of the head), unusual facial features, and lowered IQ (Streissguth, 1979; Streissguth, Barr, & Martin, 1983; Streissguth et al., 1989). Babies with this pattern of characteristics are said to suffer from **fetal alcohol syndrome** (FAS) (Rosett et al., 1983). Although occasional or moderate drinking was earlier thought to have no negative effects on the fetus, researchers now doubt there's any safe level of alcohol consumption, and they recommend total abstinence during pregnancy.

Cigarette smoking has also been studied intensively in recent years, since smoking is so widespread. Cigarettes have been associated with several adverse conditions in newborns, including low birth weight. The direct effects of nicotine in the mother's bloodstream have also been observed in the fetus. Both breathing and movement patterns become more rapid and agitated in the fetus when the mother's nicotine level is high (Erikson et al., 1983).

Some research has been directed at determining whether children whose mothers smoked during pregnancy had any long-term social or cognitive disabilities. No evidence of this has been found, at least in middle-class samples (Lefkowitz, 1981). But cigarette smoking does pose a health hazard to children. Infants whose parents smoke are twice as likely to develop pneumonia or bronchitis during their first year as are infants whose parents don't smoke (Greenwood, 1979). This higher risk is probably due to exposure to smoke after birth rather than to any prenatal influence.

As mentioned in Chapter 1, most of the evidence that cigarette smoking affects prenatal development is correlational. Much of the evidence comes from studies of children born with particular problems. Researchers try to discover common habits among the mothers of these children to see if they're different from the general population in some way. When they do find a correlation, such as the one between cigarette smoking and low birthweight, they haven't actually proved causation. The commonalities discovered among the mothers may not be the cause of the problem; something else may be. Perhaps more anxious mothers smoke cigarettes, for example. Anxiety might cause both smoking and low birthweight.

Researchers can't perform the experimental studies necessary to prove causation because it would be unethical. In their correlational studies, they do try to control for every other possible factor so that smoking seems to be the *likely* cause. In any event, since no evidence exists that smoking is beneficial

FIGURE 3-23
A child born with fetal alcohol syndrome has a typical appearance and impaired mental functioning. This condition is just becoming widely recognized, and women are now advised to abstain completely from alcohol during pregnancy.

TABLE 3-2
Environmental Factors Associated with Impairments During Prenatal Development

Agent or Condition	Effects
Rubella (German measles)	Blindness; deafness; heart abnormalities; stillbirth
Cytomegalovirus (CMV)	Microcephaly (smaller than normal head); motor disabilities; hearing loss
Syphilis	Mental retardation; physical deformities; in utero death and miscarriage
AIDS virus	Death, often within two years of birth
Addictive drugs	Low birthweight; possible addiction of infant to the drug; hypersensitivity to stimuli; higher risk for stroke and respiratory distress
Smoking	Prematurity; low birthweight and length
Alcohol	Mental retardation; growth retardation; increased spontaneous abortion rate; microcephaly; structural abnormalities in the face; lowered IQ
Irradiation	Physical deformities; mental retardation
Inadequate diet	Reduction in brain growth; smaller than average birthweight; decrease in birth length; rickets
Tetracycline	Discoloration
Streptomycin	Eighth cranial nerve damage (hearing loss)
Quinine	Deafness
Barbiturates	Congenital malformations
DES (diethylstilbestrol)	Increased incidence of vaginal cancer in adolescent female offspring; impaired reproductive performance in same population
Valium	Cleft lip and palate
Accutane (13-cis-retinoic acid, a new drug used to treat acne)	Small or absent ears; small jaws; hydrocephaly; heart defects
Endocrine disorders	Cretinism; microcephaly
Maternal age under 18	Prematurity; stillbirth; increased incidence of Down's syndrome
Maternal age over 35	Increased incidence of Down's syndrome
Malnutrition	Lower birthweight; abnormal reflexes and irritability; altered brain growth
Environmental chemicals (e.g., benzene, formaldehyde, PCBs, etc.)	Chromosome damage; spontaneous abortions; low birthweight

SOURCES: Berger & Goldstein, 1980; Brown, 1979; Cohen, 1984; Dobbing, 1984; Greenburg, Pelliteri, & Barton, 1957; Herbst, 1972; Herbst et al., 1975; Joos et al., 1983; Lenz, 1966; Meredith, 1975; Naeye, 1983; Naeye, Blanc, & Paul, 1973; Plummer, 1952; Siegel, Fuerst, & Guinee, 1971; Snyder, Schonfeld, & Offerman, 1945; Streissguth, Barr, & Martin, 1983; Walters, 1975; Zeskind & Ramey, 1978.

to the fetus, many women take the safest course and stop smoking during pregnancy.

Other agents and conditions known to affect prenatal development are listed in Table 3-2. As mentioned earlier, most of them are dangerous early in pregnancy. German measles may affect eyes, ears, and brain during the first three months of pregnancy but do no harm later. Thalidomide taken early in pregnancy prevented the formation of arms and legs in fetuses, but taken later, when the limbs were already formed, it caused no damage. Some drugs, like alcohol, cause structural damage early and stunted growth later (Rosett et al., 1983).

Perinatal Problems

Perinatal problems are those that stem from some event or condition that occurs in the last two months of prenatal development, when the baby is basically structurally complete, or during the birth process or in the moments immediately following birth. These problems have the potential to be just as devastating as prenatal ones. Here we look at the three major perinatal problems.

INSUFFICIENT GROWTH. One of the major tasks of the last two months of prenatal development is growth. Of the 7 pounds the average baby weighs at birth, about 3 are gained in the eighth and ninth months. Sometimes, late in pregnancy, the placenta becomes unable to provide the nourishment the fetus needs to reach its full size and weight. Other times a problem in the fetus itself prevents it from properly using the nourishment provided by the placenta. The fetus doesn't gain as much weight in the last few months as it should and is smaller than expected at birth. Sometimes other problems are present as well. Babies who are born small even though they're full term are referred to as **small-for-date** babies.

LACK OF OXYGEN. The main danger to the baby during birth and immediately afterward is oxygen deprivation, or **anoxia**. The baby may not get enough oxygen if the umbilical cord is compressed during delivery, if breathing doesn't start immediately after birth, or if breathing is impaired by respiratory distress in the first days or weeks of life. Respiratory distress usually results from premature birth.

Anoxia affects the lower centers of the brain most severely, where motor functioning is controlled (see Figure 3-24 for a diagram of the brain). Anoxia during or just before birth can cause cerebral palsy, a disorder of the motor system (Paneth, 1986). Children with cerebral palsy have problems speaking and controlling their muscles.

INFECTIONS. Any infection of the mother's reproductive tract can be contracted by the baby during birth or even before birth. The four most serious infections are syphilis, gonorrhea, herpes simplex virus, and AIDS. Syphilis can infect and kill the fetus during the prenatal period. If the baby is born alive, it will have syphilis. Penicillin given to the mother during pregnancy will cure the disease in both mother and fetus.

FIGURE 3-24
The human brain. The cerebral cortex is the center of thinking processes. Lower brain structures, such as the cerebellum, play roles in coordinating motor movements.

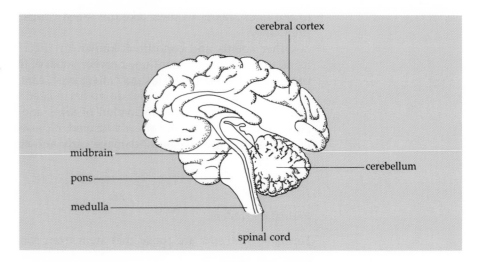

FIGURE 3-24
The human brain. The cerebral cortex is the center of thinking processes. Lower brain structures, such as the cerebellum, play roles in coordinating motor movements.

Gonorrhea can infect the baby during delivery and cause blindness. It can be present in the mother without any symptoms, so the danger to the baby may not be apparent. Because of this uncertainty, laws have been passed requiring that all newborns be treated with silver nitrate drops in their eyes soon after birth. Silver nitrate destroys the gonorrheal bacteria.

Herpes simplex virus can also be transmitted to the baby during delivery if the mother's infection is in the active phase. If this is the case, the baby is delivered by cesarean section to keep it from contacting the virus in the birth canal. Herpes can damage the baby's eyes and brain, and no cure has yet been discovered for the infection. (In adults the virus causes open sores on the skin or mucous membranes but no organ damage.)

Currently, the most serious infection affecting newborns is acquired immune deficiency syndrome (AIDS). This fatal disorder of the immune system, first identified in the United States in the early 1980s, is transmitted in blood and semen. The AIDS virus can be passed to a fetus by an AIDS-infected mother, because viruses from her body can cross the placenta into the developing child.

The population most at risk for this fatal disease are children whose mothers are IV (intravenous) drug abusers or sexual partners of IV drug abusers. These women often acquire the disease by sharing dirty needles with someone who already has the virus. Because drug addiction and the poverty associated with it are more common among blacks than whites in the United States, a high proportion of the women infected by dirty needles are black, and black babies are at the greatest risk for being infected with the AIDS virus. Currently, 57 percent of children under age 5, most of whom were infected by their mothers, are black; 24 percent are Hispanic; and 19 percent are non-Hispanic white (Johnson, 1988).

Like other aspects of child development, prenatal and perinatal problems have a social dimension as well as a biological one. Our discussion shows this to be true: some babies are reaping the benefits of the most advanced scientific research and receiving medical treatment costing hundreds of thousands of dollars. Other babies are being thrown away to drug addiction and AIDS on the threshold of life. No treatment will ever give them the same chances that normal babies have. Only education, prevention, and wide-ranging social changes will solve these devastating problems for future generations.

PRENATAL DIAGNOSIS AND GENETIC COUNSELING

Like Lindsay, the woman we met at the beginning of this chapter, many couples now know well before birth whether their baby has a genetic or chromosomal defect. Modern technology has given us the tools and knowledge to assess prenatal development quite accurately, but accompanying these advances have come moral and ethical dilemmas that never existed before. As we pointed out in Chapter 1, scientific research can provide knowledge and techniques, but it can't provide the wisdom to use them the best way. Human beings still have to make hard choices—and make them earlier than ever—about what kind of children they want to have.

Prenatal Assessment Techniques

Several techniques are now used to examine fetuses and detect prenatal problems. **Ultrasound** is a technique in which sound waves are bounced off the fetus's body and converted into a visual image of the fetus on a TV monitor.

FIGURE 3-25

A sonogram (ultrasound image) of a 16-week-old fetus. Shown in an upright position, the fetus is facing toward the right and slightly away from the viewer. The back of the head and the back are highlighted on the left side of the image; the top of the head, forehead, and cheek can be seen on the right; and the ear is visible in the middle of the head. Amniocentesis revealed that this fetus was a healthy female.

RESEARCH FOCUS

Prenatal Assessment Techniques

Physicians and parents have rushed to take advantage of prenatal assessment techniques as they've been developed. One of the first to be commonly used was ultrasound. In this technique, very high frequency sound waves, far beyond the hearing capacity of the human ear (thus the name *ultra*sound), are bounced off the fetus in the uterus. Sound waves are deflected or absorbed at different rates, depending on the density of the object they strike. For example, they bounce off bone but are absorbed by soft tissue, water, or blood. These differences can be converted into electrical signals, which can in turn be converted into a visual image (Garrett & Robinson, 1970).

In prenatal diagnosis using ultrasound, a technician passes a hand-held transducer over the mother's abdomen. The transducer emits pulses of ultrasound. The deflected ultrasound waves are converted into an image of the fetus on a TV monitor. The image reveals several things about the fetus—position in the womb, size and gestational age, and whether any anatomical problems are present. For example, the image will reveal an abnormally large head, an improperly formed spine, or a heart with certain defects. The newest ultrasound techniques also reveal less gross problems, such as a cleft lip or palate (Seeds & Cefalo, 1983).

Ultrasound appears to be a very safe procedure. To date, no harmful effects have been associated with its use. However, no benefits have been associated with it either. For this reason, it's used only for specific purposes, not as a routine procedure in all pregnancies (Shearer, 1984).

Where ultrasound gives a picture of the fetus, amniocentesis provides a genetic profile. In this procedure, a technician extracts a sample of amniotic fluid from the mother's uterus through a needle inserted into her abdomen. The fetal cells in the fluid are cultured in a lab for several weeks, and then their genetic, chromosomal, and biochemical make-up is analyzed. If a problem is apparent, the parents can decide whether to continue or to terminate the pregnancy.

Amniocentesis can reveal a variety of genetic and chromosomal abnormalities, including Down's syndrome, Tay-Sachs disease, and sickle-cell anemia. Many hospitals routinely advise all mothers over age 35 to have an amniocentesis because of their higher probability of passing on a genetic disorder. The procedure can also be used to determine the fetus's maturity. For example, if a physician wants to deliver a baby as soon as possible because the mother's health is endangered by the pregnancy, amniocentesis can reveal if the fetus's lungs are mature enough for the baby to survive outside the uterus (Kogon et al., 1986).

Amniocentesis is a relatively safe procedure (Chayen, 1978; Kelley & Gilman, 1983). It's even safer if ultrasound is used to determine the position of the fetus so the needle isn't stuck into the unborn infant or the placenta (Mennuti et al., 1983). The main drawback of amniocentesis is timing. It can't be performed until the fetus is at least 14 to 16 weeks old, because until then there isn't enough amniotic fluid to permit extraction. Then the cells have to be cultured for an additional three to five weeks before they can be analyzed. By the time the results are available, the woman is in her twentieth or twenty-first week of pregnancy—her fifth month. If she chooses to have an abortion, a saline procedure has to be used. A suction abortion, which is safer, can no longer be performed at this late date.

A new technique, known as chorionic villus sampling (or chorionic biopsy), is under investigation as an alternative to amniocentesis. In this procedure, a tube is inserted into the uterus and a small amount of chorionic tissue is extracted. Tissue from the chorion, part of the fetal support system in the uterus, is genetically identical to the fetus itself, because both originated from the zygote. Any genetic or chromosomal abnormality in the chorionic cells would indicate an abnormality in the fetus too.

Chorionic sampling can be performed as early as the ninth or tenth week of pregnancy, a full month earlier than amniocentesis (Martin et al., 1986; Saltus, 1987). Results are available within one to seven days. This procedure is still being investigated, however. Potential problems include maternal bleeding, infection, and premature rupture of the membranes (Martin et al., 1986). If these safety issues can be resolved, chorionic sampling will be preferable to amniocentesis, because parents will be able to receive information about their child six weeks earlier than they can now (Hogge, Schonberg, & Golbus, 1986).

It can reveal the number of fetuses in the womb, the position of the fetus, and certain problems in anatomy such as cleft palate.

Amniocentesis involves the extraction of some amniotic fluid from the uterus through a needle inserted into the mother's abdomen. The fluid surrounding the fetus contains fetal cells with the same genetic and chromosomal make-up as the fetus itself. From analyzing the fluid, technicians can detect a variety of abnormalities, including Down's syndrome, Tay-Sachs disease, and sickle-cell anemia. These techniques and another new technique, **chorionic villus**

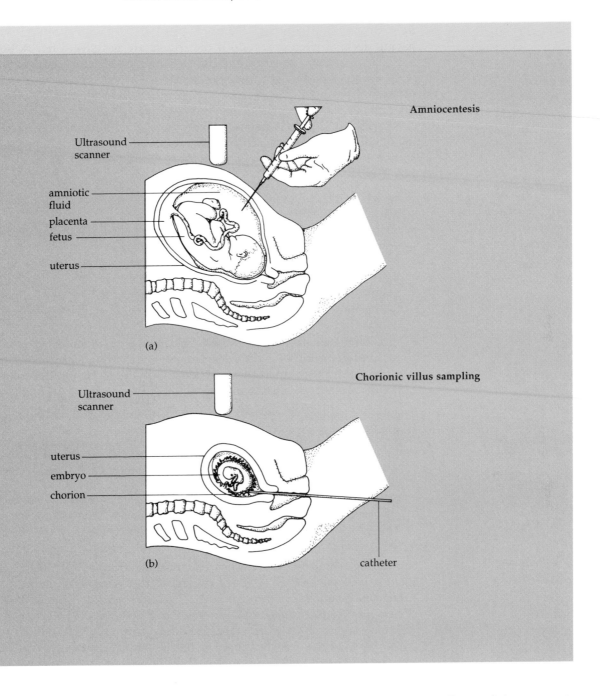

Amniocentesis

Ultrasound scanner

amniotic fluid

placenta

fetus

uterus

(a)

Chorionic villus sampling

Ultrasound scanner

uterus

embryo

chorion

(b)   catheter

sampling, are discussed in detail in Research Focus—Prenatal Assessment Techniques.

Ethical and Social Issues Related to Prenatal Assessment

When a fetus is assessed, the obvious implication is that the pregnancy may be terminated if a defect is found. This isn't always what happens, of course. Some parents use the information to prepare themselves to accept and care for a child with a disability. Many parents go into prenatal testing without having decided what they'll do if the results are negative. They're hoping, naturally, that there won't be any decision to make. But, in general, parents who wouldn't terminate a pregnancy under any circumstances don't seek prenatal assessment. That's why the choice to have an amniocentesis, for example, implies that parents might also choose to terminate the pregnancy.

The difficult decisions associated with prenatal assessment have wide-ranging moral, social, and political implications for both the parents and the larger society. Consider just some of the questions that lie right under the surface of this issue:

- Which genetic disorders are likely to cause severe enough problems to warrant termination of a pregnancy?
- Can a civilized society decide that individuals below a certain level of development are incapable of living a worthwhile life?
- If so, what level of development is sufficient to ensure a worthwhile life? Worthwhile in what terms and from whose point of view? Who decides?
- Should more research be devoted to treatment methods for people born with genetic disorders, or should such births be prevented altogether? Who decides?
- If research on treatment methods is to be pursued, which disorders should receive top priority? If a disorder that occurs more frequently in a particular ethnic or racial group is given higher priority than another disorder, what are the social and political consequences of this choice?

The ethical aspects of prenatal diagnosis have been summed up as follows (Campbell, 1984, p. 1634):

> Some . . . see this enhanced information as a clear moral gain, allowing the avoidance of suffering, the weeding out of conditions which natural selection would in any case discard, the earlier termination of pregnancies where the outcome for the fetus is inevitably fatal, and the continuation of those clearly established as normal. Others, however, fear the reappearance of a eugenic philosophy which regards all less than perfect human beings as inferior and promotes what would be better described as 'ante-natal' euthanasia.

Although some people are concerned that the technology of prenatal assessment will be put in the service of eugenics—the "science" of improving the human race genetically through such policies as prenatal "mercy killing"— the opposite side of the coin is an issue too. Some parents will choose *not* to terminate a pregnancy even when a serious problem is detected (Campbell, 1984). Who should bear the economic burden for the care of a severely handicapped child born after prenatal diagnosis revealed the problem? The parents? The government? Where should the money come from?

Money, of course, is a critical element in all these questions. In the future, according to one researcher, we may see a "zero-sum system" adopted, in which medical budgets are closed (Bloom, 1984). The total amount of money allocated for medical purposes each year would be limited to a particular sum, and within that limit, different medical services would compete with each other for funds. If more money were spent on intensive care for extremely ill neonates, for example, less money would be spent on immunization programs for all children. Or if more money were spent on all pediatric services, less money would be spent on care for the middle-aged or elderly (such as heart by-pass or transplant surgery, kidney dialysis, breast mammography, nursing home care, and so on.)

If recent history is any guide, children's services won't compete very successfully against services for the rapidly growing elderly population. And if the total amount allocated to medical care is increased, some other area has to be reduced. What will it be? Defense? Education? Social Security? And who will make *that* decision?

Changing Attitudes Toward Children

There's one other implication of using prenatal assessment techniques—a change in attitude toward the children that are born. In earlier times (up to about 1970!), parents were largely the victims of fate, and there wasn't much they

FIGURE 3-26
Do parents have the right to perfect children? Do children have the right to a healthy start in life? Our society faces many difficult issues involving children as we embark on the last decade of the twentieth century.

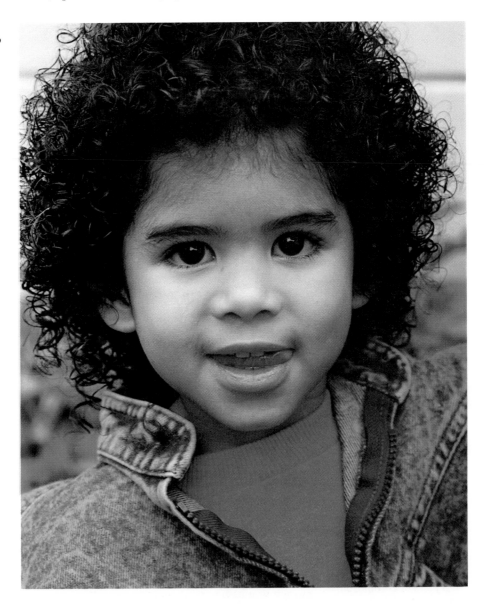

could do about it. If they had a normal child, they thanked their lucky stars, and if they had a disabled child, they grieved and managed the best they could. Now parents have more control over the health of their babies, and they increasingly expect, as a right, to give birth to perfect babies. If they don't, some parents are likely to sue the obstetrician who failed to mention some risk or recommend some test.

This attitude can also be seen later when the child gets to school. Many parents have the same high expectations for learning and achievement that they had for a healthy baby. If something does go wrong, they may believe that the knowledge exists to solve every problem, which is not always the case. Since many parents today are having only a few carefully planned children, they may invest all their hopes and dreams in one or two small human beings.

Unrealistic expectations like these make life hard for everyone. Children are pressured, parents are tense, and teachers and pediatricians face demands they can't meet. Despite great advances, there are still very real limits to scientific knowledge and technology, and these have to be accepted. Perfect children just can't be guaranteed.

OVERVIEW

Child development begins well before birth. In a sense, it begins even before conception if we take into account the parents' history, their health and habits, and the genetic material they may pass on to their children. Our knowledge about all these aspects of child development has increased so rapidly in the last 25 years and technological advances have been so dramatic that pregnancy and birth are radically different experiences today than they were a generation ago. But these advances have introduced new ethical and social dilemmas, and greater opportunities have brought greater responsibilities. The challenge of the future will be to use our sophisticated knowledge to protect and nurture every child from the start of life.

CHAPTER REVIEW

GENETICS: THE BASIS OF BIOLOGICAL INHERITANCE

- Every person on earth is unique, largely because of individual genetic inheritance. But how much people are affected by their genetic make-up, as opposed to their experiences, is a matter of debate, a question referred to as the nature-nurture controversy.
- Biological traits are transmitted from one generation to the next on genes, sequences of DNA, which are carried on chromosomes. Human body cells contain 23 pairs of chromosomes.

- A dominant gene always expresses its own characteristic; a recessive gene expresses its characteristic only when it's paired with another recessive gene.
- A child's genes come from two cells, one contributed by the father and the other contributed by the mother. Germ cells (ova and sperm) differ from body cells in the way they divide. Germ cell division, called meiosis, results in a new cell that contains only 23 single chromosomes.

- Individual genetic differences are the result of the crossing over that occurs during meiosis.
- The sex of a child is determined by the sex chromosomes it inherits. A female inherits an X chromosome from each parent; a male inherits an X from his mother and a Y from his father. Sex-linked characteristics are traits encoded by recessive genes on the X chromosome that can be expressed in males because there isn't a second X chromosome to override them.

- Fraternal twins occur when two different eggs are fertilized. Identical twins occur when a single fertilized egg divides after conception.
- Multiple births often occur when a woman has taken fertility drugs, which stimulate the ovaries to release more than one egg. Multiple births are linked to maternal age; they also occur more frequently in certain populations.

PRENATAL DEVELOPMENT

- In the past, many people thought the embryo was completely formed when implanted and simply increased in size until birth. Others advocated an epigenic, or developmental, theory of prenatal development.
- For couples who can't conceive a child, many treatments are available, including surgery, fertility drugs, and more radical approaches such as in vitro fertilization and surrogate motherhood. Sometimes infertility can't be treated.
- Once a child is conceived, it develops over a 38-week-long period, which we usually divide into three stages.
- The period of the ovum, from conception to week 2, begins in one of the fallopian tubes and ends when the embryo becomes firmly implanted in the uterine wall. If the embryo becomes implanted in the wall of

the fallopian tube, the result is an ectopic pregnancy, which must be ended surgically.
- The period of the embryo, from the second to the eighth week, is the time when all the major body structures are formed. The organism is especially susceptible to environmental influences during this time.
- The period of the fetus, from the ninth week to birth, is a time of growth and further development. The body systems begin to function, and the external genitalia develop.
- Different parts of the body grow at different rates, but the head is more fully developed throughout the entire prenatal period.
- Babies born as early as the twenty-fourth or twenty-fifth week of gestation have survived, but all premature babies face formidable problems.

BIRTH

- The birth process occurs in three stages. During the first and longest stage of labor, the cervix dilates and the baby moves down into the mother's pelvis. During the second stage, the baby moves down through the birth canal and out of the mother's body. The third and final stage is the expulsion of the placenta.
- A variety of conditions can result in birth by cesarean section, delivery of the baby through an incision in the abdominal wall. The rate of cesarean deliveries has increased to almost 25 percent in this country, a rate many people consider far too high.
- Prior to the early 1970s, birth was treated as a medical emergency. Women were heavily sedated and gave birth in hospital delivery rooms. Babies were taken to a nursery after delivery and brought to the mothers at scheduled feeding times. The father and any siblings had little or no contact with the baby during the hospital stay.
- In the early 1970s parents, physicians, midwives, and childbirth educators began to lobby for more parental involvement in the birth process and for the use of

less medication during labor. Research findings and changing social practices, such as an increase in breastfeeding, also contributed to changes in childbirth practices.
- Today, many parents take childbirth education classes in which they learn special breathing and relaxation techniques to use during labor, reducing the need for pain-relieving drugs. Women are often assisted by their husbands or partners, and they may labor and deliver in special birthing rooms if their deliveries are uncomplicated.
- If the baby is full term and healthy, the mother can usually keep the baby with her immediately afer birth. Rooming-in is available in most hospitals, and fathers and siblings have contact with the new baby before it comes home.
- Mothers stay in the hospital for two or three days following a normal, uncomplicated delivery, and women who have had a cesarean section stay from five to seven days.
- Some women who have normal, low-risk pregnancies

choose to give birth at home or in alternative birth centers assisted by a midwife or physician. Home births have both advantages and certain risks.

- The main benefit of the new childbirth practices is the reduced use of medication. There are also psychological and emotional benefits to giving birth in a relaxed setting and having the father involved during the birth.
- Early contact between mother and baby is important, but studies have shown that mothers who couldn't have contact with their babies immediately after birth have no trouble establishing a strong emotional attachment once they do have contact.

PROBLEMS IN EARLY DEVELOPMENT

- Problems that originate before the seventh month of development are called prenatal; problems that originate between the seventh month and a few minutes after birth are called perinatal.
- Prenatal problems can be genetic, chromosomal, or environmental.
- Most genetic problems result when the child inherits an abnormal recessive gene from both parents. The most common genetic diseases are sickle-cell anemia, cystic fibrosis, phenylketonuria, and Tay-Sachs disease.
- Rh disease is a genetically related disorder that occurs when an Rh-negative mother gives birth to an Rh-positive baby. A serum now controls the disease.
- Chromosomal problems occur when errors are made during meiosis. The most common chromosomal abnormality is Down's syndrome, which is more common in mothers under age 20 and over age 35.
- Environmental problems occur when a fetus is exposed to teratogens, including viruses, prescription and illegal drugs, alcohol, and environmental chemicals.
- The three major perinatal problems are insufficient growth, insufficient oxygen, and infections.
- Insufficient growth occurs when the placenta fails to nourish the fetus adequately, resulting in a small-for-date baby.
- If a baby receives insufficient oxygen during or just after birth, the lower centers of the brain may be affected, causing cerebral palsy.
- Infections can be passed from the mother to the baby during or before birth. The four most serious infections are syphilis, gonorrhea, herpes simplex virus, and AIDS.

PRENATAL DIAGNOSIS AND GENETIC COUNSELING

- Advanced techniques for detecting prenatal problems include ultrasound, which gives a picture of the fetus, and amniocentesis and chorionic villus sampling, both of which provide a genetic profile.
- These new techniques have created ethical and political questions, such as how to decide when a prenatal problem is severe enough to warrant termination of a pregnancy.
- Prenatal assessment techniques have also affected parents' attitudes, in some cases leading to unrealistically high expectations that modern technology can create perfect children. New knowledge can enhance the chances of having healthy babies, but it can't guarantee them.

KEY TERMS

nature-nurture controversy	meiosis	embryoblast	Down's syndrome
genes	sex-linked characteristics	trophoblast	teratogens
chromosomes	zygote	ectopic pregnancy	fetal alcohol syndrome
recessive gene	fraternal twins	period of the embryo	small-for-date baby
dominant gene	identical twins	period of the fetus	anoxia
germ cells	prenatal development	crowning	ultrasound
somatic cells	epigenic theory	rooming-in	amniocentesis
mitosis	fallopian tube	prenatal	chorionic villus sampling
	gestation	perinatal	

SUGGESTIONS FOR FURTHER READING

Brigitte, J. (1980). *Birth in four cultures*. Montreal, Canada: Eden Press.
    A very interesting and readable book written by an anthropologist. Brings a cultural perspective to the birthing process.

Butler, D. (1980). *Cushla and her books*. Boston: The Horn Book.
    The story of family care for a child born with physical handicaps. Very moving and informative.

Dorris, M. (1989). *The broken cord*. New York: Harper & Row.
    This compelling book is the story of a child (now grown up) who suffers from fetal alcohol syndrome. Written by his adoptive father, it not only reviews the current research on FAS but gives a clear picture of the kind of devastating brain damage associated with maternal alcohol abuse during pregnancy.

Institute of Medicine (1985). *Preventing low birthweight: Summary*. Washington, DC: National Academy Press.
    Presents an overview of the problem and what is known about its causes. Discusses policy steps that should be taken to help reduce the number of babies born with low birthweight.

Lane, D., & Stratford, B. (1985). *Current approaches to Down's syndrome*. New York: Praeger.
    This book provides detailed information about many aspects of Down's syndrome, including typical physical characteristics and problems and educational programs. Includes research on language, motor, and play behavior.

Pollock, L. (1987). *A lasting relationship: Parents and children over three centuries*. London: University Press of New England.
    This book uses diaries, memoirs, autobiographies, and letters to provide a portrait of children from the early 1600s to the mid-1800s. The first section covers views of pregnancy and childbirth. Fascinating reading.

part two

INFANTS AND TODDLERS

A child is born; a new life has begun. Prenatal development now complete, the baby appears in the world with many qualities determined and many more still unknown. In the next few years, the child will encounter an infinite variety of new sensations and experiences; personal traits and abilities will unfold; and inner and outer influences will work together to create a complex, unique human being. The importance of these early years cannot be overestimated. By the time they're 3 or 4 years old, children are launched on a course that only a great deal of hard work will alter. Much of what they will be in life is determined now. Perhaps more than any other period of childhood, infancy and toddlerhood require our best efforts to understand, to protect, and to nurture.

chapter 4

THE NEONATE

Lew Harding was finally coming back down to earth. His adrenaline had been pumping ever since his wife had gone into labor some time the previous night. He'd gotten her to the hospital, helped her relax and breathe through contractions for 8 hours, and watched her give birth to their first child, just 15 minutes ago. He had been stunned by the intensity of Susan's experience and deeply moved when the baby was born. Now he was just beginning to relax. The baby was lying on Susan's stomach under heated blankets, and he and Susan were gently rubbing the baby's back.

But as he watched his little son, Lew began to experience another feeling—worry, turning rapidly to alarm. The baby in front of him looked not at all like the baby he had imagined so many times or like the pictures in the books. Patrick's skin was bright red, chafed and creased at the wrists and elbows, and covered with a white coating that looked like old soap. His black hair was matted against his head, and there also seemed to be a coating of fine black hair all over his body. His eyes were swollen shut, his nose was flat, one of his ears was pasted forward on his cheek, his chin was nonexistent, and his head was pointy!

Lew looked up quickly to ask someone if the baby was all right. A nurse met his eyes and smiled. "Congratulations, Mr. Harding," she said. "Your son is perfect!"

Lew turned quickly back to his new family. Now, as he gazed at Patrick, he began to wonder why he'd been worried. The longer he looked, the more beautiful his son became.

If you've never witnessed a birth, you might also be surprised by the way Patrick looks. The round, rosy face you might imagine as that of a newborn is actually the face of a baby 4 or 5 months old. Patrick's appearance is quite different. He retains many features, now unnecessary, that suited him very well in his warm, dark, wet life in the womb. He also bears the marks of his long, hard journey from the uterus to the outside world. It takes some time—

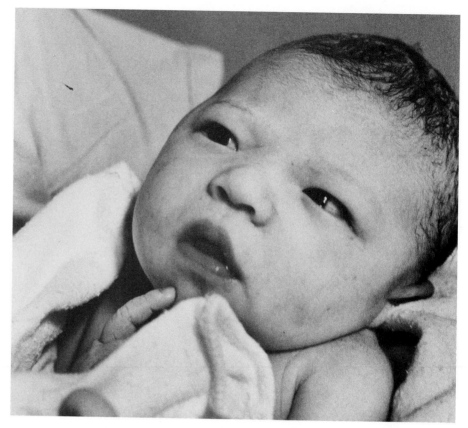

anywhere from a few days to a few weeks—for newborns to adjust to life in their new surroundings. During this time, the newborn is known as a **neonate,** and the period of adjustment is known as the **neonatal period.**

Neonates have a lot to do in their first few weeks of life outside the womb. They have many physiological adjustments to make, a social life to begin, and the wide world to observe. This chapter focuses on what neonates are like and what changes they go through in this early period. The very different experience of the premature baby is also considered. Finally, the practical concerns doctors and parents have during the earliest period of the baby's life are discussed.

PHYSICAL CHARACTERISTICS

Appearance

Why does Patrick look the way he does? There's a reason for everything about his appearance. The white, greasy covering on his skin, called **vernix caseosa,** is accumulated sebum, a secretion from glands surrounding the hair follicles in his skin. Vernix forms a protective barrier between his skin and the fluid in his mother's womb. It also provides lubrication during the birth process and protects his skin from infection once he's born.

FIGURE 4-2
The fontanelles, or soft spots, in a young baby's skull will close as the bones grow and fuse. The process is usually complete by the time the child is 2 years old.

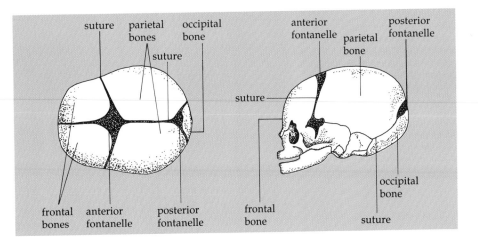

Patrick's misshapen head is a result of the squeezing that occurred as he passed through his mother's pelvis during birth. As explained in Chapter 3, the bones in the newborn's skull aren't completely formed and can be squeezed together, or **molded,** even to the point of overlapping. Molding permits the baby to have a larger, more mature brain at birth. Even if Patrick's head were an inch larger before molding than his mother's pelvis, his head could still fit through. The open spaces, or **fontanelles,** in the incompletely developed skull are covered with a tight web of skin and tissue that protects the brain from injury (Figure 4-2). The two diamond-shaped "soft spots" on the head will close sometime during the first two years of life as the bones harden and grow together.

Patrick's eyes are swollen shut probably from the pressure exerted on his face during birth. His ear and nose also were temporarily flattened. Puffiness in his face and eyes was caused by the accumulation of fluids when he was in a head-down position before birth. Additional puffiness is created when the silver nitrate drops are put in his eyes after birth to protect him from gonorrhea, which he could have contracted during delivery if his mother had been infected.

Patrick's color is deep red because his capillaries show through his thin skin. As he gains weight and builds up a thicker layer of fat under his skin, the intense redness will fade away. Patrick's appearance will change in some other ways as well in the next few weeks. His head will gradually assume a normal rounded shape, the puffiness will disappear from his eyelids, and the fine hair on his body, known as **lanugo,** will fall out. Still, he will be recognizable as a newborn because of other more enduring physical characteristics, which we consider next.

Body Proportions

When the nurse held Patrick before placing him on his mother's stomach, she made sure she supported his neck with her hand. If she hadn't, Patrick's head would fall backward and he wouldn't be able to bring it up again. This is not just because his neck muscles are weak (Prechtl, 1982); it's also because his

FIGURE 4-3
Body proportions change radically as children develop and mature. The head accounts for as much as 50 percent of body length prenatally and for about 25 percent at birth. After the first year, other parts of the body—trunk and legs—grow faster than the head. By adulthood, the head accounts for about 10 percent of overall body length.

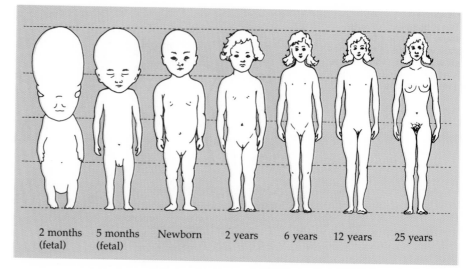

| 2 months (fetal) | 5 months (fetal) | Newborn | 2 years | 6 years | 12 years | 25 years |

head is very large and heavy compared to the rest of his body. As mentioned in Chapter 3, the head grows faster than other parts of the body during the prenatal period. The head of an adult is about one-tenth of the adult's height, but the head of a newborn is almost one-fourth its total body length (Figure 4-3).

Just as the top of the newborn's body is more fully developed than the lower portion, the top of the newborn's head also is more fully developed than the lower portion. Patrick's jawbones are underdeveloped, he has practically no chin, and his neck is very short. His head sits almost directly on top of his very narrow shoulders. As he grows, his facial features and body proportions will gradually evolve into those of the older baby and child.

Physiology: Feeding and Digestion

Patrick will be so sleepy at first that it may be hard for his mother to keep him from repeatedly falling asleep while she's nursing him. When he does nurse, he may gag frequently on mucus in his throat. However, his mother doesn't have to worry about his eating much in his first few days of life. He was born with stores of **glycogen,** a starch that his body can easily transform into sugar when he needs energy. He also has reserves of extra fat and fluids. The ability of newborns to survive for up to a week without food was demonstrated a few years ago when babies were found alive in the rubble of a hospital leveled by an earthquake in Mexico.

Although he's been nurtured through his mother's body for nine months, Patrick is able to eat food and absorb nutrients at birth. His digestive system produces enough enzymes to digest and absorb both proteins and sugars. He may be less able to absorb saturated fats efficiently, however (Katz & Hamilton, 1974). Since cow's milk is higher in fat than human milk, it's not as perfectly suited to babies as their mother's milk.

It's convenient that Patrick won't start eating in earnest right away, because his mother won't start producing milk for one to three days after his birth. Since late in her pregnancy, however, she's been producing **colostrum**, a thin, yellowish liquid high in protein and low in fat—perfectly suited to Patrick's nutritional needs and digestive capacities. Colostrum also contains **immuno-globulins,** antibodies for specific foreign agents that protect the young infant from infectious diseases. Mothers' milk continues to contain antibodies, and babies often seem to resist colds and other infections for a good six months after birth. Since premature babies are more vulnerable to disease than full-term babies, some experts have urged that all premature babies receive human milk (Goldman & Smith, 1973).

One of the first things the nurse will do after Patrick's parents have held him for a while is weigh and measure him. If he's average, he'll weigh about 7½ pounds and measure about 20 inches long. But in his first few days, he'll actually lose some weight—up to 10 percent of his birth weight would not be unusual—because his body is using up some of the stored glycogen, throwing off fluids, and excreting feces. Bottle-fed babies, who are fed on their first day, start gaining weight sooner than breastfed babies, who have to wait for their mothers' milk to flow. Premature babies gain weight more slowly because they can't eat very much at a feeding.

Although all newborns have a limited capacity at each feeding, they make up for it by eating frequently, usually every two and a half to four hours. Smaller babies may eat less but a little more often. At various times in the past, doctors and child development specialists advised parents to keep their babies on strict feeding schedules in the belief that regularity was best for babies and parents alike and that being responsive to the baby's demands would spoil the baby. Today, most parents recognize the importance of responding to the baby rather than following a rigid schedule.

Of course, this means that newborns need to be fed at night, and someone has to get up to feed them. Although some babies apparently sleep through

FIGURE 4-4
The perfect food . . . a perfect fit. At birth, the mother is producing colostrum, a source of important antibodies that protect the newborn from infectious diseases. Within a few days, she starts producing milk.

the night right from the start, most need one or more night feedings for a few months or more. New parents often mention lack of a good night's sleep as the single most stressful aspect of having a new baby. To solve this problem, some mothers keep the baby in their bed or in a cradle right next to their bed so they can feed the baby at night without having to get up. Parents whose baby is bottle fed or will sometimes take a bottle can take turns getting up on alternate nights for feedings. Other parents rely on daytime help with the new baby, with other children, or with household chores from friends, relatives, or a housekeeper. However they deal with the lack of sleep, most parents are greatly relieved when they awaken one morning to find that the baby has slept through the whole night.

Respiration and Circulation

When Patrick took his first breath, his lungs filled with air and he let out a healthy cry. But later, as he settled down into his first long sleep period, his parents might have been alarmed if they had been watching him. His breathing would have been rapid and shallow for a time and then punctuated by long, deep breaths. Sometimes he might have stopped breathing altogether for a few seconds, a normal and apparently harmless occurrence known as **apnea.** He would also have coughed and sneezed a lot because of the mucus in his nose and throat.

It's not surprising that it takes some time for Patrick's breathing to become regulated. Before birth he got his oxygen from his mother, through the placenta. His blood didn't even pass through his lungs when he was a fetus but bypassed them through a vessel called the **ductus arteriosus**. Immediately after birth, this vessel closed as air filled his lungs, and from that point on, he obtained his own oxygen from the air (Wennberg, Woodrum, & Hodson, 1973).

This change in source of oxygen can cause a problem for some newborns. Because oxygen obtained directly from the air is richer, the baby needs fewer red blood cells to carry the oxygen through his body. The baby's body therefore destroys some unneeded red blood cells. This is a process that occurs naturally to some extent at all times. The destruction of the red blood cells produces a by-product called **bilirubin,** which is metabolized in the liver. The newborn's body can't handle the bilirubin very efficiently, and sometimes the liver can't produce enough of the enzyme that converts the bilirubin into a form that can be excreted. Then the baby's bilirubin level goes up, causing **hyperbilirubinemia,** a yellowing of the skin commonly known as *jaundice*.

Within a few days, most newborns are able to produce enough of the enzyme to break down the bilirubin, and the jaundice disappears. But some babies who have moderate jaundice and a rising bilirubin level are treated with special lights, a treatment known as **phototherapy** (Slater & Brewer, 1984). Phototherapy helps convert bilirubin accumulated in the skin into a more water-soluble form that can be excreted by the liver without further metabolism. The level of bilirubin goes down more quickly than it would without the lights (Cashore & Stern, 1982). Currently, a new technique is being explored to treat hyperbilirubinemia. It involves the use of an enzyme that slows the body's breakdown of red blood cells. This gives the baby's body more time to clear the blood of bilirubin as it builds up (Kappas et al., 1988). Jaundice is dangerous because the baby's blood can become overloaded with bilirubin and allow it to pass into the brain. When bilirubin gets into the brain, it can stain brain cells—a condition known as **kernicterus**—and cause brain damage (Cashore & Stern, 1982).

Other conditions increase the risk of serious hyperbilirubinemia and jaundice in the newborn, including Rh incompatibility, which was discussed in Chapter 3, the use of general anesthesia during labor and delivery, and bruising during birth. When general anesthesia is used, the drugs enter the baby's bloodstream and have to be metabolized by the baby's body. The processing of the drugs in the liver competes with the processing of the bilirubin. When the baby is bruised during birth, blood and fluid leak into tissues and blood cells are broken down. This increases the number of red blood cells the baby's body has to dispose of, thus raising the level of bilirubin.

Temperature Regulation

The temperature of the room in which Patrick was born was approximately 80 degrees. Even so, the nurse covered him with a warm blanket as soon as he was born. Then his mother held him closely against her body, and his father rubbed his back. Although it wasn't necessarily their purpose, this helped to keep him warm too. Patrick needed all this warmth because newborns aren't able to maintain a normal body temperature by themselves until they're about 8 or 9 weeks old.

FIGURE 4-5
Newborns have to be kept warm because they can't yet regulate their own body temperatures. Swaddling them in blankets also restrains their arms and legs and soothes them, perhaps because it recreates the confining security of the womb.

FIGURE 4-6
Some newborn reflexes have obvious survival value, such as rooting (top left) and sucking (top right), both of which help the baby obtain nourishment. The purpose of other reflexes isn't as clear—the tonic neck reflex (center left), the Moro, or startle, reflex (center right), the toe grasp (bottom left), and the Babinski reflex (bottom right).

We don't know exactly why newborns have trouble keeping warm. Some researchers think the temperature-regulating mechanism in the brain is immature or that it works differently than the adult mechanism. Others note that the ratio of the baby's body surface to its mass is so high that heat escapes rapidly from the surface. Still others point out that the baby's body has very little fat under the skin to provide insulation (Mestayan & Varga, 1960; Perlstein et al., 1974; Sinclair, 1975). Whatever the cause, we do know that babies have to be kept warm. When they're taken out of the bath, they should be quickly wrapped in a towel to prevent cooling from evaporation, and when they're taken outside in cold weather, even briefly, they should be dressed in a hat and coat.

It's hard to tell when babies are too hot or too cold because they don't shiver or perspire the way adults do (Klaus & Fanaroff, 1973). Parents have to keep track of what the temperature is and judge the baby's comfort to some extent by what they themselves are wearing. If a parent thinks a baby may be too cold, holding the baby is an excellent course of action with several benefits. It enhances temperature regulation (Phillips, 1974; Rovee-Collier & Lipsitt, 1982); it soothes a baby who's upset and whose crying is using up energy needed to maintain growth; and it enhances social interaction and learning, as discussed more fully later in this chapter.

MOTOR CAPABILITIES

Reflexive Behavior

Patrick appeared to be quite helpless at birth, but actually he has some inborn motor responses, or **reflexes**, that help him survive. If his mother touched or stroked his cheek, his head would turn toward her hand and his lips and tongue would move. This **rooting reflex** gets him in a good position to get mother's nipple into his mouth. The sensation of the nipple in his mouth triggers the **sucking reflex,** a complex behavior involving a combination of pressure and suction. Patrick also has a **gag reflex** that helps him clear mucus from his throat, and he sneezes and coughs reflexively.

If Patrick were placed face down on a surface and his nose and mouth became obstructed, he would be able to engage in a series of reflexive actions that would prevent him from suffocating. He would raise and turn his head, raise his shoulders, and extend and flex his arms and legs in movements that resemble crawling. This reflex makes it possible to put a newborn like Patrick on his stomach in bed without danger of his smothering in bedclothes. The existence of this and other reflexes indicates that even newborns can protect themselves to a certain extent (Brazelton, 1969). This "crawling" reflex can get the baby into trouble too, however. Parents who believe their baby is too young to move may leave the baby unattended on a bed. If the baby's face is repeatedly obstructed and the baby reflexively "crawls" each time, he can end up tumbling off the bed.

Newborns have other reflexes as well. The function of these reflexes isn't as apparent, but they do indicate the state of the baby's neurological well-being. If these reflexes are present, the baby's nervous system is presumed to be intact and working properly. One of these is the **tonic neck reflex.** If the doctor were to test Patrick for this reflex, she would lay him on his back and

TABLE 4-1
Examples of Infant Reflexes

Reflex	Description	Developmental Course
Blinking	If a light is shone in the baby's eyes, she closes them.	Permanent
Rooting	If the baby's cheek is touched or stroked, she turns her head toward the stroked cheek and moves her lips and tongue to suck.	Gone by 4 months
Sucking	When a nipple or other object is placed in the baby's mouth, she sucks on it using both pressure and suction.	Voluntary by 2 months
Gagging, coughing, sneezing	When mucus or other material blocks the baby's air passages, she clears them automatically.	Permanent
"Crawling"	When the baby is placed face down in such a way that her nose and mouth are obstructed, she raises and turns her head and shoulders and alternately extends and flexes her arms and legs.	Voluntary maneuvers take over by 3–4 months
Tonic neck	If the baby is laid on her back and her head is turned to one side, she stretches out her arm and leg on the side that she is facing and flexes her other arm and leg.	Gone by 4 months
Moro	If the baby is startled by a loud noise or by her head dropping back suddenly, she throws out her arms, fans her fingers, extends her neck, cries, and then brings her arms back to her chest and closes her fingers as if clasping something.	Weak by 5 months, gone by 8 months
Babinski	When the baby's foot is stroked from the heel to the toe, her toes fan out.	Gone by 12 months
Grasping	When the palms of the baby's hands are stroked or pressed, she closes her fingers around the object in a strong grasp. When her feet are pressed just below the toe, she curls her toes down.	Gone by 12 months, beginning to weaken by 3 months
Stepping	If the baby is held upright so one foot just touches a surface, she makes stepping motions as if walking.	Gone by 3 months

turn his head to one side. Patrick would stretch out his arm and leg on the side he's facing and flex the arm and leg on the other side.

A loud sound or a sudden dropping back of Patrick's head would elicit the **Moro,** or **startle, reflex.** He would throw out his arms, fan out his fingers, extend his neck, let out a cry, and then bring his arms back to "embrace" or clasp his chest (Dargassies, 1966). The Moro reflex is triggered when internal receptors sense movement in the neck muscles. Babies sometimes startle themselves during crying episodes and become even more frantic.

If the doctor stroked the outer edge of the soles of Patrick's feet, she would elicit the **Babinski reflex**—his toes would fan out. If she stroked or put pressure on the palms of his hands, she would elicit the **grasping reflex.** This **palmar grasp** is so strong that the doctor could lift Patrick from his back if he were lying on a flat surface. She could also elicit a toe grasp if she pressed on the bottom of Patrick's feet just below the toes.

The purpose of these reflexes isn't clear, but they were probably useful at some time during human evolutionary history. They diminish during the first few months of life as the brain matures. The lower brain centers (midbrain, pons, medulla, and cerebellum) come under the control of the higher brain center, the cerebral cortex, which inhibits reflex action. (For a diagram of the brain, refer to Figure 3-24 in Chapter 3.) It's hard to elicit a startle reflex by 6 months of age, for example, and by 8 or 9 months it's usually impossible. The Babinski reflex is usually gone by 4 months. If reflexes persist beyond the time when they typically disappear, it may indicate that the brain isn't functioning normally. (See Table 4-1 for descriptions and developmental courses of selected reflexes.) One of the early signs of cerebral palsy, for example, is the persistence of the tonic neck reflex, the Moro reflex, and the palmar reflexes (Barabas & Taft, 1986).

Voluntary Movements

Although Patrick has a variety of reflexes, he doesn't have much control over his voluntary movements. During the last few weeks in the womb, his muscles developed a considerable amount of muscle tone, or **tonus**, the continuous tension normal in muscles at rest (Dargassies, 1966). In the fetal position, his legs were crossed at the ankles and bent at the knees so they touched his abdomen. His arms were bent at the elbows and raised up, and his fists were clenched.

After birth, his movements are like the gradual unwinding of a tightly wound spring. His arms and legs jerk and flail, and he has trouble getting his fingers or hand to his mouth. As he gains control over his muscle activity, he becomes more successful at reaching his target with less excess motion.

BEHAVIORAL STATES

Newborns are typically awake and alert when they're born, but after about an hour they fall into a long, deep sleep (Wolff, 1965; Stratton, 1982). They might remain asleep for a day or more, possibly to give their body a chance to adjust to all the changes they're going through (Brazelton, 1961). After this sleep, their behavior will be organized into recurring patterns of wakefulness and sleep called **behavioral states.** At some times they'll be alert, at other times they'll be in one kind of sleep or another, and at still other times they'll be crying.

Researchers define behavioral states by looking at specific variables, which usually include eye movements, position of eyelids (open or closed), regularity of breathing, brain wave patterns, and motor activity (Prechtl & O'Brien, 1982). Various schemes have been devised to classify and assess babies' behavioral states, but the one shown in Table 4-2 is useful because it labels the states with descriptive terms, including regular sleep, irregular sleep, drowsiness, alert inactivity, waking activity, and crying (Wolff, 1966). During the alert inactive state, the baby is calm, bright-eyed, attentive, and particularly receptive to stimuli from the environment. After the first few days, the baby spends more and more time in the alert inactive state.

FIGURE 4-7
Researchers identify babies' behavioral states by observing a variety of different characteristics, including skin color, muscle tone, rate of breathing, and vocalization, but even the casual observer can identify drowsiness, crying, and alert inactivity. In the alert inactive state, the baby can observe, learn, and interact with adults.

Regularities in Behavioral States and Variations Among Infants

Behavioral states are organized and cyclical; they don't occur randomly (Prechtl & O'Brien, 1982). In other words, we can predict which state will follow the baby's present state. For example, alert inactivity often follows waking activity, and drowsiness often follows crying. Even though they follow the same pattern, however, all babies don't spend the same amount of time in the various states. Some babies cry more than others, some sleep more than others, and some are more alert than others. We don't know exactly why this is, but genetic factors may account for some of the differences. Method of delivery may also be a factor. Babies whose mothers were anesthetized during the birth tend to be less active and alert, at least for the first few days. (For further discussion, see Research Focus—Effects of Obstetrical Drugs on Newborns.)

Childrearing practices may also influence the baby's states. For example, swaddling (wrapping the baby tightly in a blanket) keeps babies from losing control of their arms and legs and startling (Brazelton, 1969; Friedman, Jacobs, & Werthmann, 1981). Hospital nurses usually wrap babies tightly because they know it keeps them calmer. Parents, of course, quickly unwrap the blankets because they want to look at the baby. But they also hold the baby, which restrains the arms and legs and keeps the baby calmer.

TABLE 4-2 Behavioral States in the Newborn

State	Motor Activity	Muscle Tone	Skin	Eyes	Face	Respiration	Vocalization
Regular sleep	No movement of limbs and trunk; startle reflexes present	Relaxed	Pink, but pale	Closed; no movement	Relaxed	Regular; breaths 36 per minute	
Irregular sleep	Movement of trunk and limbs between periods of rest	Moderate degree of tension	Flushed during activity	Closed, but movements present	Grimaces such as smiles and frowns	Irregular rhythm; 48 breaths per minute	
Drowsiness	More movement than during regular sleep but less than during irregular sleep	Moderate degree of tension		Eyes open and close; dull, glazed, and unfocused		Generally regular	Occasional high-pitched squeal
Alert inactivity	Inactive	Moderate degree of tension		Eyes are open, bright, shining, attentive; eyes move together in horizontal and vertical plane		Faster than during regular sleep	
Waking activity	Activity occurs in spurts	Higher degree of tension	Flushed during activity	Eyes are open but not bright and shining		Irregular	Moans, grunts, whining, but no sustained crying
Crying	Very active	Considerable tension	Flushed bright red	May be open or closed; tears in some babies	Grimaces	Fast and irregular	Crying

SOURCE: Wolff, P. (1966). *The causes, controls, and organizations of behavior in the newborn. Psychological Issues, 5 (Whole No. 17),* 1–105.

Behavioral States, Attachment, and Learning

Whatever the individual baby's pattern, it does have an influence on the mother-child relationship. It's now widely acknowledged that the baby affects the mother as much as the mother affects the baby (Bell, 1971; Crockenberg, 1981). An extremely irritable baby or a baby who doesn't respond very strongly can have a negative effect on the mother, just as a baby who is responsive and calm can have a positive effect.

In Chapter 8 on the social and emotional development of infants and toddlers, we discuss in greater detail the importance of the mother-child relationship and the factors that influence it. Here, we mention just that a positive, nurturing relationship probably keeps the baby calmer and better able to take advantage of sights and sounds in the environment. Holding the baby up to the shoulder, for example, often stops crying and induces the alert inactive

RESEARCH FOCUS

Effects of Obstetrical Drugs on Newborn

Until the mid-nineteenth century, women delivered their babies without drugs or medication to relieve the pain of labor and delivery (Butarescu, 1978). Then in 1847, Scottish physician James Y. Simpson introduced the use of chloroform as an anesthetic for his obstetrical patients. Many people were outraged, because, they claimed, the Bible decreed that childbirth should be painful. But in 1853, Queen Victoria delivered a son under chloroform, and from then on the use of obstetrical drugs grew steadily.

Today, we know that drugs given to the mother quickly cross the placenta and enter the fetus (Ploman & Persson, 1957; Marx, 1961; Bonica, 1967; Morishima et al., 1966). We also know something about how drugs affect the newborn. This information, along with greater interest in prepared childbirth, has led to a decrease in the use of drugs during childbirth. Women are taking less medication than was common in previous years, and many women are having completely unmedicated births.

What are the effects of obstetrical drugs on newborn babies? First and most obviously, drugs make babies groggy at birth. Babies born to nonmedicated mothers are generally alert at birth, and they remain in the alert inactive state longer than babies of medicated mothers before falling asleep (Desmond et al., 1963). Babies born to medicated mothers suck less vigorously and for shorter periods of time than babies born to nonmedicated mothers. These differences have been found to last for one to four days (Brazelton, 1970; Kron, Stern, & Goddard, 1966; Richards & Bernal, 1972).

Babies born to medicated mothers also habituate more slowly to sounds, are less able to track objects with their eyes, exhibit less control of their behavioral states (Murray et al., 1981), and have poorer muscle tone and slower reflexes (Conway & Brackbill, 1970;

Aleksandrowicz & Aleksandrowicz, 1974). Some differences are noticeable for as long as a month after birth. In fact, some effects don't peak until the twenty-eighth day after birth and presumably persist for an unknown period of time after that.

According to one study, the clearest difference between babies from medicated and nonmedicated births is in **consolability,** the ease with which a baby stops crying when talked to or held (Brackbill et al., 1974). Nonmedicated babies are cuddlier and more readily consoled. These characteristics, along with the length of time the baby is alert and attentive after birth, have the potential to influence the parent-child relationship in important ways.

Critics have faulted the research methods used in some of these studies (Federman & Yang, 1976), and effects of drugs lasting longer than one month haven't been demonstrated by any studies. But mothers' subjective experiences of their babies play a role in infant development just as physical condition does. And in some studies nonmedicated mothers have reported their babies to be more social, more rewarding, and "easier" than medicated babies have been reported to be. As one researcher points out, "Although direct biochemical drug effects may wear off in the first days . . . the mother's early impressions may remain to influence how rewarding she finds her baby and the manner in which she responds to her baby's initiatives . . ." (Murray et al., 1981).

As with all aspects of child development, no single event—whether it's separation immediately after birth, an extended hospital stay, or a groggy baby—determines the long-term outcome for a parent-child relationship. But if there's an accumulation of such events, particularly when parents are considered "at risk" for having problems interacting with the baby, the scales may be tipped toward future difficulties.

---

state, in which the baby is most likely to observe the surroundings (Korner & Grobstein, 1966; Hunziker & Barr, 1986). Thus, babies' behavioral states affect both the kinds of relationship they develop with their mothers and the kinds of opportunities they have for learning in their early months.

SENSORY ABILITIES

Vision

Patrick's eyes were open when he was born, and he seemed to be looking around the room. When his eyes came to rest on his mother's face, she smiled broadly at him in response. She wasn't sure how much he could see, but she thought he was looking right at her. And she was right—although his vision wasn't as good as an adult's, he could see her face quite well.

As recently as 30 or 40 years ago, parents were told their newborns couldn't see, but now we know this is absolutely untrue. If an object is held in front

FIGURE 4-8
This premature newborn is being held at just about the right distance to form the best visual image of Mom's face.

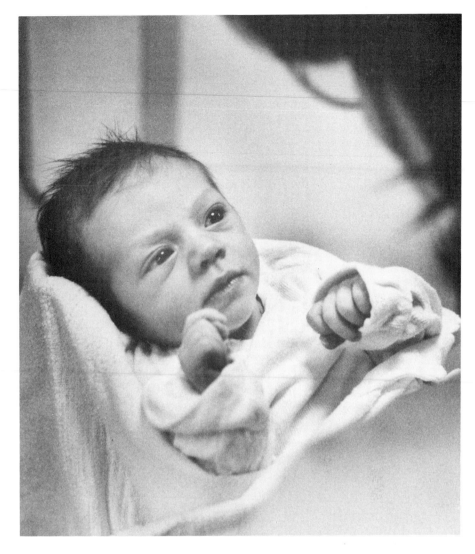

of a baby until the baby's eyes fixate on it, and then the object is moved, the baby will gaze at the object and track it. That is, the baby's eyes, or head and eyes, will move to keep the object in view (Salapatek, 1968; Brazelton, 1973a). Babies have also been shown to have **binocular vision;** that is, they can look at an object with both eyes at the same time. However, if an object is held very close to their face, they don't have this ability (Slater & Findlay, 1975).

Newborns' vision is limited in two areas—acuity and accommodation. **Acuity** refers to the resolving power of the eye, the sharpness of vision. It is measured in older children and adults with an eye chart. Babies don't have the same visual acuity as adults until about 6 months of age (Fantz, Ordu, & Udelf, 1962). **Accommodation** refers to the ability to change the shape of the lens to bring objects at varying distances into focus. Babies' eyes can accommodate as well as adults' eyes by about 2 months of age (Banks, 1980). Until then, they can focus clearly only on objects that are about 7 to 8 inches from their faces (Haynes, White, & Held, 1965). Not coincidentally, this is about the distance to the mother's face when the baby is nursing.

Hearing

Patrick could hear quite well at birth, too. In fact, it's likely that he heard a lot before birth, both the sounds of his mother's body and the muffled sounds of the world outside. As mentioned in Chapter 3, some women report that their babies jump or kick in the womb in response to a loud noise, and some mothers believe that their newborns recognize their voices.

If someone rings a bell or shakes a rattle, newborns turn toward the sound and look alert, as if searching for its source (Brazelton, 1969; Muir & Field, 1979). They are also able to distinguish between high and low sounds and loud and soft ones (Hirschman & Katkin, 1974). Researchers have learned these things about newborn hearing by using a process involving **habituation.** First, they expose the baby to a sound to which the baby responds. Then they repeat the sound several times until the baby stops responding to it. Now the baby is habituated to the sound. Finally, they introduce a different sound. If the baby becomes alert again, they know that the baby senses the difference between the two sounds.

Habituation can be explained by assuming that the baby is building a store of information—a "mental model"—about a stimulus (Sokolov, 1963; Cohen & Gelberg, 1975). When the model is refined enough to match the stimulus itself, the baby stops paying attention to the stimulus. When a new stimulus is introduced, it no longer matches the model, and the baby starts building a new model. This activity requires more attention.

Taste and Smell

Was Patrick born with a "sweet tooth"? Yes, it seems he was. Newborns have been shown to prefer a sweet fluid to fluids with other tastes, and they even prefer sugar water to plain water (Desor, Mallen, & Andrews, 1975). This means that Patrick is well adapted to his mother's milk, since human milk is higher in sugar than cow's milk and tastes quite sweet.

Newborns have also shown their relative dislike for sour, bitter, and salty tastes by sucking less when offered fluids with those tastes (Lipsitt, 1977). They also indicate their dislike of certain smells, such as ammonia, by grimacing and turning their heads away. Habituation studies have been used to determine that babies are able to distinguish different odors right from birth (Lipsett, Engen, & Kaye, 1963). Because they have a well developed sense of smell, babies quickly learn to recognize the smell of their own mothers' milk and bodies (Cernoch & Porter, 1985).

Pain

A less pleasant sensation to contemplate is pain. Newborns do experience pain, such as from a pinprick in the heel for the PKU test that is administered routinely after birth. Baby boys experience pain during circumcision, and some doctors give the baby a shot of novocaine to anesthetize the penis before this procedure, although the shot itself is painful. As neonates grow older and their nervous systems become more developed, their sensitivity to pain increases (Lipsitt & Levy, 1959). Girl babies are more sensitive to pain than boy babies, probably because they're more mature physically at birth.

Visual Perception

We know that Patrick could see at birth, but that doesn't tell us what he saw or how he perceived the world. Does he have a particular way of organizing visual stimuli? Does he see things the way an adult does? Does he have preferences? The answers to all these questions is yes. Visual perception is discussed in detail in Chapter 5 on the physical development of infants and toddlers, but here we briefly discuss newborns' perception.

PREFERENCE FOR PATTERN AND CONTRAST. Researchers approached the question of newborn perception by observing how long they look at different stimuli. Psychologist R. L. Fantz (1963) was the first to demonstrate that babies can notice the difference between patterned and unpatterned visual displays. He showed babies six different stimuli, three patterned (a face, concentric circles, and a piece of newspaper) and three unpatterned (white, yellow, and red). The babies—aged 10 hours to 5 days—looked at the patterned displays longer than the unpatterned ones; of the patterned displays, they liked the face best (Figure 4-9).

Other studies have shown that babies prefer contrast. These studies featured displays with large differences in brightness between background and foreground. It was found that babies fix their gaze on the edge of figures and are particularly interested in the area where black and white meet (Salapatek & Kessen, 1966).

VISUAL PERCEPTION AND THE NATURE-NURTURE ISSUE. If babies exhibit visual preferences at 10 hours, we know that these preferences are innate. There's no way they could have learned to like patterns and contrasts through experience. How this preference works as an adaptation for survival is quite remarkable. Babies are drawn to people's eyes when they see a face because of their pref-

FIGURE 4-9
Using these visual displays, R. L. Fantz found that newborns preferred to look at patterns rather than solid colors and that of all the patterns, they preferred to look at the most complex—the smiling human face. We can't know exactly how they perceive the face, but we can say that this inborn preference plays a role in helping them establish attachments with adults.

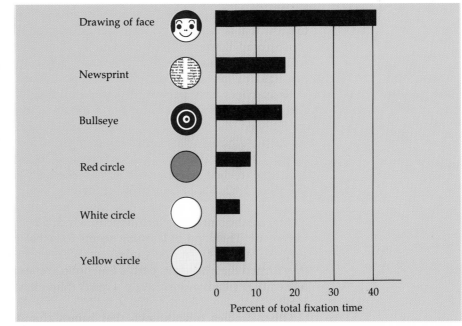

erence for patterns and contrasts. Parents are quick to return their newborn's gaze and often interpret the baby's attention as a sign of recognition. This is one of the earliest ways the attachment between parents and baby begins to grow. Of course, nothing works to ensure the survival of the baby so much as a strong attachment with a caring adult, just as nothing endangers the baby as a lack of attachment does.

LEARNING

Newborns have been eagerly studied for many years by researchers and theorists in child development. As in the perception studies just discussed, newborns are prime candidates for investigations of various aspects of the "nature-nurture" controversy—questions of whether preferences and reactions are innate or learned—because they haven't yet experienced many environmental influences. We now realize that human behavior is the result of complex interactions between the individual and the environment, so these studies provide us with important information.

Studies of the relatively simple behavior of newborns helps developmentalists understand how behavior is organized and how this organization changes with time and experience. For example, a preference for visual contrast is present at birth, but visual preferences several months later will reflect not only the innate preference but the experiences—the specific visual patterns—to which the baby has been exposed. The baby's behavior has been reorganized by experience.

Behavioral Studies of Newborn Learning

Learning is another area of interest to researchers. What can newborns learn? How do they learn it? Does newborn learning provide evidence for one or another of the major child development theories? Many behaviorists have tried to show that newborns can learn things through classical conditioning. If you recall from Chapter 2, this technique involves the pairing of a new stimulus with another stimulus that automatically elicits a certain response. After repeated pairings, the new stimulus alone elicits the response.

Researchers have paired the ringing of a bell or gentle forehead stroking with giving a baby sugar water or a nipple. If the baby could be classically conditioned, the bell or stroking alone would later elicit sucking after repeated pairings. Although classical conditioning is difficult with newborns because they don't stay awake and alert for very long periods of time, researchers have been able to elicit sucking with stimuli like bells and stroking (Rovee-Collier & Lipsitt, 1982; Blass, Ganchrow, & Steiner, 1984).

Other researchers have tried to show that babies can learn through instrumental conditioning, the technique in which a response is followed with reinforcement. This kind of learning seems to be easier for newborns (Sameroff, 1972; Millar, 1974). In one study, researchers gave newborns a nipple when they turned their heads as part of the rooting reflex. They found that the babies turned their heads more often as a result (Siqueland & Lipsitt, 1966; Papousek, 1967).

Other studies have shown that babies change their sucking response, depending on whether a nipple provides food (Rovee-Collier & Lipsitt, 1982).

RESEARCH FOCUS

Learning in Young Infants

Many studies have confirmed that infants can learn from both classical and operant conditioning methods, but some research has touched on more interesting issues. What motivation lies behind learning? What deeper lessons do infants learn from our responses to their efforts? What can we do to improve infants' ability to learn? These are some of the questions that have been raised by research on infant learning.

In one experiment, for example, researchers were interested in establishing learning in babies using operant conditioning. To do this, they turned on a light when the baby turned her head 30 degrees to the right of midline (Papousek & Bernstein, 1969). Young infants learned how to make the light go on by turning their heads, and their head turning increased when they learned this behavior. But, surprisingly, head turning declined soon after they mastered the task.

The researchers then decided to present the light only after more complex head turning, such as a turn to the right followed by a turn to the left. When infants found that the usual head turning failed to turn on the light as it had before, they began a flurry of head turning, apparently trying to find out how to get the light to come on again. But once they had succeeded in turning on the light several times in a row with the more complex pattern, head turning again declined.

These results suggest that babies are motivated to learn by opportunities to solve problems, not simply by primary reinforcement such as food or stimulation. Although this experiment is from the behavioral tradition, its findings bear out some of Piaget's ideas. Children want to learn things just because they're interesting. It follows that we can motivate them more by making learning interesting than by rewarding them with candy or gold stars.

Another study showed that individual learning experiences build on one another and that babies can use prior learning experiences to learn something new (Papousek, 1967). In this experiment, a bell sounding meant that head turns to one side would be reinforced, and a buzzer sounding meant that head turns to the other side would be reinforced. Every day, a few trials of this task were given to two groups of infants the same age. One group had previously mastered a similar discrimination task, but the other group hadn't. The group without prior training took twice as many trials to learn the task as the group with prior training. The earlier learning experience made it easier for the infants to learn a new discrimination.

Babies may be learning something more important than the mechanics of a particular situation when their actions cause changes in the environment. They may be learning they can make interesting things happen in the world. Babies whose actions don't produce results may learn "helplessness" instead (Maier, Seligman, & Solomon, 1969). Two correlational studies have supported this idea. In one, researchers observed mothers and their 5-month-old babies at home and correlated their observations with the infants' test scores on an assessment instrument known as the Bayley Scales of Infant Development (discussed in Knowledge in Action: Infants and Toddlers, following Chapter 8) (Yarrow, Rubenstein, & Pedersen, 1971; 1975). They found that babies whose mothers responded promptly to their crying had higher scores on three clusters of items—goal orientation, reaching and grasping, and effective action on the environment. Learning that their crying got results may have helped these babies understand that they could make things happen. A second study found that babies whose mothers responded quickly when they were hungry and who were sensitive to their needs during feeding had higher scores on IQ tests (Ainsworth & Bell, 1973).

Because both of these studies were correlational, we can't be certain about the relationship between responsive parenting and infant development. But experimental studies have demonstrated that when animals receive feedback contingent on their actions in one task, they're better able to learn a second, unrelated task (Finkelstein & Ramey, 1977; Ramey & Finkelstein, 1978). In another experimental study, monkeys whose feeding was contingent on what they did were observed to explore more, cling to each other less, and emerge more quickly from a cage to play in a playroom than monkeys whose feeding wasn't related to their own actions (Mineka, Gunnar, & Champaux, 1986).

We can't conduct experimental studies with human infants to see if responsive parenting improves their ability to learn, but we can draw some conclusions from the correlational and experimental evidence that we do have. It seems that the responsiveness of the environment may provide some of the baby's most important lessons. Babies whose efforts produce results learn "I can"; babies who get no response learn "I can't."

If the nipple is attached to a bottle of milk or sugar water, babies squeeze the nipple with their tongues and cheeks *and* suck on it. If the nipple is attached to a pacifier, they just squeeze it. Experiments like this show that babies can respond to the environment in intelligent ways and learn from experience. Further questions about infant learning have been raised and addressed by other studies; some of these are discussed in Research Focus—Learning in Young Infants.

Piaget's Approach to Newborn Learning

Piaget was also interested in what newborns could learn, although he didn't approach learning from a behavioral point of view. He believed that babies continually modify their behavior on the basis of experience and thus respond differently to different kinds of situations. He noted, for example, that different objects are sucked in different ways: some things are sucked, some are spit out, some are sucked at one time and not another. This rudimentary "thinking" leads to more complex behavior, although babies' intelligence is based on sensorimotor experiences for the first two years of life. In other words, babies know about the world only through their physical and sensory interactions with objects. They can't represent what they know symbolically with words. (Sensorimotor intelligence is discussed in detail in Chapter 6 on the cognitive development of infants and toddlers). Whether we feel more comfortable with a behavioral or a cognitive-developmental point of view, we can see that babies are able to learn, right from the start.

THE PREMATURE BABY

Tina stared in disbelief at her second child, born prematurely and lying in an incubator. Tubes connected Elizabeth to air and food—and life. She was so tiny she would fit in a large man's hand, and her bones showed clearly under her skin. Her eyes were shut; no flicker of awareness crossed her wizened face. She looked like some strange creature only distantly related to a newborn baby.

Tina's first child had been so healthy, so alert, that it never occurred to her she might give birth prematurely this time. The doctors told Tina that she and her husband might be able to hold Elizabeth and help feed her within a week, although she would be attached to the respirator for at least three weeks and in the hospital for five weeks more after that.

As Tina looked at her daughter, she felt a numbing emptiness. She wanted to hold her right now and awaken the feelings she had felt toward her son when he was born. It was going to be a long eight weeks.

Elizabeth wasn't as lucky as Patrick. Instead of spending 37 to 40 weeks in the womb, as nature intended, she was born after only 30 weeks. Premature babies—those born before the thirty-seventh week of gestation—account for almost 7 percent of all births, and the percentage is rising. Modern medical technology has made survival possible for babies born earlier and earlier. The problems facing such babies and their families are formidable. Some people question the wisdom and morality of saving some of these tiny babies, at tremendous cost, only to have some of them face a lifetime of disabling medical problems. Some of these physical problems are considered here, along with the long-term consequences of prematurity.

Small-for-date babies are also smaller than average but for different reasons. These babies are full term but weigh less than 5½ pounds, or 2500 grams. Their small size may be due to a variety of factors, but two of the chief causes are poor maternal nutrition during pregnancy and abnormalities of the placenta that prevent it from providing proper nourishment to the fetus (Lubchenco, Delivotia-Papodopoulos, & Searle, 1972). Small-for-date babies are vulnerable to complications, or "at risk," during the neonatal period and later

FIGURE 4-10
Premature babies face many physical problems, including the risk of brain hemorrhage and the likelihood of lung disorders, but once they get through the earliest months of infancy, many catch up with their full-term peers.

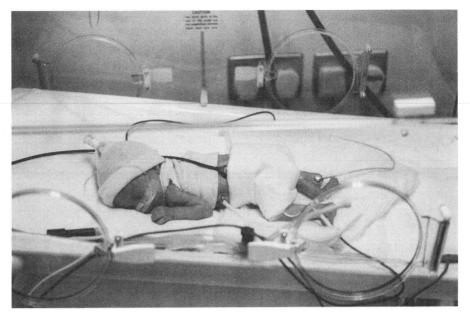

as well, but their problems aren't the same as those of premature babies. Many small-for-date babies—and some premature babies—recover completely from their early problems.

Physical Problems of Premature Babies

Because they're not fully developed, premature babies are vulnerable both during birth and postnatally. They're particularly susceptible to **hypothermia,** a dangerous drop in body temperature, and they must be kept in incubators, where the temperature can be carefully controlled.

A major problem for premature babies is the danger of brain hemorrhages, especially in those born earlier than the thirty-second week of gestation. The arterial system in the brain is not yet completely formed by this time, and certain stress conditions can cause an artery to burst (Tarby & Volpe, 1982). Severe hemorrhages result in death 50 percent of the time; mild to moderate hemorrhages result in death up to 15 percent of the time. Babies who do survive brain hemorrhages may suffer brain damage.

Premature babies are also likely to have respiratory problems. About 15 percent suffer from a serious breathing disorder known as **hyaline membrane disease.** If you recall from Chapter 3, lung development begins early in the prenatal period, but the alveoli, or air sacs, at the very ends of the branches of the lungs aren't completely formed until late in the prenatal period. The alveoli produce **surfactant**, a substance that keeps the lungs from collapsing when the breath is expelled. Surfactant is lacking in premature babies (Kogan et al., 1986), so their lungs tend to collapse when they breathe and they can't get enough oxygen. Hyaline membrane disease is a potentially fatal disease. The younger the baby, the more serious the condition is likely to be, since surfactant isn't produced until the thirty-fourth to thirty-eighth weeks of prenatal life (Hallman & Gluck, 1982).

Because babies with respiratory distress syndrome (RDS) can't get enough oxygen from the air, they're treated with concentrated oxygen. When this treatment was begun in the 1940s and 1950s, doctors didn't realize that high levels of oxygen could damage the blood vessels in the eye and cause **retrolental fibroplasia blindness** (RLF blindness). The lives of many premature babies were saved but at the cost of their eyesight.

Today, doctors monitor oxygen levels in the baby's system very carefully to make sure the baby isn't getting too much, and RLF blindness has been greatly reduced. But when very premature babies need oxygen for a long period of time, it's still hard to prevent blindness. There is some evidence that excessive oxygen isn't the only factor involved. For example, premature babies' low level of antioxidants, such as vitamin E, may prevent them from using and binding oxygen the way normal babies can. There may be other factors at work as well, and research is underway to tackle this problem anew (Lucey & Dangman, 1984). Given the ever-increasing number of premature babies who survive, there's a critical need to understand and effectively treat both hyaline membrane disease and RFL blindness.

Long-Term Effects of Prematurity

It's clear that a premature baby like Elizabeth isn't off to the best start. But what's likely to happen to her later? Will she catch up physically? Will she have emotional problems as a result of being separated from her parents at birth for medical treatment? Will she develop learning problems or have trouble in school?

Children who were born prematurely do catch up to their genetically intended size as they grow. And premature babies are not destined to have disrupted attachment relationships with their mothers because of separation at birth, as we mentioned in Chapter 3 and discuss in detail in Chapter 8. Newer hospital policies that allow contact between premature babies and their parents are helping families to build strong relationships and avoid later emotional problems.

Many studies have followed premature babies to see if and how their later development is related to their earlier condition. One study compared the development of premature and full-term babies at 4 months, 8 months, 1 year, 2 years, 3 years, and 5 years (Field, Demsey, & Shuman, 1983). Relationships were found between the preterm child's development at 5 years and (1) mother-child interaction ratings at 4 months; (2) motor development at 8 months; (3) mental development at 2 years; and (4) years of maternal education. There were consistent differences between the premature and the full-term groups, but researchers couldn't predict how any individual preterm child would do.

Another study focused on the link between premature birth and the child's risk of developing a learning disability (Siegel, 1983). The children were assessed early in infancy and then tested at age 5 for signs of learning disabilities. They were also rated on a "risk index," which included such factors as mother's reproductive health (e.g., cigarette smoking during pregnancy), infant's physical characteristics at birth (e.g., birth weight), and demographic information (e.g, mother's educational level). This study found a positive relationship between low infant scores, a high number of risks, and poor performance at 5 years. A more recent study found that most babies born prematurely show

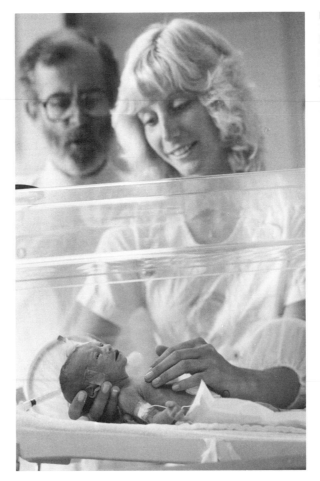

FIGURE 4-11
In the past, premature babies were deprived of normal human contact because its importance to their growth and well-being wasn't recognized. Special efforts are now made to ensure contact between mother and baby, with all its physical and emotional benefits for both of them.

no learning difficulties at age 8, although their rate as a group was 25 percent higher than that of their full-term peers (Cohen & Parmelee, 1988).

These and other results point strongly in one direction. In the words of one researcher who reviewed several studies of the long-term effects of prematurity, "the single most potent factor influencing developmental outcome turns out to be the cultural environment of the child, as expressed in socioeconomic status and parental educational level" (Sameroff, 1981, p. 392). In other words, social factors like the mother's educational level—rather than the baby's physical condition at birth—are the best predictors of long-term outcome for premature babies (Cohen & Parmelee, 1983).

Prematurity in and of itself, then, doesn't lead inevitably to later difficulties, although premature babies *as a group* are more likely to encounter problems (Taub, Goldstein, & Caputo, 1977; Drillien, Thomson, & Burgayne, 1980; Cohen & Parmelee, 1983). If we compared one hundred 5-year-olds who had been premature with one hundred 5-year-olds who had been full term, we would find that more preterm children had problems. But we wouldn't be able to predict *which* of the preterm babies would do poorly by considering only the physical aspects of prematurity. Recent research indicates that even brain hemorrhage doesn't lead inevitably to severely impaired functioning (Sostek et al.,

1987). Responsive parenting can mitigate many of the potentially harmful effects of premature birth, as we discuss in Chapter 8.

THE NEWBORN IN THE WORLD

As you can see, quite a lot of information is available about newborns. But how does all this knowledge actually help physicians and parents protect and nurture a baby? How does it help at that moment when the red-faced, crying infant at last appears in the world? And how can parents use the knowledge available from research when they begin life at home with their baby? These are the questions addressed in this final section on the neonate—knowledge in action.

Assessing the Newborn

Most newborns are like Patrick—healthy in every way. Some are like Elizabeth—premature and obviously in need of immediate medical attention. Still others have problems that may not be readily apparent but that require intervention. To make sure the needs of all newborns are met, doctors and researchers have developed various methods of assessment, or assessment instruments,

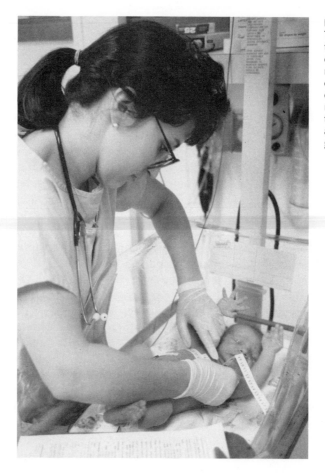

FIGURE 4-12
This physician is measuring the newborn as part of an overall assessment. She also measures his heart rate and observes his breathing, skin color, muscle tone, and responsiveness to stimulation. If he's pink and generally vigorous, he'll probably get a 10 on the Apgar scale.

TABLE 4-3
The Apgar Scale

Sign	Criterion*	Score
Heart rate (beats/ minute)	100 or more	2
	Less than 100	1
	Not detectable	0
Respiratory effort	Lusty crying and breathing	2
	Any shallowness, irregularity	1
	Not breathing	0
Reflex irritability	Vigorous response to stimulation (e.g., sneezing or coughing to stimulation of nostrils), urination, defecation	2
	Weak response	1
	No response	0
Muscle tone	Resilient, limbs spontaneously flexed and resistant to applied force	2
	Limpness, lack of resistance	1
	Complete flaccidity	0
Skin color	Pink all over	2
	Partially pink	1
	Bluish or yellowish	0

Observations made at 60 seconds after birth.
SOURCE: Apgar, V., Holaday, D. A., James, L. S., Weisbrot, I. M., & Berrien, C. (1958). Evaluation of the newborn infant—second report. Journal of the American Medical Association, 168, 1985–1988.

as they are called. These instruments help doctors evaluate the newborn's physical well-being, and they also provide information of interest to researchers. For example, studies like those described previously involving premature babies looked at whether babies' conditions at birth, as measured by assessment instruments, predicted future development.

ASSESSMENT INSTRUMENTS. Probably the best-known assessment instrument is the **Apgar scale** (named for the physician who invented it), which measures the newborn's physical well-being. The baby's Apgar score is determined in the delivery room at one minute and at five minutes after birth. The baby is scored from 0 to 2 for heart rate, respiratory effort, muscle tone, reflex irritability, and color (see Table 4-3). The five scores are added up to give a total score ranging from 0 to 10. The higher the score, the better the baby's condition (Apgar, 1953).

Another assessment instrument can be used to assess the baby's neurological condition. The best known of these is the **Neurological Examination of the Full-Term Newborn Infant**, developed in 1964 by Prechtl and Beintema and revised in 1977 by Prechtl. This test, often referred to as the Prechtl, is used to evaluate babies within ten days of birth and has two parts: (1) an observation period during which spontaneous movement and posture are noted, and (2) an examination period during which reflexes and other motor behavior are checked. As mentioned earlier, the presence or absence of the various reflexes provides information on the baby's neurological functioning.

A third kind of assessment instrument is used to obtain behavioral information, although it typically assesses neurological well-being too. The most comprehensive of these is the **Brazelton Neonatal Behavioral Assessment Scale** (Brazelton, 1973a). This test, known as the BNBAS or the Brazelton, is given on the third day of life and, ideally, on several subsequent days as well.

It provides information about the baby's general neurological condition, capacity for self-organization, and reactions to a caregiver.

Specific items on the BNBAS involve the baby's behavioral state, the major reflexes, and habituation to repeated visual, auditory, and tactile stimuli. It also assesses the baby's orientation to the human face and voice, activity level, and muscle tone (Brazelton, 1973a; Jacobson et al., 1984). For example, one part of the test involves ringing a bell loudly overhead when the baby is awake and lying on a flat surface. The baby will usually startle the first time the bell is rung. The tester then rings the bell again. This time the baby startles but typically not as much as the first time. The baby habituates to the sound of the bell, so that after a few rings there is little or no reaction. To score the baby, the tester notes how many presentations occurred before the baby stopped reacting. The longer it takes for the reaction to stop, the poorer the rating. A long time may indicate that the baby has difficulty in processing information and learning.

Brazelton stresses the importance of taking the baby's behavioral state into account when giving this test. Results obtained when a baby is drowsy or crying wouldn't be comparable to results obtained when another baby is in an inactive alert state, which is the ideal state for testing. If a baby starts to cry, the tester must stop testing and hold the baby or provide some other comfort. If the baby becomes less irritable, the testing can continue; otherwise it has to stop, at least for the time being.

Specific assessment instruments have also been devised to diagnose hearing loss in newborns. The **High Risk Registry** is used to find out from the mother whether there's a family history of hearing loss or if she was exposed to a disease like German measles during pregnancy. If it seems there may be a problem, the baby is given other tests, such as the **Crib-O-Gram** or the **Brain Stem Evoked Response** test. Both of these tests record the baby's brain waves on special apparatus to see if sounds are registering in their brains (Downs, 1978; Stein et al., 1983; Murray, 1988). Babies are also observed to see if they respond to sounds.

ASSESSMENT ADEQUACY. What do physicians learn from these early tests? In general, they're able to detect both life-threatening conditions and risks for later problems. When potential problems are identified, steps can sometimes be taken to provide more support for development in the baby's environment.

Unfortunately, it's often difficult to know which behaviors actually predict future problems. Neurological exams like the one developed by Prechtl simply measure reflexes, noting whether or not they occur. Newer tests, like the Brazelton, measure babies' reflexes as well as other characteristics, including their ability to inhibit response after a stimulus is repeated several times, to escape a stimulus, to quiet or console themselves, and to orient toward or seek out stimulation. The Brazelton scale is a better predictor of later functioning than basic neurological exams. This may be because the behaviors it measures are important to mother-child interactions, which continue to influence development for years. (See Chapter 8 for further discussion of this topic.)

Some of the other assessment instruments have additional problems. The Brain Stem Evoked Response has a high number of false positives—a hearing loss is reported when in fact there's been none. Apparently other brain activity, such as that caused by birth trauma, can interfere with the testing (Stein et al., 1983). The Apgar is criticized because it measures only the most general aspects of physical well-being and reveals only the most obvious difficulties. Timing is a problem too. The Apgar is administered at one and five minutes after birth, but studies indicate that a baby's functioning two hours after birth may be radically different from what it was immediately after birth (Desmond et al., 1963). The later score may be a better predictor of future behavior. And again, the baby's behavioral state can influence the results of a test, but many tests don't take this into account.

It may be that different instruments are just appropriate for different purposes. The Apgar gives a quick assessment of physical condition immediately after birth. Neurological exams like Prechtl's reveal clinically important neurological problems during the neonatal period. The Brazelton scale may be most useful for predicting long-term problems related to difficult parent-child interaction (Prechtl, 1982). As long as their appropriate uses and limitations are kept in mind, all of these assessment instruments can provide useful and important information about newborns.

Living with the Newborn

We've seen what Patrick and Elizabeth are like as newborns and how they're treated and evaluated at birth. But what will it be like when their parents take them home? What is it like to live with a newborn? Newborns spend most of their time sleeping at first. During their brief waking periods, they'll eat and have an opportunity to look around and get acquainted with their new families. In our culture, they'll also spend a fair amount of time crying. This is the behavior that will probably be most difficult for their parents to deal with. (For a discussion of infant crying, see Research Focus—How Much Does a Baby Have to Cry?).

SOOTHING THE NEWBORN. Parents of older babies often say they can tell why their baby is crying. Does this mean that babies actually cry differently for different reasons? Apparently it does. One study of infant crying distinguished three kinds of cries: the basic, or hungry, cry; the angry cry; and the pain cry (Wolff, 1966; 1969). A baby who is startled or who is being overstimulated, for example, might give an angry cry. A baby with colic (gastrointestinal pain) would give the pain cry.

All the mothers in this study responded immediately to the pain cry and were worried or alarmed by it. All the mothers responded to angry cries too, but they weren't worried about this kind of cry. The basic or hungry cry usually got a quick response from first-time mothers, but experienced mothers sometimes waited a while before responding.

The important questions for parents or others who care for babies, of course, is what to do to quiet a crying baby. It depends on what the baby is crying about. Hunger cries can be stopped by feeding the baby, although holding the baby or putting a pacifier in the baby's mouth might stop the crying for a short time. (An angry cry may follow soon if some food doesn't supplement the pacifier! This is inappropriate "stimulation.") A crying baby who is undressed and flailing about can often be soothed by swaddling or by being held closely so the limbs stay in control. A pacifier can also soothe a baby and inhibit

RESEARCH FOCUS

How Much Does a Baby Have to Cry?

"There's nothing wrong with him—he's just crying to let off steam."
"She always gets fussy at this time of day—just when I'm trying to get dinner started."

All babies cry, but how much crying is "normal"? In the United States, babies cry more and more until they're 6 weeks old, and then their crying gradually decreases. American babies also cry more in the afternoon and evening. Most people in our country expect babies to cry a certain amount; they consider it normal.

It occurred to one pair of researchers that the amount of crying considered "normal" might vary from culture to culture (Hunziker & Barr, 1986). They observed that babies seem to cry considerably less in cultures where they were carried extensively, usually by their mothers. They wondered if increasing the amount of time babies were carried would change the typical crying pattern found in the United States. Here, parents usually pick up their babies *after* they start crying, but there isn't a great deal of carrying of babies who aren't crying.

Hunziker and Barr set out to test this hypothesis. They recruited a number of mother-infant pairs and assigned them randomly to one of two groups: a control group with no increased carrying and a treatment group with increased carrying. The mothers in the treatment group were asked to carry their babies at least three hours a day and not just in response to crying. The extra carrying was to be spread throughout the day and was to be in addition to the time they normally held the baby during feeding. Infant carriers were provided for the treatment group. The researchers collected baseline date from both groups, so that initial rates of crying for all babies were known.

The babies in the control group increased their crying until the characteristic six-week peak. The babies in the supplemental carrying group, however, never increased their crying, and the six-week peak never occurred. Crying began to decrease after the third week of life, which was the week the supplemental carrying began. In addition, although babies in both groups cried the most in the late afternoon and early evening, the carried babies cried significantly less than the control group babies. They cried 54 percent less than the control group babies during the sixth week and 47 percent less during the eighth week.

Hunziker and Barr suggested that increased carrying "provided postural change, repetitiveness, constancy and/or rhythmicity, close proximity between mother and infant, and involvement of many sensory modalities" (p. 645). They also suggested that the increased carrying may have given mothers more information about their babies, which made them more skillful at understanding what was wrong and at soothing their babies when they did cry. Finally, since holding induces the inactive alert state, babies may

have been less fussy because they were interested in observing their surroundings.

The researchers concluded that the amount of infant crying considered normal in the United States is "only normal in the sense of being typical for infant caregiving practices in our society" (p. 646). They recommended that parents soothe their babies by increasing carrying rather than by giving a supplemental bottle, as many parents do.

One way parents can increase carrying is by keeping the baby in an infant carrier. Carriers of all kinds have become popular in recent years. For very young infants, these carriers are typically designed as pouchlike sacks that the parent straps onto the front of his or her own body. Parents have their hands free while they're holding the baby, and the baby experiences the security and warmth of the parent's body. This kind of closeness has benefits for both parent and baby.

FIGURE 4-13
When this newborn awakens from her first long sleep, she may be an "easy" baby—readily comforted with a good meal and some gentle rocking—or a "difficult" baby—inconsolable despite all her parents' efforts. But all babies cry sometimes, and parents often have to learn what soothes their baby through simple trial and error.

diffuse motor activity, which can leave a baby upset and awake (Wolff, 1966).

Many times babies are dry, fed, and being held, but they continue to cry. It's difficult to know what's causing the crying or what to do to stop it. At this point, parents have to become more ingenious. Sometimes recordings of a heart beating or of the sounds of the womb will soothe the baby. The noise of a rattle or a bright light placed in the baby's visual field will also inhibit crying, but only briefly in the very young baby. Parents may try rocking the baby in a rocking chair, pushing her in a stroller, or even taking her out for a ride in the car.

The type of activity that makes a baby stop crying begins to change after about the second week of life (Wolff, 1965). Up to this point, direct physical activities, such as feeding, swaddling, or giving a pacifier, work best. Psychological interventions, such as talking or offering the baby a bright object, don't work as well. By the end of the second week, however, babies are more interested in the environment, and sights and sounds often make them stop crying and become alert. There seems to be an intricate interplay between mental stimulation and the baby's emotional state.

At all ages, the most effective way to stop crying is to pick the baby up (Korner & Grobstein, 1966; Korner & Thoman, 1972). When babies are picked up, they not only stop crying but become alert and begin to look around.

Although this alert inactive state is usually quite infrequent in young babies, it is induced by picking them up. (See Research Focus—How Much Does a Baby Have to Cry? for another approach to handling crying.) How the parent responds to and soothes a crying baby affects not just the baby's emotional state but the baby's early learning as well. Since babies are most receptive to stimulation in the alert inactive state, parents who pick up their crying babies give them a chance to observe and learn about their world. There is even some evidence that crying reduces the flow of blood to the brain, a finding that underscores the importance of soothing a crying baby (Brazy, 1988).

ADJUSTING TO INDIVIDUAL DIFFERENCES. Despite research findings, it's not easy to know exactly how to begin a healthy relationship with a newborn. Research evidence and everyday observation indicate that newborns differ, right from the beginning, and that these differences are innate. Some babies simply cry more than others or respond more readily to soothing or stimulation (Brazelton, 1969; Korner, 1971).

These individual characteristics have important influences on parent-child relationships and on infant learning. A baby who is difficult to soothe, for example, can make a parent feel incompetent, anxious, frustrated, and worn out. These feelings can affect the parent's approach to the baby, which may in turn affect the baby's responses.

Some parents might have trouble adapting to their baby because the baby isn't what they hoped for or expected. An active, outgoing mother and father may be disappointed with a quiet, passive baby. A parent who expected a calm baby may have trouble coping with a lively one. But most parents do adapt and learn ways to interact that work with their baby, as indicated in the following example (Brazelton, 1969, p. 21):

> Daniel was hard to rouse from his deep sleep. He was wheeled into Mrs. Kay, breathing deeply and noisily, moving little. . . . Then, as if with a start, he shot from sleeping to an unapproachable state of screaming. He cried with a loud, piercing bellow that continued until he was quieted. Quieting him demanded a vigorous approach on the part of Mrs. Kay. . . .
>
> He could not be quieted with her crooning, with quiet rocking and cuddling, or with a bottle alone. His crying could only be broken into by a combination of tight swaddling of his extremities, plus vigorous rocking, plus the bottle nipple held in his mouth at his soft palate until he stopped crying to breathe and felt it there.
>
> His mother felt foolish and unhappy about the means that were necessary to quiet him, but she found they were successful, and after the second day of these maneuvers, she found that he could even be played with and enjoyed after one of his feedings.

Although Daniel wasn't the kind of baby Mrs. Kay expected, she was able to adjust to her new son. It's the parents' ability to adapt to the baby, rather than any particular characteristics of the baby, that best predicts the long-term course of the baby's emotional and intellectual development (Belsky, 1984; Sroufe, 1983). Although babies differ in temperament right from the start— and "difficult" babies are at higher risk for later problems because they require nearly ideal parenting—no specific temperament or trait predisposes a baby to future difficulties. As discussed in greater detail in Chapter 8, parents most effectively support their baby's development by accepting and responding sensitively to whatever kind of person their newborn turns out to be.

OVERVIEW

The neonate is clearly different from the fetus, but she's also different from the older infant. Her first days and weeks are a period of transition between one mode of existence and another. The body systems that functioned in conjunction with the mother's body now begin to support life on their own. The physical characteristics appropriate for prenatal existence evolve into traits suitable for life outside the womb. The baby's senses awaken to the sights, sounds, tastes, smells, and feel of the world around her. Perhaps most importantly, she becomes a partner in a relationship with someone who cares for her. In this relationship, if all goes well, she will develop a strong emotional attachment that will nurture her throughout her childhood and influence her for her entire life.

CHAPTER REVIEW

PHYSICAL CHARACTERISTICS

- A white greasy coating called vernix caseosa protects the neonate's skin before, during, and after birth.
- Two diamond-shaped fontanelles allow the bones of the skull to squeeze together, or mold, as the baby passes through the mother's pelvis.
- Newborns' eyes and faces are often swollen and puffy from the accumulation of fluids and from silver nitrate drops in the eyes. Their skin is bright red because they have so little subcutaneous fat.
- The newborn's head is very large in proportion to her body, and the top of her head is more developed than her chin, jaw, and neck.
- Newborns are able to absorb nutrients right from birth. Mothers produce colostrum, an antibody-containing liquid perfectly suited to the newborn's needs. Breast milk, high in protein and low in fat, is the ideal food for infants.

- The average neonate weighs $7\frac{1}{2}$ pounds and measures 20 inches long.
- Newborns require frequent, small feedings, and most need night feedings for a few months or more.
- The neonate's breathing is characterized by rapid, shallow breaths interrupted by periods of long, deep breathing and even brief periods of apnea.
- The respiratory system takes time to adjust to breathing oxygen-rich air, and a by-product called bilirubin often accumulates in the blood. The liver has difficulty metabolizing and excreting the bilirubin, and the baby often develops hyperbilirubinemia, or jaundice, which sometimes requires treatment by phototherapy to protect against brain damage.
- Newborns can't maintain their own body temperatures until they're about 2 months old, and care has to be taken to keep them warm.

MOTOR CAPABILITIES

- Babies are born with innate responses known as reflexes that help them survive.
- Newborns have a rooting reflex, which allows them to find the nipple, and a sucking reflex, which allows them to suckle and ingest food. The gag reflex prevents them from choking on mucus or extra milk.
- A "crawling" reflex prevents newborns from suffocating if their mouths and noses become obstructed.

It can also result in enough movement to topple them off a bed if they're left unattended.

- Other reflexes include the tonic neck reflex, the Moro, or startle, reflex, the Babinski reflex, and the grasping reflexes. As the baby matures, reflexes gradually disappear; their presence or absence at different times is a good indicator of the infant's neurological functioning.
- Newborns have little control over voluntary responses.

BEHAVIORAL STATES

- When newborns awaken from their first long sleep after birth, their behavior is characterized by recurring periods of wakefulness and sleep known as behavioral states.

- Typical behavioral states include regular sleep, irregular sleep, drowsiness, alert inactivity, waking activity, and crying. These states are cyclical; they don't occur randomly.

- Infants' overall behavioral patterns, including how long they spend in each state, are probably influenced by heredity and by their parents' responses to them. Their patterns, in turn, affect the parent-child relationship. A baby who spends a lot of time crying is more difficult to care for and requires more creative parenting.

- The initial parent-child interaction is affected by obstetrical drugs. Pain-relieving drugs given to mothers in labor quickly cross the placenta and enter the fetus. Newborns of medicated mothers tend to be less alert, less responsive, and less consolable than the newborns of nonmedicated mothers.

SENSORY ABILITIES

- Newborns can see right from birth, focusing best on objects about 7 or 8 inches from their face.
- They have binocular vision and can track a moving object. Their visual acuity is as good as an adult's by about 6 months, and their eyes can accommodate as well as an adult's by about 2 months.
- Babies can hear at birth and even in the womb. They respond to new sounds and then gradually become accustomed to everyday noises, incorporating them into their repertoire. Researchers use this process of habituation to conduct studies on their hearing and other senses.

- Newborns prefer sweet tastes over sour, bitter, and salty tastes. They can distinguish odors right from birth and soon learn to know the smell of their mother's milk.
- Newborns feel physical pain; their sensitivity to pain increases as they mature.
- Babies like to look at patterns, especially the pattern of faces, as well as areas of contrast. These preferences are innate and support the development of parent-child attachment.

LEARNING

- Newborns have been shown to be capable of learning through both classical conditioning and instrumental conditioning.
- Piaget believed that babies are continually learning about their environment and modifying their behavior based on what they experience.

- Research indicates that babies are motivated to learn by opportunities to solve problems. These opportunities may have long-term implications for whether they learn that they're powerful or helpless in their interactions with the world.

THE PREMATURE BABY

- Babies are considered premature if they're born before the thirty-seventh week of gestation. About 7 percent of all babies are born prematurely, and more and more premature babies are surviving due to advances in medical technology.
- Premature babies, prone to hypothermia, have to be kept in incubators. They're also at risk for brain hemorrhages because the arterial system of the brain isn't completely developed.
- About 15 percent of all premature babies develop hyaline membrane disease, a serious lung disorder caused by undeveloped alveoli and a lack of surfactant.

- When premature babies with respiratory distress are treated with oxygen, the levels have to be carefully monitored to prevent retrolental fibroplasia blindness.
- There are long-term differences in development between premature and full-term infants as groups, but it's difficult to predict the outcome for any individual premature child.
- The strongest factor affecting the outcome for a premature baby appears to be the social and emotional environment provided by her family as she grows rather than her physical condition at birth.

THE NEWBORN IN THE WORLD

- Babies are assessed at birth to see if they require any medical or developmental intervention.
- The Apgar scale is used to assess the baby's physical condition.
- The Neurological Examination of the Full-Term Newborn Infant is used to evaluate the baby's neurological condition.
- The Brazelton Neonatal Behavioral Assessment Scale provides information about the baby's neurological condition and behavioral patterns.

- Newborns' hearing is also tested if they are at risk for hearing loss.
- All the neonatal assessment instruments have their limitations, but they do provide important information about newborns.
- Babies cry differently, depending on whether they're hungry, angry, or in pain.
- Prior to the end of the second week, direct physical intervention soothes a crying baby most effectively.

Later, the baby may be soothed by different sights and sounds.
- The most effective way to stop crying at all ages is to pick up the baby, thus inducing the alert inactive state. Carrying the baby in an infant carrier also seems to reduce crying.
- Newborns have different personalities right from the start, but no specific temperament or trait predisposes a baby to future social or emotional problems.

KEY TERMS

neonate
neonatal period
vernix caseosa
molding
fontanelles
lanugo
glycogen
colostrum
immunoglobulins
apnea
ductus arteriosus
bilirubin

hyperbilirubinemia
phototherapy
kernicterus
reflexes
rooting reflex
sucking reflex
gag reflex
tonic neck reflex
Moro reflex
Babinski reflex
grasping reflex
palmar grasp

tonus
behavioral states
consolability
binocular vision
acuity
accommodation
habituation
hypothermia
hyaline membrane disease
surfactant
retrolental fibroplasia
   blindness

Apgar scale
Neurological Examination
   of the Full-Term
   Newborn Infant
Brazelton Neonatal
   Behavioral Assessment
   Scale
High Risk Registry
Crib-O-Gram
Brain Stem Evoked
   Response

SUGGESTIONS FOR FURTHER READING

Brazelton, T. B. (1969). *Infants and mothers.* New York: Dell.
   This book discusses the entire first year of life, but the first four chapters focus on the neonate. Good discussion of individual differences among infants, with stress on the need to adapt to the individual baby.
Goldberg, S., & Devitto, B. A. (1983). *Born too soon: Preterm birth and early development.* San Francisco: W. H. Freeman.

Contains good descriptions of premature infants and discusses ways to interact with premature infants.
Gottfried, A. W., & Gaiter, J. L. (Eds.). (1985). *Infant stress under intensive care.* Baltimore: University Park Press.
   This book contains much interesting information about the physical setup and operation of neonatal intensive care units. The ethical dilemmas involved in caring for very ill infants is discusssed. Technical in spots, but useful.

chapter 5

PHYSICAL DEVELOPMENT IN INFANTS AND TODDLERS

"Dr. Marquez will see Sabina now, Mrs. Austen," the pediatric nurse called from the open door, and Ursula began picking up her baby paraphernalia and putting it into the diaper bag she carried with her everywhere.

"Put the puzzle back on the table, Sarah," she said to her 15-month-old. "It's time for Sabina to see the doctor." As Ursula gathered her things, Sarah picked up the two remaining puzzle pieces from the floor and placed them on the frame of the puzzle she had been trying to put together. Then she leaned forward on her hands to raise herself from her sitting position. Once up on her feet, she squatted down, with knees bent, to pick up the puzzle with both hands. She carried it to the low toy table in the corner of the waiting room.

Ursula, meanwhile, had made her way to the door leading to the examination rooms and was holding it open for Sarah with the side of her body. She held 6-week-old Sabina in an upright position against her shoulder, supporting the back of her head with her other hand. Sarah toddled quickly to her mother and reached up to take hold of the diaper bag strap, which hung from Ursula's shoulder. She'd learned in the past six weeks that her mother didn't have a free hand for her to hold when she was carrying Sabina up against her shoulder, so she latched on to the strap or to her mother's skirt or leg.

In the examination room, Ursula placed Sabina on the table and began to undress her. Sarah stepped up on a small stool beside the table to get a better look. She put her finger in her sister's hand, and Sabina's fingers closed tightly around it. She probably would have held on to Sarah's finger for some time if Ursula hadn't had to get the sleeve of her sleeper over her hand.

Sabina didn't seem to like being undressed. She began to cry. Her hands were squeezed into tight fists, and her arms waved in jerky arcs. Ursula leaned over to try to talk her out of her distress. Sarah stepped down from the stool and walked over to the large medical scale, which she stepped up on. Beside it was a sturdy wooden chair, and Sarah decided to climb onto it next. She reached across the seat, taking hold of the far side with her hands and then pulling herself up and across it. When she had pulled her legs up far enough, she bent her knees under herself and sat up on them. Then she turned toward the back of the chair, put her hands on its top, and stood up. She was reaching up to get hold of a blood pressure cuff that was mounted on the wall behind the chair when her mother caught sight of what she was doing.

"Sarah! Get down from there!" she called. "That's not a toy. And you might fall!"

Sarah turned around to face her mother, but she didn't sit down. Ursula scooped Sabina up from the table and walked over to the chair. Taking Sarah's hand with her free hand, she said, "Sit down right now." Sarah bent her knees to lower herself down onto the chair seat. "This is not a place to play. You may sit and watch, but you can't touch things. Here, find one of your books in the bag." As Sarah began to search in the diaper bag, Dr. Marquez came through the door.

"Well, hello, Sarah," she said. "Did you get up on that big chair all by yourself?"

"I'm afraid so," Ursula replied, with just a touch of dismay in her voice.

Ursula had her children so close together that she has two infants to care for at the same time. Although we call both these girls infants, they are very different in appearance and abilities. The changes that take place in babies in their first few years of life are truly phenomenal, and physical changes are probably the most astonishing. A person who hasn't seen a baby in a few weeks or months will probably remark, "Look how she's grown!" A person who hasn't seen a baby for a year or so since birth might not even recognize the child.

FIGURE 5-1
The 1-month-old and the 2-year-old may both wear diapers, but the 2-year-old has rapidly emerged from infancy and become a very different person than she was at birth. Every month brings impressive advances in the first years, when the growth rate is the highest it will ever be in the child's life.

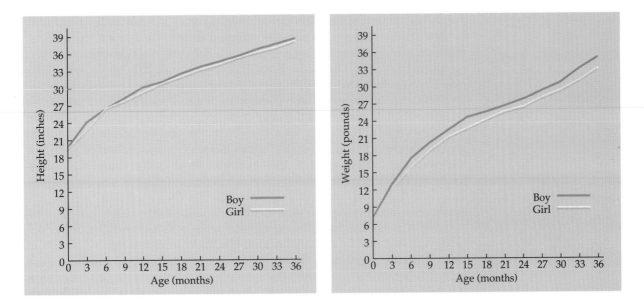

FIGURE 5-2
Height and weight for boys and girls from birth through 36 months of age. Children of the same age naturally vary in size. The graphs show heights and weights for children who are average (fiftieth percentile). Between birth and 9 or 10 months, the slope of the line is quite steep, reflecting the rapid rate of growth during this time. After 1 year of age, the slope flattens out. If prenatal growth were shown, the slope of that line would be even steeper than that for the first nine months after birth.

In this chapter we discuss the dramatic growth and the changes, both inward and outward, that occur during infancy and toddlerhood. We also focus on the exciting new motor skills that allow infants and toddlers to reach and grasp and eventually to move around with ever-increasing agility and speed. Finally, we discuss the achievement that comes at the end of toddlerhood and that separates toddlers from preschoolers in so many people's minds—toilet training.

HOW DO THEY GROW?

Increases in Weight and Length

The most obvious difference between the two girls in the examination room is that Sarah, at 15 months of age, is so much bigger than Sabina, who is only 6 weeks old. If you picked them up, you might guess that Sarah weighed two or three times what Sabina weighed. You would be right—babies usually double their birth weight in their first six months and triple it by their first birthday. This means an increase in weight from about 7 to about 21 pounds.

In their second year, weight increases by about a third, with the average 2-year-old weighing about 28 pounds. Although the baby has continued to grow, the rate of growth has not been as fast. In the third year the growth rate slows down even more; the average 3-year-old weighs about 32 pounds. The growth charts shown in Figure 5–2 illustrate these changes graphically. Notice that the curves are very steep the first year and flatten out somewhat after that.

Babies' increase in length parallels their increase in weight—they grow quite a lot in their first year and then less in the following years. The typical baby grows from about 20 inches at birth to 25½ inches at 6 months, to 28½ inches at a year, to 33 inches at 2 years (Lowrey, 1978).

VARIATIONS IN GROWTH. Although it's useful to refer to typical increases in weight and length, some infants and toddlers grow more than average or less than average. This kind of variation can be due to several different factors, including heredity and nutrition. If a fetus is cramped in the womb, or if the mother's nutrition is inadequate during pregnancy, a baby may not grow as much as it can during the prenatal period. If nutrition is adequate after birth, such a baby may catch up by growing much faster than average in the first months of life. This situation often occurs when a baby has a small mother and a large father (Tanner, 1970). Crowding of the large fetus in the uterus triggers a mechanism that slows prenatal growth, but after birth the child continues toward her genetically determined potential. Other factors can also influence growth in the postnatal period, such as the quality of food available and the infant's ability to adapt to feeding.

PREDICTING ADULT HEIGHT FROM TODDLER DIMENSIONS. We can say with a fair amount of certainty that a 2-year-old girl who is 33 inches tall will be 66.33 inches tall, or 5 feet 6 inches, as an adult. Toddler dimensions provide a reliable index of adult height, and multipliers have been determined for these calculations (Garn, 1966). For boys, the multiplier is 2.06; for girls, it's 2.01. Thus, if a 2-year-old boy is 35 inches tall, we would predict his adult height to be 72.1 inches, or 6 feet. The multiplier is smaller for girls than for boys because girls have a faster rate of physical maturation. A 2-year-old girl is already closer to her adult height than a boy the same age would be.

EFFECTS OF GROWTH RATE ON APPETITE. Very young infants seem to be hungry all the time, crying to be fed every three or four hours. Toddlers, on the other hand, pick at their food, and their parents sometimes worry that they're not getting enough nutrients. This difference in appetite is a normal reflection of the slackening growth rate by 2 years. Toddlers are growing at a much more leisurely pace than young infants, and they aren't so hungry. Toddlers would often rather play with their food than eat it. Parents do well to serve small portions of nutritious food to their young children and to accept their smaller appetites with a relaxed attitude.

Tissue Growth

Size isn't the only physical difference between younger and older infants. Toddlers are stronger and have more stamina; their appearance and body proportions are radically different from those of younger infants; and they can move in ways that younger infants can't. All of these physical characteristics reflect neurological changes and patterns of tissue growth in the first years of life.

BODY FAT. Subcutaneous fat, the layer of fat just below the skin, begins to form in the fetus about 6 weeks before birth. Premature babies don't have the benefit of this layer, as mentioned in earlier chapters, so they look unusually scrawny at birth. Subcutaneous fat accumulates rapidly in the first nine months of life and then more slowly after that, making the baby look rounded and filled out.

In the past, especially before antibiotics were discovered, many babies contracted infectious diseases that led to emaciation and death. The more fat reserves babies had, the better they were able to survive these diseases. People wanted babies to be fat because they thought they were healthier.

Then, for a while, experts were concerned that very fat babies were more likely to grow up to be fat adults. It was suggested that the number of fat cells in a person's body was determined by how much the person ate in the first year of life (Winick, 1974). But subsequent research has shown that the cell-number hypothesis of obesity isn't very accurate and that most fat babies don't become fat adults (Dobbing, 1984). Today, there's not as much concern about very fat babies as there was a few years ago. On the other hand, there's no advantage to be gained from overfeeding a baby.

MUSCLE AND BONE. No new muscle cells are formed after birth, but during infancy changes do occur in muscle fibers already present. One change is that the proportion of water in the fibers decreases and salts and proteins increase. This gives the baby greater strength and stamina.

Bones are changing too. At birth, babies have soft bones composed mostly of cartilage. Through the process of **ossification**, minerals are gradually deposited and the cartilage turns to bone. As the bones in the baby's skull harden and fuse, the fontanelles gradually close. The large fontanelle at the top of the head usually closes completely by about 2 years (Wennberg, Woodrum, & Hodson, 1973). As bones grow and become stronger, the support structure of the body changes, and the child eventually is able to learn to walk. Bone growth continues throughout childhood and adolescence (Stoner, 1978), making it essential that childen have adequate minerals, especially calcium, in their diet. (For a discussion of the development of the teeth, see Health Focus—Teething and the Care of Teeth.)

Because some bones and bone parts ossify before others in a regular pattern, ossification provides an index of children's physical maturity. The extent of ossification can be determined by X-rays, since the ossified areas are denser and show up on the X-ray film. Maturity studies using this technique have confirmed that girls mature faster than boys physically. At birth, girls are ahead of boys in skeletal maturity by about four weeks. By age 5 or 6, the gap has widened to a year (Tanner, 1970). Today, the X-ray technique is not used to do maturity research, because X-rays are known to be dangerous.

THE BRAIN. At 15 months, Sarah is well into the "brain growth spurt," which extends from the last three months of prenatal life through the first year and a half of postnatal life. During this time, more than half of the adult brain weight is achieved (Dobbing, 1984). By 5 years of age, the brain is almost at full adult weight (Tanner, 1978a). (See Table 5-1 for a breakdown of this weight gain.)

Brain cells begin to develop early in the prenatal period (Figure 5-5). **Neurons,** or nerve cells, which make up about 10 percent of the brain, develop

TABLE 5-1
Growth of the Brain

Age	Percentage of Weight of Adult Brain
Birth	25
6 months	30
12 months	60
20 months	75
5 years	90

FIGURE 5-3
The human brain is highly developed at birth, with the most rapid growth, especially of the cerebral cortex, having taken place in the last trimester of pregnancy. If a woman has an inadequate diet during pregnancy, it may be reflected in her child's mental abilities.

between the second and fifth months of prenatal life (Dobbing, 1984). **Dendrites** and **axons**, the fibrous extensions from these cells, continue to grow after the child is born. These fibers carry impulses to and from the cells.

The rest of the brain consists of **glial cells**, which begin to appear about three months before birth and continue to multiply for several years after birth. These cells support the nerve cells and may have some nutritional and regulatory functions as well (Thompson, 1967). They also produce **myelin**, a fatty substance that forms a sheath around nerve fibers and greatly increases the speed with which impulses are transmitted. **Myelination** of some parts of the brain begins before birth, but most is completed postnatally. Myelination of certain parts of the brain isn't complete until several years after birth (Konner, 1982).

IMPLICATIONS OF BRAIN GROWTH PATTERNS. The brain, then, begins to develop early in fetal life and continues developing for several years after birth. What are the implications of this long development period? Probably the most

HEALTH FOCUS

Teething and the Care of Teeth

"Ouch!" squealed Cathy one afternoon as she nursed 7-month-old Evan. "That hurt!" She slipped her finger into the side of his mouth to break the suction and ran her finger along his slippery bottom gum. Right in the middle she felt the hard edges of his first two teeth.

"You're getting teeth!" she exclaimed. "I didn't even notice!" Evan smiled up at her. "Well, I'm happy about your teeth," she went on, "but no more biting!"

Whether it's accompanied by pain and fretting or by no signs of discomfort at all, teething begins at about 7 or 8 months of age. By their first birthday, children have four teeth on the top gum and two on the bottom. By 1½ they usually add six more, and by age 3 they have their full set of 20 deciduous, or baby, teeth.

First molars don't come in until 10 months, second molars not until 20 months at the earliest, so babies have to be fed minced or chopped meat and cooked vegetables. Not until they have their full set of teeth, between 2½ and 3 years, can they really chew meat very well.

EFFECTS OF DIET AND FLUORIDE ON TOOTH DECAY
Even young babies can get dental caries—over 8 percent of children between 18 and 23 months have them, and by 3 years, almost half of all children have them (Miller & Rosenstein, 1982). The development of caries is influenced by diet and by fluoride in the drinking water. Sugar in sticky form, such as in chewy candy, cake frosting, and chewing gum with sugar, is the most pernicious form of sugar, as opposed to non-sticky forms found in fruit juice, milk, ice cream, and so on (Herrmann & Roberts, 1987). Bathing the teeth in sugar, by sucking lollipops, for example, is particularly conducive to tooth decay. When babies fall asleep sucking a bottle of milk or juice, they're likely to have "nursing bottle" caries, a particular pattern of cavities in those teeth most directly exposed to the flow of liquid from the bottle (Crall, 1986).

Water fluoridation reduces tooth decay by as much as 50 to 70 percent (Shelton, Ferratti, & Dent, 1982), and fluoride drops or tablets have the same effect where the water isn't fluoridated (Herrmann & Roberts, 1987). Frequent brushing—at least twice a day—also helps to fight tooth decay. Parents should begin cleaning their babies' teeth as soon as they erupt, at first with a wash cloth, then with a soft toothbrush.

TOOTH BRUSHING AND VISITS TO THE DENTIST
Toddlers can learn to brush their own teeth, although they don't have the coordination or skill to do a very

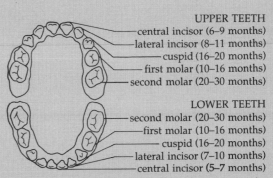

UPPER TEETH
- central incisor (6–9 months)
- lateral incisor (8–11 months)
- cuspid (16–20 months)
- first molar (10–16 months)
- second molar (20–30 months)

LOWER TEETH
- second molar (20–30 months)
- first molar (10–16 months)
- cuspid (16–20 months)
- lateral incisor (7–10 months)
- central incisor (5–7 months)

Teeth erupt in a regular pattern, often beginning with the two central incisors in the lower gum. The 20 baby teeth are usually in place by the time the child is 3 years old.

good job. A parental supervising technique that ensures clean teeth without interfering with the child's budding confidence is saying, "You did a good job with that one, and that one, and that one," while checking (and quickly rebrushing) each tooth.

Dentists often recommend that parents bring children in for a visit at about the age of 3. Children can look at the dentist's tools and get a demonstration of how the chair goes up and down. The dentist looks at the teeth, perhaps touches each one with a dental tool, and records the teeth on a dental chart. With a particularly cooperative child, the dentist might be able to do some quick scraping of plaque. With children who are more hesitant, the dentist might be able to give a fluoride treatment, which consists of having the child bite down on some toothpastelike material that contains fluoride.

EFFECT OF THUMB SUCKING ON THE TEETH
Parents often worry that thumb or finger sucking will harm the alignment of a child's teeth. These habits do affect the alignment of the baby teeth, pushing the upper front teeth forward and the lower front teeth back. But if the habit stops by the age of 5 or 6, the teeth self-correct (Schneider & Peterson, 1982). Parents therefore don't need to worry about thumb or finger sucking in the toddler or take any drastic action to stop it. Of course, parents who provide an emotionally secure and intellectually stimulating environment for the toddler's play and development will be laying the foundation for the day when thumb and finger sucking will disappear.

important is that good nutrition must be maintained throughout this entire period to ensure proper brain development. It's particularly important that pregnant women have adequate diets during periods when fetal brain cells are growing rapidly. The mother's diet is not as important to the formation of the neurons early in pregnancy as it is to the formation of the nerve fibers

FIGURE 5-4
Brain cells continue to increase in size and number during the first year of life and beyond, as can be seen in these drawings made from photomicrographs (photos taken with the aid of a microscope). Both nutrition and sensory stimulation must be adequate during this important time to ensure proper growth and development of the brain. (From Conel, 1939–1963.)

1 month   3 months   6 months   15 months

and glial cells in the later months of pregnancy (Dobbing, 1984). A good diet is also important for many metabolic processes in the brain. These processes are controlled by enzymes, and if the nutrients needed for the production of these enzymes aren't available, brain function can be impaired. (For a discussion of a government program designed to prevent nutritional problems in infants, see Public Policy Focus—The WIC Program.)

Since the brain keeps developing after birth, factors in the environment can affect it too. Research has shown that a stimulating environment can produce more growth of brain cells and can lead to better brain functioning (Greenough, Black, & Wallace, 1987). Studies with rats have shown that environmental factors have a direct impact on the weight of the brain cortex, the chemistry of the brain, and problem-solving abilities (Rosenzweig, 1984). Stimulation apparently has a similar, if not greater, effect on human babies. Babies who have been malnourished, for example, but who were later brought up in stimulating environments often seem to develop normally. Babies who were both malnourished and deprived of stimulation end up with impaired intelligence (Grantham-McGregor, Schofield, & Powell, 1984). Even when the brain presumably has been affected in some physical way by malnutrition, a rich, caring environment seems to be able to compensate for disturbances, or at least specific correlates of early malnutrition are difficult to pinpoint. As with other aspects of development, many factors, including both nutrition and stimulation, interact to form the intellect (Dobbing, 1984; Dobbing, 1987). Unfortunately, children who are malnourished are often the very ones who also receive less than optimal stimulation. Under such circumstances, it's difficult to disentangle the separate effects of each variable (Galler, 1987).

All parts of the brain don't mature at the same time. Lower brain structures, such as the midbrain, the pons, and the medulla, develop earlier than higher structures, such as the cerebral cortex. These lower structures control functions such as reflexes and balance. Within the cerebral cortex, different parts

PUBLIC POLICY FOCUS

The WIC Program

Children's health is a matter of such consequence to the larger society that many different government assistance programs have been established over the years to support good health and nutrition in children. One of the most successful of these is the Special Supplemental Food Program for Women, Infants, and Children, commonly known as the WIC program. As the only nutrition program that provides both food and health services, the WIC program is unique (Egan, 1977). It serves pregnant women, nursing mothers, infants, and children under the age of 5 who meet low-income guidelines and who are judged to be at risk for health and nutrition problems.

Established in 1972, the program provides a specified amount of food to the participants each month. Only certain foods are made available, including iron-fortified infant formulas, iron-fortified cereal, fruit or vegetable juices high in vitamin C, milk, cheese, and eggs. These foods were selected because iron-deficiency anemia, insufficient vitamin C, and low protein intake are common among the at-risk population. They also provide the nutrients necessary for healthy prenatal development, rapid growth during infancy and early childhood, and protection against disease (Select Committee on Hunger, 1988).

Between 1973 and 1976, the WIC program was associated with several health improvements (Egan, 1977, p. 237):

- Infants in the program gained weight and grew more quickly than similar infants not enrolled in the program.
- Fewer infants had anemia, and the mean blood hemoglobin concentration of infants in the program increased.
- Women gained more weight during pregnancy than similar women who weren't in the program.
- Newborns weighed more at birth than similar newborns not in the program.
- Participants took greater advantage of health services than they had prior to enrolling in the program.

Research has shown that enrollment in the WIC program improves the intake of essential nutrients in populations of women at risk for deficient diets (Farrior & Ruwe, 1987).

Like all publicly funded programs, the WIC program is reviewed periodically and is subject to the political and social views of changing administrations. But because of its success, the program would probably be one of the last nutrition programs to be cut back or discontinued. It appears to be an effective way to prevent nutritional problems when they're most likely to lead to serious impairment of physical and mental growth.

FIGURE 5-5
Two eager parents, massage, a brightly colored toy—is she being overstimulated? Apparently not, at least for the moment, judging by her smile. Although overstimulation doesn't lead to the same problems as lack of stimulation, it can be unpleasant for the baby and can lead to emotional difficulties if it becomes a regular pattern. If a baby is being overstimulated, she'll tell her parents it's time to stop by looking away, frowning, or crying.

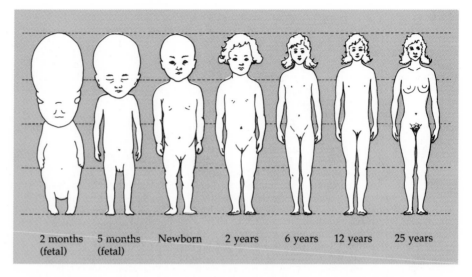

| 2 months
(fetal) | 5 months
(fetal) | Newborn | 2 years | 6 years | 12 years | 25 years |

of specific areas, such as the motor area, mature at varying rates (Tanner, 1978a). This is why babies master various physical skills in a specific sequence. They can hold their heads up before they can sit up, for example, and they can sit up before they can walk.

Changes in Body Proportions and Shape

The shape and proportions of a toddler's body are quite different from those of a young infant's body. The head is the fastest growing part of the body early in development both prenatally and postnatally, but then this growth slows down. At other times, the legs and trunk grow very fast. As with the brain, different parts of the baby's body grow at different rates. The various kinds of body tissues grow at different rates too, giving the child a different appearance at different ages.

A toddler's head is still larger in proportion to her body than an older child's or an adult's, but she's not nearly so top heavy as a young infant. Toddlers have also lost some of the "baby fat" that accumulates during the first nine months, and their bodies have more muscle and bone. By age 3, they look considerably leaner than they did at age 1.

Toddlers continue to be chubby around the middle, however, because the trunk grows slowly during infancy and early toddlerhood. At the same time, the internal organs grow quite a lot. The organs push out and the underdeveloped abdominal muscles can't hold them in. Toddlers keep their swaybacked silhouette until they're 3½ or 4 years old. By then their trunks have grown enough to provide more room for their organs.

Children start walking when they're 12 or 13 months old, but they walk with short steps and a wobbly gait. They can keep their balance only by placing their feet very far apart. This is the accommodation babies and toddlers make to compensate for their big heads. As the trunk and legs stretch out during the preschool years, the child's center of gravity moves ever lower, and balance improves. The toddler's characteristic stance and walk gradually evolve into the surer, more graceful movements of the preschooler.

FIGURE 5-7
The toddler is easily recognized by his characteristic body shape. As his trunk grows and his abdominal muscles become stronger, he'll be able to tuck that tummy in.

DEVELOPMENT OF MOTOR ABILITIES

We saw at the beginning of the chapter that a 15-month-old like Sarah can walk, step up, climb onto furniture, pick up puzzle pieces, and engage in a number of other useful actions. A 6-week-old like Sabina is limited to waving her arms in the air and a few other gestures. What are the developments that give Sarah her comparatively impressive motor skills?

During infancy, great advances in physical abilities occur. Motor development proceeds in two directions: (1) from the center of the body out to the arms, hands, and fingers, and (2) from the top of the body downward. Development in the outward direction is known as **proximodistal** (literally, "near" to "far") development; this trend leads to ever-increasing skill in using the hands. Development in the downward direction is known as **cephalocaudal** (literally, "head" to "tail") development; this trend eventually leads to using the legs to stand and walk.

Fine Motor Development: Reaching and Grasping

Young infants can wave their arms in the air, but they can't direct them toward a target much less get hold of it. Gradually, their abilities improve. By about 2½ months, they're reaching for objects by swiping at them, and by about 4½

FIGURE 5-8
This 2-month-old has become strong enough to lift her head when she's on her stomach, her first big motor achievement and one that reflects the cephalocaudal trend in development.

FIGURE 5-9
Between 9 and 12 months the baby perfects her pincer grasp, which allows her to pick up small objects (and, most likely, put them in her mouth).

months, they're able to reach for and grasp an object. However, an infant can do this only if both the object and her hand are in her visual field. If she can see the object but not her hand, or her hand but not the object, she won't attempt to reach for it. Not until 5 months of age does a baby reach for an object when her hand isn't in view.

At first, a baby grasps an object awkwardly by surrounding it with her fingers and pressing it into the palm of her hand. Later she uses her thumb to help hold the object. By about 9 months, she's able to grasp small objects by using just her thumb and index or forefinger. This is known as a **pincer grasp** (Figure 5-10).

To use a pincer grasp, babies have to be able to separate the forefinger from the other four fingers. Once they can do this, they can also point to objects in the environment. This skill is useful for language development. The child can point to an object and make a sound using a rising intonation, meaning, "What is that?" (Language development in infancy is discussed in detail in Chapter 7.)

By the time babies are 1 year old, they're playing with blocks and attempting to build towers. Not until they're 15 months old, however, will they be able to place blocks precisely where they want them. This is because they haven't mastered letting go of objects. A 6-month-old finds it impossible to control letting go because the palmar grasp hasn't yet disappeared. This reflex is gone completely by 1 year, and between 1 year and 18 months the child learns to let go of objects voluntarily.

With this difficulty behind them, babies gain immensely in coordination, strength, and steadiness. They're able to build sturdy towers by the time they're 2 years old. They're also able to snap pop-beads together, make marks on paper with some control, and work simple puzzles with two to four pieces. They're even able to string large beads if the end of the string is stiff enough to pass completely through a bead.

Factors Affecting Reaching and Grasping Development

When we discuss landmarks like the disappearance of the palmar grasp and the emergence of the pincer grasp, you may think that motor development is completely a matter of maturation. And, if you recall from Chapter 2, the proponents of the maturation theory of development took much of their evidence from the realm of physical development. However, we know now that although motor development is *largely* under the control of maturation, experience plays a role as well (Konner, 1982). Studies of blind babies have given us some of this knowledge, and additional information has come from studies in which the environments of sighted babies were modified.

STUDIES OF REACHING AND GRASPING IN BLIND BABIES. Blind babies attempt to reach and grasp early in life when they hear a sound. But the sound doesn't tell the baby how far away the object is, and more often than not the baby fails to touch the object. Soon the baby stops reaching (Bower, 1977). In her studies

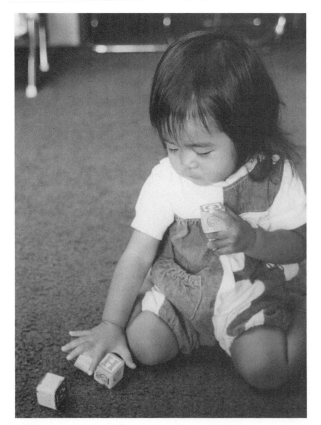

FIGURE 5-10
The 15-month-old can play with blocks more easily than she could just a few months earlier. With her growing manual control, she can pick blocks up and put them down where she wants them.

of blind babies, psychologist Selma Fraiberg (1975) found that the ability to reach for an object on the basis of sound alone requires a higher level of conceptual development than does reaching for an object on the basis of sight *and* sound. Sound alone doesn't convey the sense that something is an object and can be grasped. Blind babies have to acquire this concept, as the following observations from Fraiberg's studies show (Fraiberg, 1975, p. 48):

> For a perilously long time in the first year of life the blind baby behaves as if the musical toy in his hand is one object and the sound of the musical toy "out there" is another object . . .

Fraiberg created an environment that would help these blind babies acquire the concepts they needed to continue developing their motor skills:

> Toys that united tactile and sound qualities were sought out by us and the parents to encourage a sound-touch identity for objects. . . . Through the devices of a special play table and a playpen we created "an interesting space" in which a search or sweep of the hand would guarantee an encounter and interesting discovery. . . . Even the motor patterns for reaching may not appear in a blind baby who has no incentive to reach.
>
> Then, one day . . . the sound of the bell would motivate the hands. A grasping-ungrasping motion would appear. . . . There was not yet reach, but we knew the idea was emerging. A few days later, a few weeks later . . . without vision, a baby would discover that the sound that we call "a bell" and the bell which he could not experience in his hand were "out there" in space.

Since blind babies don't have the same physical equipment as sighted babies, the environment has to be adapted to their abilities to ensure their development. Fraiberg's studies help us realize that the development of motor skills is not simply a matter of maturation. The stimulation and feedback babies get from the environment is a crucial factor, even in physical development.

STUDIES OF REACHING AND GRASPING IN MODIFIED ENVIRONMENTS. Further evidence for the role of experience in motor development comes from a study done by psychologist Burton White (1971). Working with infants just a few months old, White added visual stimulation to their environments. He gave them multicolored sheets on their mattresses, additional time on their stomachs (a good position from which to view the world), and large stabiles (stationary mobiles) above their cribs.

One group of infants received the stabile during their second, third, and fourth months. A second group received an attractive pacifier centered on a disk at both sides of the crib during their second month and the stabile during their third and fourth months. A control group didn't receive any additional stimulation.

Babies in both experimental groups began reaching and grasping with the hand out of view at about 130 days of age (4½ months), a month earlier than the norm. Babies in the control group didn't reach and grasp until about 170 days of age (5½ months), which is right in line with the norm. Again we see that the environment has an effect on what might seem to be a purely biological development.

An interesting side effect of this study was that the babies who received the stabile in their second month cried at first more than any other group. The

FIGURE 5-11
The development of creeping. One milestone of locomotor development is broken down here into 14 steps. The baby's persistence pays off first with crawling (step 9) and then with creeping on the hands and feet (step 14).

stabile may have been too stimulating—too novel or frightening—for them. When parents want to provide additional visual stimulation for their baby, they're wise to give the baby a choice. A mobile can be hung at the side of the crib, for example, rather than directly over the baby's head. The baby's reactions are probably the best guide to how much stimulation is too much. If the baby expresses extreme surprise or fear, or if she frequently looks away from it, the stimulation is probably too novel. If she gazes continuously, the level of stimulation is probably just about right.

Locomotor Development: Up and About

A baby's first unassisted steps are usually celebrated as the major achievement of infancy, coming, as they do, at the end of the first year. Walking is an important milestone of infancy, but it's preceded by an equally impressive—and orderly—series of developments. Before they can walk, babies have to be able to stand. Before they can stand, they have to know how to sit; and to sit, they have to be able to hold their heads up. The cephalocaudal trend in development means that the head, neck, trunk, and leg muscles come under control in a head-to-tail order. The cephalocaudal development of **locomotor skills** (skills used in moving from place to place) is shown in two classic illustrations done by researchers working in the 1930s. Figure 5-11 shows the development of creeping (Ames, 1937), and Figure 5-12 shows the development of walking (Shirley, 1933). Today, babies seem to reach these milestones earlier than they

FIGURE 5-13
Milestones of locomotor development (left). The cephalocaudal trend in development can readily be seen in this chart. As the baby's brain and muscles mature, her achievements center on progressively lower parts of the body, leading eventually to walking.

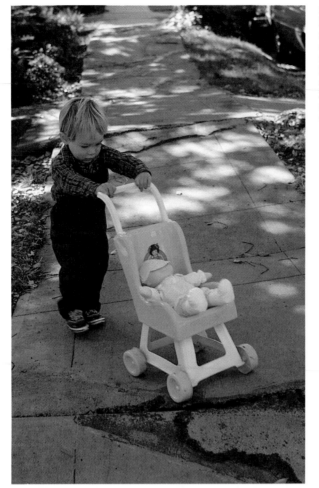

FIGURE 5-14
Beginning walkers can steady themselves and gain experience moving in an upright position with the help of push toys. Even an experienced walker like this 2-year-old may appreciate a doll carriage when the sidewalk is unpredictable.

did in the 1930s, perhaps because of better nutrition or more opportunities to move around on the floor. The order in which they achieve them, however, remains the same.

A baby who has just started walking has to give her full attention to remaining upright and taking a few steps. As she gains experience, she begins to move faster and with more abandon and ease. The difference between these two levels of skill can be seen in children's abilities to use two different kinds of toys. A baby just starting to walk can use a push toy; a more experienced walker can also use a pull toy.

A baby pushing a toy, such as a plastic lawn mower, can use it to help balance herself as she walks along behind it. Her arms are extended out from her body, which also helps her balance, and her eyes are directed ahead of her. A child pulling a toy behind him, on the other hand, has one arm down, holding the string. He usually wants to look at the toy, so he has to twist his trunk to turn part of his body around. Both the arm position and the turning can throw a child off balance, so only an older walker can manage a pull toy.

Factors Affecting Locomotor Development

Like the fine motor skills, the locomotor skills emerge according to a built-in biological timetable. And like the fine motor skills, they emerge normally only with appropriate stimulation and feedback from the environment. Evidence for this relationship comes from some of the same sources as the evidence about the development of reaching and grasping.

STUDIES OF LOCOMOTOR DEVELOPMENT IN BLIND BABIES. Fraiberg's work with blind babies provides information about locomotor development as well as fine motor development, illustrating how heredity and experience are intertwined (Fraiberg, 1975, p. 48):

> In normal development when control of the trunk is achieved in a stable sitting posture, there is a smooth transition to bridging and creeping. In our sample, most of our babies achieved stability in sit well within the range for sighted babies. Then, something that should appear on the developmental timetable did not appear. The baby did not creep!

> The sighted child will reach for the out-of-reach toy which propels him forward. It is the visual incentive that initiates the creeping pattern. At every point where vision would normally intervene to promote a new phase in locomotor development we had to help the blind baby find an adaptive solution. The prone position, for example, is not an "interesting" position for the blind baby. . . . The blind baby, without . . . incentives, may resist the prone position. We build in "interest" in prone through speaking to the baby, through dangle toys or other devices.

> Practicing pulling to stand and cruising will be more "interesting" in the familiar space of a playpen with favorite toys offering sound-touch incentives. And one day, sometime between 13 and 19 months, the blind baby steps out into the vast black space to his mother's voice across the room and the news is telegraphed to us that he is walking!

FIGURE 5-15
The child raised in an unstimulating environment suffers in many ways. She's likely to have motor delays from lack of opportunities for practice, mental deficiencies from impaired brain development, and emotional disturbances from inadequate emotional attachment. Awareness of the importance of stimulation has led to many changes in institutional practices, reducing the number of situations like this one.

STUDIES OF LOCOMOTOR DEVELOPMENT IN INSTITUTIONAL SETTINGS. Many studies have shown that babies' motor skills are delayed when they're raised in non-stimulating environments, especially in institutional situations. A study by psychologist Wayne Dennis (1960) focused on orphans in three institutions in Iran. In one institution, which Dennis labeled Institution I, lived 600 children under the age of 3 with one attendant to care for every eight children. Babies who couldn't yet sit up spent their time lying on their backs in their cribs. They were never propped up or given toys. They were even fed in their cribs with bottles propped up on pillows.

When babies managed to pull themselves into a sitting position, they were placed on the floor while they were awake, but still they were given no toys. Not surprisingly, only 42 percent of the children between 1 and 2 years could sit up, and none could walk. In fact, only 8 percent of the children between 2 and 3 years could walk. When they turned 3, most of these children went to Institution II, where conditions were just as bad. Only 15 percent of the children between 3 and 4 years at Institution II could walk.

Institution III had been opened as a model of improved child care. The babies with the most retarded development at Institution I had been transferred to Institution III very early in infancy. Here, there was one attendant for every four babies. Babies were held when they were fed, placed on their stomachs or in a sitting position in their cribs, put in playpens when they were 4 months old, and given toys. At Institution III, 90 percent of the children could sit alone by 2 years of age (as compared with 42 percent at Institution I), and 15 percent could walk (none could walk at Institution I). By age 3, all children could walk alone (compared to 8 percent at Institution I). Dennis attributed this more normal development to the better child care at Institution III, especially the practices of placing the babies prone in bed and on the floor. In this position, babies can push up and learn to sit up, roll over, and crawl.

Studies have shown that retarded motor development in early infancy can be overcome later if the baby is placed in better conditions (Dennis, 1960; Kagan, Kearsley & Zelazo, 1978). But Dennis's institutional study demonstrates conclusively that child care practices do have an effect on motor development. In our society, most parents provide the environment and experiences that foster rapid motor development. This leads us to believe that normal development occurs spontaneously and inevitably. This isn't true; children's development depends in part on the conditions we provide for them.

Motor Development: Maturation or Experience?

Some earlier studies seemed to demonstrate that motor skills would emerge on schedule no matter what experiences a child had. In a classic experiment on maturation and learning, maturational theorists Arnold Gesell and Henry Thompson (1929) compared the stair-climbing skill of children with and without stair-climbing experience. They used identical twins in their experiment so that differences in behavior couldn't be attributed to genetic or biological differences. They gave one twin daily practice climbing stairs for six weeks, beginning at 46 weeks of age. By the fourth week of practice, this twin could climb the stairs alone, and at the end of six weeks, at 52 weeks of age, he could climb them in just 26 seconds.

FIGURE 5-16
This 14-month-old can manage a big step not only because his bones and muscles have reached a certain size and strength but because he's had ample opportunities to crawl, pull up, stand, and walk. Maturation is the crucial factor—he couldn't have taken this step at 10 months—but experience influences the timing of motor developments.

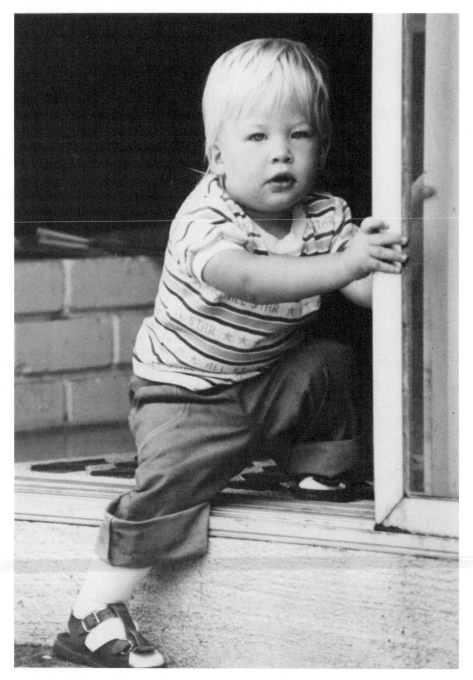

The other twin had never climbed stairs. The researchers introduced him to stairs at 53 weeks of age, and on his first attempt he climbed them in 46 seconds. Two weeks later, at 55 weeks, he could climb them in just 10 seconds. In other words, without any experience of stairs at all, he equalled or surpassed his brother's performance at a particular age.

The conclusion researchers drew from this and similar studies was that maturation alone was responsible for motor development. What these researchers didn't take into account was that the ability to climb stairs might be influenced not just by practice in climbing stairs but by practice in other motor skills as well. The twin who hadn't had any practice climbing stairs *had* had just as much practice crawling, creeping, and walking as his brother. The researchers demonstrated that learning a behavior doesn't require a specific experience, but they didn't prove that the behavior will occur without any experiences at all (Bower, 1974). Again, although maturation plays a primary role, experience does influence the development of motor skills. (For a discussion of a question that hasn't received as much attention, see Research Focus—Effects of Motor Development on Other Areas of Development.)

DEVELOPMENT OF BLADDER AND BOWEL CONTROL

Sarah and Sabina, the sisters we met at the beginning of the chapter, are different in many ways, but in one way they're alike: they're both in diapers. Sarah won't be able to be toilet trained for another 15 to 20 months, at age 2½ or 3, although she may begin to show an interest in it by the time she's 2½.

Just as children gain control of the muscles of the upper and lower body in a certain order, they also achieve control over the **sphincters**—the smooth,

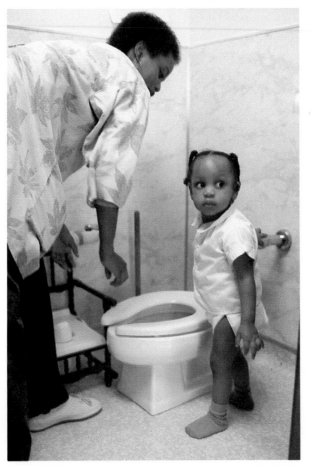

FIGURE 5-17
If toilet training is begun before the child has the physical maturity to control her bladder and bowel functions, a very difficult struggle may ensue. Interest in using the toilet is a good first sign that a child is becoming ready for toilet training.

RESEARCH FOCUS

Effects of Motor Development on Other Areas of Development

Quite a lot of research has been devoted to investigating the factors—both inborn and environmental—that influence motor development. As we've seen in this chapter, experimenters have manipulated the environment in many ingenious ways to see how changes affect motor skills. Not nearly so much research has been designed to test how the development of motor skills affects other areas of development. But it seems clear that greater mobility and agility must have a profound impact on the rest of the child's life. The information that we do have suggests that motor development does affect other aspects of development in important ways.

In some early animal studies, researchers found that kittens who were prevented from walking had impaired visual development (Held & Hein, 1963). Other studies showed that locomotion was a critical step in providing feedback necessary for normal social development in some species (Schneirla, 1957; Schneirla & Rosenblatt, 1961; Schneirla, Rosenblatt, & Jobach, 1963).

Human studies have indicated that infants' avoidance of drop-offs, as demonstrated in the visual-cliff experiments (see Chapter 6) (Gibson & Walk, 1960), is learned quickly after infants have some experience crawling (Campos et al., 1978). Infants' spatial knowledge probably increases after they begin moving around independently because they experience so many different spatial orientations (Acredolo, 1978). And, as every parent surely knows, babies who move around independently change the terms of their interactions and relationships with adults (Bowlby, 1969b; Green, Gustafson, & West, 1980). These studies suggest that cognitive, perceptual, and social development are all affected by advances in motor skills.

A study designed specifically to probe the effects of locomotion on other behavior involved the use of mechanical walkers (Gustafson, 1984). Babies who weren't yet crawling independently were placed in a walker in a laboratory equipped with several wall posters, a popular "activity center" toy mounted on the back of a chair, and toys in a pan on a shelf. Babies were observed to see how much they traveled around the room; what they looked at and for how long; what objects they manipulated and how they manipulated them; and how much they vocalized, smiled, gestured, or fussed.

Babies traveled much more in the walkers than they did when they weren't in them. They entered more areas of the playroom and approached the activity center and the adults more often (their parents were present as well as a research assistant). They looked more at the people and at non-toy aspects of the room, such as the wall posters, when in the walkers. They also smiled more and directed more vocalizations toward adults.

A second group of infants was also investigated. These were babies who were already crawling inde-

Motor developments rearrange both the baby's experiences and the parents' lifestyle.

pendently. For this group, placement in the walker didn't lead to as many changes in behavior. However, there were some differences between their behavior when out of the walkers and the behavior of the noncrawlers when the noncrawlers were in the walkers. Out of the walkers, the babies who could crawl spent more time close to adults, manipulating them physically. They crawled into adults' laps and played with their faces, hair, and jewelry. The babies in the walkers couldn't get as close to the adults, so they spent more time manipulating features of the room.

This researcher suggests that the ability to move around independently affects babies' social interactions, language development, and cognitive and perceptual development. But he cautions against parental attempts to speed up normal motor development to accelerate development in other areas. There is no evidence to suggest any long-term advantages to such attempts. The implication from this research is simply that locomotion, when it occurs, will result in a major reorganization of infant experiences and behavior. Unless motor development is delayed excessively by poor environmental conditions, we can assume that this reorganization will occur for all individual children in their own good time.

circular muscles of the bladder and bowel—at a certain time in an overall pattern. Control of these muscles comes after control of the lower trunk and legs.

In young infants, the sphincter of the rectum or bladder relaxes reflexively, permitting the contents to escape. As infants mature physically and neurologically, they learn to inhibit these reflexive actions. This requires an awareness of the sensations associated with a full rectum or bladder, which depends on the maturation of the cerebral cortex. The cephalocaudal order of development applies not just to the motor area of the cerebral cortex; it also applies to the sensory area. Sensory development of the leg area in the brain is not fully achieved until age 2 or even a little later (Tanner, 1978).

Bowel control comes first, often beginning late in the second year. Control of the bladder comes later, first during the day and then also during the night. Boys achieve control later than girls because they're less mature physically. Girls may be toilet trained by age 2½; boys may not be ready until age 3. It usually takes several months for childen to gain control of these functions. Sometimes it takes even longer, especially if parents misjudge physical readiness and start too soon or try to push the child. It may take several years for some children to gain complete night control. And all children occasionally have relapses (for example, when they're sick, tired, absorbed in play, or "off-schedule" on a family trip).

Toilet training is a subject that's been considered exhaustively by doctors, theorists, and other child care experts. Many techniques and approaches—often with conflicting advice—have been devised for parents and other caregivers. Toilet training is discussed further in Knowledge in Action: Infants and Toddlers, following Chapter 8.

OVERVIEW

Young infants are relatively weak and helpless, but in their first weeks and months of life they grow and develop faster than they ever will again. In the first six months, they double their birth weight, develop more fat, stronger muscles, and harder bones, and begin to acquire fine motor and locomotor skills. In the second half of the first year, they acquire a few teeth, start to move out and about, and finally, around the time of their first birthday, begin to walk. In their second and third years, they spend a good part of every day practicing their new motor skills. By the end of the third year, we have to look hard to find a hint of the infant's face or body in the rambunctious toddler, who is taller, leaner, stronger, and eager to tackle the preschool play yard.

CHAPTER REVIEW

GROWTH

- Babies triple their birth weight by their first birthday and then grow more slowly in their second and third years. Length also increases rapidly at first and then proceeds at a slower rate.

- Variations in growth among different babies can result from either genetic or nutritional factors. Babies whose growth was limited in the prenatal period will catch up to their genetic potential after they're born, given adequate nutrition.

- As the growth rate slows down, toddlers' appetites diminish, and they're able to eat less.
- Body tissue grows and changes in a particular pattern. Subcutaneous fat accumulates rapidly in the first nine months, giving babies their rounded look; muscle fibers lose water and gain in salt and protein, making them stronger; and soft, cartilagenous bones begin to ossify, providing the support structure needed for walking. The fontanelles on the top of the head are fully closed by the time children are about 2 years old.
- Teething begins at about 7 months, and babies have their full set of 20 deciduous teeth by the time they're 3 years old. A lifetime of healthy teeth can begin in toddlerhood with proper brushing, a good diet, fluoride treatments, and regular trips to the dentist.
- The brain is about one-quarter of its adult weight at birth. The "brain growth spurt," when more than half the adult brain weight is achieved, takes place between the last three months of prenatal life and the first year and a half of postnatal life. The brain reaches almost its full adult weight by the time the child is 5 years old.
- Adequate nutrition, both prenatally and postnatally, is crucial to proper brain growth and functioning, as is environmental stimulation during infancy.
- Different parts of the brain mature at different times, causing physical abilities to appear at different times but in a specific sequence.
- The proportion of fat to muscle and bone decreases in the second and third years of life, giving toddlers a leaner look. But because of rapid growth and undeveloped abdominal muscles, they keep their protruding tummies and swaybacked silhouettes until they're about 4.
- Toddlers are still top heavy, although not as much as infants. Their body proportions cause them to walk with quick, short steps—their characteristic "toddle."

MOTOR DEVELOPMENT

- Motor development proceeds in two directions: (1) from the center of the body out to the fingers, known as proximodistal development, and (2) from the top of the body downward, known as cephalocaudal development.
- Proximodistal development results in reaching and grasping with the hands and fingers. At first, babies swipe at objects; later they reach if they can see both the object and their hand; by about 5 months, they reach even if they can't see their hand. Once babies acquire the pincer grasp (at about 9 months) they can pick up objects, and after they lose the palmar reflex, they can voluntarily let objects go (between 12 and 18 months).
- Although the emergence of reaching and grasping is largely controlled by maturation, experience plays a part as well. Research has shown that babies develop these skills earlier if there are stimulating objects in the environment that they want to grasp.
- When babies have mastered standing up and controlling their leg muscles, they can learn to walk. They reach developmental milestones somewhat earlier than babies did years ago, but the order in which the locomotor skills are achieved remains the same.
- Like fine motor development, locomotor development is largely controlled by biological maturation but is also influenced by environmental factors. Stimulation and opportunities to move around are necessary for normal motor development. Delayed motor development in early infancy can be overcome if the environment is improved.
- Research has shown that the development of motor skills affects other areas of babies' development and experience, including their social interactions, language development, and cognitive and perceptual development. But researchers caution against trying to speed up motor development, since it occurs for all children, given adequate stimulation, in their own time.

BLADDER AND BOWEL CONTROL

- Toddlers can become toilet trained only after a certain level of neurological and motor development has been reached. They also have to gain control of the sphincter muscles of the bladder and bowel.
- Bowel control is usually achieved before bladder control. Girls are typically ready earlier, about age 2½, than boys, who aren't ready until about age 3. Night control isn't achieved until after daytime control, sometimes several years later.
- If the child is ready, toilet training takes several months, although there are many accidents and relapses. For some children, it takes much longer.

KEY TERMS

ossification	axons	myelination	pincer grasp
neurons	glial cells	proximodistal trend	locomotor skills
dendrites	myelin	cephalocaudal trend	sphincters

SUGGESTIONS FOR FURTHER READING

Caplan, F. (1978). *The first 12 months of life*. New York: Bantam.
Extensive discussion of physical development during infancy.

Cratty, B. J. (1986) *Perceptual and motor development in infants and children* (3rd ed.). Englewood Cliffs, Prentice-Hall.
Includes detailed information about early brain growth, how brain development affects movement capability, the reflexes found in infants, and the factors that affect movement development.

Tanner, J. M. (1978). *Fetus into man: Physical growth from conception to maturity*. Cambridge, MA: Harvard University Press.
Provides a thorough discussion of physical growth at all stages of life.

chapter 6

COGNITIVE DEVELOPMENT IN INFANTS AND TODDLERS

Adam, 24 months old, sits in his high chair, waiting for his lunch. His mom has given him a blue felt-tip marker and a white piece of paper to occupy him until his lunch is ready, and he eagerly puts marker to paper. He begins by making a patch of circular marks in the upper left portion of the paper. He pauses to inspect it for a moment and then creates another patch to its right. A second pause for inspection is followed by a third circular creation, placed practically on top of the first one. Then he begins to draw horizontal lines, from left to right. The first line begins in the right-hand circular patch, another begins above that patch, and another is placed at the very top of the upper left portion of the paper. He makes several more horizontal lines lower on the paper.

Next, a different sort of experiment—vertical lines. Adam adds two, slowly and deliberately, on the left side of the paper. Then he draws one line straight through the middle of the first circular patch and another line diagonally down from the patch. Finally, he adds a series of "combination" lines. One starts as a vertical line, drawn from the top, but then turns and makes its way horizontally to the right before looping around to make a tiny, irregular circle. It continues horizontally, then around, to create a larger circle, and still doesn't stop. It continues upward, then bends to the right horizontally. Adam adds several more lines now that combine the separate vertical, horizontal, diagonal, and circular lines that he used when he first began to draw. At last, apparently finished, he sits back and looks with satisfaction at his creation.

From Adam's apparently random scribbling, shown in Figure 6-1, we can tell quite a lot about his cognitive development. First, he didn't make a line or shape just once; he repeated them several times. He also seemed to be varying his movements in a systematic way, as if experimenting to see what differences he could create. After he had made different types of lines separately—horizontal, vertical, diagonal, and circular—he joined them into complex lines and then experimented with several combinations.

Adam's behavior is typical of a child in a certain stage of cognitive development. Regardless of the materials themselves, whether paper and pen, a spoon, a musical toy, or a toy containing tiny beads that scatter when shaken, the 18- to 24-month-old takes a predictable approach. He experiments and watches; then he repeats what he's discovered. A drawing that looks like a meaningless scribble to the unknowing eye can turn out to be a fairly sophisticated "thinking" piece. The same is true of other materials. A spoon isn't just thrown from the high chair: first, it's dropped; then, it's tossed straight out; finally, it's flipped in the air. The child-scientist is at work.

It's not easy to interpret or understand cognitive development in children, and it's particularly challenging in infants and toddlers, who can't tell us what they know or think. Probably the best known approach to cognitive development in children is that of Jean Piaget, whose theories we described in Chapter 2. In this chapter, we discuss his theory and study of the intelligence of the infant and toddler.

Another fruitful approach to infant cognitive development is the study of visual perception in babies. This research gives us a somewhat different, though equally fascinating, picture of the baby as a very active intellectual being. We can also study thinking and knowing in children by observing their play—an open book in which we can read what's going on in their minds. In this chapter,

FIGURE 6-1
Adam's experiments with a felt-tip marker give us telling clues about his intellectual development.

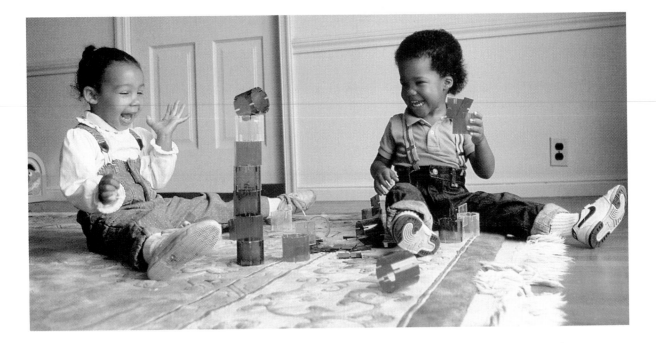

FIGURE 6-2
These 2-year-olds are learning about their world and what they can do to it through experimentation. Observing their play gives us important information about infant and toddler thinking.

we discuss all three of these approaches for a comprehensive view of infant and toddler cognitive development.

VISUAL PERCEPTION

People have long been interested in how babies see the world and how they process visual images. Do babies see our faces? Are they born with depth perception? Can they organize the world into meaningful pictures, or is it a blur of colors and shapes? A wide variety of studies has addressed these and other questions, and we discuss some of these studies here.

Preferences for Certain Patterns

We saw in Chapter 4 that even newborns have definite preferences when they gaze at objects. They like to look at patterned displays rather than nonpatterned ones; they like circles and ovals, such as the shape of the face; and they like areas of high contrast, such as edges where black and white meet.

HOW PREFERENCES EVOLVE. As babies get older, they prefer patterns that are increasingly "complex." ("Complexity" is defined differently by different researchers, as we discuss below.) For example, babies prefer patterns with more elements. Checkerboard patterns, like those shown in Figure 6-3, are often used in studies to see how babies' visual preferences change as they get older.

In one such study, checkerboard patterns of 4, 64, and 576 squares were shown to groups of babies aged 3 weeks, 8 weeks, and 14 weeks (Brennan, Ames, & Moore, 1966). Since young babies can't focus very well, the researchers thought the youngest babies might see the 576-square pattern only as a

FIGURE 6-3
Examples of stimuli used in infant perception complexity studies. Researchers found that younger babies preferred the checkerboard with the fewest squares, and older babies liked checkerboards that were increasingly complex. But we can't tell exactly what it is about the increasingly complex patterns that makes babies prefer them.

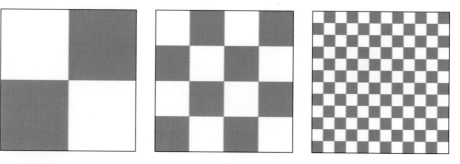

SOURCE: Hershenson, M. (1964). Visual discrimination in the human newborn. Journal of Comparative Physiological Psychology, 58, 270–76.

patch of gray. They added a fourth pattern, a plain gray square, to see if the babies looked at it for the same length of time as the 576. If looking time was the same, it could be assumed that they didn't perceive the most complex pattern as a pattern.

The researchers found that the 3-week-old infants could definitely see the most complex pattern, but it wasn't their favorite. They liked the least complex pattern best, followed by the intermediate pattern. The 8-week-olds liked the intermediate pattern best, and the 14-week-olds preferred the most complex pattern. Clearly, preferences for different patterns change with age. As babies get older, they prefer to look at patterns with more and more elements.

THE PROBLEM OF DEFINING "COMPLEXITY." Despite many studies like this, researchers do not agree on what it is about a particular pattern that makes babies of different ages like or dislike it. The definition of "complex" is one of the problems. Is complexity a matter of the number of elements? The number of angles? The arrangement of elements or angles? Is a regular, symmetrical pattern more or less complex than an asymmetrical pattern with the same number of elements? No one can agree.

For any given stimulus—checkerboards, alternating black and white lines, angles, and so on—researchers can determine what is preferred by younger babies versus older babies. But calling a stimulus more or less complex isn't enough to explain the reasons for babies' choices. (Banks & Salapatek, 1983). For example, if we increase the squares in a checkerboard, we increase not just the number of elements but also the amount of contrast in the pattern. We don't know which quality the baby actually prefers. That's why researchers hesitate to say simply that older babies prefer increasingly complex patterns.

Luckily for babies and parents, this problem doesn't affect child care practices very much. In our society, babies have a lot to see in their environment, and they can choose what they want to look at. Most babies' cognitive development is just fine, although they're giving some researchers a very difficult puzzle to sort out.

Changes in Scanning Behavior

Another aspect of infant perception is scanning behavior, that is, how babies move their eyes across a pattern and settle their gaze on one part of it or another (Figure 6-4). Investigations have revealed that scanning behavior changes as babies get older. Newborns tend to fixate on one feature of a stimulus, such as one angle of a triangle. Older babies, about 2 months old, scan several parts of the figure (Salapatek & Kessen, 1966; Salapatek, 1975).

Similarly, if a dot or a line is inserted inside the outline of a triangle or a square, 1-month-olds fixate on the outline and ignore anything in the middle of the figure. But 2-month-olds fixate on the dot or line inside the figure (Salapatek, 1975). When the complex stimulus of the face is used, the same behavior occurs. The 1-month-old looks at the outline or border of the face, such as the hairline (Haith, Bergman, & Moore, 1977). The 2-month-old looks within the face to the eyes. This development coincides nicely with the onset of smiling, discussed in Chapter 8. The baby looks at the parents' eyes and simultaneously smiles; the parents feel that the baby recognizes them and returns their affection. This feeling enhances the development of attachment (also discussed in Chapter 8)—an excellent survival strategy!

Why does scanning increase with age? One hypothesis is that very young babies process information quite slowly and have limited energy for giving attention to external stimuli. Looking at one spot on a stimulus exhausts their energy, and they're unable to look any further. In contrast, older babies, may process each area faster and then have time to move from one area to another before they get tired of looking.

To test this hypothesis, one researcher gave newborns more than one chance to look at a stimulus (Leahy, 1976). When they saw the stimulus the second time, these babies did look at it for a shorter period of time. However, they didn't use their "extra time" to move around the figure to look at other spots. They just looked away from the pattern. From this behavior, Leahy concluded that it's not just the ability to process information faster that makes older babies do more scanning. It may be this ability in combination with some other factor, such as the ability to search for something new to look at.

FIGURE 6-4
Babies' visual scanning behavior changes as they get older. At 1 month, babies look mainly at the borders of a figure, or the outside edges of a face. By 2 months, they're looking inside the figure and, if it's a face, especially at the eyes.

1 month old   2 month old

FIGURE 6-5
Only babies about 3 or 4
months old prefer the normal face to the scrambled
ones. Older babies seem to
be intrigued by the unusual
faces, and very young babies
don't show any preference
at all.

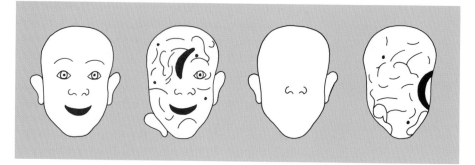

Changes in Preferred Faces

We can extend what we know about babies' scanning behavior to explain their preferences for faces. When newborns and 1-month-olds are shown pictures of faces with normal features and with scrambled features as in Figure 6-5, they don't indicate that they like normal faces any better than scrambled ones. Considering how they fixate at the edges of figures, it's not surprising that they don't show a preference for the normal arrangement of facial features. They probably haven't formed a very stable idea of what a face should look like.

By 3 or 4 months of age, babies show a definite preference for the normal face over a partially scrambled or totally scrambled face. They clearly scan and analyze the internal features. Then again at about 1 year, babies look longer at a scrambled face than a normal face. Perhaps they're attracted by the novelty of the arrangement of features, or they may be comparing it to what they know about normal faces and trying to figure it out (Haaf & Bell, 1967; Wilcox, 1969).

Do Infants Have Depth Perception?

Another question about what babies see and know is whether they have depth perception, that is, the ability to tell how far away something is or to understand a drop from one plane to another. A classic study, involving a "visual cliff," revealed that babies can perceive a drop-off in surface level (Gibson & Walk, 1960). In this study, babies 6 to 14 months old were placed on a special surface that appeared "shallow" on one side and "deep" on the other. The deep side was covered with glass so babies could crawl across it just as they had crawled across the shallow side. Their mothers stood on the far side and encouraged them to crawl across to them. The babies in this study would not crawl across the deep side even after they felt the glass on top of the drop.

Gibson concluded that depth perception is innate and that fear of cliffs is innate as well. Other researchers have suggested that although depth perception might very well be innate, fear of cliffs is more likely to be learned quickly from experience once the infant begins to crawl about (Campos et al., 1978). Further study is needed to determine which of these views is correct.

Perception as a Clue to Infant Thinking

Studies of infant perception have also led to discoveries about how babies think. Some researchers wondered if babies could form **concepts,** which are ideas about general sets of characteristics that apply across many different individual cases. For example, a child who understands the concept "dog" will be able to recognize several different kinds of dogs as members of the category "dog." Babies can't tell us if they recognize dogs as dogs, of course, so we have to infer that understanding from their responses.

To see if babies form concepts, researchers used the principle of habituation. As you recall, babies stop responding to a stimulus after a certain number of repetitions, indicating they've become habituated to it. In this study babies were shown several different instances of a given category, such as the same adult face in different orientations (profile, full face, three-quarter face, and so on) (Cohen & Strauss, 1979). Once the babies were habituated to that face, two new stimuli were shown, one that could be part of the same category and one that couldn't. If babies recognize a new stimulus as a member of the same category, they should remain habituated, that is, show no increase in looking time. But a totally new stimulus that's not a member of the category should elicit longer looking time.

Studies like this indicate that babies can indeed form concepts. Babies who are 30 weeks old recognize a new orientation of a face as an example of the same face they've been viewing. They recognize a totally different face as not

FIGURE 6-6
The visual cliff experiment was designed to determine whether depth perception is innate, but it has been used to learn about other aspects of child development as well. For example, researchers have studied infants' ability to read emotions in other people's faces by observing how they respond to their mother's expression as they approach the "deep" side. If mothers appear pleased, babies are more likely to cross; if they appear angry or afraid, babies are less likely to cross.

a member of this face category by becoming more alert and looking at it longer (Cohen & Strauss, 1979). Other researchers are trying to determine just what elements babies are noticing when they form notions about categories and concepts (Sherman, 1985; Younger, 1985). These assertions about what babies know and how their thinking develops lead us to our discussion of Piaget, who approached these questions from a different point of view.

SENSORIMOTOR INTELLIGENCE: PIAGET'S STUDIES OF INFANTS AND TODDLERS

Piaget's theory and research span the entire childhood period. Through careful observations, ingenious experiments, and tireless questioning and listening, Piaget built a theory of how children think and acquire knowledge. As mentioned briefly in Chapter 2, he believed that cognitive development progresses through a series of stages. During each of these stages, there are certain ways that information is obtained from the world and certain ways that knowledge is organized. In other words, each stage is characterized by a particular way of thinking.

Piaget labeled the period of infant intelligence the **sensorimotor period.** He chose this name because behavior during this period consists of simple coordinations between what babies sense and how they react physically. Babies don't think the way older children or adults do. They don't gain knowledge or insight by sitting back and contemplating what might happen. They act, look, taste, smell, hear, and feel. Through these strategies—acting and sensing—babies build intelligence during the sensorimotor period.

Dimensions of Infant Intelligence

Piaget proposed that within the sensorimotor period, which extends from birth to about 2 years of age, babies pass through six levels, or substages. He observed and described several different aspects or dimensions of infant intelligence. For each of these dimensions, he described the developments that occur during the various substages. Three of the dimensions Piaget described are discussed here. The first is one he called "means for achieving desired environmental events"; the second is imitation; and the third is object permanence. These dimensions are described in detail to explain Piaget's work and give its flavor. Some of the objections that other researchers have raised to Piaget's work are also discussed.

MEANS FOR ACHIEVING DESIRED ENVIRONMENTAL EVENTS. As the name suggests, this dimension of intelligence involves figuring out ways to make things happen. Another name for it might be problem solving. During the six stages of this dimension, babies become progressively more skilled at influencing the environment.

- *Stage 1: Reflexes (birth to about 1 month).* At this stage, babies' behavior is dominated by the use and progressive organization of the reflexes. The baby has the reflex to suck, for example, and a nipple or finger inserted in the mouth elicits the sucking response and maintains it. It doesn't take long for babies to learn that sucking provides food. If they're hungry and get a

FIGURE 6-7
The intriguing sensation of his tongue on his lips gives this 1-month-old information about himself and his actions, and he repeats it to experience the sensation again. Piaget called this kind of experience a primary circular reaction.

pacifier instead of a nipple, they'll quickly stop sucking. They've begun to "think," based on their prior experience with things inserted in their mouth. What they think in turn affects what they do.

- *Stage 2: Primary Circular Reactions (1 to 4 months).* A circular reaction occurs when something a baby does leads accidentally to an interesting result. The baby tries to achieve the result again by repeating the original action, which again leads to the interesting result, which again makes the baby repeat the action, and so on. This reaction is called circular because an action-event-action sequence is repeated over an extended period of time. The sequence is called *primary* because it involves only the baby's own body, not any objects in the environment.

A primary circular reaction may involve actions that were once reflexive, but it develops beyond this primitive level. Thumb sucking is a good example of this kind of reaction, as described by Piaget and his colleague Barbel Inhelder (Piaget, 1969, pp. 7–8):

> Fortuitous or accidental thumb sucking may occur as early as the first day. The more advanced sucking is systematic and dependent on a coordination of movements of arms, hand, and mouth. . . . It is quite clear that this is a genuine case of acquisition in a broad sense, since there exists no reflex or instinct for sucking one's thumb.

Another primary circular reaction occurs when a baby touches his tongue to his lips, notices the sensation, touches them again, notices it again, and so on. Cooing, too, is an example of this type of reaction. The baby makes a sound, hears or feels it, makes it again, and so on.

- *Stage 3: Secondary Circular Reactions (4 to 8 months).* These circular reactions are called "secondary" because they involve objects in the environment,

FIGURE 6-8
The discovery that banging his feet on his mattress produces some interesting changes in the environment leads this 5-month-old to continue banging his feet and observing the changes—a secondary circular reaction.

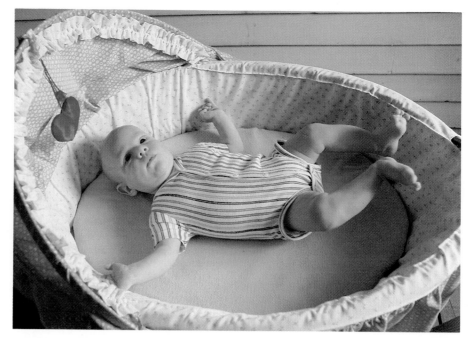

not just the baby's body. In the following example, Piaget had attached a hanging toy to a string and tied the string to the baby's arm (Piaget, 1952, p. 161):

[At 3 months] I attached a string to the left arm after six days of experiments with the right. The first shake is given by chance: fright, curiosity, etc. Then, at once, there is coordinated circular reaction: this time the right arm is outstretched and barely mobile while the left swings . . .

The baby notices that when he moves his arm, the toy moves, so he moves his arm again to make the toy move again.

A common secondary circular reaction occurs when a baby shakes his crib to make a mobile move. He accidentally makes the mobile move the first time, notices it, and then tries to make it move again. In the process, he discovers that banging his legs or feet on the mattress makes the mobile move. He bangs his feet, watches, bangs his feet, watches. The reaction is circular—it involves an action-event-action sequence. But unlike the primary circular reaction, this reaction involves something beyond the baby's own body.

- *Stage 4: Coordination of Secondary Circular Reactions (8 to 12 months).* In this stage, Piaget saw what he considered the first acts of true intelligence. The baby in this stage can intentionally perform an action with a goal in mind. In primary and secondary circular reactions, the first action occurs accidentally. The thumb gets into the mouth, the tongue touches the lips, the mobile moves—all by accident. The baby notices and tries to make it happen again.

But now the baby conceives of the action, the goal, in his own mind. He then pursues this goal with some familiar means. The action the baby takes to reach the goal isn't new, but the idea to do it is. In the following example,

Piaget placed a piece of paper on the hood of his son's bassinet. Laurent had already had experience with a string attached to the hood, and he used the string to get the paper (Piaget, 1952, p. 214):

> Laurent, at 6 months and one day, tries to grasp a big piece of paper that I offer him and finally place on the hood of his bassinet (and on the string connecting the hood with the handle of the bassinet). Laurent begins by stretching out his hand, then as soon as the object is placed, he reacts as he always does in the presence of distant objectives; he shakes himself, waves his arms, etc. . . . After having behaved thus for a moment, he seems to look for the string hanging from the hood, then pulls it harder and harder while staring at the paper. At the moment when this is ready to fall off the hood, Laurent lets go the string and reaches toward the objective, of which he immediately takes possession. Several sequential attempts have yielded the same result.

In this case, the paper didn't come down accidentally the first time. After several unsuccessful attempts to reach the paper, Laurent sized up the situation and *thought* of a way to achieve his goal. He took hold of the string, pulled it, and knocked the paper down. His thinking consisted of "schemes," or ways of behaving, that were already in his repertoire.

Laurent coordinated two familiar actions to get hold of the paper—pulling the string and picking up the paper. The object of his efforts was in the environment rather than part of his own body, and these two factors account for the name Piaget gave this stage—coordination of secondary circular reactions.

We often see this kind of action in 8- to 12-month-olds. For example, we'll see a baby crawl to an object (first action) and then grasp it (second action) when it's within reach. Or, if a baby wants a toy that's blocked by some other object, we might see the baby push the object away (first action) and then pick up the toy (second action). In both these cases, the babies think of putting together two actions to achieve a goal.

- *Stage 5: Tertiary Circular Reactions (12 to 18 months).* In this stage, babies seem to be less interested in achieving their goal than they were just a few months earlier. Now they're interested in experimenting with ways to achieve it. In the course of these experiments, they often invent or discover new ways to act on the world, as Laurent did in the following example (Piaget, 1952, p. 283):

> I place my watch on a big red cushion (of a uniform color and without a fringe) and place the cushion directly in front of the child. Laurent tries to reach the watch directly and not succeeding, he grabs the cushion which he draws toward him as before. But then, instead of letting go of the support at once, as he has hitherto done, in order to try again to grasp the objective, he recommences with obvious interest, to move the cushion while looking at the watch. Everything takes place as though he noticed for the first time the relationship for its own sake and studied it as such. He thus easily succeeds in grasping the watch.

Adam, the boy we met at the beginning of this chapter, was in this stage of cognitive development. He was more interested in experimenting, discovering, and repeating actions than in drawing a particular picture. Another kind of Stage 5 behavior involves the dropping experiments most parents recognize (Piaget, 1952, p. 269):

> Laurent is lying on his back but nevertheless resumes his experiments of the day before. He grasps in succession a celluloid swan, a box, etc., stretches out his

arm and lets them fall. He distinctly varies the positions of the fall. Sometimes he stretches out his arm vertically, sometimes he holds it obliquely, in front of or behind his eyes, etc. When the object falls in a new position (for example on his pillow), he lets it fall two or three times more on the same place, as though to study the spatial relation; then he modifies the situation. At a certain moment the swan falls near his mouth: now, he does not suck it (even though this object habitually serves this purpose), but drops it three more times while merely making the gesture of opening his mouth.

Younger babies also drop spoons from high chair trays, but they don't experiment with trajectories. They simply pick the spoon up, let it fall, and listen for the crash. They'll repeat this sequence for as long as someone is willing to pick up the spoon. But it's not until Stage 5 that babies experiment with how they drop the spoon.

- *Stage 6: Invention of New Means Through Mental Combinations (18 to 24 months).* This stage marks the end of the sensorimotor period and the beginning of the period in which the child uses mental representation to solve problems. If the child wants something but doesn't have a way to get it, he invents a way to get it. And the child invents this way not by physical means as in the past, such as trial and error or groping, but by "insight." It's not the idea of the goal that marks this stage as different from previous ones—that was the achievement of Stage 4 thinking; it's the fact that the child creates the means to achieve the goal by thinking, rather than by actions, that makes this stage different. Consider Laurent in the following example (Piaget, 1954, p. 335):

Laurent is seated before a table and I place a bread crust in front of him, out of reach. Also, to the right of the child I place a stick about 25 cm long. At first Laurent tries to grasp the bread without paying attention to the instrument, and then he gives up. I then put the stick between him and the bread; it does not touch the objective but nevertheless carries with it an undeniable visual suggestion. Laurent again looks at the bread, without moving, looks very briefly at the stick, then suddenly grasps it and directs it toward the bread. But he grasped it toward the middle and not at one of its ends so that it is too short to attain the objective. Laurent then puts it down and resumes stretching out his hand toward the bread. Then, without spending much time on this movement, he takes up the stick again, this time at one of its ends (chance or intention?) and draws the bread to him. He begins by simply touching it, as though contact of the stick with the objective were sufficient to set the latter in motion, but after one or two seconds at most he pushes the crust with real intention. He displaces it gently to the right, then draws it to him without difficulty. Two successive attempts yield the same result.

When Laurent picked up the stick the second time, he seemed to adjust the position of his hand by insight. He seemed to know in his mind that this position would be more effective than the way he held it previously. He also didn't need to grope at the bread with several different actions. After seeing that just making contact had no effect, he immediately moved the stick in a more effective way.

In Laurent's adjustments of action, we can see the budding ability to think— to judge and anticipate, to select an action that will have a desired result. Children at this stage no longer have to respond to accidents in the environ-

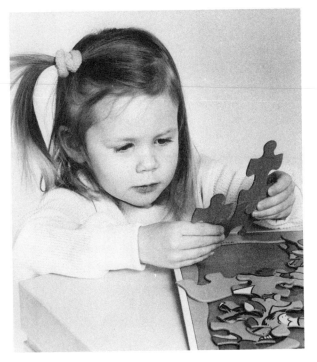

FIGURE 6-9
Before she was 2 years old, this child would have attempted to do a puzzle by acting on it, forcing pieces together at random. Now that she's 2, she can approach a puzzle by thinking—looking, comparing, and choosing pieces that appear to match. Even though this puzzle is much too difficult for her, she demonstrates a more advanced way of trying to solve problems, typical of the last stage of sensorimotor intelligence.

ment to make things happen. They have a kind of knowledge and intelligence that allows them to take much more control of their world. For example, in playing with a shape box (a toy with holes of different shapes and pieces that fit in each one), they can inspect the individual pieces and decide where they go. They no longer have to solve the puzzle by trial and error, trying a piece in every hole until they find the one where it fits.

This new ability to relate things to other things and to imagine actions in the mind results in more efficient behavior, because action can now be guided by thought. A Stage 6 child who is drawing on paper with a marker copies forms from the environment. Instead of experimenting, he thinks about how to move the marker before he begins, discovering movements that create interesting lines and then repeating them. Although the drawings of a Stage 6 child may not be accurate from an adult point of view, they're guided much more by thought than ever before.

IMITATION Another dimension Piaget investigated was **imitation,** the acquisition of a new behavior by copying it from someone else. The newborn isn't capable of imitation, according to Piaget, but in Stage 2 (primary circular reactions, 1 to 4 months), the first glimmerings of imitation appear. Piaget called this behavior **pseudoimitation** (literally, "false imitation"), because it has two requirements that aren't necessary in real imitation. A Stage 2 baby will repeat an action made by an adult on two conditions: first, the action must be something the baby can already do, and second, the baby must have recently performed the action.

Pseudoimitation occurs, for example, when an adult interrupts or joins in with a baby's vocal play. The baby says "aah," the adult says "aah," the baby

FIGURE 6-10
A 1-year-old can imitate her mother's whooping noises quite quickly and accurately, but if she doesn't imitate and learn this behavior right now, she won't be able to imitate it an hour later. This child is probably in the stage Piaget called tertiary circular reactions.

says "aah" again, and they continue as if taking turns. But because it's really the adult who's doing the imitating, Piaget didn't consider this type of behavior real imitation.

In Stage 3 (secondary circular reactions, 4 to 8 months), babies can imitate a specific behavior they've never performed before, but it must involve familiar schemes. They can put an old action to a new use. For example, if a baby is banging on her high chair tray with a spoon and her mother responds by banging on the bottom of a pot with a spoon, the baby would be able to bang on the pot if her mother gave it to her. The baby already knew how to bang. She quickly learned how to bang on a pot after she saw her mother do it.

In Stage 4 (coordination of secondary circular reactions, 8 to 12 months), imitation increases. New actions can be imitated if they resemble actions the baby already knows how to perform. For example, at this age a baby can learn to wave good-bye. It might be a novel behavior, but it resembles a lot of the motions she already makes with her hands and arms. Even so, she has to see several demonstrations of the motion and make several attempts to copy it before she'll have it down. In Stage 5 (tertiary circular reactions, 12 to 18 months), babies can imitate more novel actions, and they learn them more quickly.

In the first five stages, children imitate actions only immediately after they've seen them. In Stage 6 (18 to 24 months), they become capable of **deferred imitation,** as Jacqueline does in the following example (Piaget, 1954, p. 63):

> Jacqueline had a visit from a little boy . . . whom she used to see from time to time, and who, in the course of the afternoon got into a terrible temper. He screamed as he tried to get out of a playpen and pushed it backward, stamping his feet. Jacqueline stood watching him in amazement, never having witnessed such a scene before. The next day, she herself screamed in her playpen and tried to move it, stamping her foot lightly several times in succession.

Now babies begin to imitate everything they see and hear. Parents have to start being careful about what they say or do in front of their children at this age, because the child is likely to be capable of repeating it at any time, in any place.

OBJECT PERMANENCE A third dimension of infant intelligence investigated by Piaget is **object permanence.** This is the knowledge that objects exist even when we can't see them. As adults, we know that something we see on two different occasions existed somewhere, unseen by us, in the meantime. A typical 6-month-old doesn't make this same assumption. If a 6-month-old watches a favorite toy being covered up with a cloth, she won't pick up the cloth to get the toy—out of sight, out of mind. But a typical 1-year-old will search for the hidden toy. The 1-year-old has object permanence; the 6-month-old doesn't. Let's follow the development of object permanence through the six stages:

- *Stage 1.* Newborns will follow a moving object continuously with their eyes over a short arc in an attempt to keep it in view. But if it goes out of sight, they don't keep searching for it. We assume there's no object permanence at all at this age.
- *Stage 2.* Babies 1 to 4 months old will continue to stare at the place where an object disappeared as it left the field of vision. For example, if we slowly move a red ball back and forth in front of a 3-month-old's face, the baby will move his head and eyes to follow it. But if we move the ball all the way around behind the baby, his eyes will linger for a moment at the spot where he last saw the ball before it disappeared. Then he will look away. The baby's lingering glance suggests some notion that the ball still exists, but this awareness is fairly fleeting.
- *Stage 3.* Babies 4 to 8 months old begin to reach and grasp for objects in the environment, and they will search for a partially hidden object. If we partially cover a baby bottle with a cloth so that only the bottom of the bottle shows, the baby will search for the bottle. But a Stage 3 baby won't search for a completely hidden object, and Piaget took this to mean that objects have not yet become permanent for the baby in this stage.

FIGURE 6-11
A 9-month-old baby will search under a cloth for a completely hidden toy, indicating that she knows it exists even when she can't see it. But her grasp of object permanence is still somewhat tenuous, and she can easily lose track of exactly where an object as been placed.

- *Stage 4.* Babies 8 to 12 months old first begin to search for completely hidden objects placed under a screen. But even at this stage, the baby's notions of object permanence are uncertain. Piaget found that if he hid a toy under one screen, then took it out in full view of the watching baby and hid it under a second screen, the baby would look for it under the first screen. Even though the baby saw him hide it under the second screen last, he seemed to retain the first image more strongly. This mistake is known as the **perseveration error.**

- *Stage 5.* The 12- to 18-month-old baby has very strong notions of object permanence. Piaget found that even if he used three screens, hiding the toy first under one, then under another, then under the third, the baby would go right to the last screen where she saw the toy disappear. But some situations still confuse the Stage 5 child. If the screens themselves are moved around, along with the hidden toy, the baby looks under the screen that's in the position where the toy was originally left. Not finding it there, she simply gives up the search.

  The child in this stage is also confused if the tester hides the toy in his hand or in a box before he places it under the screen. The child sees only the hand or the box pass under the screen; she doesn't see the toy placed there. If the first screen she tries doesn't reveal the toy, she gives up. The technique of concealing the object in something else before placing it under the screen is known as **hidden** or **invisible displacement.**

- *Stage 6.* The 18- to 24-month-old baby isn't fooled by switching screens or by hidden displacement. If she doesn't get the right screen the first time, she flips up the others until she finds the toy, as if to say, "It's got to be here somewhere!" Apparently, her new ability to imagine actions in her head allows her to understand the unseen path of the toy. She now has a strong and durable concept of object permanence.

Other Interpretations of Piaget's Tasks

Other researchers have had different perceptions of the situations Piaget put babies in and the tasks he asked them to do. Their different views have led to a certain amount of controversy over Piaget's interpretations and conclusions. None of these researchers disputes how babies respond to Piaget's tasks. When they repeat his experiments, the results are exactly the same. The controversy is over the tasks themselves and how to interpret babies' responses to them. Many researchers believe babies have the notion of object permanence, for example, long before Piaget thought they did. Different kinds of tests and tasks indicate that this may be true.

MODIFYING THE OBJECT PERMANENCE TASKS. One researcher, who had doubts about the timing of object permanence, tried hiding the toy *behind* a screen rather than *under* it, as Piaget usually did (Brown, cited in Bower, 1974). He found that a Stage 3 baby (aged 4 to 8 months) would search for an out-of-sight toy that was behind a screen but not for one that was under a screen. Apparently, the difficulty is not so much that these babies think unseen objects don't exist but that they can't figure out how two objects can be in the same place at the

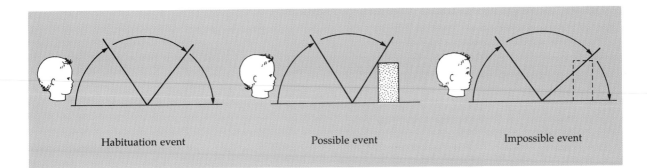

Habituation event   Possible event   Impossible event

FIGURE 6-12
In Baillargeon's experiment (1987), babies didn't have to look for a hidden object to demonstrate their grasp of object permanence. They only had to show surprise at an "impossible event"—a screen moving through a space where they had previously seen a box standing. Baillargeon found that babies showed surprise at a considerably younger age than the age at which babies search for a completely hidden object in Piaget's tasks.

same time. Babies this age don't yet understand the concept "under." When the screen is placed on top of the toy, they see that the screen itself now clearly occupies the space. They're stumped about where the toy could possibly be, and they don't lift the screen to look under it. These babies do have the concept "behind." When the toy is placed behind the screen, they search for it even though it's completely hidden. This behavior indicates that Stage 3 babies know an object still exists even when it's out of sight.

TESTING OBJECT PERMANENCE WITH HABITUATION TECHNIQUES. Another group of researchers changed the traditional task even more dramatically (Baillargeon, Spelke, & Wasserman, 1985; Baillargeon, 1987). They wanted to test for object permanence without relying on the baby's ability to search for the object. They devised quite an ingenious apparatus to do this:

> . . . a box was placed on a surface behind a wooden screen. The screen initially lay flat, so that the box was clearly visible. The screen was then raised, in the manner of a drawbridge, thus hiding the box from view. Infants were shown two test events: a possible event and an impossible event. In the possible event, the screen moved until it reached the occluded box, stopped, and then returned to its initial position. . . . In the impossible event, the screen moved until it reached the occluded box—and then kept on going as though the box were no longer there! The screen completed a full 180-degree arc before it reversed direction and returned to its initial position, revealing the box standing intact in the same location as before.

If the babies expected the box to be there even when they couldn't see it, they would be surprised to see the screen continue moving into the space supposedly filled by the box. If they didn't expect the box to be there—out of sight, out of mind—they wouldn't be surprised.

The researchers measured surprise with a habituation technique. They showed the babies the screen moving all the way back and forth until the babies became habituated to it and no longer paid attention. If the babies paid more attention to the moving screen after they saw the box put in place, it would indicate surprise. And surprise would indicate that they understood how strange it was—in fact, impossible—for the screen to be able to move into the space filled by the box. Surprise would reveal that they had object permanence.

The 5-month-old babies in this experiment did pay more attention to the impossible event. They assumed the box was still there when they couldn't

TABLE 6-1   Summary of Three Dimensions of Sensorimotor Development

Stage	Development of Means to Achieve Desired Environmental Events	Imitation	Object Permanence
1. Reflexes Birth–1 month	Elaboration of reflexes		Follows object with eyes over short arcs
2. Primary circular reactions 1–4 months	Use of means to produce interesting effects involving own body	Pseudoimitation	Glance lingers where an object disappears
3. Secondary circular reactions 4–8 months	Use of means to produce interesting effects involving objects in environment	Imitation of familiar schemes	Uncovers partially hidden object
4. Coordination of secondary circular reactions 8–12 months	Novel coordinations of familiar schemes	Imitation of somewhat novel schemes	Uncovers hidden object but shows perseveration error
5. Tertiary circular reactions 12–18 months	Progressive modification of familiar schemes to produce novel schemes as means to an end; groping	Imitation of novel schemes	Uncovers hidden object but shows switching error
6. Invention of new means through mental combinations 18–24 months	Insight without groping	Deferred imitation	Uncovers object hidden through invisible displacement

see it, and they were surprised to see the screen move past the upright position. This study suggests that babies just entering Stage 3 (age 4 to 8 months) do have object permanence, even though Piaget thought it didn't begin to develop until Stage 4 (age 8 to 12 months).

These researchers believe that Piaget asked the wrong question. They think the problem is "not to establish whether young infants believe objects are permanent" but to "determine what they know about the displacements and transformations of objects, and how they attain and represent this knowledge" (Baillargeon, Spelke, & Wasserman, 1985, p. 206). In other words, the issue is what babies know about how objects can be moved and changed rather than whether they know objects continue to exist when they can't see them.

The Enduring Value of Piaget's Work

Although Piaget's theoretical interpretations and behavioral timetables have been questioned, his data on the order in which behavior develops have held up. Table 6-1 shows the relationships among the three dimensions of sensorimotor development discussed in this chapter. A child may not reach a particular stage at the same time in all three dimensions (Uzgiris, 1973). For example, a child may be in Stage 4 in her object permanence skills, such as uncovering a hidden object, before she reaches Stage 3 in imitation skills, such as imitating familiar sounds (Schickedanz, 1976). Within any one dimension, however, very few babies show behavior of a higher stage before they show behavior of a lower stage (Brainerd, 1978). For example, no baby would be able to solve a problem by insight before she could solve it by trial and error. In this aspect of cognitive development, no one has been able to challenge Piaget's findings.

COGNITIVE DEVELOPMENT AND PLAY

Piaget observed that at about 2 years of age a new way of thinking, which he called **representational thinking,** begins to emerge. Children are able to think about the world even when they aren't experiencing it directly, and they start to use symbols to represent things. Nowhere do we see a more enthusiastic celebration of this new ability than in pretend play.

Mark and Samantha are playing with toys on the living room rug. In his chubby hand, 10-month-old Mark clutches a red plastic ring from a set of stacking rings. Nearby, Samantha, age 3½, holds her baby doll in her arms and feeds it with a toy bottle.

Mark looks at his red ring, passes it from one hand to the other, chews on it briefly, and taps it on the floor. Samantha looks up at Mark and then down at her doll. She carefully places the doll on the floor and reaches over to take the ring out of Mark's hand. In exchange, she offers him the orange ring from the stack. He releases the red ring and accepts the orange one without making a fuss. Samantha picks up her doll again and says, "Here's a bracelet, baby. I just bought it for you at the store."

Mark and Samantha were playing next to each other, but their minds were miles apart. To Mark, the red ring was an object to explore: What does it look like? How does it feel and taste? What kind of sound does it make when tapped on the floor? These are the burning questions for a 10-month-old.

Samantha, on the other hand, was interested not in what the object was but what she could pretend it was. Her thoughts went beyond reality into a world created by her imagination, where objects can be what you make of them. The red ring could become a very special object, a bracelet fashioned by her mind, bought on a trip to an imaginary store. Flights of fancy like this are the hallmark of pretend play, the remarkable intellectual feat of the toddler.

The Significance of Pretend Play

The ability to engage in pretend play, or **pretense** as it's sometimes called, marks a revolution in the child's way of thinking. The child now has the ability to use one thing to stand for another. We also see this capacity for **symbolic representation** in the emergence of language at about the same time. The child becomes able to use words to stand for things. Both pretend play and words start to emerge around the first birthday or soon after.

The toddler—the child between 18 and 36 months of age—brings pretend play into full bloom, but the roots of pretense extend back somewhat into infancy, as we will see. We also look ahead a bit to the preschool years to see how pretend play becomes **sociodramatic**—filled with roles and acted out in combination with other players. For the toddler, however, pretend play is rarely coordinated with the play of a real-life partner. It seems that the combination of pretense and social interaction is far too complicated for the toddler to manage.

Analyzing Pretend Play

Pretend play emerges at about 1 year and continues as the child grows. But a 2-year-old doesn't pretend the same way a 4-year-old does. Pretend play changes dramatically as the child's understanding and cognitive abilities develop. People who have observed and described children's play have often noted three different kinds of changes, or trends, that occur. They've called these trends decentration, decontextualization, and integration.

Decentration has to do with the child's role in the pretend play. As she gets older, she slowly becomes able to remove herself from center stage and to take on the role of other, imaginary characters. **Decontextualization** has to do with the objects used in the play and refers to the child's increasing ability to substitute one object for another. She can take an object out of context and pretend it's something it's not. **Integration** has to do with the content and action of the play. It refers to the child's ability to combine actions in increasingly complex sequences. Following is a more complete discussion of these three dimensions of play as they change over the course of several years.

DECENTRATION. When Samantha was 1 year old, she often pretended to feed herself or to be asleep. When babies do this, they may smile or giggle, which helps their parents know they're pretending (Bretherton, 1984). One distinguishing feature of this pretense is that it involves no one but the child herself. Another feature is that the content of the play—what the child pretends— comes from her daily life (Fein, 1981; McCune-Nicolich, 1981; Fenson, 1984).

When Samantha got a little older, she began to feed her doll rather than herself and put the doll rather than herself to bed. Children between about 15 and 21 months of age begin to include others as the recipients of their

FIGURE 6-13
Tea parties are a favorite form of pretend play among toddlers, especially when they include real cookies. The trend toward decentration can be seen in the child who feeds her bear rather than herself. This 2½-year-old probably also makes her bear feed himself.

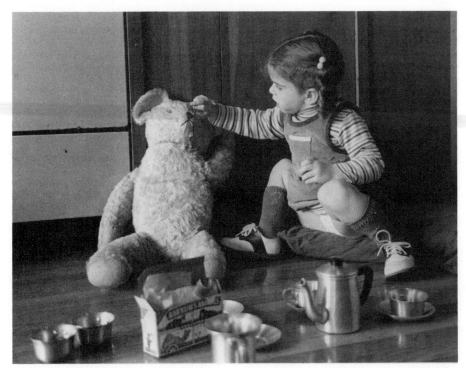

playful actions (Fenson & Ramsey, 1980; Fein, 1981). The other player, however, remains passive. The doll doesn't "come alive" or act on its own (Bretherton, 1984). The child doesn't make the doll talk, arrange its arms and legs as if it were moving, or give it a will of its own. The child does things *to* the doll. At about the same time, the child starts to include objects in her play, such as a cup for stirring imaginary food (Fenson & Ramsey, 1980).

When she was about 2 years old, Samantha began to put a spoon in her doll's hand and make it look as if it was feeding itself. At this age, children begin to make their dolls come alive (Fenson & Ramsey, 1980). They give them a cup or a comb and pretend they're drinking or combing their hair. They no longer just do things to the doll; they make the doll do things to itself. The child has removed herself somewhat from center stage, thus the name for this trend, *decentration*. Children seem to animate their dolls first by making them talk—in some cases, as early as 20 months—and later by making them move (Fenson, 1984).

At the same time, children begin to assume the roles of others in their play (Bretherton, 1984). They do this in two ways: They include activities that don't come from their own real-life activities, and they pretend to be other people. At this point, we might have seen Samantha "reading" a newspaper and heard her say, "Mommy read paper." In other words, "I'm pretending to be a mommy who's reading the paper."

Later still, Samantha went "camping out" in her room with her dolls. She set up a play tent with a blanket and put the dolls in it. One doll served hot cocoa with marshmallows to the other in a plastic cup, and then they went to sleep in sleeping bags in the tent. When Samantha's dad came into her room, Samantha wanted to serve him pretend cocoa too. At this higher level of

FIGURE 6-14
The youngest toddlers, like this 15-month-old, can play at pouring and drinking only if the pretend objects look very much like the real objects they represent. More far-fetched substitutions stretch the toddler's imagination beyond its limits.

decentration, the child is able to create two roles, either for herself and a doll, for two dolls, or for herself and another person. To do this, she has to be able to stand back a bit and consider one role in relation to another. This ability appears between 24 and 30 months of age (Bretherton, 1984; Miller & Garvey, 1984).

Between ages 3 and 6, children become much more skilled at playing out pretend roles. They can give roles to an increasing number of dolls or figures (Watson & Fischer, 1977), and they can coordinate their role with an increasing number of real players. Pretend play becomes more and more elaborate up to the age of 6, when it begins to diminish.

DECONTEXTUALIZATION. When Samantha pretended to feed herself at 1 year, she used a real cup for this pretend action. Very young pretenders, aged 12 to 20 months, need real objects, or at least realistic replicas of these objects, to support their pretend play (Fein, 1975; Fenson, 1984). They can't pretend a cube or a leaf is a cup, for example.

By 20 to 24 months of age, most children have begun to substitute one object for another (Fein, 1975; Ungerer et al., 1981). This is part of the decontextualization trend—objects can be taken out of context and used as something they're not. At first, substitutions are limited. The child may be able to use a stick to pretend to feed a realistic doll, but she may not be able to pretend both that a block is a doll and that a stick is a spoon. When too many transformations, or changes from reality, are required, it puts a damper on the play of the youngest pretenders. Children under age 3 can accept a substitution only if plenty of other things in the play situation are realistic (Fein, 1975).

Substitution also depends on how much an available object resembles the object needed in the pretend play. Children under 26 months will substitute one object for another if it looks like the needed object (Fenson, 1984). Children from 26 to 34 months old are most likely to use substitute objects, and they use them freely, no matter how unlikely the substitute seems to be (Ungerer et al., 1981). Older children choose less defined, more ambiguous substitute objects for their play. For example, a 4-year-old would probably resist using a plastic golf club as a fishing pole, because a golf club has a very specific function for him. But he could use a rolled-up newspaper as a fishing pole; this object has no clearly defined or contradictory use in his life. This research finding suggests that older preschoolers' pretend play can be enhanced when they have access to "raw" materials such as blocks, paper tubes (from paper towels, toilet paper, or gift wrapping), an assortment of paper, and a supply of tape.

The creation of imaginary objects is another aspect of pretend play that appears in older toddlers and continues during the preschool years. It occurs first when other objects support the presence of the imaginary objects (Fenson, 1984). When Samantha went camping out, for example, she pretended more than that her dolls were alive and her plastic cups were real. She also pretended there was hot cocoa with marshmallows in the cups. The cups obviously supported the idea of hot cocoa.

Later, children invent imaginary objects without support from the rest of the situation (Fenson, 1984). For example, a child might look across the room and say, "Now you sit over there, doggy." Or a child might knock on a pretend

FIGURE 6-15
By 3 years of age, children can readily substitute one object for another in their pretend play. The pervasive imaginary gun can be nearly anything that comes to hand—a stick, a stone, a crayon, even a shoe or a lunchbox.

door to enter a particular area of a nursery school play room. In these cases, the imaginary objects are created "out of thin air."

INTEGRATION. When Samantha was playing in the living room, she was involved in several actions: holding her doll, feeding it, and giving it a bracelet. Younger children can't manage so many actions; they use only one, perhaps feeding or combing hair, applying the action to themselves or to a doll. As pretend play develops, children invent several actions and put them together. These combinations and sequences change as children get older (McCune-Nicolich, 1981; Fenson, 1984).

Younger children, aged 15 to 24 months, are most likely to use **single-scheme combinations.** This kind of action sequence involves one action applied

TABLE 6-2   Stages of Pretend Play

Age	Symbolic Level	Examples
10–12 months	*Presymbolic scheme:* The child shows understanding of the object and uses it meaningfully. However, there is no pretending. What is done with an object is dictated by its characteristics, not by the child's imagination.	Child picks up lid to a cooking pot, looks at it, and puts it on the pot.
12–14 months	*Auto-symbolic scheme:* The child begins to pretend. Activities are self-centered in that actions (1) are from the child's own daily actions, and (2) are directed toward the child's own body. This level includes the meaningful object use from the previous level, along with a pretending—playful—quality.	Child pretends to drink from a cup. Child pretends to sleep.
15–21 months	*Single-scheme symbolic games:* The child now extends pretend play beyond himself or herself in two ways. 1. The child applies pretend action to others. 2. The child begins to use actions that are not part of his or her typical repertoire.	Child pretends to feed a doll or his or her mother. Child pretends to read a book to a doll. Child makes a toy dog go "woof-woof."
19–24 months 24 months and beyond*	*Combinatorial symbolic games:* The child now begins to combine action sequences. These can be of two types: 1. Single-scheme combinations relate one action to a number of recipients. 2. Multi-scheme combinations involve different actions related to one another in a sequence.	Child drinks from a cup and then gives a doll a drink from a cup. Child feeds doll, puts doll to bed. Child gives doll a bath, dresses doll, then feeds doll.

*Beginning at about 24 months, object substitution—decontextualization—begins to take place; a block might be used as a cup, for example.

SOURCE: Adapted from McCune-Nicolich, L. (1977). Beyond sensorimotor intelligence: Assessment of symbolic maturity through analysis of pretend play. Merrill Palmer Quarterly, 23 (2), 89–99.

to several things. The child might pretend to feed her doll and then pretend to feed her mother.

Children over 24 months begin to put more than one action together in sequence; these action sequences are called **multischeme combinations** (Fenson & Ramsay, 1980; McCune-Nicholich & Fenson, 1984). Now the child applies a series of different actions to the same object. This is what Samantha was doing in the living room—holding her doll, feeding it, giving it a bracelet. As children get older, they can combine more and more actions. This is the trend in play known as integration.

Another aspect of children's play that observers have noted is **theme**—the content of the play. The child's actions can relate to one theme or to more than one theme. A multischeme combination relating to the theme "putting baby to bed" might consist of the following actions: rocking the doll; putting the doll into bed; covering the doll with a blanket; and kissing the doll good-night. A multischeme combination on the theme "feeding the baby" might consist of these actions: putting the doll in the high chair; putting a bib on the doll; offering the doll some food from a spoon; reheating the doll's food in a pan because it was too cold; dumping the reheated food back onto the doll's plate; feeding the doll again; wiping the doll's face; and taking the doll out of the high chair.

If the child feeds the doll and then puts the doll to bed, she has combined two themes, each of which involved a multischeme combination. This kind of complex play involving two themes isn't really possible for children until they're about $2\frac{1}{2}$ or 3 years old (Bretherton, 1984). Extensive action sequences combining three or more themes aren't observed until children are age 3 or older.

Developmental Stages of Pretend Play

We've seen that children's pretend play begins during the second year of life and develops in terms of three dimensions—decentration, decontextualization, and integration. One researcher has analyzed the changes that occur in each of these three areas and organized them into a summary of the developmental stages of pretend play (Nicolich, 1977). She suggests that there are several stages, or symbolic levels, of pretend play during early childhood. These stages are shown in Table 6-2.

The toddler's cognitive achievements show up in more areas than pretend play. But we focus here on this one achievement because it's such a dramatic one. It also illustrates more than any other change the impact of the child's ability to use symbolic representation. After all, symbolic representation (or mental representation, in Piaget's terms) is the cognitive ability lacking in the infant. This is why Piaget referred to the period of infant intelligence as the "sensorimotor period."

As children's capacity for representational thinking emerges and increases, their thinking and acting take on many new qualities, as seen in the changes that occur in their pretend play. Other aspects of early representational thinking are apparent late in the toddler years and in the preschool years. These are covered when we discuss cognitive and language development in preschool children. But whether we consider pretend play, Piagetian stages of development, or changes in perception and concept formation, it is apparent that the transformations in thinking and understanding that occur in the first few years of life provide a solid foundation for a lifetime of intellectual growth.

OVERVIEW

Human beings are born with tremendous potential to learn, but it takes many years—virtually all of childhood—for this intellectual potential to be fully realized. Children spend their earliest years rapidly expanding their knowledge and developing their problem-solving skills. Their visual preferences and behaviors change in significant ways, their senso-rimotor intelligence builds through several stages, and their pretend play evolves from the 1-year-old's first pretense to the 4-year-old's elaborate symbolic play. If all goes well, the unfolding of cognitive abilities that begins in infancy continues into later childhood and beyond, establishing the pattern for a lifetime of learning.

CHAPTER REVIEW

VISUAL PERCEPTION

- Babies like to look at patterns and areas of contrast, and as they get older, they prefer to look at increasingly "complex" patterns, although researchers don't agree on how to define that complexity.
- Newborns fixate on one feature of a visual display, but by 2 months, babies scan from one point to another. At 1 month, babies look at the outline of a figure, but at 2 months they look at whatever is inside the figure.
- Researchers theorize that scanning behavior changes with age because young infants process information slowly and don't have the energy to pay attention to stimuli for very long.

- Babies' preferences for faces change too. When given a choice between normal and scrambled faces, newborns and 1-month-olds show no preference. Babies 3 and 4 months old prefer the normal face, but 1-year-olds prefer the scrambled face.
- We still don't know whether babies are born with depth perception, although they do show a fear of heights once they begin to crawl.
- On the basis of habituation studies, researchers conclude that babies are able to form concepts.

SENSORIMOTOR INTELLIGENCE

- Piaget suggested that infants build intelligence and learn about the world during their first two years by sensing and acting.
- According to Piaget, infants pass through six substages of development during the sensorimotor period, as follows: Stage 1: reflexes (birth to 1 month); Stage 2: primary circular reactions (1 to 4 months); Stage 3: secondary circular reactions (4 to 8 months); Stage 4: coordination of secondary circular reactions (8 to 12 months); Stage 5: tertiary circular reactions (12 to 18 months); and Stage 6: invention of new means through mental combinations (18 to 24 months).
- Piaget described several dimensions of infant intelligence, including means for achieving desired environmental events, imitation, and object permanence.
- The dimension of intelligence referred to as means for achieving desired environmental events involves solving problems or learning to make things happen.
- Another dimension of infant intelligence, imitation,

involves learning a new skill by copying it from someone else.
- Object permanence refers to the ability to remember that an object still exists even when it can't be seen. Babies begin to demonstrate object permanence during Stage 4, although they tend to think an object is located in the first place they saw it hidden, a mistake known as a perseveration error.
- Researchers sometimes use the technique of hidden or invisible displacement to test object permanence, but this technique doesn't fool the Stage 6 child.
- Some researchers believe that babies have object permanence well before Piaget said they do. They suggest that infants have trouble locating objects because their spatial and temporal concepts aren't yet well defined.
- Although the timing of some of Piaget's stages may be open to question, his description of the order in which cognitive skills emerge has stood the test of time.

COGNITIVE DEVELOPMENT AND PLAY

- The capacity for symbolic representation—using objects or words to stand for something else—emerges at about 1 year of age. Pretend play is the hallmark of the toddler years.
- Changes take place in children's pretend play as their cognitive skills increase. These changes have been referred to as decentration, decontextualization, and integration.
- Decentration refers to the child's gradual removal of herself from center stage in her play.
- Decontextualization refers to the child's increasing

ability to take an object out of context and pretend it's something it's not.
- Integration refers to the child's ability to combine actions in increasingly complex sequences.
- Multischeme combinations involving more than one theme (the content of the play) are seen in the play of older toddlers and preschoolers.
- Pretend play illustrates the child's growing ability to use symbolic representation, the ability lacking in the infant.

KEY TERMS

concept
sensorimotor period
imitation
pseudoimitation
deferred imitation

object permanence
hidden or invisible
  displacement
representational thinking
pretense

symbolic representation
sociodramatic play
decentration
decontextualization
integration

single-scheme
  combination
multischeme combination
theme

SUGGESTIONS FOR FURTHER READING

Gottfried, A. W., & Brown, C. C. (Eds.) (1986). *Play inter-actions: The contribution of play materials and parental involvement to children's development.* Salisbury, NC: Lexington Press.
  Includes chapters on mother-child interaction, affect and play, and the roles of physical and social environments. This book will interest the student who is serious about understanding play.
Piaget, J. (1952). *The origins of intelligence in children.* (Margaret Cook, Trans.) New York: International Universities Press.
  The original Piagetian discussion of sensorimotor intelligence. Slow reading for those who aren't accustomed to reading Piaget.
Rubin, K. H., Fein, G. G., & Vandenberg, B. (1983). *Play.* In P. H. Mussen (Ed.), *Handbook of child psychology.* (Vol. 4, 4th ed.). New York: Wiley.
  This chapter provides a thorough review of children's play.
Sawyers, J. K., & Rogers, C. S. (1988). *Helping young children develop through play.* Washington, DC: National Association for the Education of Young Children.
  A very practical book written to help caregivers provide for children's play.

chapter 7

LANGUAGE DEVELOPMENT IN INFANTS AND TODDLERS

"Dat?" Colin asks, as he points up to the sky.

"That's an airplane," his mother tells him. "It's making a loud noise, isn't it?"

"'Pane? 'Pane?" Colin says, as he continues to follow the airplane with his eyes.

"Yes, that's an airplane. It's a very noisy one, isn't it?"

"Vroom, vroom," Colin answers back.

"That's right. The plane is going 'vroom, vroom,' like a car . . . like you do when you play with your cars."

"'Pane . . . vroom . . . vroom."

"Uh-huh. The plane is going vroom, vroom, just like your cars."

Colin, who is 17 months old, is just beginning to talk. He can say a few recognizable words, and he can vary his intonation to indicate if he is asking a question or making a statement. Quite recently, he has begun to join two or three words to form a very primitive sentence: "Pane . . . vroom . . . vroom." Colin's mother is used to hearing him talk and can interpret what he says. Their shared history also helps her understand what Colin means when he says something like "vroom, vroom." She knows that he makes this sound in a very loud voice when he plays with his toy cars and that after she mentioned the airplane's noise, Colin was trying to tell her that the plane's noise reminded him of the car noise.

Learning to talk is one of children's most remarkable accomplishments during the first few years of life. Newborn babies are able to communicate by crying and gazing, but they can't use words. But 12 months later, a word or two spills out of the mouth of almost every baby. Just a year after that, at the age of 2, most toddlers are using rudimentary sentences. This chapter discusses infants' and toddlers' language development milestones—the different

FIGURE 7-1
At 4 months of age, this baby pleases both herself and her mother with her cooing, open vocalizations. The mother's delight encourages the baby and makes it likely that she'll say more.

ways they understand and produce speech before they can do either one exactly the way adults do. This discussion is rounded out with an examination of several explanations, or theories, of language development.

MILESTONES IN LANGUAGE PRODUCTION

There are two sides to children's language behavior: the **productive** side, or the speech they produce, and the **receptive** side, or the speech they understand. We'll take each side in turn, starting with language production, as we describe language behavior from birth up until about $2\frac{1}{2}$ years of age.

Vocal Behavior During the First Year

Vocal behavior during the first year of life is called **prelinguistic** because it contains no actual words. The relationship between this early speech and later speech is still not known. It includes crying and cooing, babbling, and intonation variations.

CRYING AND COOING. The first vocalization is uttered at birth when the infant cries. Other, noncrying, vocalizations appear soon after birth. They seem to emerge at first out of "fake crying"—the type of crying that parents commonly call "fussing." This cry is not the high-pitched, screeching sort of cry that babies use when they're terribly mad, hungry, or in pain. It's lower in pitch

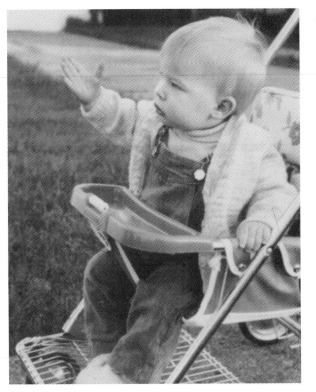

FIGURE 7-2
This 9-month-old practices both vowel and consonant speech sounds by babbling and even accompanies his speech with gestures. Within a month or so he'll be able to separate his index finger from the rest of his fingers to point to interesting objects while he babbles.

and quieter, with more drawn-out, moaning sounds (Wolff, 1969). Once the baby makes these sounds accidentally while fussing, she apparently reproduces the individual sounds in the circular pattern described in the discussion of Piaget's primary circular reactions in Chapter 6.

This first type of noncrying vocalization is called *cooing*. Initially, coos consist mostly of "open" sounds, or vowels (Cruttenden, 1970; Menyuk, 1977). Examples of these sounds include the "aaaah" you make for the doctor who inspects your sore throat and the "oooooo" you make when your favorite baseball player strikes out. The few consonantlike sounds that appear in early cooing are produced primarily by stopping air with the very back of the throat (/k/ as in *k*ite; /g/ as in *g*oat) or with the lips (/w/, /p/) (Cruttenden, 1970).

BABBLING AND INTONATION PATTERNS. By 4 or 5 months of age, infants begin to include a larger number of both vowel and consonant sounds in their cooings. Then at 8 months of age, they begin to combine these sounds into consonant-vowel strings such as "mamamama" or "dadadadada." Vocal behavior consisting of this type of syllable combination is called **babbling.** For several months, infants produce long strings of babble. Then, at about 10 or 12 months of age—about the time that most infants say their first real word—they shorten their babbles to one or two repetitions of the syllable. For example, the infant says "da-da" rather than "dadadada" (Menyuk, 1977). These wordlike forms are sometimes called **protowords** (Kamhi, 1986).

Infants also begin to vary the intonation of their vocalizations during the second half of their first year. For example, they sometimes babble with a raised or lowered pitch. These intonation patterns correspond to the signals older children and adults use for asking a question versus making a statement. Variations in intonation increase during the infant's second year (Bruner, 1975; Tonkova-Yampolskaya, 1969, cited in Rosenblith & Sims-Knight, 1985). Pointing, accompanied by a babble with a questioning intonation is a fairly common behavior in children 10 to 14 months old (Lemish & Rice, 1986).

Vocal Behavior During the Second Year

Colin's speech is well beyond the babbling stage. Children start to use specific utterances to refer to objects and express intentions soon after their first birthday. At this point, speech is used meaningfully and is considered to be linguistic rather than prelinguistic.

FIRST WORDS. Babies usually say their first real word at about 12 months of age (see Research Focus—Children's First Words). First words often approximate adult sound patterns, as when "boo" is used to refer to boots and "ku" is used to refer to cookies. But sometimes, children use a totally different sound sequence than the one used by adults to refer to an object or action, such as "ga-ga" to refer to a blanket (Winitz & Irwin, 1958; Carter, 1975). It's not the child's use of a conventional sound sequence that defines an utterance as a word; it's the child's consistent use of a particular sound sequence to refer to a specific object or action. If a child always calls his blanket "ga-ga," then he is using "ga-ga" as a real word.

As young children learn words, they often use them differently than adults do. Sometimes they **underextend** the meaning of a word, not using it as broadly

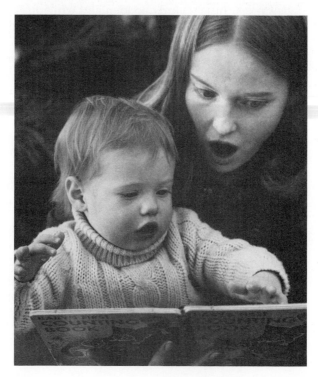

FIGURE 7-3
A baby's first word appears at about 12 months, often to name some familiar object in the environment. The baby's acquisition of speech represents an exciting transformation for her and for everyone in her life. Verbal communication now begins to be a mutual enterprise.

RESEARCH FOCUS

Children's First Words

Christina loved the cheese her mother often gave her for lunch. Her first word was "cheese," although she didn't say it very clearly. Sometimes she would say "cheese" as soon as she was put in her high chair for meals. Other times she would go to the refrigerator door and say, "cheese, cheese."

When Tod started talking, his first word was "light." He usually said it when a light was turned on in the room. "Water" was Nicholas's first word. During the hot summer when he was 11 months old, Nicholas often visited his grandmother, who watered her garden with a hose. He "helped" with this chore and played with the hose for hours on end, filling and refilling buckets and pans with water. When he was inside the house, Nicholas often went to the door, reached for the doorknob, and said, "Water, water."

What do Christina's, Tod's, and Nicholas's first words have in common? A study conducted by Katherine Nelson (1973), a language researcher, may provide an answer to this question. She recorded the first words used by 18 children between 1 and 2 years of age and found they could be categorized into five groups:

1. Nominals (nouns), or words used to refer to things. Subgroups within this category include specific nominals (proper nouns)—words used to refer to one example of a category ("Mommy," "Spot")—and general nominals (common nouns)—words used to refer to all members of a category ("doggie," "key," "milk").
2. Action words, or words that describe, demand, or convey action or that express or demand attention ("bye-bye," "up," "hi").
3. Modifiers, or words that refer to properties or qualities of things or events ("pretty," "hot," "all-gone," "more").
4. Personal-social words, or words expressing affective states or social relationships ("please," "ouch," "want," "thank you").
5. Grammatical function words ("what," "where," "is," "for").

Nelson found that for the 18 children she studied, more than half of their first 50 words were general nominals. And, of these, most were names of things that the children acted on in some way. Nelson suggests that children ignore things that simply exist, such as tables, carpets, grass, and sidewalks. They notice and learn the names of things that do something or that they do something to. Christina's "cheese," Tod's "light," and Nicholas's "water" are consistent with this idea—they can all be acted on.

Why should action matter? It may be because action produces change, change produces novelty, and novelty—the discrepancy between what a child already knows and what actually happens—catches the child's attention. When a baby hears the sound of the cuckoo clock, she may stop what she's doing to look at it. Her mother or father may follow her gaze and say, "Clock? Did you hear the clock? Do you see the clock?" The baby hears the name for the object that's attracted her attention and learns to associate the object with the name.

Parents do seem to follow their baby's line of regard—the direction the baby is looking—from as early as the baby's fourth month (Scaife & Bruner, 1975). This tendency helps ensure that parents and baby are paying attention to the same thing and that the baby associates the names with the appropriate object. It also explains why children's first words are so often the names of things that act or can be acted on: These are the things that catch children's attention.

---

as an adult might. At other times they **overextend** the meaning of a word, using it more broadly than is common. For example, a child might use the word "shoes" only to refer to mommy's shoes because it was in this context that she first learned the word. In this case, she's underextended the word's meaning. Or a child might call a horse a dog, because it has four legs and hair like a dog. In this case, the child has overextended the word's meaning. Much of what occurs in language learning during the early years involves expanding and contracting the meaning of known words to cover new situations.

Children's understanding and use of some words seem to change as their cognitive skills advance. For example, between 12 and 18 months, toddlers use certain words in "social" ways, which engage others in interactions. They use "there" to draw someone's attention to an object, "more" to ask for help in doing or getting something, and "no" to refuse suggestions or complain about someone's actions. Between 18 and 24 months, they use these same words to comment on actions and plans. They use "there" to mark their success when they complete an action or attain a goal, "more" to indicate that they're planning to repeat an action, and "no" when they change their minds about an action or when they try to do something but fail. Later still, they use these words in more standard linguistic ways. They use "there" to indicate the location of an object ("There dog."), "more" to refer to a greater quantity of an object ("More juice."), and "no" to deny that something is true ("Dog no go.") (Gopnik & Meltzoff, 1985).

The earlier, more social use of "there," "more," and "no" seems to occur during Piaget's sensorimotor Stage 5, in which children solve tasks by trial and error. Their use of these words to comment on their actions and plans seems to be correlated with the cognitive shift to sensorimotor Stage 6, in which they become able to solve tasks by insight. In other words, changes in cognitive development apparently are accompanied by new understandings and uses of words already in the child's vocabulary.

Changes in word use are also influenced by factors other than cognitive development. For example, some changes probably occur when children observe how adults use words. Other changes occur when children receive direct feedback about their own word use: "That's not a doggy, that's a horsie." We discuss changes in word use in greater detail later in this chapter.

LANGUAGE PRACTICE. The appearance of words doesn't mean that a baby stops babbling. Word development and babbling interact with each other in early language behavior. Researchers have even suggested that children produce two kinds of speech during the first-words period: meaningful speech using "real" words and babbling speech using a combination of meaningful words and nonmeaningful sounds. Children use the meaningful speech to talk to

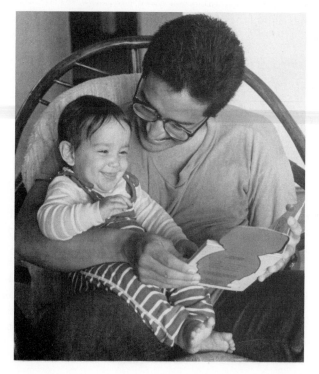

FIGURE 7-4
Because his dad reads to him, this baby will babble using two different intonations. Some of his babbling will sound like conversation, and some will sound like a person reading a book.

people. They use the babbling speech to practice speech sounds and words that will soon show up in their "talking" speech (Elbers & Ton, 1985).

Soon after the first-words stage, at about 14 to 18 months, another kind of practice appears as well. This type of practice involves the intonation patterns of sentences, also known as the **suprasegmental** features of speech. (*Suprasegmental* literally means "above the parts" and refers to the overall sound pattern of language.) The child is now practicing the sound of people talking in her language. The content of her sentences is nonsense; she's using babble, not words. Still, this **expressive jargon**, as it's called, sounds remarkably like "real" talk because it captures the overall rhythm and flow of actual speech.

Two kinds of expressive jargon can be distinguished among infants whom adults have talked with and read to: **conversational babble** and **book babble**. Each kind appears in the appropriate social context. When the child is "talking" to himself, with another person, or with a doll or stuffed animal, he uses conversational babble. But when he's "reading" a book, he uses book babble, which has unique suprasegmental features (Schickedanz, 1986).

HOLOPHRASES. Once infants or toddlers can vary intonation, they can express several different intentions even though they can utter only a word or two. For example, if a baby says the word "milk" with a rising intonation, she might mean "Is that milk?" or "Can I have milk?" A falling intonation might mean "That is milk," or "Give me some milk." A single word that expresses a more complex thought or sentence is called a **holophrase**.

A fairly common holophrase in 14- to 18-month-olds is "Dat?", which Colin used when he spotted the airplane in the sky. This holophrase, meaning "What is that?" often appears suddenly after the child gains the insight that things have names. The child typically points to an object when uttering "Dat?" Given a willing adult partner, this naming game can go on for quite a long time and often results in rapid acquisition of words (Nelson, 1973; Kamhi, 1986).

The use of holophrases depends very much on adult partners who can interpret what the baby means. We saw that Colin's mother paid close attention to both the immediate situation and Colin's intonation. She also referred to her knowledge of his past use of sounds and language. Some parents can apparently interpret their children's intentions before the holophrase stage. One mother responded differently to her 6-month-old when the baby used different pitches to vocalize. The baby used higher-pitched vocalizations when playing with objects than when vocalizing to his mother. The mother looked at him when his pitch dropped, apparently to see if he was "talking" to her. The baby's vocalizations also began more sharply when he was reaching for objects that were out of his grasp than when he was reaching for accessible objects. The mother responded to the sharper vocalizations by moving the object toward the child (Bruner, 1975).

MULTIWORD UTTERANCES: TODDLERS' TELEGRAPHIC SPEECH. Children usually begin to combine words into primitive sentences when they are between 18 and 24 months of age. They begin to say things such as "Doll cry," "Jamie go," "Daddy car," "No eat," or "Mommy up." Although the number of words they include in their sentences is limited, toddlers can communicate quite a few meanings and relationships with these two- and three-word utterances. For example,

FIGURE 7-5
The speech of 2-year-olds can often be understood only in context. If this child says, "Eat cracker," his father will gather that he's referring to the goat's appetite. If the child utters the same words when sitting in his high chair, his father will probably give him something to eat.

TABLE 7-1
Meanings Expressed by Toddlers in the Two-Word Stage

Category of Meaning	Example
Identification	That plane See man
Location	Kitty here Bottle [on] chair
Recurrence	More juice Tickle again
Nonexistence	Nomore cookie Milk allgone
Negation	No bed
Possession	Sarah book
Agent, action, object	Mommy throw Throw ball
Attribution	Big clown Go truck
Question	Where bottle? What that?

Adapted from A First Language: The Early Stages, *R. Brown, 1973, Cambridge: Harvard University Press.*

they can indicate where something is, who it belongs to, what someone is doing, and what they want or don't want to do (Schlesinger, 1974; Bloom, Lightbown, & Hood, 1975). These and other meanings expressed by toddlers in the two-word stage are given in Table 7-1.

Despite the fairly extensive variety of relations that children can express with their two- and three-word utterances, these utterances still are not completely formed. When adults interpret what a toddler says, they often need to "read" the extralinguistic context—the situation "outside" or "beyond" the language—to know exactly what the toddler means. The burden of determining what the child means is considerably less during this stage than it is during the prelinguistic and holophrase stages of language development, when children use either no actual words or only one at a time. When language is confined to just one word, as many as 50 percent of the children's communications are unclear to mothers (Golinkoff, 1986). Toddler talk, with its two- and three-word constructions, is easier to understand, but statements still can't stand on their own without cues from the situation.

Toddlers' speech has been called **telegraphic**, because children this age omit words that are not essential to their meaning. Toddlers change an adult sentence like "Mommy is going to the grocery store" to "Mommy go store." Adults do this when they send a telegram and have to pay for every word. The person who receives the telegram has to fill in the missing words to understand the message. When toddlers talk in their two- and three-word sentences, adults have to interpret their "telegrams." Parents often repeat the toddler's utterance and add words that are missing—responses known as expansions (Brown & Fraser, 1964). If a toddler says, "Mommy milk?" the mother might say, "Is this mommy's milk? Yes, it's mommy's milk." Adults respond in other ways too, and we discuss these later in this chapter.

MILESTONES IN LANGUAGE PERCEPTION

The other side of children's language behavior is the receptive side, the speech the baby perceives or understands. When do babies recognize the sound of human speech? When do they start to understand?

Speech Perception

PERCEPTION OF SPEECH SOUNDS AND INTONATIONS. Infants hear all kinds of sounds, not just the sound of speech; there's the hum of the air conditioner, the patter of rain, the creaking of the crib. But the human voice has special significance for the baby. By the second week of life, a crying infant is quieted by a voice more effectively than by other sounds (Wolff, 1969). Even infants 1 or 2 days old seem to be able to sort out the human voice from other sounds in the environment and pay attention to it, if it's cast in the Baby Talk register (discussed below).

Very young babies can also discriminate between various speech sounds, as indicated by habituation studies. Infants as young as 1 month old can differentiate the voiced and voiceless stop consonants /b/ and /p/ (Eimas et al.,

1971; Eimas, 1974). They can also tell the difference between /d/ and /t/ and between /b/ and /g/ (Moffit, 1971; Trehub & Rabinovitch, 1972), and they differentiate pairs of vowels, whether they are presented in combination with consonants (/pa/, /pi/) or as vowels alone (/a/, /i/) (Trehub, 1973).

The fact that infants can hear differences between speech sounds at such an early age suggests that this language ability is innate. However, young infants can't detect all contrasts in sounds (Eilers, Wilson, & Moore, 1977), and the ones they can detect may be influenced by their language experiences, such as the native language to which they're being exposed (Streeter, 1976). So, we really can't say for certain how much language ability is innate and how much is a result of experience on the basis of early ability to perceive speech sounds.

Infants also perceive or understand the suprasegmental features of language—the intonations—when they hear others talk. Infants as young as 8 months of age can differentiate between rising and falling intonation patterns, that is, between statements and questions (Kaplan & Kaplan, 1970).

Since babies recognize different sounds and intonations from an early age, it's not surprising that they recognize and respond to a way of speaking referred to as Baby Talk (often abbreviated BT). Baby Talk, also known as Motherese, is a specific linguistic register that many adults seem to use when talking to babies. It involves speaking in a higher pitch than is typical in adult-to-adult speech, varying intonation more, and using shorter sentences. For example, a mother inquiring about her child's apparent distress might ask, "Does your tummy hurt?" rather than, "Do you have abdominal pain?" Similarly, a mother would probably say, "That's Mommy's," rather than "That's mine," so the child wouldn't have to figure out the referent of the pronoun "mine" (Mann & Boyce, 1982).

Many studies have confirmed the existence of Baby Talk and have demonstrated that babies not only can distinguish it from adult talk but prefer to listen to it. When given the opportunity to choose between a tape of Baby Talk and a tape of adult talk by turning their heads to one side or the other, they choose to listen to Baby Talk (Fernald, 1985). We discuss the implications of this "dialect" below, when we describe theories of language development.

LANGUAGE COMPREHENSION. Babies' and toddlers' language comprehension is typically more advanced and varied than their language production. They understand quite a few words when they can say only two or three (Goldin-Meadow, Seligman, & Gelman, 1976). And they understand multiword utterances when their own productive language is at the holophrase stage. In one study, children who could produce only one-word utterances could respond to such requests as "Kiss Teddy," "Throw ball," and "Smell truck" (Sachs & Truswell, 1978).

In everyday situations, there are many multiword utterances that children in the holophrase stage seem to understand ("Wave bye-bye to grandma," "Give the book to mommy"). But the child receives many clues to their meaning from the context in which the sentences are said—grandma getting in her car and waving, mommy holding out her hand toward the book. It's doubtful that children would understand the meaning of all that's said to them in the absence of this contextual support.

SOCIAL ASPECTS OF LANGUAGE DEVELOPMENT: LEARNING TO BE A CONVERSATIONAL PARTNER

Language acquisition isn't just a matter of learning how to speak and understand words and sentences. Language is fundamentally a social activity, and learning how to hold a conversation is part of learning how to talk. There are rules, commonly accepted ways of interacting, that we follow when we carry on a conversation with someone else. For example, we use strategies for getting a conversation going and for taking turns. We also have ways of maintaining the topic of conversation and of signaling that we're changing the topic.

Between about 2 and $2\frac{1}{2}$ years, toddlers begin to use specific verbal strategies for opening conversations: (1) They talk about what their listener is doing, ask a question, or give a command; (2) they get the listener's attention by looking at him or her; (3) they stand relatively close to the listener; and (4) they use attention-getting gestures and verbalizations, such as "Hey!" or "Guess what?" (Mueller et al., 1977).

These strategies are remarkably similar to the approaches mothers take in communicating with their infants, beginning late in the first year. When they want to interact, for example, mothers first follow their infants' gaze to see what they are looking at. Then they provide labels for the object and comment about it (Collis & Schaffer, 1975; Collis, 1977). When babies are about 9 months old, mothers begin to point to call their babies' attention to things they're talking about (Murphy & Messer, 1977). At first, babies aren't very skillful at following their mothers' pointing, and mothers often try to bring objects closer to their child if they can. Mothers work hard to establish joint reference or joint attention with their babies when they want to communicate with them.

Book-reading routines provide an ideal situation for mothers and babies to practice establishing joint attention. One mother attracted her baby's attention

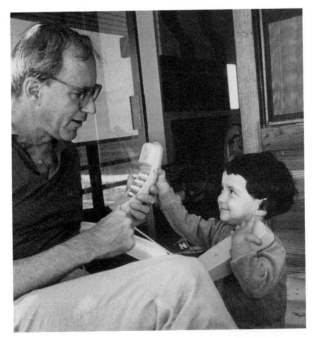

FIGURE 7-6
"Phone, Grandpa!" At 20 months, this toddler has a good idea of how to get someone's attention, but it will be quite some time before he's mastered the subtle give-and-take of true conversation.

with such verbalizations as "Look!" followed by a question like "What is that?" (Ninio & Bruner, 1978). The mother answered her own questions at first, because the baby wasn't yet able to talk. But as soon as the baby could talk, the mother paused and allowed the baby to respond.

By the time they're toddlers, children already have a long history of verbal interaction in which they've seen and practiced different kinds of attention-getting devices. Given mothers' typical strategies, it's no wonder that toddlers attempt to open conversations by such tactics as standing close, commenting on what the listener is doing, and saying "Hey!" and "Guess what?"

Once toddlers have someone's attention, they have to pursue the conversation, and this is harder to do. They know how to take turns, in the sense that they can avoid interruptions and simultaneous starts, but they don't know how to take the lead in maintaining a dialogue. What they say during their turn doesn't push the conversation forward. They respond to questions and comments, but they don't ask questions or link their comments to their partner's previous remarks (Kaye & Charney, 1980; Kaye, 1982). It's the adult who takes this responsibility, leading the dialogue and making long conversations possible.

THEORIES OF LANGUAGE DEVELOPMENT

We've seen quite a lot so far about what babies and toddlers can say and understand. But how is it that they learn language at all? Do human beings have an innate ability to understand the symbols and representations of the world contained in language? Are they born with the power to express themselves in words and sentences? Or do they simply learn "language behavior" from their parents the same way they learn to eat with a spoon or put on their socks? Like theories of other aspects of child development, theories of language development vary in the emphasis they place on internal versus external factors—the nature-nurture controversy. Behaviorist theories claim that language is learned primarily from contact with the environment. Nativist theories claim that language comes primarily from within. We turn now to a closer look at the major theories of language development and the evidence that supports or undermines each one.

Behaviorist Theory

Behaviorist, or learning, theory explains language development exclusively in terms of environmental factors. Following the lead of B. F. Skinner, behavioral theorists claim that children gradually learn how to speak and understand their language because they're reinforced for doing so.

Some aspects of language learning are obviously influenced by the environment. The language we learn as our mother tongue, for example, is the one we hear around us in our environment. Human beings don't have an innate language the way animals do—different species of birds, for example, sing different, genetically determined songs regardless of where they live (although even birds' songs are partially learned, it now seems). But what interests theorists is the very ability to learn a language—any language. They disagree about the extent to which humans have a specific neurological make-up that facilitates language learning. Behaviorists give less importance to these internal characteristics than they do to external factors when they explain language development.

The major learning mechanisms proposed by behaviorists are imitation, reinforcement, and punishment. They suggest that children learn to speak by imitating what they hear and repeating it in appropriate situations. When they do this, adults lavish praise and attention on them, which increases the likelihood that they'll do it again. When they use language incorrectly, adults' responses are not so reinforcing.

This explanation doesn't account for some things that actually happen in language development, however. Children generate words and sentences that adults never model for them. They say "mouses" instead of "mice," for example, and "What it is?" instead of "What is it?" These creative constructions can't be explained by direct imitation or other behaviorist mechanisms. To generate words and sentences never before uttered in their presence, children seem to induce grammatical rules from things they *have* heard. Behaviorist theory doesn't have a way of explaining such inductive learning.

The other behaviorist mechanisms of reinforcement and punishment don't seem to play a great part in language development either. Most parents don't explicitly approve correct pronunciation and grammar or disapprove incorrect forms. They look past the form to focus on what the child is trying to communicate. Grammatical errors are ignored, but errors of fact are pointed out as shown in the following example (Brown, Cazden, & Bellugi, 1969, pp. 57–58):

> In general, the parents fit propositions to the child's utterances, and then approve or not, according to the correspondence between propositions and reality. Thus "Her curl my hair" was approved because mother was, in fact, curling Eve's hair. However, Sarah's grammatically impeccable "There's the animal farmhouse" was disapproved because the building was a lighthouse, and Adam's "Walt Disney comes on, on Tuesday" was disapproved because Walt Disney comes on, on some other day.

More recent research has demonstrated that parents do provide some feedback to their children about how well they're speaking, and we discuss this research later in the chapter. Although these studies are offering some support for the behaviorist position, it still appears to be inadequate as a complete explanation for language development.

Nativist Theory

Nativist theory stands at the opposite end of the nature-nurture continuum from behaviorist theory. To a nativist, language development depends not on what is in the environment but on what is in the child. In this view, the child is endowed with an innate language acquisition device (LAD). This is a metaphor for a specific neurological structure that enables children to derive a grammar from the language they hear (McNeill, 1966).

Noam Chomsky launched this view of language development when he sharply criticized the behaviorist views about language learning (Chomsky, 1959; 1965). Chomsky and other nativists made the observations just mentioned—that imitation doesn't explain children's creative utterances and that

FIGURE 7-7
According to Noam Chomsky, the human language faculty is a specific innate endowment, a "mental organ," that "grows" in the mind once it has been triggered by experience. Children are born knowing how to construct grammar, Chomsky claims, just as birds are born knowing how to fly. What they learn from experience is the specific language that will be their mother tongue. Chomsky's nativist view is diametrically opposed to the behaviorist view, which asserts that children acquire language the same way they learn other behaviors, mainly through imitation and reinforcement.

parents don't explicitly approve or disapprove children's grammar. They also argued that the way parents provide language to children doesn't fulfill the behaviorist requirements for learning, which are simplicity and step-by-step sequencing of information. And parents often use less-than-perfect grammar themselves when talking to their children. Chomsky felt it was unlikely that children could learn a grammar according to behaviorist mechanisms, given the "sloppy" nature of parents' input. Therefore, he argued, children's knowledge of grammar must be innate, part of their species-specific endowment.

Support for the nativist view comes from information about the universal nature and orderly progression of language development in every culture. No matter what the specific language, development follows certain paths and language forms appear in the same sequential order in virtually all children. In every different environment, children acquire a grammar for their mother tongue. These facts suggest that language ability is due to something within the child rather than something about the environment.

Challenges to the strong nativist view of Chomsky and others have come from various sources. Some cognitive theorists have questioned the notion of a special language acquisition device to account for language development. They believe that the basic cognitive schemes constructed during the sensorimotor period can provide the basis for language.

Other critics have focused on the Baby Talk register as a special teaching device parents may use to help their children learn language. They object to the nativist claim that the language addressed to children is poorly formed, pointing out that BT may particularly suit the needs of babies. Still other critics have argued parents do provide feedback to their children about their speech, even though it's not explicit. Following are brief discussions of these three additional theoretical views that have challenged the strong nativist position.

Challenges to a Strong Nativist Theory

THE COGNITIVE UNDERPINNINGS VIEW. Some cognitive theorists argue that children learn about the structure of the world through their actions during the sensorimotor period. Children's knowledge comes from the combined forces of maturation, equilibration (Piaget's notion of how the individual balances new information with existing cognitive schemes), and experience gained through action. As discussed in Chapter 2, experience is considered vital in this cognitive-interactionist view. Children are capable of biologically given intellectual processes, but without experience of the world they would have nothing from which to construct knowledge. Children create knowledge, according to this view; knowledge isn't transferred to them passively through the sequenced lessons and learning mechanisms proposed by behaviorist theory. Both inner and outer forces are at work, placing this view of learning somewhere in the middle of our theory continuum.

Cognitive underpinnings theorists suggest that children's sensorimotor knowledge of ordered relations, such as the relationship between agent, object, and action, provides a basis for understanding grammar (Bruner, 1975). The knowledge they've gained about the world during their first two years—that they can make certain things happen by certain actions, for example—gives them a grasp of such grammatical propositions as "I shake the rattle" or "She rolls the ball." A summary of the cognitive underpinnings view is provided by Roger Brown (1973, p. 200):

In sum, I think that the first sentences express the construction of reality which is the terminal achievement of sensorimotor intelligence (the permanence of form and substance of immediate objects), and the structure of immediate space and time does not need to be formed all over again on the plane of representation. Representation starts with just those meanings that are most available to it, propositions about actions, schemas involving agents and objects, assertions of nonexistence, recurrence, location, and so on.

This cognitive "determinism" view, so called because it suggests that language inevitably follows from certain innate cognitive developments, has been challenged too. Critics have pointed out that even if these cognitive understandings are present, the exact expression of them varies from one language to another. The same meaning is coded by different sequences of subjects, objects, and verbs in different languages (Slobin, 1982). Children with two years' worth of sensorimotor knowledge still have to learn how to express their understandings in specific linguistic forms. The understandings themselves don't provide any clue about how these meanings are coded in language.

One cognitive theorist uses a "waiting-room" metaphor to describe the possible relationship between cognitive and linguistic development (Slobin, 1982, p. 169):

> Each linguistic form in this metaphor has its own waiting room. The entry door is opened with the underlying notion as key; the key to the exit door is the appropriate linguistic form. The child receives the entry key when he or she discerns the existence of a given notion—primarily on nonlinguistic grounds, but perhaps at times with some prompting from established linguistic knowledge. The entry is thus determined by conceptual acquisition of the sort generally referred to as *cognitive development*. . . . The child must figure out just what aspects of the particular notion are encoded in the language, and what means are used for the encoding. The solutions take varying amounts of time and effort, depending on linguistic features, but finally the child leaves that particular waiting room with the appropriate "semantactic" key in hand. The important point of the waiting-room metaphor is its two doors: the cognitive entry door and the linguistic exit.

Even though cognitive development might provide the necessary *basis* for language learning, it appears that something additional is required. It's this language-specific learning that remains a theoretical puzzle.

THE CASE OF MOTHERESE. Other critics of a strong nativist view of language development have pointed to Baby Talk, or Motherese, as a way young children may learn language. New research has shown that Motherese is composed of short, grammatically well-formed utterances, cast in a high pitch (Ferguson, 1977; Furrow & Nelson, 1986). Contrary to what Chomsky and others thought, Motherese is not sloppy or ill formed. These theorists suggest that this simplified register serves a teaching function and that the baby's experience of conversational give-and-take in Motherese plays an important role in language development.

On the other hand, it's not clear exactly what the role of Motherese might be. It may serve a communicative function but not a teaching one. In other words, Motherese may get the baby's attention and permit more of the mother's message to be understood (Newport, Gleitman, & Gleitman, 1977; Fernald, 1984) without actually teaching the baby anything about grammar.

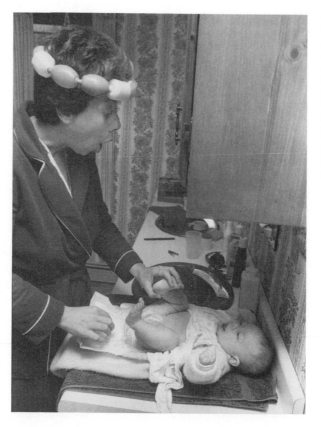

FIGURE 7-8
To get through the 4 a.m. diaper change, this mother uses Baby Talk and more. Adults often exaggerate their expressions when they use this special register, increasing the baby's interest and pleasure in the interaction. Although the role of Baby Talk in teaching language isn't clear, the preference of babies for its sound is well documented.

Knowledge of grammatical relations may still be due to innate predispositions (Wexler, 1982). So we're not really sure what the role of Motherese is in language development.

IMPLICIT FEEDBACK. More questions about the nativist view have been raised by further study of the feedback that parents give their children about their speech. A major study that documented the absence of parents' disapproval for poor grammar (Brown & Hanlon, 1970) has recently been challenged by new research. In one study, mothers' responses to their 2-year-olds' utterances were examined. Children's utterances were categorized as ill formed or well formed, depending on whether or not they contained grammatical errors. Mothers' responses were categorized as explicit or implicit. Explicit responses could consist of approval ("That's right" or "Good") or disapproval ("No, that's not right"), as long as the response to the grammar was directly stated. Implicit responses contained unspoken feedback about grammar. They could be repetitions, in which the mother repeated what the child said, as if to confirm it; clarifying questions, such as "You want the doll's hat?"; and "move ons," in which the mother began a new topic or added to the last one without questioning or repeating the child's previous statement (Demetras, Post, & Snow, 1986).

The researchers found that parents didn't provide explicit approval or disapproval of children's grammar, as the earlier Brown and Hanlon study had also shown, although they did respond explicitly to whether or not the child's statement was true. However, parents' implicit responses *did* vary, depending on whether the child's statement contained grammatical errors. When the child's utterance was well formed, the most common parental response was a move on. When the utterance was not well formed, the most common response was a clarifying question. Furthermore, within the repetition subcategory, parents responded differently to well-formed and ill-formed utterances. They followed well-formed utterances with exact repetitions, but they followed ill-formed utterances with extended repetitions (repetitions with something added) or contracted repetitions (repetitions with something deleted). Exact repetitions can be seen as a form of confirmation, and extended or contracted repetitions can be seen as corrections of a sort. It appears that children do receive feedback from their parents about the correctness of their grammar, although it's implicit rather than explicit.

The discovery that parents provide implicit feedback, or reinforcement, has weakened the strong nativist view of language development and strengthened the behaviorist view. However, the negative feedback that children get for grammatical errors isn't consistent or specific. Parents don't always follow ill-formed utterances with an implicit correction, nor do they point out exactly what was wrong with a child's utterance when they repeat it in an altered form. It's hard to see how a child could learn from such vague and erratic responses, although they may not be as erratic as they seem at first. Researchers have suggested that mothers may implicitly correct only those language structures they perceive the child to be mastering at that particular time. They may ignore more complicated errors until later in the child's development (Demetras, Post, & Snow, 1986).

At this point, we simply can't say for certain what role, if any, parental feedback plays in language learning. But we can say that the three theoretical challenges discussed in this section—the notion of cognitive underpinnings, the claims about Motherese, and the discovery of implicit feedback—have undermined the strong nativist view of language learning. There is currently a renewed interest in taking a closer look at how external factors affect children's language development. The complete answer to the question of how language is acquired probably lies somewhere in the middle of the nature-nurture continuum.

OVERVIEW

Spoken language, that uniquely human achievement, emerges over the course of the first few years of life. Babies listen, attend to certain noises, show preferences for certain tones, and soon begin to produce the sounds of their native tongue. By the second half of their first year, they're babbling in the rising and falling intonations of questions and statements, and by the end of that year, they're forming words. A year later they're putting words together into sentences and beginning to initiate conversations. How do they do it? Is it a matter of learning to imitate the sounds they hear other human beings make and being rewarded for it? Or do they have a genetically inherited ability to derive grammar from the speech they hear, an ability that emerges according to a developmental timetable? Research hasn't yet provided a clear answer to this question, but what remains clear is that learning to talk—the linguistic hallmark of the infant-toddler period—is a formidable accomplishment.

CHAPTER REVIEW

MILESTONES IN LANGUAGE PRODUCTION

- Children's productive language behavior is the speech they produce. Their receptive language behavior is the speech they understand.
- Babies' vocalizations during the first year are called prelinguistic because they typically don't contain any words. Crying and cooing are forms of prelinguistic language.
- Babbling, a type of vocalization consisting of vowel-consonant strings, emerges at about 4 or 5 months. By about 10 or 12 months, babies shorten their babbling to one or two syllables that begin to sound like real words, called protowords. They also vary their intonation patterns, so their babbling resembles the inflections used in their language.
- Most babies say their first real word at about 12 months, and their speech is now considered linguistic.
- Young children often use words differently than adults do, underextending the meanings to refer to too few cases or overextending them to refer to too many cases. Their understanding and use of words change as they progress to new cognitive levels.
- Babies continue to babble after they can say words, perhaps using the real words to communicate and the babble to practice sounds.
- Between about 14 and 18 months, children practice the intonation patterns of sentences in their language, known as the suprasegmental features of speech. Babies who have been read to and talked to produce two kinds of this expressive jargon—conversational babble and book babble.
- Once children can vary intonations, they can use holophrases, which are single words that represent more complex thoughts or sentences. Children using holophrases need an adult who can interpret their meaning.
- Between 18 and 24 months, children begin to combine words into primitive sentences. Toddlers' speech is referred to as telegraphic, because they leave out words that aren't crucial to their message. Adults have to interpret their statements, often by repeating them and filling in the missing words. Adults' responses to both holophrases and telegraphic speech aid in the child's language development.

MILESTONES IN LANGUAGE PERCEPTION

- Infants can perceive the difference between human speech and other sounds very early in life, but it's difficult to determine how much language ability is innate and how much is learned. Infants can also distinguish intonations when people talk.
- Babies' ability to recognize speech and intonation probably make them receptive to the higher-pitched, lilting tones of Motherese, or Baby Talk, a "dialect" that they seem to prefer.
- Babies and toddlers comprehend more language than they are able to speak. Their comprehension is assisted by context clues.

SOCIAL ASPECTS OF LANGUAGE DEVELOPMENT

- Toddlers use strategies for opening conversations that resemble mothers' approaches to communicating with their children. Mothers typically establish a common object of attention and then label the object. Toddlers stand close, comment on what the listener is doing, and say "Hey!" or "Guess what?"
- Toddlers aren't very skilled at the complex give-and-take necessary to carry on long conversations, and adults have to take the lead in dialogues.

THEORIES OF LANGUAGE DEVELOPMENT

- Behaviorists believe that babies acquire language through the learning mechanisms of imitation, reinforcement, and punishment. This theory doesn't account for certain grammatical errors children make that they've never heard modeled. Furthermore, most parents don't reinforce correct grammar; instead, they respond to the truth value of their children's utterances.

- Nativists believe that human beings are born with a specific neurological structure, or language acquisition device (LAD), that enables them to learn language. Championed by Noam Chomsky, this theory is supported by the universal nature of language development in every culture.

- One challenge to the strong nativist view comes from cognitive theorists who claim that the basic schemes constructed during the sensorimotor period provide the basis for language and that the notion of a special neurological device is unnecessary. They believe that once babies have knowledge about agents, objects, and actions, they can translate this knowledge into an understanding of grammatical forms like the sentence. This theory doesn't explain how children learn to express these understandings in the specific grammar of their native language.

- Another challenge to the strong nativist view comes from those who point to Baby Talk as a way mothers teach babies language. However, the role of Baby Talk in language development remains unclear.

- A third challenge to the strong nativist view comes from recent studies of parents' feedback to their children about their speech. Although parents don't explicitly correct their children's grammar, they do provide implicit feedback by "moving on" when grammar is correct and repeating or asking clarifying questions when grammer is incorrect. Children can be seen as learning language through these parental reinforcements.

- The complete explanation for language acquisition probably lies somewhere in the middle of the behaviorist-nativist continuum.

KEY TERMS

productive speech	protowords	suprasegmental	book babble
receptive speech	underextend	expressive jargon	holophrase
prelinguistic	overextend	conversational babble	telegraphic speech
babbling			

SUGGESTIONS FOR FURTHER READING

Brown, R. (1973). *A first language.* Cambridge, MA: Harvard University Press.

A classic. Essential reading for students seriously interested in learning about early language behavior. Technical but understandable, even to those with minimal background.

Lee, D. (1986). *Language, children and society: An introduction to linguistics and language development.* New York: New York University Press.

This is a book for the beginner, as its title implies. Of particular interest is the chapter on meaning, which focuses on how children learn language through social interaction with adults.

Lindfors, J. W. (1987). *Children's language and learning.* (2nd ed.). Englewood Cliffs, NJ: Prentice-Hall.

A comprehensive overview of language development at a beginning level. Language acquisition theories, as well as the details of language behavior during infancy and toddlerhood, are discussed.

Reilly, A. P., & Stark, R. E. (Eds.). (1980). The communication game. In *Pediatric Round Table: 4.* New York: Johnson & Johnson.

Written for parents and practitioners in the medical and child care fields, this small book discusses normal language development as well as screening for language difficulties. Includes many short pieces contributed by researchers well known in their fields.

c h a p t e r 8

SOCIAL AND EMOTIONAL DEVELOPMENT IN INFANTS AND TODDLERS

It's the first day of play group! Excitement and confusion fill the brightly colored room as parents and 2-year-olds explore activities. Wooden puzzles dot the tabletops in one corner, and two boys head for them eagerly. Dumping the pieces out on the table makes a loud "ker-plop!" Then comes the hard part—putting the puzzles back together. After a few tries, Juan turns to his mom, who is sitting nearby watching him, and says, "Where this goes?" "Try it here," she suggests, pointing to an empty spot. He smiles as the piece slips in.

Daniel is also trying to reassemble his puzzle. He tries to force a piece into a spot, then throws it down and tries another, then a third. His mom picks up the first piece, hands it to Daniel, and says, "This will work. All you have to do is turn it around." But Daniel shouts, "No!" and pushes her hand out of the way. He selects a different piece and tests it in the same unyielding spot.

In a few minutes, Juan has his puzzle back together. He sits back to admire it, saying, "All done! I do again!" But Daniel has abandoned his puzzle, leaving the empty frame on the table and the pieces on the floor. He's in the block corner now, and his mother calls to him, "Daniel, come here! You're going to have to finish this puzzle. I'm not going to pick up this mess for you!" But Daniel doesn't look at her or answer; he keeps playing with the blocks.

By the end of the morning, Juan is tired and happy. He leaves hand in hand with his mother, chattering about the morning. But Daniel has worked himself into an angry frenzy. He darts out of the room ahead of his mother, ignoring her calls to wait or to say good-bye to the teacher. She chases after him, shouting, "Daniel, stop! Get back here right now, young man!"

When all the children are gone, the teacher turns back to the disordered room. Putting toys away, she muses, "I wonder if Daniel was having a bad day or if there's a problem in his relationship with his mother. They definitely seem to be at odds." Closing the door behind her as she leaves for the day, she thinks, "If he still seems to be this angry after the first week, I'll talk to her to see how she perceives his behavior and how long he's been this way. They may need some help learning more positive ways of interacting. Judging from past experience, I'd say there's a lot of work ahead for Daniel and his mother, and for me too."

The teacher might not have known what was making Daniel act this way, but she suspected that something had gone wrong in his relationship with his mother. It wouldn't be surprising if she were to discover, as she got to know them, that the trouble started a long time ago, back in the early part of his infancy. Perhaps Daniel and his mother had never quite gotten along with each other, never quite "clicked." Perhaps instead of building a comfortable give-and-take relationship, they had become locked in a struggle that eroded their good will and wore them both down. We would say they had experienced a problem in their attachment relationship.

Attachment is the strong emotional tie babies and their mothers (or other primary caregivers) develop for each other. It's hard to underestimate the importance of attachment to the child's development, including social, emotional, cognitive, and even physical aspects, in cases of extreme disruption. The quality of the attachment relationship influences whether the child is likely to become independent, confident, flexible, and positive, on the one hand, or withdrawn, rigid, easily frustrated, and negative, on the other hand. This chapter explores various aspects of attachment—how it forms, what each partner brings to the relationship, and what the connections are between attachment history and the child's later development. Several other topics are addressed in this chapter as well. Moving from the relationship between infant and mother, infants' and toddlers' interactions with each other and their growing ability to play together are explored. Like so many other features of development, the child's social "style" with other children is strongly influenced by attachment history.

The development of empathy in young children—their ability to respond to others' distress—is also considered. Finally, sex-typed behavior is discussed, particularly the role parents play in teaching their children to act "like boys" or "like girls." Taken together, these topics provide a comprehensive picture of the emotional and social underpinnings that shape children's personalities and the way they interact with others as they grow.

ATTACHMENT

To begin to understand attachment, let's look again at the case of Daniel. Picture him not as an angry 2-year-old but as a newborn. He interacts with his mother for many hours every day, and his attachment to her forms out of these interactions. The quality of this attachment becomes a crucial factor in his social and emotional development. From the way he interacts with his mother, he learns patterns of interacting with others. From the way he feels about her, he learns ways of feeling about himself and others.

If his mother responds to him in ways that are comforting, satisfying, and interesting, he develops feelings of confidence, enthusiasm, and trust. In Erikson's terms, he learns that he is "all right." If she does not respond in this

FIGURE 8-1
The attachment relationship has many faces. This child shows her attachment to her mother by seeking safety and comfort after receiving an inoculation. The mother shows her attachment by holding and soothing her daughter, providing comfort in a nurturant way.

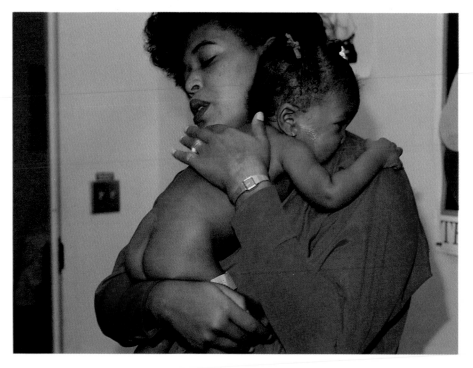

way, he associates his initial expectations with feelings of disappointment, sadness, and anger. He fails to develop a sense of trust in her; he feels uneasy and dissatisfied; and he decides he is "not all right." Because he has not established a secure attachment to his mother as an infant, he may have difficulty separating from her as a toddler. It may be hard for him to begin to gain a sense of autonomy—a sense of himself as an independent person. Without a solid base from which to explore the world, he may be fearful and passive or angry and aggressive with other people. And because so much of learning hinges on social interaction, the same factors that cause disruptions in attachment may have an effect on his cognitive functioning as well. A child with a disrupted attachment is often unable to stick with tasks or to seek or accept help.

There are many theories about how and why an emotional tie develops between parent and child. In this chapter, we consider three of them—the psychoanalytical, the behavioral, and the ethological—and the evidence available that supports or challenges them. We discuss the first two theories together and then go on to the third, which is now the favored explanation. Next, we focus on details of the two sides of the attachment relationship, the infant's and the adult's. Finally, we explore how attachment history is related to other areas in the child's life.

Theories of Infant Attachment

THE PSYCHOANALYTICAL AND BEHAVIORAL EXPLANATIONS. Both psychoanalytical and behavioral theories propose that babies become attached to adults who satisfy their basic needs, especially hunger. Traditional Freudian psychoanalytic theory is based on this notion of **drive reduction**. According to this theory, inner needs (hunger, for example) create tension, which in turn generates a drive to reduce the tension. The individual seeks to reduce the drive by satisfying the need (by eating, for example). The adult who gratifies a baby's needs becomes associated with the pleasurable sensations that result. Psychoanalytical theory also assumes that each person has a limited amount of mental energy for attachments, so a baby becomes attached to only one person, preferably the mother. Later, the child comes to identify with the parent of the same sex, but only after having worked through conflicts associated with this first emotional tie with the mother. According to Freudian theory, a person's sexual identity is likely to be disrupted if early attachment is disrupted.

The first relationship with the mother is also assumed to be extremely important for personality development and as a model for later love relationships. The first attachment is seen as an enduring part of the psyche. According to Freud, the mother and father continue to be present in the individual's mind as objects of love, admiration, and fear long after the actual parent-child relationship is over.

Early behavioral theorists also explained attachment in terms of drive reduction: The adult who feeds a baby becomes a **secondary reinforcer.** If you recall from the discussion of behavioral theory in Chapter 2, a secondary reinforcer is something or someone who takes on reinforcing properties as a result of having been associated with a primary reinforcer, which, in the case of hunger, is food. Babies become attached to their mothers because they associate them with being fed.

Unlike psychoanalytic theory, however, behavioral theory has never used ideas like "mental energy" and thus has never claimed that the mother is the baby's only attachment figure. A baby might become attached to several adult caregivers if all of them are involved in feeding. In addition, in behavioral theory the first attachment is not considered central to all others. In fact, behavioral theory suggests that later relationships may depend as much on the circumstances surrounding them as on the first relationship with the mother.

THE ETHOLOGICAL EXPLANATION. The ethological explanation for attachment, first proposed by John Bowlby in 1969, claims that infants are **preprogrammed**— genetically "wired"—to form attachment to the adults who best ensure their survival. **Ethology** is the study of animal behavior, particularly the aspects of behavior having to do with ecology and evolution. The ethological explanation for attachment focuses on the ways young animals, including young humans, keep in touch with their mothers (Waters & Deane, 1982). Babies do this by sending signals to their mothers, and mothers respond by reacting to the signals. Babies prefer adults who read their signals accurately and respond to them appropriately. Although signals often revolve around feeding, attachments are not necessarily based on this situation. Babies may develop strong atttachments to adults who have never fed them or provided them with other basic physical care.

The ethological explanation accounts both for the way babies try to stay near their mothers and for the way they separate to explore. Babies must be able to explore if they are to learn about their environment and become independent, but they also need to be kept safe from danger. As the human species evolved, both babies and mothers needed to learn to send and read signals about feeding, danger, and so on if they were to survive. Those who learned

FIGURE 8-2
According to the ethological explanation for attachment, babies become attached to adults who correctly read their signals, ensuring their safety and supporting their efforts to explore. This little girl is being kept safe—an adult holds her hand to prevent her from falling down—at the same time that she's being allowed to find out about her environment. A proponent of the ethological explanation would say that the conditions for a healthy attachment relationship are being provided by a sensitive adult.

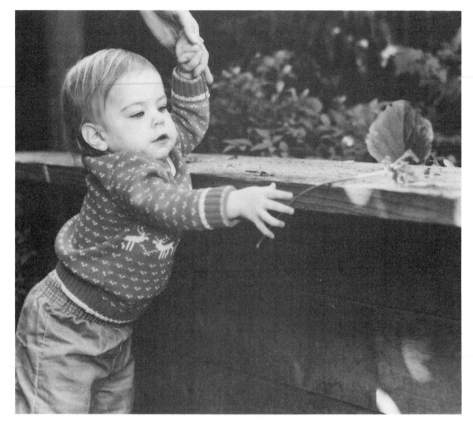

the best were the ones who survived and passed on their genes to succeeding generations.

The ethological theory predicts that babies will become attached most strongly to the adults who respond the best to their signals. Although the theory is based on studies of animal behavior, it doesn't claim that babies have an innate attachment to their biological mothers. What it does suggest is that babies are born with certain capabilities for building relationships with adults. It also assumes that adults have to be able to respond to the subtle signals babies send if these relationships are to work.

EVIDENCE FOR THE THEORIES. Research has not supported the drive reduction explanation for attachment that lies at the heart of both the psychoanalytical and behavioral theories. It was struck down first when Harry Harlow, a psychologist at the University of Wisconsin, conducted studies with baby monkeys to determine why they became attached to a caregiver (Harlow, 1958). He used two types of surrogate (substitute) mothers, one made from a tube covered with terry cloth and the other made of wire mesh. The baby monkeys were fed from a bottle placed on the wire mesh surrogate; the cloth mother provided only "contact comfort." If the monkeys showed a preference for the surrogate who fed them, it would support the drive reduction explanation for attachment, because it would indicate that they developed an emotional tie to a caregiver who fed them. If they showed a preference for the cloth mother, it would not support this explanation.

FIGURE 8-3
In Harlow's experiments, monkeys spent more time clinging to the terry cloth surrogate mother who provided contact comfort than to the wire mesh mother who provided food. These findings undermined the belief that feeding alone is the crucial factor in the formation of attachment.

As it turned out, the baby monkeys spent more time on the cloth mother, and when a frightening wind-up toy was placed in their cage, they ran to the cloth mother for protection. This experiment undermined the drive reduction and secondary reinforcement explanations for attachment, because they're both based on the satisfaction of hunger. (Harlow's experiment didn't rule out the possibility that there's a drive for contact, but ethological theories haven't focused on this possibility, because they tend to stress interconnecting needs and behaviors, not isolated ones.) Further evidence against the secondary reinforcement hypothesis came when a study reported that 30 percent of the infants in the study were attached to an adult other than the one who took care of them most of the time. Additionally, 22 percent of the infants were attached to someone who had never performed any basic caregiving activities for them at all, such as feeding or diapering (Schaffer & Emerson, 1964). More recently, cases have been reported in which foster children were found to be attached to their biological parent, even though they were cared for almost exclusively by their foster parents (Gaensbauer & Harmon, 1982).

Right now, the best explanation we have for infant attachment is the ethological one—babies come into the world equipped to build relationships with people who will take care of them. They send signals to adults, and they build the strongest relationships with adults who respond most sensitively to these signals.

Several questions come to mind at this point in our discussion. First, how do we know when an infant has become attached to an adult? What does the baby do that indicates attachment? Second, what are the signals babies send to adults, and what are the so-called sensitive responses? Finally, what makes

FIGURE 8-4
Babies can become attached to adults other than the people who feed them or take care of them most of the time. Attachment depends more on sensitive responses to signals sent back and forth between the baby and the adult. This woman knows exactly how to interact sensitively with her great-grandson. She cradles him at just the right distance from her face, affectionately returning his friendly gaze.

some adults respond sensitively and others respond insensitively? A discussion of these questions follows.

Infant Attachment Behavior

THE STRANGE SITUATION. How do we tell if a baby has become attached to a particular adult, and how can we judge the quality of the attachment? A standard method has been devised to study and describe attachment behavior in babies between 1 and 2 years of age. The so-called strange situation was developed by Mary Ainsworth and colleagues in 1969. It involves seven episodes and three participants—mother, baby, and stranger.

The experimental procedure begins with the mother and baby being introduced to the laboratory playroom. Then the mother and baby are left alone in the room, but the mother doesn't play with the baby (episode 1). Next, a stranger enters, talks with the mother a bit, and then focuses her attention on the baby (episode 2). The mother leaves, introducing episode 3, in which the baby is separated from the mother, leaving the stranger and the baby alone. Soon, the mother returns (episode 4); this is the first reunion. The mother talks to the baby and comforts the baby if she is distressed. (If the baby is very distressed at any point, the experiment is terminated.) Then the mother leaves again. Episode 5, the second separation, follows. This time the baby is left completely alone, and the stranger, not the mother, enters the room first after this separation (episode 6). Finally, the mother returns, and the stranger leaves (episode 7).

Secure attachment

Anxious/ambivalent attachment

Anxious/avoidant attachment

(a)   (b)   (c)

FIGURE 8-5
Observations of many mother-baby pairs in the strange situation led researchers to formulate three types of attachment behavior. When attachment is secure, the baby separates from the mother to explore the toys and is happy to be reunited with the mother after she leaves the room and returns (a). In anxious/ambivalent attachment, the baby clings to the mother while she's in the room and, although distressed, rejects her when she returns (b). In anxious/avoidant attachment, the baby doesn't seem to care when the mother leaves or returns and doesn't seem to prefer the mother to the stranger (c). Studies have shown that the quality of the mother-child attachment is related to many aspects of the child's future development.

Several features of infant attachment become apparent in the strange situation. The researcher or observer can see to what extent the baby uses the mother as a secure base for exploration, how much the baby prefers the mother to the stranger, and how likely the baby is to consider the mother a haven of safety when frightened (Connell & Goldsmith, 1982). From observing many babies in the strange situation, researchers have identified and described three major patterns of response. These patterns, which indicate the quality of babies' attachment to their mothers, have been labeled **secure attachment**, **anxious/ambivalent attachment**, and **anxious/avoidant attachment**. (A fourth pattern, labeled disorganized/disoriented, is currently under investigation, but it hasn't yet been related consistently to any specific pattern of parenting [Carlson et al., 1989]).

In the first pattern, the baby separates from the mother to explore the toys in the playroom but periodically touches base with her. When she leaves, the baby is moderately distressed and either cries or plays in a more subdued way. When she returns, the baby greets her warmly. In the second pattern (anxious/ambivalent, also called resistant), the baby stays close to the mother and doesn't explore the toys. When the mother leaves, the baby reacts with great distress; when she returns, the baby seeks her and rejects her at the same time (that is, the reaction is ambivalent).

In the third pattern (anxious/avoidant), the baby readily separates from the mother to explore the toys and doesn't seem to prefer the mother to the stranger. When the mother leaves, the baby shows no concern, and when she returns, the baby ignores or avoids her. Details of the behaviors associated with the three patterns are shown in Table 8-1.

What do these different patterns of attachment tell us? As the labels imply, one of the patterns is considered optimal or normal, and two are considered deviant. Each pattern seems to reflect different patterns of behavior by the parents. When parents respond sensitively to the baby's signals, the baby tends to become securely attached. When parents respond inappropriately, or not at all, the baby tends to form an anxious attachment of one kind or the other. A discussion of parent's responses follow, but before we do that, let's take a closer look at how babies signal their needs to their parents.

THE INFANT'S EARLY SIGNALS. Some of the newborn's signals are subtle, but others aren't subtle at all. Probably the least subtle and most powerful signal is crying. Adults find infant crying unpleasant (it's been found to raise people's blood pressure), and they usually move quickly to do something about it. As mentioned in Chapter 4, many parents can tell from listening to the crying whether their baby is hungry, angry, or in pain. Their judgments are based on how suddenly the crying starts, how loud and high-pitched it is, and how long it lasts (Wolff, 1969). Considering the context of the crying as well—for example, when the baby was last fed—the parent decides what's causing the crying and begins to do something about it.

Most parents respond to a crying baby by picking her up and holding or rocking her. This not only soothes her (Korner & Thoman, 1972; Hunziker &

TABLE 8-1   Patterns of Attachment Observed in 12- to 18-Month-Olds in the Strange Situation

	Exploratory Behavior before Separation	Behavior during Separation	Reunion Behavior	Behavior with Stranger
Secure	Separates to explore toys; shares play with mother; friendly toward stranger when mother is present; touches "home base" periodically.	May cry; play is subdued for a while; usually recovers and is able to play.	If distressed during separation, contact ends distress; if not distressed, greets mother warmly; initiates interaction.	Somewhat friendly; may play with stranger after initial distress reaction.
Anxious/ambivalent (resistant)	Has difficulty separating to explore toys even when mother is present; wary of novel situations and people; stays close to mother and away from stranger.	Very distressed; hysterical crying does not quickly diminish.	Seeks comfort and rejects it; continues to cry or fuss; may be passive—no greeting made.	Wary of stranger; rejects stranger's offers to play.
Anxious/avoidant	Readily separates to explore toys; does not share play with parent; shows little preference for parent versus stranger.	Does not show distress; continues to play; interacts with the stranger.	Ignores mother—turns or moves away; avoidance is more extreme at the second reunion.	No avoidance of stranger.

SOURCE: Compiled from Ainsworth, M. D. S., & Wittig, B. A. (1969). Attachment and exploratory behavior of one-year-olds in a strange situation. In B. M. Foss (Ed.), Determinants of infant behavior (Vol. 4). London: Methuen.

Barr, 1986) but also tends to induce the alert inactive state, which was discussed in Chapter 4. She opens her eyes and searches with them, often fixating on her parent's eyes if the parent is looking at her. If you recall, babies like to look at patterns such as the one provided by the face and eyes (Brazelton, 1973; Als, 1977).

The baby now uses another very powerful signal—gazing. This steady, intent attention to another's face indicates that the baby wants to engage in a social interaction. The parent will probably gaze back at the baby and smile or speak; the baby may smile or coo in return. Parents like this eye contact— it makes them feel that the baby is enjoying their company. They'll often gaze back at the baby as long as the baby gazes at them (Robson, 1967). Gazing between parent and baby can go on for much longer than is typical between adults. Even when they're not engaged in gazing, adults like to look at babies' faces because they find them "cute" (Lamb, 1982).

Babies signal their wish to reduce stimulation or end the interaction by looking away. Gaze aversion is an expression that often indicates disgust (Izard & Dougherty, 1982). Sensitive parents do something different when the baby looks away. Of course, starting to cry again is another way the baby says, "That's enough."

Besides crying and gazing, babies have other inborn ways to make adults pay attention to them and interact with them on their terms. When they're eating, for example, babies suck in rhythmical bursts and then pause. Mothers often jiggle babies during the pauses, and in the first few weeks, they learn that short jiggles make the baby start sucking again. This biologically based sucking pattern, with its alternating bursts and pauses, keeps the mother actively involved in the feeding. She sees that her attention is important to the feeding process, and she watches the baby's face closely. The baby often gazes back at her, and this, too, keeps her attention. When the baby is done eating, the mother may wish to continue this pleasing interaction in some other situation, such as playing. The turn-taking nature of the feeding inter-

FIGURE 8-6
Infants gaze more intently and for longer periods of time than do adults, unless the adults happen to be falling in love with each other.

action may help mothers learn to observe their baby closely and adjust their responses to the baby's behavior (Kaye, 1982).

As the newborn matures, another powerful signal appears—the **social smile**. It begins to appear on the baby's previously expressionless face by about 2 months of age. (See Research Focus—The Developmental Course of Smiling.) One day, often after some searching of the mother's or father's face, the baby's eyes light up and her face breaks into a smile. News that "the baby smiled today" is thrilling for parents, who may need a boost at this point in their sometimes thankless daily routine with their newborn. This smile is their reward; it makes them feel that there is truly a relationship between them and their baby (Robson, 1967). Smiling is the baby's way of saying that all is well with the interaction that's going on at that moment. When the smile starts to fade and the baby sobers, something is going amiss. Smiling and sobering, gazing and gaze aversion are the signals with which the baby regulates her interactions with her parents in the early months.

This may not seem like much in comparison with the virtually infinite variety of signals older children and adults use to communicate, but it's enough for the sensitive parent. How do these signals and cues work in action? Consider the following examples of parent-infant interactions (Stern, 1977, pp. 3, 110–111): In the first example, the mother adjusts what she does to the level desired by the baby. The baby, too, is skillful: When the mother reduces stimulation below the level he wants, he smiles more broadly to get her to raise it again. In the second example, the mother misreads the baby's signals or chooses to ignore them. She continues with strong stimulation even after the infant breaks her gaze to signal she wishes to stop or slow down.

EXAMPLE 1:

While talking and looking at me the mother turned her head and gazed at the infant's face. He was gazing at the ceiling, but out of the corner of his eye he saw her head turn toward him and turned to gaze back at her. This had happened before, but now he broke rhythm and stopped sucking. He let go of the nipple and the suction around it broke as he eased into the faintest suggestion of a smile. The mother abruptly stopped talking and, as she watched his face begin to transform, her eyes opened a little wider and her eyebrows raised a bit. His eyes locked on to hers, and together they held motionless for an instant. The infant did not return to sucking and his mother held frozen her slight expression of anticipation. This silent and almost motionless instant continued to hang until the mother suddenly shattered it by saying "Hey!" and simultaneously opening her eyes wider, raising her eyebrows further, and throwing her head up and toward the infant. Almost simultaneously, the baby's eyes widened. His head tilted up and, as his smile broadened, the nipple fell out of his mouth. Now she said, "Well, hello! . . . hello . . . heeelloooo!", so that her pitch rose and the "hellos" became longer and more stressed on each successive repetition. With each phrase the baby expressed more pleasure, and his body resonated almost like a balloon being pumped up, filling a little more with each breath. The mother then paused and her face relaxed. They watched each other expectantly for a moment. The shared excitement between them ebbed, but before it faded completely, the baby suddenly took an initiative and intervened to rescue it. His head lurched forward, his hands jerked up, and a fuller smile blossomed. His mother was jolted into motion. She moved forward, mouth open and eyes alight, and said "Oooooh . . . ya wanna play do ya . . . yeah? . . . I didn't know if you were still hungry . . . no . . . noooooo . . . no I didn't . . ." And off they went.

RESEARCH FOCUS

The Developmental Course of Smiling

Newborns are often seen smiling in their sleep, but these spontaneous smiles are triggered by changes in their internal sleep states and are known as **endogenous smiles** (Emde & Gaensbauer, 1981). Between 6 and 8 weeks of age, the *social smile* appears—a smile given in response to something outside the baby. The baby smiles more and more frequently over the next few months (Wolff, 1969; Anisfeld, 1982; Konner, 1982).

At first, the social smile is indiscriminate: The baby smiles at familiar and unfamiliar adults alike, as long as they make some friendly gesture, such as gazing, smiling, or talking. But at about the fourth month, things begin to change. The baby begins to search the faces of unfamiliar people and to sober a bit toward them (Emde, Gaensbauer, & Harmon, 1976). By 6 to 8 months of age, the baby's reaction may be so intense that he cries if a stranger approaches (Konner, 1982; Lamb, 1982). The baby's smile is now a very selective social smile, reserved only for familiar people. Unfamiliar people are likely to make the baby cry. When a baby reacts this way to a stranger (usually between 6 and 18 months of age), he's showing *stranger anxiety*.

What makes a baby smile? Does the baby learn to smile by seeing smiles, or is the impulse to smile innate? It seems that it's the latter. Evidence comes from a study of smiling in premature babies. Researchers hypothesized that smiling is an innate capability, programmed to emerge at a certain point in the baby's development, and they calculated this point in weeks from conception rather than weeks from birth. They suggested that babies born 8 weeks prematurely would smile not at 6 weeks, when full-term babies smile, but at 12 to 14 weeks, when their developmental age would match that of 6-week-olds. This is exactly what they found (Anisfield, 1982). Further support for a biological view of smiling comes from research showing that social smiling begins at about the same time that certain portions of the brain develop. (See Konner, 1982, for an excellent discussion of this topic.)

It turns out, then, that one of the baby's most powerful social signals isn't especially social in origin. But the baby's intention isn't what's important at this point. What matters is how the parent perceives and responds to the signal—and parents read the smile as a friendly social gesture. Commenting on the parent's point of view, one researcher writes (Kaye, 1982, p. 196), "fantasies are not to be disparaged. Fantasies, are, in fact, part of the evolved apparatus with which parents are provided (the evolution in this case being cultural, not only genetic), so that they treat the infant as a person from the start. . . . Parents capitalize on certain aspects of the newborn organism that, so far as we can tell, evolved for that very purpose, so as to involve the infant in social frames." In other words, smiling is another behavior that may have evolved to help ensure the survival of the baby—and the species.

The newborn smiles mysteriously to herself (top); the older baby smiles at her parents (bottom).

EXAMPLE 2:

The dance they had worked out by the time I met them went something like this. Whenever a moment of mutual gaze occurred, the mother went immediately into high-gear stimulating behaviors, producing a profusion of fully displayed, high-intensity, facial and vocal infant-elicited social behavior. Jenny invariably broke gaze rapidly. Her mother never interpreted this temporary face and gaze aversion as a cue to lower her level of behavior . . . Instead, she would swing her head around following Jenny's . . . She would reinitiate the same level of stimulation with a new arrangement of facial and vocal combinations. Jenny again turned away . . . Again, instead of holding back, the mother continued to chase Jenny . . . She moved closer, in an apparent attempt to break through and establish contact. She also escalated the level of her stimulation even more by adding touching and tickling to the unabated flow of vocal and facial behaviors. . . .

With Jenny's head now pinned in the corner, the baby's next recourse was to rapidly swing her face from one side to the other right past her mother's face. When her face crossed the mother's face, in the face-face zone, Jenny closed her eyes to avoid any mutual visual contact and only reopened them after the head aversion was established on the other side. All of these behaviors on Jenny's part were performed with a sober face or at times a grimace.

These examples show that babies can be real partners in even the earliest social interactions, regulating their parents' actions and responses with their repertoire of signals. The examples also show that having the repertoire doesn't necessarily guarantee the best interaction. Parents must be able to read and respond to the signals. What happens to the relationship when parents are insensitive to their baby? This is the question we look at next.

THE RELATIONSHIP BETWEEN INFANT ATTACHMENT AND PARENT BEHAVIOR. The parent's overall pattern of behavior toward the baby determines the kind of attachment the baby will develop for the parent. We saw earlier, in discussing the strange situation, that some babies are securely attached to their mothers and others are anxiously attached. We now know that babies become securely attached when their parents give them responsive feedback. This means that they (1) pay attention to the baby's signals; (2) interpret the signals accurately; (3) give appropriate feedback; and (4) respond contingently, that is, they respond promptly enough for the baby to feel that his signals caused the response (Ainsworth et al., 1978). Responsive parents also cooperate with the baby's ongoing activity rather than intruding or interfering. Mothers of securely attached babies "are more responsive to their infant's cries, hold their babies more tenderly and carefully, pace the interaction contingently during face-to-face interaction, and exhibit greater sensitivity in initiating and terminating feeding" (Crockenberg, 1981, p. 857).

Parents of anxiously attached babies act quite differently. They may ignore the baby's signals, or they may respond but in inappropriate ways. For example, a mother may take the opportunity to read the newspaper every time she feeds the baby, holding him loosely and not noticing his gaze. A father may consistently ignore the baby's hungry cries in the middle of the night to get some extra sleep. A parent might bounce a baby vigorously when the baby prefers to be cuddled or end a feeding when the baby only wants to rest or, as we saw in Example 2, continue to stimulate the baby when the baby wishes to stop.

FIGURE 8-7
Something's going wrong when a child pulls away from a mother who's trying to offer comfort. Is it a momentary mismatch of signals, or is there a larger pattern of anxious attachment?

More serious problems in attachment occur when a parent's behavior is more disturbed. For example, some mothers dislike physical contact with their babies or treat them in an angry or threatening way (Bretherton et al., 1986). Some mothers have "restricted affect," meaning that they express fewer emotions than other mothers, especially positive, joyful ones (Ainsworth et al., 1978; Main, 1981). Some mothers even mock their babies' behavior, speak sarcastically to them, handle them roughly, and "stare them down." Babies treated this way are likely to have severe problems in their emotional and social development.

One researcher has suggested that sensitivity in parenting has two dimensions: responding versus not responding, and responding appropriately versus responding inappropriately (Lamb, 1982). The first dimension probably affects the baby's sense of power and effectiveness in the world. Babies whose parents respond to their signals learn that what they do matters. Children whose parents are insensitive to their signals may come to exhibit "learned helplessness," the sense that they have little effect on the world.

Babies whose parents don't respond contingently or consistently may show the ambivalent (or resistant) pattern of anxious attachment. The response they receive is appropriate when it comes, but they're not sure when it's going to be given or if it will come at all. Because they can't be sure the parent will give the desired comfort, they seek it but then resist it, as if anticipating disappointment.

The second dimension of sensitivity in parenting—responding appropriately versus responding inappropriately—in combination with the first may affect the development of the child's trust in others. Babies whose parents respond to them appropriately learn to expect that people will react to them in desired ways. Babies whose parents respond inappropriately, who find they can get a response but aren't sure what it's going to be, may tend to show the avoidant pattern of attachment. They stop sending signals and may even try to avoid the parent, perhaps as a protection against getting an inappropriate response. Children showing the resistant pattern of attachment seem to involve their mothers in power struggles almost as a goal (Sroufe, 1981); avoidant children, on the other hand, seem to want to get away from the mother's sphere of influence.

At this point we don't fully understand the links between specific maternal behavior and the two anxious patterns of attachment. Still, we can see overall patterns, and the two dimensions just described offer a promising way of exploring them further. Since we do know that the quality of parenting in the early months is vitally important to the child's long-term development and future happiness, we need to be alert to situations in which a parent and child seem headed for trouble.

ATTACHMENT REACTIONS: STRANGER ANXIETY AND SEPARATION DISTRESS. During the second half of the first year—between 6 and 12 months—babies add a whole new set of actions to their repertoire: they begin to move around. They learn to cling, creep, crawl, and finally walk. Now they don't have to wait for their parents to come to them or just watch them as they move away. They can follow them around. At about the same time, babies start to discriminate sharply between familiar and unfamiliar adults (as described in Research Focus—The Developmental Course of Smiling). When approached by someone they don't know, they sober and may even cry, a response known as **stranger anxiety**. Babies also become capable of gaining information about new people and situations by **social referencing**, as described in Research Focus—"How Do You Feel About Her, Mom?" Social Referencing in Infants.

By late in the first year, somewhere between 8 and 10 months of age, babies start to be able to express on their faces emotions such as joy, surprise, and anger (Hiatt, Campos, & Emde, 1979; Stenberg, Campos, & Emde, 1983). Now they can put together facial expressions, sounds, and motion to produce the full-blown attachment reactions that parents (and babysitters) know so well. When they see their parents after a separation, they greet them with joy and stretch out their arms or crawl to them. When they're separated from their parents, or when they're concerned that a separation may be coming, they show **separation distress**—they sober, cry, and cling or try to follow. (Knowledge in Action: Infants and Toddlers discusses the implications of this development for parents placing their infants in day care.) The older infant and the toddler show attachment by walking or running to keep in contact with the parent. With the acquisition of language, the child adds words to the protest: "Mommy! Daddy! Stay here! I go!" These kinds of scenes are practically the hallmark of the toddler years, when separation distress is at its height.

In sum, then, babies come into the world well equipped to interact with adults and to regulate those interactions. But the "amazing newborn" has an

RESEARCH FOCUS

"How Do You Feel About Her, Mom?" Social Referencing in Infants

Ten-month-old Anthony is playing with brightly colored plastic rings on the living room floor when the doorbell rings. His mother gets up from the sofa to answer it. She has been expecting a visit from a new neighbor. When this virtual stranger enters the room, she stops for a moment to chat with Anthony. "Well, hello there, big boy," she says, as she kneels down on the floor. "What are you doing?"

Anthony, meanwhile, has stopped playing and clutches the yellow ring in his hand. He looks toward his mother, who sits down once again on the sofa. She smiles at Anthony and says, "Say hi to Mary Beth, Anthony. Say, 'Hiiii, Mary Beth.'"

Anthony looks at this new person, Mary Beth; he looks hard, as if concentrating on figuring out who she is or what she's going to do. Then he casts a glance back toward Mom, who is still smiling as she talks now with Mary Beth about how old Anthony is. Anthony looks back toward Mary Beth, as if led there by the direction of his mother's gaze. Anthony slowly raises the hand that holds the ring, and then he extends it toward Mary Beth. "Oh, what a pretty yellow ring!" Mary Beth exclaims. "Does it go on this post?" Mary Beth reaches for the post as she asks and tilts it toward the ring that Anthony holds out to her. Anthony looks up at Mary Beth for a moment and glances at his mom once more. Then he slips the ring over the end of the post, and his face breaks into a smile.

WHAT IS SOCIAL REFERENCING?

Anthony used his mother's facial expressions to gain information about a new situation. Anthony didn't know Mary Beth, and he wasn't quite sure how to respond to her. Should he be friendly, or should he retreat to his mother's arms? Anthony's strategy of using information about how another person feels about a third event—in this case, Mary Beth—is called *social referencing* (Clyman et al., 1986). It involves scanning the face of a familiar and trusted person to pick up information about a new situation. From that person's emotional reaction to the situation, the child can form his response. Babies 8 or 9 months of age and older often use this strategy. As they get older, they get better at interpreting and using the information their parent provides (Walden & Ogan, 1988).

STUDIES OF SOCIAL REFERENCING

Social referencing has been documented in many studies of how babies react to situations when their mothers change their facial expressions. In one study mothers were asked to pose different expressions as their babies were presented with a new toy (Klinnert, 1981). When mothers looked happy or joyful, their babies were more likely to accept the toy. Babies' reactions to strangers have also been shown to be related to their mothers' facial expressions (Boccia & Campos, 1983; Feinman & Lewis, 1983). In still another situation, mothers' facial expressions have been observed to influence babies' willingness to cross over the "visual cliff." (If you recall from Chapter 4, this is a laboratory apparatus, originally designed for the study of infant depth perception, in which a drop in surface level is covered with a transparent sheet of glass or plastic). When babies get close to the part of the surface where the cliff appears, they hesitate. Often they look up at their mothers for clues about this novel situation. In studies of social referencing, researchers asked different mothers to show such emotions as interest, anger, or fear as their babies approached the cliff. The results were clear: When mothers looked pleased or interested, babies were much more likely to cross the cliff than when mothers looked angry or afraid.

BABIES' ABILITY TO READ FACIAL EXPRESSIONS

When babies engage in social referencing, it indicates that they recognize and can respond to the facial expressions that reflect various emotional states. Babies start discriminating facial expressions by the time they're 4 or 5 months old, but they probably don't attach appropriate, or any, meanings to different expressions (Appel & Campos, 1977). Somewhat later, between 6 and 9 months of age, they begin to respond differently to different expressions, which indicates they understand some of the meanings attached to the expressions. A baby might cry, for example, on seeing an angry face or smile on seeing a joyful one. At this point, they start to be able to communicate with someone else, via emotional expressions, about an uncertain third event (Campos et al., 1983).

amazing parent as well. "Left to their own devices," says one child development specialist, "infants' intrinsic amazingness would not amount to much" (Kaye 1982, p. 196). The parent is the crucial element in the relationship. The baby's signals—gazing, smiling, crying, and sobering—get the parent going, and then the give-and-take of the interaction keeps them both going, if all proceeds smoothly. But what ensures that things get going on the parent's side? And what happens if they don't? These questions are discussed next.

FIGURE 8-8
Stranger anxiety—acute fear of anyone unknown who approaches too closely—reaches its height between the middle of the first year and the middle of the second. This 8-month-old is very distressed when held by a man he doesn't know but immediately comforted when returned to his mother.

Theories of Attachment: The Parent's Side

Newborns turn life upside down. They wake every few hours to be fed, leaving their parents sleepless and irritable. They sometimes may cry many hours a day, challenging the patience and ingenuity of even the most resourceful adult. Old family patterns break down and new ones emerge as the baby takes her place in the household. All of this is stressful for parents. But they're helped through the difficult parts of parenting by their own feelings of attachment to their baby.

Like infant attachment, maternal attachment has been a subject of great interest in the study of child development. What causes maternal attachment to form? Three explanations for its development have been proposed: the biological explanation; the parental history explanation; and the social system explanation. Each of these is discussed below.

THE BIOLOGICAL EXPLANATION. The biological explanation, also known as the critical period explanation, claims that maternal attachment is based on hormones. The theory is that hormones released at the end of pregnancy or soon after birth "prime" the mother to bond with her baby. **Bonding** refers to the dramatic and immediate emotional tie that mothers feel toward their newborn babies, according to the proponents of this explanation (Klaus & Kennel, 1976). It is triggered in the hormonally primed mother by contact with her baby within a **critical period** immediately after birth, according to the explanation, when the hormones are at their highest level. If the mother bonds with the

FIGURE 8-9
Proponents of the biological explanation for maternal attachment believe that the moments after birth are a critical period for bonding between mother and baby. Although these moments *are* special, as this mother and baby show, the evidence indicates that attachment develops over a longer period of time and depends on factors other than contact during a critical period.

baby during this early period, her love will continue to grow, and she will be able to provide the responsive care needed to ensure the baby's attachment to her.

The biological theory of maternal attachment originated in research on lower animals. Studies of sheep, goats, and rats showed that mothering was disrupted when the young were separated from their mothers immediately after birth, even for only one or two hours (Collias, 1956; Hersher, Moore, & Richmond, 1958). Mothering wasn't disrupted, or the disruption wasn't as serious, when some contact was allowed before mothers and young were separated. The identification of a critical period for maternal attachment emerged from these studies.

Other studies investigated maternal behavior in rats. Researchers found a higher level of maternal behavior in pregnant rats than in nonpregnant rats, and when blood plasma from pregnant rats was injected into nonpregnant rats, these rats also exhibited maternal behavior (Rosenblatt, 1965). This research established a hormonal basis for maternal behavior in rats.

General interest existed in investigating whether the findings from animal studies could be applied to humans. One research group in particular wanted to know if there was a causal relationship between severe disruption in maternal attachment—the kind that results in child abuse—and separation at birth. Physicians who cared for premature newborns in the neonatal intensive care unit of a large city hospital noticed that an unusually high number of these children returned to the emergency room as child abuse victims. They wondered if the mothers of these babies had been unable to bond with them because they were separated during a critical period for bonding.

In pioneering studies to test the critical period theory in humans, these physicians and their colleagues (Klaus et al., 1972; Klaus and Kennell, 1976), as well as other groups of researchers, manipulated the amount of contact between mothers and their newborns in hospitals. Some mothers were kept on traditional schedules, which involved contact mainly at regular feeding times; others were given contact immediately after birth and for increased periods of time in the days that followed (Leifer et al., 1972; Hales et al., 1977; Carlsson et al., 1978; Rode et al., 1981).

Results from these studies were mixed. Some studies found that attachment seemed stronger in the mothers who had more contact, but other studies found no long-term differences. In general, the studies did not provide strong evidence for a critical period during which bonding must take place. Hormones probably play a more important role in animal behavior than they do in human relationships. In humans, maternal attachment seems to depend not on one critical event but rather on many different factors occurring over a period of time. Early contact between mother and baby is probably beneficial to the relationship, but the evidence indicates that it's not essential to the formation of attachment (Goldberg, 1982; Svejda, Pannabecker, & Emde, 1982).

THE PARENTAL HISTORY EXPLANATION. Other theorists and researchers have suggested that maternal attachment is closely related to the mother's history—her earlier experiences in life. A mother's ability to form a close, nurturing tie with a baby is seen as a function of her personality and of the way she was cared for when she was a child. This explanation comes from observations and studies of disrupted attachment, such as in cases of neglect and abuse, rather than from observations of healthy mother-child relationships. Mothers who have no positive attachment to their children are seen as lacking in par-

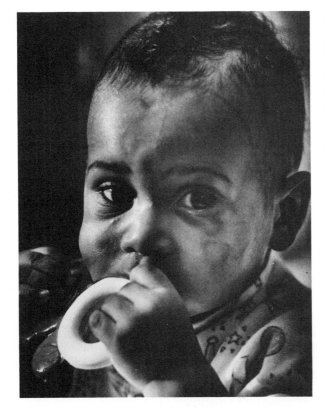

FIGURE 8-10
When maternal attachment fails, children are placed at tremendous risk. This child was found in a shopping cart outside a supermarket after he was abandoned by his mother on a cold winter night. Although no simple theory explains attachment and no easy solutions are possible when things go wrong, our society attempts to protect and help the children of these troubled relationships.

enting skills, knowledge about children, or the ability to act responsibly because of their own immaturity. Sometimes these mothers have psychological problems or personality disorders.

In support of this theory, it can be said, first, that abusive parents as a group are more likely to have been poorly parented than nonabusive parents (Oliver & Taylor, 1971; Green, Gaines, & Sandgrund, 1974). Additionally, mothers who suffer from certain psychoses often have difficulty being effective parents (Fraiberg, 1974; Musick, Clark, & Cohler, 1982). And it has generally been confirmed that past childhood relationships, at least the reconstructed memories of those relationships, influence how individuals parent their own children (Ricks, 1985). However, parents' childhood histories don't completely explain maternal attachment behavior. After all, not all abused parents abuse their own children. And although some abusive and unresponsive mothers do have personality disorders, other mothers who fail to develop an attachment to their babies don't suffer from such problems. Parental history and personality characteristics may provide part of the explanation for maternal attachment, but they don't account for it completely (Parke & Lewis, 1981).

THE SOCIAL SYSTEM EXPLANATION. Because no single factor completely explains maternal attachment, some researchers have considered that many factors might be working together. They have proposed a model, known as the interaction/social system explanation, suggesting that maternal attachment is a function of several interacting factors: (1) characteristics of the mother (such as personality traits and psychological well-being); (2) characteristics of the baby (such as health, degree of development at birth, activity level, and so on); (3) characteristics of the family (such as number of children, role of the father in child care, economic resources, and so on); and (4) social supports beyond the immediate family (such as extended family, friends, medical resources, and so on).

These factors are thought to interact to determine the kind of attachment the mother forms as well as the extent of her ability to nurture attachment in the baby. As an example, consider the case of the premature baby. Premature babies overall are more difficult to parent than full-term babies. They signal their needs less clearly, avert their gaze more often, and smile less (Brown & Bateman, 1978; Crnic et al., 1983). Adults find their cries more unpleasant and their faces less attractive or cute (Frodi & Lamb, 1978). All these characteristics mean that the premature baby can't contribute as much to a relationship as the full-term baby. But if the premature baby is born to a mother with some parenting skills, a healthy personality, a stable relationship with a partner, a supportive extended family, a network of friends, and a secure economic situation, the baby's initial deficiencies probably won't stand in the way of the mother's forming an attachment.

On the other hand, if an extremely robust and "easy" baby is born into a situation that's not ideal or to a mother who's barely able to keep an interaction going, the baby might be able to contribute enough to make the relationship work. But when a difficult baby is born into difficult circumstances, there probably will be trouble ahead (Vaughn et al., 1979; Crockenberg, 1981). It's the combination of circumstances—not one or another single factor—that determines the quality of the mother-baby attachment.

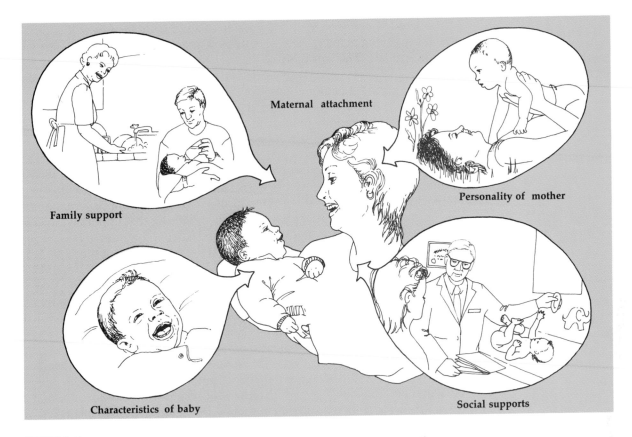

Maternal attachment

Family support

Personality of mother

Characteristics of baby

Social supports

FIGURE 8-11
The social system theory of maternal attachment suggests that four different factors affect the quality of the mother-child relationship.

Even under ideal circumstances, there's still a period of adjustment when a new baby enters a family, and it can take some time for a satisfying give-and-take relationship to be worked out. This is the time when the attachment is forming. It's also the time when disruptions in attachment can take root. Such disruptions can range from mild to severe—from a somewhat "poor fit" to a situation in which child abuse occurs.

Since many factors are involved in the development of attachment, it follows that infant **temperament**—the inborn characteristics that account for differences in crying, cuddliness, activity level, and so on among babies—is not a critical factor in the relationship. Temperament characteristics at birth often don't last, and they don't predict the baby's later behavior nearly as well as the mother's parenting does (Egeland & Farber, 1984).

Infant temperament does predispose babies to express themselves in certain ways, however, regardless of the quality of their attachment. Two securely attached babies may respond differently when they're reunited with their parents after a separation, for example, one crying and the other calling out a happy greeting (Belsky & Rovine, 1988). Any baby who has a so-called difficult temperament may be "at risk for developing attachment problems," because such a baby needs parenting under ideal circumstances, which not all mothers can provide. When a relationship does seem to exist between early temperament and later poor attachment, it's probably because a difficult baby has challenged an overtaxed mother (Sroufe, Fox, & Pancake, 1983).

The social system explanation for maternal attachment focuses on the complex interweaving of many factors, both those that create stress and those that provide support. The balancing of these elements seems to "buffer" parenting, because if one part of the system is weak, another part can compensate for it. However, if something must go wrong in the system and only one part can be intact, it will be best if that part is the parent. The most vulnerable situation occurs when the only strong part of the system is the baby (Belsky, 1984).

The social system model is currently the favored explanation for maternal attachment. In its complexity, it reflects what we see in real families, where nothing happens in a vacuum or in isolation. It also makes sense from an ethological point of view. If we think of maternal attachment in terms of its role in preserving the species, we realize that nothing that important would be left to only one or two determining factors.

Implications of Early Attachment

Now that we've viewed attachment from both the baby's side and the mother's side, we need to consider how early attachment affects the child's emotional and social development. If a baby is found to be anxiously attached in the strange situation at 1 year, what kind of child might she be at 2 years? What will she be like later in life? Overall, studies have shown that the quality of the early attachment has long-lasting effects on the child's social and cognitive development. Table 8-2 gives a sampling of some of the studies that have reported on the later behavior of children whose attachment was evaluated in infancy.

As the table shows, children who were securely attached as infants grow into toddlers and preschoolers with a positive attitude, a friendly interest in other people, and a confident approach to problems. Children who were anxiously attached as infants, on the other hand, have a much harder time getting along in the world. Like Daniel, whom we met at the beginning of the chapter, they tend to become extremely difficult children who are negative and aggressive with people and tasks. They evoke reactions from others that keep them in negative relationships and that prevent them from developing more positive social behavior. According to one researcher, "not all anxiously attached children later show acting-out behavior problems, but a young child manifesting such problems in an extreme form is likely to have a history of avoidant or resistant attachment relationships" (Sroufe, 1981, p. 15). Taken together, these studies paint a rather bleak picture for children whose early attachments are anxious. If other factors or events trouble these children's lives (divorce, poverty, accidents, and so on), the picture becomes even more bleak.

The question, of course, is what can be done to help these children. The first line of defense should be prevention. Neonatal intensive care units in hospitals, for example, are making valiant efforts to involve parents in the care of even the smallest premature babies. This involvement helps parents learn to read their babies' signals and gain confidence in caring for them.

Hospital staff and other professionals can identify parents who may be at risk for parenting difficulties, even if their baby is full term. These parents can be offered counseling, parent support groups, or home visits by a nurse or social worker. Older children in the family can be provided with day care or

TABLE 8-2   Later Behaviors of Children Whose Attachment Was Assessed in Infancy

Behavior of Children Who Were Securely Attached as Infants	Behavior of Children Who Were Anxiously Attached as Infants	Current Age	Study
When separated from mothers, cried less and played more than anxiously attached peers.	Cried more, played less.	$1\frac{1}{2}$	Jacobson & Willie, 1984
More likely to engage in play session with stranger; IQ, language, and social relations intercorrelated and related to stimulating and positive maternal behavior.	Less likely to play with stranger.	2	Clarke-Stewart, Vanderstoep, & Killian, 1979
Engaged in more pretend and imaginative play; accepted mothers' suggestions in problem solving; showed more enthusiasm and persistence in problem solving.	Engaged in less symbolic play; ignored mothers' problem-solving suggestions.	2	Matas, Arend, & Sroufe, 1978
Approached problems with enthusiasm; were more persistent; used mothers to help them.	More likely to throw tantrums, act aggressively, ignore mothers' suggestions.	2	Sroufe, 1982
More likely to engage in purposeful behavior, be more involved in activities, and get along well with peers.	More likely to be aggressive with peers, to be on the fringes of activities, and to use materials in destructive rather than purposeful ways.	$3\frac{1}{2}$	Sroufe, 1982
More flexible in handling feelings and impulses; more independent in helping selves and managing social relations; more compliant; showed more empathy.	More likely to create problem behaviors and exhibit aberrant behavior.	3	Sroufe, 1981
Appropriately independent: sought contact with teacher when ill or hurt or when they needed help, but otherwise functioned autonomously.	Showed emotional dependence that interfered with autonomous functioning; needed teacher's constant attention and support.	3	Sroufe et al., 1983
	Toddlers in day care setting who were abused as infants showed anxious attachment; they were more aggressive, more inhibited in approach to adults, and more resistant to friendly overtures than peers who were not abused.	2–3	George & Main, 1981
At lower risk of becoming bullies or the victims of bullies at school during the preschool years.	High risk for becoming a bully or a victim of a bully at school during the preschool years.	4–5	Troy & Sroufe, 1987
At lower risk for developing attention-deficit disorder with hyperactivity in kindergarten.	At increased risk for developing attention-deficit with hyperactivity in kindergarten.		Jacobvitz & Sroufe, 1987

other programs to relieve the demands on the mother while she's dealing with a new baby. Extra support and help during the first few months can help a mother and baby get off to a good start. Additional programs are available for parents who are known to be at very high risk for parenting difficulties. One such program, designed for mothers with mental illness, is described in Knowledge in Action: Infants and Toddlers.

Even parents having no special problems and a typical baby need support in parenting, especially with a first child. Parenting classes and other support services are now offered by community agencies, local school districts, and private groups. Legislation for parental leave from jobs, which has recently been discussed at the federal level, is intended to ensure that parents have every chance to establish strong relationships with their children.

When preventive measures haven't been available or effective and a toddler or preschooler has obvious difficulties in relating to others, then help must be given directly to the child as well as to the parents (George and Main, 1981). Therapeutic day care is one way to help such children. Specially trained staff are necessary because the behavior of these children is hard to understand and manage. The following excerpt is an example of the kind of changes that can occur under the right circumstances (Sroufe, 1981, pp. 23–24):

> E.L. is a good example of this reachability of young disturbed children. His malicious, antisocial behavior, his apparent pleasure at other's distress, and his fearless contesting of wills with the teacher had all the marks of incipient sociopathy. His elaborate deviousness and his swaggering style seemed to confirm that he was beyond reach. But in fact, of course, no 4-year-old can "pull off" being a sociopath. And beneath the swagger was a desperately needy child . . . The teachers quickly learned to see opportunities for closeness with E.L. and explicitly disconfirmed his feelings of low self-worth by not rejecting him. As often as possible, the teachers prevented E.L. from engaging in hostile behavior. And when it was necessary to separate E.L. from other children, which was often the case early in the term, a teacher would stay with him. Having difficulty confirming his image of himself as bad, and being totally unable to confirm the belief that he was unworthy, E.L. had little choice but to change his behavior. He formed a strong attachment to the male teacher and made remarkable progress toward learning to meet his basic needs for closeness. . . . The "veneer of toughness" E.L. was building would have, of course, been much "thicker" in later years . . . But I have no doubt that in the preschool years the vast majority of these troubled children could be helped in a fundamental way toward healthier development. One unfortunate implication of our data is, however, that without help these children are likely to carry forward patterns of maladaptation into later childhood and even adulthood.

THE EMERGENCE OF PROSOCIAL BEHAVIOR

One of the characteristics we sometimes observe in securely attached children is **empathy**, the ability to understand how another person is feeling. Babies at first are purely self-centered. They're unable to realize that others have their own points of view and their own emotions. When children start to show empathy, we know that certain social understandings are beginning to dawn on them.

We see empathy when a child hugs or pats a friend who's crying. This type of behavior involves at least three things: (1) the ability to perceive the distress, (2) some idea of what might be causing the distress and what might be done to help, and (3) the willingness and emotional wherewithall to go to someone's aid. Researchers have been interested in when children start to notice that someone is sad or hurt, what they do once they notice, and what kinds of differences in capacity for empathy exist from one individual to another.

FIGURE 8-12
Prosocial behavior includes sharing, helping, cooperating, and showing empathy when someone else is distressed. Although toddlers don't very often go to the aid of a distressed person, that doesn't mean they don't have affectionate feelings toward each other. This warm hug may pave the way for a nurturant friendship later on.

One study reported that 12-month-olds responded to another's distress about half the time, although their response consisted of crying, frowning, or looking toward their mothers (Radke-Yarrow, Zahn-Waxler, & Chapman, 1983). They couldn't take any action, but they clearly noticed the distress and were aroused by it. By 18 months, children began to try to do something for the distressed person, such as touching or patting. By 2 years, children sometimes offered an object, said something supportive, or went to get help. If their first efforts didn't work, they tried something else. By 2 to 2 1/2 years, children could communicate verbally about emotions and knew how to provide comfort with words, such as, "Baby crying. Kiss. Make it better," "I love Mommy. I want to hold Mommy," and "No cry, Mom. It will be all right" (Bretherton et al., 1986, p. 536).

Although children are capable of empathic responses before the age of 2, whether they actually respond is a different matter. Children aged 2 to 4 at day care centers have shown surprisingly low rates of response to other children's distress. This may be because they expect the teachers to take care of the crying child, which they usually do. At one day care center children responded to only 26 percent of the incidents of crying and ignored the other 74 percent (Phinney, Feshbach, & Farver, 1986). But when they did respond, most of their actions were prosocial and included approaching, commenting, mediating, or consoling (see Table 8-3). In a few cases, children stared at or chastised the crying child. In another day care study, ignoring was again the most frequent response to other children's sad, angry, or hurt feelings (Denham, 1986). But there were enough incidences of sharing, helping, and looking

TABLE 8-3
Responses of Children to Peer Crying at Day Care Center

Category	Definition
Stare	Child stands near crying child and watches but takes no action and remains silent.
Approach	Child walks over to child and observes silently.
Comment	Child talks about the episode with another child or gives the teacher information about the child who is crying.
Mediate	Child tries to remove the source of pain or conflict or takes the crier to the teacher.
Console	Child offers physical or verbal comfort by patting or hugging the crier, offering an object, or apologizing when the child has caused the distress.
Ignore	Child appears unaware of or ignores crying, even when close by.

SOURCE: Compiled from Phinney, J. S., Feshback, N. D., & Farver, J. (1986). Preschool children's response to peer crying. Early Childhood Research Quarterly, 1(3), 211. Adapted by permission.

concerned to indicate that prosocial responses do begin to develop during these years.

As we see in these studies, there are wide differences in children's responses to others' distress. Children have also been observed to leave the scene where a child is crying or even attack the crying child (Radke-Yarrow, Zahn-Wexler, & Chapman, 1983). Varying responses among different children may reflect how much the child's own needs were being met at the moment, the reaction the child has received to prosocial gestures in the past, and the general level of nurturing among the adults serving as models for the child. (For a discussion of the effects of models on preschoolers' prosocial development, see Chapter 12).

Perhaps more important to children's development of empathy is their own attachment history. If a parent has been responsive to a child's distress, the child will tend to be more competent in responding to the distress of someone else (Roberts & Strayer, 1987). If the parent has been relatively non-nurturing, the child will tend to be unresponsive to others' distress (Crockenberg, 1985).

All in all, we can say that prosocial responding to others' distress *begins* in the late toddler period. It continues to develop throughout childhood and beyond. As children mature, they learn how to recognize that others are unhappy and what situations are likely to create unhappiness. They also become more skillful at providing comfort. But, as we have seen, the seeds of empathic understanding are present in children well before they're 2 years old.

BABY TO BABY: PEER INTERACTION AMONG INFANTS AND TODDLERS

Rebecca, a bouncy 16-month-old, arrives in the pediatrician's office in her mother's arms. Her mother finds a chair in the crowded waiting room and sits down with Rebecca on her lap. She reaches into her purse and takes out a small stuffed rabbit, which she places in front of Rebecca. But Rebecca doesn't grab it. In fact, she doesn't seem to know it's there. She's turned around, looking behind her, at a baby sitting on another mother's lap across the room. Rebecca's mother taps her softly on the head with the stuffed rabbit to get her attention. Rebecca turns around, sees the rabbit, and takes hold of it. But she doesn't play with it. Instead, she immediately turns around again to look at the same baby she was staring at before. Then she waves her rabbit-filled fist up and down as she squeals a greeting to her peer. The other baby looks serious for a moment, and then her face breaks into a smile too. She slaps her hands against her lap and gives out a friendly squeal in answer to Rebecca's greeting.

Babies notice and interact not just with adults but with other babies as well. Like Rebecca, they're curious and interested in what their peers might be like. But since they're not yet very skilled at social interactions—we've seen that infant-adult exchanges are kept going by the adult partner—babies' peer interactions are different from parent-child interactions. We look more closely now at this aspect of social and emotional development.

Signals, Responses, and Interaction

Babies start to watch other babies and send them social signals as early as 10 months of age. They might smile, laugh, or vocalize to them, more often than not from a distance. Or they might cry or fuss while watching another baby. Occasionally, they might touch or strike another baby (Eckerman, Whatley, & Kutz, 1975). Many times the interactions among infants and toddlers involve a toy. Toddlers often offer a toy to another child, reach for the toy the other child is playing with, or attempt to play with a toy while the other child is playing with it (Bronson, 1981). Some of the social signals observed in a group of toddlers are listed and defined in Table 8-4.

Of course, real social interaction requires not just a signal but also a response, and infants and toddlers aren't very adept at responding. By far their most frequent response to a social gesture from another infant or toddler is to ignore it (Bronson, 1981). They also might look at the other child or passively grasp an offered toy. Sometimes they hit, poke, or pull hair. Responses that seem to

TABLE 8-4
Social Signals Directed by Infants and Toddlers to Peers

Category	Definition
Offer	Child holds out a toy to peer.
Deposit	Child places an object in peer's lap or at peer's feet.
Offer-withdraw	Child holds out a toy to peer, then retracts it as peer starts to accept.
Join gesture	Child acts on peer's toy; e.g., child hits drum held by peer.
Play gestures	Examples included throwing a ball toward a peer, taking a book to a peer, pushing a rocking boat in which a peer sat, squatting near a peer to watch peer's play.
Affiliative gestures	Child kisses, pats, hugs peer.
Point to peer Reach for peer's toy Touch peer Touch peer's toy Smile/laugh Verbalizations	

SOURCE: Compiled from Bronson, W. C. (1981). Toddler's behaviors with agemates: Issues of interaction, cognition, and affect (pp. 49–52). Norwood, NJ: Ablex. Adapted by permission.

reciprocate the social intention of the other child are fairly rare in the first or second year of life.

When a child of this age does respond to a social gesture, it's most often a single response with no further interaction following. Sometimes a second "contact burst" occurs between the same two children, involving a different toy or theme. Parallel play, in which two children play with similar toys near each other, is very rare at this age, as are "contact chains," in which children engage in a series of back-and-forth actions and reactions—true social interaction (Bronson, 1981).

What we see, then, is that children up to about 2 years of age don't yet have much ability to sustain social interaction with peers. Interactions do increase when children are brought together more than once and have a chance to become acquainted with each other (Rubenstein & Howes, 1976; Mueller & Brenner, 1977). They also sometimes get caught up in **social games,** group activities that involve taking turns, repetition, and imitation, along with lots of smiling and laughing (Fein & Rivkin, 1986). The following examples of social games illustrate this typical kind of social interaction. In the first example, several children in a nursery get involved in crawling around together near a changing table (Drucker, 1975, pp. 521–522). In the second example, two 22-month-old boys discover the fascination of spinning a wheel on an overturned doll carriage (Fein, 1984, p. 97).

EXAMPLE 1:

John (16 months) . . . crawls under the changing table and pushes his leg through to Michelle, who is on the other side. She crawls into the bathroom and he follows her in; then he crawls out and she follows him, crawling out; he crawls through the curtain, past Alicia and out the other side of the table, turns around, looks back, and they're off. Michelle is playing peek-a-boo with him, and Orin goes under the table too. John crawls in and crawls right through the curtain—he laughs, seems to be having a great time. Then he sits there watching, continues

FIGURE 8-13
Infants and toddlers have limited understandings of group activities and are easily distracted, so moments of shared fun tend to be fleeting. But at least for the moment, these young toddlers are playing a game together and enjoying each other's company.

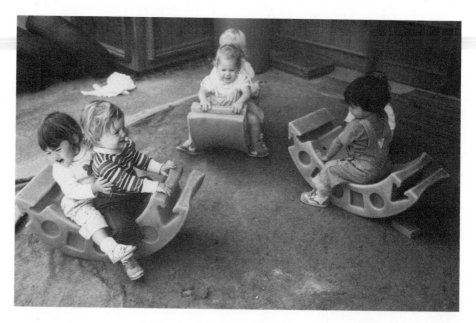

to watch, crawls toward Michelle, past her under the curtain and through to the other side of the table, turns around and laughs and talks to Alicia. Looks at Alicia and then crawls toward her, past her. He crawls into the bathroom and out, back under the table, sees Alicia, and they're laughing at each other. He crawls over next to her and laughs, sits up and laughs. She crawls in the other direction and he calls "Baba," but she doesn't look. He sits there quietly watching her, crawls out and back again, crawls through the curtain and sits up and smiles, crawls to Alicia and says "Hi," says a few things to her, and they are looking at each other, babbling at each other, talking to each other, and they both laugh.

EXAMPLE 2:

David approaches the overturned doll carriage. After exploring the spokes of the wheel, he discovers that the wheel can be made to spin. Sam wanders over, watching David's motion on the wheel and the resulting spin. David looks up at Sam, grinning. The wheel is no longer spinning, and Sam timidly puts his hand on it, giving it a push. He laughs, looks at David, who is smiling broadly. As the spin slows down, David gives it a push, and when it slows again, looks at Sam who again makes it spin. The children continue to take turns, but soon they begin to overlap. After five turns, Sam moves the wheel continuously, studying its motion. David fingers the spokes, then wanders off to another toy.

Certain aspects of these interactions made it possible for the children to sustain several rounds of play. The actions were repetitive, and they resembled games parents often play with their children—peek-a-boo, chase, and taking turns. Once the children established a **shared meaning**—an understanding about the content of the game (Brenner & Mueller, 1982)—they could coordinate and maintain the action. If pretend play had been involved, these children probably couldn't have managed it. Children between 2 to 3 years of age begin to be able to engage in pretend play (see Chapter 7), but play is fairly solitary until about age 3. Here is an example of solitary pretend play in a $2\frac{1}{2}$-year-old boy (Fein, 1984, p. 130):

> (Alan sits on a chair, a mop extended over the edge of the table. Richard, another child, is sitting on the floor nearby reading a book. Richard occasionally glances at Alan, but there is no interaction between them.)
> ALAN: "I'm gonna get a fish." (He raises the mop, commenting on his catch and the wetness of the sea water. Taking the mop with him, he crosses the room and picks up the broom.) "I want to row." (He tosses the mop and broom over his head.) "I got my boat over here." (Walks back to the table.) "Eee, ooh. I'm in the boat . . . I'm gonna get two fish, fish." (He extends both mop and broom over the edge of the table.)

Alan's play will gradually change to include others. At some point not too far in the future, Alan and Richard will be able to understand and agree on a joint project and go off into an imaginary world together.

Peer Interaction and Attachment History

We know that children's attachment history has a powerful effect on their social and emotional development. How does it specifically affect their relationships with other children? By the time children are in elementary school, some of them are popular and preferred as playmates and others are disliked and rejected. (Popularity in middle childhood is discussed in greater detail in Chapter 16.) The ones who are popular are often children who have positive, friendly personalities and who don't engage in much aggressive, hostile, or harassing behavior. This kind of social "style" seems to be related to a child's attachment history.

Toddlers who were securely attached as infants seem to be more positive toward other children than toddlers with histories of anxious attachment (Pastor, 1981). They're friendlier and more cooperative, more outgoing, and more flexible in struggles over toys. Toddlers with secure attachment histories also seem more comfortable with symbolic play (Slade, 1987). They can pretend play for longer periods of time, and they spend more time planning and creating make-believe scenes. Their greater ability to plan may be related to a greater capacity to delay action and control their impulses. These are skills that serve children well later on. Older children who are popular seem to be good at sizing up ongoing play situations and accurately timing their bids to be included.

There also seems to be a connection between attachment history and the tendency to be a bully or a victim. A recent study of 4- and 5-year-olds found that victimizers, or bullies, had anxious/avoidant attachment histories at 12 and 18 months (Troy & Sroufe, 1987). Furthermore, most victims—children who are consistently passive in the face of aggression—had anxious/ambivalent attachment histories. In fact, in all of the cases in which a child with an avoidant attachment history was paired with a child with an ambivalent attachment history, one victimized the other. Children with secure attachment his-

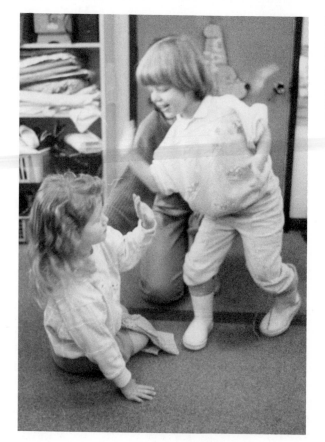

FIGURE 8-14
If her bullying behavior is part of an overall pattern, this girl may need help in changing her feelings about herself and others. Behavior problems often stem from an anxious attachment relationship.

tories tended not to be victims or victimizers—they didn't exploit or bully others, but they also didn't respond passively when others tried to bully them. We see again that the effects of early parent-child attachment reverberate on and on in the child's life, long after infancy and toddlerhood are over. We might even say they become embedded in the personality. Clearly, it's worth all our efforts to make sure the early attachment relationship is a good one.

SEX-TYPING IN INFANCY

Today, Benjamin is 4 weeks old. His mother puts him in his cradle for a nap and then sits down to write some thank-you notes for baby gifts. As she mentions each gift in the notes, it dawns on her that Benjamin received very different baby presents than his older sister received 3 years ago. Back then, there weren't any soft hammers or squeezable choo-choo trains, nor was there a sturdy metal dump truck to put away for later. And she couldn't recall a single item of clothing that had been blue. Everything was pink, white, or pale yellow. "Well," she thought, "the birth announcement did say, 'IT'S A BOY!'"

The first thing most parents ask about their baby is whether it's a boy or a girl (Itons-Peterson & Reddel, 1984). This information is proclaimed on the birth announcement along with other vital statistics like weight and length. There's no question but that everyone is interested in the baby's gender, but does this information then influence how they act toward the baby? Do people treat boy babies differently than girl babies? And if they do, what are the consequences of this different treatment?

We've all seen 2- or 3-year-olds acting "like boys" or "like girls." At a nursery school, for example, we would probably see more boys than girls playing with trucks and cars, building with blocks, or chasing each other outdoors. We would probably see more girls than boys caring for dolls, having tea parties, or playing house.

Where do they learn to act this way? It's clear that many of these apparently sex-appropriate behaviors aren't "built into" the biological make-up of boys and girls but are acquired during childhood. The question is whether children learn these different behaviors because their parents—consciously or unconsciously—treat them differently right from the day they're born.

How Adults See Boy and Girl Babies

Adults do seem to have different perceptions and expectations of boy and girl babies. A number of studies have shown this to be true. In some studies with actor babies (babies who were not the children of the adults being observed), adults were misled about the baby's sex and their reactions to the baby were observed. When a 6-month-old boy was presented as a girl to some women and as a boy to others, they played differently with him depending on how he had been labeled (Will, Self, & Datan, 1976). The women who thought he was a girl offered him a doll rather than a train or a fish. The women who thought he was a boy offered the train. In another study, adults encouraged "boys" to walk, crawl, or engage in physical activity more than they encouraged "girls" (Smith & Lloyd, 1978).

Parents perceive their own babies differently too, based on whether they're boys or girls. When one group of parents rated their newborns on a questionnaire, they made clear distinctions between the sexes. Although the babies didn't differ in their newborn measurements or their Apgar scores, girls were judged to be weaker, prettier, softer, and more delicate, and boys were judged to be firmer, more alert, stronger, hardier, and better coordinated. Fathers' ratings showed even more differences for the sexes than mothers' ratings did (Rubin, Provenzano, & Luria, 1974).

These studies confirm that adults do perceive and treat babies differently based on their sex, but some flaws are apparent in these experimental situations. When actor babies are involved, the brief interaction with a strange child might be expected to evoke a stereotypical reaction (Frisch, 1977). And when parents are new and inexperienced, they may be forced to rely on sex role stereotypes when answering questions about their newborns (Rubin et al., 1974). It's probably more important to know whether parents treat their own children in stereotypical ways over longer periods of time.

How Parents Treat Their Own Boy and Girl Babies

Many studies have found no differences in how parents treat their boy and girl babies, but other studies have turned up some differences. For example, fathers have been observed to play in more active, physical ways with their

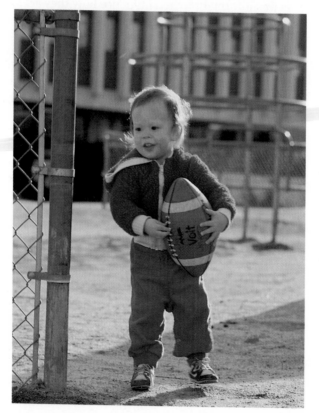

FIGURE 8-15
A football, a brisk day, warm sweats—what more could a boy want? By selecting a football as a toy, the parents of this 22-month-old tell him that outdoor physical play and rough-and-tumble games are acceptable behaviors for him. The perceptions and expectations of adults shape children's sex-typed behavior in subtle ways throughout childhood.

sons than with their daughters (Parke & Suomi, 1980; Power & Parke, 1982). Boys and girls have also been found to have different toys, most of them presumably bought by their parents (Fein et al., 1975). And mothers have been observed to respond differently to their sons' and daughters' emotions. When their infant girls showed pain, mothers matched their expressions with furrowed brows, but they almost totally ignored their infant boys' expression of pain. When their boys showed anger, on the other hand, mothers responded with expressions of concern and sympathy, but they met their girls' anger with a return of anger (Haviland, 1982). Although at this point we can only speculate about the effect of these reactions, it seems logical to conclude that they teach boys to hide their pain and show their anger and girls to show their pain and hide their anger—the stereotypes of "masculine" and "feminine" emotional expression.

The mixed results of these studies don't give us clear answers to our questions about the origin of the sex-typed behavior we see in children and adults. We can note that the studies that turned up no differences in how parents treat their boy and girl babies are the ones in which researchers were observing basic, daily caregiving and social interaction. The studies that did report differences focused on activities like playing and shopping for toys or clothes. It may be that the job of taking care of a baby is so demanding that it overrides all other considerations. Most parents are so busy that they treat their babies just as babies, not as girl babies or boy babies.

However, the few occasions when they do treat them differently may be important, such as when they respond to the expression of emotions. This is exactly the subtle kind of teaching and learning we would expect when we're dealing with something that seems so innate, so much a part of one's basic nature, as sex-typed behavior. Future research in many areas of child development, psychology, and biology will probably shed more light on how boys and girls come to adopt the behaviors that fit the sex roles accepted in their society.

OVERVIEW

When infancy and toddlerhood are over, a 3-year-old has emerged. Most of us think of this child as very, very young, and of course she is. But a lot has happened in those three years, a lot that will influence the child and those she touches in all the years to come. It isn't that what she is at this age is impossible to change in any way—it isn't. But change will come hard and will take great effort, if the course now set is to be altered. What is already there will need to be—and will demand to be—taken into account.

We would run into the most difficulty trying to

alter the effects of a history of anxious attachment, although even this is not impossible. And apparently it is well worth the effort to try, given the wide-ranging implications of a child's attachment history. As we have seen, general stance toward life, personality characteristics, patterns of peer interaction, responses to others' feelings, and general cognitive functioning are influenced by attachment history. It's safe to say that not a single other aspect of a child's experience will be able to exert such a profound influence on the child's life. And that's worth thinking—and doing—quite a lot about.

CHAPTER REVIEW

ATTACHMENT

- Attachment, the emotional tie between infant and mother (or other primary caregiver) is a crucial factor in the social and emotional development of the growing child.
- Early theories of attachment assumed that infants develop a preference for the adult who feeds them. Both psychoanalytic and early behavioral theories were based on notions of drive reduction and secondary reinforcement.
- Ethological explanations of attachment focus on the aspects of this behavior that would have enhanced chances of survival as the species evolved. They suggest that adults who are skilled in reading and responding appropriately to babies' signals are the ones most likely to foster healthy attachments.
- Harlow's study of surrogate mothers among monkeys discredited the secondary reinforcement explanation of attachment. Ethologists have used this study as support for their view.
- Infant attachment is assessed in a standard laboratory procedure known as the "strange situation," which highlights the way infants use their mothers for both safety and exploration.
- Three basic patterns of attachment—one normal and two deviant—emerged from experiments involving the strange situation: secure, anxious/ambivalent, and anxious/avoidant. Securely attached infants use their mothers as a home base from which to explore and as a source of comfort when they're distressed. Infants exhibiting the anxious/ambivalent pattern show extreme distress when separated from their mothers but can't accept comfort from them when they return. Infants exhibiting the anxious/avoidant pattern rarely interact with their mothers during play and show no distress when separated.
- Crying, gazing, and averting the gaze are among the earliest social signals at the infant's disposal. Smiling emerges by 2 months of age, apparently as a result of maturational rather than social factors.
- The child usually exhibits "stranger anxiety"—wariness of unfamiliar adults—between 6 and 18 months of age.
- It has been suggested that the anxious/ambivalent pattern of attachment may result when parents fail to respond contingently to a baby's signals. The anxious/avoidant pattern may result when parents routinely respond inappropriately to a baby's signals.
- Social referencing—scanning the face of a familiar and trusted person to pick up information about a new situation—begins at about 9 months. Infants can discriminate facial expressions by the time they are 4 or 5 months old, but they don't know their meaning until they are between 6 and 9 months old.
- On the parent's side of attachment, the hormonal theory suggests that maternal attachment is a result of bonding with the baby in the first hours after birth. This theory has not been supported by research.
- A mother's history has an effect on her parenting behavior, but it's not the sole determining factor in the kind of attachment she forms with her baby.
- The currently accepted social system theory suggests that many factors interact with each other to influence attachment. Characteristics of the parent seem to have a stronger influence on parenting behavior than do characteristics of the baby or those of the environment. Temperament—the child's inborn characteristics—can influence the attachment relationship, but it's not necessarily a crucial factor.
- Children with anxious attachment histories are at a higher risk of becoming emotionally dependent, aggressive, noncompliant, easily frustrated in the face of challenging tasks, and inattentive and hyperactive.

THE EMERGENCE OF PROSOCIAL BEHAVIOR

- Signs of empathy—the understanding of another person's feelings—reflect the child's social and emotional development.
- At 12 months, babies tend to respond to the distress of others by showing distress themselves. By 18 months, they begin to focus on the distressed person and try to provide comfort. By 2 years, children share, help, and look concerned often enough to indicate that the seeds of empathy are present by this age.
- When parents have been nurturant and responsive to their child's distress, the child is better at responding to others' distress.

PEER INTERACTION AMONG INFANTS AND TODDLERS

- Children between 12 and 24 months of age have a repertoire of social signals that they can use with peers, but true social interaction is rare in this age group.
- Children under 3 years enjoy social games, which involve actions familiar to them from their games and play with adults.
- Pretend play is usually solitary prior to the age of 3.

- Social "style" seems to be related to attachment history. Toddlers with secure attachment histories are more positive toward peers than are toddlers with anxious attachment histories. They engage in more planning during pretend play, sustain their play episodes for longer periods of time, and tend to be neither bullies nor victims in later social interactions.

SEX-TYPING IN INFANCY

- Sex role development is the learning that results in children's acting "like boys" or "like girls."
- Adults perceive babies differently, depending on whether they're labeled boys or girls.
- When basic caregiving is examined, few, if any, gen-

der-related differences in how parents treat their babies have come to light.
- An important area in which boys and girls do seem to be treated differently is emotional expression.

KEY TERMS

attachment	anxious/ambivalent attachment	stranger anxiety	empathy
drive reduction		social referencing	social games
secondary reinforcer	anxious/avoidant attachment	separation distress	shared meaning
preprogrammed		bonding	
ethology	social smile	critical period	
secure attachment	endogenous smile	temperament	

SUGGESTIONS FOR FURTHER READING

Bretherton, I., & Water, E. (1985). Growing points of attachment theory and research. *Monographs of the Society for Research in Child Development, 50,* 1–2.
This research collection includes studies on topics such as social development in institutionalized infants, the impact of out-of-home infant care, and culture and attachment.

Izard, C. E. (1982). *Measuring emotions in infants and children.* New York: Cambridge University Press.
This book provides detailed information about ways to measure infant emotions and includes many pictures of babies' facial expressions.

Plomin, R., & Dunn, J., (Eds.). (1986). *The study of temperament.* Hillsdale, NJ: Lawrence Erlbaum.
A number of chapters in this book treat different aspects of temperament—the presumably inborn personality characteristics of children.

Stern, D. (1977). *The first relationship: Infant and mother.* Cambridge, MA: Harvard University Press.
A very readable book about the development of attachment; includes material on behaviors of the infant and the caregiver and things that can go wrong in mother-infant interactions.

INFANTS AND TODDLERS

"Good morning! How are you doing today?"

"Good morning! I'm doing just fine! How about you?"

Jasmine and Monica exchange greetings as they leave their homes with their babies. Jasmine has a 6-month-old daughter, Jenna, and works full time for a large advertising agency. Her next-door neighbor, Monica, has a 9-month-old daughter, Ellie. Monica is a full-time, at-home mother right now, although she worked as a scientist in a major research center before Ellie was born.

Jasmine is headed for work, but first she'll take Jenna to the day care center that her advertising company owns and operates as an employee benefit. Monica is setting out for the early stimulation program her daughter attends three mornings a week. Ellie, retarded at birth, is enrolled in a special program intended to maximize her potential. Monica may leave Ellie with the program staff while she runs errands, or she may stay at the center to observe the staff as they work with her daughter. Once a week, the center holds an informal discussion session for parents and staff, and she often attends that. Monica relies heavily on the program for support in raising her daughter and for respite from the extra stress of having a child with developmental delays. Jasmine also relies heavily on Jenna's program for the day care that allows her to lead the life she's always dreamed of, as both a mother and a business executive.

Infant and toddler education and care programs can serve many different purposes. Some parents use them because their children have special needs. Others use them as a way to nurture their child's development and provide stimulation that's not otherwise available in the child's environment. Still others use them because they work full time or they're finishing their own education.

Regardless of a program's specific purpose, the overall goal of infant and toddler programs is to provide the best conditions for the development of their young clientele. How do the people who design these programs know what the best conditions are? They're guided by the kind of research discussed in earlier chapters of this book. Many programs have made the development of cognitive abilities and language skills a top priority. They include moderately novel stimulation in their activities to keep babies' interest and to promote learning. They're sensitive to the importance of responsive caregiving when they're with the children. These programs increasingly reflect the latest findings in child development research.

Infant and toddler education and care programs are only one "real-life" area in which child development research has important implications and applications. The previous chapters have discussed many kinds of research and described many facets of knowledge about children. This chapter describes knowledge in action—how that knowledge about children can be used. Knowledge gained from research makes it possible to plan appropriate education and care programs for children. It provides the tools to assess children for possible developmental problems. It guides and supports adults' efforts to keep children healthy and safe, to feed and toilet train them, and to provide them with appropriate toys and playthings. These areas of applied knowledge are addressed in this Knowledge in Action section.

INFANT AND TODDLER EDUCATION AND CARE PROGRAMS

Twenty years ago, only 25 percent of mothers with babies under 1 year of age were in the work force in this country. In 1988 the figure was at 53 percent (Hymes, 1989). Financial pressures, changing social conditions, new cultural ideals, and special needs all contribute to the ever-growing demand for out-of-the-home education and care for young children.

Over the years, some programs have become prominent as models of outstanding care for both the average child like Jenna and the child with special needs like Ellie. Here, we discuss five such programs, which have focused on the following concerns: (1) how to provide appropriate day care; (2) how to prevent language and cognitive delays in children who live in poverty conditions; (3) how to assist parents of children with disabilities; and (4) how to help parents whose personal problems put their children's emotional development at risk.

The five programs described here are aimed at children who are economically disadvantaged, who have cognitive or physical disabilities, or who are at risk for developmental delays and emotional difficulties because of a parent's severe mental problems. They've provided models for many of the care programs we see today, both for typical and for atypical children.

The Florida Parent Education Infant and Toddler Program

The Florida Parent Education Infant and Toddler program, begun in 1966 at the University of Florida, was designed to help children whose families were economically disadvantaged. Developed by Dr. Ira Gordon, the program emphasizes parent education. Parents are trained to teach their own babies, rather than taking the babies to a program where professional educators teach them. This is a common feature when programs serve children who may be

FIGURE 1
As the demand for good child care has grown, the number of programs available has increased and the quality of their facilities has improved. One important feature of a model program is an outdoor area with safe, sturdy equipment, opportunities to improve motor skills, and lots of space to play.

at risk for developing delays because of a family's economic situation. Focusing on the parents as the babies' primary teachers makes it more likely that the effects of the program will be carried over into the home and will continue after the child "graduates" from the program.

RESEARCH UNDERPINNINGS. Dr. Gordon relied heavily on Piaget's conception of sensorimotor intelligence when he developed the program. He devised activities for parents to engage in with their babies that would support the babies' cognitive growth. He especially wanted to help parents solve what has been called "the problem of the match" (Hunt, 1965)—the need to give children experiences that challenge them but that don't go beyond their level of skill and understanding.

Dr. Gordon also recognized that babies should learn that they can make things happen. In Chapter 8, we discussed what happens when babies don't get responses to their efforts—they develop "learned helplessness," the feeling that what they do has no effect on the world. Dr. Gordon designed activities that would help babies gain feelings of mastery and competence.

SAMPLE ACTIVITIES. Two sample activities from the Florida Parent Education program demonstrate how Dr. Gordon translated research findings into specific activities for babies and their parents. The first is called "Look Ma, No Hands." Here are the instructions (Gordon, 1970, p. 16):

> Baby will be delighted to learn he can make some things happen, even when he can't touch them.

> You can use either the cradle gym, or you can fasten a mobile to the crib, or you can tie some colorful pieces of cording or other fabrics to the top bar of the crib over the baby's feet, where he can see them.

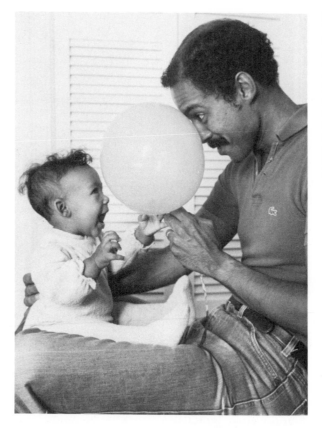

FIGURE 2
The simplest interaction can be a delightful challenge for a baby. The game of spotting Dad through a balloon helps this 7-month-old with her budding grasp of object permanence. However, a different kind of peek-a-boo would be preferable and just as much fun. Babies shouldn't play with balloons because they can bite, swallow, and choke on them.

Bounce the crib mattress with your hand near his feet to make the objects move.

Take one of his feet, and gently tap it on the mattress to set the objects in motion. He'll see that movements on the mattress cause an interesting action, and he can do it on his own, when he wants to.

This activity enables babies to act on their environment and see the effects of their actions. You'll recognize the action and effect as an example of Piaget's sensorimotor Stage 3, secondary circular reactions.

The second activity is called "Hide and Seek." The instructions are as follows (Gordon, 1970, pp. 32–37):

Begin with a simple game using a toy and some soft covering material, such as a blanket. Attract his attention to the toy and then partly hide it under the blanket so that baby can still see a part of it.

Then say, "Where did it go?" "Find the toy."

If he's puzzled and doesn't seem to know how to retrieve it, show him how. If he ignores the toy after it is hidden, play with it yourself in front of him, but don't demand his attention or any action. He will, on his own, get interested in what you are doing. Partly hide it again until he's able to get it himself.

Play the same game, but hide the toy completely under the soft materials.

Repeat this for fun a number of times and then leave the child with both toy and blanket . . .

A third approach to hide-and-seek is to place one of his favorite objects in a box or other container where he can no longer see it. Be sure the container is easy to open. Ask him, "Can you get it now?" . . .

Remember, don't tease, don't frustrate and don't force. Watch for the child "turning off."

When he discovers the toy is in the container, he'll enjoy putting it in, closing the box, opening it, taking it out, and then he can be left to repeat this for his own continued learning and amusement.

This activity involves object permanence, another concept from Piaget's work. The instructions emphasize various aspects of parent-child interaction discussed in earlier chapters—verbalization while the parent interacts with the baby; careful observation of the baby's behavior; variation in the kind and level of stimulation given; and responsiveness to the baby's signals. All of these components contribute to a healthy, nurturing parent-child relationship. The relationship, in turn, supports the baby's cognitive development.

The Mother-Child Home Program

As the name implies, the Mother-Child Home Program is based in the home rather than at a center or school. This orientation reflects the program's philosophy that the parent is the child's first and most important teacher. Having the program at home gives the parent the opportunity to learn effective ways

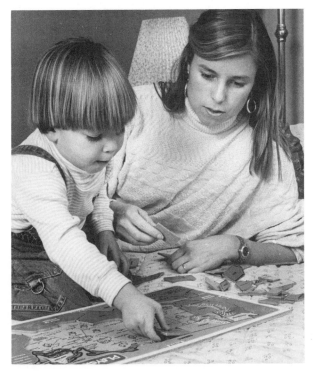

FIGURE 3
A wooden puzzle gives this toddler practice with both his problem-solving abilities and his fine motor skills. Equally important is the positive interaction he's having with an interested adult. This is the kind of activity at the heart of the Mother-Child Home Program.

TABLE 1
Criteria for VISM Toys

Criteria	Names and Descriptions of Toys	Criteria Met by Toys
Verbal 1. Induces language 2. Permits language	*Block cart* Wooden wagon, colored blocks with holes, rods that fit into holes	All but 6, 15
Perceptual 3. Strong colors 4. Geometric forms 5. Space organization 6. Size differences 7. Sound differences 8. Tactile differences 9. Form matching	*Hammer and pegs* Pegs fixed into wooden bench can be pounded through to under side; bench can then be reversed	All but 5, 6, 11, 13
	Mail box Copy of corner mail box; colored wood beads are dropped through top holes into bin	All but 15
Motor 10. Specific skills 11. Fitting parts 12. Hitting 13. Pulling 14. Lifting 15. Diffuse motor discharge	*Transportation puzzle* Jigsaw puzzle, each piece a different vehicle	All but 7, 12, 13, 15
	Two plush hand puppets Animals, movable mouths	All but 5, 6, 9, 12, 15
	Circus puzzle Jigsaw puzzle of circus tent, circus scene beneath	All but 7, 12, 13, 15
Conceptual 16. Problem solving 17. Intelligible goal 18. Intrinsic reward 19. Imaginative uses 20. Social concepts 21. Sex neutrality 22. Ethnic neutrality	*Cash register* Simple copy with cash drawer and bell activated by crank	All
Other 23. Low anxiety potential 24. Safety 25. Durability 26. Easy care for mother	*House puzzle* Jigsaw puzzle of street and outside of house; inside of house and buried *utilities* shown under pieces (fewer pieces than same puzzle used with 3-year-olds)	All but 7, 12, 13, 15

SOURCE: Levenstein, P. (1977). The mother-child home program. In M. C. Day and R. Parker (Eds.), The preschooler in action: Exploring early childhood programs (2nd ed) (pp. 28–49). Boston: Allyn & Bacon. Copyright © 1977 Phyllis Levenstein. Reprinted by permission of the author.

of interacting with the child. It also recognizes that children are often more receptive to learning experiences if they're introduced in a familiar setting by someone they know. This program, developed by Phyllis Levenstein in New York State, is also aimed at economically disadvantaged families.

PROGRAM ORGANIZATION AND ACTIVITIES. The Mother-Child Home Program is for toddlers. Parent and child enroll when the child is age 2, and they stay in the program until the child is age 4 (one year into the preschool period). The curriculum, or content of the program, focuses on language and conceptual development. Each week during the school year, a trained home visitor comes to the home with a toy or book that the child can keep forever. The home visitor reads the book or shows the child how to play with the toy, at the same time encouraging the parent to participate in the session.

The criteria for selecting the toys and books are listed in Tables 1 and 2, along with suggested toys and titles. These materials are called Verbal Interaction Stimulus Materials (VISM) because their primary purpose is to promote

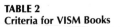

TABLE 2
Criteria for VISM Books

Criteria	Titles and Authors of Books by Subject Groups (in Order of Presentation)
1. Contents geared to children's age and interest; interesting to mothers; leads to verbalized associations; widens experience 2. High literary standards 3. Language simple, rhythmic, with some repetition 4. Reading level within ability of all mothers 5. Content, illustrations, and general format attractive to both sexes and any ethnic group 6. Illustrations profuse, large, colorful, detailed, rich source of labeling and classification 7. Low anxiety potential 8. Durability	*2- and 3-Year-Olds* Runhardt, D. *Pat the Bunny* Brown, M. W. *Good Night Moon* Rojankovsky, F. (Illus.) *The Tall Book of Mother Goose* Keats, E. J. *The Snowy Day* Zion, G. *All Falling Down* Krauss, R. *The Carrot Seed* Keats, E. J. *Peter's Chair* Eastman, P. D. *Are You My Mother?* Keats, E. J. *Whistle for Willie* *2-Year-Olds* Tresselt, A. *Rainy Drop Splash* Tresselt, A. *Wake Up Farm* Gag, W. *Millions of Cats* *3-Year-Olds* Brown, M. W. *The Runaway Bunny* Seuss, Dr. *The Cat in the Hat* MacGregor, E. *Theodore Turtle*

SOURCE: Levenstein, P. (1977). The mother-child home program. In M. C. Day and R. Parker (Eds.), The preschooler in action: Exploring early childhood programs (2nd ed) (pp. 28–49). Boston: Allyn & Bacon. Copyright © 1977 Phyllis Levenstein. Reprinted by permission of the author.

language development. The toys and books are classics, available today in toystores, bookstores, and libraries and present in most preschools.

PROGRAM RESULTS. Children enrolled in this program have gained long-term positive benefits. They do better in elementary school than similar children not enrolled in the program. We can pick out various aspects of the program that probably contribute to its success—the emphasis on the parent's participation in the child's play, the provision of appropriate toys and books, the focus on reading.

Another factor for success is probably the age of the children. Toddlers are energetic, busy, willful—even the most resourceful parents don't always know what constructive experiences to offer them. The program gives concrete ideas and models of positive interaction at an important time in children's lives. It begins in time to help set the stage for learning during the toddler and preschool years. The model provided by the Mother-Child Home Program is widely used today.

The Family Development Research Program

Like the first two programs discussed here, the Family Development Research Program was designed to help children from economically disadvantaged families. But unlike those programs, the program is center based in this model. Babies are brought by their parents to an infant-toddler classroom where trained teachers work with and care for them. Parent education and support are also an important part of the program, although the program assumes that adults other than parents can play a vital role in providing education and care for young children. The Family Development Research Program, developed at

TABLE 3
The Family Development Research Program Infant Curriculum: Selected Items

Development of prehension skills

- Reaching for toys
- Shaking toys
- Grasping and handling objects of different sizes and shapes

Development of object permanence

- Playing peek-a-boo
- Finding toys after visible displacements under screens
- Putting toys into containers and finding toys under containers

Development of means for achieving desired environmental ends

- Reaching over obstacles for toys
- Using a string vertically to obtain a toy tied to the string
- Putting a chain into a box

Development of new schemes in relation to objects

- Hitting two toys together
- Stretching an elastic bracelet
- Adorning oneself (with pop-it bead necklace, for example)
- Drinking from a cup

Development of causality (understanding the distinction between act and external result)

- Ringing a bell to make a sound
- Turning a key to make a mechanical toy run
- Working a jack-in-the-box

Developmental achievement of the construction of the object in space (conceiving of a single, objective space within which all objects are contained and interrelated)

- Finding a toy by its sound
- Bunching a chain and putting it into a box
- Nesting several boxes
- Creeping around a barrier, such as a rocking chair, to retrieve a ball rolled underneath the chair

Development of gestural imitation

- Imitating a familiar visible gesture, such as pat-a-cake
- Imitating a familiar invisible gesture, such as an eye wink

Development of verbal learning

- Imitating baby sounds
- Imitating familiar sounds, such as "la-la"
- Labeling objects, people, feelings, actions, places, times, etc.

Physical development and exercises

- Stretching and flexing legs
- Doing somersaults
- Bouncing body to music
- Bending to pick up objects

Development of sense organs

- Producing and listening to sounds (e.g., music boxes, rattles, wrist bells, records, tapes)
- Producing tactile experiences (e.g., feel boxes, fur collars, nylon net, styrofoam)
- Tasting new foods and new textures of familiar food

SOURCE: Adapted from Lally, R., & Honig, A. (1977). *The Family Development Research Program,* in C. Day & R. Parker (Eds.), The preschool in action *(pp. 149–194). Boston: Allyn & Bacon.*

Syracuse University in the 1970s, has been a model for many infant day care programs begun since that time. Jenna's day care center, for example, could have been modeled on this program.

RESEARCH UNDERPINNINGS. The Family Development Research Program is based on the cognitive theories of Piaget and the social-emotional theories of Erikson. Program planners also relied on research in infant language development and in attachment. Every baby is given one primary caregiver, who takes care of most of the baby's feeding, diapering, and comforting. This ensures that the babies receive responsive care from someone who knows them well. Each adult has responsibility for four babies.

PROGRAM ACTIVITIES. The program emphasizes the importance of daily caregiving routines, such as feeding, diapering, and putting the baby to sleep. It also stresses responsive social encounters and in-context language experiences. By making the daily "living" and "loving" environment a rich learning environment as well, the program integrates socioemotional and cognitive development. For example, caregivers are reminded to talk to babies when they change their diapers, and mirrors are put on the walls by changing tables so babies can see themselves. An outline of the "formal" infant program, for children between 6 and 15 months of age, is given in Table 3. (Detailed descriptions of infant activities are given in Honig & Lally, 1972).

The Marin County, California, Program for Atypical Infants

Sponsored as part of the community mental health services, this early intervention program was designed for babies with special needs. It serves physically handicapped and mentally retarded babies, emotionally disturbed babies, and babies who are at risk because of such factors as low birth weight or mental illness in their mother (Nielsen et al., 1975).

The program includes several subprograms. There are weekly home visits, group meetings for parents and children, and group meetings for children alone. Children enrolled in the last subprogram come to the center several mornings a week for a therapeutic day care program.

Development in many areas is emphasized—sensorimotor, language, motor, and feeding. To support sensory development, for example, teachers provide various tactile experiences. Childen can walk (or crawl) on carpeted and tiled areas of the floor and on grass and foam rubber as well. They're given various materials to feel—wet and dry sand, corn meal, warm and cool water. Babies are allowed to play with edible materials such as pudding, whipped cream, or mashed potatoes.

To encourage language awareness, teachers introduce new sounds for back-and-forth language play and associate words with actions and objects. To support motor development, they provide appropriate activities, depending on individual babies' handicaps—swinging one in a blanket or hammock, for example, and helping another explore a space. Teachers also help parents recognize the different signals their handicapped babies may give, and they encourage them not to give up when responses aren't typical.

Ellie attends a program similar to this one. As an atypical infant with moderate retardation, she has not yet begun to sit up independently or use her hands to explore the world in the active way that normally developing infants will. Her approach to the world is quite passive, both because she lacks the motor skills needed for active exploration and because her retardation makes her less curious and less capable of thinking of things to do.

One infant caregiver works directly with Ellie, trying to encourage her to respond to and act on the world. One morning, for example, Ellie's caregiver held a brightly colored rattle in front of her and shook it. The color of the rattle, as well as its sound, caught Ellie's attention. When she looked at it, the caregiver raised her hand so that she could take hold of the rattle. Then she moved the rattle toward Ellie's mouth so she could mouth it. After giving Ellie a few minutes to explore the rattle in this way, the caregiver moved it so that it was a little bit out of the direct range of Ellie's gaze. Then she shook the rattle again. Ellie turned her head and eyes to catch sight of the rattle, and the caregiver again raised Ellie's hand to the toy. All these maneuvers are designed

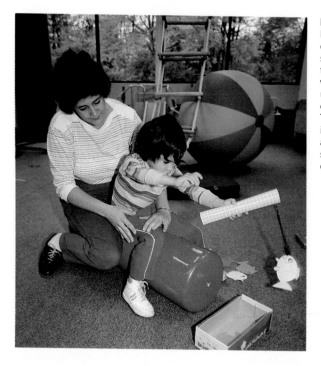

FIGURE 4
Programs for children with disabilities are designed to serve their needs. Trained teachers or therapists often work with children individually on special equipment or in appropriate activities. This game provides practice in balance and coordination and enhances the child's sense of control and competence.

to increase Ellie's repertoire of actions on objects and to raise her interest in attending to and exploring the world around her.

The Threshold Mothers' Project

This program, funded by the National Institute of Mental Health and developed by a psychiatric rehabilitation agency in Chicago, focuses on the children of mentally ill mothers. These children are more likely than other children to have attachment disruptions and cognitive impairments. The program has three facets: It treats the mothers alone, the babies alone, and the mothers and babies together (Musick, Clark, & Cohler, 1981).

Mothers attend weekly therapy sessions, receive training in parenting, and take a child development course. Children attend a therapeutic nursery five mornings a week. Language and emotional development are the main concerns here. Once a week, each mother participates in the nursery program, where she can observe the positive interactions modeled by the staff.

Every few months, each mother-child **dyad** (pair) participates in a video-taping session. The staff analyzes the tapes with the mother, helping her understand her interactions with her child. These tapes can be used to sensitize the mother to her child's cues and help her respond to the child's needs.

Day Care for Children without Special Needs

The five programs just described are designed for children with special needs of one kind or another. But what about the children like Jenna—ordinary children from ordinary families who need day care because their parents work? This is the fastest-growing population of children in need of educational programs today and the group most teachers of young children are likely to have in their programs. What are their needs, and what are their programs like?

Jenna's day care center has a large playroom for each age group. In Jenna's infant room, there are many toys, including colorful plastic balls; push and pull toys; a "climbing/crawling" area with ramps and tunnels; simple shape boxes; some picture books with cardboard pages; a low, unbreakable mirror; and numerous rattles and other manipulatives that babies can feel, look at, and mouth.

The infant caregivers spend their day playing with and talking to the infants, feeding them, and rocking or patting them to sleep. Each infant is assigned to one of the three caregivers for primary care, although all caregivers interact with all the babies. Because different babies are on different schedules, all these activities go on throughout the day. Not until the babies graduate to the toddler classroom is there a daily schedule for eating, playing, and napping that's more or less followed by all the children.

Finding suitable day care is a difficult problem for many working parents. More and more businesses are providing some help, either in the form of company-run centers like Jenna's or in the form of information and referral services to help parents locate appropriate care. Other companies provide day care vouchers—payments the parents can use toward day care services not associated with the company. Voucher programs typically pay only a portion of the day care costs and are adjusted to give more help to workers with lower salaries. Some employers give special consideration to parents whose children are sick and can't go to day care, allowing them time off or flexible hours (see Public Policy Focus—Sick Child Day Care).

PUBLIC POLICY FOCUS

Sick Child Day Care

When children get sick, as they often do in the first few years of life, someone has to take care of them. This isn't a problem when a parent is available at home. But when parents are working and children normally go to day care centers, their illnesses pose a difficult problem for parents, day care regulators, and public health officials.

Several strategies have been suggested to solve this dilemma for working parents. Obviously, very sick children need and deserve to have their parents' attention, and work policies need to be flexible enough to handle such situations. But when children are just mildly sick—when they need a quieter day or a little more attention than is available in their usual day-care setting—other arrangements may be possible. Some solutions that have been suggested include the following:

- *Special rooms within day care centers.* These rooms would keep sick children isolated from other children in the center and would be staffed by a specially trained person. Several children could be accommodated in the same room. This solution has the advantage of keeping sick children in their regular day care center.

- *At-home sick child services.* The child would stay at home but would be cared for by a visiting adult rather than by a parent. Although expensive, this solution would allow children to remain in their familiar home environment.
- *Special family or group care facilities for sick children.* Sick children would go to a special child care facility that served their day care center or day care home. These facilities would be attended only by sick children. This solution would be the most stressful for the child. No one likes to be taken care of in an unfamiliar place by unfamiliar people. A sick child is likely to find this arrangement especially intolerable (Fredericks & Kendrick, 1985).

Children are sensitive and vulnerable when they're sick, and a quiet, familiar environment helps them recover their sense of well-being. Although the suggestions listed here have some promise, none of them meets all the needs of the sick child. The best solution probably is for employers to allow parents to take time off or work flexible hours so they can stay at home and care for their sick children themselves.

RESEARCH FOCUS

How Does Day Care Affect Parent-Child Attachment?

It used to be that textbooks about child development hardly mentioned mother-child interaction. Freud's work in the early part of the twentieth century changed all that. Now we know that the mother-child relationship is crucial to all areas of development, and many people have wondered how appropriate full-time day care is for young infants. There isn't any question but that this practice runs counter to traditional doctrines of motherhood and domesticity in our society. Mothers have long been idealized as the keepers of a refuge against a cold outside world. Now women are shrugging off this role. They're going out into the world, and they're taking their babies with them (Lasch, 1977; Grubb & Lazerson, 1983). What effect do these new practices have on attachment?

HOW DOES DAY CARE AFFECT ATTACHMENT?

Researchers interested in how day care affects attachment posed the question, Is there a difference in attachment behavior between babies reared at home and babies in full-time day care? One of the first studies to document such a difference used the strange situation to assess attachment behavior in two groups of babies (Blehar, 1974). In this study, more of the children in the day care group than in the home-reared group were judged to be anxiously attached to their mothers.

Many studies followed (Brookhart & Hock, 1976; Doyle, 1975; Kagan, 1978). Overall, they showed no significant deleterious effects from the day care experience (Clarke-Stewart & Fein, 1983; Rutter, 1981). But studies continued; and in the early 1980s, two studies again found a difference in attachment in day care versus home-reared infants (Schwartz, 1983; Vaughn, Gove, & Egeland, 1980). Day care infants showed a greater tendency to avoid their mothers upon reunion after separation. Several recent studies have found similar differences between day care and home-reared infants (Belsky, 1988).

If you recall from Chapter 8, anxious attachment in babies is a worrisome thing. Older children with histories of anxious attachment have more social and cognitive problems than other children. They're more noncompliant toward adults and more aggressive toward peers. These correlates of early attachment his-

Special equipment can provide safety and comfort for very young infants in day care, such as this sleeping area for babies up to a few months of age. But full-time day care is not recommended for babies less than 1 year old.

tory make the discovery of anxious attachment in day care infants especially troubling.

HOW STRONG IS THE EVIDENCE? HOW SERIOUS IS THE PROBLEM?

These concerns do need to be put into perspective. In studies where increased avoidance has been found, 50 percent of the full-time day care infants did *not* show more avoidance toward their mothers upon reunion than home-reared infants. Thus, it seems that it's not the daily separation itself that produces the increased avoidance.

It also appears that increased avoidance is not correlated with the type of day care facility the child attends (Belsky, 1988). Increases in avoidant behavior

---

Even though the demand for day care for children without special needs is a fact, there's considerable debate over its merits. Many people question the wisdom of separating infants from their mothers for long periods of time early in life. (For a discussion of the day care debate, see Research Focus—How Does Day Care Affect Parent-Child Attachment?) In our society, where care has traditionally been provided for infants and toddlers only when their famhave been found in high-quality, university-based programs, in family day care homes, and in day care centers. Apparently, something other than the care itself is responsible for the various effects. (An alternative explanation is that the quality or location of the day care experience *is* responsible for the different effects, but our current measures of quality aren't fine-tuned enough to pick up these differences.)

What accounts for the different attachment patterns found among day care infants? Some researchers point to what they call **family process variables**—the different attitudes, beliefs, and patterns of behavior in different families, such as the mother's attitude toward working or her assumptions about how her working affects her child. For example, one researcher suggests that a mother who feels guilty about working might try to pack more interaction into the short amount of time she has available to spend with her baby. This concentrated dose of stimulation might be more than the baby can tolerate, leading the baby to show avoidant behavior (Belsky, 1988). If this were the case, it wouldn't be the separation itself but the mother's attitude toward the separation that affects the infant's attachment behavior. Because not all working mothers feel guilty and because infants differ in their ability to handle stimulation, the effects associated with full-time day care would show a fair amount of variability across infants.

Another fact from the research helps put the situation in perspective. Although more day care infants showed avoidance, the amount of avoidance observed in some studies wasn't enough to change the infants' overall attachment classifications. In other words, the day care infants had secure attachment patterns overall, although their behavior at reunion showed more avoidance than did the behavior of home-reared infants (Thompson, 1988).

At this point, it's unclear why more avoidance is apparent in day care infants. Maybe their parents encourage them to be more independent, or maybe they're more accustomed to routine separations and reunions (Thompson, 1988). It's also unclear exactly what the differences mean. Avoidance in populations of day care infants may have a different meaning than it would in home-reared populations. Only follow-up studies done in the years ahead will clarify this.

WHAT SHOULD PARENTS AND DAY CARE CENTERS DO?

Right now, full-time day care for infants under 1 year of age is considered a **risk factor** for attachment disruption. It doesn't inevitably lead to attachment disruption, but it's associated with a greater probability of disruption than home rearing. Babies in part-time day care—less than 20 hours per week—don't show changes in attachment behavior, nor do babies who begin day care after 1 year of age.

Given the current research findings, parents should probably try to avoid full-time day care for infants under 1 year of age. At the same time, policy makers can take a number of steps to help. They can make sure women's jobs are still available after adequate maternity leave; they can support job-sharing and part-time work for mothers and fathers; and they can provide incentives for employers to set up child care in the workplace, enabling parents to see their children, however briefly, during their work day.

Day care workers and other professional caregivers can also help parents maintain close relationships with their children. They can encourage parents to linger in the morning to let their children see their interest in their day. Day care staff who view parental concern as an affront to their professional competence need to rethink their attitudes. Parents should probably show their children that they wish they could stay with them even though they know they must go, rather than leave abruptly as if they didn't care.

Day care staff and parents also need to work out effective ways to communicate with each other about the child. They have to share the information that helps explain the child's behavior. This kind of information is the basis for responsive caregiving, which underlies secure attachment.

When parents bring their baby in the morning, for example, they should tell the staff when the baby was last fed and changed, whether a new tooth is coming in or a new food was introduced, and so on. Then when the baby cries, the staff won't have to try everything before they find the cause of the discomfort. At the end of the day, the staff can give similar information to the parents. This kind of open exchange enhances adult responsiveness to the baby both at day care and at home.

ilies can't care for them (Grubb & Lazerson, 1983), some people find day care for babies living in so-called normal family situations unnecessary or inappropriate. Working parents respond that they must work to survive economically, that the role of full-time parent is too narrow and limiting, or that both parents are entitled to a career. Given the complexity of the issue, this debate is likely to continue for some time.

INFANT AND TODDLER ASSESSMENT

> One morning in July I was driving [the] children to their half-day nursery play session, and as I honked in front of Joshua's, his dad opened the back door to get a peek at Zach.
>
> "Hi, you rascal," he said, sticking his head in right next to Zach in his car seat. Zach was awake, but he did not even look at John. . . . The car motor was running. I felt the uneasiness spread. . . .
>
> In New York that summer to see my parents, the visit was fraught with tension. . . . Before we left New York, my father asked me when I was going to see the pediatrician. "Zach really doesn't hold his head up very well, Fernie. Ask the doctor about that the next time you go."
>
> *From Kupfer, F. (1982). Before and After Zachariah (pp. 31–32).*

As it turned out, Zachariah had severe brain damage caused by a rare genetic disease. Zach's parents had him examined and evaluated many times, but it was months before they got any definitive word about the extent of his retardation or the prospects for his future. Assessing development—observing what a child can and can't do—is easy enough, but interpreting the observations is something else. It's often hard to decide exactly what a specific performance means, especially when it comes to predicting the child's development in the future.

How do we know when a baby isn't developing normally? There's a fair amount of normal variation among individual children for the emergence of behaviors such as holding up the head, smiling, sitting up, walking, talking, and so on. But when things don't happen within a certain range of time, as was the case with Zach, we're likely to want to assess the child. Assessment results can help in devising plans for children with problems so they can develop to their full potential.

In this section, we discuss four different assessment tools—tests designed to elicit specific behavior from children. From the children's responses, information about their current level of functioning is obtained. After we describe these tools, we discuss the issue of why assessment is easy and prediction is hard.

The Denver Developmental Screening Test

The Denver test is widely used to screen children for a broad range of developmental problems. It can be used with children ranging in age from a few weeks to 6 years. The test is divided into four areas of development. In the personal-social domain, testers observe appropriate-age behaviors such as smiling, playing pat-a-cake, or using a cup or spoon. In the fine-motor domain, they test for such behaviors as grasping a rattle, building a tower, or drawing a person. In the language domain, they test for vocalizing, turning toward a voice, imitating sounds, saying specific words, and so on. In the gross motor domain, they observe holding up the head, standing, walking, hopping on one foot, and so on.

A child's development is assessed in terms of norms—the average ages at which children can perform the specific behaviors on the assessment test.

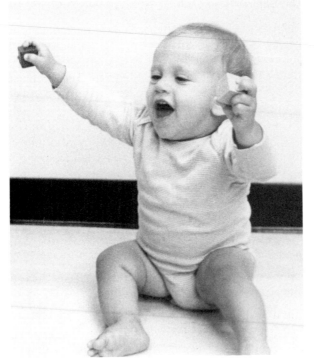

FIGURE 5
For a 9-month-old, the fine-motor domain of the Denver Developmental Screening Test includes assessing the child's control and coordination in handling blocks. The Denver's activities are fun for the baby but carefully designed to reveal developmental delays.

These norms have been established by studying hundreds of children. The scoring sheet provided with the Denver Test indicates the ages at which 50, 75, and 90 percent of children pass each item. A child who is delayed in passing clusters of items is judged to be in need of further evaluation to determine if significant developmental problems are present.

The Bayley Scales of Infant Development

The Bayley Scales are used to assess development in children from early infancy up to about 3 years. Devised by Dr. Nancy Bayley at the University of California at Berkeley, the scales have been revised several times since they were first used in the 1930s.

Children are tested on a motor scale and a mental scale. The motor scale includes items such as pulling up, creeping, walking, going up and down stairs, and balancing. The mental scale includes items that measure small motor skills, such as using the hands to build towers or to put pegs in pegboards. The mental scale also tests sensory abilities, such as the child's response to sound and light, and it measures language abilities and adaptability (Bayley, 1969).

The Bayley Scales are widely used to assess children's initial level of development when they enter an early intervention program. Information from the test is used to plan a program for the individual child. The test can also be administered after children have been in programs to see how effective the programs are.

The Uzgiris-Hunt Ordinal Scales of Psychological Development

The Uzgiris-Hunt Ordinal Scales are narrower in focus than the Denver or the Bayley. They measure sensorimotor development in children from birth up to about age 2 or $2\frac{1}{2}$. This test is based on the work of Piaget and uses his conceptualizations of infant intelligence. There are several different subscales in the test, each measuring development in a specific sensorimotor area. For example, one scale assesses the child's development of means to achieve desired environmental events, which was discussed in Chapter 6 on cognitive development. Another measures development of object construction, and a third measures development of verbal imitation (Uzgiris & Hunt, 1975).

The Uzgiris-Hunt Scales are often used to evaluate the effectiveness of educational programs for infants. They can also be used to evaluate a child's current level of development. For example, a tester would be able to find out if a child was at Stage 3 or Stage 4 in a particular dimension of sensorimotor intelligence and plan the child's program accordingly.

The Gesell Developmental Schedules

You'll probably recognize Dr. Gesell's name by now, recalling from Chapter 2 that he was a maturational theorist. The Gesell Developmental Schedules, which are based on research conducted by Dr. Gesell and others at the Yale University Clinic of Child Development, was one of the first assessment tools to be developed, and it is still used today. Like the other tests described here, it assesses children's performance in terms of norms—that is, in comparison to the performances of other children the same age (Gesell, 1954).

This test can be given to children between 4 weeks and 5 years of age. It measures motor, adaptive, language, and personal-social behavior. The motor subscale measures posture, **prehension** (reaching and grasping), locomotion, and coordination. The adaptive subscale measures a child's ability to learn from past experiences and initiate new ones. The language subscale measures both productive and receptive language skills. And the personal-social subscale measures a child's reactions to people and observance of social conventions.

Summary of Assessment Instruments

All of the assessment instruments provide norms—age references—that indicate the typical age range during which particular behaviors emerge in children. Results of assessments can indicate if a child is developing normally, within the typical age range. The tests can also be used to evaluate the effects of specialized programs—to see, for example, if early intervention programs alleviate developmental delays in economically disadvantaged children or children with disabilities.

All these tests and more probably were administered to Zachariah. Yet his parents were unable to find out what, if anything, was wrong with him for many anxiety-filled months. Assessment instruments have very definite limitations, and we turn now to an explanation of what they are.

Issues in Assessment

The biggest problem with infant assessment is prediction. If we were to assess 100 babies at 1 year of age, ranking them in terms of developmental maturity, and then test them again at 5 years of age, we would find quite a few changes in ranking. Infant assessment simply doesn't predict later problems very well, which of course is what we often would like to know (Honzik, 1983).

One reason for this poor showing is that infant/toddler assessment relies so heavily on motor and sensorimotor skills. Later intellectual functioning and achievement in school, on the other hand, rest heavily on language skills. These are the very skills that have not yet emerged in very young children (Bornstein & Sigman, 1986).

For example, neither a normal 1-year-old nor a 1-year-old with moderate mental retardation would have much language ability. A test given to both of them at this age might show very few differences between them. But at age 3, when the normal child's language has emerged and the retarded child's has not, an assessment would show significant differences. And the assessment at age 3 would reliably predict later differences in school achievement, because language is so crucial to school performance. We see, then, that infant/toddler assessment can't pick up variability in the very area that is most vital to later academic achievement (Harris, 1983).

A second problem with infant/toddler assessment instruments is that they're so heavily normed in terms of chronological age. In other words, they show the typical ages at which behaviors emerge in most children. What they don't account for is the very wide variation that occurs among perfectly normal children in the emergence of specific skills. Since we know this variation exists, we often can't say whether a child with developmental delays has a slow developmental timetable or whether the child has serious problems. This is no doubt what happened with Zachariah. The doctors who examined him saw that he was delayed, but they couldn't at first say why.

The younger a child is, the more difficult it is to say whether a problem exists. Consider walking as an example. The normal age range for the emergence of this behavior is 9 to 14 months. A child who hasn't walked by 13 months might be a worry to his parents or doctor, because most children do walk by this age. But it would be hard to know the significance of this behavior at 13 months. If the child still isn't walking by 18 months, however, the meaning of his behavior at 13 months becomes clearer.

A related problem with assessment instruments is that they necessarily include items that are easy to score and exclude items that are hard to score. Behaviors like habituation time—time it takes for attention to an event to subside—and goal-directedness are more difficult to assess than are reaching and grasping or initial orientation to a stimulus, which are the items typically administered in infant tests.

Right now, infant/toddler assessment instruments are the best predictors when a child's scores are very low. Of course, these are the very children whose problems are readily apparent to parents and experts alike, without the aid of a test. Although better tests may be available in the future, the results of assessments currently should be viewed with caution, especially if scores are only slightly below normal.

LIVING WITH THE YOUNG CHILD

It was 2 o'clock in the morning, but instead of sleeping soundly in their bed, Frank and Donna McKinney were up with their 18-month-old daughter, Kimberly. Early in the evening, Kimberly had been cranky and had refused to eat her dinner. She had been listless and uninterested in playing. Frank and Donna chalked it up to fatigue, since they'd been out all evening at Donna's mother's house.

Kimberly had begun to cry at about 1 A.M., and Donna had gone to see what was the matter. When she reached down to smooth Kimberly's hair, Donna realized that she was very hot. She got the thermometer and took her temperature under her arm. It was an alarming 105 degrees. Calling to Frank to come help, Donna quickly took off Kimberly's sleeper to allow heat to escape from her body. Frank got the acetaminophen from the medicine cabinet and managed to get a dropperful of it into Kimberly's mouth.

Kimberly was crying hard now. Donna picked her up and carried her into the living room. Frank decided to get a damp washcloth to sponge Kimberly's body and try to cool her through evaporation. After 15 minutes, they thought she was getting cooler. The thermometer read 103. Frank stopped sponging, thinking that the acetaminophen was probably beginning to take effect. They considered calling the doctor but decided to wait a little longer. Within half an hour, Kimberly's temperature was down to 101, she had taken a drink of water, and she was beginning to doze off.

"I'll rock her for a while," Frank offered. "If her fever goes up again, we'll call the doctor. Why don't you get some sleep?"

"Okay," said Donna. "Can you stay home with her tomorrow morning and then work later in the afternoon? I could go to work early and then take the afternoon as half a sick day."

"I have to turn in a report in the morning. Can you drop it off for me?"

"Not if I want to get to work early myself. Maybe Bob could stop by on his way to your office and take it in."

"Good idea."

Donna went back to bed, but she couldn't fall asleep. She wasn't worried about Kimberly, who seemed to be getting better already. She was trying to figure out all the arrangements she'd have to make tomorrow to accommodate this unscheduled event— calls to her office, to Frank's office, to the day care center, to her pediatrician. Whenever Kimberly got sick, it threw a wrench into their busy, carefully choreographed life. Well, thought Donna, that's just how it is once you have a baby. I didn't know it then, but, ohhh, life used to be so simple.

Living with a young child *is* complicated. It requires patience, resourcefulness, and information about children. Individuals who live with infants and toddlers—whether parents or professional caregivers—have a number of practical, everyday concerns. They need to know how to comfort babies, how to keep them safe and healthy, and how to approach feeding and toilet training in toddlers.

We discussed ways to comfort a baby in Chapter 4 on the neonate, because that seems to be the primary concern during the early weeks of a baby's life. Here, we address the other issues—health, safety, and play.

Ensuring Health in the Infant and Toddler

Children are relatively healthy during their first two years of life. In fact, they have fewer illnesses at this time than at any other time during childhood. During the first six months, a baby has passive immunity gained from the mother in utero. Breastfed infants gain added immunity, because breast milk carries the mother's antibodies. Infants' low illness rate is also due to their relatively low exposure to other children.

Once this exposure increases during the preschool years, children suffer from a rash of illnesses, ranging from the common cold to chicken pox. In fact, the highest incidence of illness in children occurs during the preschool years, when they're first exposed to many other children and haven't built up their own immunities. Sharing toys in preschools makes contagion more likely too.

When children under 2 years do get sick, the illness can be more serious than illnesses in older children, mainly because of their small body size. Infants have narrow air passages that easily become blocked from respiratory infections, and they dehydrate—lose water—rapidly when they vomit or have diarrhea. These conditions require careful monitoring and prompt medical attention in young infants. (For a discussion of another medical problem in infants, see Research Focus—Sudden Infant Death Syndrome.)

COMMON CHILDHOOD DISEASES. Childhood diseases are often grouped into four categories: respiratory (colds, bronchitis, tonsillitis, and so on), communicable

FIGURE 6
Children become sick more often as soon as they're exposed to other children on a regular basis. Special arrangements have to be made for sick children who normally attend day care or preschool. The sick child is fragile and needs to be in a quiet, familiar place to rest and get well. A thumb, a blanket, and a stuffed toy help too.

RESEARCH FOCUS

Sudden Infant Death Syndrome

Probably nothing fills parents with more dread than the thought of finding their infant dead in her crib. This fear becomes reality in Sudden Infant Death Syndrome (SIDS). Two out of every 1,000 infants—about 8,000 infants in all—die of SIDS each year in the United States. Currently, this disease is the major killer of infants between 1 and 12 months of age (Merritt & Valdes-Dapena, 1984).

THE MYSTERY OF SIDS

SIDS usually strikes infants between 2 and 4 months of age, at night, while they are asleep. Most have no apparent illness. In fact, the mystery of the disease is that it suddenly strikes apparently healthy infants (Kelly & Shannon, 1982).

The cause of SIDS is still unknown, but researchers suspect that some kind of assaults on the brain stem—where breathing is controlled—during the prenatal or perinatal period may be responsible (Kelly & Shannon, 1982). There might have been slight oxygen deprivation, for example. Viral infections are also suspected in some cases (Williams, Uren, & Bretherton, 1984).

Even though we don't know the cause of SIDS, we can say that some infants are more likely than others to be victims. Several risk factors have been identified, based on analysis of the characteristics of previous victims (Krongrad & O'Neill, 1986). Groups considered to be at risk for SIDS include the following:

- Infants born to mothers who are less than 20 years old
- Infants born to mothers who smoke cigarettes
- Infants born to mothers who abuse narcotic drugs
- Premature infants
- Small-for-date infants
- Infants who are twins or triplets
- Infants with a sibling who was a SIDS victim
- Male infants who have some of the above risk factors

APNEA MONITORING

High-risk infants may be monitored, at the hospital and at home, for sleep apnea (periods when breathing stops). Apnea is associated with some, although not all, cases of SIDS (Ariagno, 1984). Infants may be judged high risk because they had a sibling who was a SIDS victim, because they showed abnormal breathing patterns in the hospital nursery, or because their parents reported that they found them blue, pale, and apparently not breathing at some point (Krongrad & O'Neill, 1986). The monitor is attached to the infant during sleep. If the infant stops breathing, an alarm sounds to alert the parent.

Parents of infants at risk for SIDS have tremendously high levels of anxiety about their child. They usually feel they have no choice but to use a monitor, and yet it doesn't completely relieve their fears. The equipment is expensive, so it places a financial burden on the family. An evening out of the house is hard to arrange, because babysitters have to know how to use the monitor and how to resuscitate a baby who has stopped breathing. Parents who are monitoring their baby need the understanding and support of their doctor and home monitor staff (Smith, 1984), as well as the help of their friends and relatives. One mother who had lost a child to SIDS described the monitoring experience with her second child (Silvio, 1984, p. 231):

> Jerry and I learned quickly the meaning of monitoring. We became the constant companions of our baby, Ashley. Monitoring meant that we were always within hearing range; it meant that routines such as going to get the mail or watering the flowers were not done while she was sleeping. In short, it meant a total adjustment in our lifestyle, not to mention the adjustment to our budget. The bottom line, though, was that the monitor could give us the chance to save her life if it became necessary, the chance we wish we had had with Adam. It gave us a feeling of security knowing that without keeping a constant eye on her, she was doing fine. I learned a great deal from my adjusted lifestyle. I learned to appreciate the constant companionship of Ashley and the rest of our family. I learned how to take a shower while listening for the alarm. I became quite skilled at vacuuming while keeping a constant eye on the remote alarm. I learned that monitoring can be very trying at times and that the value of a night out did not compare to the value of my child's life. I soon realized that adjusting to monitoring was much easier than adjusting to the loss of a child.

The tragedy of SIDS will go on until research tells us what causes it and how we can prevent it. Until then, apnea monitoring, although far from ideal, is our best hope for sparing families the trauma of infant death.

(mumps, German measles, whooping cough, and so), gastrointestinal (those that affect the stomach and intestines and cause vomiting and diarrhea), and accidents.

Adults who were children 30 or 40 years ago often remember having had every childhood disease imaginable and spending long periods of time sick in bed. Children today are immunized against many communicable diseases.

FIGURE 7
Regular physical check-ups are important for infants and toddlers. They give the pediatrician the chance to answer parents' questions, spot any problems that may be developing, and immunize the child against such life-threatening diseases as polio and diphtheria. Toys, games, and friendly adults help the child develop positive associations with the visit.

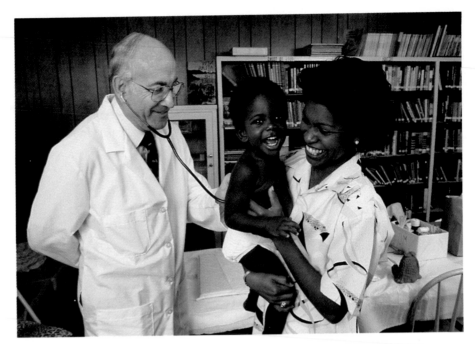

One shot, known as the DPT immunization, protects against diphtheria (an upper respiratory illness), tetanus (an infection causing contraction of facial muscles), and pertussis (an upper respiratory illness, commonly known as whooping cough). Another shot contains the vaccines against measles, mumps, and rubella (German measles). Children are also immunized against polio and hemophilus influenzae B, the organism primarily responsible for meningitis. Immunizations are given during regular checkups at 2 months, 4 months, 6 months, 1 year, and 18 months (influenzae type B). "Booster" shots are given at 18 months and again when the child is 5 years old.

THE DEBATE OVER IMMUNIZATION. Immunization is a surprisingly controversial issue. Public health officials are anxious for as many children as possible to be immunized to control the spread of disease. Although we refer to them as common, childhood diseases are serious and can cause permanent disabilities and death. In the late 1970s, the problem of nonimmunized children in the schools became so serious that a federally funded program, the Childhood Immunization Initiative, was begun to increase the number of immunized children in the United States. At the time the program started, 40 percent of children under 5 years were not immunized. Within a few years, less than 10 percent of the children in this country had not been immunized (Bumpers, 1984). Since then, many states have passed laws requiring that children be immunized before they attend day care, preschool, or elementary school.

Despite the obvious benefits, many parents have resisted having their children immunized. Their primary concern has been the safety of the vaccine. In extremely rare cases, a child has contracted the disease itself from the vaccine. More often, children have reactions to vaccines, consisting of fever,

HEALTH FOCUS

Sickness at Day Care Centers

Parents who take their babies to day care often worry that they'll catch colds and other contagious diseases there, and they're right to be concerned. Day care children do get sick more often than babies who stay at home. For working parents, having a sick child is a serious problem, one that we discuss in another focus box. How can parents and day care centers alike reduce the risk of illness for children?

SOME DAY CARE CENTERS HAVE MORE ILLNESS
Certain types of day care centers have higher rates of infectious diseases than others. One type is the center that serves non–toilet trained children under 2 years of age. At this age, children mouth everything, come in close contact with each other, and eat with their hands. Germs pass easily from one child to another.

Large day care centers also have more disease, simply because children come in contact with larger numbers of other children. Centers that allow drop-ins—children who can't attend their regular center because they're sick—have higher rates of infection as well. Finally, centers that employ immigrants from certain countries seem to have higher incidences of tuberculosis in their children. This problem can be controlled if day care centers insist on proof of negative tuberculin skin tests before they hire new employees.

WHAT KINDS OF DISEASES DO CHILDREN GET?
Even if parents don't use day care centers with these features, they can still expect their children to get sick. It's virtually impossible to protect children who attend day care centers from contagious diseases. Parents may see any of a wide range of illnesses, including respiratory infections, meningitis, hepatitis, gastro-intestinal infections, and cytomegalovirus (CMV) infections.

People get respiratory infections—colds, bronchitis, pneumonia, and so on—from close contact with an infected person. The bacteria and viruses that cause these diseases are in the saliva and mucus secretions and are spread when people talk, cough, sneeze, or pass on germs with their hands. Tissues and towels used to wipe children's noses and hands can carry the germs.

Meningitis, an inflammation of the meninges, the membranes covering the brain and spinal cord, can cause brain damage and even death in children. It's caused by the bacteria hemophilus influenzae B and, like the common cold, is spread through respiratory secretions.

Hepatitis is a viral infection of the liver. It's transmitted orally and through the feces. In some cases, hepatitis causes the skin to turn yellow, but many children don't have any symptoms. When this is the case, the disease can spread until many children and adults are infected (Smith, 1986). Close to 30 percent of all hepatitis type A outbreaks in the United States can be traced to day care centers (Marwich & Simmons, 1984).

Gastrointestinal infections—often labeled "the flu" and characterized by vomiting and diarrhea—are also spread orally and through the feces. CMV infections are viral. Children with CMV infections usually don't have any symptoms, but the disease still has to be controlled. Pregnant women and women of child-bearing age who contract CMV are at risk for having babies with birth defects.

headache, nausea, and other flulike symptoms, which occur as the body begins to develop antibodies toward the diseases the immunizations prevent. The reaction rate for the pertussis vaccine is particularly high, although most reactions aren't severe (Frenkel, 1986).

Physicians often respond to these concerns by asking parents to put them in perspective. They point out that the risk of dying in a traffic accident is 1 in 8,000; the risk of dying from pertussis itself, if the child has not been immunized and contracts the disease, is 1 in 1,000; and the risk of dying from a pertussis immunization is 1 in 2,000,000. Pediatricians do, however, follow guidelines for administering the pertussis vaccine to individual children. If a child has had a very strong reaction to the vaccine at 18 months, for example, the doctor will probably not give the booster shot at age 5.

Many other diseases can't be prevented by immunization, but they can be controlled through good hygiene. A full discussion of this topic is provided in Health Focus—Sickness at Day-Care Centers.

This is obviously a list of serious diseases. How can day care centers reduce the risk of sickness for the children in their care?

HOW CAN DAY CARE CENTERS CONTROL DISEASE?

Health experts have recommended the following procedures for controlling the spread of disease in day care centers:

- Day care staff should frequently *wash their hands* with soap. Hand washing is the most effective way to prevent infections. Workers should wash their hands when they arrive at the center; before eating, preparing, or serving food; and after diapering a child, wiping noses, or being outside. Children should wash their hands after using the toilet, before meals, and after playing outside. Hands shouldn't be washed in a sink where food is prepared.
- Workers should *change diapers carefully* as soon as they're soiled. The changing table should be covered with a disposable surface and used only for changing diapers. The table top should be cleaned and disinfected after each use. Diapers should be properly disposed of in plastic bags and put in a plastic-lined trash can with a lid. The diaper-changing table should be near a sink so caregivers can wash their hands immediately after changing a diaper.
- Day care staff should *wash and disinfect toys and equipment* daily. They should disinfect high chair trays after each use.
- Centers should *establish and stick to a sick child policy*. They should maintain a regular enrollment and not allow any drop-ins. Children with fever, diarrhea, or other signs of infection should not be allowed to attend the center. Children who become ill at the center should be isolated from the other children until a parent can take them home.
- Centers should require that all children between the ages of 2 and 5 be *vaccinated against hemophilus influenzae B*, the virus that causes meningitis. Some doctors recommend this vaccination as early as 18 months for children in day care.
- Day care centers should make sure they *employ enough people*. When workers are extremely busy, they tend to forget about washing hands, cleaning the diapering area, and so on. Centers should also *avoid overcrowding among the children*, since this increases contact and the spread of germs. Day care *staff should be educated* about how diseases are transmitted and how they can be controlled. (The National Centers for Disease Control in Atlanta provides excellent training material.) Finally, all centers should have a pediatrician or nurse as a health consultant to provide training and advice when diseases do break out.
- Parents should *keep sick children home* from day care, despite the inconvenience and disruption in their working life. Some possible solutions to this dilemma are discussed in Public Policy Focus—Sick Child Day Care.

Ensuring Health in the Older Toddler

People who live with toddlers face two major health-related challenges: feeding and toilet training. How these two aspects of child care are handled has long-range consequences for the child's well-being, so they're worth careful consideration.

FEEDING THE TODDLER. Two trends affect the toddler's eating behavior: a decrease in appetite and an overwhelming urge to explore the world. Together, they create fairly messy and prolonged feeding times, during which remarkably little food is consumed. Adults often wonder if toddlers are getting enough nutrients—and if the dining room rug is going to survive.

We saw in Chapter 5 that toddlers' appetites decline because their growth rates slow down so drastically. They don't need or want large amounts of food. Adults can manage toddler feeding in a positive way by offering small portions

FIGURE 8
The toddler is too busy feeding himself to care about mealtime decorum. He's getting more than sustenance right now—he's learning that he has the ability to do things for himself. Messy meals are the small price his parents pay for his growing sense of autonomy.

of nutritious food at mealtimes and limiting between-meal snacks. Toddlers are likely to be more interested in attractively served foods and in foods that adults appear to be enjoying. But none of these tactics will work with children who simply aren't hungry. Loading up their plates only sets up power struggles between children and adults. Adults need to understand and accept the toddler's small appetite.

Toddlers' desire to explore food can be satisfied by offering "finger" foods, such as slices of apple or banana, small pieces of bread, or bits of dry cereal. Because these foods can be easily managed by the child, they also support the toddler's emerging sense of independence.

Parents who want to curtail extreme messiness have to take the time to manage their toddlers' mealtimes. They can teach their children to handle only finger foods, for example, and to stir and smear other foods in the dish or on the high chair tray. They can also teach them not to turn cups upside down. For their part, they can serve the toddler's food on nonbreakable dishes, use cups with lids, and feed the toddler over a washable floor. They can also be diligent about removing the child from the high chair promptly when she indicates that she's done, since keeping her there with food on her tray only encourages her to play with it or throw it on the floor. Despite all precautions, however, toddlers are messy eaters. They often emerge from meals covered with food from their hair to their shoes. Again, adults are wise to accept a certain amount of mess from their curious toddlers.

TOILET TRAINING THE TODDLER. A second major issue in the toddler years is toilet training. Between ages 1 and 2, most toddlers begin to be aware of how it

FIGURE 9
When bathrooms are clean and toilet training is systematic and humane, children can readily be toilet trained at their child care center as well as at home. Most parents experience at least one moment when they despair of ever training their child, but child care providers know from experience that virtually all children will eventually be trained.

feels when the bladder is full. This is the first stage of readiness for bladder control (Doleys & Dolce, 1982). But the bladder still releases urine reflexively in children this age. The child can't retain urine and can't anticipate the need to use the toilet. Children may indicate that they have a full bladder by dancing around or holding the genital area at this stage, and children who show these signs are often ready to get to the toilet and take appropriate action.

By about age 3, and sometimes earlier in girls, children become able to retain urine for a short period of time after sensing that the bladder is full. At this point, the child can consciously control the bladder muscles so urine isn't reflexively released. This is the second stage of readiness for bladder control. Now children can begin to anticipate the need to use the toilet, and parents or caregivers can help them get there in time.

This is the point at which parents usually teach their children to use the toilet, and many different approaches to toilet training have been proposed over the years. In the 1970s and 1980s, a social learning approach using reinforcement and modeling promised that children could be toilet trained "in less than a day." It's probably wise to modify any system to fit individual children, keeping in mind that praise and encouragement are the best teaching tools and that scolding and punishment are not only inhumane but counterproductive.

Children become dry at night after they've achieved daytime control, usually 6 to 12 months later. In one study of Dutch children, girls were wetting the bed twice a month between ages 4 and 5, but by age 5, they were wetting the bed significantly less. By contrast, about 15 percent of the boys were still wetting the bed about twice a month at age 5. Not until they were 8 years old did the boys' rate of bed-wetting fall to the girls' 5-year-old level (Verhulst et al., 1985). These differences are largely due to girls' faster physical development, which by age 5 is almost a full year ahead of boys'.

The inability to control bladder function during the night after the age of 4 is known as **enuresis**. According to various studies, 15 to 20 percent of 5-year-olds and 5 percent of 10-year-olds are still wetting the bed, with boys again having the harder time. There are several possible reasons for enuresis. Some children have deep-sleep patterns that prevent them from waking to go to the bathroom before it's too late. Others have a genetic predisposition toward immaturity in bladder control. Still others might not have received daytime training or might not have learned toileting behavior well enough (Doleys & Dolce, 1982). Older children who still wet their beds often feel embarrassed or ashamed, especially if they've received negative reactions from their friends or parents. Experts urge families to seek medical or psychological help to prevent these secondary consequences if they do have an enuretic child.

Children typically achieve bowel control several months before they achieve bladder control. This is mainly because the sensations are easier to detect and the expulsion of the waste is easier to control. But some children—one to two out of every one hundred 4-year-olds—have trouble gaining bowel control, a difficulty known as **encopresis**. This problem, again more common in boys than in girls, can have serious consequences and requires medical attention (Rappaport & Levine, 1986).

Teachers and other caregivers can help all the children in their care avoid toileting problems by letting them use the bathroom when they need to. Since children are usually very sensitive to the condition of bathrooms, adults can also help by keeping bathrooms fresh and clean.

Keeping Infants and Toddlers Safe

Think for a moment about the picture we've drawn of older infants and toddlers. They're mobile, they're energetic, and they're fiercely independent about doing things themselves. They want to try everything, explore everything, touch and taste everything. At the same time, they're still clumsy physically, and they have very limited ideas about how the world actually works. It shouldn't be surprising then that toddlers easily get into trouble, some of it very dangerous trouble. About 4,000 children under 4 years of age die each year in the United States from accidents (Caldwell, 1984). (For a discussion of burns in young children and how to prevent them, see Safety Focus—Burns in Young Children).

Not all children are equally likely to have accidents. There are more accidental deaths among boys, black children, urban children, and children living in poverty (Butler, 1984). To prevent tragedies, everyone living with infants and toddlers must make sure the environment has been designed with the child's safety as a top priority. Certain precautions can help keep children safe:

- Never leave a baby unattended on a bed, on a table, or in a crib with the side down. Even newborns can move reflexively and plunge over the edge.
- Place gates at the tops and bottoms of stairs and in doorways to areas that are off limits to children.
- Place barriers around stoves, floor grates, and radiators. Babies might be able to roll close enough to touch a hot surface but then not be able to move away.

SAFETY FOCUS

Burns in Young Children

Burns are a serious threat to infants and toddlers, ranking third (behind auto accidents and drowning) as a cause of death in children (McLaughlin & Crawford, 1985). About 1,300 children die of burns every year in the United States. House fires cause the most deaths, and hot water causes the most nonfatal burns.

How can children be protected from burns? Several simple precautions can help. Tap water set at 160 degrees Fahrenheit takes just two seconds to cause a third-degree burn (the most serious burn). Water set at 120 degrees Fahrenheit, by contrast, takes ten minutes to cause the same burn (Caldwell, 1984). Obviously, if hot water heaters are set no higher than 120 degrees Fahrenheit, many serious burns can be avoided. A simple device, easily installed by a plumber, can regulate the mix of hot and cold water that comes out of a faucet. Child care centers in many states are required to install such devices and to keep them set so that water temperature is within acceptable limits.

In the kitchen, many children are burned by spills of hot liquids such as coffee, tea, or cooking fat. The same danger exists in child care centers when caregivers carry hot cups of coffee into the children's play areas. A bump from a child can easily make some of the liquid spill onto a child who is underfoot.

A new type of kitchen scald has recently started to appear. When baby bottles are heated in microwave ovens, the liquid inside can become extremely hot without the outside of the bottle getting very hot at all. (The heat only gradually gets conducted to the outside container.) Adults should always test the contents of the bottle on their wrists before feeding the baby. Safer methods of heating bottles (such as setting them in a pan of hot water) should be used in day care centers, where distractions can easily cause workers to forget to test the temperature on their wrists.

Adults can protect children from kitchen scalds by keeping them out of food preparation areas. At home, gates can be put up in kitchen doors, or a child can be placed in a high chair with toys on the tray to get him out from underfoot where he could trip the adult.

If a child is burned by a hot liquid, an adult should pour cool water on the burn *immediately*. This cools the hot liquid and the affected tissues and prevents the burn from going still deeper. Adults should not remove a child's shirt or pants before holding the child under cold running tap water.

Burns from electrical current are another category of burn. They don't occur very frequently, but when they do, they're usually serious. They often occur when a child sucks on the end of an extension cord that has been left plugged into a wall socket (Crikelair & Dhaliwal, 1976). Obviously, extension cords should always be unplugged and put away when not in use. Adults should also use plastic plugs in unused wall sockets to prevent infants and toddlers from putting objects into the holes, another way they get electrical burns.

Chemical burns usually occur when children drink caustic substances such as lye or household bleach. The peak age for this injury is 24 months (Wasserman & Ginsburg, 1985). Doctors are now seeing chemical burns caused by the miniature batteries used in cameras, hearing aids, and camera flash attachments (McLaughlin & Crawford, 1985). Like everything else the infant or toddler comes across, these tiny batteries seem fair game for mouthing and swallowing. Good poison prevention procedures can prevent chemical burns. All dangerous substances should be kept behind locked doors or out of reach, with the toddler's ingenuity and persistence taken into account.

Adults can protect children from sunburn by limiting exposure to the sun, using sunscreen, and keeping the sun off children's faces with hats. Child care center playgrounds should be designed with areas of shade so that children can play outdoors without constant exposure to direct sunlight.

Adults can lower the danger of house fires by installing smoke alarms in their homes and by holding family fire drills to teach children what to do in case of fire. These same measures increase safety in day care centers. All states have fire codes that must be followed in buildings where groups of young children are housed. They often specify that children must be on the ground floor, where they have the easiest access to the outside. Additional procedures may be required where there are nonmobile infants. For example, special aprons with large, deep pockets have been designed for emergency evacuations. Caregivers can carry two babies in their arms and tuck more into the pockets of the aprons. Training and practice reduce the likelihood that children in any setting—home, day care center, or school—will be seriously injured in a fire.

- Don't use tablecloths on tables. Babies pull themselves up on tablecloths and can pull dishes and hot food down on themselves.
- Store medicine in locked cabinets or well out of a child's reach. Buy medications in the smallest available quantity, and keep purses out of reach.
- Strap infants and toddlers into government-tested car seats when driving them in cars. Never hold a child in your lap while a car is moving. In the

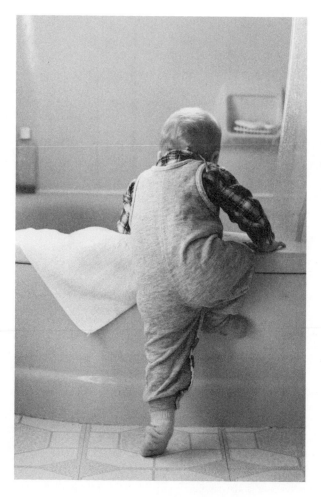

FIGURE 10
If he manages to climb onto the edge of the tub, he could be hurt falling off. If there were water in the tub, the outcome could be far more serious. The world is new to the child, and curiosity will lead him into situations his parents never even dreamed of before. Adults have to be especially careful when babies first become mobile and are trying new feats every day.

event of an accident, holding onto a 10-pound infant in a car going 30 miles per hour requires the same strength needed to lift a 300-pound weight. If you're not wearing a seat belt and are holding an infant, your body will continue to move forward at the speed the car was moving before impact. The infant would be crushed between your body and the interior of the car (Robertson, 1985).

- Keep small objects out of reach of children under age 3, and don't give them raw carrots, nuts, popcorn, or hard candy. They can easily choke.
- Inspect toys carefully for small parts that could come loose and be put in the mouth. Many toys are now labeled if they have small parts and are unsuitable for children under age 3.
- Inspect hand-me-down furniture to make sure it's free of lead-based paint and other hazards, such as spaces where a young child's head could become stuck.
- Don't put babies to bed wearing jackets with drawstring hoods. The strings could strangle them.
- Don't use talcum powder, which contains a substance that damages the lungs.
- Keep cleaning solvents, laundry detergents, furniture polishes, and all other

toxic substances in locked cabinets or in places inaccessible to infants and toddlers.
- Keep the number of the poison control center near your telephone.
- Keep a bottle of ipecac syrup on hand. Use it to induce vomiting in the event of accidental poisoning, but don't use it if caustic substances or petroleum products have been ingested.
- Use plastic covers over electrical outlets.

It's important that toddlers be able to explore their environment. They learn what the world is like by being active participants in it, and they achieve a sense of mastery by making things happen. Children's sense of themselves can be distorted when parents constantly have to say, "No! Don't touch!" They can become fearful and uncertain or, on the other hand, angry and defiant. Although it requires work and attention, it's far easier in the long run to adapt the environment to the child than to try to make the child fit into a hands-off home.

Toys for Infants and Toddlers

Living with a young child is by no means all worries over health and safety. Playtime can be fun for both child and adult, and many toys are made that support play at the various skill levels of infancy and toddlerhood. We look at some of them here before we close with a few words about playing with young children.

TOYS FOR VERY YOUNG INFANTS. Most toys for babies are designed to provide sensory stimulation. Crib mobiles have become popular as research on babies' visual perception and sensorimotor intelligence has sifted down to the popular level. The best mobiles have designs on the bottoms of the figures (not just on the sides), so the baby (not just the parents) can see them. Babies will be most interested in them if they have sharp contrasts in color or design. Mobiles should be removed when babies can reach them, since most of them aren't made to be handled or mouthed. Babies also like to look at themselves and other interesting sights reflected in nonbreakable mirrors attached to the sides of their cribs.

Rattles are another popular toy for young infants. A 3-month-old will grasp a rattle (although she won't be able to let go of it voluntarily), look at it, put it in her mouth, feel it with her free hand, and shake it. She'll like the sound it makes and the puzzle of who or what is making the sound.

TOYS FOR CRAWLERS AND BEGINNING WALKERS. When babies start to crawl, they enjoy pushing a colorful ball in front of them. They like the changing colors or patterns and the moderately predictable path of movement. Another good push toy for crawlers is a nonbreakable mirror attached between two wheels. As the mirror moves, it reflects a variety of stimulating displays to catch the baby's attention.

Babies who have begun to walk can use musical push toys, such as the popular plastic lawn mower. As mentioned in Chapter 5, these toys help the top-heavy toddler stay upright and balanced. Pull toys are for more experienced walkers.

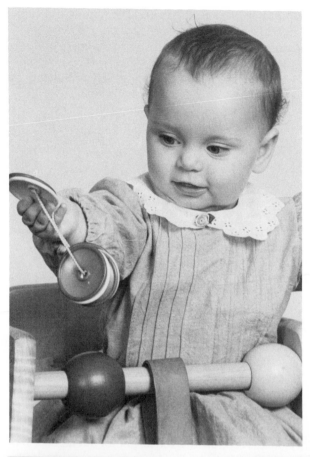

FIGURE 11
Brightly colored plastic disks on a circle of string make a good toy for a 9-month-old. She can hold it and shake it, watch it move, listen to its sounds, try it out for taste, and throw it on the floor to see how it sounds when it lands.

FIGURE 12
Doing puzzles helps toddlers learn shapes and colors, understand how space is organized, develop problem-solving strategies, and improve their fine motor control. If they work on puzzles with other children, they also practice their social and language skills. In addition to their other benefits, puzzles are sexually neutral, easy to take care of, and durable—the perfect toddler toy for home or child care center.

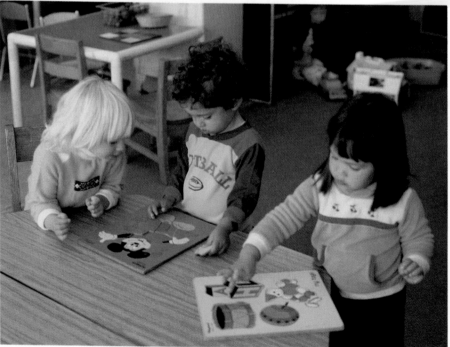

TOYS FOR TODDLERS. With their improving fine motor coordination, toddlers start to enjoy simple puzzles, boxes with shapes to sort and fit, stacking toys, small blocks, and crayons and paper. Dolls and stuffed animals give them something soft to hug, and old hats, purses, shoes, and clothes suggest roles to toddlers who are just beginning to play pretend games. Play dishes and pots and pans will be used too.

BOOKS. Even very young infants like the rhythm of nursery rhymes and children's songs. Older babies like looking at pictures of familiar objects and naming the objects. Books for babies are made of heavy cardboard, cloth, or plastic to withstand the mouthing, chewing, and sucking to which babies subject them.

By about age 2, children can enjoy actual stories, which the younger baby can't tolerate. Toddlers like stories about familiar events such as taking a bath, sitting on the potty, or getting ready for bed. Bedtime stories often become a ritual during the toddler period. As nursing or a pre-bedtime bottle becomes a thing of the past, the bedtime story can take its place. This ritual can form the basis for a childhood of warm relationships and a lifetime of enjoyable reading.

SOCIAL PLAY. Perhaps the favorite play of babies of all ages is social play with adults. Babies love old favorites like "tickle the tummy," "ah-boo," and "peek-a-boo." Adults can keep the games interesting by varying the pace of the tickling or booing and their facial and vocal expressions. They should also be careful to watch for gaze aversion and sobering—signs that the baby has had enough stimulation and wants to stop the game.

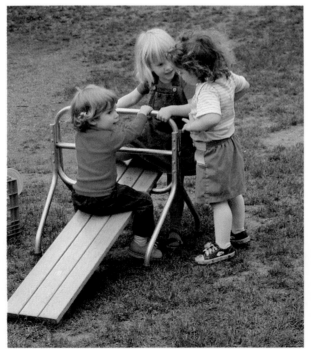

FIGURE 13
Two children can play together cooperatively on a teeter-totter, and a third can be included in friendly conversation. An important benefit of child care programs is that children can be taught positive ways of interacting with their peers and shown a variety of constructive ways to resolve disagreements.

Young toddlers like to be with other children, but they can't sustain interactions. Adults can help them be together happily by providing duplicate toys as well as equipment that can be used by several children at the same time, such as sandboxes, water tables, playhouses, rocking boats, and climbing structures. This kind of play equipment helps keep struggles over objects to a minimum and encourages parallel and joint play.

Adults have to supervise toddler play because toddlers aren't able to settle disagreements among themselves constructively. When toddlers want a toy another child is using, they're likely to grab it out of the child's hands. It's helpful if an adult can offer an identical toy, but this isn't always possible. When it's not, adults have to take the time to explain to toddlers, "That's Laurie's toy—she doesn't want to share it right now," or "It's Maria's turn—you'll have to wait for your turn. Let's look for something else for you to do until she's finished." With help like this, toddlers can begin to learn how to play together in relative harmony.

OVERVIEW

Individuals who live and work with infants and toddlers have many important practical concerns. They may wonder about child care: What should a program provide in order to nurture and support a young infant? An older infant? A toddler? Given all we know about attachment relationships, is child care appropriate at all for young infants? They may wonder about assessment: Is it significant if a child doesn't walk by 14 months? If he doesn't talk by 24 months? Or they may have questions about health, safety, or play: If a child has a reaction to a vaccine, should she get the booster shot? If she's not toilet trained by age 3, is there cause for alarm? These are the kinds of questions and concerns that can be addressed by applying research findings to everyday life with children.

KNOWLEDGE IN ACTION REVIEW

INFANT AND TODDLER EDUCATION AND CARE PROGRAMS

- Over 50 percent of mothers with babies under 1 year of age are in the work force today.
- The Florida Parent Education Infant and Toddler Program supports the cognitive and emotional growth of children from economically disadvantaged families. Its activities are based on Piaget's stages of sensorimotor intelligence.
- The Mother-Child Home Program focuses on the cognitive and language development. Home visitors bring books and toys to the home and help parents interact constructively with their children.
- The Family Development Research Program is based on the theories of Piaget and Erikson. Many child care centers use this program as a model.
- The Marin County, California, Program for Atypical Infants serves babies with special needs, such as mental retardation or a physical disability, and includes a therapeutic day care program.
- The Threshold Mothers' Project focuses on the children of mentally ill mothers and includes activities that help sensitize mothers to their babies' signals.
- Parents of all children in day care face problems when their children are sick, and no truly satisfactory solutions have yet been devised. The best solution is probably for employers to allow parents to take time off when they have a sick child.
- Babies in full-time day care show more avoidance toward their mothers than babies raised at home. The meaning of this behavior isn't clear. Full-time day care for infants under 1 year of age is considered a risk factor for attachment disruption.

INFANT AND TODDLER ASSESSMENT

- The Denver Developmental Screening Test tests for problems in personal-social, fine motor, language, and gross motor development.
- The Bayley Scales of Infant Development assess children from early infancy to 3 years of age on both a motor and a mental scale.
- The Uzgiris-Hunt Ordinal Scales of Psychological Development measure sensorimotor development in children from birth to 2 or $2\frac{1}{2}$ years of age. This test is often used to evaluate infant educational programs.
- The Gesell Developmental Schedules are used to assess motor, adaptive, language, and personal-social behavior in children between 4 weeks and 5 years of age.
- Assessment instruments indicate whether children are developing normally—within the norms—for their age, but they don't predict problems very well because later functioning depends heavily on language skills, which haven't emerged yet in infants. Infant assessment instruments also don't account for the wide variation among normal children, nor do they include items that are hard to measure and score.

LIVING WITH THE YOUNG CHILD

- Natural immunities and limited exposure to other children make the first two years of life relatively healthy ones, but illnesses in children under 2 years can be serious.
- Sudden Infant Death Syndrome is a mysterious disease that can strike infants while they're sleeping. When a child is judged to be at risk for SIDS, parents can use a device that monitors the child for sleep apnea.
- Once children are exposed to other children, they contract a variety of illnesses. The most common ones are respiratory infections, gastrointestinal viruses, and communicable diseases.
- Most children are immunized against diphtheria, pertussis, and tetanus (the DPT shot); measles, mumps, and rubella; polio; and bacterial meningitis.
- Public health officials want to make immunization universal, but many parents worry about the safety of vaccines. The benefits of immunization do outweigh the risks and side effects.
- Babies who attend day care centers get sick more often than babies who stay at home, and parents should select centers that follow strict sanitary and health procedures.
- Feeding and toilet training are two health-related challenges facing those who live and work with toddlers.
- Toddlers have small appetites and an urge to explore everything in their world. Their needs are best suited by small portions and foods and dishes that allow them the greatest independence.
- The first stage of readiness for toilet training occurs between 1 and 2 years of age, when the toddler becomes aware of the sensation of bladder fullness. At about age 3 (earlier in girls), the child can consciously control the bladder muscles so that urine isn't released reflexively.
- A popular social learning approach uses reinforcement and modeling to teach toileting behavior.

- Children become dry at night after they achieve daytime control. The inability to control bladder function at night after the age of 4 is called enuresis.
- Children typically achieve bowel control several months before they achieve bladder control. Some children, usually boys, have encopresis (difficulty with bowel control), a condition that requires medical attention.
- Inquisitive, mobile, and motivated by a desire for independence, toddlers easily get into trouble and require constant supervision. Accidents are the leading cause of death among children aged 1 to 4.
- Burns are a serious threat to young children. Adults must protect them against burns from hot water, electrical current, chemicals, sunburn, and house fires.
- Adults should "baby proof" children's environment rather than restrict their explorations of it.
- Toys for young infants are designed to provide sensory stimulation. Crawling babies like toys they can push with their hands. Beginning walkers enjoy push toys that help them steady themselves as they learn to walk.
- Toddlers enjoy toys that require fine motor coordination and items that can be used as props for their emerging pretend play.
- Young infants like looking at colorful picture books and hearing nursery rhymes. Older infants like books full of familiar objects they can name. Toddlers love actual stories about familiar events.
- The favorite play of all babies is social play with their parents or caregivers. Adults have to keep alert for signs of overstimulation.
- When young toddlers play together, adults can provide duplicate toys and equipment that can be used by more than one child, and they can help toddlers understand and handle their interactions with other children.

KEY TERMS

dyad
family process variables

risk factor
prehension

enuresis
encopresis

SUGGESTIONS FOR FURTHER READING

Brazelton, T. B. (1984). *Neonatal behavioral assessment scale* (2nd ed.). Philadelphia: J. B. Lippincott.

A complete discussion of the Brazelton scale for neonates.

Butler, D. (1979). *Cushla and her books*. Boston: The Horn Book.

A case study of a child born with a number of disabilities. The "intervention" described is home based and delivered by the child's parents. Gives an inside view of the challenges presented by disabled children and how experiences can sometimes be adapted to their advantage.

Godwin, A., & Schrag, L. (1988). *Setting up for infant care: Guidelines for centers and family day care homes*. Washington, DC: National Association for the Education of Young Children.

This little volume discusses the nitty-gritty of providing care for the youngest of children. Gives a good overview of what's involved.

Gonzales-Mena, J., & Eyer, D. (1989). *Infants, toddlers, and caregiving*. Mountain View, CA: Mayfield.

This practical text focuses on the special relationship between the young child and the caregiver. It provides problem-solving strategies and care-giving principles.

Gunzenhauser, N. E., & Caldwell, B. M. (Eds.) (1986). Group care for young children. *Pediatric Round Table: 12*. Skillman, NJ: Johnson & Johnson.

This small volume contains chapters on the current use of child care, care for disabled children, special programs for children of women who are in prison, health in child care settings, and corporate support of child care. Provides a good overview of contemporary needs, issues, and programs in a very readable fashion.

Reynolds, E. (1990). *Guiding young children: A child-centered approach*. Mountain View, CA: Mayfield.

A practical guide for caregivers in day care and family care. The book describes how to set up and maintain a child-centered facility, how to relate to the child, and how to provide for the child's intellectual and physical growth and social-emotional security.

MILESTONES IN INFANT AND TODDLER DEVELOPMENT

AGE	PHYSICAL	COGNITIVE	LANGUAGE	SOCIAL-EMOTIONAL
0–6 mos.	Holds head up when on stomach Rolls over from front to back Reaches for objects Exhibits many reflexes	Demonstrates primary circular reaction stage of sensorimotor intelligence Scans within a face Shows preference for contrast in visual displays Prefers looking at normal face	Cries and coos Recognizes human voice, prefers "Baby Talk" Can discriminate /d/ from /t/	Signals needs with crying and gazing Becomes attached to caregiver Smiles in sleep Smiles at people but indiscriminately
6–12 mos.	Demonstrates fewer reflexes Gets first tooth Sits up Develops pincer grasp Creeps, crawls Stands holding on	Demonstrates secondary circular reaction Demonstrates coordination of secondary circular reactions Imitates new behavior if scheme is familiar Searches for completely hidden object Looks longer at scrambled face	Repeats consonant-vowel syllables Varies intonation Says protowords Says first word	Smiles selectively Begins to use social referencing Shows stronger anxiety Responds to distress of other by showing distress, crying
12–18 mos.	Walks Climbs stairs	Demonstrates tertiary circular reactions Includes others as recipients of play behaviors	Uses holophrases Uses expressive jargon	Experiences peak of separation distress
18–24 mos.	Begins to run	Demonstrates invention of new means through mental combinations Finds hidden objects through invisible displacement Shows deferred imitation Activates toy or doll in pretend play	Uses telegraphic speech Understands multiword utterances	Demonstrates less separation distress Begins to show empathic responses to another's distress
24–36 mos.	Jumps Begins to ride a tricycle	Shows ability to substitute objects in pretend play Shows greater ability to substitute objects in pretend play Shows ability to integrate themes in play	Uses verbal strategies to start a conversation Uses less telegraphic speech	Begins to respond verbally to another's distress Includes others in pretend play

part three

PRESCHOOL CHILDREN

Remarkable changes occur between the ages of 3 and 6. The 3-year-old, perhaps still in diapers, becomes the eager preschooler of $3\frac{1}{2}$ and 4 and then the more confident kindergartner of 5 and 6. In the course of these years, magical thinking, with its confusion of animate and inanimate, real and pretend, gives way to a somewhat more rational comprehension of the world. Preschoolers' charming coined words and invented linguistic forms are replaced by nearly perfect grammar. And the awkward social gestures of the inexperienced playmate evolve into the complex social skills that underlie true friendships. All of these advances help prepare the child for the great leap into formal schooling that will take place at the end of this period. In the meantime, these years are for experiencing life with all the senses open, learning about social relationships beyond the family, and discovering the world through play.

chapter 9

PHYSICAL DEVELOPMENT IN PRESCHOOL CHILDREN

"Push us, push us," sang out a trio of girls on swings.

"I can't push all of you," called Monique, one of their teachers, as she came across the nursery school yard toward them. "Someone's going to have to pump."

"Oh, I know how to pump. My brother teached me," said one. She backed up against the swing and then plopped onto it as it swung forward. She thrust her short legs out in front of her awkwardly.

"That's right," said Monique. "Your legs go out as you go forward and back as you go back."

"I want to try," said one of the other girls. "Me, too," said the third. Monique watched as they struggled to coordinate their movements with the swings. "You're getting it," she called to them.

As they practiced, Monique kept an eye on other activities in the yard. Two children were climbing a jungle gym, and a third was hanging upside-down by her knees from the top bar, about 4 feet above the sandy ground. "Hang on tight, Alice," Monique called out. Nearby, a child was standing on top of a seesaw, trying to find the midpoint where it would balance. She shifted her weight back and forth, raising and lowering her arms like a windmill.

Monique looked over at the sandbox. Four children were digging canals and filling them with water from a hose. In some places, the canals were so wide they had put boards across them as bridges. They ran back and forth across the boards, or jumped over the canals, to repair their sandy aquaducts.

"It's one of those perfect mornings," thought Monique as she surveyed the busy scene. "I better enjoy it while it lasts."

Preschoolers *are* busy, both outdoors and indoors. The preschool years can very aptly be called the play years. Children spend a lot of time running,

FIGURE 9-1
Preschoolers are more skilled physically and more confident than they were a year or so earlier. This metal dinosaur makes a challenging climber for a group of 3- and 4-year-olds.

chasing, galloping, balancing, and climbing. Indoors, they paint, build, string beads, cut with scissors, do simple puzzles, and color with crayons. Both their large and small motor skills have improved immensely since they were toddlers. Let's take a closer look at their appearance and what they can do with their bodies.

APPEARANCE AND GROWTH

It's easy to see the difference in physical appearance between toddlers and preschoolers (Figure 9-2). Preschoolers have a different silhouette than toddlers. They're longer and leaner, and their heads aren't so large in proportion to their bodies. During the preschool years, children's legs and trunks continue to grow faster than their heads, producing this change in body proportions. Preschoolers' stomachs don't protrude so much any more, either. The lengthening of the trunk and the increase in muscle tissue that occurs between ages 3 and 6 gradually provide the space and resistance the body needs to keep the large internal organs tucked in.

Although their appearance changes quite a lot, preschoolers don't actually grow very much—at least not compared to babies. The slowdown in growth rate that began during the toddler years continues in the preschool years. The growth rate now is the slowest it's been in the child's short life.

FIGURE 9-2
The legs and trunk grow faster than the head during the preschool years. By age 6, the child's body proportions have begun to approach those of an adult.

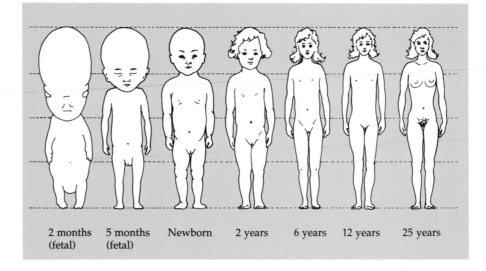

| 2 months (fetal) | 5 months (fetal) | Newborn | 2 years | 6 years | 12 years | 25 years |

Of course, the child does gain weight and grow taller. Weight gain during the preschool period amounts to about 3 pounds per year (compared to 14 pounds gained between birth and 1 year), or 9 pounds in all. The average child weighs 31 pounds entering the preschool period; 35 pounds at age 4; 38 pounds at age 5; and 43 pounds at age 6, the end of the preschool period (Figure 9-4).

Increases in height follow the same pattern. The child grows about $2\frac{1}{2}$ inches per year from the age of 3 until the age of 10 (Lowrey, 1978). Compared to the gains of 10 inches between birth and 1 year, $4\frac{1}{2}$ inches between 1 and 2 years, and $3\frac{1}{2}$ inches between 2 and 3 years, these increases are very moderate. At age 3, the average child is 37 inches tall. By age 6, the average child is 45 inches tall.

FIGURE 9-3
The preschooler has lost her baby fat and her toddler tummy. Her longer trunk and legs give her a more mature body shape and appearance.

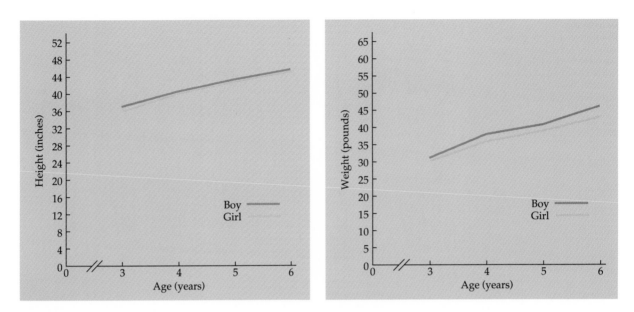

FIGURE 9-4
Height and weight for children 3 to 6 years of age. The graphs reflect height and weight for children who are average (fiftieth percentile). Growth is slower during the preschool years than it was during toddlerhood.

As we pointed out when discussing physical development in the toddler, slower growth means a smaller appetite. Preschool children usually don't eat very much, and sometimes they eat very little indeed. Children sometimes have a one- or two-month period of hearty eating followed by a period when they're not interested in food. These periods, exasperating as they can be for parents, correspond to bursts of faster and slower growth. Children are simply responding to the demands of their bodies.

As with toddlers, parents do well to accept the child's small appetite as normal. They should curtail non-nutritious, between-meal snacks and offer children wholesome foods when they see that they're eating less. If children have a choice of nourishing foods, their appetites can be the guide to how much they should eat.

MOTOR DEVELOPMENT

How do preschoolers use their stronger, more coordinated bodies? And how can adults help them to develop their motor skills in appropriate ways? We look more closely now at the development of preschoolers' fine and gross motor skills, as well as at the implications of these developments for parents and teachers.

Fine Motor Development

Toddlers learn how to use their hands and fingers to grasp, let go, wave, and point. But toddlers don't have much flexibility in the way they use or move their fingers. Preschoolers gain much more control over their hands and fingers. They become adept at a variety of nursery school activities, including putting pegs on pegboards, cutting and pasting, drawing with markers or crayons, doing simple sewing, and making wooden bead necklaces.

FIGURE 9-5
With their advancing fine motor control, these preschool girls are able to pick up small toys and figures and place them where they want them. An average boy the same age would be less skilled, because boys mature more slowly than girls.

Preschoolers also learn to dress themselves. They can button large and easily accessible buttons, zip up and snap their trousers (if the snaps aren't too stiff), pull on their socks and shoes and take them off, and maneuver their way in and out of a T-shirt or sweatshirt. Connecting the two ends of a zipper on a jacket or coat presents quite a challenge to the young preschooler, but many 5-year-olds have mastered this task. Other aspects of getting dressed are beyond the abilities of preschoolers, and they'll ask for help with these—tying shoelaces, buttoning small buttons, wrapping and tying scarves, and snapping large, stiff snaps.

This improvement in fine motor skills corresponds nicely with preschoolers' desire to be independent and help themselves. If parents choose their clothes wisely, young preschoolers can begin to dress and toilet themselves. This means parents should avoid clothing with tiny buttons, difficult snaps, openings in the back, and strings to tie.

Naturally, parents and teachers have to be available to teach, supervise, and help when children are learning how to dress themselves. Preschoolers don't always think about putting on their snowpants before their boots, for example, or zipping up their jackets before they put on their mittens. They may get tangled up in overalls and bathing suit straps. They don't have the motor skills to brush their teeth very thoroughly or to wipe themselves very well after going to the bathroom. But they're definitely launched. By the end of the preschool years, if guidance has been good and opportunities plentiful, the child has become a fairly competent and independent person. (For a discussion of how parents and teachers can help children with disabilities achieve independence too, see Special Education Focus—Adapting the Environment to the Disabled Child.)

SPECIAL EDUCATION FOCUS

Adapting the Environment to the Child with Disabilities

Parents and teachers often have to restrain themselves from rushing to help young children who are struggling with buttons and zippers, forks and spoons, combs and toothbrushes. It's even harder for adults to watch the struggles of children with physical disabilities. Children work very hard to master the daily tasks of taking care of themselves, and children with disabilities, including those with impaired motor control or limited use of their arms or legs, are no exception. How can adults help these children attain the fullest possible measure of independence and self-sufficiency?

One thing parents can do is make sure their child's clothing is adapted to specific needs. It should fit properly, allow easy movement, be strong enough to withstand abrasion from braces or other mechanical aids, and have openings and fasteners the child can reach. A preschooler may be able to dress herself as well as her able-bodied age-mates if her shirt is fastened in the front with Velcro instead of buttons. She may be able to zip a zipper if a large ring, such as the kind used to hold papers together, is inserted through the tab at the end. And she may be able to get her coat on by herself if she sits down with the coat in her lap and flips it over her head. A child with delayed physical development will be top-heavy and will fall over if she tries to flip her jacket while standing.

Some simple adjustments in equipment and tools can also help the preschooler with disabilities do the same things the other nursery school children do. For example, a child who has poor wrist rotation (a common problem among children with Down's syndrome) may be able to pour her juice from a pitcher if the lid is attached so the spout is 90 degrees from the handle rather than opposite it. A child with poor balance or muscle tone may be able to use a toilet more confidently if there's a low stool in front of it where she can rest her feet. Children who have difficulty grasping objects can be given eating utensils and toothbrushes with extended or thickened handles (Schleifer, 1987).

Children with disabilities often have poorer coordination and slower reaction time than other children. They can benefit from practicing T-ball—batting a ball from a stationary holder rather than a ball that's moving. Movable playground equipment can be taken apart and the pieces placed flat on the ground. Children who couldn't otherwise use parts of play structures can practice walking across them when they're on the ground.

Teachers often have one or more mildly disabled children in their regular classrooms, and their presence can be a positive experience for all the children. Teachers can help them be part of the group by meeting their needs in many large and small ways. Of course, a great deal of special equipment and clothing is now made for children with disabilities, and many parents and teachers take advantage of it. A good source for information about these materials is the journal *The Exceptional Parent* (605 Commonwealth Avenue, Boston, MA 02215).

Gross Motor Development: Locomotor Skills

At the beginning of this chapter, a variety of motor activities that would be impossible for toddlers were mentioned—balancing on a seesaw, hanging upside-down from a climber, and jumping over canals in the sand. Preschoolers owe a great deal of their agility to their lower center of gravity. The **center of gravity**—the point in the body around which the weight is evenly distributed—is very high in the newborn, near the bottom of the breastbone. As children grow, their center of gravity moves down. By the time they're age 5 or 6, it's below the navel (Lowrey, 1978). This lower center of gravity provides a firmer foundation for balance and movement, allowing preschoolers to improve both their locomotor skills and their upper body and arm skills.

WALKING AND RUNNING. Preschoolers' days are full of movement, including twisting, turning, running, bouncing, and jumping. What are the specific skills they acquire during this period? As toddlers, they learned to walk, of course, and they started running between ages 2 and 3. They appeared to run before age 2, but in this early kind of running, the feet never actually left the ground at the same time. Between ages 2 and 3, they started moving quickly enough for both feet to leave the ground for an instant. By age 3 they run, but they can't change direction while staying on the go and they can't stop

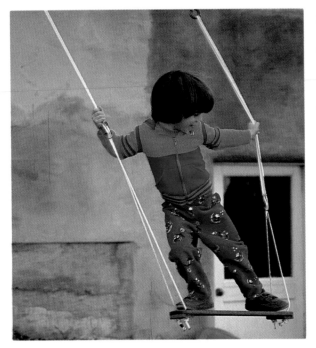

FIGURE 9-6
To swing sideways, a child has to shift his weight, coordinate two different pushing motions, and keep his balance at the same time. The preschooler loves to experiment with interesting new ways to use familiar equipment, whether it's a swing or his body.

quickly. By age $4\frac{1}{2}$ or 5, preschoolers perfect these skills (Cratty, 1986).

Toddlers have to keep their legs spread wide apart to balance themselves as they walk. Young preschoolers begin to narrow the base on which they walk; they can place one foot in front of the other to walk a line drawn on the floor. By age 4, they can walk a curved line, which is even harder because they have to place one foot in front of the other and turn at the same time. Still more difficult is walking a balance beam (a board raised off the ground), which narrows the base of support even more. Children have to place one foot in front of the other and at the same time make adjustments in how their weight is distributed to each side. Preschoolers have a hard time walking a balance beam—they usually have to step off to the ground several times to regain their balance (Cratty, 1986).

JUMPING. The children digging canals in the sandbox were accomplished at jumping, another locomotor skill preschoolers master. Before they're 2 years old, children jump from a low height by stepping off with one foot, keeping the other foot in contact with the higher surface. By age 2, they can jump with both feet suspended off the ground for a moment.

By age 3, children are getting higher when they jump off a low height, but they "wing" their arms—throw them back behind them— and lean backward rather than forward. This makes for an awkward jump that tends to leave them off balance when they land. By age $4\frac{1}{2}$, they learn to move their arms forward and up at take-off for a two-footed jump, leaning forward as they go into the air. To leap over obstacles, they start by leading with one foot; later they can jump over things with both feet together. By age 5, most children have a whole repertoire of jumps they can perform. The movements involved in jumping and other locomotor skills are illustrated in Figure 9-8.

FIGURE 9-7
These children are doing surprisingly well for their age on a curved balance beam. This task is a challenge for preschoolers because they're still developing their sense of balance and their large motor skills. As the motor areas of the brain develop and the center of gravity moves lower, balance improves.

CLIMBING. Climbing is another playground skill that preschoolers master. They've been climbing stairs practically since they could walk, although as toddlers they went up stairs by climbing a step with one foot and then the other before attempting the next step. This kind of climbing is called **marked-time climbing.** By the beginning of the preschool period, children can walk up stairs by alternating feet. Walking down stairs is still a challenge, though, because of the different balance problem. Children usually don't alternate feet going down stairs until they're about 4 years old.

The same sequence of climbing skills is used on play equipment. Children use marked-time climbing to get up ladders, climbers, and jungle gyms before they climb with alternate feet. And they can get up before they can get down. At the beginning of the school year, preschool teachers have to watch for children who have climbed up bars by themselves but can't figure out how to get down. Teachers usually can talk them down, giving them verbal instructions about how to retrace their steps. Gradually, preschoolers come to feel comfortable on climbing structures. The girl at the beginning of this chapter who was hanging upside-down from a climber was an older preschooler, probably about 5 years old.

COORDINATING MORE DIFFICULT MOVEMENTS. Other, more difficult, activities seen in the nursery school play yard include hopping, skipping, and galloping. These locomotor skills require better balance and coordination than the more basic skills. Hopping, for example, narrows the base of support to one foot and requires good balance. By age $3\frac{1}{2}$, children can hop a few steps on one foot; by age 5, they can hop eight to ten steps. Rhythmic hopping—hopping on alternate feet—requires balance and coordination beyond the ability of most 5-year-olds.

Galloping and skipping are hard because they require coordination and shifts in balance. Galloping involves an uneven rhythmic movement with a lead foot, but since the legs don't alternate, coordination isn't as much of a problem. Most 4-year-olds can gallop. Skipping requires alternation of the feet and coordination of a step forward and a hop; it's a relatively difficult skill to learn. Most children can't skip until they're about 6 years old (Cratty, 1986).

FIGURE 9-8
Movements involved in selected motor skills. The skillful execution of a broad jump involves extending the arms at takeoff, lifting off at a forward angle, and landing with flexed knees and arms thrust forward. Many children can broad jump at 5 or 6 years of age (a). Hopping involves making a springing push into the air on one foot. Most 4-year-olds can hop (b). Skipping involves a combination of a skip and a hop on alternating feet. Most children are at least 6 years old before they can skip (c).

The development of the large motor skills during toddlerhood and the preschool years are summarized in Table 9-1.

Preschoolers are eager to try any physical activity they see other children doing. Most 3-year-olds can ride a tricycle; most 6-year-olds can ride a bicycle. Older preschoolers can maneuver a scooter quite well, but they have to wait until they're older to handle a skateboard. Older preschoolers can even begin to learn to roller skate, ice skate, kick a soccer ball, and ski.

SUPPORTING MOTOR DEVELOPMENT. As was the case with babies and toddlers, preschoolers' physical abilities and motor skills emerge according to a biological timetable. Their bodies grow, they develop more muscle tissue, and the motor areas of their brains continue to mature. They become capable of running, climbing, jumping, and skipping when their bodies and brains are ready. But, as with babies and toddlers, these developments are supported by stimulation from the environment and opportunities for practice. Preschoolers flourish when they have a place to stretch their bodies and their minds.

TABLE 9-1 Large Motor Skills

Age	Walking	Running	Jumping	Pedalling	Climbing	Throwing
8 months–1 year	Walks in a wide stance like a waddle				Climbs onto furniture and up stairs as an outgrowth of creeping	
1–2 years	Walks in a toddle and uses arms for balance (does not swing arms)	Moves rapidly in a hurried walk in contact with surface	Uses bouncing steps off bottom step of stairs with one foot		Tries climbing up anything climbable	Throws items such as food in a jerky sidearm movement
2–3 years	Walks upstairs two feet on a step	Runs stiffly; has difficulty turning corners and stopping quickly	Jumps off bottom step with both feet	Sits on riding toy and pushes with feet	Tries climbing to top of equipment, although cannot climb down	Throws ball by facing target and using both forearms to push; uses little or no footwork or body rotation
3–4 years	Walks with arms swinging: walks up stairs alternating feet; walks downstairs two feet on step; walks straight line	Runs more smoothly; has more control over starting and stopping	Springs up off floor with both feet in some cases; jumps over object leading with one foot	Pedals and steers tricycle	Climbs up and down ladders, jungle gyms, slides, and trees	Throws overhand with one arm; uses body rotation; does not lose balance
4–5 years	Walks up and down stairs alternating feet; walks circular line; skips with one foot; gallops; walks balance beam	Displays strong, speedy running; turns corners, starts and stops easily	Jumps up, down, and forward	Rides trike rapidly and smoothly	Climbs up and down ladders, jungle gyms, slides, and trees	Uses more mature overhand motions and control but throws from elbow
5–6 years	Walks as an adult, skips alternating feet	Shows mature running, seldom falls, displays increased speed and control	Jumps long, high, and far; jumps rope	Rides small bicycle	Displays mature climbing in adult manner	Steps forward on throwing arm side as throws

SOURCE: From Beaty, Janice J. 1986. Observing development of the young child, p. 148. Columbus, OH: Merrill.

Many parents wonder if they should support their children's motor development even more by participating in some of the many movement and pre-gymnastics programs that have sprung up in recent years. In these programs, children walk on balance beams, crawl through tunnels, tumble on mats, roll on balls, climb ladders, and interact with other children. For older children, real gymnastics classes are available.

Although these programs provide a stimulating, cheerful environment, practice in locomotor activities, and opportunities for learning and social inter-

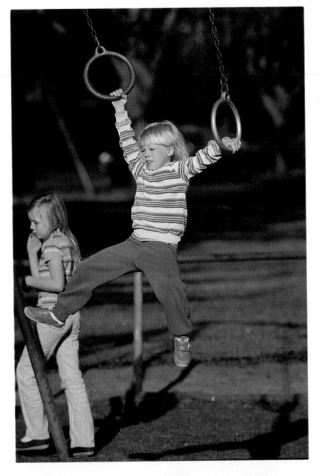

FIGURE 9-9
Swinging on rings requires strength in the muscles of the arms, the upper body, the abdomen, and the legs. The child swings her lower body like a pendulum and moves from ring to ring by throwing her weight back and forth. This favorite activity of 5- and 6-year-olds also requires timing, coordination, and blister-resistant hands.

FIGURE 9-10
Gymnastic training can help young children gain flexibility and strength and learn specific skills, such as how to do a back bend or a cartwheel. But it doesn't speed up physical development or the acquisition of motor skills in very young children. Under normal circumstances, motor skills appear in sequence in all young children without special training or classes.

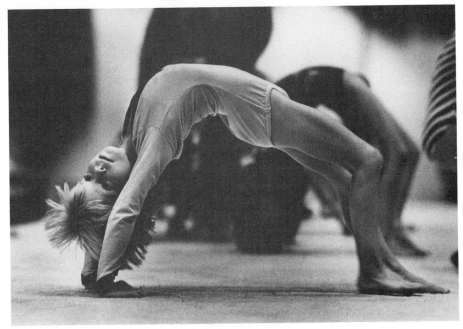

PUBLIC POLICY FOCUS

Making Playgrounds Safe

Skinned knees, scraped elbows, bruises, and bumps—these are the battle scars all children wear at one time or another as they work at developing their physical skills. Parents and teachers usually find that a few words of sympathy, along with a bandaid, some antiseptic wash or spray, or an ice cube wrapped in a wash cloth, are enough to ensure a speedy recovery. These occasions of being hurt and healed are actually an important part of the child's learning experience.

But sometimes children suffer more serious injuries at play, many of them the needless result of unsafe conditions at playgrounds. Approximately 150,000 children per year are seen in hospital emergency rooms for injuries sustained on playgrounds. Most injuries are caused by swings and swing sets. Climbing equipment comes in second, followed by slides and seesaws. Other injuries are caused by protruding bolts and sharp edges on play equipment and by play equipment that entraps a body part. The most serious injuries (and the most deaths) are caused by falls from a height (Greensher & Mofenson, 1985).

What should adults look for in a safe playground? The Consumer Products Safety Commission (1981) has proposed safety standards for playgrounds, although these standards haven't become mandatory. For surfaces under play equipment, the association rates concrete, asphalt, brick, and packed earth as very hazardous and unacceptable. Minimally acceptable are gravel, wood chips, 2-inch-thick gym mats, and 1⅛-inch-thick rubber mats. The only acceptably safe surface is sand to a depth of 8 to 10 inches.

A research lab also conducted tests to investigate the relative safety of various playground surface materials. They wanted to determine the heights from which a child could fall before the critical limit for receiving a concussion was exceeded, expressed

as 50 G (G = gravity) (Reichelderfer, Overbach, & Greensher, 1979). As shown in the accompanying figure, a child would have to fall from over 11 feet to receive a concussion if the surface below were sand, but from less than a foot if the surface were concrete or asphalt.

The association suggests that safety zones surround play equipment like swings so that children don't run into the path of moving swings. Low bushes, railroad ties partially sunk in the sand, or some other border barrier should be used to mark the zones. They also recommend that structures built over a certain height have protective railings or be completely enclosed to prevent falls. Designers of playground equipment must remember that young children are thrilled to be 4 or 5 feet off the ground—10 or 12 feet is unnecessary.

Adults can also inspect equipment for exposed bolts, rough or rusty surfaces, or deteriorated parts. Broken glass, crushed soda cans, and other trash in sand or wood chips are particularly hazardous, and children should never go barefoot where these dangers are evident. Splinters from all wood chips are unpleasant; those from redwood chips quickly become inflamed.

Even when playgrounds are very safe, young children need supervision and guidance in using them. A safety zone around a swing won't do much good if children don't know they're not supposed to run through it. Children have to be taught not to climb over railings, not to rough-house at the top of a slide, and not to ride tricycles off set paths. But when the equipment is safe, adults can concentrate on helping the children play safely.

What can adults do to make playgrounds safer for children? A demonstration project in New York State illustrates what's possible (Fisher, Harris, & VanGuren,

action, there's no evidence that they significantly improve children's motor skills. Most children develop their motor skills by using whatever they find at hand—at home, in their local playground, or in their nursery school play yard. (For a discussion of what to look for in a safe playground, see Public Policy Focus—Making Playgrounds Safe.) As long as there's space to run, a few things to climb on, and a soft place to fall, children attain a fair degree of skill at motor activities by the time they leave their preschool years. But if parent and child enjoy other activity opportunities—like pregymnastics—that's fine too.

Gross Motor Development: Upper Body and Arm Skills

"OK, Tessa, I'm going to throw it again. Get ready." Rick stands about 5 feet away from his daughter and gently tosses a soft ball to her.

Tessa stands with her arms extended straight out in front of her body. As Rick throws

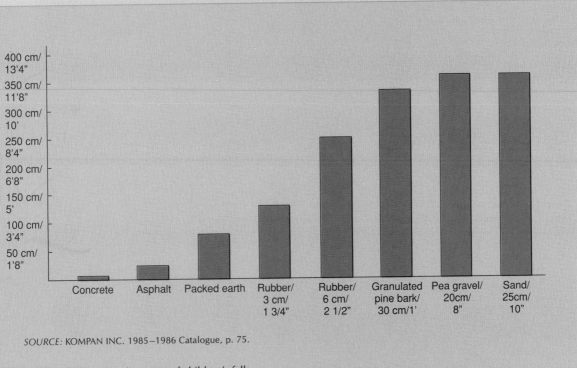

SOURCE: KOMPAN INC. 1985–1986 Catalogue, p. 75.

Effect of surfacing on seriousness of children's falls.

1980). The people who undertook this project inspected the playgrounds in one community, gave seminars and provided literature about playground safety to community personnel, and dispensed information to the public through the local newspapers. As a result, the community made significant changes in the local playgrounds. They covered hard surfaces under play equipment with softer materials and reduced other hazards by 42 percent. Local hospitals subsequently reported that playground-related injuries had dropped by 22 percent. Clearly, training personnel and providing information to the public are important steps in improving safety in local playgrounds.

the ball, she continues to look at his face rather than looking at the ball, and as the ball approaches her, she turns her head to the side and squeezes her eyes shut.

"Ohhh, you missed! Throw it back." Tessa runs to get the ball. She extends her arm up above her head and throws the ball onto the ground in front of her. Rick picks it up and gets ready to throw it again.

"OK, are you ready?" Tessa smiles and nods. "Put your arms out in front of you. Now, this time, try to watch the ball, OK? Keep your eye on the ball." He tosses the ball. Tessa watches Rick's face again as the ball approaches, and again turns her head away and shuts her eyes as it bounces softly against her chest.

"Ohhh, almost! Try again!"

Anyone who has played catch with a young child will recognize this scene. As long as the child is having fun and the adult understands her limitations, a ball game is a positive experience for a preschooler. But some ball skills are very difficult to master, and older children and adolescents are still learning and practicing them. Preschoolers have their hands full learning the rudiments of throwing and catching a ball.

FIGURE 9-11
Throwing a ball isn't as easy
as it looks. Skill develops
over a number of years and
progresses through the
stages shown here.

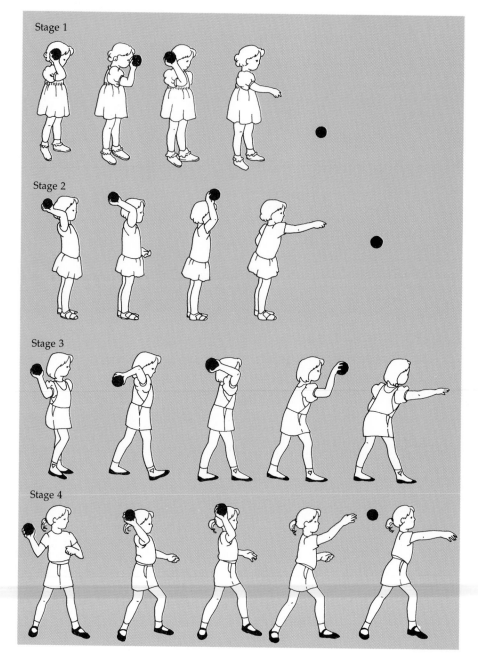

THROWING A BALL. The groundwork for ball playing is laid even before the
preschool period. Infants enjoy rolling a ball forward once they can sit up. In
the second year of life, children start to throw or toss objects in the air from
a sitting position during Stage 5 of the sensorimotor period (see Chapter 6).
Older toddlers stand and toss a ball with both hands, shifting their weight
very little as they let go of it.

Once a child like Tessa starts using a one-handed strategy for throwing, we
can observe a four-stage pattern of development (Williams, 1983). At first, she

holds her body stiffly and throws the ball with a simple, fast arm extension. She doesn't rotate her body or "get behind the ball." In the next stage, she twists her shoulder a bit to follow her arm as it moves forward, but she doesn't shift her body weight or change her footing.

In the third stage, she takes a step forward with the leg on the throwing-arm side of the body as she extends her arm and releases the ball. She rotates her shoulder slightly but doesn't turn her body much. Finally, she starts to rotate her body, first twisting it back as she pulls her arm back, then twisting it forward as she throws. As she rotates her body, her arm moves through quite a wide arc, increasing the ball's velocity. Illustrations of this developmental process are shown in Figure 9-12.

It takes anywhere from three to five years for a child to move from the first to the fourth stage in ball throwing. At age 3, a child is usually at the first stage; by age 6 to 8, the child has usually attained a rudimentary stage 4. Although school-age children and adolescents continue to develop their throwing skills, the basics are mastered during the preschool period.

CATCHIING A BALL. Catching also develops in stages. It begins when babies sit and capture a ball that rolls between their legs. Young children find it easier to catch a large ball tossed straight at them than a smaller ball thrown up like a fly ball (Randt, 1985). Even so, they extend their arms stiffly to try to trap the ball with arms, hands, and body rather than reaching to grasp the ball with their hands. Like Tessa, they're unable to follow the ball with their eyes and often turn their faces away in a protective gesture as the ball approaches.

Somewhat later, they start to watch the ball as it approaches and to use just their hands to grasp it. Later still, usually at about age 5, they place their feet wide apart on the ground in anticipation of needing to move to one side or the other to catch the ball. When they actually close their hands around the ball, they pull their arms back to cushion the force of the throw against their

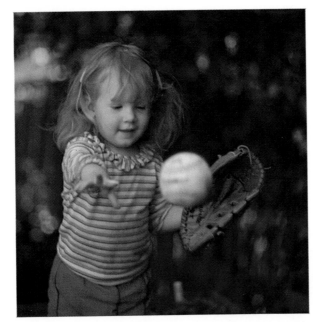

FIGURE 9-12
A young preschooler needs more than a glove to play a good game of baseball. She lacks the coordination and muscle strength necessary for effective throwing and the nervous system development necessary for accurate catching. Those skills will come in time.

bodies (Cratty, 1986). Only older children and adolescents are able to execute such maneuvers as jumping and extending one gloved hand to catch a fly ball.

REACTION TIME. In addition to the physical skills needed to catch a ball, children have to develop the mental agility to respond to the throw. The time it takes the child to respond is called **reaction time.** Reaction time consists of the time it takes for the child to assimilate the stimuli (such as the appearance of an oncoming ball); the time it takes for the child to make judgments about the throw; the time it takes for the child to decide which movements to make to catch the ball; and the time it takes the mental plan to reach the muscles (Cratty, 1986).

Even a ball thrown slowly from a short distance requires a judgment the instant it's in the air if the child is going to catch it (Whiting, 1969). As we saw, reaction time in a 3-year-old like Tessa is very slow. It improves quite a lot between ages 3 and 5, but it still lags way behind the reaction time of older children and adults. A lot of older children's skill at throwing, catching, and batting can be attributed to their faster reaction time.

Like the locomotor skills, the upper body and arm skills of throwing and catching develop as the child grows. The center of gravity changes, muscle tissue increases and fat decreases, and the nervous system matures, producing better coordination and improved reaction time. All the child needs from the environment is a ball, a willing companion, and plenty of opportunities for practice.

OVERVIEW

The chubby toddler with her protruding tummy and waddling walk gives way now to the leaner, more coordinated preschooler who can run, climb, and jump with relative ease. The preschool yard is filled with children pedalling tricycles, pushing each other in wagons, scrambling up play structures, and pursuing imaginary bad guys and monsters. Preschoolers' improved large and fine motor control allows them to do many things for themselves that they couldn't do just a year earlier. With their greater desire for independence, this development suits them just fine. By the end of the preschool years they've gained so much in physical abilities and motor skills that they're ready to take on the elementary school physical education program.

CHAPTER REVIEW

APPEARANCE AND GROWTH

- Preschoolers are longer and thinner than they were as toddlers, and their heads are more in proportion to their bodies.
- They continue to grow at a slowed-down rate, gaining about 3 pounds a year and growing about $2\frac{1}{2}$ inches a year.

- Preschoolers often don't have very big appetites. They should be given a nutritional diet and not be pressured to eat.

MOTOR DEVELOPMENT

- Children gain more control over their hands and fingers during the preschool years and use this ability in many fine motor activities, such as drawing, cutting, pasting, and stringing beads.
- They also gain the ability to dress and toilet themselves, fine motor skills that mesh well with their emerging desire to be independent. Parents can support this quest for independence by providing manageable clothes as well as any necessary help and supervision. When children have disabilities, parents and caregivers may have to make certain adaptations in the environment to help them become independent.
- The preschooler's center of gravity has moved down to the abdomen, providing a more secure base for balance and locomotor activities.
- Preschool children are adept at running, jumping, and climbing. Movements requiring more coordination, such as galloping, hopping, and skipping, take them longer to master. Their balancing skills also improve during this period.
- Motor skills emerge as more muscle tissue develops and as the brain matures. These skills are nurtured by a stimulating environment and opportunities to practice. Playgrounds are important places for preschoolers, although adults should make sure they're safe and free from hazards.
- Preschoolers begin to master the basics of throwing and catching a ball. By the age of 6, the typical child can get her body behind the ball to throw it and can maneuver to catch it. Children's reaction time also improves during the preschool years, so they're able to respond more quickly when catching or batting a ball.

KEY TERMS

center of gravity
marked-time climbing
reaction time

SUGGESTIONS FOR FURTHER READING

Clarke, J. E., & Humphrey, J. H. (Eds.) *Motor development: Current selected research* (Vol. 1). Pennington, NJ: Princeton Book.

This book includes chapters on the motor skills involved in such tasks as catching a ball and jumping. Other chapters discuss timing and fine-tuning of skills. This volume is for the student who is very interested in motor development in preschool and school-age children.

Cratty, B. J. (1986). *Perceptual and motor development in infants and children* (3rd ed.). Englewood Cliffs, NJ: Prentice-Hall.

This highly readable classic provides a thorough discussion of physical growth and motor development.

Chapters on hands, visual perception, and the effects of exercise provide interesting information.

Engstrom, G. (1971). *The significance of the young child's motor development.* Washington, DC: The National Association of Young Children.

This short booklet discusses the importance of motor development in the preschool child. Included are useful pictures of sequences of movements young children make in throwing a ball and in jumping from a height.

Sinclair, C. B. (1973). *Movement of the young child: Ages two to six.* Columbus, OH: Merrill.

This book provides a thorough, but readable, overview of many physical skills that develop in young children.

chapter 10

COGNITIVE DEVELOPMENT IN PRESCHOOL CHILDREN

Margaret and her dad are playing a board game. Margaret, who is 4, rolls the dice.

"A five and a two," she says as the dice come to rest. Then she starts to count out the dots, pointing to each one with her finger, to find out how many spaces to move her token. "One, two, three, four, five, six, seven."

Next, Margaret's dad takes his turn. He rolls a four and a three. "Seven," he says, as he starts to make his move.

"Hey! You can't do that," Margaret protests. "You have to count the dots."

"Well, four dots and three dots are seven dots," her dad replies.

"No," Margaret insists. "You have to count to see."

Her dad complies, but since he thinks Margaret is questioning his ability to add, he starts with the four as a given. "Four," he says, pointing to one die. "Five, six, seven," he continues, pointing to the dots on the other die. "See? Four and three do equal seven."

"But you have to count that one, too," Margaret persists, pointing to the die with four dots.

"I do?" asks her dad. "Why?"

"To see how many it is," she explains, sounding a little exasperated.

"Oh, I see," her dad answers. "Okay. I thought we already knew that it was four."

"No, we didn't," Margaret says, as she watches to make sure her father counts all four dots.

"One, two, three, four, five, six, seven," her dad counts out loud. "Did I do it right that time?"

"Uh-huh. Now you can move."

Margaret's behavior is fairly typical of most preschoolers. On the one hand, her cognitive abilities seem quite sophisticated. She can recognize the pattern of five dots at a glance, and she can count accurately at least to seven. On the

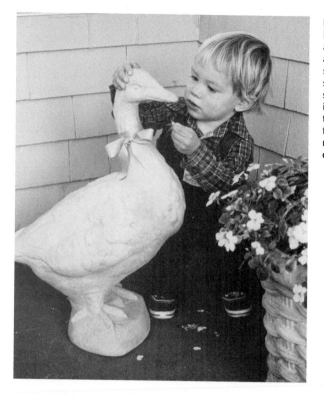

FIGURE 10-1
Distinctions between appearance and reality aren't apparent to young preschoolers. It makes as much sense to this boy to feed a stone duck on the porch as it does to feed a live one at the duck pond. In the next few years he'll develop a much clearer sense of the difference between the two.

other hand, she doesn't exploit the knowledge she has. She can say, "That's a four," at the same time that she says, "We have to count to see if it's four." Her knowledge about one situation doesn't extend to another situation.

Preschoolers have pieces of knowledge, but they don't have an overall framework into which they can fit the pieces. Their knowledge is fragmented and tied to certain contexts. Their thinking seems inflexible and illogical. They lack some of the basic assumptions on which adults base their understanding of the world.

Despite these limitations, preschoolers have made some important advances since they were toddlers. Their thinking is now **preoperational** rather than sensorimotor; that is, they can represent objects and events mentally—they can think—in ways that weren't possible before, even though they don't apply the logic that's characteristic of older children's thinking.

In this chapter, we examine the typical thinking of preschoolers. We see, for example, that they rely on appearances rather than on ideas, that they can focus on just one relationship at a time, and that they often see things primarily from one point of view—their own. We begin by looking at the cognitive skills and abilities that they have and the ones they don't have yet. We explore their difficulties with seemingly simple tasks such as judging whether quantity changes when spacial arrangement changes, creating an ordered series, classifying items into categories, understanding another person's physical perspective, and counting. We then consider children's thinking about thinking itself—about thoughts, dreams, ideas, false beliefs—and the mental abilities that make their thinking unique. From these discussions, we arrive at an overall picture of the child's cognitive development between ages 3 and 6.

UNDERSTANDING THE CONCEPT OF NUMBER

As with cognitive development at other ages, much of our knowledge about the abilities of preschoolers comes from the work of Piaget. Additional ideas and data come from researchers who questioned Piaget's methods and challenged his findings, researchers known as neo-Piagetians. Here, we discuss Piaget's classic contributions before turning to some of the criticisms of Piaget's work and to more current research.

Perhaps the most famous of Piaget's experiments are his investigations of conservation. No matter how we arrange ten blocks, for example, they will always be ten blocks. And no matter how we distribute a cup of water, it will always be one cup. When children understand that rearrangement of a substance or a group of objects doesn't affect its quantity, we say that they have **conservation**, meaning they can think in such a way as to arrive at a logical conclusion about what does and does not affect quantity. Piaget investigated several different areas of conservation, including conservation of number and conservation of continuous quantity, or mass.

Conservation of Number

In the classic Piagetian number conservation task, the experimenter arranges eight to ten objects in a row and asks the child to make a second row with just as many objects as the first row. Most 3-year-olds and even some young 4-year-olds are unable to do this task. They pay attention to the length of the row and make sure their row begins and ends just opposite the model, but they use either more or fewer objects than the model in constructing their row (Figure 10-2a). When the child performs this way, the experiment has gone as far as it can.

If, on the other hand, the child is able to create a second row equal to the first row by matching the objects one-to-one, the experimenter can proceed with the second part of the task. Now the experimenter changes the distribution in one of the rows so that it becomes either longer or shorter than the other (Figure 10-2b). The child is told to watch what the experimenter does,

FIGURE 10-2
In the Piagetian conservation of number task, the experimenter asks the child to create a row with the same number of objects as the row created by the experimenter (a). If the child can do this (b), the experimenter rearranges the row and asks the child if it still has the same number of objects as before. Most preschoolers answer no, basing their response on appearances rather than logical thinking.

and afterward, the child is asked if the two rows still have the same number of objects or if one has more or less than the other.

Less advanced children say that the new row contains a different number of objects. Some children focus on the density of the rows; they say the shorter row contains more objects. Other children focus on the length of the rows, and they say the longer row has more objects. Most children between ages $4\frac{1}{2}$ and 6 deny that the two rows could have the same number after they've been rearranged.

By 6 years of age, most children say that the two rearranged rows still contain the same number of items. When asked why they think this is so, they usually give one of three explanations: (1) No item was taken away or added (that is, they explain it by **identity**); (2) the longer row has big gaps (they explain it by **compensation;**) or (3) the displaced row could be put back the way it was in the beginning (they explain it by **reversibility**). According to Piaget, any one of these responses indicates that a child can conserve number. Children typically begin to respond to the conservation of number task in terms of logic—what they think about the rows—rather than in terms of perception—how the rows look—when they're about 6 or $6\frac{1}{2}$ years old.

Conservation of Continuous Quantity

Whereas the conservation of number involves individual objects or units, the conservation of continuous quantity involves mass. The Piagetian task with which this cognitive ability is investigated involves two large identical beakers (referred to here as beaker 1 and beaker 2) filled with colored water. The experimenter asks the child to look at them to be sure that they contain the same amount of liquid. The child can pour liquid from one to the other, if necessary, until they are exactly the same. When the child has agreed that the quantities in the two beakers are identical, the experimenter pours the water in beaker 2 into another beaker of a different shape or into several small containers (Figure 10-3). The child is then asked if beaker 1 contains the same amount of liquid as beaker 3 (if the beaker is used) or as the small cups (if cups are used).

Three-year-olds and young 4-year-olds think that the liquid that has been transferred into a different container has also changed in quantity. Between ages $4\frac{1}{2}$ and 6, children sometimes say that the quantity of the transferred liquid is the same as before, especially when the liquid is now in a different-shaped beaker. But when the containers are very different, as they are when cups are used, these children revert to saying that the quantity has changed. It's not until children are 6 or 7 years old that they disregard what they see and instead rely on logic. They explain the apparent discrepancy by saying, "This container is wider, but it isn't as high," or "There are more little cups, but they don't hold very much," or "We could pour all these back into this one."

As you can see, preschoolers typically are unable to demonstrate conservation on the Piagetian conservation tasks. However, there is some debate about preschoolers' understandings: Some critics say that preschoolers are more competent than the Piagetian tasks reveal (Gelman & Gallistel, 1978). They've found that changing the tasks affects how children perform on them. To clarify the issue in this debate, we elaborate briefly on how Piaget explained preschoolers' difficulties on the conservation tasks.

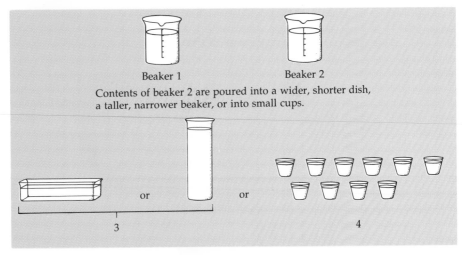

FIGURE 10-3
In the Piagetian conservation of continuous quantity task, the experimenter pours water from one beaker into a beaker of a different shape or into several cups. Most preschool children think the amount of water is different at the end of this procedure.

Beaker 1   Beaker 2

Contents of beaker 2 are poured into a wider, shorter dish, a taller, narrower beaker, or into small cups.

or   or

3   4

Piaget's Explanation: Preoperational Thinking

Piaget described many aspects of children's cognitive development in terms of mental operations. Mental operations are specific processes of reasoning we go through in our minds. Thinking that a taller, thinner container of water is equal to a shorter, fatter container of water is an example of a mental operation—a logical comparison or multiplication, in this case. According to Piaget, preschoolers have certain limitations in their operational abilities that make it impossible for them to think about things in this logical way. For example, they tend to **center**—focus mentally—on only one aspect of a relationship at a time, to the exclusion of all other aspects, perhaps the tallness of one container of water and the shortness of a second container. What they cannot do is focus on both tallness and thinness versus shortness and fatness. The conservation tasks require that *two* relationships be compared and coordinated, and this is the thing that preschoolers typically can't do.

Another limitation of preschoolers' thinking is its **irreversibility**. After observing an action, preschoolers can't play it backward in their heads to reconstruct how things were originally. They focus more on states—how things look at the end of a particular action—than on transformations—how one state changes to another and is related to it. When a child watches the experimenter spread out a row of pennies so they're no longer directly opposite the pennies in another row, the child doesn't realize the action of spreading out the pennies could be reversed. If the child watches someone else put the pennies back, or if the child does it himself when asked, he will then say that the rows once again contain the same number of pennies. The child thinks only about pennies opposite each other or pennies not opposite each other. The transformation connecting these two states escapes him.

Piaget referred to the preschool child's thinking as **preoperational**; that is, it's not characterized by such operations as coordinating two aspects of a relationship (such as length and density of rows of pennies) or reversing an action to coordinate two different positions of the same objects (such as close together and spread out). The child who can conserve, on the other hand, is said to be thinking at a **concrete operational** level. A child at this level can apply

FIGURE 10-4
Preschool children don't have a problem accepting the notion that Santa Claus delivers toys to every child in the world in one night, nor do they question how reindeer can fly. These 3-year-olds aren't old enough to wonder if this is the "real" Santa. Their concern is what to say when it's their turn and how Santa will respond.

logical thinking to a situation, as long as the data can all be seen and the situation is therefore concrete.

Children usually become capable of concrete operational thought by 7 years, the age at which many new mental functions appear and many new activities are introduced at school. This age has traditionally been recognized as marking the "dawn of rationality." By age 7, many children have figured out through logic that Santa Claus, the Tooth Fairy, and the Easter Bunny (probably) don't exist. This is in contrast to the thinking of a 6-year-old who responded indignantly when told by a 9-year-old that "your mom and dad" perform all those duties. "Santa Claus *does* exist," she stormed. "I *know*, because how could your mom and dad get all the way to the North Pole?!"

Critiques of Piaget and Approaches to the Conservation Tasks by Neo-Piagetians

Piaget's discoveries about the limits of children's thinking have been generally accepted, but some people have questioned the ages at which he found various understandings in children. They believe, for example, that children really understand conservation earlier than Piaget's tasks indicated. They have looked carefully at the tasks to see if another explanation exists for the children's performance. Some critics suggest that the standard procedure used in administering the tasks was influencing children's expectations and leading them astray.

For example, the child is told to "watch closely while I do something." A statement like this may lead the child to believe that a significant change is being made, which isn't really the case. In children's everyday life, people rarely call their attention to something insignificant. When they're told to "watch carefully," it's usually because something important is going to happen. But in the task, quantity *doesn't* change. They may understand this, but they may take the experimenter's words as a cue that a trick of some kind is going on. If this is the case, then the experiment is measuring not just their concept of number but also their social awareness—their knowledge that sometimes people try to fool other people.

One researcher decided to change the conservation task to reduce the likelihood that children were being influenced by false expectations (Donaldson, 1978). She used a stuffed animal named Naughty Teddy to intrude on the task and "mess up" one of the rows of cubes. The exasperated experimenter then invited the child to put Naughty Teddy back in his box, and she resumed the experiment, saying, "Now, where were we? Ah yes, is the number in this row the same as in this row?"

In Piaget's standard experiment with 4- to 6-year-olds, only 13 out of 80 children could conserve number, but in the Naughty Teddy experiment, 50 out of 80 did so. The researcher concluded that young children know more about the logic of number than Piaget's task suggests. If their expectations aren't biased by the experimenter's statements, we can discover more about their actual knowledge.

Other researchers agree with this assessment and have devised a variety of alterations on the standard test. In one study, children were asked about the equality of the rows only once, after the transformation, instead of both before and after. Children again demonstrated more understanding than in the standard test (Rose & Blank, 1974). Other researchers have reduced the number of objects used in the tasks and changed the task format (Gelman & Gallistel, 1978). Under these conditions, they found that preschool children do realize when quantities have been changed and when they've just been rearranged.

Still other critics have objected not so much to the way early parts of the task are presented as to Piaget's requirement that children be able to explain their answers. If they couldn't give one of the three reasons mentioned previously to explain why the two quantities were still the same, Piaget didn't believe they could conserve number. Critics suggest that this rigorous requirement brings in verbal and expressive abilities and obscures children's understanding of number (Brainerd, 1977).

How Much Do Preschoolers Really Understand?

Despite the validity of the critics' comments about the Piagetian tasks, Piaget did put his finger on a significant difference between the thinking of preschoolers and that of 6- or 7-year-olds. Younger children's thinking is not as logical, not as "connected," as older children's. Consider this incident:

4-year-old Andy was setting a table for snack time at his preschool. On one side of the table, he accidentally put an extra place setting, leaving a chair on the other side without a napkin and cup. "I don't have enough," he told the teacher.

"Well, we counted out six cups and six napkins, and there are six chairs at your table," answered the teacher, "so it should work out."

"But I don't have enough," Andy protested. "Come look."

The teacher saw the problem and picked up the extra cup and napkin that Andy had positioned between two chairs on one side of the table. "Where do these go?" he asked Andy.

Andy straightened the place settings, making sure there was one in front of each chair. "Oh," he said, "Those go here. Now we have enough."

An older child would probably have viewed this situation differently. If he had counted out six napkins and six cups and had come up one place setting short, he might have thought, "I know I had enough. Where did I goof up?" After surveying the table, he might have said, "Oh, I see. I made a mistake over there." But Andy assumed the number of cups and napkins—not their arrangement—was the problem. Even after putting the place settings in the right place, he said, "Now we have enough," rather than "I made a mistake," as if the rearrangement itself had created a different number of items.

In their everyday behavior, whether setting tables or counting the dots on dice, preschoolers do demonstrate a limited understanding of number. Both Piaget and his critics have given us valid information about their mental competence in this area. Drawing on both sources, we conclude that preschoolers can often function at quite a high level if we're careful about how we organize the situation and if we're willing to give a helping hand.

UNDERSTANDING THE CONCEPTS OF SERIATION AND CLASSIFICATION

Some of the same kinds of limitations in thinking are obvious when we look at preschoolers' ability to create a series by placing different objects in order by size (a process called **seriation**). As with the concept of number, Piaget did the ground-breaking work, but others have added refinements to his conclusions.

Piaget's Standard Seriation Task

The seriation task involves arranging about ten sticks, all a little different in length, into a graduated series. This task is impossible for most 4-year-olds and young 5-year-olds. They might put the shorter sticks together in one pile and the longer ones together in a second pile (Figure 10-5a). Or they might focus only on the tops or only on the bottoms, creating a pseudoseries (Figure 10-5b).

The task is somewhat easier for 5- and 6-year-olds. They can make a series, but they get there through a process of trial and error. They still can't think of two aspects of each stick at the same time—its length in relation to the last one placed in the series and its length in relation to the rest of the sticks in the pile. They tend to select a stick that's longer than the last one but also longer than some of the remaining ones. Only when they pick up another stick and discover it's shorter than the last one do they discover their error and make an adjustment. Piaget called this approach **intuitive**—based on a vague notion of what's involved in seriating—and **empirical**—discovered as they go along.

Children aged 6 and 7 can solve the problem **operationally**. They select each successive stick correctly by thinking about how long or short it is in relation both to the sticks already used and to those that remain. They think, "The next one has to be longer than the last one but shorter than all the others." Unlike the preoperational child, who can only make one comparison and make it on the basis of how things look, the operational child can make two comparisons, using mental operations.

FIGURE 10-5
In the Piagetian seriation task, children are asked to arrange a number of sticks in order from smallest to largest. Preschoolers often create series like those shown here. Most children younger than 6 or 7 are unable to select the stick that comes next except through trial and error.

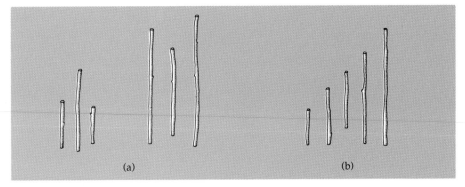

(a)　　　　　　　　　　　　　(b)

The Nesting Cup Task

Other information about children's ability to create a series comes from research that wasn't specifically designed to test Piaget's findings. Psychologist Judy DeLoache (1985) was interested in how children correct their errors when they encounter a problem. She devised a study involving ten nesting cups (a series of graduated plastic cups that fit inside each other) of the kind parents frequently buy for babies and toddlers. She wanted to see how children between $1\frac{1}{2}$ and $3\frac{1}{2}$ years approach the task of getting all the cups to nest inside each other.

The youngest children in the study, those under $2\frac{1}{2}$ years, often responded with force when they couldn't insert one cup inside another. They pushed, banged, or used some other way to force the fit. They also sometimes put down one of the cups they held and tried another. The idea that the two they already held could be reversed didn't occur to them. A third strategy was also seen: Regardless of whether the child had already fit several cups together, once a problem was encountered, the child took the whole series apart and started over!

Older children, those between $2\frac{1}{2}$ and $3\frac{1}{2}$, were less likely to use brute force or to dismantle the series once they encountered a problem. Often, they simply reversed the two cups they had, putting the smaller one into the larger instead of the larger into the smaller. This maneuver suggests that they understood the size relationship of the two cups to each other. An even more sophisticated strategy involved insertion. This involved taking apart the stack of cups assembled so far until the point was reached at which the new cup could be inserted. Both of these approaches—reversing and inserting—involve reordering and are similar to the trial and error approaches of 5- and 6-year-olds in Piaget's seriation task.

Of the 40 children in the study, 18 actually created a correct series. Given the age of these children, the results are surprising. In the standard Piagetian task, children much older than this are just starting to be able to seriate.

The Two Tasks Compared

Why do we see this big discrepancy between the two tasks? The answer, again, seems to involve the variables of the testing situation. The nesting cups can't be placed incorrectly; it's physically impossible. But the sticks used in the

FIGURE 10-6
Research findings differ on the ages at which children have the cognitive ability to perform such tasks as creating an ordered series. In Piaget's task, children younger than 4 were unable to create a series, but 5- and 6-year-olds could seriate through trial and error. In DeLoache's experiment, many 3½-year-olds were able to seriate through trial and error. Whatever the actual ages, it's clear that the understandings needed to perform the task develop considerably during the preschool period. A 5-year-old (right) has a much better grasp of the problem and how to solve it than a 2-year-old (left).

Piagetian task can be put anywhere; they don't physically resist the child's mistake. Children have to notice an error on their own before they can rearrange the sticks. Some of the mistakes children make with the sticks may be due to a failure to notice things about the different sticks, not to an inability to make a series by operational processes. Furthermore, many children have experience with the cups, and they may already know that they have to pay close attention if they're going to get them all inside each other.

The nesting cups test highlights the big differences between preschoolers' abilities and those of toddlers. The Piagetian tasks were administered to preschool and older children, not to children under age 3. They make us focus on what preschoolers *can't* do rather than on what they can do. The nesting cups experiment helps us put preschool cognitive abilities in better perspective.

Classification

A third dimension of logical thinking that researchers have studied in children is the ability to classify—separating objects and grouping them in classes according to certain attributes. To see what's involved in this process, consider this task:

> On a table are a large red felt circle, a large blue felt circle, a large blue felt square, a little red felt square, a little blue felt square, a little red felt circle, a paper clip, an elastic band, and an eraser. Organize the materials.

FIGURE 10-7
In hierarchical classification tasks, experimenters are interested in whether children can create superordinate and subordinate categories, such as those shown here. Preschoolers aren't very skilled at organizing or classifying, which is one of the reasons a conversation with a 4-year-old may take some surprising turns.

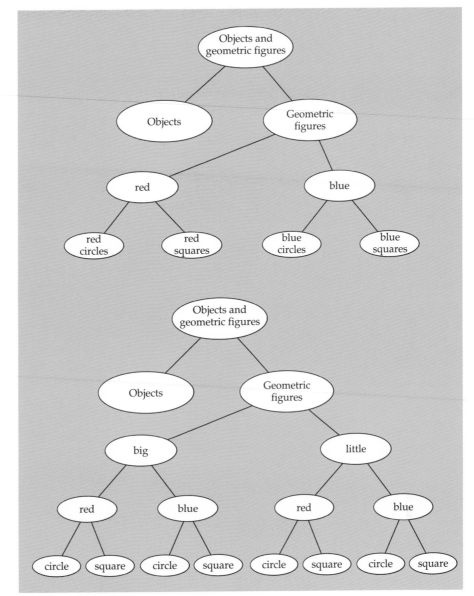

First, you might separate the shapes from the objects. Then you might work within the class of shapes to create finer categories. You could put the red shapes together and the blue shapes together and then divide these groups further into circles and squares or big shapes and little shapes. Groupings like these can be represented schematically as shown in Figure 10-7. This process is known as hierarchical classification because subclasses are created within classes.

When we classify, we create categories, or classes, in our minds. Shapes become red shapes and blue shapes, or big shapes and little shapes, or circles and squares. A classification system is constructed and imposed on objects—

it's not inherent in the objects themselves, although objects' attributes determine the classes we're able to construct.

Children under 4 years of age would have trouble classifying the shapes and objects in this task. They can group objects into collections but not into true classes, which are groups defined by a stable attribute (Inhelder & Piaget, 1969). They might start with one defining attribute in mind, such as color, and then switch to another one, such as shape. They would start with a red square, follow it with a red circle, and follow that with a blue circle. Preoperational children are guided less by thinking—by keeping an idea of an attribute in mind—than by what they see in front of them and have in their hands.

Sometimes young children "organize" these shapes and objects by making a picture with them (a house, a bridge, an airplane). They group them not according to any specific attribute but by what fits with the picture they want to make. No defining "class" characteristic is selected at all.

Children between 5 and 7 years of age can make classes based on a single, defining attribute. They can put all the red shapes together, or all the squares together, without losing track of the attribute they're working with. They even organize subclasses within classes, such as red squares, blue squares, and yellow squares. But children this age have trouble thinking about **class inclusion**, about the fact that both red circles and red squares are members of the larger class, red. This difficulty is particularly noticeable if they're asked questions such as, "Would we have any red objects left if we lost all of the red circles?" To answer questions like this, children have to think about parts (red circles and red squares) in relation to the whole (all the red things). Children are unable to comprehend questions like this until they're 7 or 8 years old (Ginsburg & Opper, 1988).

FIGURE 10-8
This boy is able to separate marbles from plastic gears, indicating that he has some sense of how objects can be classified on the basis of their attributes. But he probably wouldn't be able to think in terms of abstract categories or of the attributes themselves. Because his thinking is preoperational, his grasp of classification is still confined to hands-on experiences.

Aerial view

UNDERSTANDING PHYSICAL POINT OF VIEW

The last dimension of logical thinking that we consider here is the ability to understand that another person's physical perspective might be different from one's own and to figure out what that perspective might be (Piaget & Inhelder, 1967). The apparatus Piaget used in this task consists of a three-dimensional display of three mountains, which differ in height, color, and landscape features (Figure 10-9). The child is asked to walk around the display and to look at it from all vantage points. The child is then seated on one side of the display opposite a doll who faces it from the other side and asked to select the doll's view of the display from among a series of ten photographs.

The youngest children (4-year-olds) select photographs at random. By age 5, children usually select the photo showing the view they see. By age 6 or 7, children seem to realize that the doll can't see what they see, but they rarely pick out the correct photo. Not until the age of 9 or 10 do they reliably select the doll's actual view. From these results Piaget concluded that preschoolers are unable to take another's point of view.

This task, like some of the other Piagetian tasks, has been criticized by other researchers. Modifications in the task have shown preschoolers to be somewhat more competent than Piaget found. For example, when children are asked to rotate a model to show what the doll sees, they perform better than when they're asked to pick out a photo (Huttenlocher & Presson, 1973).

Children's performance on completely different tasks also indicates that even 2- and 3-year-olds have some awareness of different perspectives. For example, when asked to hide an object so that an adult could not see it, they made it invisible to an adult (by placing it behind a screen) while keeping it within their own view (Flavell, Shipstead, & Croft, 1978).

Preschool children are certainly more aware of their own perspectives than of the perspectives of others, and in this sense we can say they're egocentric. But as with other abilities, Piaget may have underestimated their ability to see things from another's point of view.

ARITHMETICAL SKILLS AND UNDERSTANDINGS

Research on conservation, seriation, classification, has given us insight into the limits of preschoolers' logical thinking. But these aren't the kinds of problems young children normally have to deal with as they play games or live their everyday lives. The cognitive tasks they're more likely to encounter involve counting or adding simple sums. The way they perform these tasks also reveals how their cognitive functioning differs from older children's.

Early Counting

Carlos was counting the chairs set up around a small table to see if there were enough for himself and four other 3-year-olds. "One, two, three, four, five, six, seven," he counted, before his teacher interrupted. "Whoa there, Carlos! I think you counted some of those chairs twice. Start again, and this time I'll keep my hand on the chair you began with. Then you'll know where to stop."

Counting isn't the simple skill it may at first appear to be. By definition, it involves enumerating units to arrive at a total number of units. It also involves giving a stable, consistent meaning to each of the conventional counting words (called **tags**). We might see toddlers and young preschoolers pointing to objects and reciting counting words, but this behavior doesn't mean they're really counting. The skills and understandings required for true counting are just being acquired by preschoolers. On their way to these achievements, they make a number of typical errors.

THREE KINDS OF COUNTING ERRORS. Carlos made a counting error that's very common among preschoolers. He counted items more than once because he failed to notice which ones he'd already counted and which he hadn't counted. Sometimes children neglect to count some items because they skip over them. In either case, this **partitioning error** involves a failure to separate counted items accurately from uncounted items (Gelman & Gallistel, 1978).

Sometimes children start saying tags (number words) before they touch or point to the first object, say them faster than they touch or point, or keep on saying them after all the objects have been accounted for. In these **coordination errors**, they fail to match their numerical recitation to the objects they're counting (Baroody, 1987). Preschoolers playing board games often make these errors. They move their playing piece down the board path at a different rate than they say the tags.

A third kind of counting error preschoolers commonly make is using unconventional tags ("one, two, three, four, a, b, c") or using conventional tags in nonstandard order ("one, two, three, six, eight, ten"). If they use the same nonstandard sequence in successive counts, we can say that they're really counting; they're just not using the conventional tags. If they use one nonstandard sequence one time and a different one the next time, they're not really counting. They're simply using counting words as labels or names for objects (Gelman, 1982).

AGES ASSOCIATED WITH THE COUNTING ERRORS. When 2-year-olds start to count a group of objects, they make a partitioning or coordination error almost imme-

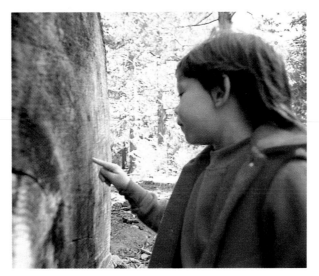

FIGURE 10-10
Counting tree rings is an ambitious task for a 5-year-old. Even if he counts slowly and uses his finger to keep track of the rings he's already counted, it will be hard for him to avoid the common preschool counting errors. And with a tree this old, he may not know or remember the names of all the numbers he'll need. In just a year or two, he'll be much more skillful at counting accurately.

diately. Most 4-year-olds can count about five objects accurately before they begin to make errors (Gelman & Gallistel, 1978; Saxe, Guberman, & Gearhart, 1987). Many 5-year-olds can count 20 objects accurately if the objects aren't in disarray (Baroody, 1987).

When objects are in disarray, and when there are a lot of them in a group, children have to order the objects mentally in some way to count them without making partitioning or coordination errors. Understanding the need to establish some order is probably tied to an increased understanding of the meaning of counting. Unless children realize that counting implies **hierarchical inclusion**—the idea that 1 is included in 2, 2 is included in 3, and so on—they're not likely to be careful about counting each object once and only once (Kamii, 1982).

Even 5-year-olds have trouble counting large groups of disorganized objects (Fuson, 1988). Objects arranged in a straight line are easier for children to count than objects arranged in a circle, because the beginning and end of the group are clear. Movable items like cubes and buttons are also easier to count than immovable items like dots on the face of a die. They can be moved away from the group as they're counted, making them distinct from the items still to be counted. Like the teacher who helped Carlos count by putting his hand on the first chair Carlos counted, parents and preschool teachers can modify situations to help children learn to obtain more accurate counts.

The ability to use the conventional tags for numbers is also tied to age. Many 3-year-olds know and use the first five tags and can recite them in order, (Saxe, Guberman, & Gearhart, 1987), but after this they jump ahead: "One, two, three, four, five, seven, ten" (Gelman & Meck, 1983). Most 4-year-olds can recite the conventional tags up to about 15 (Saxe, Guberman, & Gearhart, 1987), but they tend to make errors when they get to the teens: "twelve, fifteen, sixteen, thirteen, twenty." Because some of the teen numbers do not match their one-to-ten counterparts (we say "thirteen" rather than "threeteen," for example, and "fifteen" rather than "fiveteen"), the teen tags are hard to remember and use in the correct sequence (Baroody, 1987).

FIGURE 10-11
Younger preschoolers don't realize that counting the number of objects in a group gives them the answer to the question, How many objects are there?

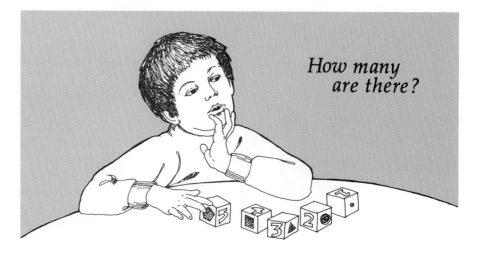

Understanding Simple Arithmetical Relations

As mentioned previously, one of the understandings involved in counting is hierarchical inclusion. Older children and adults know that counting implies that 1 is included in 2, 2 in 3, and so on, and that this implies further that 3 is more than 2 and 2 is more than 1. Relationships as simple as "greater than" and "less than" are not self-evident to young children. Some 3-year-olds are just beginning to understand these relationships with small numbers and can tell you, for example, that 3 is more than 2 (Schaeffer, Eggleston, & Scott, 1974).

By 4 years, children can make many accurate comparisons between numbers under 10 when asked which number of a pair is larger. The greater the difference between the two numbers—4 compared with 9, for example, rather than 8 compared with 9—the more accurate they are. By the time they're 5 years old, children are more accurate than they were at 4 years, especially with numbers that are only one number apart (Baroody, 1987).

THE CARDINALITY RULE. Another understanding involved in counting is the **cardinality rule**, or the **cardinality principle**. This rule refers to the understanding that the last number we say when we count a group of items is the total number of items in the group. When 3-year-olds count a group and are then asked how many items there were, they often count the group again. They don't realize that the last number they counted to indicates how many there were altogether. Four-year-olds begin to answer the question, How many? by saying the last word they counted to, but they may not really understand cardinality—they may simply have learned to repeat the last word they said.

Margaret, the child at the beginning of the chapter, didn't have a full understanding of the cardinality principle. She understood one part of it—that counting up to 4 indicated the total number of dots on the die. This is the "count-to-cardinality" meaning of the cardinality principle. But she didn't understand the reverse—that the number 4 represents a count of 1 to 4. She made her father count the dots rather than assuming that the number 4 implied this counting sequence. This is the "cardinality-to-count" meaning of the principle (Fuson, 1988).

COUNTING ALL AND COUNTING ON. Until young children understand both sides of the cardinality rule, they **count all** when they combine two groups of items, such as the dots on the faces of dice. If, like Margaret, they roll a 4 and a 3, they count, "one, two, three, four, five, six, seven," rather than starting with 4 (which they do recognize) and **counting on**—"five, six, seven." They're not being stubborn—they simply don't believe that the 4 they see is the same as the 4 to which they count.

The counting-all strategy is typically replaced by the counting-on strategy when children are between ages 5 and 7 (Fuson, 1982). Counting on, in turn, is gradually replaced by known number facts and by regrouping combined with counting on. For example, children who have played games with dice learn that $2 + 3 = 5$, $2 + 4 = 6$, $6 + 4 = 10$, and $6 + 6 = 12$. Later, when confronted with numbers whose sums are greater than 10, such as $6 + 6$, they might approach the problem by first taking 4 from one 6 to convert the other 6 to 10. Then they would add the 2 and 10 to get 12. This higher-level approach departs from using a known fact—$6 + 6 = 12$—in a sophisticated way, one that can be applied to the situation in which 6 and 8 or 18 and 4 are added, for example. The child clearly understands the composition of numbers—the various ways a given number can be divided into two sets—and can take numbers apart and put them together in very efficient ways.

These calculations are out of the reach of most older preschoolers, especially if the numbers are written down. To figure out a problem this way, a child first must understand that the written number symbols represent counting sequences up to the numbers represented, which requires knowledge of counting and of the cardinality rule. The child also has to understand each number's relationship to other numbers, such as how 6 is related to 10 and to 2. Finally, the child has to know that the number 12 is composed of 10 and 2. Almost all these understandings are beyond the preschooler's grasp. It's not until first or even second grade—again, at about age 7—that children are able to deal with numbers this way.

UNDERSTANDING THINKING

We've looked now at several aspects of young children's cognitive abilities and skills. A topic we haven't discussed is what children think about thinking—about what thoughts are, what dreams are, where knowledge comes from, and so on. This domain of children's knowledge has recently been referred to as children's "theory of mind" (Astington, Harris, & Olson, 1988). Again, Piaget has contributed a great deal to our understanding of children's theory of mind.

Childhood Realism: Piaget on Dreams

When Piaget investigated childhood realism, he concluded that young children do not separate mental and physical phenomena. They attribute thoughts and feelings to inanimate objects, such as rocks, chairs, blankets, and blocks, and they attribute a physical reality to thoughts. Piaget referred to the tendency to give thinking abilities to inanimate objects as **childhood animism** and the tendency to give physical reality to thoughts as **childhood realism**.

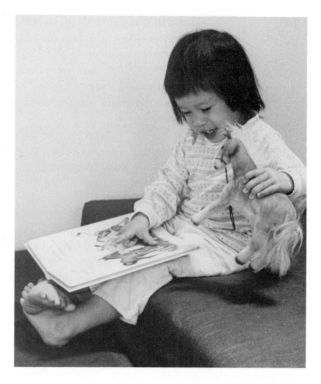

FIGURE 10-12
"Look at the horsies, Horsey." A 4-year-old can share a book with a toy horse because she doesn't think about whether it can have experiences the way she can. Piaget referred to the tendency to attribute consciousness to nonconscious things as childhood animism.

He came to these conclusions in part from interviewing children about their dreams, asking the following questions (Piaget, 1969):

- Do you know what a dream is?
- Where do dreams come from?
- Where do dreams happen? Where is the dream when you are dreaming?
- Could someone else see your dream?
- What do you dream with?
- Why do you dream? What sends dreams?

With these questions, Piaget probed the extent to which children viewed dreams as thoughts or as real things. If a child said that someone else in the room could see the dream, for example, Piaget considered this good evidence that the child thought that dreams existed in the external world rather than merely in the mind. Similarly, if the child said the dream was in front of her eyes, he assumed the child didn't know that dreams are thoughts.

Piaget suggested that children progress through three stages of development in their understanding of dreams, ranging from the child who makes no distinction between dreams and external reality to the child who distinguishes them fully. These stages are shown in Table 10-1, which also indicates

	Origin	Location
Stage I	External	External
Stage II	Internal	External
Stage III	Internal	Internal

TABLE 10-1
Summary of Developmental Stages in Children's Understanding of Dreams

where the child thought the dream came from (origin) and where the child thought the dream took place (location).

For example, consider the following interview of a 6-year-old, whom Piaget classified as Stage I (Piaget, 1969, p. 94):

> Where do dreams come from? — *They come from the night.* — How? — *I don't know.* — What do you mean by "they come from the night"? — *The night makes them.* — Does the dream come by itself? — *No.* — What makes it? — *The night.* — Where is the dream? — *It's made in the room.* — Where does the dream come from? — *From the sky.* — Is the dream made in the sky? — *No.* — Where is it made? — *In the room.*

Now consider the interview of a $9\frac{1}{2}$-year-old, classified by Piaget as Stage II (Piaget, 1969, p. 108):

> Where do dreams come from? — *When you are asleep, you think someone is beside you. When you see something in the day, you dream of it at night.* — What is the dream? — *Oh, anything.* — Where does it come from? — *I don't know. It comes by itself.* — Where from? — *Nowhere.* — Where is it made? — *In the room.* — Where? — *When you are lying down.* — Where is it made, in the room or inside you? — *In me . . . outside.* — Which, do you think? — *Outside.* — Where does the dream come from, from the room or from you? — *From me.* — Where is it, outside or in you? — *Beside me.* — Where? — *In my room.* — How far away? — (*points to 30 cm in front of him.*)

This boy didn't think the dream originated outside of himself, but he did locate it outside of himself. Finally, a child aged 11 years and 1 month demonstrated that he understood dreams are created in the head and remain there. Consider his interview for a typical Stage III response (Piaget, 1969, p. 119):

> You dream "with the head," and the dream is "in the head." — It isn't in front? — *It's as if you could see.* — Is there anything in front of you? — *Nothing.* — What is there in your head? — *Thoughts.* — Do the eyes see anything in the head? — *No.*

RECENT RESEARCH ON CHILDHOOD REALISM. As with other Piagetian work, contemporary researchers have critically examined his conclusions and attempted to test children's understandings in different ways. Two psychologists at the University of Michigan, Henry Wellman and David Estes, conducted several experiments to see if childhood realism—the belief that thoughts have a physical reality—is as prevalent as Piaget claimed (Wellman & Estes, 1986). All of their experiments had essentially the same results, regardless of the specific task presented to the children, so a description of one experiment suffices to explain their work.

Children were shown eight pairs of cards and told various things about the characters depicted on the cards. For example, the researcher might point to one card and say, "This boy likes cookies very much. He's very hungry right now, and he's thinking about a cookie." Then he would point to the other card in the pair and say, "See this boy here? He likes cookies too. Right now, he's hungry, so his mother *gave* him a cookie." (Wellman & Estes, 1986, p. 912). As the experimenter worked his way through the sets of cards, he changed the terms for the mental activities from *thinking*, to *remembering*, to *pretending*, to *dreaming*. In this way, he tested not only whether the child could distinguish mental things from physical things but whether the terminology had any effect on what the child seemed to understand.

After the experimenter told the children what a pair of characters were doing, he asked them questions about them. For example, he might ask, "Which boy can *see* a cookie?" "Which boy can *not* touch a cookie?" "Which boy can *eat* a cookie?" Then the children were told that the characters were having friends over to play. They were asked questions such as "Whose friend can eat the cookie?" and "Who can put the cookie away to eat the next day?" Finally, the children were reminded about what the character on each card was doing and asked to sort the cards into two boxes, one for "real" things and one for "not-real" things.

The researchers found that the terminology used—*think, remember, pretend,* or *dream*—made no difference in whether the child understood the difference between the real and the not-real situations. They did find that 5-year-olds performed better than 4-year-olds, and 4-year-olds performed better than 3-year-olds. But surprisingly, even the 3-year-olds performed quite well on both tasks, correctly answering questions about the characters 72 percent of the time and correctly sorting the cards 83 percent of the time. (The 5-year-olds performed correctly 92 and 91 percent of the time, respectively.)

In contrast to Piaget's findings, the children—even the 3-year-olds—didn't say that a dream (for example, a cookie that a boy was dreaming about) could be seen. The researchers wondered if this was because they misunderstood some of the questions. When they said that a boy was thinking or pretending about a cookie, did the children understand that to mean that the boy actually had a real cookie but just didn't have it on his person at that moment? If they thought this, they might have said the boy couldn't see the cookie or touch it because it was too far way, not because it was nonexistent. But subsequent experiments with different tasks yielded results that were as good as, if not better than, the results from the first experiment. Children even did extremely well when they were asked to identify nonexistent items, like a pencil that cries and a flower that talks.

ACCOUNTING FOR THE DIFFERENCES. Why did the children in Piaget's studies have such a hard time distinguishing thoughts and dreams from real entities when the much younger children in the contemporary study did so well? First, Wellman and Estes (1986) suggest that Piaget's questions were often misleading. If children are asked, "What are dreams made of?" they might assume, based on the adult's question, that dreams are made of some material. Or they might think that the adult wants them to describe the dream in terms of actual objects. Their answer in this case would be metaphorical rather than an indication that they think dreams actually have substance.

Wellman and Estes also point out that they may have been probing a different mental construct than Piaget was. They asked children questions about a thought or a dream involving an object, such as a cookie. Piaget asked them about dreams in abstract form, about the idea of a dream rather than a dream about a specific thing. Dreams or thoughts always have content, Wellman and Estes point out, and are "therefore difficult to talk about in themselves, removed from their contents, even for adults." (Wellman & Estes, 1986, p. 921). The children in Piaget's study might have known that dreams are abstract, non-material things, but they might have been unable to talk about them without reference to physical comparisons. This may have led Piaget to believe they were unable to understand the abstract concept of a dream.

At this point, it's difficult to say exactly how much children understand about what exists in physical reality and what exists in the mind. But the trend is to question the extent to which children really are the "realists" Piaget thought they were. Even 3-year-olds seem to have a reasonable grasp of the insubstantial nature of thoughts when the question or task is a familiar one from their own experience.

Distinguishing Appearance from Reality

The Gilbert family were on their way to the Natural History Museum's latest exhibit, called "Return of the Dinosaurs." Sitting in the back seat, 5-year-old Jacob chattered away excitedly about the show.

"Boy, moving dinosaurs that look real! I can't wait. I hope they have a big tyrannosaurus rex, and a triceratops, and a pterodactyl . . ."

"I'm sure they'll have them all," said Arthur, his dad. "I'm curious about how they do this kind of thing with computers. It'll be interesting to see."

No one noticed that 3-year-old Noah was hunched up in the corner of the back seat, clutching his blanket and sucking his thumb. When they got to the museum, Helen, his mom, turned around and said in surprise, "Noah, what's wrong? Don't you feel OK?"

He looked at her miserably and said, "I don't want to see any old dinosaurs. I want to go home!"

"Oh, Noah, they're not real!" she said. "They're just pretend. There's no such thing as a dinosaur any more. They lived millions of years ago. These dinosaurs are made of metal, and motors make them move. They can't hurt you!"

Noah allowed himself to be pried out of the back seat, and he cheered up as he walked into the museum and saw an exhibit of baby chicks in an incubator. After he watched them for a while, he asked if they could go to the space capsule exhibit they'd seen the last time they came.

"No!" said Jacob. "Let's go see the dinosaurs!"

"Yes, let's see the dinosaur exhibit now," agreed Helen. But Noah started to whimper, and Arthur had to pick him up and carry him. When they got to the dinosaur exhibit, he looked around for a second and then hid his face against his dad's shoulder.

"Noah, look," said Arthur. "These dinosaurs are just big motors covered with paper and material. They look like real animals, but they aren't. They're pretend. Here, look."

But Noah wouldn't look. Instead, he started to sob.

"He's trembling all over," said Arthur in surprise. "He's really scared. I better take him out. We'll go to the space exhibit and meet you later."

Why is a 5-year-old able to enjoy an animated display like this and a 3-year-old frightened by it? The reason is that younger children simply can't distinguish appearance from reality the way older children can. They respond to what they see. A huge gray creature with sharp teeth and claws and a moving head *is* a dinosaur to a 3-year-old, and it *is* dangerous. In the same way, a person wearing a gorilla costume and mask *is* a gorilla to a 3-year-old—even if the child sees the person put the mask on! (This is why Halloween can be a truly terrifying experience for very young children.)

When do children begin to be able to distinguish appearance from reality? Some recent studies have confirmed that at age 3, there's very little ability to make this distinction. In one study, 3-year-olds were shown various objects

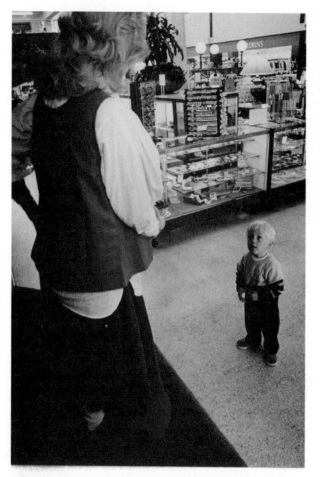

FIGURE 10-13
A mannekin presents an incomprehensible puzzle for a 3-year-old. Young children rely on appearances for their information about the world, and when appearances are contradictory, they're bewildered. One problem seems to be that they can't think two thoughts about something at the same time. In this case, the child can't think of the mannekin as an inanimate object (as he suspects) at the same time that he thinks of it as a woman (as he sees with his eyes).

both as they really were and as they appeared behind colored filters (Flavell, Green, & Flavell, 1986). One object was a toy seal that was partly covered with a filter; another was a glass of milk covered by a red filter; and another was a small white fish that swam behind a larger, blue, transparent fish. In a fourth task, children wore colored glasses.

Before the tasks were presented, the children were trained in making appearance-reality distinctions with puppets. They were shown a Charlie Brown puppet first dressed as himself and then dressed up in a ghost costume. When the puppet was disguised as a ghost, the children were told, "When you look at this with your eyes right now, it looks like a ghost. It looks like a ghost to your eyes, but it isn't. It's really and truly Charlie Brown. Sometimes things look one way to your eyes (costume is put on again) when they really and truly are a different way (costume is removed)" (Flavell, Green, & Flavell, 1986, pp. 7–8). When the tasks were administered, the children were asked, "How does the object look to your eyes right now?" and "How does the object really and truly look?"

Only about half of the children were able to answer the questions correctly, although the rate was higher when they were asked about the seal, whose real color was always partially visible. Because these tasks seemed so easy, the researchers tried the experiment again but gave the children more training first. The results remained the same. The researchers then included some older children in the experiment and found that 6- and 7-year-olds could make the appearance-reality distinctions quite easily.

These researchers also tested the 3-year-olds on their ability to distinguish between real and pretend objects. They showed them a real coffee mug and a real kitchen knife, for example, as well as a plastic (pretend) cucumber and a plastic ice cream bar. While the child inspected each item, the researcher said, "Right now this looks like a real cucumber (coffee mug, ice cream bar, and so on). Is it a pretend cucumber, or is it a real cucumber?"

The children did much better on these tasks than they did on the color appearance-reality tasks. The results (18 out of 24 children responded correctly) were similiar to results obtained by Wellman and Estes in their study of children's understanding of real versus thought-about (pretend) objects just discussed. Part of the children's success in identifying real and pretend cucumbers and ice cream bars may have come from the fact that they inspected these objects and were familiar with them. Noah's difficulty in understanding that the dinosaurs were pretend may have been partially due to his refusal to get close enough to inform himself about them.

FIGURE 10-14
Hands-on experience helps preschoolers distinguish "real" from "pretend." It takes many such experiences before children are willing or able to override the evidence of their senses.

Distinguishing Other Aspects of Mind: Thinking about Thinking

Very young children also have difficulty making distinctions between two different thoughts and holding two different thoughts about the same object in mind. For example, in one study, children were shown a familiar candy box that they would expect to contain candy. But when it was opened, the children saw that it contained pencils instead. When asked what they thought was in the box at first, before it had been opened to reveal its acutal contents, 3-year-olds often reported that they thought the box contained pencils. They seemed to be unable to focus on two different representations (thoughts) formed at different points in time—that they first thought the box contained candy and then thought that the box contained pencils. The 4-year-olds did much better at distinguishing their two different representations, and the 5-year-olds did better still (Gopnik & Astington, 1988). As in the conservation tasks, the child focuses on the two different end states—the appearance of the material at the end of the change—rather than on the transformation that links the two states.

The researchers also asked the children what another child, who hadn't seen the pencils, would think was in the box. This question was asked to probe children's understanding of "false beliefs," the idea that someone can have an incorrect belief about something, such as that a box contains candy when it actually contains pencils. When asked this question, the 4- and 5-year-olds showed a fairly good understanding of the possibility of false beliefs, but 3-year-olds did not (Gopnik & Astington, 1988). They responded that the other child would think there were pencils in the box. Apparently, 3-year-olds have a hard time realizing that other people might be ignorant of some fact that they themselves know. This characteristic of 3-year-olds' thinking has been confirmed by other researchers as well (Juergen, Wimmer, & Perner, 1986).

Very young children are also amazingly unaware of the source of their own knowledge. When they know something, they can't say whether they actually saw it with their own eyes, whether someone specifically told them about it, or whether someone gave them clues and they drew an inference about it (Gopnik & Graf, 1988). Overall, they seem to be unaware of the source of thoughts themselves. Instead, they focus on the object represented by a thought.

A related difficulty is young children's inability to distinguish another person's visual perspective from their own, which we described earlier in this chapter. When asked how something would look to someone in a different position, they describe how it looks to them. For example, in one study, a doll was placed between the child and another person, with the doll's face toward the child. When the researcher asked the child what the other person was looking at, the child reported that the other person saw the doll's face. Children aged 4 and 5 in this experiment had much less difficulty than younger children distinguishing their own view from the view of the other person (Flavell et al., 1981).

The Limits and the Growth of Understanding in Preschool Children

One common thread running through all the research findings about young children's abilities to think about thinking is that 3-year-olds just aren't capable of thinking about an object in two different ways at the same time. They form one representation about an object and answer all questions in terms of that one thought (Flavell, Green, & Flavell, 1986). Older children and adults can have two representations of the same object, even though the object itself isn't two different things. For example, an object can't really be a rock and a sponge at the same time, but it can *appear* to be a rock even though it's a sponge. We can think these thoughts about a rocklike sponge; 3-year-olds can't.

Children 3 years old and younger aren't very aware that people have thoughts, nor are they aware that thoughts are subjective rather than physical entities. Thus, they don't know that a person's thoughts can change from one time to another or that different people can have different thoughts. The mental distinctions required in understanding two different thoughts about the same object—distinctions concerning reality versus appearance, real versus pre-

FIGURE 10-15
Preoperational thinking lends the child's world its "magical" quality. Children believe in elves and fairies, witches and spells, animals that talk and wear clothes. From an adult point of view, the earliest years are almost like a dream from which children awaken as the age of reason dawns at about age 7. But during these years, they often surprise and delight us with their original ideas about how the world works.

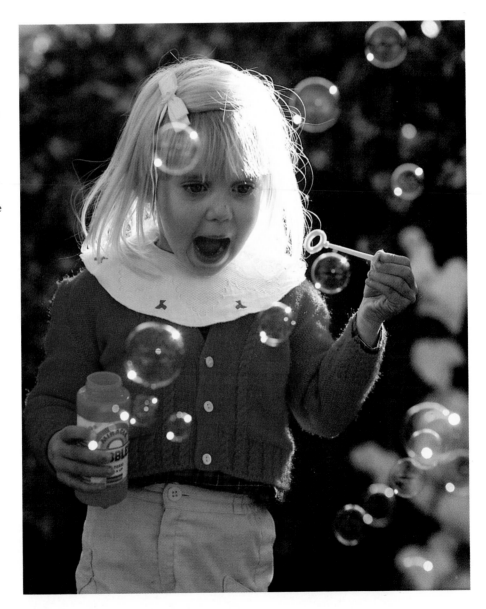

tend, false belief versus correct belief—are probably literally unthinkable to a 3-year-old (Flavell, Green, & Flavell, 1986). As they mature biologically, and as they gain experience, children become capable of more sophisticated ways of thinking.

Perhaps children begin to get their first sense of the distinction between thoughts about real things and pretend thoughts about the same things when they engage in pretend play, starting at about 1 year of age. Pretend play is a favorite activity of 3-year-olds, and experience gained from this kind of play could account for the vastly better performance of 4- and 5-year-olds on most tasks requiring them to consider two different representations of objects.

Children also play increasingly with other children from about the age of 3 on. This social interaction introduces them to the fact that different people can have different thoughts about the same object. "That's my magic carpet," one child says about a doll's blanket. "No, it's my tablecloth," says another, grabbing it from the first child. "We'll eat first, and then we'll go for a ride." Perhaps when they first encounter two different pretend thoughts about the same real object, children begin to become aware of the distinctions between thoughts and things thought about and between different thoughts about the same thing (Gopnik & Astington, 1988).

Whatever the reason, a remarkable transformation in thinking occurs between the ages of 3 and 5—one of the most important of all the many changes that occur during these years. Without the ability to realize that thoughts are subjective and changeable, human beings would be unable to think the way they do—to reflect about their thinking, to correct their misperceptions and misunderstandings, to allow their ideas to change and evolve, to accept that other people may have different ideas than they do about the same thing, to understand many forms of art and music. We see hardly a glimmer of such understanding in 3-year-olds. A year or two later, the foundations for these understandings begin to appear. The school-age child and the adolescent will sharpen these abilities, but in a 5-year-old who knows that an animated dinosaur isn't real, we see the dawning of the revolution in thinking that is to come.

OVERVIEW

The preschool years are the prime years for "magical thinking." Children are likely to have a doll or toy they consider "real," and impossibilities such as talking animals and flying reindeer aren't a problem for them. Their thinking, referred to as preoperational, tends to be untouched by logic and is guided instead by appearances, by particular contexts and situations, and by certain limited cognitive abilities. These limitations shouldn't obscure the remarkable advances preschoolers have made from the sensorimotor thinking of toddlerhood, however, as well as the significant improvements they make during the preschool years. By the end of this period, they have some understanding of the differences between real and pretend, between fantasy and reality, and between their own thoughts and those of others.

CHAPTER REVIEW

UNDERSTANDING THE CONCEPT OF NUMBER

- One of the important areas of cognitive development investigated by Piaget was conservation, the understanding that a quantity doesn't change when arrangement or distribution changes.
- Piaget found that conservation of number doesn't emerge until children are about 6 or $6\frac{1}{2}$ years old. By this age, they realize that rearranging the objects in a group doesn't affect how many objects there are. Preschoolers, on the other hand, judge the group by its appearance.
- Conservation of continuous quantity also becomes established by age 6 or 7. Before this, children believe that the quantity of water in a beaker changes when it's poured into a beaker of a different size or shape.
- Piaget tested children in other areas of conservation, such as length, area, and weight, and found that these understandings are generally beyond the preschooler's abilities.
- Piaget referred to preschoolers' thinking as preoperational, meaning that they don't use the logical mental operations that older children and adults use to make sense of their experiences. Limitations in their operational thinking—such as their tendency to center (focus on only one aspect of a relationship at a time) and their inability to reverse transformations mentally—make it impossible for preschoolers to think logically.
- Some researchers who believed that children are able to conserve at an earlier age than Piaget found have modified his experiments to see just what they're testing. Their results indicate that many children do have conservation of number during the preschool years, but they can easily be confused, distracted, or misled by the experimenter.
- Despite these findings, a significant qualitative difference in thinking does exist between the preschool child and the school-age child, with the preschool child much less able to think logically.

UNDERSTANDING THE CONCEPTS OF SERIATION AND CLASSIFICATION

- Young preoperational children are unable to arrange objects in a graduated series, mainly because they can't focus on more than one characteristic of an object at one time. Older preschoolers form a series using trial and error, an approach Piaget called intuitive and empirical. School-age children approach this task operationally.
- Different findings about children's ability to seriate comes from experiments with nesting cups. Research showed that $3\frac{1}{2}$-year-olds were able to construct a series through trial and error when the materials were familiar and supported their efforts.

CLASSIFICATION

- Separating and grouping objects into hierarchical classes is difficult for children under age 4. Between ages 5 and 7, children can classify objects based on a single attribute, but they still can't think in terms of class inclusion. Not until they're 7 or 8 years old do children really master classification.

ARITHMETICAL SKILLS AND UNDERSTANDINGS

- Counting and doing simple sums are the kinds of cognitive tasks preschoolers typically encounter.
- Preschoolers learn the conventional number words, or tags, and begin to acquire the skills needed for true counting.
- Preschoolers typically make three kinds of errors—partitioning errors (not separating objects counted from those not counted), coordination errors (not saying the tags at the same time they point to the object counted), and use of unconventional tags.

- Until children understand that counting implies hierarchical inclusion, they have difficulty avoiding these errors. When objects are in disarray, they're also harder to count.
- Some 3-year-olds are just beginning to understand the concepts of "greater than" and "less than"; 4-year-olds are able to make more accurate number comparisons; and 5-year-olds are quite accurate.

- Young preschoolers don't understand the cardinality rule—that the last number counted represents the total number of items in a group. To find out how many objects there are in a group they've counted, they count all the objects again. Between ages 5 and 7, children find totals by counting on, and beyond age 7, they use known number facts and regrouping combined with counting on.

UNDERSTANDING THINKING

- Children's thoughts and ideas about the nature of thinking are sometimes referred to as children's "theory of mind."
- Piaget investigated children's theory of mind by interviewing children about their dreams. He found that young children tend to attribute thoughts and feelings to inanimate objects, a tendency he named childhood animism, and to attribute physical reality to thoughts, a tendency he named childhood realism.
- Piaget suggested that children go through three developmental stages as they grow before understanding that dreams are distinct from reality. They don't reach the final stage until about 11 years of age.
- Recent experiments have demonstrated that many children, as young as 3 years old, understand the difference between physical reality and what one thinks, dreams, or pretends. These researchers believe that Piaget's questions may have misled the children and may have been too abstract for the children to answer on the basis of their own experience. The current thinking is that children are aware of the difference between reality and nonreality at a much younger age than Piaget believed.

- At age 3, children have little ability to distinguish appearance from reality, although they do better if they can examine the real and pretend objects.
- Young preschoolers have difficulty distinguishing between two different thoughts (for example, what they thought about one thing at two different points in time). They also fail to understand the concept of false beliefs, the idea that someone could have an incorrect belief about something. By age 4 or 5, children understand these ideas fairly well.
- Young preschoolers don't really understand where their own knowledge comes from, nor are they able to understand that the visual perspectives of others may differ from their own.
- Experience with pretend play probably helps children learn to distinguish between the real and the nonreal. Playing with other children also helps them to realize that other people can have different thoughts than they do.
- Experience and neurological maturation together account for the better understanding of reality versus appearance that is apparent in 4- and 5-year-olds.

KEY TERMS

preoperational thinking	concrete operational	class inclusion	cardinality rule,
conservation	thinking	egocentrism	cardinality principle
identity	seriation	tags	count all
compensation	intuitive	partitioning error	count on
reversibility	empirical	coordination errors	childhood animism
center	operational	hierarchical inclusion	childhood realism
irreversibility			

SUGGESTIONS FOR FURTHER READING

Donaldson, M. (1978). *Children's minds.* New York: Norton.
This researcher/author thinks the Piagetian tasks underestimate preschoolers' reasoning ability. This readable book presents some of the research that has been conducted to support this conclusion.

Gelman, R., & Gallistel, C. R. (1986). *The child's understanding of number.* Cambridge, MA: Harvard University Press.
These authors stress the development of counting skills in preschool children. As such, the book is a contrast to Piaget's work and may be interesting to the student who wishes to take a broader look at children's cognitive development in relation to mathematics.

Ginsburg, H. P., & Opper, S. (1988). *Piaget's theory of intellectual development* (3rd ed.) Englewood Cliffs, NJ: Prentice-Hall.
This readable book discusses Piaget's theory and stages of development. Constructs such as conservation and seriation are covered.

Kamii, C. (1985). *Young children reinvent arithmetic.* New York: Teachers College Press.
This author uses a Piagetian framework as a basis for developing a program of mathematics education.

chapter 11

LANGUAGE DEVELOPMENT IN PRESCHOOL CHILDREN

When 4-year-old Kate came home from nursery school one day, her dad asked what she had done at school. "Oh, nothing," she replied.

"Well, I know you did something," her dad continued. "You brought a painting home, so you must have painted today."

"No, I painted a picture the last day. Today, I didn't paint. I clayed with clay."

"Oh, I see. You played with clay. What did you do after you played with clay?"

"Mmmmmmmmm. Well, I think that is when Jessica teached me how to staple papers together for a book."

"You and Jessica were using a stapler?"

"Yes! You press it very hard—very, very hard—and the staples stick in the paper. Then, you pull the stapler away. The papers stay sticked together because the staple you put in there holds them."

"I hope you didn't stick your finger."

"No, we didn't."

"That's good. A staple in the finger hurts."

If we hadn't already known Kate's age, we could have pegged her as a preschooler quite easily, because her language is typical of children between the ages of 3 and 6. She no longer speaks the way a toddler does, but she doesn't yet speak as well as a school-age child either. In this chapter, we look at the characteristics of preschoolers' language and the origin of the peculiar kind of mistakes they make. We also examine the development of preschoolers' language comprehension. Finally, we discuss emergent literacy—the beginning stages of written language development.

RESEARCH FOCUS

The Grammatical Morphemes Young Children Acquire

Children's oral language emerges in a definite, predictable way. A child who now says, "Daddy go," will soon be saying, "Daddy going," and later, "Daddy is going." With each new utterance, the child has learned a new morpheme and made a linguistic leap. The following list includes 14 morphemes that young children learn to use, in the order in which they learn to use them (Brown, 1973).

Name of Morpheme	*Example*
Progressive (-ing)	Daddy going.
Locative (in)	Bat in room.
Locative (on)	Hat on head.
Regular plural (-s)	Boys there.
Irregular past	Ran home.
Possessive (-'s)	Adam's shoe.
Uncontractible copula*	Susan is here.
Articles (the, a)	The pail has a hole.
Regular past (-ed)	Daddy walked home.
Regular third person (-s)	He runs.
Irregular third person	He does that.
Uncontractible auxiliary	She is running.
Contractible copula	She's afraid.
Contractible auxiliary	She's running.

That is, the child doesn't form contractions with the copula ("is").

ORAL LANGUAGE DEVELOPMENT

Language Production: What Preschoolers Can Say

Kate's language is quite different from her language of just a year or two earlier. As a toddler, her statements were telegraphic—short and incomplete. She might have said, "Mommy sock," for example, to mean "This is Mommy's sock." Now, her sentences are grammatically complete and contain many more words and morphemes. A **morpheme** is the smallest unit of meaning in a language. It can be a word, or it can be a smaller group of letters that changes the meaning of a word, such as the word endings "ing" or "ed." Preschoolers learn many morphemes, and they learn them in a specific sequential order (see Research Focus—The Grammatical Morphemes Young Children Acquire for a list of some of these morphemes).

Despite these advances in language ability, however, Kate's speech is still imperfect. What marks it as essentially different from the speech of older children and adults is her use of words that she's coined herself.

ACQUIRING MORPHOLOGICAL RULES. Kate has learned **morphological rules**—the rules of word formation in her language. In fact, we can even say that she's overlearned them. Kate thinks that all English verbs, for example, are changed to the past tense by adding the morpheme "ed" to the end. She doesn't know that some verbs are irregular and that their past tense is formed by using a

RESEARCH FOCUS

The Words Children Create

Preschoolers are notorious for their invented words. Once they catch on to a particular usage, they tend to generalize it to other cases they perceive to be similar. When we know the model they had in mind, we can see that their statements aren't so strange. One researcher made extensive studies of children's invented words in English, French, and German, and some usages she reported are given here (Clark, 1982, pp. 402–406). In the third column, we've added a model that could explain the child's choice.

All of these statements are based on the notion that nouns can also be used as verbs. Given the complexity of sorting out exceptions to general rules in English, it's no wonder that we still hear invented words in the language of 6- and 7-year-olds.

SITUATION	INVENTION	MODEL
Child was referring to cheese that had to be weighed.	"You have to scale it first."	"You have to drill it first."
Child was hitting a ball with a stick.	"I'm sticking it and that makes it go really fast."	"I'm batting it to make it go really fast."
Child was using tongs to remove spaghetti from a pan.	"I'm going to pliers this out."	"I'm going to hammer this out."
Mother was sweeping child's room.	"Don't broom my mess."	"Don't mop the floor."
Child was putting crackers in soup.	"I'm going to cracker my soup."	"I'm going to dye my hair."
Child was putting beads in play dough.	"I think I'll bead it."	"I think I'll salt it."
Child wanted chocolate syrup in milk.	"Will you chocolate my milk?"	"Will you salt my eggs?"

different word altogether. Because she's heard "walk" and "walked," she says "run" and "runned." Once children learn that most words can be **inflected**, or changed in form, according to certain rules, they **overgeneralize** the rules, applying them even when they're inappropriate. Kate will notice the exceptions to the rules as time goes on, and she'll begin to use them instead of her own invented words. But it will be another two or three years before the last traces of her tendency to overgeneralize will vanish altogether.

Preschool children overgeneralize rules not only for forming verb tenses but for creating plurals, for forming superlatives, and for using nouns as verbs (Branigan & Stokes, 1976; Garvey, 1977). For example, most preschoolers refer to teeth as "tooths," to feet as "foots," and to mice as "mouses." Overgeneralizing from a statement like "Giving a hug is the nicest thing you can do," they say that jumping on the bed is the "funnest" thing you can do. And they say they "clayed" with the clay, because they assume this is similar to saying they hammered with the hammer or sawed with the saw. (Other examples of rule overgeneralization are listed in Research Focus—The Words Children Create.)

Before children learn any morphological rules—when they're $2\frac{1}{2}$ years old, for example—they use the correct forms of the common irregular nouns and verbs (Brown, 1973), because they're imitating what they've heard. As they learn rules and start to overgeneralize, they begin to make mistakes. Children typically learn the irregular past before the regular past (see Research Focus—

The Grammatical Morphemes Young Children Acquire). Thus, at age $2\frac{1}{2}$, Kate repeated what she heard and said "ran" and "went"; by age 4, she's learned the morpheme "ed" for forming the regular past, so now she says "runned" and "goed." Later still, she will sort out the exceptions to the rule and once again say "ran" and "went." This is a good example of something we often see in development: New skills and abilities lead to errors or problems that didn't exist before. Kate's language emerged at a whole new level once she acquired some morphological rules, but a new kind of mistake appeared too.

CREATING SENTENCES. Just as there are rules in our language for inflecting individual words, there are also rules for forming different kinds of sentences. When asking a question, for example, we invert the order of the subject and verb—we say, "Where is she going?" rather than "Where she is going?" It takes some time for children to master the rules of sentence construction. Their early sentences are different from adults', particularly their questions and negative statements. At first, they form questions by combining a "wh" word with a primitive sentence: "Where dolly?" "Where man?" As they get older, the structuring of their questions changes in a predictable pattern (Menyuk, 1969, p. 73):

1. Where goes the wheel?
2. Where the wheel goes?
3. Where the wheel go?
4. Where does the wheel goes?
5. Where does the wheel go?

Negative sentences are another challenge. At first, children just combine "no" with a word or short sentence: "No break." "No eat." Later, they start to include subjects and verbs in both questions and negative sentences: "I no eat." "Where dolly is going?" Eventually, by about $3\frac{1}{2}$ to 4 years of age, they learn how to rearrange words within sentences: "Where is the dolly going?" Preschoolers also learn which part of a verb to change to indicate tense. For example, in the sentence "Where does the wheel go?" they learn to change "do" to "does" rather than "go" to "goes."

Another problem area for preschoolers is the use of comparative adjectives. At first, children double-mark words for comparison, using both the adjective and the adverb "more" (Gathercole, 1985): "I had my birthday yesterday, so now I'm more older than you are." Later, during the school years, children learn to drop the superfluous "more" from these sentences.

CORRECTING CHILDREN'S GRAMMAR. Kate's father didn't correct her grammar, although he did model the correct forms himself. Sometimes adults wonder if they should go further than this and correct children directly. The research literature indicates that adult efforts to get children to correct their speech aren't very successful. In the following examples, we can see how resistant children are to changing the language forms they've used (Gleason, 1967, cited in Cazden, 1972, pp. 4–5):

A child said, "My teacher holded the baby rabbits and we patted them."
I asked, "Did you say your teacher held the baby rabbits?"
She answered, "Yes."
I then asked, "What did you say she did?"
She answered, again, "She holded the baby rabbits and we patted them."
"Did you say she held them tightly?" I asked.
"No," she answered, "She holded them loosely."

In this second example, a more direct approach was used (McNeill, 1966, p. 69):

CHILD: *"Nobody don't like me."*
MCNEILL: *"No, say 'Nobody likes me.'"*
CHILD: *"Nobody don't like me."*
  (eight repetitions of this dialogue)
MCNEILL: *"No. Now listen carefully; say 'Nobody likes me.'"*
CHILD: *"Oh! Nobody don't likes me!"*

Most parents respond to their children's early grammatical errors the way Kate's dad did. They talk naturally with children, concentrating on getting their meaning and judging the truth of what they say. In the second example just given, in fact, one might wish that the researcher had paid more attention

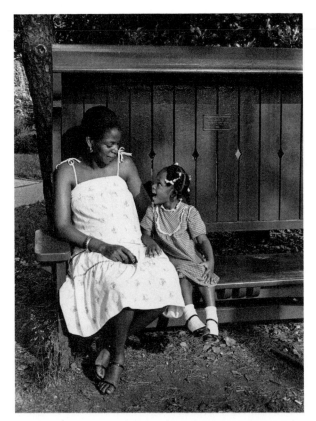

FIGURE 11-1
Children learn language from their parents in the course of everyday life, without direct instruction. Research shows that parents seldom correct their pre-schoolers' grammatical errors, listening instead for the content of the child's speech. Being listened to uncritically probably enhances not only language development but cognitive and emotional development as well.

to what the child was saying instead of trying to correct his grammar. Parents' responses to sentences containing errors do differ somewhat from their responses to sentences that don't have errors, however, as was noted in Chapter 7. It's possible that this varying feedback serves a "correction" function, although we don't know that it does. In any event, children appear to correct their mistakes over time, even though most adults don't call mistakes to their attention in any direct way. The best type of "instruction" seems to consist of exposure to natural, meaningful language in which the correct use of rules is constantly demonstrated.

Language Comprehension: What Preschoolers Can Understand

Preschoolers' comprehension of spoken language has increased dramatically from toddlerhood. The average 3-year-old understands about 900 words—an impressive gain from the 100 or so understood by the average 18-month-old (Moskowitz, 1978). But some word meanings and some elements of **syntax** (sentence construction) still elude them. We look now at preschoolers' typical trouble spots in language comprehension.

UNDERSTANDING WORD ORDER. The meaning of sentences in English depends on the order of the words in them. When we hear, "John hit the ball," we know that John is the subject and the ball is the object of his action. Even though the sentence is reversible—it would make sense if interpreted as, "The ball hit John"—we interpret it correctly because we know the rules of word order. At what age do children begin to understand how word order determines the meaning of sentences?

Several studies have been designed to answer this question. In one, researchers asked $2\frac{1}{2}$-year-olds to match pictures with sentences they had just heard, such as "The dog bites the cat" (Fraser, Bellugi, & Brown, 1963). In another study, children between the ages of 2 and 3 were asked to act out sentence meanings (Bever, Mehler, & Vallian, 1974). A third study investigated how children's understanding of word order was related to the length of their own spoken sentences (deVilliers & deVilliers, 1973). All of these studies showed that children between the ages of 2 and 3 begin to understand how word order determines meaning. The third study mentioned also showed that the length of the child's own sentences is a better indicator of understanding than is the child's age alone. Children with less mature speech were likely to interpret "Make the truck push the car" as "Make the car push the truck."

Although children on the brink of the preschool years understand that word order determines meaning, at first they understand only active sentences— those following the subject-verb-object word order. They find it impossible to understand passive sentences, such as "The ball was thrown by John." The response of 2-year-olds to passive sentences is correct only 50 percent of the time, which means that they're only guessing, just as we do when someone flips a coin and we call out "heads" or "tails" (Bever, 1970; deVilliers & deVilliers, 1973). It's not until late in the preschool period—at about 5 years of age—that children finally understand passive sentences. The exception is cases in which incorrect interpretation makes the sentence unlikely. For example, even a 3-year-old will correctly interpret the sentence "The baby was fed by her mother," because babies don't feed their mothers. In these cases, however, children are

FIGURE 11-2
Word order is elusive for 3-year-olds. If told to "make the car push the truck," this child is just as likely to make the truck push the car.

FIGURE 11-2
Word order is elusive for 3-year-olds. If told to "make the car push the truck," this child is just as likely to make the truck push the car.

using their knowledge of events rather than their knowledge of language structure to determine the meaning of the sentence. Only when a sentence makes sense both ways, such as "The cat was chased by the dog," do we see that the younger preschooler doesn't understand the passive construction (Strohner & Nelson, 1974).

Another trouble spot for preschoolers is the use of the verb "promise." Overgeneralizing from sentences using other verbs, such as "tell," they misunderstand who the person is who's doing the promising (Chomsky, 1969). For example, in the sentence "Amy told Susan to be quiet," Susan is the one who is to be quiet. But in the sentence "Amy promised Susan to be quiet," it's now Amy who is to be quiet. Because of this difficulty, a preschooler may not be able to understand a sentence like "You promised Emily to share the blocks." A parent or teacher who realizes a child doesn't understand can help by rephrasing the sentence—"You said Emily could play with some of your blocks."

UNDERSTANDING LOCATIVE EXPRESSIONS. Locative expressions—words such as "in," "on," "under," and "beside"—provide information about where something is located. Young preschoolers are just beginning to master the meaning of these words as they're used in such phrases as "in the box," "on the sofa," and "beside the chair."

In one well-known study, the objects pictured in Figure 11-3 were used to probe children's understanding of locative terms (Clark, 1978). The objects were shown to children so that only two relationships were possible at a time. Objects 1 and 2 allowed the relations "in" and "on"; 3 and 4 allowed "in" and "under"; and 5 and 6 allowed "on" and "under."

Children interpreted instructions differently, depending on which objects they were shown. If children saw any kind of container, such as objects 3 and 4, they always placed something in it, even when the instructions contained other locatives such as "on" or "under." Similarly, they interpreted any instruction to mean "on" when the object had a supporting surface, even if they were asked to place something under or in it.

Clark's study showed that children don't understand the meanings of any of these words until they're about $2\frac{1}{2}$ years old. Instead, they interpret sen-

FIGURE 11-3
Objects used by Clark to test young children's understanding of locative expressions. The children in the study always placed something "in" a container, such as object 3 or 4, even when instructed to place something "under" it, demonstrating that they pay more attention to clues in the situation than to specific word meanings.

FIGURE 11-4
Young children learn language at first from action and context. This teacher is showing a child how to clean up at the same time that she's helping the child learn locative expressions: "Put the toys IN the bin," "Put the bin ON the shelf."

tences containing locative expressions in terms of what's available in the situation. When children do begin to understand the actual meanings of the words, they learn "in" first, followed by "on" and then "under."

Other locative expressions are even harder to learn. Children don't master the words "beside," "between," "front," and "back" until they're $4\frac{1}{2}$ or 5 years old, and when they do learn these terms, they learn them in the following order (Johnston & Slobin, 1979):

- beside
- between
- front (when the object itself has a front)
- back (when the object itself has a back)
- back (when the back depends on the position of the person in relation to the object)
- front (when the front depends on the position of the person in relation to the object).

Parents and teachers of preschoolers often find that children are puzzled by instructions involving locative expressions and need to be shown what is meant. For example, a preschool teacher who tells a child that the crayons are on a shelf between the paste jars and the scissors rack might find that the child approaches the shelf but doesn't direct her gaze to the right spot, even when the teacher repeats the instruction. A child who behaves this way probably doesn't understand the word "between." The teacher may need to approach the shelf and say, "Here are the crayons, right here (pointing at them) between (with emphasis) the scissors and the jars of paste." Or, if the teacher can't go to the shelf, she might say, "Find the jars of paste." Then she might add, "Now find the scissors." In the process of moving from one item to the other on the shelf, the child would discover the crayons. At this point, the teacher might comment, "Oh, good—you found the crayons, right there between the jars of paste and the scissors."

ACQUIRING WORD MEANINGS. The meaning of a word isn't always obvious to a child; in fact, it may take repeated associations over the course of many years for children to realize exactly what a particular word means. The words "more" and "less" are a case in point. Children don't understand the use of the word "more" to refer to the greater of two amounts until they are about $3\frac{1}{2}$. They have a better understanding of "more" with countable objects such as pennies or blocks than with uncountable quantities such as clay or sand (Gathercole, 1985). By the age of $4\frac{1}{2}$, children's use of "more" is accurate with both countable items and mass quantities, although by age 5, they tend to prefer using "more" when they mean greater in number and "bigger" when they mean greater in amount or mass.

It takes children even longer to understand the word "less." When asked which of two quantities is less, children will sometimes point to the quantity that actually is more. Perhaps they know at first only that "less" also refers to quantity, and they use it interchangeably with the other quantity word they know. Only later—at about age $4\frac{1}{2}$—do they distinguish the two terms, using "more" to indicate the greater of two quantities and "less" to indicate the smaller. Preschoolers also tend to confuse other opposites, such as warm/cold and bigger/smaller.

FIGURE 11-5
Children learn vocabulary, word meanings, and many other language understandings when adults involve them in their activities, such as making an apple pie. A parent teaches naturally by making statements like, "Let's put the apple peels in the garbage" or "Please get me the bowl with the blue stripe from the cupboard."

If children have a hard time understanding words for opposites, they have an even harder time grasping words for things that are similar. This is probably because they fail to sort out features of objects or situations that indicate when they should use one term rather than the other. The greater the number of features there are to sort out—size, shape, color, content, function, and so on—the longer it seems to take children to see the difference.

For example, 3-year-olds use "glass" and "cup" almost interchangeably, regardless of whether the container is tall or short, has a handle or doesn't, or is made of glass, ceramic, or plastic (Nelson & Nelson, 1978). In labeling the container, they pay very little attention to context—whether it's filled with ice water or hot cocoa, for example. Children 4 and 5 years old, on the other hand, consider both physical form and context in deciding which word applies, using the word "glass" for taller containers filled with ice water, for example. By 6 to 8 years of age, children refer to containers that are twice as high as they are wide as "glass" regardless of what they hold. By age 10, children add the observation that shorter containers may be called "glass" when they hold cold drinks. From this example, it is clear that children's understanding of word meanings continues to evolve well beyond the preschool years.

CONTEXT AND COMPREHENSION. In our discussion of language comprehension, we've mentioned several times that children read the context of language—the situation at hand—to obtain clues about the meaning of words and sentences. In fact, if young children were forced to rely only on words, they would understand very little. Early language learning is **context bound**, that is, language is understood not in terms of linguistic structures alone but also in terms of the extralinguistic context (Bates, 1979). Later, language becomes more **decontextualized**, that is, less dependent on context, although neither spoken nor written language can ever be understood completely out of context (Cazden, 1987). The shift is from concrete, immediate contexts to "contexts of the mind," from almost total reliance on the situation to an ability to understand on the basis of both linguistic structures and background knowledge.

Because the younger preschool child's understanding of linguistic structures is limited, the child is still very dependent on context. But even the older preschool child, as well as the much older school-age child, is still building "contexts of the mind." Because of this, it's vitally important that children's experiences, and especially preschoolers' experiences, be broad and real, based on a wide range of meaningful activities. Preschoolers need to experience not just how things look but how they feel and move, how they taste, sound, and smell, to build that rich and lasting storehouse of information and knowledge crucial to an understanding of the spoken and written word.

WRITTEN LANGUAGE DEVELOPMENT

A teacher was reading Maurice Sendak's Where the Wild Things Are *to Matt and Amy, two 4-year-olds, in the library area of the preschool classroom. When he got to the pages with pictures but no print, Matt told him to turn past them, saying, "You can't read these—you have to turn to where the words start again."*

Amy objected. "No!" she said. "He has to read all of the pages."

"He can't read those pages," protested Matt. "They don't have any words on them."

"Yes, he can!" repeated Amy.

At this point, the teacher suggested that he talk about the pages with pictures but no words and then begin reading where the words start again. Matt and Amy accepted his compromise.

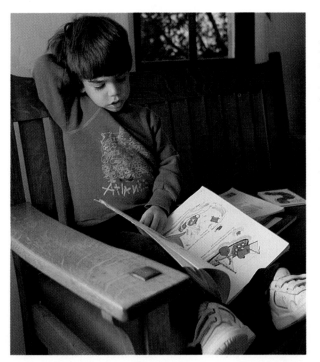

FIGURE 11-6
In our society, many children are exposed to books almost from birth and have very sophisticated understandings about them by the time they're in the preschool years. This boy may be learning one of the most important early literacy lessons—that even though books have pictures, reading involves getting meaning from print.

These two children are at different levels in their understanding of print. Amy doesn't think there's any difference between text and pictures at all. To her, a page with pictures but no print can be "read." Matt, in contrast, thinks that pictures and text serve different functions. The text tells the story and is read; the pictures illustrate or confirm the text. It's common for young preschool children to assume at first that the pictures in a book, not the print, are what you read (Ferreiro & Teberosky, 1979). As they gain experience, they gradually come to understand that reading involves getting meaning from print.

In the past, people thought that preschoolers were incapable of understanding very much about written language. Now we know that they understand quite a lot about it. Because of this discovery, the term **emergent literacy** has replaced the term **reading readiness.** The latter term implied that children needed to learn many things before they could begin to have "real" reading experiences. The former term suggests that even very young children engage in "real" reading and writing activities. What changes as they get older is the way they read and write, not the basic nature of what they attempt to do (Teale & Sulzby, 1986).

In this section, we discuss some of the current knowledge about emergent literacy in preschoolers. We also discuss some of the different home experiences and activities that seem to foster the highest level of literacy development.

Understanding Print

When Jonathan, age 4, reads Eric Carle's *The Very Hungry Caterpillar* out loud to himself, he doesn't miss a word of what's actually printed in the text. He even sounds like a person who's reading a story. Jonathan had heard this story read many times, of course. Furthermore, the book has a **predictable text** (Rhodes, 1981)—a text with many repetitions— which makes it an easy book to learn and remember. Given a totally unfamiliar book, Jonathan probably would be at a loss. But in many ways he *is* reading the book, and although he's not yet a beginning reader, he deserves to be called an emergent reader rather than a nonreader. This is an important early stage in the long process of learning how to read. A closer look at this process, which extends well into the school years, is provided in Research Focus—Stages of Storybook Reading.

DISTINGUISHING WRITING FROM NONWRITING. Jonathan knows that some things he sees in *The Very Hungry Caterpillar* are words and some things are pictures. Matt, too, knew that some pages in *Where the Wild Things Are* had pictures but no words on them. Recognizing writing and distinguishing it both from pictures and from other kinds of marks are some of the early literacy skills children acquire. How and when do they become capable of making these distinctions?

In a study designed to answer the question of how preschoolers recognize writing, children ranging in age from 3 to $6\frac{1}{2}$ were shown various combinations of letters, numbers, pictures, and doodles printed on cards (Figure 11-8) (Lavine, 1977). Children were asked to sort the cards into two piles, one of writing and one of marks that weren't writing.

Actual writing samples were recognized by 80 percent of the 3-year-olds, 90 percent of the 4-year-olds, and 96 percent of the 5-year-olds. Even when children couldn't name letters or words, they knew that writing was writing.

FIGURE 11-7
Displays used by Lavine (1977) to see if children could distinguish writing from nonwriting. Even 3-year-olds were found to be highly print aware.

Children apparently recognize writing at first by its linearity (it's arranged in lines) and variety (letters don't repeat more than two times in a row). Later, they recognize the letters themselves. The high rate at which even 3-year-olds were able to distinguish general features of writing indicates that many children are "print aware" at a very early age.

FIGURING OUT HOW ALPHABET LETTERS CODE WORDS. Once children begin to notice and recognize writing, they may next try to figure out how printed words are related to what they say and hear. In English, each letter of the alphabet represents a **phoneme**—an individual speech sound—within a word (with the exception of some silent letters and letters that are combined to represent one sound, such as "th," "ch," and "ei"). There isn't any reason for children

RESEARCH FOCUS

Stages of Storybook Reading

When we imagine a young child reading a book, we usually think of a 6- or 7-year-old who reads the text fluently by deciphering the print and referring to inner knowledge about context and language structures. This image is basically correct for a fluent reader, but such a child has been "reading" in other ways for quite a long time. The earlier attempts and strategies we refer to as emergent reading behavior prepare the child for more mature, independent reading.

Researchers have traced the development of storybook reading through the emergent to the beginning reader stage (Rossman, 1980; Sulzby, 1985). Sulzby has identified five developmental stages of storybook reading, as shown in the accompanying diagram. Sulzby found that when children first read their favorite storybooks, they look at the pictures rather than the print (top of diagram). Their first picture-based reading attempts often are not given in story form. The children simply label the pictures or comment about what is happening in them.

If and when they read the pictures in story form, they might tell the story in one of two ways (second tier of diagram). If they use an oral languagelike approach, they may direct comments to a listener, as if carrying on a conversation (dialogic storytelling). Or they may not make comments, but they sound as if they were telling a story rather than reading one (monologic storytelling). In this case, they could just as easily be giving a blow-by-blow account of an ongoing event in the world as reading a story from a book.

If children use a written languagelike approach to telling the story, they don't direct comments to the listener or tell the story in a conversational way. They sound more like they're reading, although within this category some children might mix elements of reading and storytelling and others might give a word-for-word rendition of the book. Even though they are using written languagelike speech, however, these children are not necessarily watching the print in the book.

Eventually, children do start to pay attention to the print (third tier of diagram). Once they do, they might focus on a specific aspect of the print, such as words they know, words that begin with the first letter of their name, or words with letters whose sounds they know. Other children have memorized the text and run their fingers along as they read, trying to match what they see with what they say. Sulzby refers to any of these approaches as aspectual, meaning that children focus on just one aspect of the print (fourth tier of diagram).

Whatever the child's specific approach to reading at this stage, its distinguishing characteristic is that the child "doesn't have it all together" (Sulzby, 1985, p. 472). Children at this stage often become self-conscious and refuse to try to read for a period of time. When they're paying attention to the print, they sound less fluent than when they're "reading" the pictures. This is another example of an apparent regression occurring as the child advances in insight—in this case, about how reading really works.

Finally, children begin to combine strategies instead of focusing on just one aspect of the print. At first, they have a hard time using different strategies as complements to one another, so their strategies are "imbalanced" (fifth tier of diagram). They are not yet independent readers (that is, readers with balanced strategies). **Independent readers** use context to predict what's coming next; they use the pictures to confirm their predictions; and they go back and make corrections when something doesn't make sense. Children whose strategies aren't balanced, by contrast, often pay too much attention to context, making up words that make sense instead of reading what's actually there. Or they pay so much attention to sounding out the words that what they read doesn't make sense at all. This is the **beginning reader** stage of reading, and it sounds the way children reading out loud in old-fashioned first-grade reading groups used to sound. Gradually, children learn to use different cues in a flexible, "checks and balances" sort of way, and their strategies become balanced. At this point, they can be considered competent, fluent, independent readers.

Preschoolers usually read by paying attention to the pictures. Children are often at the "imbalanced" stage of reading during the greater part of first grade, moving to an initial type of fluency by the end of first grade. Children become more fluent readers during the second and third grades (Chall & Snow, 1988).

---

to assume that the English **orthography** (system of writing) works this way; in many other languages, it works differently.

In Chinese, for example, each character represents an idea, not a sound within a word. Students learning to write Chinese must memorize thousands of different characters (Taylor, 1981). In Japanese, characters represent syllables; this reduces the number of characters needed, since a single syllable can appear in many different words. But fewer characters still are needed for an

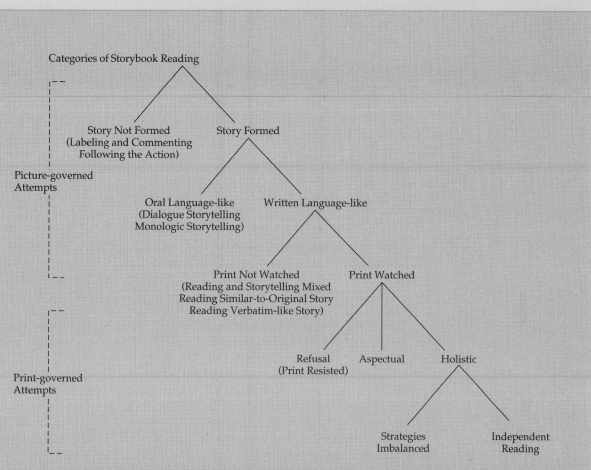

Categories of Storybook Reading

Story Not Formed
(Labeling and Commenting
Following the Action)

Story Formed

Picture-governed
Attempts

Oral Language-like
(Dialogue Storytelling
Monologic Storytelling)

Written Language-like

Print Not Watched
(Reading and Storytelling Mixed
Reading Similar-to-Original Story
Reading Verbatim-like Story)

Print Watched

Refusal
(Print Resisted)

Aspectual

Holistic

Print-governed
Attempts

Strategies
Imbalanced

Independent
Reading

SOURCE: *From Sulzby, E. (1985). Children's emergent reading of favorite storybooks: A developmental study.* Reading Research Quarterly, 20 *(4), 464. Reprinted by permission.*

Although a few children are **early readers** (reading at age 5), it is generally quite difficult by third grade to distinguish early readers from children who became fluent readers during the course of first grade.

We see from these studies that learning to read takes place during both the preschool and the school-age years. It actually takes a very long time, although it seems to occur over a short period of time because we usually focus on just one stage. In fact, oral language and written language are alike in this respect: They are both acquired over the course of many years.

alphabetically based system such as English. This is because just a few characters, combined in different ways, can be used to represent a small set of phonemes and to create all the words in the language (Taylor, 1981).

When children begin to make the connection between the sounds they hear in spoken language and the words they see in books, they typically think that each letter represents a syllable. For example, a child named Adam might write his name as "AD," because he has divided it into two parts—A-dam.

He hears two syllables and selects a letter to represent each one. Similarly, a child trying to read a familiar storybook title might point to one letter for every syllable she hears:

A child dictating a story to a teacher or parent tends to think the adult has written down more than he has; the adult constantly has to say, "Just a minute—you're going too fast."

The young child's tendency to use this **syllabic hypothesis** when trying to match speech to print is understandable, given that syllables are much easier to hear than phonemes (Ferreiro, 1986; Schickedanz, 1987). Apparently, the peaks of acoustic energy that fall at syllable centers provide cues that make it easy for the listener to pick them out of the stream of speech (Liberman et al., 1974). What probably pushes the child to give up the syllabic hypothesis and think about speech at the phonemic level is the continual mismatch between speech and print—there are just too many letters left over. To account for all the letters in her name, for example, the child must consider that each letter represents something smaller than a syllable.

When children begin to think about individual speech sounds in language, they've gained what we call **phonemic awareness** and **phonemic segmentation skill.** Now they learn to associate each letter of the alphabet with specific sounds, a knowledge that underlies the ability to read and write (Bradley & Bryant, 1983; Tunmer & Nesdale, 1985). They may show that they have high levels of phonemic awareness by recognizing rhyming words or by announcing that "'milk' begins just like 'mommy' and 'mouse.'"

Children begin to write differently once they've gained the ability to segment words phonemically. Since they're starting to think about individual sounds in words, they use more than one letter to represent a one-syllable word, such as "KT" or "KAT" for "Kate." Preschool children's spelling may not be conventional, but it usually indicates that they're on the right track.

The age at which phonemic segmentation skills appear varies among different groups of children. It has been observed in children as young as $3\frac{1}{2}$ (Read, 1975), but it also has been found to be absent in 6-year-olds (Ferreiro & Teberosky, 1979). The timing seems to be related to the kind of opportunities children have to read and write. When there are many opportunities, phonemic segmentation skills appear earlier; when there are fewer opportunities, they appear later.

LEARNING TO RECOGNIZE LETTERS OF THE ALPHABET. Besides learning that letters represent phonemes, children also have to learn to recognize the individual letters of the alphabet. As adults, we recognize the letters of our alphabet instantaneously. To appreciate the difficulty of this task, which we mastered so long ago, we only have to examine a writing sample from a language that uses an alphabet we're not familiar with, such as Greek or Russian. Suddenly the letters are indistinguishable, and we don't know one from another.

Children face a similar challenge when they first begin to learn the letters of their own alphabet. How do they begin to sort the letters out? This process

FIGURE 11-8
This girl knows that putting marker to paper produces results that please both her and her parents. Access to the tools of literacy gives children important early experiences with reading and writing. When access is limited at home, preschools can often make up the difference.

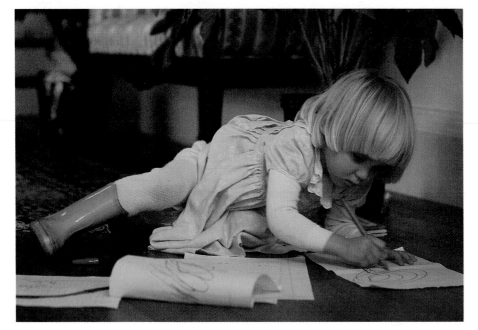

seems to involve the gradual differentiation of distinctive features. **Distinctive features** are the characteristics of a set of similar things (such as our alphabet) that make that set different from other sets (such as the Greek alphabet). At the same time, distinctive features are combined in different ways within the set to make individual units (in this case, the letters) different from each other.

The distinctive features of our alphabet are characteristics such as whether a line is straight or curved, whether curves are open or closed, and whether straight lines are diagonal, horizontal, or vertical (Gibson, 1969). For example, some letters are closed (D, O), and others are open (C, L); some letters have curved lines (C, S, O), and others have straight lines (L, E, T); and some straight-line letters contain diagonal lines (K, N, M), and others don't (L, E, T).

When children first begin to recognize letters of the alphabet, they often consider letters "the same" that share some distinctive features. For example, if you give children two sets of letters with instructions to put letters that are "the same" together, they might very well place "D" with "O", because both letters are closed figures containing curved lines. They might confuse "E" and "F" because both are made from straight horizontal and vertical lines. They might confuse "M" and "N" because both are made from straight diagonal and vertical lines. But they would rarely pair "O" with "L" or "M" with "O," because in both cases, the letters have no distinctive features in common.

Distinguishing letters from each other requires that the child pay attention not to how they're the same but to how they're different. This kind of learning probably runs counter to how children (and human beings in general) have to deal with much of their world. A lot of learning requires that we form categories of things that are similar. We can't cope with a world full of separate and unrelated things; we make the world more manageable by lumping similar things together and responding to them as a group.

FIGURE 11-9
This boy is practicing the alphabet by matching the letters in his hand with the letters on the pegboard. Because the letters of our alphabet share so many distinctive features, it's hard at first to sort them out. Z shares straight horizontal lines with E, F, L, and T and diagonal lines with M, N, V, W, and X.

FIGURE 11-10
Seeing high-interest words in context helps children learn how to recognize letters, associate sounds with them, and begin to understand what's involved in reading. Even words like "Bubblicious" can promote emergent literacy.

This is exactly how children first approach the alphabet letters. They note similarities and ignore differences. This allows them to discriminate among certain letters but not others. Gradually, with more exposure to alphabet letters and their different, distinctive sounds and uses, children begin to see each letter as different from all the others. When children grow up surrounded by **environmental print**—the written language they see all around them in stores, on the street, and so on—it's not uncommon for them to know most of the upper-case alphabet letters by the time they're 4 or 5 years old.

One distinctive feature that is especially difficult for children to sort out, however, is orientation in space—whether a letter faces right or left, up or down. This feature is what makes the letters "W" and "M," "p" and "q," and "b" and "d" different. All of the other distinctive features of these letter pairs are identical. **Reversals**, or errors in a letter's orientation, are common in children's writing, even during the first grade. One reason children find this distinctive feature difficult to notice is that it contradicts all their previous experience with three-dimensional objects.

To understand the child's problem, imagine that you are going to a cupboard to get two identical coffee mugs. There are four mugs on the shelf: (1) a tall, brown, plastic mug sitting upside down with its handle to the left: (2) a short, brown, ceramic mug sitting upright with its handle to the right; (3) a second tall, brown, plastic mug sitting upright with its handle to the right, and (4) a second short, brown, ceramic mug sitting upside down with its handle to the left (Figure 11-11).

Chances are you would select mugs 1 and 3 or mugs 2 and 4 as a pair, completely ignoring whether the mugs were upside down or whether their handles were turned to the left or the right. This example shows that orientation is not used as a distinctive feature in distinguishing three-dimensional objects. When children first begin to look at print, all their previous experience has involved objects, and although they see that some letters are reversed versions of others, they assume that the differences don't matter any more than they did with the physical objects.

A child who deliberately wrote his name both "frontwards" and "backwards" considered both versions to be his name, just as a chair is still a chair whether it's right side up or upside down. At the same time, he recognized other kinds of errors—starting his name with two A's, for example—as mistakes. He didn't consider a mirror-image version of his name wrong—just "backwards"—until a year and a half after he recognized that other errors made his name wrong (Schickedanz, 1987).

Learning the letters of the alphabet and the sounds they represent used to be considered the only, or at least the most important, "prereading" skill that children had to acquire. Now we know that this is only one of many things

FIGURE 11-11
Which two cups would you pick as "identical"?

FIGURE 11-12
Mirror writing is common among preschoolers and shouldn't be taken as a sign that a child has a learning disability. Children who write this way simply haven't acquired a strong sense of where to begin and which way to head when they start to write.

an emergent reader and writer must learn. We also know that knowledge of letter names is not a "prereading" skill in the sense that the child can't engage in reading and writing activities until letter names are mastered. Children do engage in these activities long before they know any specific alphabet letters. They "read" stories in familiar storybooks (Sulzby, 1985), respond to labels and signs (Mason, 1980), and "scribble-write" messages (Clay, 1987) before they have much, if any, knowledge of letter names. Learning the letters is just one part of the long-term, complex process of learning to read.

Creating Print

Reading is one part of literacy; writing is the other. To learn to write, children have to master many skills, both physical and cognitive. They also have to learn the conventions—established ways of doing things—of writing in our language. Two conventions that preschoolers usually confront are the formation of letters and the arrangement of print on a page.

LEARNING PRINT CONVENTIONS: HOW LETTERS ARE FORMED. Many children will write—represent a message with marks—long before they can form or even recognize most alphabet letters. The marks they use often include **scribble-writing**, or chains of zigzags or loops across a page, and **mock letters**, which resemble actual alphabet letters and indeed would make good candidates for a twenty-seventh or twenty-eighth letter of our alphabet, should we ever need one.

FIGURE 11-13
Examples of preconventional writing: (a) Continuous scribble-writing; (b and c) mock letters; (d) conventional letters with a few mock letters intermingled; (e) individual scribble marks.

Several examples of both scribble-writing and mock letters are shown in Figure 11-13.

Children often mix scribble-writing, mock letters, and conventional letters as they learn to write, using one, then another, then the first again (Clay, 1987; Schickedanz, 1987). Many children who can write conventional letters turn to scribble-writing in certain situations, such as when creating a very long story.

Temporarily reverting to an earlier, more comfortable strategy—in this case, scribble-writing—is not uncommon in childhood. We see the same thing when beginning walkers drop to their hands and knees to crawl when they want to get somewhere in a hurry.

LEARNING PRINT CONVENTIONS: HOW WORDS ARE ORGANIZED ON A PAGE. Another aspect of writing that children must learn is how print is organized on a page. Does it go from right to left, from left to right, or both, sweeping back and forth on alternate lines like a computer printer? And how is the page filled vertically? From top to bottom or from bottom to top?

There isn't any one absolute, right way to arrange print on a page. There are simply conventions in every language. Some languages, like Hebrew, are written from right to left; others, like Chinese, are written from top to bottom in columns. Still others, like English, use a left-to-right, top-to-bottom organization.

The writing done by young preschool children often appears quite disorganized, and it is. Most preschoolers don't know how print is placed on a

(a)

(b)

FIGURE 11-14
Examples of preconventional writing by a 5-year-old who hasn't yet mastered such print conventions as starting at the top of the page and leaving spaces between words. His messages are, "I love you, Mommy, I love you forever" (a); "Dear Badgie, I miss you. Love, Adam" (b); "Dear Bullfrogs, Hi. I think I can visit at Beaver Camp" (c). In the last message he ran out of room, so he finished up on the other side of the paper with mirror writing.

(c)

page in our language. They also lack the concepts of space that would enable them to stick with specific conventions even if they knew them. For example, children often mix orientations when writing, perhaps writing the first few letters of their name from left to right across the top of a page and then turning the page to write more letters from left to right across the new top of the page. The finished product is written in several orientations, and the reader has to rotate the page to read it. Children who mix orientations this way often lack a spatial concept that Piaget called **projective** (1967). A person who has projective spatial understandings knows that there are different points of view and can adopt a view and stick with it. Children who mix points of view in the same writing sample often don't know that there are specific points of view or that their writing contains contradictions (two sides of the paper treated as the top, for example). Mixed orientations can be seen in the writing samples in Figure 11-14.

Once children are able to adopt a point of view and stay with it consistently, they still have to realize that certain specific conventions are considered "right" in our language. One 5-year-old who had invited an adult to write a book with him asked the adult if they could write from left to right so they wouldn't be "confusing to each other." This child realized that internal consistency was a good idea, but he didn't realize that left-to-right organization is the accepted convention in our language. He thought the organization of writing on the page was something you decided each time you sat down to write.

Another print convention involves strategies for marking where one word ends and the next begins. Dots, slashes, hyphens, and special letters have all been used in different languages to indicate word endings. In English, of course, we separate words with a space. Young children—preschoolers, kindergartners, and even early first graders—typically string their letters together without any spaces between words (Figure 11-14). Sometimes they invent their own ways to show where words end, such as slashes or dots. As with other literacy skills, in time they notice how other writers separate words, and they adopt the convention in their own writing.

The Social Context of Emergent Literacy Development

Everything in child development takes place in a context—in some kind of setting—and emergent literacy is no exception. The development of reading and writing skills occurs in the context of home, school, and community. It's probably been obvious in our discussion so far that we're making some assumptions about what materials and experiences are available to the preschool child. Children can't develop story-reading strategies without hearing storybooks read. They can't learn how to create print if they never have access to writing materials. Many studies have shown that high levels of written language development in preschoolers are associated with easy and frequent access to literacy activities (Durkin, 1966; Read, 1975; Ferreiro & Teberosky, 1979; Bissex, 1980; Schickedanz & Sullivan, 1984).

It's probably also obvious that different homes provide different literacy experiences for children, and research has supported this assumption too. In some homes, parents do more talking and explaining; they read and write

FIGURE 11-15
Literate homes help children
view themselves as readers
and think of reading as an
enjoyable, natural choice
from an early age. These
children have been told to
keep their clothes clean
while they wait for a party to
begin—an ideal time for a
book.

more; and they provide more literacy activities and toys for their children. There are differences in literacy experiences from household to household even at the same socioeconomic level (Anderson, Teale, & Estrada, 1980).

Children whose early literacy experiences at home are schoollike have a better idea of what to expect when they get to school. If they've had lots of storybooks read to them, for example, they're familiar with the kind of books that will be in their classrooms. Children who haven't had this experience will be less familiar with books, although they might be very experienced at reading print on food cartons or store fronts.

Some parents seem to interact with their children in a more schoollike way, too, and this may help the children understand some of the more abstract features of written language. For example, all children might recognize a stop sign in context, but some are more likely to know that the word "stop" begins with "s" just as the words "Susan" and "soup" do (Dickinson & Snow, 1987). Perhaps some parents ask their children to display their knowledge more than others do, asking, "What does that sign say?" or "What letter does the word 'stop' begin with?" This kind of schoollike experience probably helps children think about writing in an analytical way.

Some of these differences in early literacy experiences tend to be associated with socioeconomic status (SES), with higher SES parents providing more schoollike experiences than lower SES parents. Higher SES parents may interact this way more with their children because they're less preoccupied with worries about housing, food, medical bills, and so on. We know that when parents have something on their minds, it's harder for them to give attention to their children. One researcher observed how parents' interactions with their children changed when they were asked to fill out a form (Zussman, 1980). He found that they interacted less frequently and less positively while they were concentrating on the form. If a preoccupation as trivial as this can affect parent-child interactions, it's not surprising that economic stresses can have a significant impact.

But despite differences in the literacy experiences that children have at home, all children in a literate world such as ours come to school knowing quite a lot about written language. If teachers find that some of their children haven't had as many early schoollike experiences as others, they can often provide them with the background experiences and knowledge they need to succeed in school.

Parental Behavior During the Emergent Literacy Period

Since early experiences do make a difference when children get to school, what can and should parents do to support literacy development? Contrary to what might be expected, parents don't have to set out deliberately to teach their young children to read and write. Parents obviously do give their children information about reading and writing, but it's not in the form of organized lessons. Instead, literacy experiences occur as the family lives its life. A shopping list has to be made before a trip to the supermarket, a letter has to be written to grandma, a check must be written to pay a bill, and some positive way must be found to make children want to get ready for bed. It's in the course of getting these things done that children's literacy experiences occur (Heath, 1983; Schickedanz & Sullivan, 1984; Teale, 1986). A mother gives her son a piece of paper and a pencil to make his own shopping list or to write his own letter to grandma. She hands her daughter a deposit slip from the checkbook to scribble on. Parents establish storybook reading as a bedtime routine. In these ways, children learn that reading and writing are a natural part of their lives.

Because parents don't set out to teach literacy skills to their children, they overlook the child's mistakes and incomplete knowledge. When a child hands them a scribbled note and explains, "It says, 'I love you,'" they accept it without criticism. When a child recites a memorized storybook and says, "I read it all by myself," they allow the child's assertion to stand. Parents' "teaching" of emergent literacy skills is very different from most of the formal teaching that goes on in school. **Whole language** approaches to reading and writing, which are popular in schools right now and which we discuss in Chapter 15, are modeled after literacy learning as it occurs in the home.

OVERVIEW

There isn't much guesswork involved in figuring out what preschoolers are saying. Unlike toddlers, who say only part of what they mean, preschoolers can "tell all." But they haven't perfected all language forms yet. They still have to sort out the complexities of syntax and the exceptions to all the rules that they've miraculously picked up. These tasks begin during the preschool years and are completed in the school years. Preschoolers rely heavily on extralinguistic context to understand language, and broad, rich experiences help them build inner "contexts of the mind." Preschoolers learn a great deal about written language as well, usually without the kind of specific lessons we typically associate with school. But early schoollike literacy experiences do give children an advantage later in learning to read. Providing these experiences to more children will be one of the challenges of the 1990s.

CHAPTER REVIEW

ORAL LANGUAGE DEVELOPMENT

- Preschoolers' speech is no longer telegraphic. Their sentences are longer and more complete than those of toddlers.
- Preschoolers overgeneralize morphological rules, producing the coined words and ingenious usages for which they're famous.
- Word order rules for formulating questions and negative sentences are gradually acquired by preschoolers.
- Children learn correct speech not from being corrected but from being exposed to correct usage in a natural, meaningful way.
- An understanding of the meaning coded by word order in active sentences emerges between 2 and 3 years of age, but an understanding of passive sentences is not attained until about age 5.
- Understanding the locative expressions "in," "on," and "under" emerges at about age $2\frac{1}{2}$, but "beside," "between," "front," and "back" are not understood until age $4\frac{1}{2}$ or 5.
- It can take children many years to acquire some word meanings.
- Preschoolers use extralinguistic context to figure out what is being said; rich experiences help them to build "contexts of the mind."

WRITTEN LANGUAGE DEVELOPMENT

- The term emergent literacy has replaced the term reading readiness to describe all the literacy activities children engage in prior to becoming conventional readers and writers.
- Children's reading strategies evolve over a long period of time. At first, children often think that pictures in books are what one reads; only later do they realize that reading involves getting meaning from print.
- Learning that letters of the alphabet code phonemes rather than whole words or syllables is one thing that children must figure out about print.
- Children as young as 3 years old recognize print and can distinguish writing from nonwriting.
- Recognizing letters of the alphabet involves the gradual differentiation of distinctive features. One of the hardest features for children to sort out is orientation in space, a difficulty that accounts for the frequency of letter reversals by young children.
- Scribble-writing, mock letters, mixed orientations, and lack of space between words can be seen in children's writing attempts before they master print conventions.
- High levels of written language development are associated with easy and frequent access to literacy activities during the preschool years. Children who have had many schoollike experiences tend to be more successful when they start school.
- Parents support literacy development with the many reading and writing experiences that occur naturally in the home every day.

KEY TERMS

morpheme
morphological rules
inflected
overgeneralize
syntax
context bound
decontextualized

emergent literacy
reading readiness
predictable text
independent reader
beginning reader
early reader
phoneme

orthography
syllabic hypothesis
phonemic awareness
phonemic segmentation
   skill
distinctive features

environmental print
reversals
scribble-writing
mock letters
projective
whole language approach

SUGGESTIONS FOR FURTHER READING

Clay, M. (1987). *Writing begins at home*. Portsmouth, NH: Heinemann Educational Books.

This short book is full of samples of preschoolers' writing. It's an excellent introduction for anyone unfamiliar with young children's writing.

Lindfors, J. W. (1987). *Children's language and learning* (2d ed). Englewood Cliffs, NJ: Prentice-Hall.

This basic text provides an excellent survey of all areas of language development. Included in this second edition is information on written language development.

Muma, J. R. (1986). *Language acquisition: A functionalistic perspective*. Austin, TX: Pre-Ed.

This book reviews and summarizes considerable bodies of research and is for the student who is seriously interested in studying language acquisition.

Newman, J. M. (Ed.). (1985). *Whole language: Theory in use*. Portsmouth, NH: Heinemann Educational Books. Providing information about the theoretical and research base for the whole language approach to literacy development, this contributed volume contains practical information for teachers who wish to implement this approach.

Schickedanz, J. (1986). *More than the ABCs: The early stages of reading and writing*. Washington, DC: National Association for the Education of Young Children.

This short paperback provides an overview of research on emergent literacy and suggests ways that parents and teachers can support young children's curiosity about written language.

chapter 12

SOCIAL AND EMOTIONAL DEVELOPMENT IN PRESCHOOL CHILDREN

Two children were playing on an outdoor play structure at a birthday party. Laura, 4 years old, was swinging, and Aaron, 6, was climbing on a ladder nearby. They were talking and laughing in a friendly way. Suddenly, Martina, $3\frac{1}{2}$ and a classmate of Laura's at nursery school, burst out of the house and came running across the grass.

"I want to swing, I want to swing," she called out. As she got to the play structure, she gave Laura a shove and grabbed the swing away from her.

"I had it, Martina," Laura protested.

Martina held onto the swing and glared at Laura for a moment. Then she raised the swing behind her and let it go in Laura's direction. The swing hit Laura in the face, and she burst into tears. As she ran off, Martina jumped onto the swing.

"Martina," Aaron called from the ladder above the swing, "if you don't give Laura back the swing, I'm going to spit in your hair." Martina squinted up at him and hesitated. At the same time, a parent started across the grass toward the play structure with a tearful Laura in tow.

"Martina," she called out, "you'll need to wait for your turn to use the swing. Laura was using it."

As Martina scooted off the swing, the parent said, "Come with me. I want to talk to you. I saw you hit Laura with the swing. It gave her a bump on her head. Why did you do that?"

"Because I wanted the swing. I wanted her to leave so I could have it."

"You need to learn a better way to get a turn. What do you think you could do?"

Martina looked down at the ground without answering.

"Let's go back and talk to Laura. We're going to go tell her that you want a turn on the swing and ask her how much longer she thinks she's going to be using it."

With support and coaching from the parent, Martina was able to tell Laura that she wanted a turn and to ask how long she'd have to wait. Laura said that she didn't know how long it would be.

"Well, we'll be over in the sandbox while we wait," said the parent. "Come tell us when you're finished, in case we don't see you get off. And, remember, Martina needs a turn before the party is over."

"Okay," Laura agreed.

With their improved motor skills and cognitive abilities, preschoolers are able to engage in much more complex social exchanges than they could as toddlers. And very often, they get themselves hopelessly entangled in social difficulties from which only adults can rescue them. Very young children have neither the skills nor the experience that are needed for smooth social interactions. They acquire some of these skills through socialization during the preschool period. **Socialization**, if you recall from Chapter 8, is the process by which children learn the values and behaviors accepted in their society. Children have to learn how to act in social situations—how to share and be fair; how to express themselves and solve problems without hurting or depriving other children; and how to trust, enjoy, and care for people both inside and outside their family. They learn to behave in ways that adults—and ultimately they, themselves—will consider acceptable.

Between ages 3 and 6, children make great strides in controlling their aggressive impulses, in thinking about others besides themselves, and in resisting doing what they know they shouldn't. How do they learn these things? How do they become socialized? And what are the best ways for adults to help children become responsible, caring people with an appropriate measure of self-control? These are the issues addressed in this chapter on the social and emotional development of preschool children.

FIGURE 12-1
Even though their most important relationships are still with their parents and other family members, preschoolers find fun and friendships with their peers. Support and guidance from adults help preschoolers work out interpersonal difficulties in a positive way.

FIGURE 12-2
She teaches him how to behave because she loves him. He listens because he cares so much about her and her opinion of him. The most effective socialization is based on a high-quality attachment relationship.

SOCIALIZATION PROCESSES

Socialization results from learning, and many of our current approaches to socialization are based on both learning and social learning theory. As described in Chapter 2 on theories of child development, learning theory focuses on processes such as reinforcement and punishment. Social learning theory focuses on imitation of models, or what we call observational learning.

If you were asked how you think children learn social behaviors, you might answer that they learn by being rewarded, punished, or having some of their inappropriate behavior ignored; by watching what others do; and by being told about expectations. These techniques are at the heart of the three main socialization processes—reinforcement, punishment, and extinction; observational learning; and verbal instruction—that are discussed in this section.

These socialization processes don't operate in a vacuum. Their effect involves and depends on a child's history of relationships with adults, especially the critical attachment relationship with the parents, as we saw in Chapter 8. A child's orientation to adults and her feelings toward them are strongly influenced by the nature of her attachment relationship. This, in turn, affects the extent to which she imitates adult behavior, responds when adults reinforce or punish her actions, listens when they explain the reasons for an admonition, and feels dissatisfied with herself when she fails to meet their expectations.

Other factors, including the child's level of cognitive development and her temperament, also influence the effect of various socialization attempts and the ease or difficulty with which adults are able to deal with the child in specific situations. This is why we also discuss how biology and the child's level of cognitive development influence the application of socialization processes and the effects they have.

Reinforcement, Punishment, and Extinction

One Saturday morning while playing in the family room, Susan, age 3, turned the knob of the TV and watched the screen as it lit up. Then she turned it off and on again. She was intrigued by the dot of light that appeared and spread across the screen. She turned the knob off and on again and again. In the next room, her dad heard what was going on and came in to investigate.

"Susan, where's your play dough?" he asked. "Weren't you going to make some cookies this morning out at the picnic table?"

Susan ran to get her play dough and pushed open the back door. Her dad went outside with her and helped her set up her place mat and cookie cutters. Then he settled into a nearby chair to continue his reading.

After a while he looked over and said, "Looks like Christmas cookies." He got up and went over to the table. "Can I have a bite?" He took an imaginary bite, and Susan laughed in delight. She continued playing with the play dough for the next hour, apparently having forgotten all about the TV knob.

A learning theorist would say that Susan's responses in this situation were reinforced. **Reinforcement** is defined as a consequence to a response that increases the probability that the response will occur again in the same situation or a similar one. The interesting light appearing on the screen reinforced Susan's turning of the TV knob; her father's attention reinforced her playing with the play dough.

FIGURE 12-3
Preschools can structure their programs to include many socialization opportunities. This little girl has asked another child to pour her some milk, and she thanks him when he complies. The teacher can reinforce their actions by complimenting them on a job well done.

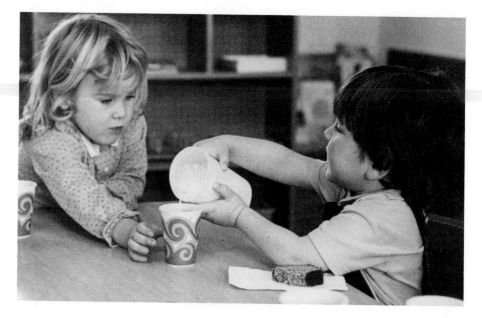

Susan's dad showed thought and skill in his response to what she was doing. He didn't simply tell her to stop fiddling with the TV knob, for example. He redirected her instead to an interesting alternative activity, one in which she was likely to stay engaged for some time. This helped her to avoid becoming involved in other play activities that might create additional problems. The play dough activity was also one for which her father could easily provide positive reinforcement in the form of attention, even though he needed to do some reading in his book. Effective socialization depends in large part on the skill of adults in organizing situations and redirecting behavior so that they can give positive reinforcement.

Another parent might have slapped Susan's hand or sent her to her room to teach her not to play with the knob. If Susan's knob-turning behavior decreased after these kinds of actions, we would say that they were punishers for her behavior. **Punishment** is defined as a consequence that decreases the probability that the response will recur.

Learning theory distinguishes two different kinds of punishment. One kind adds stimuli to the environment, such as a slap on Susan's hand. The other kind removes stimuli from the environment, often those that were previously reinforcing the behavior. Sending Susan to her room, where she couldn't play with the TV or the other toys in the family room, would be an example of this kind of punishment.

Punishments of the second kind—in which reinforcers are removed—are referred to as **response costs** (Reese & Lipsitt, 1970). In other words, they're the costs to the child as a result of his or her response. When children are sent to their rooms at home, or when they're sent to sit somewhere by themselves at school, away from the major activities going on in their classroom, the procedure is called time out from positive reinforcement, or, more commonly, **time out**. Because children's normal environments at home or school have so many interesting activities and social interactions with other people, taking them out of these environments for misbehavior usually serves as a punishment.

A third way to reduce inappropriate behavior, besides reinforcement and punishment, is to arrange the environment so the child receives no reinforcement at all for the behavior. In Susan's case, her dad might have unplugged the TV. When she turned the knob, she wouldn't have seen any spreading light that would have made her want to repeat her action. When a behavior doesn't produce any interesting consequences, it often disappears. This process is called **extinction**. In the classroom, a teacher who ignores obnoxious behavior is attempting to use extinction.

CHOOSING AN APPROPRIATE METHOD. Although all three of these approaches can get results, one is considered the learning technique of choice—reinforcement. Both extinction and punishment have serious drawbacks. Extinction isn't used very often, because it's difficult for adults to ignore children's misbehavior. Some misbehavior can't be ignored because it hurts or endangers other people or the misbehaving child. And parents and teachers know that many times, children need practical ideas about what they *should* do instead of the thing they're doing that's getting them into trouble. Susan's dad sensed that she needed a suggestion about something else to do besides play with the TV knob. He directed her to an engaging activity that took her outside, away from the TV, where she wouldn't be tempted to turn the knob again.

Susan's dad may also have known that punishment has its drawbacks. One of them is that it can backfire and produce exactly the opposite effects of the desired ones. We've all witnessed scenes like the following:

> Kevin approaches the TV set and turns the dial. His father, Edward, looks up from his book and tells him, "No!" Kevin stops playing with the dial, and Edward returns to his book. Kevin again turns the TV dial, but Edward doesn't notice right away. Finally, Edward notices and intervenes again, once more telling Kevin, "No!" He returns to his book, and Kevin begins to play with some toys. Kevin then approaches the TV, turning to look at his dad. Edward looks back at him. Kevin smiles broadly and turns the dial. Edward intervenes, says, "No!" again, picks Kevin up, and puts him down on the other side of the room. Kevin runs to the TV, laughing in delight, and turns it on. Edward by now is very angry and spanks Kevin hard.

In this situation, Edward's responses reinforced Kevin's behavior rather than punishing it—they increased his involvement with the TV rather than decreasing it. Kevin was pleased that he'd found a way of getting his dad's attention. The "class clown" often behaves this way. The teacher's attention serves to reinforce the child's misbehavior, making it increase. A no-win situation quickly develops, with the teacher often escalating punishment to a harsher level, as when Edward spanked Kevin for playing with the TV dial. But escalation to physical punishment has definite problems.

DISADVANTAGES OF PHYSICAL PUNISHMENT. One problem with physical punishment is simply that we can't explain or teach very much to a crying child. The period of time following misbehavior is often a unique one for instruction, and learning during this period may generalize to other situations. We can use this time to help the child understand why the behavior was inappropriate or what a person should or could do in that particular situation. But if the child is upset or in pain, the opportunity for learning is wasted. An explanation might reduce the inappropriate behavior just as well as the punishment.

A second problem with punishment—and with time out—is that it may reduce exploration and initiative, especially if it comes without warning. A child in a new situation must be given the chance to find out what behaviors work and what behaviors are considered inappropriate. Consider the following example:

> Two preschoolers were each attempting to look in a small, round mirror they were both holding. They started tugging it back and forth.
>
> "Let *me* have it," shouted Katie.
>
> "*I* want it," Andy responded.
>
> Katie's mother came over and took the mirror. She put it on the table and showed them that if they stood back a little, they could both see themselves at the same time. The two children played happily together for the next several minutes as they both looked in the mirror.
>
> Later, Andy relayed the incident to his mother, who asked him why he hadn't shared the mirror with his friend in the first place. "Well, I didn't know *how* to do that before Katie's mom 'splained it to me," he said.

If Katie and Andy had been punished for quarreling with spanking, yelling, time out, or loss of use of the mirror, they may have learned that the only way to avoid punishment is to avoid new situations altogether. Children who are treated this way may become timid, hesitant, and fearful. Or they may develop only a limited repertoire of responses when they find themselves again in conflict situations over toys. When Katie's mom demonstrated a way for both children to use the toy, she may have not only helped them solve their current problem but given them the idea that sometimes a way can be found to use a toy together. Obviously, children learn more when they don't avoid situations out of fear and when adults provide suggestions for alternative behavior.

A third problem with punishment is that it can create hostility and resentment, making the adult an **aversive stimulus** for the child. An aversive stimulus is something a person seeks to avoid. A punishing adult will become particularly aversive if the child thinks the punishment is harsh, unnecessary, or motivated by anger rather than concern for the child's well-being. If Katie and Andy had been spanked for quarreling, they may have had such feelings of hostility and resentment. After all, as Andy explained, they didn't know how to share the mirror until an adult provided an idea. The fact that they played cooperatively with the mirror after being shown how indicated that they hadn't really wanted to fight with each other. They were simply two young children without the means to solve a problem.

A very serious problem with punishment is that it can lead to child abuse. Some parents have reported that child abuse occurred in disciplinary situations that simply went too far (Gil, 1970). The principles of social learning apply to adults too—if physical punishment works, it can reinforce the parent for hitting. And if the punishment used is severe, or it's seen as coming from anger or hostility, so that the parent becomes an aversive stimulus, then any positive reinforcement the parent tries to initiate will have limited effect. Praise, for example, only works if the child likes the person who is giving it.

A vicious cycle can be set up this way. The parent begins to control less by using rewards and more by using punishment. But the level of punishment necessary to have an effect increases, because punishment too is enhanced when a child cares about the person who delivers it. In a nurturant parent-child relationship, for example, a small amount of punishment can go a very long way. But if the child is resentful and angry toward the adult, mild forms of punishment—which serve mostly to inform the child of how serious an adult is about some expectation—don't work. The angry and resentful child resists the parent's authority (Brehm, 1981). In these cases, physical punishment often is escalated to the point at which it really hurts. And because an angry and resentful child is often willing to absorb quite a lot of physical hurt rather than submit to the adult, the adult feels compelled to increase the hurt. The result can be child abuse.

Punishment is also dangerous because it provides the child with a model of aggressive behavior. A correlation between parents' use of physical punishment and children's aggressive behavior has been heavily documented (Eron, Walder, & Lefkowitz, 1971; Trickett & Kuczynski, 1986). Since the evidence is correlational, we don't know which way the association works, that is, we don't know if more aggressive children lead parents to use more physical punishment or if more physical punishment produces more aggressive chil-

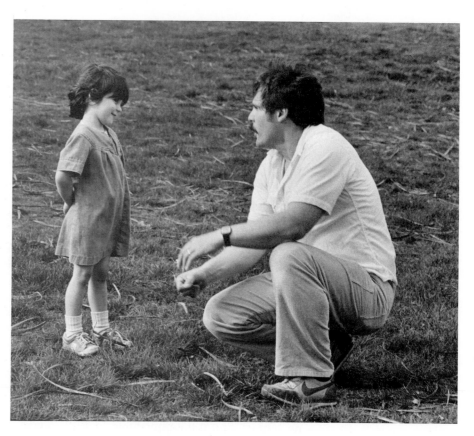

FIGURE 12-4
A parent who wishes to teach his child a lesson she'll remember uses reasoning, not physical punishment. This father has a serious message for his daughter, even though she's not quite sure how to respond. Punishment is a less effective way to teach because it models aggression, creates resentment, and destroys trust between parent and child. In vulnerable parents it can lead to child abuse.

dren. But we do know that a lot of aggression can be learned by imitation, and the assumption that physical punishment produces more aggressive children is consistent with these findings.

As we describe in more detail below, the most effective disciplinary strategy with children has been found to be **induction**—reasoning with them to inform them about how their misbehavior affects others and why they need to change their actions. Power-assertion techniques, including mild punishment, often have a role in induction because they can be effective at getting children to stop what they're doing and pay attention to what adults are saying to them. One researcher asserts that "too little power assertion or love withdrawal may result in children's ignoring the parent. Too much power assertion or love withdrawal produce fear, anxiety, or resentment in children, which may interfere with the effective processing of the induction" (Hoffman, 1984, p. 304).

Physical punishment, no matter how mild, always models aggressive behavior. For this reason, we believe it's wise to avoid it. But adults don't need to tolerate situations where their admonitions are ignored. Parents and teachers of young children often need to intervene physically in situations, such as when they must restrain a child who is kicking someone or when they must carry a child to a chair where they can discuss the child's misbehavior. And if induction is not effective, adults probably need to use loss of privileges or time out, especially if the child clearly has the ability to understand the situation and is felt to be capable of behaving as expected.

Observational Learning

Another socialization process by which children learn the ways of their society is **observational learning.** Everyone has seen children imitating the adults they know—their parents, teachers, neighbors, and people who work in their community. Their motivation to imitate others has been explained in various ways. Freud, for example, believed that imitation occurred because of children's identification with the parent of the same sex. During the phallic stage of psychosexual development, boys compete with their fathers for their mother's attention. This creates what Freud called the Oedipal conflict. The little boy even contemplates killing his father, but because this is too frightening, he decides instead to become like his father—to adopt many of his behaviors, attitudes, and beliefs. This is the process Freud labeled **identification.**

Social learning theorists don't argue with the fact that children imitate their same-sex parent. But they don't think we need constructs like the Oedipal conflict to explain it. They think children imitate behavior because of incentives—reinforcement and punishment—and because of the model's status or value. A parent who is nurturant and who helps a child solve conflicts by serving as a source of good suggestions, for example, is likely to be held in high esteem by a child and to be considered a desirable model.

The social process by which one person demonstrates behavior that another imitates is called **modeling.** Many studies have shown that when children watch another person act a certain way and receive reinforcement for it, they're likely to imitate the person's actions (Bandura, 1977). They're more likely to imitate a person whom they perceive as being similar to themselves, because they think it's possible to become like the model. Nurturance and help given

FIGURE 12-5
Observational learning accounts for much of the sex-typed behavior we see in children. These 5-year-olds discussing the merits of Wonder Woman have already identified some powerful models of female appearance and behavior in our society.

to the child by the model influence the child's relationship with the model, which in turn influences whether the child wants to become like the model.

It doesn't require much imagination to realize that when girls see their mothers reinforced for looking pretty, they want to look pretty too. And when boys see their fathers reinforced for acting tough, they're motivated to act the same way. Today, our society is providing a much wider variety of models for children, so that girls have assertive, successful women to imitate and boys have articulate, nurturing men in their environment. But a tremendous amount of sexually identified behavior is deeply engrained, so adults still model traditional behaviors for children in many areas. This may be why we see girls and boys acting in stereotypical ways by the age of 3, as discussed in Chapter 8 on infant and toddler social-emotional development. Regardless of whether we explain imitation in psychoanalytical terms or in social learning terms, the fact that children learn this way is beyond dispute.

Verbal Instruction

A third way we can give children some idea of appropriate and inappropriate behaviors and their consequences is simply to tell them. In many situations, verbal instruction is the quickest and most effective method of socialization.

FIGURE 12-6
A backup on the climber and a child still sitting on the bottom of the slide pose two challenges to playground harmony. But when the teacher helps by reasoning and giving verbal instruction, children can begin to learn to negotiate and solve problems.

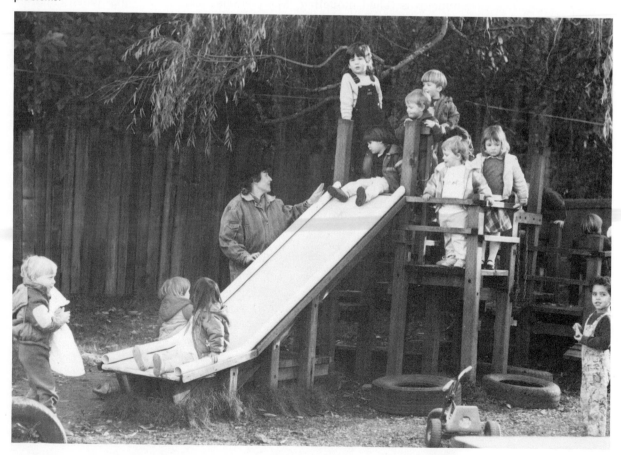

It not only discourages inappropriate behavior but teaches and encourages positive alternative behaviors, such as in a situation like the following:

> During a free play period in school one day, Joann and Amelia began chasing each other around a table. As they bumped into other children's activities and their laughter got louder and louder, their teacher came over to them. She took hold of both their hands and said, "Let's stop the running. You might hurt someone or fall down and hurt yourselves. Let's find something else to do. There's clay on the art table, or you could play in the block corner or read a book in the library area."
>
> "Let's build with blocks," said Joann. "We can make cages for animals!"
>
> "Okay," agreed Amelia.
>
> "Good idea," said their teacher as they hurried off. "I want to see those cages when they're done."

Joann and Amelia's teacher used verbal instruction to involve them in some positive activity that was incompatible with running around the classroom. The teacher's concrete suggestions helped the girls find something else to do. Studies have shown that once children are engaged in an activity, they're likely to increase their involvement with that activity in the future (Staub, 1979). In this case, now that they have experience with the blocks, Joann and Amelia are more likely to play with the blocks another day. Their teacher can make their block play even more interesting by providing additional props, such as animals to go in the cages.

Verbal communication can also be used to lead children to see themselves in certain ways. A parent might say, "You're such a good helper. I don't know what I'd do without your help. It would take me forever to fold all this laundry by myself." Or a teacher might say, "You're such good listeners. I don't think I've ever seen such good listeners as you are today." Children often respond to this kind of comment by seeing themselves in these favorable terms and trying to live up to the image in the future (Miller, Brickman, & Bolen, 1975; Jensen & Moore, 1977).

Comments like these must be made sincerely, however—when children *are* helping or listening well (gauged in terms of their level of development, of course). Children usually know whether they're behaving well in terms of a standard, and if they're praised when they're not behaving well, they'll see no reason to improve.

Another kind of verbal communication can influence children's behavior as well. **Exhortation** informs children of what they should do or what behavior is desirable. Two kinds of exhortation—power-assertive and inductive—were distinguished in one study (Smith et al., 1983). A parent using power-assertive exhortation might say, "I'm going outside to get the newspaper. I want you to listen for the telephone while I'm gone." A parent using inductive exhortation might say, "I would like to go outside to get the newspaper, but I won't be able to hear the telephone if it rings while I'm away."

In this study, children were given opportunities for prosocial behavior such as helping to move chairs, helping to look for a lost pen, and teaching someone how to make a picture. Children in the group receiving power-assertive exhortation were told to help. Children in the group receiving inductive exhortation were given a description of the need and of the effect of their behavior if they

FIGURE 12-7
An 8-year-old demonstrates the results of effective socialization. She realizes that someone is hurt, has the desire to help, and knows what to do. The 3-year-old might have pro-social impulses but probably wouldn't be able to provide very effective help. Socialization goes on all the time—being nurtured by an older child provides the 3-year-old with an important model of prosocial behavior.

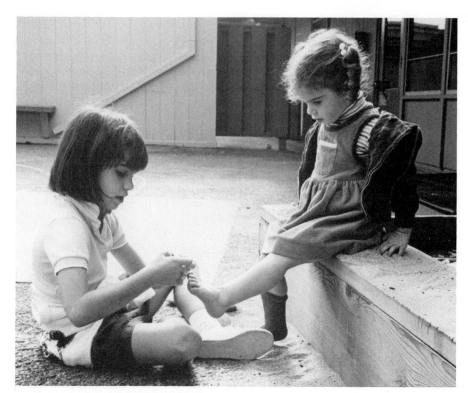

decided to help. None of the children suffered any consequences if they didn't help.

The researchers expected the inductive approach to be more effective than the power-assertive approach in getting children to help and share. They knew that a history of power-assertive parenting is usually associated with noncompliant behavior in children and that induction is associated with cooperation. The study showed, however, that the two types of verbalization were equally effective. Children in both groups cooperated and helped. The researchers explained this discrepancy by noting that parents who use power-assertive exhortations also often use punishment, such as spanking or denial of privileges, if children don't do what they tell them to do. It's probably the whole pattern of power-assertive disciplinary practices that makes their children less cooperative than other children.

What this study showed is that verbal instruction alone *can* be effective in getting children to behave in the ways adults want them to. But other studies have shown that verbal communications combined with reinforcement and modeling are typically more powerful than words alone.

Other Factors Influencing Socialization

How children behave in a particular situation depends on more things than how they've been socialized. Another important factor is their level of cognitive development. A child who's been encouraged to help in the past, and whose previous helpful behavior has been reinforced, still might not help in a new situation. She may not understand that help is needed, or she may not

FIGURE 12-8
Helen Keller was difficult to socialize as a child because her parents couldn't communicate with her. When Annie Sullivan joined the household to be Helen's teacher, she found her completely unsocialized and behaving more like an animal than a person. Here, Patty Duke and Anne Bancroft portray the moment in *The Miracle Worker* when Helen realized that water has a name and that human beings communicate through language.

know what kind of help she might offer. This knowledge is a matter of cognitive development. As children get older, their level of **social cognition**—the ability to understand other people's problems and feelings—gets higher. With more understanding, it becomes easier for children to respond in socially appropriate ways. A higher level of social cognition doesn't automatically result in better behavior, however. Other aspects of children's experiences, such as the values they are taught and how socialization processes have been used by their parents, influence whether they use their cognitive abilities in prosocial or antisocial ways.

Genetic and biological factors also influence children's behavior. If a child has a genetic problem or birth defect that impairs his intelligence or ability to communicate, it's harder for him to learn what adults try to teach him. Children born with "difficult" temperaments influence their parents' responsiveness and choice of socialization techniques—how much they reward or punish their children, for example (Thomas & Chess, 1977). The parents' reactions to the child in turn affects the child's future reactions to them.

Some earlier studies reported a correlation between particular inherited characteristics and specific patterns of behavior (Sheldon, Hartle, & McDermott, 1949; Glueck & Glueck, 1950)—for example, between a muscular body build and aggressive behavior—but these associations are no doubt due to the combined effect of biology and socialization. A very large, very active, and very determined baby boy, for example, might induce his large, active, and equally determined parents to play with him roughly and discipline him firmly. As with so many other aspects of child development, no single factor determines children's behavior.

AGGRESSION: HOW IT'S LEARNED, HOW IT'S CONTROLLED

"I'm rubber,
You're glue,
Whatever you say bounces off me
And sticks to you."

"Sticks and stones
Will break my bones,
But names will never hurt me."

In the child's timeless response to insults and name calling, we see the movement from physical aggression to verbal aggression that occurs late in the preschool years. Physical aggression peaks in most children when they're 2 or 3 years old and then begins to decline. Verbal aggression continues well into the school years and beyond. Preschoolers still tend to respond to verbal insults with hitting, but by the time they're in elementary school, they're much more likely to respond with words (Parke & Slaby, 1983). Toddlers and young preschoolers use more **instrumental aggression**—aggression intended to gain some object or privilege (Hartup, 1974)—and older preschoolers and school-age children rely on their rapidly growing verbal skills to get what they want as well as to insult and hurt.

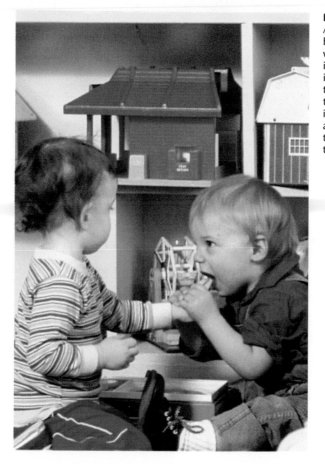

FIGURE 12-9
A very young child tries out biting, probably just to see what will happen. Aggressive impulses seem to be innate in human beings, but how they're expressed and controlled are learned behaviors. If the other child cries and the teacher intervenes, this boy will be less likely to try this experiment again.

Whatever its form, aggression in children is generally considered unacceptable to adults and is one of the main targets of their socialization efforts. Often, parents and teachers are perplexed about the best way to discourage aggression and encourage other ways of expressing feelings and solving problems. One father realized he needed to rethink his approach when he gave his daughter a slap on the hand and said, "Don't hit!"

How do children come to be aggressive? Is it an inborn trait, or do children learn it? There's no doubt that biology plays some role in aggressiveness. Some children seem to be born with stronger emotions, more volatile personalities, or less ability to control their impulses, all of which might make them more difficult to socialize than other children. But a great deal of aggressive behavior is learned, and it's learned according to some of the same principles we've been discussing—reinforcement, punishment, and observation of aggressive models. In this section, we discuss the processes by which children learn aggressive behavior and some of the ways adults can help them control it. In the next section, we discuss more of the ways that adults help children learn prosocial behavior.

Reinforcement, Punishment, and Aggression

Dolores is playing with her dolls in the living room near her little sister, Isabella. Isabella is using a small wooden mallet to play a toy xylophone. Dolores stops playing to listen to the sounds her sister is making. Then she reaches over and grabs hold of the mallet. Isabella, surprised, resists, gripping the mallet more firmly and scrunching up her face in anger. But Dolores persists. She pushes Isabella with her free hand and pulls harder on the mallet. Isabella releases her grip on the toy, and Dolores starts playing her sister's xylophone.

REINFORCEMENT. Dolores succeeded in taking away her sister's toy by force, and her success this time is likely to reinforce her aggressive tactic. The extent to which children are reinforced—or punished—for aggression influences whether they learn to be aggressive or nonaggressive.

In addition to material rewards, such as possession of a toy, aggression can yield **intrinsic reinforcement**—nonmaterial changes in the child's environment. For example, with just a little aggression, children can make other children cry and move away, objects fly across the room and shatter, and adults come running. Aggression can quickly produce a little excitement in an otherwise boring environment (Roedell, Slaby, & Robinson, 1977). The child feels a sense of power and becomes the center of attention, even though it's negative attention.

Aggression sometimes increases when children are initially gathered together into a group, apparently because their aggression is reinforced. In a study of preschool children's free play, one researcher found that 80 percent of children's aggressive actions were rewarded by victims' giving up objects or leaving the field (Patterson, Litman, & Bricker, 1967). Because they were successful, the aggressors were encouraged to aggress again. Children who weren't aggressive at the beginning of the year became more aggressive if they were frequent victims. Apparently, they imitated aggression to defend themselves, and then they found that it worked when they wanted to get objects them-

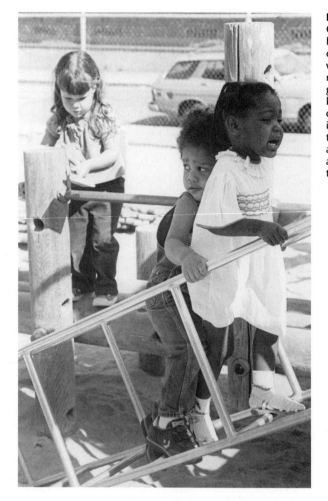

FIGURE 12-10
Crowding another child on a ladder is a fairly subtle form of aggression. This boy may want to get ahead, or he may just want to harrass the girl, but in either case, he knows he shouldn't be doing it. If children succeed in getting what they want through aggression, their aggressiveness will increase and other children will imitate it.

selves. The only children who didn't become more aggressive were those who failed in their first attempts at defensive aggression.

Studies like this underscore exactly how reinforcement increases behavior—if a behavior works, it will increase. Teachers have to be particularly alert in the first weeks of a nursery or kindergarten school year to situations in which aggression is used to obtain objects. If the few children who initiate these tactics when they enter school aren't prevented from using them, the tactics will be adopted by other children. Teachers should do their best to make sure aggressive practices—grabbing toys, pushing ahead, taking someone else's turn, and so on—don't work. If teachers have more than one of each item, and if equipment is available that several children can use at the same time, the number of occasions in which children are inclined to use aggressive tactics will be reduced.

PUNISHMENT. Adults often punish children for aggressive behavior, but punishment is the least effective strategy for helping children become less aggressive, especially if it's the only or the primary strategy used. As explained

FIGURE 12-11
When time out is used carefully, it can be an effective way to punish misbehavior and make the child interested in learning more positive ways of acting. This child has been told he can return to the circle when he's ready to be with the group again, a technique that helps him take responsibility for his behavior.

earlier, physical punishment models aggression and can lead to anger, resentment, and increased noncompliance. Severe physical punishment is actually associated with very high levels of aggression in children, perhaps because of the combined effects of modeling and resentment. If a child's aggressive behavior continues after parents and teachers have tried such tactics as induction and reinforcing good behavior (discussed in the next section), they may need to use punishment in the form of time out from positive reinforcement.

Although time out can be an effective procedure for controlling aggression, it has to be used wisely. Like any other form of punishment, it should not be used for a first infraction, when the child might not have known that some behavior was wrong or how he could have behaved in a more appropriate way. Redirection and induction should be given a chance first. If the adult is satisfied that the child can't be excused on the basis of naivete or ignorance, then time out might be appropriate.

Even here, the punishment must be reasonable. If a teacher, for example, denies a misbehaving child the opportunity to participate in a special activity that had been planned for the class later in the day, the child no longer has any incentive to behave well for the rest of the day. In addition, the child might become so frustrated and resentful about losing the privilege that he acts even more aggressively.

To avoid these situations, teachers should explain any contingencies that are associated with special activities—or even with routine activities. Adults should also keep in mind that denial of privileges or participation works best when it's related to a specific offense. For example, if a child is harrassing a classmate during free time, it makes more sense to restrict the child's privileges by confining him to an isolated area of the classroom for a few minutes than to tell him he can't go on a scheduled trip to the park later in the day. If a child misbehaves at the park, then it makes sense to decide that there will be no trip to the park the next day.

It's also a good idea to use the minimum removal of privileges, the minimum *response cost*, necessary to end the misbehavior (Roedell, Slaby, & Robinson, 1977). The teacher makes the point that the child must stop behaving inappropriately toward another child by removing him from the free play interaction for a few minutes. A longer period of time out may not be needed to get the child to stop this behavior. Five minutes can seem like a very long time to a child who is waiting to return to the center of classroom or household activities. Some parents let the child himself decide how long the time out

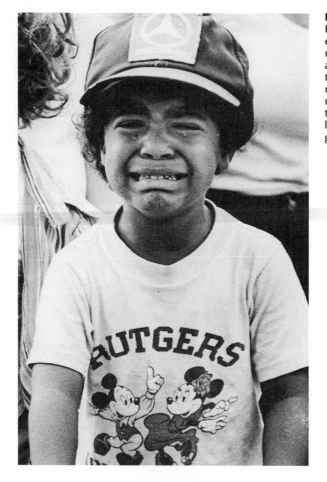

FIGURE 12-12
Physical punishment isn't an effective socialization technique. A child who is crying after a spanking often feels too much pain, anger, and resentment to process any messages his parents were trying to give him. The only lesson he may learn is not to get caught the next time.

will be, telling him he can come back when he's able to be with others in a positive, constructive way.

Minimum response cost may work better than more severe punishment because the child's anger and frustration are minimized. With his self-esteem intact, his emotions under control, and his feelings for the adult still positive instead of hostile, the child is able to learn from the experience and may even identify with the adult's positive standards (Lepper, 1973).

Observational Learning and Aggression

There's no question that children learn aggression by observing it in others (Bandura & Walters, 1963). Even when an aggressive model isn't reinforced, children may learn the aggressive response and use it when they think it may lead to reinforcement. Obviously, these facts have important implications for how children learn aggression from family members and friends as well as from movies and TV. In this section, we examine how these processes influence aggressive behavior in children.

THE FAMILY AS A MODEL OF AGGRESSIVE BEHAVIOR. Most parents use physical punishment to discipline their children. This type of parenting gives children

FIGURE 12-13
All siblings fight, but families differ in their tolerance of aggression. Some parents would find this level of violence acceptable, but many wouldn't. Children who are allowed to be aggressive at home bring their aggressive behavior to preschool with them, where they have to learn other ways of interacting.

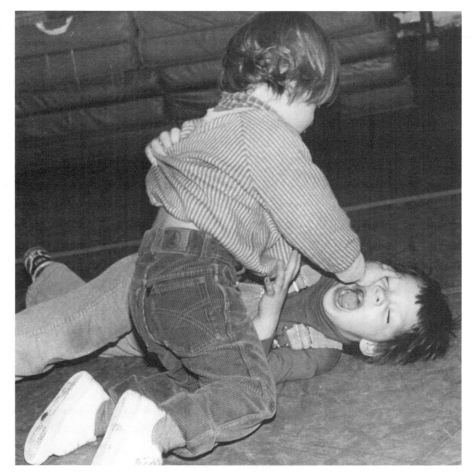

impressive models of aggressive behavior. Many parents also model verbal aggression, telling their children they're stupid or saying things like, "I'm going to kill you if you don't start listening to me."

Children also witness violence between their parents. In a national survey taken 10 years ago, about 4 percent of the respondents—1.8 million couples—stated that one or more episodes of physical violence, such as hitting, beating, or threatening with a weapon, had occurred between them over the course of the previous year (Straus, Gelles, & Steinmetz, 1980). If milder forms of aggression, such as pushing, slapping, or throwing an object, are included, the percentage jumps to about 12 percent, or 5.4 million couples. Obviously, huge numbers of children have the opportunity to witness violence between their parents.

Even when parents don't model aggression, children often learn aggressive behavior from their brothers and sisters. Aggression between siblings is the most common kind of aggression in families (Straus, Gelles, & Steinmetz, 1980). Older siblings are usually the aggressors, but younger siblings quickly learn from them (Dunn & Kendrick, 1982; Parke & Slaby, 1983).

TELEVISION AS A SOURCE OF AGGRESSIVE MODELS. The ever-present television set is another powerful source of aggressive models in the family. It's common knowledge that children watch a lot of TV, but the statistics are still startling. Virtually every household in the United States has at least one television (Nielson Television Index, 1982). Many parents regulate the number of hours their children are allowed to watch it (Huston et al., 1983), but many more place no restrictions whatsoever on TV viewing (Lyle & Hoffman, 1972). When households have cable TV, the amount of viewing appears to increase even further (Kerkman et al., 1983).

Children begin to watch TV systematically at about $2\frac{1}{2}$ years (Schramm, Lyle, & Parker, 1961). Between the ages of 2 and 5, they watch anywhere from 13 to 27 hours per week, or 2 to 4 hours per day (Nielson Television Index, 1981; Anderson et al., 1985). Some studies have shown that TV viewing peaks during the kindergarten year and then declines during the school years (Calvert & Wright, 1982). Other studies have reported that viewing continually increases during the school years and peaks in early adolescence (Liebert, 1986). Today's home video games, which children play on the TV and which are often extremely violent, have no doubt increased the number of hours children spend in front of the television screen, or at least they haven't helped reduce them.

The discrepancy in time spent watching TV reported by different studies may reflect the different populations included in the studies. Some of the subjects may have been from lower socioeconomic-status (SES) families, for example, which is associated with higher levels of television viewing (Comstock et al., 1978; Ross, Wartella, & Lovelace, 1982). Or the studies that reported lower TV viewing during the school years might have included communities that had more after-school activities available for school-age children. Whatever the precise number of hours children spend in front of the television, we know that they watch it a lot. By the time the average child is 15 years old, she will have spent more time watching television than going to school (Liebert, 1986).

FIGURE 12-14
Although cartoons may seem benign, they are among the most violent shows on TV. In many shows, violence is used by both the heroes and the villains, giving children universal models of violent behavior.

Violence on television has been studied extensively. Violent incidents averaged about 8 per hour in prime-time programming and about 17 per hour in cartoons in 1972, a period of increased public concern about violence and TV. By 1978, the average number of violent incidents in cartoons had climbed to about 25 per hour (Gerbner, 1972; Gerbner et al., 1979). Research on this excessive violence has turned up both correlational and causal relationships between filmed models of aggression and children's aggressive behavior.

The correlational studies showed that children of all ages who see more violence on TV tend to behave more aggressively. In one study, researchers found that preschoolers—boys and girls—who watched more action-adventure programs exhibited behavior marked by aggression, anger, and sadness (Singer & Singer, 1981). The researchers thought the relationship might be due to other factors, since lower SES and lower IQ are associated with higher levels of aggression. But the relationship held up, even when they controlled for these two factors. All the children who watched more TV, regardless of IQ or SES, were more aggressive.

Since lower IQ and lower SES children reportedly watch more TV than their counterparts (Chaffee & McLeod, 1972), it appears that their greater TV viewing contributes to their higher level of aggressive behavior. In other words, lower SES and lower IQ children are more aggressive; since they also watch more TV, and we know TV models violence, their increased aggression may be due, at least in part, to their greater TV viewing.

Correlational studies tell us about associations, but experimental studies give us conclusive evidence that viewing TV violence increases aggression in the viewer. In one ambitious study of cause-and-effect (Friedrich & Stein, 1973), researchers divided nursery school children into three groups and showed them television programs of three different types: aggressive cartoons, such as "Batman" and "Superman"; prosocial programs, such as "Mr. Roger's

Neighborhood"; and neutral programs, such as nature films. Each group watched a 20-minute program of a particular type every day for four weeks. Baseline data on children's interactions during free play were collected before the study began, and researchers observed the children's behavior every day during the study.

After four weeks, they found that among the children who were initially above average in aggression, those who were in the group that saw the violent TV shows showed more aggression than those who watched the other programs. All the children in the group that saw the violent films showed less self-control in waiting for materials or adult attention, regardless of their initial level of aggression. And these same children had more difficulty obeying.

Other studies have also reported that children who are already aggressive are especially susceptible to TV violence. A study involving Lebanese children found that for these children, exposed to the violence of war in their country every day, TV violence was a very powerful stimulus for eliciting violent behavior (McHan, 1986).

Children have been observed to increase aggression after watching only one violent TV show (Ellis & Sekyra, 1972). Children who watched a violent sequence from the TV series "The Untouchables" were more willing to do

FIGURE 12-15
War gives children powerful real-life models of aggression. The effects of growing up surrounded by violence can be seen in the faces of these Lebanese boys.

things they believed were hurting other children than children who watched an athletic competition (Liebert & Baron, 1972). Overall, the evidence is conclusive: Watching violence on TV is causally related to aggression.

CHILDREN'S UNDERSTANDING OF TV VIOLENCE. The evidence for the effect of TV violence on aggressive behavior in children is even more disturbing if we consider what young children understand as they watch TV. In some TV shows, the "bad guy" is punished after the last commercial to discourage the modeling of negative behavior. But young children might not make the connection between the villain's motives and deeds and the negative consequences. This is especially true of preschoolers, whose cognitive abilities aren't developed enough for them to understand why TV characters are violent or what the consequences of the violence are (Leifer & Roberts, 1972).

A dramatic example of this lack of understanding came from a study of preschoolers' reactions to the assassination attempt on President Reagan in 1981 (Rowland, Robinson, & Jacobson, 1982). The vast majority (91 percent) of these children, aged 3 to 5, were aware of the event. Most had seen it on TV, and many had seen it repeatedly in replays on news broadcasts. But when they were questioned, 53 percent of the children said they approved of the man shooting the president, and 40 percent said they thought the man who shot the president was brave. Children from lower SES families responded even more in this manner.

When asked to explain what happened to President Reagan, one child answered, "He got killed. No, not really, he just got shot like J.R." (referring to a character on the TV series "Dallas"). Another said the assailant "pretended to shoot him." Clearly, these children did not have the ability to understand the meaning of televised events and the relationships depicted in them. They also could not distinguish television reality (news) from nonreality (action shows). (Children's ability to distinguish reality from fantasy on television is also discussed in Chapter 15).

Realizing their young children's limitations and vulnerability, some parents watch TV shows with them and explain or comment on the action. But watching TV with an adult who criticizes violent behavior doesn't seem to affect young children's later behavior. The children will copy the adult's verbal criticism without modifying their aggressive behavior. In contrast, aggression in 10-year-olds is affected by watching violent TV shows with an adult companion who criticizes the violence.

Even when children imitate the "bad guys" less because they understand that they're bad and that they're punished for their violence, they still have plenty of models of violence among the "good guys." TV heroes use violence just as much as the criminals and enemies—they just use it for prosocial purposes. This type of violence may be even harder for children to understand and sort out. The hero who "verbalizes socially sanctioned norms may well be teaching the observer how to be brutal and what to verbalize" while being brutal (Bryan & Schwartz, 1971).

LONG-TERM EFFECTS OF WATCHING TV VIOLENCE. The effects of viewing TV violence appear to be deep and long-lasting. Children seem to become desensitized to violence and accept it more willingly. In one experimental study, researchers showed one group of third- and fourth-grade children a violent cowboy movie and another group a nonviolent film (Drabman & Thomas, 1974). They then asked the children to observe a group of younger children and to seek adult help if the children began to fight. The group who had seen the cowboy movie were less likely to summon help when the children fought.

Another study reported correlations between high TV use and desensitization to violence (Cline, Croft, & Courrier, 1974). Researchers tested groups of 5- and 12-year-old boys for their emotional reactivity, measured by their pulse rate and other physiological signs of arousal, while they were watching a violent film. Boys of both ages who were high users of TV had milder physical reactions to the violence than boys who didn't watch much TV. They seemed to have grown accustomed, in both mind and body, to observing violence without much reaction.

With violence being accepted and promoted so enthusiastically in our society, how can parents and teachers help children to control their aggressive impulses? One of the best approaches to discouraging aggression is to teach and encourage prosocial behavior. This is the area of socialization we discuss next.

PROSOCIAL BEHAVIOR

Prosocial behavior is behavior that benefits others rather than, or in addition to, oneself; it includes helping, sharing, comforting, and cooperating. Children may have an inborn inclination to be helpful, nurturing, consoling—and some children definitely show more of these characteristics than others—but most prosocial behavior, like most aggressive behavior, is learned. And many of the same socialization processes are at work—reinforcement, verbal instruction, observational learning, and practice. A child's level of cognitive development also plays an important part. In this section, we discuss how parents and teachers can support children in this aspect of their development.

Reinforcement, Punishment, and Prosocial Behavior

When adults notice and praise children's prosocial efforts, children are motivated to act that way again in the future. Smiles, approving looks, and simple comments like "Good job!" can be just as reinforcing to children as elaborate rewards. Adults often overlook children's positive behavior, perhaps because it seems like normal courtesy to them, at the same time that they're quick to criticize misbehavior. If they get in the habit of expressing their appreciation of children's thoughtfulness, helpfulness, and other prosocial attempts when they occur, they'll increase the likelihood that they'll occur again. One parent occasionally said to her 3-year-old, "Thank you for saying thank you!"

Teachers can also build opportunities for helping into the structure of their classroom day. For example, children can help prepare and serve the snack for the class, with different children counting out cups and napkins, making juice, and distributing crackers each day. Children enjoy this kind of responsibility, and the teacher has the chance to comment on how well they're working together.

Punishment is not an effective way to teach children prosocial behavior, for all the same reasons that it's ineffective in discouraging aggression. There's usually a way to support sharing and cooperating without resorting to punishment. Consider the following example:

> One day during the first week of nursery school, Emily was sitting at a table drawing with crayons. Karen sat down nearby and pulled a piece of paper toward herself. Then she reached over to get a crayon from the box Emily was using.
>
> "No, they're mine!" Emily snapped, grabbing them away. "You can't have any!"
>
> "But I want to draw," Karen protested.
>
> The teacher approached. "Emily," she said, "could Karen use the red crayon while you're using the blue one? Then you could both draw."
>
> "Well, okay," Emily slowly replied. She pushed the crayons toward Karen. After a few moments, she looked over at Karen and said, "What are you going to draw?"

Now imagine that instead of suggesting a way to share the crayons, the teacher took the crayons away from Emily, saying, "Those crayons belong to the whole class. If you can't share them, you can't use them at all!" It's easy to see that Emily would learn very little about prosocial behavior from this harsh lesson.

Verbalization and Prosocial Behavior

If, after Emily shared the crayons, the teacher made positive comments to her about her behavior, she would teach the prosocial behavior even more effectively. "You really are a good sharer," she might say. "You know just how to make sure you and Karen both have fun." As we saw earlier, attributing positive characteristics to a child can make the child want to live up to the image in the future.

It also helps when parents and teachers explain why someone's behavior is appropriate: "Emily shared the crayons with Karen, so Karen had a chance to color too. Everyone in the classroom is happier when more children are able to play." Exhortations to share—simply telling children to do it—aren't very effective in getting children to share, especially when they're out of the range of watchful adults (Elliott & Vasta, 1970).

We did see earlier that exhortations to share or help were effective in eliciting prosocial behavior in children (Smith et al., 1983). But because of evidence from other studies, we might wonder how long those children would continue to share or help without being guided to understand exactly why a person was in need and exactly how their helping contributed positively to the other person's welfare.

Observational Learning and Prosocial Behavior

Verbal instruction, especially of the inductive type, is effective in helping children learn prosocial behavior, but seeing prosocial behavior modeled is even more effective. Some kinds of models and modeling situations, however, are more effective than others. An elaborate study undertaken with preschoolers showed that adults who are warm and nurturant are the best models. It also showed that seeing helping modeled in real-life situations is more effective than seeing it depicted in fictional situations, such as books, films, or puppet plays (Yarrow, Scott, & Waxler, 1973).

RESEARCH FOCUS

How Children Learn to Help Others

Many people have wondered what the best way is to teach children to help others. One group of researchers set up a study with preschoolers to find out (Yarrow, Scott, & Waxler, 1973). They began by collecting baseline data on the children's helping behavior. Children were tested individually to see how they responded to pictures of animals, adults, and children in distress. For example, one picture showed a child being hit on the head by a swing. The child was asked "What's happening in this picture?" and "If you were there and saw that happening, what would you do?" Real-life incidents of distress also occurred during the pretesting session. For example, the tester knocked a vase of flowers to the floor, and a kitten tangled in yarn was brought into the room. The child's responses to the pictures and incidents were recorded and rated in terms of helping behavior.

In the next phase of the experiment, an adult interacted with groups of eight to ten children in a playroom for half an hour a day for two weeks. Half the groups interacted with a nurturing adult who offered help, gave attention and praise, and was friendly and sympathetic. The other half interacted with an adult who was not nurturing, didn't give attention, and criticized achievements.

Next, the adult who interacted with the children modeled prosocial behavior either symbolically or symbolically and in real life. The symbolic situation involved a diorama (a small box depicting a situation), in which a toy was helped—for example, a toy monkey was helped to reach some bananas. The real-life situation involved people in the room. For example, a person might enter the room and bump her head; the adult model would comfort her and ask her if she would like to sit down.

In summary, the experiment involved four sets of conditions:

1. Nurturant adult behavior paired with symbolic modeling
   (The friendly adult showed the diorama.)
2. Non-nurturant adult behavior paired with symbolic modeling
   (The unfriendly adult showed the diorama.)
3. Nurturant adult behavior paired with symbolic and real-life modeling
   (The friendly adult showed the diorama and helped the person in the room.)

A study of kindergarten children showed that the level of nurturance of the adult model is a critical factor in how actively helpful a child is (Staub, 1971). It seems that if the adult is warm and accepting, the child will attempt to help in a situation even if she doesn't know exactly what to do. If an adult is distant and unfriendly, the child is more hesitant, apparently because she's afraid her efforts will be criticized. Both these studies are discussed in detail in Research Focus—How Children Learn to Help Others.

Sharing is another prosocial behavior that's influenced by modeling. One study found that children shared significantly more after they saw a film in which a boy shared his candy with someone who didn't have any (Elliott & Vasta, 1970). Even more sharing occurred among children who saw the film and who then saw the boy rewarded with a toy and heard why he was being rewarded. In other words, the highest level of prosocial behavior resulted from observational learning combined with reinforcement and verbalization.

4. Non-nurturant adult behavior paired with symbolic and real-life modeling
(The unfriendly adult showed the diorama and helped the person in the room.)

During post-testing—the period when changes in behavior are observed—the children were allowed to play with the diorama and were also taken to a nearby house to visit a mother and baby. During the visit, several "accidents" occurred, such as toys falling out of the baby's crib. The children's helping behavior was recorded in both the symbolic situation with the diorama and the real-life situation with the baby's toys.

It turned out that only the children who interacted with the nurturant adult and who saw helping behavior modeled in both the diorama and the real-life incident increased their helping behavior in the real-life situation with the baby. This indicates that nurturant adults are more effective models than nonnurturant adults, but that nurturance alone isn't enough. Children have to actually see adults helping others in real situations to become helpful themselves. When helping is modeled symbolically, children seem to learn only the principle of helping, not the idea that they can do it too.

A study with kindergarten children turned up similar results (Staub, 1971). In this study, individual children played games with the experimenter, who was nurturant with some children—warm and friendly, smiling often, and praising the child's skill at the games—and non-nurturant with others—task oriented and unfriendly. After they played for a while, the experimenter excused himself and said he had to do one of two things: check on a child in the next room, or respond to a child's crying in the next room, which the child playing games could hear. This was the distress modeling situation.

When the experimenter returned, he explained that the child had fallen but that he had helped her up and she was all right. Then he said he had to go do some work but that the child could continue playing. He also told the child that more crayons could be found in the next room.

After he left, the child heard a crash from the next room followed by the sound of crying. This was the post-testing situation. Children who went to the next room to try to help the crying child saw the tape recorder and were told by the experimenter that he wanted to see how children felt when they heard another child cry. Children who didn't offer direct help, including those who described the incident to the experimenter when he returned, were told that someone else had helped the crying child and that she was fine.

Results indicated that children who saw the adult demonstrate helping behavior by going to the assistance of the "crying child" were more helpful than children who thought he was just checking on another child. In addition, children with whom the adult had been nurturant were much more likely to offer active help rather than just telling the adult about the crying. Even children in the nurturant group who hadn't seen helping modeled were more likely to go to the crying child's aid than were children in the non-nurturant group.

The experimenters suggest that being nurtured gives children the confidence to try to do something in new situations, even if they don't know what to do. Fear of disapproval for doing the wrong thing inhibits children who haven't been nurtured. This experiment underscores the importance of living up to the values we verbalize to children. If we protect, help, and comfort them, and if they see us helping others, they'll learn to help and care for the people in their lives.

Although studies show that helping and sharing are both influenced by modeling, sharing is not influenced by the nurturance of the model the way helping is. In fact, the more nurturant the relationship with the model, the less likely a child sometimes is to share. This phenomenon is usually explained by pointing to the difference between sharing and helping. Sharing requires some sacrifice on the part of the child. She has to give up part of something she has, and naturally she doesn't want to do this. If she doesn't do the socially accepted thing, the adult model may express disapproval of her. But if she has a warm, accepting relationship with the adult, she may not feel she needs to fear the adult's disapproval. Therefore, she doesn't feel compelled to share.

Helping is a slightly different matter. Helping often involves empathy—the understanding of someone else's feelings. When we see or hear someone else's distress, we remember what we felt like in similar situations and we feel distress too. Helping or comforting the other person relieves our own feelings

FIGURE 12-16
All of these children know they shouldn't pull the fire alarm, but one is tempted by it more than the others. Is this boy less socialized—less able to control his impulses —than his fast-footed friends, or is he just enjoying the attention and sense of power his daring gesture gives him? When adults can't put temptations out of sight or reach, they have to rely on instruction and on children's self-control.

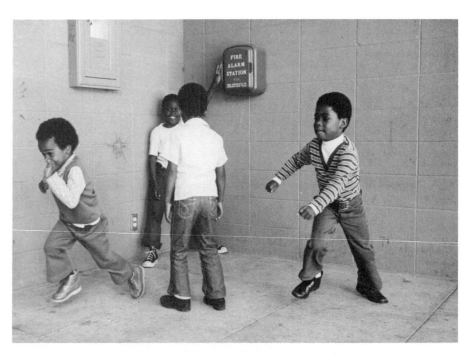

of pain or sadness, and thus it's in our own interest to help. A child often doesn't know what to do to help someone in distress, and she may worry that she'll do the wrong thing. But if she has a nurturant relationship with the adult model, she doesn't fear that the adult will ridicule or disapprove of her attempts. She can take a chance on offering help without fear of making a mistake (Grusec & Skubinski, 1970; Staub, 1971, 1975).

If this explanation is correct, nurturance has the same general effect on children in both helping and sharing situations: It encourages them to act in their own best interest without fear of consequences. The difference is that helping is usually in the child's own interest; sharing is not.

How should parents and teachers act, then? If they're nurturant, children learn to help others in distress, but they don't learn to share. Luckily, the conditions in the experiments were a little different from real life. The children in the studies never expected to see the experimenters again, and they could act just as they wished at the moment (Baumrind, 1972). But in their own lives, children have long-term relationships with adults who have definite expectations of them and whose approval is important to them. Parents and teachers show by their consistent encouragement of sharing that this is a behavior they expect children to learn.

LEARNING SELF-CONTROL

Eli, Sam, and Rebecca were trudging along the darkened street in their Halloween costumes behind their dads. It was late and they were cold and tired. The giddy excitement of dressing up and going trick-or-treating was gone, but the pleasure of eating all that candy drove them on toward home.

"Can I eat a piece of my candy, Daddy?" piped up Rebecca.

"No, not now, Becca," Mike replied. "Wait till we get home."

"Just one piece?" she wailed.

He turned around and looked at her. "You know we talked about this before. Your mom and I want to look at all your candy before you eat any. And we want to make sure you don't eat too much tonight. You'll get a stomachache." He turned back and continued his conversation with Sam and Eli's dad.

When they got to their door, Rebecca and Mike said good night to their neighbors. Looking down at his daughter in the porch light, Mike saw that she had chocolate smeared across her face.

"Hey," he said, squatting down in front of her. "I told you not to eat any candy until we got home."

Rebecca looked down at the ground. "I'm sorry, Daddy," she said. "I just couldn't wait. I had to eat one piece."

Rebecca couldn't resist the temptation of eating her Halloween candy, and her dad was disappointed that she couldn't. Developing self-control of all kinds is an important part of the socialization process, especially in an affluent society like ours where people are tempted by so many things. A lack of self-control is common among children—and adults. When we help young children learn self-control, we give them a stronger foundation for self-control later. With their greater freedom, older children often encounter formidable temptations, including alcohol and drugs. How can the socialization processes we've been discussing be used to support self-control?

Verbal Instruction and Self-Control

Rebecca's dad could have helped her if he'd suggested she think about something else on the way home. "Don't think about the candy or it'll be harder not to eat any," he might have said. "Why don't you see how many jack-o-lanterns you can count? Or we could sing one of your Halloween songs." Distractions and diversions help children control their impulses. In one study, children were told they would receive a large reward later if they could forego a smaller reward immediately (Mischel & Ebbesen, 1970). Children did everything from covering their eyes to making up games with their hands and feet to avoid taking the smaller reward. In another study, children were helped to delay taking rewards like pretzel sticks and marshmallows by being told to think about them as little brown logs and white cotton balls or clouds (Mischel & Baker, 1975).

Other researchers gave children a repetitive task to work on to win attractive rewards (Patterson & Mischel, 1976). They created a temptation dilemma for the children by placing a "Mr. Clown Box" in the same room. The clown made noises and friendly comments and lit up to show toys within the box. Children who paid attention to the clown instead of doing the task would lose out on rewards later.

Researchers gave the children two different self-instructional plans to help them resist the temptation to watch the clown. One was a temptation inhibition plan, in which the child's attention was directed away from the clown. The other was a task-facilitation plan, in which the child's attention was directed

FIGURE 12-17
A cooperative situation at preschool can help children learn to share. To continue playing their game together, these boys have to share the playdough and playdough tools. Things would probably go less smoothly if they were playing with toys from home.

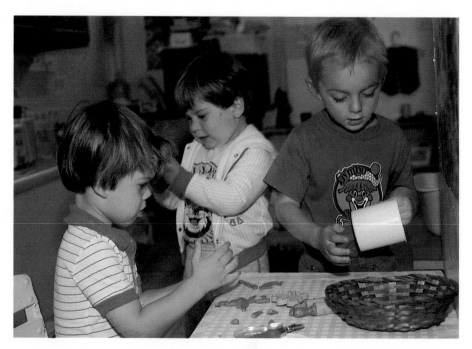

toward the task. The temptation inhibition plan was more effective in helping the child resist the temptation.

All these studies show that various strategies, ranging from putting the temptation out of sight to thinking about something besides the temptation's desirable characteristics (for example, thinking about candy as rocks), can help children resist temptations. Research has also shown that younger children don't know that these strategies might work (Glucksberg et al., 1975; Patterson, 1982). Adults can help preschoolers by instructing them in these various tactics when they see that some support may be needed.

Other Ways to Teach Self-Control

Observational learning—adult modeling of self-control—doesn't seem to have as clear-cut results as does modeling of some other prosocial behaviors we've discussed. Some studies have shown that children who see an adult model of resistance fare about the same as children who see a model of self-indulgence when it comes to controlling themselves (Stein, 1967; Rosenkoetter, 1973). But there are other ways to help children in this area of socialization.

Adults often manage children's environment to minimize the temptations in it, and they're wise to do so. Parents keep cookies and candy out of sight until they want children to have some. Teachers closely monitor students during exams. Of course, this kind of management is limited to situations where the adults have a certain amount of control. When children get older and have more freedom, they need other, more internal, means of resistance. Adults can help them develop these means by stressing the consequences their actions will have, both for themselves and for others, by modeling resistance, and by helping them think through strategies for dealing with temptations that may arise.

Parents can help young children by making reasonable demands on them. When children are successful at resisting small temptations, parents can use attribution to support their efforts ("You did such a good job leaving the cat alone as I asked you to. You're a good listener.") Attribution can motivate children to resist larger temptations in the future.

Finally, adults should be aware that self-control is strongly influenced by situations. Even adults are apt to yield when social controls and external sanctions are absent. We should "discard any simplistic notion that a person's internal moral standards persist unchanged through life without environmental support," writes one observer, "and accept the fact that internalized standards are vulnerable to external pressure and temptations" (Hoffman, 1984, p. 307). This is not to say we should give up on supporting internal controls. Rather, we should realize that *both* internal and external controls have a role to play when children—or adults—face difficult situations.

OVERVIEW

Most young preschoolers are interested in other children and eager to play with them, but they don't have much of a sense of how to make things work. They may grab toys from other children, or they may try to hoard all the blocks or play dough. They may bring a new or special toy from home to show at preschool and then not be able to let anyone else play with it. They may destroy someone else's toy, or they may take it home without asking. Sharing, helping, playing together amicably, settling disputes with words, and controlling impulses to do what they know they shouldn't are some of the behaviors children learn in the course of being socialized during the preschool years. By the end of this important and busy social period, they'll have a grasp of many of the skills they'll need to handle the increasingly complex social situations of middle childhood and adolescence. At age 6, they aren't yet completely "civilized," but they're well beyond their comparatively primitive social gestures of just a few years earlier.

CHAPTER REVIEW

SOCIALIZATION PROCESSES

- Currently favored methods of socialization are based largely on both learning and social learning theory.
- The three main socialization processes are reinforcement, punishment, and extinction; observational learning; and verbal instruction.
- The effect of the socialization process depends on the child's attachment relationship with her parents, her level of cognitive development, and her temperament.
- Reinforcement occurs when a response increases the likelihood that a child will respond the same way again in the same or a similar situation. Socialization is fostered when children receive positive reinforcement for their desirable behaviors.

- Punishment decreases the likelihood that a child will respond the same way again. Some punishments add stimuli to the environment (such as a spanking); others remove stimuli from the environment (such as time out), also known as response costs.
- Extinction involves arranging the environment so the child receives no reinforcement at all for her behavior.
- Reinforcement is considered the best learning method for socializing children. Extinction is difficult to use, since it's not always possible to ignore a child's misbehavior. Punishment has many disadvantages.
- Physical punishment can reduce a child's initiative and drive; make her timid and fearful; restrict her to a few

limited responses in difficult social situations; and create hostility between her and the punishing adult.

- The most serious problem with physical punishment is that it can lead to child abuse.
- Physical punishment models aggressive behavior. A positive correlation exists between aggression in children and the use of physical punishment by the parent.
- The most effective way to discipline children is to use induction—reasoning about how their behavior affects others and how they can change it in positive ways.
- In observational learning, children observe how adults act and then imitate their actions. When an adult demonstrates a behavior, we say the adult is modeling that behavior. Children are more likely to imitate a model who is nurturant and helpful and whom the child perceives to be like himself.

- In verbal instruction children are told what behaviors are desirable. Verbal instruction can also be used for attributing positive characteristics to children when they're behaving well.
- Exhortation is a type of verbal communication in which adults tell children what they want them to do, either using power assertion or induction. Verbal instruction combined with reinforcement and modeling is more effective than verbal instruction alone in motivating children to behave in a desired way.
- Children's behavior is influenced by their level of social cognition, the values they've been taught, the socialization methods their parents have used, and genetic and biological factors. No single factor explains how a child behaves.

AGGRESSION: HOW IT'S LEARNED, HOW IT'S CONTROLLED

- Toddlers and young preschoolers tend to use more physical aggression than older preschoolers and school-age children, who tend to use more verbal aggression; the younger groups use more instrumental aggression, which is implemented to obtain a desired object or privilege.
- Some children seem to be more volatile and to have poorer impulse control than others, but most aggression is learned.
- Children are reinforced for aggression when their aggressive behavior gets them what they want. Aggression sometimes increases when children are brought together in a group for the first time.
- Severe physical punishment is associated with very high levels of aggression in children, probably due to the combined effects of modeling and hostility.
- Time out can be an effective punishment, but it has to be used appropriately and moderately to minimize the child's loss of self-esteem.

- Much aggressive behavior is learned through observation. Aggression observed in the family includes physical punishment, verbal abuse, violence between spouses, and violence among siblings.
- Correlational studies reveal that all children, regardless of age, level of intelligence, or socioeconomic status, act more aggressively after they watch very violent TV programs. Experimental studies show that watching violent TV shows is causally related to children's aggression.
- Preschoolers don't have the cognitive ability to understand violence on TV or its consequences, nor can they distinguish between real and nonreal events depicted on TV.
- In the long run, children who watch a lot of violence on TV seem to become desensitized to it and accept aggressive behavior.

PROSOCIAL BEHAVIOR

- One of the best ways to discourage aggression is to model prosocial behavior—behavior that benefits others besides oneself, such as helping, sharing, comforting, and cooperating.
- Reinforcement promotes prosocial behavior by recognizing it and making the child want to attempt it again. Punishment of antisocial behavior is not an effective way to teach prosocial behavior.
- Verbal reinforcement of prosocial behavior helps children understand why their behavior was desirable.
- Children also learn prosocial behavior by observation

and imitation. Effective models are warm and nurturing and demonstrate prosocial behavior in real-life situations.
- Nurturant models make children more likely to help others but less likely to share with others, apparently because in each case, the child feels free to act in her own best interest. Adults have to make it clear that sharing is necessary and expected in many situations.
- Studies have shown that the best way to teach prosocial behavior is through a combination of modeling, reinforcement, and verbalization.

LEARNING SELF-CONTROL

- Learning to exercise self-control is important, especially in adolescence and adulthood, when people face potentially dangerous temptations.
- Adults can help children use diversions and distractions to control their impulses. They can guide the children's thoughts, redirect their actions, or remove the temptation from view. Helping children direct their attention away from a tempting object seems to be more effective than helping them concentrate on an alternative activity.
- Adults can help children by explaining the consequences of their behaviors and by working out strategies of resistance with them. The more internal control a child has, the more likely he is to be able to resist a temptation when external controls are absent.

KEY TERMS

socialization	time out	observational learning	social cognition
reinforcement	extinction	identification	instrumental aggression
punishment	aversive stimulus	modeling	intrinsic reinforcement
response costs	induction	exhortation	prosocial behavior

SUGGESTIONS FOR FURTHER READING

Grusec, J. E., & Lytton, H. (1988). *Social development: History, theory, and research.* New York: Springer-Verlag. This paperback book was written to be used as a text in courses on social development. It has good chapters on socialization and the family, and on the development of self-control and the problem of aggression.

Murray, J. P., & Salomon, G. (Eds.) (1984). *The future of children's television.* Boys Town, NB: Boys Town Center. This book discusses some of the positive potentials of television and some ways in which these potentials might be achieved. Provides a good range of discussion and is fairly easy to read.

Williams, T. M. (Ed.). (1986). *The impact of television: A natural experiment in three communities.* New York: Academic Press. This book is a report of a field study in which the effects of the introduction of television were probed. Very interesting reading.

PRESCHOOL CHILDREN

Serena Cortez was looking for a preschool. Her son had turned 3 in February, and now, in May, he was making headway on toilet training. Serena was expecting another child in the fall, and she wanted a regular, reliable place to take Brian a few mornings a week. Today, she had two appointments, one at the Humpty Dumpty Nursery School, a preschool for 3-, 4-, and 5-years-olds, the other at Fair Oaks School, a school that started with nursery and went through the eighth grade. Serena had gotten both names from the phone book.

At Humpty Dumpty, she met a young woman leading a group of children in some songs and games in the play yard. "Touch your knees, touch your toes, touch your shoulders, touch your nose," she sang, as the children bent and stretched to find the right part of their anatomy to touch. She invited Brian to join them while Serena went inside to meet Mrs. Wells, the director of the school.

Inside, Serena found the children sitting on the floor playing with blocks and wooden puzzles. Mrs. Wells was working with one child at a table, helping her finish a fabric-covered eyeglasses case.

"These are Mother's Day gifts," she explained to Serena. "I'm working on them individually with the children, so the other children have to play quietly. Usually at this time, I would be reading them a story or helping them do an art project at the tables. You can see the Easter pictures we did last week up on the wall."

When she had finished the project for the day, Mrs. Wells gathered the children together on the floor in front of an easel with a large pad on it. Serena sat down on a pillow with Brian on her lap. Mrs. Wells pointed to a colored square on the pad and said, "Now, what color is this?"

"Orange," called out Brian, "I think it's orange!"

"No, it's not orange," Mrs. Wells said. "Anyone else?"

"Red?"

"No, not red. We did this last week. Doesn't anyone know?"

"Blue? Yellow?"

"Yes, it's yellow. Thank you, Megan."

The lesson went on, and Serena began to feel this school wasn't for her. She wasn't sure what she wanted for Brian, but she didn't think he would be able to sit quietly and answer questions for very long. He was too active and too eager to follow his own interests.

After leaving the Humpty Dumpty Nursery School, Serena drove straight to Fair Oaks. Here, she again found children playing in the yard. A teacher sat on a nearby picnic table watching them. One girl was pounding nails into a log with a hammer, some other children were digging with shovels, some were climbing in trees, some were playing in a play house, some were in the sandbox with the hose running. Inside, Serena found more activities—children painting at easels, dressed up in gowns and high heels, petting a rabbit. At a table, a teacher was helping some children use a food mill to make applesauce for the snack.

"We get them all together for just one activity," one of the teachers explained to Serena. "At 10 o'clock we have juice and a story. That's all they can tolerate at this age. After one story, the children who want to go back to playing can go outside, and children who want to hear a second story can stay. Snack time lasts about 20 to 30 minutes. The rest of the morning they can choose to do whatever they want, either the activity we have for them here at the table—today it was making applesauce—or whatever they create themselves. One day a week we take them to the library, and several times a month we take them on nature walks around the school and the neighborhood."

Serena had to search for Brian after she finished observing the classroom. When she found him at the top of the slide looking completely at home, she realized that this kind of school was going to suit them both.

Serena encountered just two of the many kinds of programs available for preschoolers in this country. These programs have proliferated as more and more parents have joined the work force and have sought part- or full-time care and education for their children. Programs vary tremendously in such characteristics as the structure of the day, the content of the curriculum, and the role of the teachers, depending on the theoretical orientation of those who run the programs and the needs of the families and children for whom they're designed. They also vary in cost and method of funding or payment, so that not all programs are available to all families.

Education and care programs for preschoolers are just one important application of research and knowledge about children. In this chapter, we discuss the characteristics of these programs and some of the major issues associated with preschool education today. We then treat the assessment and testing of preschoolers, a hotly debated topic right now. How children are tested and evaluated is having profound effects on the very nature of early education in this country. Finally, as in Knowledge in Action: Infants and Toddlers, we discuss living with preschool children—how to make sure they're healthy, how to keep them safe, and how to support their play with toys, books, and games. Together, these topics round out our overall picture of applied knowledge about preschool development.

EDUCATION AND CARE PROGRAMS FOR PRESCHOOL CHILDREN

In 1965, 13 percent of all 3- and 4-year-olds in the United States were enrolled in preschool programs. In 1987 the figure had soared to 40 percent (Hymes, 1988). Who are the children who participate in these programs? How do parents manage to pay for the programs? And what are the programs themselves like? These are some of the questions we address in this section.

Who Are the Children in Preschool? Who Pays for Preschool?

Although many children attend preschool, not all children are equally able to take advantage of these programs. Many more children from economically advantaged families are enrolled in preschool than children from disadvantaged families. In 1987, for example, 67 percent of the children whose family incomes were over $35,000 attended preschool, compared with only 33 percent of those whose incomes were under $10,000 (Children's Defense Fund, 1987). Some publicly funded programs have been introduced to reach children from poorer families who otherwise wouldn't attend preschool. A variety of other programs serve families in different situations and children with different needs.

PROGRAMS FOR CHILDREN WITH DISABILITIES. One population particularly in need of early educational opportunities consists of children with disabilities. In 1976, Congress passed the Education for All Handicapped Children Act, a bill that provided funds to help states pay for the education of all children aged 3 to 18. Under the act, many different programs have been offered to children with different disabling conditions, including hearing-impaired and blind chil-

FIGURE 1
These preschoolers have very different experiences than young children did a generation ago. Today, almost half the children in the United States between 3 and 5 years of age participate in organized child care programs.

dren, mentally retarded children, and children with various kinds of language delays.

Many of these programs resemble preschool programs for ordinary children (described below), but they're adapted to the needs of the children they serve. A major adaptation is the ratio of adults to children. Children with disabilities often need more physical help with routine activities, such as eating, dressing, and toileting, and they often need individualized interaction to support language development and social skills. Rather than two teachers for twenty children, which is considered minimally acceptable in ordinary preschools, these programs may have one teacher for every six children, or even one teacher for every three children.

Other adaptations include the use of alternative communication systems, such as sign language or Braille, and specially designed equipment and materials for children with motor impairments, such as puzzle pieces with knobs and riding toys with straps or arm pedals. Trained staff know how to position children and to provide therapy that helps the children use the motor abilities they do have.

PROGRAMS FOR CHILDREN FROM ECONOMICALLY DISADVANTAGED FAMILIES. Another population in need of early educational opportunities consists of children from economically disadvantaged families. Many of these children attend Project Head Start, the largest of the federally sponsored programs. In 1987, 451,000 preschoolers attended Head Start programs, but this was only 16 percent of the 2.5 million children who were estimated to be eligible on the basis of income (Children's Defense Fund,1987). The government simply doesn't appropriate enough money to fund the programs needed to include all the eligible children.

FIGURE 2
Project Head Start gives children from economically disadvantaged families the same kinds of experiences their more affluent peers are having at home. These Hispanic children from San Francisco are starting their day with a nutritious breakfast.

Because of this shortfall, some cities and states, including Alaska, Massachusetts, New Jersey, New York, Oregon, and Washington, provide funding for additional programs for children eligible for Project Head Start (Mitchell, 1987). New York City has begun its own preschool program, called Take a Giant Step, concentrating on neighborhoods where many low-income families live. The Take a Giant Step program set a goal of accommodating 10,000 four-year-olds per year for four years, beginning in 1986 (Early Childhood Education Commission, 1986). However, as of 1988, the program had been able to provide programs only for the first 10,000 children due to a scarcity of physical facilities. The cost of renovating acceptable spaces has slowed down the growth of this program (Kagan & McAllister, 1988).

Other kinds of funding for preschools exist as well. When working parents fall below certain income guidelines, some states provide subsidies for full-day preschool programs for their children. When parents are enrolled in certain state and federal job-training programs, money is available for day care and preschool for their children. In a few cases, employers provide day care facilities or help employees pay part of their day care costs (as discussed in Knowledge in Action: Infants and Toddlers). Some parents participate in cooperative preschools, working a certain number of hours per week at the school in exchange for lower tuition. Of course, this solution is feasible only when one parent isn't working full time and has the hours to contribute.

Educational programs for 5-year-olds (kindergarten) are provided within the public school system for virtually all children in 46 of the 50 states (Robinson, 1987). In a major new trend, public schools in many states are providing educational programs for children under age 5. In most cases, the funds are targeted for school districts where many of the children are at risk for later school failure (Day, 1988).

The federal tax code allows child care and preschool costs to be taken as a deduction or a credit on individual income tax returns. In 1987 an Act for Better Child Care was introduced in Congress. This act was defeated, but sponsors expect to resubmit it. It calls for day care subsidies for families whose incomes are less than 15 percent of a state's median income (Children's Defense Fund, 1987). In the 1988 presidential campaign, both candidates supported proposals to help parents defray day care costs. In 1989 legislators moved to formulate a federal day care policy, to push for mandated maternity leaves and leaves for parents with newborns or sick children, and to bolster and expand preschool educational programs like Project Head Start. One of the first actions of Congress in 1989 was the introduction of a $2.5 billion day care bill (Cannon, 1989). With costs ranging from $4,000 to $10,000 per child per year, day care is out of the reach of poorer families as well as many middle income families. As the number of mothers in the work force continues to grow, day care services and their funding are sure to remain one of the major issues of the 1990s.

Characteristics of Preschool Programs and Issues in Preschool Education

TEACHER-DIRECTED VERSUS CHILD-DIRECTED PROGRAMS. The preschools Serena visited represented two different approaches to education and care for 3-, 4-, and 5-year-olds. The Humpty Dumpty Nursery School tended to take a **teacher-directed approach**, with teachers giving the children lessons with specific

FIGURE 3
In a teacher-directed preschool program, children
participate in organized
activities with specific educational aims (top). In addition
to the content of this circle
game, these children are
learning to listen, take direction, and cooperate with the
group. In a child-directed
program, children choose
what they want to do from a
variety of possible activities
(bottom). These children are
learning to take the initiative, make their own decisions, and cooperate with a
playmate. Parents make
choices about programs on
the basis of their personal
beliefs and values, their
child's needs, and simply
what's available in the
community.

content for most of the day. Programs with this orientation attempt to teach skills like counting to 10, naming alphabet letters and colors, and recognizing geometric shapes through recitation, repetition, and drill. The Fair Oaks School, on the other hand, tended to take a **child-directed approach,** with children playing freely for most of the day in such activities as block building, water play, and story reading. In programs like this, very little, if any, specific content is presented, and specific skills are not isolated or taught directly by the teachers.

Had Serena looked further, she might have encountered a third kind of program, one in which the day was divided into separate, alternating periods of teacher-directed and child-directed activities. Ideal programs are often judged to be those in which neither extreme dominates and balance is achieved in an integrated way, rather than by dividing the day into different segments. The day is filled with well-planned but child-appropriate activities around which both teachers and children interact. (For a description of such activities for 4- and 5-year-olds, see Research Focus—Developmentally Appropriate Practices in Programs for 4- and 5-Year Olds.)

WHICH APPROACH IS BETTER? Because preschool programs like Project Head Start were begun specifically to improve later school achievement among children from economically disadvantaged families, many people have followed the progress and achievement of these children and formed opinions about what and how preschool children should be taught. Overall, opinion is divided on which approach—teacher-directed or child-directed—is superior. Research results also have been mixed. For example, some studies have shown that boys enrolled in nondidactic (noninstructional, or child-directed) preschool programs did better in sixth and eighth grades than boys who had been enrolled in didactic (teacher-directed) preschools. Girls enrolled in didactic programs did better in math but not in reading in sixth and eighth grades (Miller & Bizzell, 1983).

Other studies comparing didactic and nondidactic programs showed little difference in long-term academic achievement but significant differences in social outcomes. Juvenile delinquency rates, for example, were lower for children who had been in nondidactic programs (Schweinhart, Weikart, & Larner, 1986). Many preschool programs, including Project Head Start, have not been able to show many long-term effects on achievement scores, but high-quality programs, most of them nondidactic, have demonstrated an effectiveness in reducing retention in the same grade in elementary school, placement in special education classes, teenage pregnancy, high school drop-out rates, and welfare dependence (Zigler, 1985; Schweinhart, Weikart, & Larner, 1986).

OBSTACLES TO DEVELOPING THE MOST APPROPRIATE PRESCHOOL PROGRAMS. The dilemma in developing preschool programs may be that although young children *can* learn a great many academic skills—in mathematics, reading, and writing, for example—they require a personalized, interactive context and the opportunity to use the skills they acquire if they are to stay interested and to truly understand what they're taught. It's the difference between teaching children to read numbers by rote from flashcards and helping them to learn numbers by playing a game like Chutes and Ladders. In the former, the skill is isolated and drilled; in the latter, the skill is embedded in a meaningful situation where its usefulness can be appreciated.

Developmentally Appropriate Practices in Programs for 4- and 5-Year-Olds

As we've seen, preschool children don't think the same way older children do. It's not surprising, then, that the kind of programming that educators prepare for school-age children is often inappropriate for very young children. In response to concerns about educational practices and goals, a position statement on appropriate practices for 4- and 5-year-olds was developed by the National Association for the Education of Young Children (NAEYC), the largest professional organization concerned with early education (NAEYC, 1986). The following excerpts are taken directly from the position statement.

Component	APPROPRIATE Practice	INAPPROPRIATE Practice
Curriculum goals	• Experiences are provided that meet children's needs and stimulate learning in all developmental areas—physical, social, emotional, and intellectual. • Each child is viewed as a unique person with an individual pattern and timing of growth and development. The curriculum and adults' interaction are responsive to individual differences in ability and interests. Different levels of ability, development, and learning styles are expected, accepted, and used to design appropriate activities. • Interactions and activities are designed to develop children's self-esteem and positive feelings toward learning.	• Experiences are narrowly focused on the child's intellectual development without recognition that all areas of a child's development are inter-related. • Children are evaluated only against a predetermined measure, such as a standardized group norm or adult standard of behavior. All are expected to perform the same tasks and achieve the same narrowly defined, easily measured skills. • Children's worth is measured by how well they conform to rigid expectations and perform on standardized tests.
Teaching strategies	• Teachers prepare the environment for children to learn through active exploration and interaction with adults, other children, and materials. • Children select many of their own activities from among a variety of learning areas the teacher prepares, including dramatic play, blocks, science, math, games and puzzles, books, recordings, art, and music. • Children are expected to be physically and mentally active. Children choose from among activities the teacher has set up or the children spontaneously initiate. • Children work individually or in small, informal groups most of the time. • Children are provided concrete learning activities with materials and people relevant to their own life experiences. • Teachers move among groups and individuals to facilitate children's involvement with materials and activities by asking questions, offering suggestions, or adding more complex materials or ideas to a situation. • Teachers accept that there is often more than one right answer. Teachers recognize that children learn from self-directed problem solving and experimentation.	• Teachers use highly structured, teacher-directed lessons almost exclusively. • The teacher directs all the activity, deciding what children will do and when. The teacher does most of the activity for the children, such as cutting shapes or performing steps in an experiment. • Children are expected to sit down, watch, be quiet, and listen or do paper-and-pencil tasks for inappropriately long periods of time. A major portion of time is spent passively sitting, listening, and waiting. • Large group, teacher-directed instruction is used most of the time. • Workbooks, ditto sheets, flashcards, and other similarly structured abstract materials dominate the curriculum. • Teachers dominate the environment by talking to the whole group most of the time and telling children what to do. • Children are expected to respond correctly with one right answer. Rote memorization and drill are emphasized.
Guidance of socioemotional development	• Teachers facilitate the development of self-control in children by using positive guidance techniques such as modeling and encouraging expected behavior, redirecting children to a more acceptable activity, and setting clear limits. Teachers' expectations match and respect children's developing capabilities. • Children are provided many opportunities to develop social skills such as cooperating, helping, negotiating, and talking with	• Teachers spend a great deal of time enforcing rules, punishing unacceptable behavior, demeaning children who misbehave, making children sit and be quiet, or refereeing disagreements. • Children work individually at desks or tables most of the time or listen to teacher directions in the total group. Teachers inter-

Component	APPROPRIATE Practice	INAPPROPRIATE Practice
	the person involved to solve interpersonal problems. Teachers facilitate the development of positive social skills at all times.	vene to resolve disputes or enforce classroom rules and schedules.
Language development and literacy	• Children are provided many opportunities to see how reading and writing are useful before they are instructed in letter names, sounds, and word identification. Basic skills develop when they are meaningful to children. An abundance of these types of activities is provided to develop language and literacy through meaningful experience: listening to and reading stories and poems; taking field trips; dictating stories; seeing classroom charts and other print in use; participating in dramatic play and other experiences requiring communication; talking informally with other children and adults; and experimenting with writing by drawing, copying, and inventing their own spelling.	• Reading and writing instruction stresses isolated skill development, such as recognizing single letters, reciting the alphabet, singing the alphabet song, coloring within predefined lines, or being instructed in correct formation of letters on a printed line.
Cognitive development	• Children develop understanding of concepts about themselves, others, and the world around them through observation, interacting with people and real objects, and seeking solutions to concrete problems. Learnings about math, science, social studies, health, and other content areas are all integrated through meaningful activities such as those when children build with blocks; measure sand, water, or ingredients for cooking; observe changes in the environment; work with wood and tools; sort objects for a purpose; explore animals, plants, water, wheels and gears; sing and listen to music from various cultures; and draw, paint, and work with clay. Routines are followed that help children keep themselves healthy and safe.	• Instruction stresses isolated skill development through memorization and rote, such as counting, circling an item on a worksheet, memorizing facts, watching demonstrations, drilling with flashcards, or looking at maps. Children's cognitive development is seen as fragmented in content areas such as math, science, or social studies, and times are set aside to concentrate on each area.
Physical development	• Children have daily opportunities to use large muscles, including running, jumping, and balancing. Outdoor activity is planned daily so children can develop large muscle skills, learn about outdoor environments, and express themselves freely and loudly. • Children have daily opportunities to develop small muscle skills through play activities such as pegboards, puzzles, painting, cutting, and other similar activities.	• Opportunity for large muscle activity is limited. Outdoor time is limited because it is viewed as interfering with instructional time or, if provided, is viewed as recess (a way to get children to use up excess energy), rather than an integral part of children's learning environment. • Small motor activity is limited to writing with pencils, or coloring predrawn forms, or similar structured lessons.
Aesthetic development	• Children have daily opportunities for aesthetic expression and appreciation through art and music. Children experiment and enjoy various forms of music. A variety of art media are available for creative expression, such as easel and finger painting and clay.	• Art and music are provided only when time permits. Art consists of coloring predrawn forms, copying an adult-made model of a product, or following other adult-prescribed directions.
Motivation	• Children's natural curiosity and desire to make sense of their world are used to motivate them to become involved in learning activities.	• Children are required to participate in all activities to obtain the teacher's approval, to obtain extrinsic rewards like stickers or privileges, or to avoid punishment.

SOURCE: National Association for the Education of Young Children.

FIGURE 4
If every child could have the kind of individual attention and affirmation this boy is getting from his Head Start teacher, very few children would fail. But limited financial and human resources mean that the teacher-child ratio in most preschool programs is more like 10:1.

The problem is that fairly large groups of children can be taught to read numbers from flashcards at the same time, but only three or four children can play Chutes and Ladders or other math games. And while they're playing, they need adult help and guidance. Large groups can be taught the names of letters of the alphabet or the sounds associated with them, but only a few can follow the print in a storybook as it's read. For a program to be this highly interactive and fine-tuned, one adult is needed for every three or four children in the class.

Very few preschools have such high adult-child ratios, of course, so they're not able to engage all the children in activities like these. At the same time, it's generally recognized that young children simply can't pay attention to direct group instruction for very long or learn much from it. For these reasons, most preschools forego direct instruction entirely in favor of more general, child-directed activities such as block building, water and sand play, dramatic play, woodworking, puzzles, and creative art projects like painting and working with clay. Each of these activities can accommodate four or five children, and two teachers can manage and supervise a group of 20 children as they play. Preschools with this kind of child-directed orientation usually also include some large-group activities in their daily program, such as singing and story reading.

Children can and do learn a great deal in programs like this. However, as we pointed out in Chapters 10 and 11, many economically advantaged children are learning specific academic skills at home during their preschool years in the course of playing educational games with their parents, writing and drawing with pencil and paper, and participating in routine daily tasks (Bissex, 1980; Saxe, Guberman, & Gearhart, 1987; Delpit, 1988; Schickedanz, in press). These are the very skills that children from economically disadvantaged families often don't acquire at home and that they need to learn in preschool if they are to succeed in school. Child-directed preschool programs, by the very nature of their activities and because of the low level of adult interaction, don't support the learning of specific academic skills. (For a discussion of another population with unique educational needs, see Special Education Focus—Young Gifted Children.)

THE CHALLENGES OF THE FUTURE. The challenge in the years ahead will be to devise meaningful ways to embed academic skills in child-directed activities and daily routines at preschools, especially for children from economically disadvantaged families. At the same time, preschool teachers will need to learn styles of interaction that maintain child-initiated activities and extend children's learning. (For examples, see Schickedanz, 1986, and Kamii, 1985). An additional challenge will be to reduce group size for children at risk for later academic failure to 16 or 18 children, rather than the typical 20, so they can benefit from more learning-oriented interaction with adults.

ASSESSING THE PRESCHOOL CHILD

In March, Ellen Bernstein took her son to her neighborhood elementary school to register for the kindergarten class that would start the following September. There, a staff member took Andrew into a testing room and screened him for entrance to kindergarten. When they were finished, the staff member told Ellen that Andrew would need to be tested further. "He doesn't seem to have some of the readiness skills he'll need in kindergarten," she explained. "You can schedule an appointment for another test right over there."

Ellen was surprised. Andrew seemed to her to be a bright child. He could think problems through quite well for his age, and he could remember things that had happened to him in the past in minute detail. He had memorized several of his favorite storybooks and could "read" them without missing a word. Lately, he'd been asking his parents what specific words said, and he could read many signs on the street and in stores.

As Ellen waited to schedule the appointment, she thought further about Andrew's abilities. He knew the names of the dinosaurs and which were carnivores and which were herbivores. When they played board games together, he could read the dice and count out

FIGURE 5
Fine motor control is still precarious for kindergartners, and patience has its limits. Reverting to a full palmar grasp of the marker can sometimes be the only way to deal with frustration.

SPECIAL EDUCATION FOCUS

Young Gifted Children*

At the age of 3, Zachary spent hours experimenting with the various types of equipment on the science table at his preschool. Time after time, he observed the ball rolling through the elaborate structure of tubes and tunnels. He tried to understand what was happening and why. He used his problem-solving skills in social situations, too. When Darrel stumbled into Zachary's elaborate car and track set-up in the block corner, Zachary simply moved the set-up out of Darrel's way. Then he helped Darrel begin his own car and track set-up nearby.

Four-year-old Margaret sat on a couch in her nursery school listening intently to a prerecorded story on headphones. She held a book in her lap, and her eyes followed the words on the page as she listened. Later, she read the book to a friend. Margaret could make up a story by herself and write it down with very little unconventional spelling. When she saw another child struggling to copy a letter from the chart on the wall, she helped him, saying, "You make a capital A like this."

On the first day of school, Miles bounded into the first-grade classroom reporting that he had a telescope at home to watch the stars and that he and his mom kept track of the birds that visited their bird feeder. Tests revealed that Miles had already mastered the first-grade curriculum. His teacher modified the classroom program for him and allowed him to work independently at his own level. During the year, Miles wrote and illustrated a book about birds in the area, set up a bird-feeding station outside the classroom window, and made presentations about his interests to his classmates. He occasionally tutored some of his classmates, often led small group activities, and enjoyed the rough-and-tumble play on the playground, just as the other 6-year-olds did.

WHAT ARE GIFTED CHILDREN LIKE?

Zachary, Margaret, and Miles have many of the characteristics of gifted children. These children often have large vocabularies and long attention spans; they're sometimes early readers; they exhibit curiosity; they attend to detail; and they have good memories. They

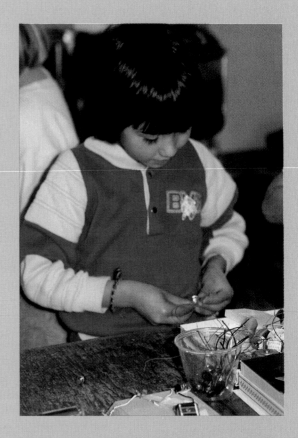

often have many mature, in-depth interests, a strong sense of right and wrong, and highly developed imaginations that allow them to create stories and songs. They may be unusually sensitive to changes in their environments, have a heightened awarenss of their own uniqueness, and make mental connections between the past and the future. Gifted children are also sensitive to other children's feelings and needs, and they're often effective problem solvers in both social and academic situations.

*Written by Dr. Carol Story, Johnson State College, Johnson, VT.

---

the correct number of spaces. He also knew many basic sums. Ellen shook her head and made the appointment.

Later, she talked to a neighbor whose child was a kindergartner that year. "They think Andrew might not be ready for kindergarten, Terry," she told him. "I'm not sure why. What does Jennifer do in kindergarten anyway?"

"Jennifer brings home a lot of papers she's done," Terry told her. "They practice writing numbers and the letters of the alphabet. They do some simple addition problems, and they have papers about the sounds the different letters make. That's the kind of thing they seem to be doing."

There are two different formal definitions of giftedness in young children that are often recognized:

- Gifted children are those youngsters possessing intellectual ability, scholastic aptitude, creativity, leadership, talent in the visual and performing arts, and/or psychomotor ability (Marland, 1972).
- Gifted children are those who apply above-average ability, creativity, and task commitment to a special area of interest (Renzulli, 1978).

HOW ARE GIFTED CHILDREN IDENTIFIED?

Parents and teachers who think a young child is gifted can confirm their judgment by observations and rating scales. A checklist for parents is the Things My Child Likes to Do Checklist (Delisle, 1979). A commonly used observational scale for teachers is the Renzulli-Smith Early Childhood Checklist (Renzulli & Smith, 1981). Teachers are also instructed to note which children direct activities or are followed by other children, which ones exhibit the characteristics listed previously, and which children rank at high levels on developmental scales (Cohen & Stern, 1983; Beaty, 1986).

Sometimes, children demonstrate their giftedness by producing a tangible product, such as a book they've written or a block structure they've made. Other times, giftedness is recognized through intelligence or creativity tests. The most widely used tests for identifying gifted children are the Stanford-Binet Intelligence Test, the WISC-R Intelligence Test, and the Goodenough-Harris Draw-A-Person Test (Harris, 1963). Creativity measures include the Torrance Test of Thinking Creatively in Action and Movement (1981) and the Wallach and Kogan Creative Battery (1965). Parents and teachers have to use these and other tests of creativity with caution because questions about their validity have been raised. Experts recommend that adults use a variety of tests, along with observation, to identify gifted children.

HOW SHOULD YOUNG GIFTED CHILDREN BE EDUCATED?

When children have been identified as gifted, parents and teachers can help them develop their individual potential in various ways. One of the more common ways is grade acceleration—the child enters second grade immediately after kindergarten, for example. This option is appropriate only when a child is emotionally and socially mature enough to cope well with older classmates. When a child is socially immature, part-time acceleration is sometimes a good compromise. The child participates with the older students for certain parts of the day, perhaps for math or science instruction, and spends the rest of the day with children the same age. Grade acceleration is rarely an option for a gifted preschooler, because most school districts require that children entering kindergarten be a certain age. Only after a child has entered kindergarten will some school districts begin to consider advanced placement.

Besides grade acceleration and part-time grade acceleration, a third way to meet the needs of gifted children is enrichment. Here, the teacher individualizes the program, broadening and deepening the content of the curriculum, to support the child's special skills and interests and provide intellectual stimulation. Miles's teacher, for example, provided an enrichment program. Because classroom teachers often don't have the time or resources to develop such programs, some school districts provide consultants the teachers can call on for assistance in designing enrichment programs. This resource is rare in school systems, however, and practically nonexistent in preschools, which are almost never part of public school districts.

In many cases, teachers and parents have to work together to provide stimulation and challenges for a young gifted child. Very often it's the parents, especially during the preschool years, who provide the child with an enriched environment. Activities outside of school can include music lessons, special courses at museums, and heavy use of libraries and other community resources. Within the family, the gifted child and her parents can explore books, games, and activities together, attend plays and concerts, travel and sight-see, learn about other peoples and cultures, and adopt an open and curious attitude toward the world, enabling the child to perceive it as a source of endless interest.

"Oh," said Ellen. "I didn't realize kindergarten was so—so formal and academic. I thought it was more a social experience, where kids learned to be together and like school. Andrew is just beginning to write his name. He can't really hold a pencil the right way yet, so it's hard for him to write."

"Maybe that was the problem," suggested Terry.

"Maybe. They did ask him to write his name. But, you know, there are so many things he can do. It doesn't seem fair to keep him out of school another year just because he can't sit and write the way some of the other kids can."

"But it might be hard on him," Terry said. "If they make the kids sit and write, and he

can't do it very well, he could start to think there's something wrong with him, or he might start to hate school."

"That's true, but it does seem unfair. He's really eager to learn, and he wants to be with other children. Why can't they teach him how to hold a pencil correctly? They used to do things like that. Now it seems they want the children to know how to do everything before they even get to school!"

Ellen had come face to face with some of the issues related to the use of tests with very young children. These assessment and screening tools are controversial—and widely used. Since many of them tap knowledge and skills thought to be related to academic functioning, they're often used to assess preschoolers for kindergarten and kindergartners for first grade. Others, including Piagetian tasks, are used in research studies to determine the correlates of various behaviors or the effectiveness of various treatments. Before discussing the concerns many people have about these tests, let's briefly examine some of the most widely used assessment instruments.

Assessment Instruments Used with Preschoolers

Three of the most common tests for preschoolers are the Metropolitan Readiness Tests, the Concepts about Print Test, and the Caldwell Preschool Inventory. A fourth category of test is the Piagetian tasks. Each of these yields information about a different aspect of children's intelligence and is used for a somewhat different purpose.

THE METROPOLITAN READINESS TESTS. The Metropolitan Readiness Tests (Nurss & McGauvran, 1986) are used to assess children's cognitive understandings and knowledge. There are two levels of tests, one simpler and given at the beginning and middle of the kindergarten year, the other more complex and given at the end of kindergarten or the beginning of first grade. Each test is divided into several subtests. Sample items from some of the subtests are shown in Figure 9.

Level 1 assesses children's knowledge in the following areas:

- *Auditory memory*. Items contain several boxes in a row with a series of pictures in each one. The teacher asks the children to close their eyes and then names the pictures in one box in the order in which they appear. Children open their eyes and mark the box containing the pictures named. For example, the teacher says, "Spoon, ball, star," and the children select the box with those pictures.
- *Rhyming*. Items contain several boxes with a picture in each one. The teacher says a word and asks the children to mark the picture whose name rhymes with the word. For example, the teacher says "floor," and the children mark the picture of the door.
- *Letter recognition*. Each item contains a row of four uppercase or lowercase letters. The teacher names a letter and asks the children to mark it.
- *Visual matching*. Items contain boxes with individual letters, series of letters, or numerals. The teacher points out a model box to the children and asks them to find the identical one and mark it.
- *School language and listening*. Items contain pictures of events that illustrate (a) the use of prepositions ("The boy is behind the tree."); (b) the use of

FIGURE 6
Sample Items from the Metropolitan Readiness Test, Level 1.

AUDITORY MEMORY

A. Now put your finger on the little black BIRD. Close your eyes. Don't peek! Listen. CHAIR CUP. Open your eyes. Mark the right box.

B. Now put your finger on the little black MOON. Close your eyes. Remember not to peek. As soon as I say the words, open your eyes and mark. Don't wait for me to tell you to open your eyes. Listen. SPOON BALL STAR.

RHYMING

A. Put your finger by the top row. The pictures are MILK, LEAF, TIE, BIKE. Listen to the word I say: LIKE. Mark the one that rhymes with LIKE, the one that rhymes with LIKE.

LETTER RECOGNITION

A. Put your finger on the little black SPOON at the beginning of the top row. Look at the letters in this row. Mark the *S* . . . the *S*.

VISUAL MATCHING

B. Put your finger on the little black CUP. Look at what is in the red box. Then mark the box that has in it just what is in the red box.

[red box]

SOURCE: Nurss, J. R., & McGauvran, M. E. (1986). Metropolitan Readiness Assessment Program (5th ed.). Orlando, FL: Harcourt Brace Jovanovich, The Psychological Corporation.

verb tenses ("The girl will cut the string."); (c) the use of passive sentences ("The boy is being carried by the girl."); or (d) a sequence of events described in a short paragraph ("Bob tore a piece of paper out of his notebook and wrote his name on it. Then he crossed out his name and wrote it again.") The teacher reads the sentence or paragraph and asks the children to mark the box that illustrates it.

• *Quantitative language.* This subtest assesses the child's understanding of words such as "more," "less," "big," and "little." Children are also tested on their ability to count; recognize numerals; match numerals to the quantity they represent; understand ordinal numbers ("Mark the fifth turtle"); determine if two groups are equal; match items in one set one-to-one with items in another set; and understand the concept of subtraction ("There were four cookies to start with. A child ate two. Mark the picture showing how many cookies were left.").

The subtests in level 2 are similar but more complex. They assess understanding in the following areas:

Beginning consonants	School language
Sound-letter correspondence	Listening
Visual matching	Quantitative concepts
Finding patterns	Quantitative operations

THE CONCEPTS ABOUT PRINT TEST. The Concepts about Print Test, also known as the Sand Test, was developed in 1976 for use with kindergarten children and children entering first grade (Clay, 1976). The only material required is a picture book entitled *Sand*. The tester reads the book to the child and asks questions about it. From the child's answers, the tester can tell if the child knows the front of the book from the back; that the reader reads print rather than pictures; that print is scanned from left to right and from top to bottom; how to match a spoken word with a printed word; the difference between a letter and a word; and that print is incorrect when it is inverted. As we saw in Chapter 11, these are some of the understandings about print that seem to be related to good reading achievement in later school years.

THE CALDWELL PRESCHOOL INVENTORY. The Preschool Inventory (Caldwell, 1970) is used with individual children between the ages of 3 and 6 to assess the effectiveness of educational programs like Project Head Start. Children are tested on three basic kinds of abilities: (1) concept activation ("Copy a circle," "Count to five."); (2) personal-social responsiveness ("What is your name?" "Show me your neck."); and (3) vocabulary ("What color is this crayon?").

THE PIAGETIAN TASKS. Piagetian tasks are often used to assess children's intellectual development. For example, a child may be administered the conservation of number task we described in Chapter 10. Required materials are simply a number of discrete objects, such as pennies or checkers. Piagetian tasks are always administered to individual children. In groups, children tend to copy what others are doing. Besides, the Piagetian researcher is just as interested in *why* a child does something as in *what* the child does, so individual discussions have to take place.

Issues in Assessing Preschoolers

Now that we've examined some of the common tests, let's return to the issues raised by Ellen Bernstein's experience. She thought Andrew was a bright child, and she wondered if the problems detected by the tests were important ones. This touches on the issue of **validity**—the question of whether a test measures what it says it does and can predict later performance as it claims. Ellen also wondered about the kindergarten curriculum and why it wasn't what it used to be. She wondered too about what the role of kindergarten was, if children were expected to come to school already knowing what she thought they were supposed to teach.

Ellen may not have known it, but testing itself is the force that often shapes school curricula and policies about entrance to kindergarten. Whether this should be so is one of the most controversial issues in early education today. We turn now to a discussion of this and related issues.

VALIDITY. The younger the child, the more serious is the problem of test validity. Young children are often unfamiliar with testing formats, don't always relate well to strangers in charge of testing, and grow and change rapidly. Their performance on tests also reflects factors other than their intellectual abilities, such as their experiences at home. For example, one child might do poorly on tests at the beginning of kindergarten because she's never been exposed to the information being tested before, and another child might do poorly because she has learning difficulties. The tests don't distinguish between these two conditions, but the children's long-term outcomes are likely to be very different. The child without exposure is likely to progress quickly, and the child with learning difficulties is likely to have to struggle. Tests given only a year later may yield radically different results than the tests given at the start of kindergarten.

All these factors threaten the validity of testing done to predict future classroom performance. Currently, readiness tests used with preschool and kindergarten children don't predict much better than chance. This means the decisions that schools make about entrance to kindergarten and first grade on the basis of tests are about as accurate as decisions they would make by flipping a coin (Peck, McCaig, & Sapp, 1988).

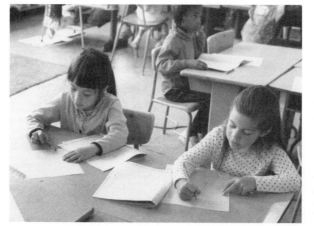

FIGURE 7
Assessment instruments are used to measure kindergartners' memory, intellectual abilities, and language development, but they also test children's ability to sit still, hold a pencil, listen to directions, and focus attention on one thing for a long time. Many 5-year-olds—especially boys—are ready for the social and learning experiences associated with traditional kindergarten but unable to succeed in a testing situation. Should they wait a year for kindergarten?

THE INFLUENCE OF TESTING ON THE EARLY CHILDHOOD CURRICULUM. With a strong emphasis on basic skills and test scores in the elementary grades these days, many early childhood programs have started to focus almost exclusively on teaching the information and skills that are contained in readiness and achievement test items. In other words, tests are determining the curriculum, and exploratory activities and play are being squeezed out.

As we discussed in Chapter 11, many experts think that young children need experiences that are broadly based, content rich, interesting, and likely to involve thinking and problem solving. Experiences provided in programs

FIGURE 8
Some kindergartens use workbooks and pencil-and-paper activities to teach math and language skills (top). Others use manipulatives and hands-on experiences (left). Evidence indicates that kindergartners, like younger children, gain deeper understandings and better problem-solving skills from hands-on experiences.

that are "test driven" are unlikely to have these characteristics. A recent report recommended that schools' early childhood classrooms—preschool through third grade—be under the direction of an early childhood coordinator rather than the elementary school curriculum director. This would protect the youngest children from the wave of testing that has swept the schools. Although testing and accountability may be appropriate for older elementary and high school students, the narrow curriculum and high pressure associated with such practices are not appropriate for younger children, in the opinion of the National Early Education Task Force of the National Association of State Boards of Education. Using didactic methods to teach abstract material is an educational approach unsuitable to the needs and abilities of preschool children (Shultz, 1988).

Andrew, for example, knew quite a lot about alphabet letters, number facts, and counting, but his poor fine-motor skills prevented him from expressing his knowledge in ways required and accepted by the school curriculum. Teachers free to do so could easily devise many experiences for Andrew that would enable him to thrive in kindergarten. Later, when his fine motor skills caught up with his intellectual abilities—perhaps in first grade—he could begin to do more written work. But the teachers in his school were probably under pressure to produce good written test scores in their classes. They wanted to make sure that all of the children would be able to perform well on the tests before they were admitted to kindergarten. This is the narrowing of curriculum approaches and content in the service of testing that worries many experts.

WHAT SHOULD THE SCHOOL'S MISSION BE? One of the most controversial aspects of testing is the use of test results to delay a child's entry into kindergarten. If a child doesn't do well on readiness tests, the school may recommend that the child be kept out of school for an additional year. Critics say that instead of doing this, schools should individualize their programs more and adjust their curricula to meet the needs of a wider range of children. But schools are under pressure to display good scores on achievement tests, and their "first line of defense" is to exclude children from kindergarten who don't appear to have a good start on mastering skills that show up on tests. The result is that children who could benefit from school are kept out for a longer period of time.

In many parts of the country during the mid- to late 1980s, school districts changed their age requirements for entrance to kindergarten so that children would be older when they started school. Districts that previously required children to be 5 years old by January 1 moved the date up to December 1 or even September 1. In a related trend, some parents, especially those who could afford an additional year of preschool, were voluntarily delaying their child's entry into kindergarten to give him (the child is more often a boy) the maturity to handle the academic material. Again, critics fault schools for both of these trends, charging that the heavy reliance on test scores is fueling narrow academic goals, unnecessary competitiveness and tension among children and parents, and inappropriate pressure on very young children. Like the issue of funding for preschool programs, the issue of testing is likely to be debated well into the 1990s.

LIVING WITH THE PRESCHOOL CHILD

"Get down off the couch, right now! Running and jumping aren't safe in the living room! Go out in the yard if you want to play like that!"

Sentiments like this are familiar to anyone who lives with or cares for preschoolers. They possess boundless energy and the agility and mobility to use it. Their parents and teachers have their hands full trying to keep them healthy, safe, and happily engaged in constructive activities. These are the topics we turn to next.

Ensuring the Health of the Preschooler

Two general areas of preschoolers' health—the communicable health problems parents and teachers may see and the eating and sleeping patterns young children are likely to have—deserve discussion.

COMMUNICABLE HEALTH PROBLEMS. Illness in the preschooler is fairly frequent but usually not very serious. As mentioned in Knowledge in Action: Infants and Toddlers, the highest incidence of illness in childhood occurs during the preschool years, perhaps because this is the age when many children first interact frequently with other children in groups, and also perhaps because children interact very directly at this age. They play together closely, share toys, and often sneeze and cough without covering their mouths and noses. Any contagious diseases are quickly passed on to other children.

Three very contagious and somewhat troublesome health problems commonly seen in preschoolers are head lice, ear infections, and chicken pox. Although they're very different in some ways, all are caused by an outside agent, so we discuss them together here.

Head lice are tiny, wingless insects. The female lays eggs, known as nits, on the shaft of the hair near the scalp. When the eggs hatch, the lice that emerge quickly burrow into the scalp to get a meal of blood from their host, leaving a toxin as they feed that causes intense itching. Special shampoos must be used to kill the lice and the nits. Nits then have to be removed from the hair with a fine-toothed comb provided with the shampoo. Hats, clothing, bedding, and all other items that might have come in contact with the lice have to be washed in very hot water or sealed in a plastic bag for two weeks. Lice need blood to survive, so they die inside the plastic bag. Insecticidal sprays are available for furniture and car upholstery, which can't be washed or sealed.

Because lice don't have wings, they're passed from one child to another by direct contact. Items like pillows, combs and brushes, and dress-up hats are all potential sources of infection in preschool classrooms. Teachers can suspect head lice if they see children scratching their heads frequently. Many schools and teachers conduct regular "head checks" to keep infestations from getting established.

Infections of the middle ear—known as **otitis media** to medical personnel—are another common annoyance in the preschool years. Young children are susceptible to these infections because of the anatomy of their faces. The **eustachian tubes**, which connect the middle ear to the throat, are in a nearly horizontal position during early childhood because the lower face develops later than the upper face. Fluid accumulates in the middle ear when the child has a cold, but it doesn't drain into the throat as it does in older children and adults. Trapped fluid provides a perfect medium for bacterial growth, and this can lead to recurring ear infections. As the lower face grows during the school-age years, the tubes assume a more vertical position and fluid drains more easily. Consequently, school-age children get many fewer ear infections than preschoolers.

Sometimes, ear infections occur so frequently that the middle ear is almost never clear of fluid. If a child has chronic ear infections, despite careful treatment with antibiotics, surgeons will sometimes insert tiny tubes into the eardrum to allow fluid to escape through the ear canal.

Ear infections not only make children feel miserable but also can impair hearing. Good hearing is especially important in early childhood when language is developing, so hearing problems at this time are serious and can have long-term consequences. Many studies have shown a relationship between a history of middle-ear infections and language delays (Tecle, Klein, & Rosner, 1984), although more recently, studies have indicated that this relationship is not as close as was once thought (Roberts et al., 1986).

Chicken pox is a common viral disease among preschool children. It has a characteristic rash, which starts out as clusters of tiny blisters that soon change into whitish pus-filled pimples, which in turn break and become crusty scabs. Usually, the worst symptom for children is the intense itchiness of the rash. Parents can help relieve some of the itching with baking soda baths.

Chicken pox is very contagious, and once it breaks out in a classroom, most children will get it. Luckily, it's rarely serious, except when a child's immune system is already impaired by some other disease, such as leukemia. Complications of chicken pox can include bacterial infection of the skin lesions and brain or kidney inflammation. Because of its danger in these few cases, and because children have to miss seven to ten days of school (the time it takes the lesions to scab over), some people have promoted work on a chicken pox vaccine (**varicella vaccine**). An experimental vaccine has been developed and tested in pilot studies but is not yet available for general use (Takahashi, 1986; Brunell et al., 1988).

EATING AND SLEEPING HABITS. Problems in eating and sleeping patterns can affect preschoolers' short- and long-term well-being and can cause quite a lot of anxiety among adults as well. Eating patterns are often a source of constant irritation to parents and other caregivers. Adults worry about both the small amount of food preschoolers seem to eat and their dislike for certain foods, especially those that adults consider nutritious.

Like toddlers, preschoolers have periods of relatively slow growth when their appetites are small. The only sensible approach when children aren't eating much is to limit non-nutritious snacks and then let their appetites be their guide. Adults can influence children's food preferences in several ways. Contrary to popular belief and practice, forcing a child to eat something she dislikes is not a good way to change her food preferences nor is bribery with a favorite food, such as dessert. In research conducted at the University of Illinois, it was discovered that children's rating of a disliked food dropped even lower when they were bribed to eat it with a desired food, and the desired food's rating rose. Thus, forcing children to eat vegetables to get some dessert

FIGURE 9
When appetites are small, parents should be sure to offer healthy snacks rather than candy bars or bags of chips. Apples are a good choice for preschoolers because they're nutritious, naturally sweet, and easy to handle.

apparently only teaches them to like vegetables less and dessert more (Olson, October, 1986).

One of the most effective ways to increase the number of foods that preschoolers like is to expose them to the food and to people who eat it. For example, when children who initially prefer one vegetable to another eat with children who have the opposite preference, they change their preference within days to match that of the other children. They still prefer it even weeks later (Olson, October, 1986). Eating with adults who like a food they dislike also increases their interest in the food, although not as much as another child's preference does. The more the exposure, the more likely it is that the child will taste the food and learn to like it.

Preschoolers' sleep habits also cause adults concern. Parents and other caregivers often worry about the amount of sleep a child gets, when a child should stop taking naps, how to get children to go to bed and to sleep, and what to do when a child wakes up crying in the middle of the night. How widespread is behavior that adults consider to be problematical?

In one study of preschoolers' sleep-related behavior at home, researchers found that bedtime routines, such as hearing stories, using the toilet, and getting a drink of water, took more than 30 minutes in over half the children. Most of the children took a comfort object, like a stuffed animal or a doll, to bed with them. Almost all of the children took at least 30 minutes to fall asleep. Some children had night lights, and the percentage of children who needed them increased between the ages of 2 and 4, before beginning to decline at age 5. Many children called to their parents for an additional kiss or drink of water after being put to bed, and almost all went through periods when they cried or called out during the night (Beltramini & Hertzig, 1983).

A second study investigated bedtime problems in children ranging in age from 15 months to 4 years. Problems included nighttime waking (defined as crying and demanding adult attention) and bedtime struggle (defined as protest and active struggle over going to bed and taking more than an hour for bedtime routines and getting to sleep) (Kataria, Swanson, & Trevathon, 1987). At the beginning of this 3-year study, 42 percent of the children had sleep problems; at the end of the study, 38 percent had sleep problems. Sleep disturbances were often associated with some upset in the child's life, such as a change in routines, an illness or accident, or a family move.

These studies and others indicate that sleep-related behavior that cause adults concern are actually quite common among preschoolers. They resist going to bed, call for a drink or a kiss after they're in bed, take a long time to fall asleep, and wake up and cry in the middle of the night, at least occasionally. What steps can adults take to make the difficult transition to sleep easier for children? Bedtime and naptime routines seem to help. A specific set of events leading up to bedtime—using the toilet, brushing the teeth, having a story read, getting a comfort object, and kissing and hugging—can help manage and prevent problem behavior, both at home and at day care centers. Dimming the lights and putting on some quiet music can also help.

At day care centers, an additional sleep problem arises from children's different napping habits. Often there isn't enough space for a separate sleeping room, nor are there staff members to supervise it. Thus, naptime has to be scheduled at the same time for everyone, even though some preschoolers take long naps, some take short naps, and some don't take naps at all. Parents may have preferences too. They may want their child to take a nap because without it the child is extremely irritable, which makes it difficult for the working parent to enjoy some time with the child in the evening. Or they may *not* want their child to take a nap, because it shortens the length of time the child sleeps at night.

Day care staff often try to accommodate these different needs and wishes by requiring all children to lie down on mats for a period during the day but

FIGURE 10
Children require less sleep as they get older, and an afternoon nap can make it hard for an older pre-schooler to fall asleep at night. If this child is still awake in 15 minutes or so, he may be able to get up and play quietly while his friends finish their nap.

allowing children who don't nap to look at books if they wish. After half an hour or so, when napping children have had a chance to fall asleep, children who are still awake may get up to engage in some quiet activities.

Ensuring the Safety of the Preschooler

Most of the safety precautions described in Knowledge in Action: Infants and Toddlers continue to apply during the preschool years. Children still can't be trusted to keep nonedible objects out of their mouths, to leave electrical outlets alone, or to adjust a water faucet to a safe temperature. In fact, preschoolers' greater motor ability and curiosity make them even more likely to get into trouble, such as exploring a medicine cabinet.

A major hazard of early childhood that we haven't yet discussed is lead poisoning. When lead enters the body, even in low concentrations, it can be toxic and can result in impaired mental functioning, overactivity, and even death. Children ingest lead in several ways. Lead-based gasolines emit lead-containing fumes, which is a problem in areas near highways. Water can be contaminated with lead from lead water pipes or lead soldering on water pipes. Some factory workers carry lead dust home on their clothing. It can mix with regular household dust and be ingested by children when they mouth toys and household objects.

By far the most common source of lead is lead-based paint, which was used in houses before World War II. Some paints were as much as 50-percent lead. When lead-based paint crumbles, young children can pick up chips and eat them, or the paint chips can be crushed underfoot and combine with house-hold dust, to be inhaled or ingested. When older homes are renovated, the

FIGURE 11
Lead poisoning is a danger for children who live in deteriorating buildings with crumbling walls and paint. When government efforts to improve conditions fall short, social service agencies can at least educate parents—especially teen parents like this young woman—about how to protect their children from environmental threats to their health.

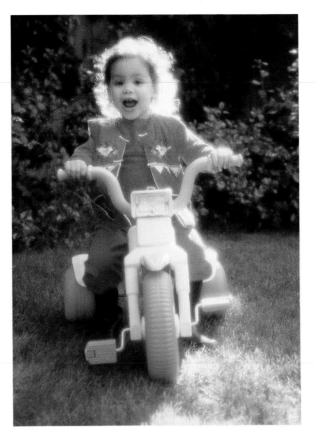

FIGURE 12
Trendy "hot wheels" have replaced the traditional trike in preschooler's life, but either one helps the child develop balance, coordination, and strength.

lead-containing airborne dust can be hazardous (Landrigan, 1981). Ironically, the deleading of older houses has actually created problems of air-borne lead particles, because safe procedures haven't always been followed (Williams, 1989).

In some Northeastern states, laws have been passed prohibiting the sale of houses or the rental of apartments to families with children under 6 years of age if the interior paint is found to contain lead. Day care centers also have to pass inspection to ensure that their spaces are lead free. Despite these measures, lead poisoning is a serious and common problem among young children, especially those who live in older, dilapidated buildings in urban areas.

Supporting Preschoolers' Play

Preschoolers have many interests and budding skills, and a tremendous range of toys and play items can be provided to support them.

TOYS REQUIRING LARGE MOTOR SKILLS. Swing sets, climbing structures, tricycles, and wagons give preschoolers a chance to use their large muscles. Large building blocks do too, because children have to lift them, carry them, and bend over to put them in place. Younger preschoolers enjoy throwing and catching balls, and older preschoolers can use a low basketball hoop and a plastic baseball and bat. They also enjoy kicking a soccer ball around.

PUBLIC POLICY FOCUS

Improving Children's Television

Children's television programming has been an area of intense struggle over the years. Public policymakers have tried to get broadcasters to reduce TV violence, to increase the number of children's shows, especially educational ones, and to limit commercials on children's shows. Broadcasters and advertisers, driven by financial pressures and goals, have successfully resisted most of these efforts. Today, our country has no coherent children's television policy. What concerns and issues are involved in this debate?

CONCERNS ABOUT VIOLENCE

Television sets were common in American homes for little more than a decade when concern arose about the amount of violence depicted on TV. In 1960 the National Commission on the Causes and Prevention of Violence issued a report, stating that violence on TV was a factor affecting children's aggressive behavior. The report rated television shows for violence and recommended that programs be rated on an annual basis. Over the years, the violence rating indicated that shows were becoming more violent.

During the 1960s and 1970s, the focus of most research on children's television was violence. As we have seen elsewhere in this book, many studies established correlations (but not causal relationships) between viewing of filmed violence and aggressive behavior. Many people were concerned not only that there were so many violent episodes in cartoons but that children were watching violent shows intended for adults. Pressure was applied to legislators to take steps to regulate TV to control televised violence, but these efforts failed. Television stations asserted that programming decisions were matters of internal policy, and some lawmakers felt that regulation would

violate the stations' First Amendment rights of freedom of speech.

CONCERNS ABOUT PROGRAMMING AND ADVERTISING

The Birth of Public Television

The Federal Communications Commission (FCC) in 1960 officially recognized children as a segment of the public needing special attention from TV broadcasters. Programming for children got a tremendous boost when the Corporation for Public Broadcasting was founded as a result of a 1967 Carnegie Commission Study. This study called for the creation of a federally funded network of public and educational television stations that would air more and better children's programs. The Public Broadcasting System (PBS) is the network within this system that carries such acclaimed shows as "Mr. Roger's Neighborhood," "Sesame Street," and "Reading Rainbow."

Action for Children's Television: Efforts to Limit Advertising

Special interest groups continued to put pressure on the commercial stations as well. In 1970 a grassroots group called Action for Children's Television (ACT) lobbied the FCC to require all stations to provide certain minimal programming for children every day. ACT also proposed that advertising be abolished during children's programs. As a result, the FCC issued their 1974 Children's Television Report and Policy Statement. This was a nonbinding ruling, establishing guidelines for broadcasters to follow in children's programming. Among other things, it instructed TV stations to use "separators" between children's shows and commercials (to help children perceive that a commercial isn't

Wide open space is well used by preschoolers, who run, jump, gallop, and roll around on the ground. In winter they like to help shovel snow with a child-sized shovel, and in fall they can rake leaves with a small rake. In spring and summer they like to fill watering cans and carry them to plants. Water and sand are all-time favorites of preschoolers, who will spend hours playing with pails, molds, sifters, scoops, funnels, and other sand and water toys.

TOYS REQUIRING SMALL MOTOR SKILLS. Children gain much greater skill with their hands during the preschool years, and they enjoy drawing and writing with markers, crayons, paint, and paper. They can also learn to use scissors now, especially if they practice on thin strips of paper that require just one snip to cut through.

Jig-saw puzzles, small construction toys, beads for stringing, simple sewing cards, play dough, and clay all give preschoolers practice with their fine motor skills. Doll clothes also require skilled use of the hands, and Velcro fastenings make them easier than ever to manipulate.

part of the show) and to stop using characters from children's shows to push products (a practice known as "host selling"). As we've seen, even school-age children lack the cognitive skills to process accurately the messages sent out by advertisers.

Although the FCC made it clear that stations would be evaluated for their compliance with this ruling at license-renewal time, broadcasters ignored many of the guidelines. In 1976 ACT succeeded in getting a different agency, the Federal Trade Commission (FTC), to consider children a special population with respect to advertising. The FTC proposed a ban on television advertising directed toward children under 8 years of age. The proposal met with so much resistance that the FTC abandoned its efforts to encourage regulation of TV commercials directed at children (Hymes, 1982).

Efforts to Improve Children's Shows: The Children's Television Education Act

More recently, efforts to develop a policy for children's television have focused on improving the educational value of shows. In 1984, Rep. Timothy Wirth of Colorado introduced the Children's Television Education Act of 1983 in the House of Representatives. This bill called for TV stations to provide a minimum of one hour of children's programming every weekday. The bill died in 1984.

Rep. Wirth, along with cosponsor Senator Frank Lautenberg, reintroduced the bill in 1985. Under the revised act, broadcasters' licenses would not be renewed if they failed to provide minimal children's programming every day. The bill also called for the FCC to investigate the effects of children's programs produced solely to promote toys or other products—the so-called "program-length commercials." These shows now take up a large part of the air time reserved for children's programs. This bill died in 1986. However, legislators remain committed to the ideals and issues addressed in the bill and intend to introduce it again sometime in the future (Kunkel & Watkins, 1985; Wirth, 1985).

WHAT SHOULD ADULTS DO?

In the absence of a public policy regarding televison for children, parents and other caregivers have to control children's TV viewing (Murray & Lonnborg, undated). Adults who are concerned about what children are watching on TV can take the following steps:

- Limit the amount of time children spend watching TV. Active play is preferable to TV watching for children of all ages. Children who don't watch much TV have been found to be more creative, social, activity oriented, and successful in school than children who watch a lot of TV. Experts recommend that adults limit preschoolers to no more than one hour a day and school-age children to no more than two hours a day.
- Screen the programs children watch, and don't allow them to watch shows that contain a lot of violence. Make adult shows off-limits, including news broadcasts, situation comedies, game and talk shows, and many documentaries. Preschoolers can't comprehend most adult programming and often find it upsetting or frightening.
- Watch television with children and explain what is "real" and what is "pretend."
- Encourage children to watch educational programs and shows with a prosocial message.
- Support citizens' groups, such as ACT, to work for public policies that will improve children's television.

MATERIALS THAT SUPPORT PRETEND PLAY. Pretend play is often the preschooler's favorite kind of play. Dress-up clothes of all kinds help support pretend play, as do baby dolls, stuffed animals, and small dolls or figures. Props help too—dishes, doll clothes, doll carriages and furniture, small kitchen appliances, empty food cartons, a cash register, shopping carts, and doctor's equipment will all be used.

BOOKS. Preschoolers love to hear stories, and they also like to look at picture books and attempt to reread them themselves. Many books are available today with cassette tapes, so children can listen to stories even when adults are busy. There are even some excellent television shows that feature the lively reading and discussion of stories and books.

There has been an explosion of new books for children and children's bookstores since the 1960s and 1970s. At that time, libraries bought 90 percent of all children's books sold. By the mid-1980s, parents were buying so many books for their children that the proportion of books purchased by libraries had fallen to 60 percent. The Association of American Booksellers for Children estimated in 1988 that children's bookstores were opening in the United States at the rate of one per month (The Boston Globe, January 1, 1989). Preschoolers can also choose from among several children's magazines, such as *Sesame Street Magazine* and *Your Big Backyard*. They feature stories, games, activities, cartoons, and instructions for making things.

BOARD GAMES. Children begin to enjoy board games during the preschool years. They can learn to play simple games in which cards are drawn or an arrow is spun on a wheel to indicate how many spaces the players move, such as Candyland, Candyland Bingo, Chutes and Ladders, and Hi-Ho Cherry-O. To play these games, children need only be able to count to ten, match colors, or have some other basic skill, although they may need adult supervision to help them count correctly and take turns. Preschoolers' games are games of chance. As we saw in Chapter 10, they won't have the cognitive skills to play games of strategy, such as Checkers, MasterMind, or Battleship, until they're well into their school years.

Board games, reading, and active play of any kind are all preferable to watching TV, which has many disadvantages for children. A discussion of attempts to improve children's television is given in Public Policy Focus—Improving Children's Television.

FIGURE 13
Items destined for the thrift shop should be rerouted to the preschooler's toy box or the nursery school dress-up area. Old hats, shoes, and clothes are all children need for hours of pretend play.

OVERVIEW

Preschoolers are active, curious, talkative, and ready for social interactions with peers. These qualities make preschool an appropriate and valuable experience for them. At the same time, children between the ages of 3 and 6 have unique characteristics and needs that make it difficult to design truly effective preschool educational programs. Their cognitive limitations, social inexperience, relatively brief attention span, and urge to use their large muscles in active play mean that schoollike situations will create more problems than they solve. Preschoolers learn best in hands-on situations where they can explore freely, initiate their own activities, and interact on a one-to-one basis with an adult—characteristics that are difficult indeed to incorporate into programs on a large-scale basis. Knowledge and research help adults design educational programs and structure living environments for the enhancement of preschoolers' growth in all domains, but public policies have to be established that support these efforts.

KNOWLEDGE IN ACTION REVIEW

EDUCATION AND CARE PROGRAMS FOR PRESCHOOL CHILDREN

- The preschool population is diverse, but special programs exist to provide educational, social, and emotional experiences to groups who otherwise wouldn't be able to take advantage of preschool.
- Preschool programs adapted to children with disabilities are provided under the Education for All Handicapped Children Act of 1975.
- Several federal, state, and city programs have been established for children from economically disadvantaged households, although funding always falls short of need. Some states subsidize preschool for working parents, and some companies provide day care facilities for their employees. Affordable day care will be a major issue of the 1990s.
- The best preschool programs are judged to be those that offer a balance of teacher-directed activities and child-directed activities throughout the day. Highly interactive educational programs for preschoolers require a very high ratio of teachers to children, perhaps one teacher for every three or four children.
- Preschoolers thrive with individualized adult interaction, hands-on experience, positive feedback, and opportunities to engage in activities that require large motor skills. All this should take place in a safe, nurturing, well-organized environment.
- Gifted children have above-average intellectual ability, creativity, or a demonstrated talent in a particular area. They need educational tasks that challenge and stimulate them. At the preschool level, these activities are most often provided by the parents.
- Children learn a lot from child-directed activities, but they don't learn specific academic skills from them. These are the very activities needed by children from economically disadvantaged families if they are to succeed later on in school. Creative teaching and reduced group size may help solve these problems in the 1990s.

ASSESSING THE PRESCHOOL CHILD

- Preschool children are sometimes tested to assess their intellectual skills, their developmental level, and their readiness for academic tasks.
- These tests are controversial. Their validity is questionable, since most of them don't predict future academic success any better than chance. Their use also narrows the preschool curriculum and squeezes out more creative, exploratory, and child-initiated activities, which are considered essential to intellectual growth.
- One result of the wave of testing is that less mature children are being kept out of kindergarten rather than given the individualized attention that would support their overall development.

LIVING WITH THE PRESCHOOL CHILD

- Preschoolers get sick fairly often, mainly because of their close contact with other children. They're at risk for getting head lice, developing ear infections, and contracting chicken pox, all of which are more annoying than causes for concern.
- Preschoolers can be picky eaters and should be given nutritious meals and snacks. Coercion and bribery aren't effective ways to get children to eat food they don't like, but exposing them to people who like other foods does help them expand their diet.
- Sleep behaviors that adults consider problems are actually common among preschoolers. Bedtime and naptime routines are often helpful, as are the understanding and patience of parents and caregivers.
- Lead poisoning is a serious environmental danger for children, and homes and day care centers should be inspected to ensure that the walls aren't covered with lead-based paint.
- Preschoolers enjoy pretend play, outdoor play, toys and activities that require fine motor skills, books, and simple board games.
- Active play is preferable to television for children. Efforts over the years to improve the quality of children's television have not been very effective, although the creation of public television is one of the successes. Concerns focus on violence, advertising, and the quality of the programming. In the absence of a national policy on children's television, the responsibility for monitoring and controlling TV viewing falls on the parents.

KEY TERMS

teacher-directed education
child-directed education
head lice
otitis media

eustachian tubes
chicken pox
varicella vaccine

SUGGESTIONS FOR FURTHER READING

Blum, M. (1983). *The day-care dilemma: Women and children first.* Lexington, MA: D.C. Heath.
This book claims that women have made advances in their careers at the expense of their children's well-being. Much day care, according to the author, is not of high quality.

Gunzenhauser, N., & Caldwell, B. M. (Eds.). (1986). *Group care for young children.* Skillman, NJ: Johnson & Johnson.
This short paperback contains many interesting chapters, including ones on the child care needs of single and low-income parents, on the opportunities for parent education in child care, on child care and public policy, and on corporate support for child care.

Kagan, S. L., & Zigler, E. F. (1987). *Early schooling: The national debate.* New Haven, CT: Yale University Press.
This book discusses the current trend of public schools providing programs for 4-year-olds. Issues such as the appropriate content and methods to use with preschools are discussed.

National Association for the Education of Young Children. (1986). *Developmentally appropriate practice in early childhood programs serving children from birth through age 8.* Washington, D.C.: NAEYC.
This booklet contains a set of standards for quality early childhood programs.

MILESTONES IN PRESCHOOL DEVELOPMENT

AGE	PHYSICAL	COGNITIVE	LANGUAGE	SOCIAL-EMOTIONAL
3 yrs.	Demonstrates true run, with both feet leaving ground Walks upstairs alternating feet Walks downstairs using marked-time climbing Can take most clothes off	Begins to demonstrate pre-operational thinking Knows conventional counting words up to 5 Can solve nesting cup problem by reversing two cups or by insertion	Understands *in, on,* and *under* Speaks in more complete sentences Distinguishes graphics that are writing versus graphics that are pictures Begins to overgeneralize rules for creating verb tenses and plurals	Might begin preschool Uses physical aggression more than verbal aggression
3 yrs. 6 mos.	Can hop a few steps on preferred foot Can button large buttons Can put easier clothes on	Can't easily distinguish reality from fantasy Can count 5 objects before working in partitioning error	Might use a syllable hypothesis to create words Rereads favorite storybooks using picture-governed strategies Often uses scribble-writing	Has difficulty generating alternatives in a conflict situation Will learn aggressive behavior rapidly if these means succeed
4 yrs.	Appears thinner due to longer trunk Can walk a curved line Walks downstairs alternating feet Can gallop Can cut straight line with scissors	Can make a row of objects equal to another row by matching one to one Puts shorter and longer sticks together in piles but can't create a series	Creates questions and negative sentences using correct word arrangement Might create "mock" letters	Watches, on average, 2 to 4 hours of TV per day
4 yrs. 6 mos.	Might begin to hold writing tool in finger grip Leans forward more when jumping from a height Can button smaller buttons	Knows conventional counting words up to 15 Is better able to distinguish reality from fantasy	Often reverses letters when writing Understands *beside, between, front,* and *back* Doesn't notice or grasp print conventions	Can't distinguish TV reality (news) from dramatic (fantasy) programs
5 yrs.	Can stop and change direction quickly when running Can hop 8 to 10 steps on one foot	Selects own view in three-mountain task Can create a series through trial and error Creates classes of objects based on a single defining attribute	Understands passive sentences Might begin to use invented spellings	Is still poor at self-control; success depends on removal of temptation or diversion by others
5 yrs. 6 mos.	Can connect a zipper on a coat Might be able to tie shoes	Can count 20 objects without making a partitioning error "Counts all" to combine two groups of objects	Might begin to make print-governed reading attempts with favorite books	Uses more verbal aggression

SCHOOL-AGE CHILDREN

The years between 6 and 12 are in many ways the most tranquil of childhood. Freud claimed that these years were a period of sexual latency, and
whether we accept his theories or not, we can see a certain quiet steadiness in children this age that didn't exist in earlier years. Physically, they
grow slowly and predictably, acquiring and consolidating motor skills that
will last a lifetime. Socially and emotionally, they become more aware of
themselves and others, refining the personal style they're coming to call
their own. Against this relatively placid backdrop, they cross the threshold
of rationality and begin to become intellectual beings. The school years
are above all a time of learning, a time when children can apply themselves to schoolwork and master the academic skills they'll need to
become educated people. Although children are developing in every
domain during these years, going to school is their defining experience,
and this is why we've chosen to refer to them in this book as *school-age
children*.

chapter 13

PHYSICAL DEVELOPMENT IN SCHOOL-AGE CHILDREN

As Steve Atkinson set up orange cones at the ends of the school playing field, he heard the children in his first P.E. class of the day coming out of their classroom. They were sturdy first graders, filled with enthusiasm.

"Today we're going to play a game of tag," Steve told the children after he led them in some warm-up stretches. "We can play either color tag or freeze tag. Which do you want?"

"Color tag!" they all seemed to shout at once.

"Okay, color tag it is."

"Steve, can me and Sharon be the chasers today?" piped up Yolanda, an energetic 6-year-old.

"Let me check my list," Steve replied. "Everyone needs to have a turn . . . yes, that looks okay, Yolanda. Any other questions? No? Okay, look at your clothes to see what colors you're wearing, and then we'll divide into two sides."

When the class was ready, Yolanda and Sharon stood whispering in the middle of the field for a moment and then turned and called out "RED!" From opposite ends of the field, children started running directly for the other side, and the two girls tagged as many as they could. One unlucky boy discovered he had red on his sneakers after everyone else was behind the lines and had to make a dash for the other side by himself. Yolanda quickly tagged him.

Sharon and Yolanda conferred again and this time called out "YELLOW!" The field once more became a blur of children running, laughing, and trying to dodge the taggers. Sometimes a child would run wide, out to the edges of the field, but most made straight for the other end of the field. Sharon and Yolanda had no trouble tagging all but two of the children in four rounds, and those two became the next taggers. By the end of the class, when Steve had them walk around the field to cool down, the children were pink-cheeked and tired, ready to return to their classroom.

Steve's next class was a group of third and fourth graders, and he offered them a choice of dodge ball, capture the flag, or elbow tag. They chose elbow tag, a more complicated game of tag that they were just becoming able to play. Steve liked elbow tag because of the combination of quick thinking and maneuvering it required. When the children were warmed up, they linked arms at the elbow with a partner and spread out over the field. Steve asked Cindy to be the first chaser, and Nathaniel agreed to be the first one chased.

As they started running, Nathaniel was able to keep ahead, but when Cindy started to close in, Nathaniel ran over to a pair of classmates and linked elbows with one of them. The other child in the pair pulled her arm free and ran off, and Cindy now ran after her. But she was starting to get out of breath, and soon she too linked elbows with a classmate. The boy on the other end of that chain became the new chaser.

As the game continued, Steve watched the children running, dodging, and stopping short only to take off in another direction after a different child. Sometimes he marveled that they were able to keep track of what was going on as well as they could. They too were ready for a rest by the end of the class.

Steve met his last morning class in the gym. The sixth graders had begun learning some basic basketball skills two years earlier, dribbling first with one hand, then with alternate hands, then dribbling around the body while remaining stationary, and finally dribbling and traveling. Later they practiced dribbling around obstacles, changing directions, and dribbling against an opponent. They'd practiced a series of throwing and shooting skills too.

Just this year they were starting to put together the understanding, coordination, and skills really required to play the game. After warm ups, Steve had them practice dribbling and shooting lay-up shots, and then they played a short game. As he watched them play, Steve noted that many of them would be joining the school's seventh and eighth grade basketball team the following year. He also noted that many of the skills they were using were built on their first experiences in games like color tag, played not so many years ago.

The school years are a period of steady physical growth and rapid skill acquisition. The somewhat chubby first grader turns into the taller, leaner, more muscular child of the later elementary school years, able to begin playing a complex game like basketball. This transformation is supported by a physical education program like Steve's, built around games and physical skill development. As children grow, their increasing strength and motor coordination in turn contribute to good health, a sense of independence, high self-esteem, and appropriate cognitive development.

This chapter covers the typical growth patterns of middle childhood as well as normal and abnormal variations in these patterns. The causes and effects of the most common abnormal variation, childhood obesity, are discussed. This is followed by a discussion of motor development, including both the fine and gross motor skills that school-age children acquire. Finally, this chapter addresses some of the implications of physical development for sports programs and the development of healthy life-styles.

HOW DO THEY GROW?

Increases in Height and Weight

Growth during the school years slows down from preschool rates. The average 6-year-old weighs about 43 pounds and is about 44 inches tall—almost 4 feet. The average 12-year-old weighs a little over 80 pounds and is about 5 feet tall.

FIGURE 13-1
First graders are typically slender, sturdy, and designed for action, as we can see around the edges of this group. Children grow slowly and steadily for most of the school years, but height and weight both start to increase rapidly toward the end of this period, when the preadolescent growth spurt begins.

If you recall, infants double their birthweight in their first six months. In contrast, it takes the average 6-year-old twelve times that long—six years—to double her 6-year-old weight (Figure 13-1).

By the time children are 6 years old, they're about two-thirds of their adult height. And by the end of middle childhood, boys have reached 80 percent of their adult height, and girls have achieved about 90 percent of theirs (Tanner, 1978). Weight gain during this period is concentrated more in muscle than in fat, so strength increases considerably. Because boys as a group have more muscle cells than girls as a group, they're stronger during the school years as well as during adolescence (Maccoby, 1980).

Changes in Body Proportions

Up to now, the head has grown more rapidly than the body, but now the growth of the head slows dramatically. If you recall from Chapter 5, the brain achieves about 90 percent of its adult weight by age 5. Brain weight equals adult levels by age 6, although many changes, including **lateralization** (dominance of one hemisphere or the other with respect to specific functions) and **myelination** (growth of a fatty sheath on the outer surface of nerve cells), will continue for several years (Cratty, 1986).

Now the trunk and especially the legs begin to grow more quickly, making the school-age child look quite long and slim. The face changes too, becoming longer and thinner. Just as the head grew more rapidly than the body during the first six years of life, the upper part of the head grew more rapidly than the lower part. Now, the lower face and jaw begin to catch up. The cheeks slim down and the face elongates. The eustachian tubes connecting the middle ear to the throat begin to assume a more vertical position, as explained in Knowledge in Action: Preschool Children. Fluids can drain out of the ear, and children tend to have fewer ear infections. The tiny plastic tubes that some preschoolers need in their ears to prevent ear infections are rarely needed by children over 7 or 8 years old.

FIGURE 13-2
The long and lanky school-age child can run, chase, and dodge with speed and skill. In a quieter moment, this 8-year-old traces out a self-portrait that reflects just how much she has grown in the last few years.

FIGURE 13-3
Body proportions continue to change during the school-age years as the trunk and legs grow more rapidly than the head. By the time the child is 12, her body proportions are very close to those of an adult.

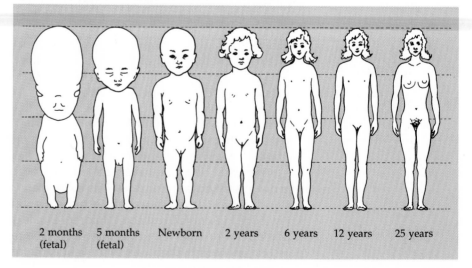

| 2 months (fetal) | 5 months (fetal) | Newborn | 2 years | 6 years | 12 years | 25 years |

The Eruption of Permanent Teeth

Losing the first baby tooth is a rite of passage into middle childhood. A few children lose one or two teeth soon after their fifth birthday, but it's more commonly a 6-year-old phenomenon. First- and second-grade classrooms are usually full of "toothless grins." The process of tooth loss continues over the entire course of middle childhood. By about age 11 or 12, all permanent teeth have erupted except for two sets of molars.

Care of the permanent teeth is especially important, since they'll last for life. Thumb and finger sucking should stop by the time the permanent teeth have come in, or **malocclusion** (improper alignment) may result. If a child doesn't give up this habit, parents may want to consider special counseling. Even without thumb or finger sucking, some children will have overbites and other misalignments of their teeth. Braces are a common sight in the older elementary grades.

Normal Variations in Growth Patterns

THE PREADOLESCENT GROWTH SPURT. All children grow at different rates, and children who are tall at age 7 or 8 may be surpassed in height by their classmates a few years later. These variations are particularly apparent toward the end of the school-age period, when the **preadolescent growth spurt** occurs (this and other aspects of puberty are discussed in detail in Chapter 17). Some children shoot up and begin to develop sexually, while others retain their

FIGURE 13-4
Wiggly teeth are a frequent topic of interest among school-age children. Sometimes a friend can't resist feeling it for himself.

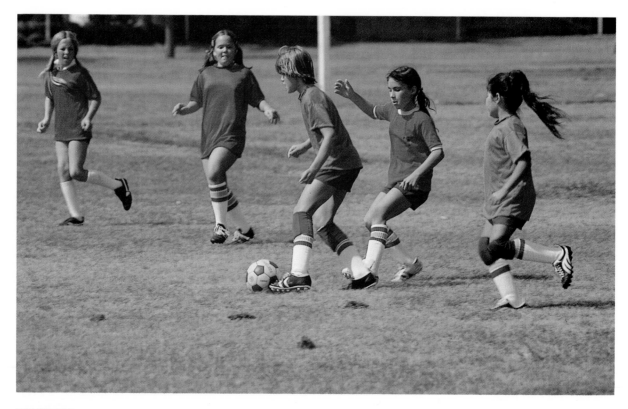

FIGURE 13-5
Normal variation in the timing of the preadolescent growth spurt means that some girls show evidence of sexual development before their friends do, often at 10 or 11 years of age. Many girls begin to drop out of sports towards the end of the school years, perhaps due partly to feelings of self-consciousness about their bodies. Since participation in physical activities like soccer has benefits throughout life, extra effort has to be put into encouraging girls to stay in sports programs.

childish proportions longer. The age at which the growth spurt occurs can vary by several years, but girls usually experience it a few years before boys.

IMPLICATIONS OF THE GROWTH SPURT. The rapid physical change of the later school-age years is both exciting and frightening to children. When one mother discovered that her sixth-grade daughter was concerned about a topic that began with the letter "D," she hastened to assure her that she and her husband had never even considered divorce, only to have the 11-year-old inform her in exasperation that the topic of interest was "development." Children's concern is heightened by the wide variation in timing of the growth spurt and in onset of puberty. If a child develops sooner or later than her peers, or if she's much taller or much shorter than the children in her class, she may feel awkward and self-conscious. The physical changes of puberty, such as the development of breasts and pubic hair, can affect how children are regarded by their peers (Aro & Taipale, 1987; Dornbusch et al., 1981).

Added to this self-consciousness about physical development is a strong desire to belong, to be like others, which typically emerges in older school-age children, along with a heightened awareness of other people's opinions, which characterizes children's thinking from about fourth or fifth grade on. All of these developments can combine to make older school-age children vulnerable to wide fluctuations in self-image and in how they feel about themselves. Adults can help by making sure children understand their physical development and emerging sexuality and by providing a supportive environment in which developmental changes are an accepted part of each child's life.

Abnormal Variations in Growth Patterns

Although there is a wide variation in children's growth patterns, some children don't grow normally during the school-age years. Some children fail to grow or grow too slowly; others put on too much weight and become obese during childhood. Both of these conditions are cause for concern.

RETARDED GROWTH. Sometimes, children just don't grow properly. Retarded growth can be caused by either social-environmental factors or by organic (physical) ones. Children whose growth is far below what is typical for their age are known as **failure-to-thrive** children. In infants, this syndrome is most often caused by parental neglect. But if conditions in the home don't improve, or if there are intermittent episodes of crisis and stress, failure to thrive can continue throughout childhood (Kempe & Kempe, 1976; Kristiansson & Fallstrom, 1987). Failure-to-thrive children are small for their age, appear undernourished, and may be lethargic or listless. The syndrome is treated by working with the neglectful parents or by placing the child in a foster home where proper care can be provided.

One organic problem that may cause retarded growth is a disturbance of the pituitary gland, which supplies growth hormone to the body. Sometimes the disturbance is due to a lesion (an injury from a disease or trauma) in the gland, which can result from an infectious disease such as meningeal tuberculosis. Radiation treatment for tumors of the middle ear or eye or for leukemia can also disturb hormonal production. When the disturbance in the pituitary gland isn't caused by a lesion, the condition is known as **idiopathic**; idiopathic pituitary conditions are inherited as recessive characteristics (Frasier, 1979).

Children with low levels of growth hormone are short for their age and often overweight for their height. Their chests and abdomens tend to be chubby, although their head size may be typical for their age (Frasier, 1979). The best indicator of a problem in growth hormone is an extreme deviation from the norm for the child's age. Children with this problem can be given synthetic hormones, but physicians have to monitor their growth carefully to control their response to these drugs (Raiti et al., 1987).

CHILDHOOD OBESITY. Obesity is the most common deviation from normal growth found among school-age children. Obesity is defined as weight that exceeds normal weight-for-height or weight-for-age by 20 percent (Neumann, 1977). Estimates of the number of overweight school-age children vary from study to study, but the condition is prevalent and on the rise (Epstein, Wing, & Valoski, 1985). During the 15-year period from 1966 to 1980, the proportion of boys aged 6 to 11 who were obese increased from 18 to 20 percent, and the proportion of obese girls increased from 17 to 25 percent. (For a discussion of why childhood obesity is particularly worrisome and how it can be treated, see Health Focus—Treating Childhood Obesity.)

What causes some children to be overweight? Surprisingly, overweight children don't always eat more than their normal-weight peers. What often does distinguish the two groups is their different levels of physical activity (Berkowitz et al., 1985). The implication is that children's obesity may be due to lower-than-average energy expenditure rather than higher-than-average calorie intake. Obese children also tend to watch more television than normal-

HEALTH FOCUS

Treating Childhood Obesity

The later in childhood a baby or child remains overweight, the greater are the chances that the child will become an obese adult. This fact underlies the urgency of getting early weight problems under control as soon as possible. Of all overweight 6-month-olds, 14 percent will become obese adults. By age 7, the odds have increased to 41 percent. By age 13, the odds stand at about 70 percent (Epstein, Wing, & Valoski, 1985).

Furthermore, obese children have some of the same health-risk factors that are common in obese adults, including high blood pressure and elevated total cholesterol levels. Overweight children can be enrolled in weight control treatment programs to help them adopt eating and exercise habits that will carry over into their adult years. The goal of these programs is to minimize health risks and maximize self-esteem and personal satisfaction.

One particularly comprehensive program has been developed by the Child Weight Control Clinic at the University of Pittsburgh School of Medicine (Epstein, Wing, & Valoski, 1985). The program has three components: diet, exercise, and behavior modification. The diet component uses a "traffic light" system to manage eating. "Go" foods can be eaten in unlimited amounts; "Caution" foods can be eaten in moderate amounts;

and "Stop" foods should be avoided.

The exercise program works on a point system. Different activities are rated according to how many calories they burn. Children are given a point goal for the week, but they can choose the exercises they prefer to reach their goal. The behavior modification component has several parts: (1) information mastery, which includes knowledge about food and diet; (2) self-monitoring, which involves keeping a log of foods eaten; and (3) contracting, which requires parents and children to earn back money paid at the beginning of the program by attending weekly training sessions.

Programs like this one obviously call for considerable commitment and investment of time by both the child and the family. Comparative studies have shown that programs involving the parents are more successful than those involving just the child. But it's important, especially for children approaching adolescence, that the child and parents attend separate training sessions, even though they're enrolled in the same overall program (Brownell, Kelman, & Stunkard, 1983). This separation gives the child independence and control and shifts responsibility for weight control to the child, who will increasingly be the one who has to maintain it.

weight children (Dietz & Gortmarker, 1984). This habit not only takes up time that could be spent in physical activities and play but increases snacking, particularly of calorie-dense food, otherwise known as junk food (Barcus & McLaughlin, 1978; Dietz, 1986).

Children put on this excess weight during middle childhood at a rate of about 5 pounds per year, which amounts to an excess of about 50 calories per day. A 20-minute bike ride would more than eat up that number of calories, and one less snack of chips and a cola drink while watching TV probably would eliminate even more. It's easy to see that for most children a little prevention, begun early in life, can keep weight gain under control.

Strong evidence exists, however, that obesity has a genetic component (Pollitt, Garza, & Leibel, 1984). There is a high correlation between obesity in parents and obesity in children. If their parents are obese, 50 percent of obese infants will become obese adults. If their parents aren't obese, only 20 percent of obese infants will become obese adults (Epstein, Wing, & Valoski, 1985). Of course, since all family members share a more or less common environment, the high correlation could be due to learning rather than inheritance or to some combination of the two factors.

Many researchers have attempted to sort out the relative effects of genetics and environment on obesity, and their results indicate that genetics accounts for between 20 and 60 percent of the variance in obesity (Brook, Huntley, & Slack, 1975; Rao et al., 1975; Garn & Clark, 1976; Foch & McClearn, 1980). In other words, researchers believe that 20 to 60 percent of the difference in

FIGURE 13-6
Heredity or life style? It's very difficult to sort out the influence of biological and environmental factors when a child is overweight. This girl may sit down to high-fat, high-calorie meals three times a day and be offered cookies and cakes at grandma's, too. She may spend more time watching TV with her family than riding her bike. But it's likely that she also has an inherited tendency to be overweight.

weight between obese groups and normal weight groups can be attributed to *something other than* eating patterns and energy expenditure through physical activity—most likely, genetic inheritance. Even though the researchers don't agree on exactly how large the role of genetics is, they all give it considerable importance.

The good news is that environmental factors also play a large role in determining if a person actually becomes obese. The bad news is that some people may indeed have a natural tendency toward obesity. But with rigorous weight-control measures, even these individuals don't have to become fat. Good habits of physical activity developed during the school-age years may play an especially important role in lifelong fitness.

MOTOR DEVELOPMENT

Rapid Acquisition of Skills

At the beginning of this chapter, we saw that children become adept at many physical games during the school-age years. They learn to play games involving gross motor skills, including soccer, frisbee, basketball, tennis, baseball, handball, hockey, volleyball, golf, or football, depending on personal incli-

FIGURE 13-7
School-age children's games and sports require more balance and coordination than younger children's activities do. Walking on stilts calls for an extra dash of determination and a well-developed sense of humor—qualities commonly present in fourth and fifth graders like these boys.

FIGURE 13-8
Children gradually acquire the fine motor control required for handwriting in first or second grade. Creating stories or writing in a journal can inspire them to practice their skills once they have the necessary control. But even when the control and skills are present, becoming an accomplished writer requires the kind of patience and perseverance we see in this boy.

nation and what's available in the community. They might swim, ski, jump rope, bowl, or run. They might take gymnastics or dance lessons. And, of course, they play a great variety of self-created and traditional childhood games.

Activities involving fine motor skills that school-age children enjoy include playing jacks, working a yo-yo, or doing origami projects. They enjoy hobbies and crafts that require small motor skills, such as weaving, sewing, and assembling and painting models. Many school-age children also begin to take lessons on the piano or another musical instrument.

The ability to control and manipulate a pencil or pen often improves rapidly during the early school-age years as children acquire a mature grip on the writing tool. Younger children often use a full-palm or fist grip on a pencil, and they keep their hand and arm up off the tabletop. They move the tool with the muscles of the upper arm rather than with the fingers. Because the distance from the pivot (source of movement) to the tool is so great, their marks are very large. As the movements begin to originate in the wrist rather than the upper arm, children are able to make smaller marks. Writing becomes smaller still when children begin to rest the side of their hand on the table top and move the tool with their fingers. With this superior control, they can make finer marks and confine their writing to a smaller and smaller amount of space.

One of the many drawbacks of including handwriting programs in the kindergarten classroom is that many children, especially slower-maturing boys, don't yet have the fine motor control required for this activity. Writing is better taught in the elementary grades, although some first-grade boys will still find it difficult. Younger children do like to draw and write, but their enjoyment will be dampened if they have to confine their creations to a restricted area, such as the lines on ruled paper. To see the dramatic change in size and precision that takes place in children's handwriting between the ages of $2\frac{1}{2}$ and $7\frac{1}{2}$, look at the samples in Figure 13-9.

Injuries Associated with Growth Patterns and Excessive Exercise

During the school-age period, many children begin to participate in organized sports, such as swim teams and Little League baseball. Although they have the cognitive and motor skills to play sports, children's bones and muscles are immature and easily injured. Immature bones are softer than the fully ossified bones of teenagers and adults, and they can be deformed from strain or squeezing. Immature muscles also can easily be strained or torn.

Prolonged use of one area of the body or of several specific areas can lead to "overuse" injuries, such as sprains, tendinitis, and stress fractures (small breaks) of bones (Harvey, 1982). It can also lead to accelerated bone growth in an overused area (Stoner, 1978). If these injuries are handled improperly, long-term disability can result. This is why restrictions are placed on the amount of time a child can pitch in a Little League game (Milberg, 1976).

Children actually lose flexibility between 5 and 12 or 13 years of age because bones grow a little faster than muscles. At first, muscles get pulled tighter as bones grow; then muscles catch up (Teitz, 1982). Warm-up exercises, which get muscles into a flexible state before hard use, are especially important during this period to prevent children from sustaining an injury during physical activity.

FIGURE 13-9
As this child's fine motor control improved, he was able to write his name smaller and smaller. His age at the time of writing the different samples (shown reduced here) was (a) 2 years, 9 months; (b) 3 years, 6 months; (c) 4 years, 4 months; (d) 5 years, 7 months; (e) 6 years, 2 months; (f) 7 years, 7 months. Not until he was well over 7 years old was his writing small enough to fit comfortably on regular lined paper.

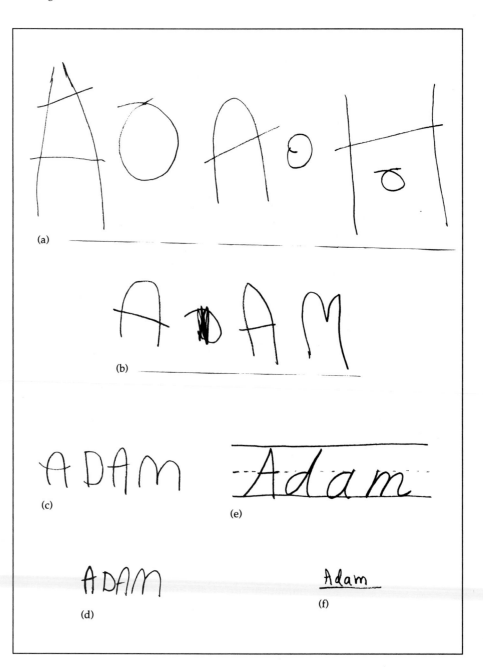

The Importance of Physical Education

A healthy body contributes to healthy growth in every other area of development. Good motor coordination and appropriate body strength can support cognitive growth and provide children with positive feelings about themselves. Participation in games and sports can help children learn individual and group social skills. Overall, physical activity can give children a sense of health and general well-being.

FIGURE 13-10
The motions used in pitching place tremendous stress on certain parts of the body, particularly the elbow and shoulder, and overuse can lead to permanent injury. Although children still learn how to pitch in Little League, pitching machines are now widely used for both practices and games.

FIGURE 13-11
Organized sports programs give children a chance to develop strength, agility, and endurance. They also provide them with the opportunity to achieve and excel.

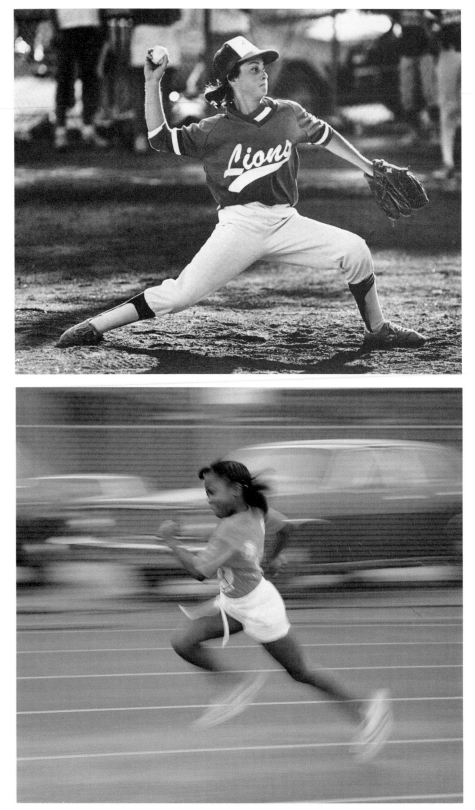

Despite the acknowledged benefits of motor skill development and physical activity, however, many schools pay very little attention to their physical education programs. Reading, for example, is often taught for an hour every day, but physical education may be taught only once a week, if at all. In 1980, the U.S. Department of Health and Human Services reported that school physical education programs aren't meeting the goal of establishing school-based programs made up of activities that go beyond competitive sports. Schools emphasize informal games and relays and short, weekly activity times. According to this report, "inadequate investment is being made in conveying the physical skills needed for active life-styles" (Ross & Gilbert, 1985). This is counterproductive to what we know is necessary for good health.

It follows that schools need to devote more of their resources to basic physical education for the elementary grades, and the public needs to support them. Other adults in children's lives can help them develop motor skills and a love of physical activity by playing games and sports with them and by encouraging them to be active. Instead of watching TV, children can play handball or jump rope on the sidewalk. They can play frisbee in the playground or basketball in the school yard. The whole family can go on a bicycle expedition, a walk around the neighborhood, or a hike in the woods. Experiences like these help children discover the pleasures of using their bodies in active ways and provide a solid foundation for the development of healthy life-styles.

OVERVIEW

It's no accident that we so often see school-age children playing sports. They now have the skills and coordination to learn and enjoy nearly every kind of physical activity. They're taller, slimmer, and stronger than they were during their preschool years, and they like to stretch their growing limbs. Those children who avidly pursue physical activities experience many cognitive, emotional, and social benefits, along with an enhanced sense of well-being. The challenge, increasingly, is to make sure the resources, support, and encouragement are available so that all children can have these experiences.

CHAPTER REVIEW

HOW DO THEY GROW?

- Children grow more slowly during the school-age years than they did as preschoolers. By the age of 6, they've reached almost two-thirds of their adult height.
- Most weight gain is concentrated in the muscles, so children increase in strength. Boys have more muscle cells than girls, which tends to make them stronger.
- The growth of the head slows, and the trunk and the legs grow more rapidly. This growth pattern gives school-age children a long and lean appearance. Facial appearance becomes longer and slimmer as the lower

face and jaw begin to come into balance with the upper part of the head.
- Most children start to lose their first teeth at about age 6, and by age 11 or 12, they have all their permanent teeth except for two sets of molars.
- All children grow at their own individual rates. Normal variations are particularly apparent toward the end of the school-age period when the preadolescent growth spurt occurs.
- Some children don't grow properly. Children who grow

much more slowly than average are called failure-to-thrive children. If their retarded growth is caused by environmental factors, it can be treated by providing counseling to the parents or placing the child in a foster home. If it's caused by physical factors, it can often be treated medically, for example, by administering growth hormone.

- The most common abnormal growth pattern in school-age children is obesity. Studies have shown that obese children exercise less and watch more television than their normal-weight peers. A correlation exists between obesity in parents and obesity in children, suggesting that this condition may have a genetic basis.

- Obese children may have to take extraordinary steps to keep their weight under control. Programs for obese children often use behavior modification techniques that help them take responsibility for their eating habits.

MOTOR DEVELOPMENT

- School-age children rapidly acquire many gross and fine motor skills, and they use and practice these skills in their sports, games, and activities. As their fine motor skills mature, their handwriting becomes smaller and more precise.

- Certain injuries are associated with excessive exercise during these years, because bones and muscles are still immature. When children overuse one part of their body, they can suffer stress fractures and sprains, which can lead to long-term disabilities. For this reason, knowledgeable adults should supervise children's sports programs.

- Children should be encouraged to participate in physical activities and physical education programs. Physical activity promotes cognitive development, increases physical strength, helps develop better motor coordination, improves self-esteem, and provides opportunities for peer interactions. It would be optimal if schools devoted some part of every day to physical education.

KEY TERMS

lateralization of the brain	preadolescent growth spurt
myelination	failure-to-thrive
malocclusion	idiopathic growth retardation

SUGGESTIONS FOR FURTHER READING

Cratty, B. J. (1986). *Perceptual and motor development in infant and children* (3rd ed.). Englewood Cliffs, NJ: Prentice-Hall.

This classic provides a thorough discussion of physical growth and motor development in language that is highly readable. Chapters on hands, visual perception, and the effects of exercise provide interesting information.

Haywood, K. M. (1986). *Life span motor development*. Champaign, IL: Human Kinetics.

This book is very readable and contains interesting material about the effects of practice on motor skills, the ease with which outstanding athletes can be identified early in life, and the extent to which body build is genetically determined.

Lewis, V. (1987). *Development and handicap*. Palo Alto, CA: Blackwell.

This book includes informative discussions of motor development often associated with certain conditions, such as Down's syndrome, spina bifida, and cerebral palsy.

chapter 14

COGNITIVE DEVELOPMENT IN SCHOOL-AGE CHILDREN

Jason and Chris were sitting at opposite ends of the dining room table with books and papers strewn around them. Chris, a second grader, had done his homework and was setting up a chess game. He was waiting for his older brother, who was in the fifth grade, to finish studying for a science test. As he carefully arranged the pawns for the third time, he said, "Are you almost done, Jason? How much longer will you be?"

"Just a few more minutes," Jason answered. "I have to go over this hard part again. It's about changing Fahrenheit temperatures into Celsius."

"Okay, but hurry up!"

"Did you check your math problems, Chris?" their mother asked as she came into the room.

"No, but I know they're all right," he replied. She began to glance over his homework. "Better check it, Chris," she said.

"Why? What's wrong?"

"Well, just go across and check them. You'll find the mistakes."

Chris took the paper and began to look it over. "Oh," he said, "here's a mistake." He found two more errors and corrected them all. By the time he'd finished, Jason was done studying. "I'll get up early and go over the definitions again," Jason said. He folded up the list he had written out and marked his place in the book with it. "Okay, Chris, let's play chess! What do you want to be, white or black?"

Children make dramatic gains in cognitive skills during the school-age years. For one thing, their thinking is more logical than the thinking of preschool children. We saw in Chapter 10 that preschoolers understand and evaluate situations largely on the basis of appearance. But by the beginning of the school-age years, children are beginning to use logic and mental operations to understand situations and to think about how things work.

For example, they begin to master the highest performance levels on some of the Piagetian conservation tasks, as shown in Figure 14-1. This means they not only realize that changing the physical appearance of something doesn't change its quantity, but they can defend their answer with one of the three explanations mentioned in Chapter 10—identity (nothing was added or taken away); compensation (the new row is longer but has big gaps, the new container is wider but not as deep); or reversibility (the new arrangement could

FIGURE 14-1
Piaget found that different types of conservation were mastered at different ages, most of them during the school-age years. Conservation is one of the hallmarks of Piaget's concrete operational stage of cognitive development.

Type of Conservation	Dimension	Change in Physical Appearance	Average Age at Which Invariance Is Grasped
Number	Number of elements in a collection	Rearranging or dislocating elements	6–7
Substance (mass) (continuous quantity)	Amount of a malleable substance (e.g., clay or liquid)	Altering shape	7–8
Length	Length of a line or object	Altering shape or configuration	7–8
Area	Amount of surface covered by a set of plane figures	Rearranging the figures	8–9
Weight	Weight of an object	Altering its shape	9–10
Volume	Volume of an object (in terms of water displacement)	Altering its shape	11–14

be put back the way it was before). The thinking of school-age children is labeled *concrete operational* in Piagetian terms, meaning that they can think logically by using specific thinking skills, as long as they can see or are familiar with what they're talking about. They still can't think in abstract terms—that ability is a hallmark of Piaget's formal operational thinking, which isn't achieved until about 12 or 13 years of age.

Metacognition is just one of the school-related topics discussed in this chapter. We also look at intelligence testing, which children usually encounter for the first time in school, and we explore the long-standing controversy over whether intelligence is something fixed at birth or something that can rise or fall with the experiences a person has in life. We also consider the issue of cultural bias in intelligence tests. Finally, we look at that all-important ingredient in any success story, achievement motivation. We consider both the factors that influence the development of motivation in children and the ways that adults can help them want to succeed. Together, these topics give a complete picture of cognitive growth during the school-age years.

METACOGNITIVE ABILITIES

Metacognition refers to the ability to think about thinking, to play with thoughts, and to monitor and deploy mental effort strategically. When a child plays chess or checkers and thinks through her moves in terms of the possible moves they open up for her opponent, she's not only thinking—she's thinking about thinking. When a child makes up a joke, or laughs at one, she's playing with thoughts. And when a child decides to study one section of a text more than others, makes a list of definitions, or reviews certain material right before the test, she's deploying mental effort strategically.

The ability to think about what someone else is thinking significantly alters the way a child relates socially to other children and adults. Now the child

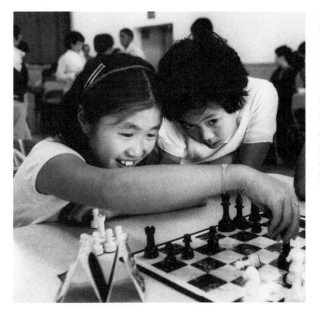

FIGURE 14-2
School-age children begin to understand chess as a strategy game because they can think about how their opponent may respond to their moves. Somewhat later, they'll be able to consider a greater number of possible responses and the implications of each response. Possibly the most brilliant chess game in the history of the game was played by Bobby Fischer at the age of 13.

can adjust her actions in terms of others. This kind of behavior, along with children's thinking about social concepts such as "justice," "friendship," and "fairness," make up the area we call **social cognition**. We consider social cognition in detail in Chapter 16, Social and Emotional Development in School-Age Children. The ability to understand jokes and riddles is a specific type of **metalinguistic awareness**, which we discuss in Chapter 15, Language Development in School-Age Children. This chapter focuses on the metacognitive abilities that allow children to monitor their own thinking and develop mental strategies to help themselves learn.

Monitoring Understanding

"Does this make sense?" "Are these instructions correct?" "Do I have all the information I need to do this assignment?" These are some of the questions a child with metacognitive monitoring ability asks while reading or listening to verbal instructions. When does this ability appear? Several studies have investigated this question.

STUDIES OF CHILDREN'S AWARENESS OF THEIR OWN UNDERSTANDING. In some of the research, children have been asked to read text materials containing inconsistencies and contradictions. In one study, two groups of children—8-year-olds and 11-year-olds—were given material to read in which some sentences didn't correspond with the titles of the passages. For example, in a paragraph entitled "A Trip to the Toy Store," they might read, "She walked down the aisle and selected some rolls of paper towels," a sentence that would make more sense in a paragraph entitled, "A Trip to the Supermarket."

Children from both age groups read more slowly when they encountered sentences that didn't seem to make sense in terms of the title of the piece. But when questioned about the material later, many more 11-year-olds than 8-year-olds talked about the problems they had detected in some of the sentences (Harris et al., 1981).

In another study, children were asked to listen to taped instructions about how to create a block building. Both kindergartners and second graders looked puzzled or replayed the tape at points where it contained insufficient information or unfamiliar words. Yet when the children were asked later about their block buildings or the instructions, which had been taped by another child, the second graders were much more likely than the kindergartners to report problems in the instructions (Flavell et al., 1981).

These and other studies show that although both younger and older children indicate by their behavior when they're having problems with understanding, only the older children can report on the inconsistencies or gaps in the instructions. Some people have suggested that younger children just might not have the verbal skills to express the problems in the messages. This isn't really a very plausible explanation because even kindergartners have a fair amount of verbal ability.

Another, more probable, explanation is that younger children lack the background knowledge and experience to know with assurance when something is wrong in their environment. They're more likely to think that they've gotten mixed up or don't understand. Older children, who are surer about what is found in toy stores and supermarkets, for example, might be more inclined to focus on the message or instructions, thinking, "Something's wrong here. What is it?" This focus puts them in a better position to pinpoint and remember a problem in the text when they're asked about it.

IMPLICATIONS OF CHILDREN'S AWARENESS OF UNDERSTANDING. Whatever the exact explanation, younger school-age children do have a harder time figuring out unclear verbal explanations or poorly written reading material, and they're particularly vulnerable to negative outcomes when confronted by them. They're less able than older children to ask clarifying questions or to use their own background knowledge and experience to "override" or correct a problem they encounter. It's essential that teachers, especially of young school-age children, communicate clearly and create a classroom environment in which children feel comfortable asking for help when they don't understand.

Teachers might also respond explicitly to pinpoint problems in the original instructions when they discover that children are confused or stumped. "Oh, I didn't want you to make a secret message with the numbered list of alphabet letters," a teacher might say. "I wanted you to use the list to find out what the mystery message at the top of your paper is. I guess when I was explaining how people could use a number code to write a secret message I didn't make clear how I wanted you to use the code today." Statements like this help all the children become more aware that when they don't understand something, the problem may be in the instructions, not in their own abilities.

Teachers should also be sensitive to the quality of their teaching materials. In one study of fourth graders' understanding of why days are longer in summer than in winter, the researchers concluded that major misunderstandings were due to the poor quality of the text. Attempts to simplify the reading level of the textbook had eliminated many "because" statements that would have made causal relationships clearer, and in many instances, the text included

FIGURE 14-3
Elementary school teachers need to be sensitive to misunderstandings that may arise from unclear instructions and gaps in children's thinking. When they establish rapport with their students, as this teacher has, they create the atmosphere for comfortable exchanges and effective communication.

irrelevant and misleading information. As a result, the children didn't learn basic science concepts from the text. In fact, they went away with misinformation and many incorrect concepts. Only the children having prior knowledge gained from books read at home or from trips to a museum were able to learn from the text (Bruce & Michaels, 1988).

Developing Mental Strategies

"How can I remember this?" "What are the important ideas here?" "What points are irrelevant?" The ability to think about information this way, as well as to direct mental effort strategically, is another aspect of metacognitive functioning. We saw that Jason, a fifth grader, had this ability—he was able to identify parts of his book that required special study strategies.

STUDIES OF CHILDREN'S MENTAL STRATEGIES. Again, younger children aren't very skillful at tasks as simple as remembering pictures from a collection they've examined. When asked to name them from memory, kindergartners say they're ready, but then they can't recall many of the items. They don't seem to organize the items into categories, make associations between the items and something else that will serve as a reminder, or go through practice runs to see if they have in fact memorized the items (Flavell, Beach, & Chinsky, 1966). Second graders, on the other hand, tend to use some of these memory strategies, although their strategies aren't as sophisticated as those of older children or adults. Of course, the more information a person has, the better able the person is to categorize it and develop associations that will help to prompt recall (Ornstein & Naus, 1978).

Younger children can be taught strategies like rehearsal, and this improves their memory considerably (Belmont & Butterfield, 1977). They can be given

FIGURE 14-4
These second graders have put together an impressive "multimedia" project about chickens, and they're justly proud of it. But if they were asked to give an oral report on their work, either spontaneously or with written cue cards, they would show a limited ability to organize their thoughts and remember the material. The more knowledge they acquire during the school years, the better context they'll have for understanding and remembering information in the future.

mnemonics (memory devices), such as "Roy G Biv" for the colors of the rainbow and "My Very Educated Mother Just Served Us Nine Pizzas" for the names of the planets. Young children show some use of strategies in familiar settings with goals that make sense to them—such as remembering where a toy has been hidden—although even here, their skills are fragile and inconsistent (DeLoache, Cassidy, & Brown, 1985).

Overall, preschool children and younger school-age children don't use memory strategies efficiently. And older school-age children don't have the skills of high school and college students. Memory isn't a separate cognitive domain apart from areas such as knowledge and concepts. The ability to remember, to store and retrieve material efficiently, is a matter of organizing the material conceptually. Thus, it makes sense that an older child, who has more knowledge and skills to use in developing a system to organize material, would be able to remember things better than a younger child, who knows and understands less.

Other metacognitive skills important to studying emerge during the later elementary school years. When asked to identify the portions of a text that were closely related to a specified theme, for example, third graders were unable to determine how relevant a passage was. Fifth graders couldn't distinguish among any of the less relevant passages (which ranged from totally irrelevant to somewhat relevant). Seventh graders could identify passages at the extremes (very relevant and very irrelevant) but couldn't make any finer distinctions. Only the twelfth graders in this study could accurately rank all portions of the text in terms of the four levels of relevance specified (Brown & Smiley, 1977).

Other study skills, such as notetaking, summarizing, and outlining, also require metacognitive abilities. Students must weed out irrelevant information, notice redundancies so they don't note the same thing twice, create categories, and use category markers such as topic sentences and headings. Fifth graders can delete irrelevant and redundant information, but they aren't very good at creating categories or using category markers provided by a text. Seventh and tenth graders are much more skillful at these activities, although poorer students, even at the college level, still have great difficulty with them (Brown & Day, 1983).

THE IMPORTANCE OF MENTAL STRATEGIES. Clearly, metacognitive abilities are crucial in many school tasks, especially once children begin to have the heavy reading assignments associated with the upper grades of elementary school and beyond. Children can't study effectively if they can't distinguish what's important and focus on it, or if they can't organize material in such a way that they can remember it. These skills develop during the school years, but there are vast differences among individuals. Even at the college level, poorer students often report, "I studied a lot and thought I knew it" after failing an exam. Teachers can support the development of metacognitive abilities during the school years by giving children material at their level, by helping them learn specific study skills such as outlining, organizing, and summarizing, and by having them try to teach some material to each other. To learn efficiently and succeed in school, students have to be aware of what they know, what it's important to know, and how to use mental strategies to sort through and master material.

INTELLIGENCE TESTS

Our discussion of metacognitive abilities highlights the importance of school for children in our society. School is the defining experience of life at this age. Going to school—learning, practicing, gaining knowledge and skills, establishing a sense of oneself in relation to other children and to adults—is what children do. And success in school is a potent factor in an individual's future success and happiness. It's no wonder that adults—both teachers and parents—are concerned about how children are doing in school, how children who are having difficulties can be helped, and how educational programs can be improved so children can learn better.

One of the ways adults discover how children are doing is by testing them. Intelligence tests are typically administered during the elementary school years to measure children's abilities to engage in different kinds of thinking. The results reflect the variation we would expect among individuals of different ages and different abilities. Subscales within tests tap different kinds of thinking and different products of thinking, such as the ability to recognize absurdities, the ability to discuss objects in terms of similarities and differences, and the ability to define words. Items are age-graded to indicate which ones are typically passed by an average child of a given age.

As mentioned in Chapter 2, the first intelligence test was developed by Alfred Binet and Theodore Simon in the early 1900s. They had been asked to

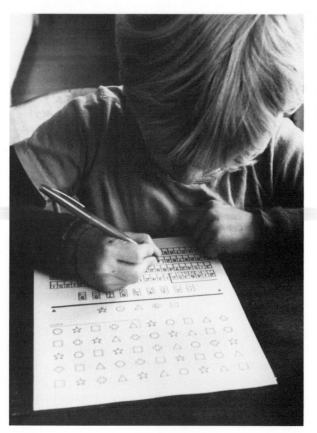

FIGURE 14-5
Many children take IQ tests, but the validity of these tests for a broad range of diverse populations is under question today. Some states prohibit the grouping of students for instruction on the basis of IQ test results.

devise a way to distinguish Parisian schoolchildren who could be expected to succeed from those who would probably fail. Binet and Simon chose tasks requiring judgment and reasoning, and they determined **norms** (typical or normal ranges) by testing a large number of children of various ages.

Binet and Simon determined a child's **mental age** (MA) by comparing the child's score to the norm for different age levels. For example, a 10-year-old who passed items typically passed by 5-year-olds was said to have a mental age of 5. The problem with using an absolute measure such as mental age is that a child of 4 with a mental age of 3 and a child of 10 with a mental age of 9 would both have an MA one year behind their age group. But these children wouldn't be equal in intelligence. A difference of one year between a child's MA and **chronological age** (CA) has a different meaning at different ages. The concept of the **intelligence quotient** (IQ) was introduced to overcome this problem (Stern, 1912). IQ is calculated according to the following formula:

$$\frac{MA}{CA} \times 100 = IQ$$

A 4-year-old who has an MA of 3 has an IQ of 75:

$$\frac{MA\,(3)}{CA\,(4)} \times 100 = 75$$

A 10-year-old who has an MA of 9 has an IQ of 90:

$$\frac{MA\,(9)}{CA\,(10)} \times 100 = 90$$

A child whose MA and CA are the same has an IQ of 100. A child whose MA is higher than his CA has an IQ over 100. Today, IQ is calculated by reference to tables of age-group norms; the ratio method isn't used any longer. As you can see from the graph showing the distribution of IQ scores in the population (Figure 14-6), most people have an IQ of about 100. Only about 3 percent of the population have IQs above 130, and an additional 3 percent have IQs below 70. (People whose IQs are lower than 70 are categorized as mentally retarded. For a discussion of this topic, see Special Education Focus— Mental Retardation.)

FIGURE 14-6
The normal statistical distribution of IQs, showing percentages of the population expected to fall in each IQ range. (Due to rounding, the total is more than 100 percent.) The largest number of people have IQs close to the average, which is 100.

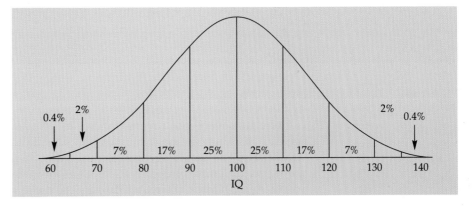

SPECIAL EDUCATION FOCUS

Mental Retardation

In 1975 Public Law 94-142, the Education for All Handi-capped Children Act, called for children with handi-capping conditions to be educated in the "least restric-tive environment," which means they should be placed with nonhandicapped children as much as possible. As a result, many children with mild and moderate mental retardation today are members of regular classrooms in public schools. The practice of placing children with disabilities in the same classroom as children without disabilities is called mainstreaming. Retarded children are taught within the classroom or out of it, as needed, for varying portions of the day. Teachers with a retarded child in their classroom have to develop a special plan to provide the best education to both the retarded child and the rest of the children in the class.

What is mental retardation? According to the Amer-ican Association on Mental Deficiency (AAMD), mental retardation is defined as "significantly subaverage gen-eral intellectual functioning resulting in or associated with impairments in adaptive behavior and manifested during the developmental period" (Grossman, 1983). Let's consider what all of this means.

"Subaverage general intellectual functioning" is defined as a score of less than 70 on one or more of the individually administered standardized tests of intelligence. "Adaptive behavior" refers to the self-help and social skills needed to get along in everyday life. Problems in adaptive behavior are harder to iden-tify than an IQ below 70, because a person is likely to function better in some environments than others. Usually, observation of the person's behavior, along with some clinical judgment made by a professional health worker, is used to identify impaired adaptive behavior. There are some standardized tests too, how-ever. One of the best known is the Vineland Adaptive Behavior Scales, which outlines the communication, daily-living, and socialization skills that should develop at given ages. For example, at ages 6 and 7, the items on the scale are "uses spoon, fork, and knife compe-tently," "initiates telephone calls to others," and "prints own first and last name" (Sparrow, Balla, Cicchetti, 1984).

"Manifested during the developmental period" means that the delays in intelligence and adaptive behavior occur before the person is 18 years old. If impairments take place after 18, the diagnosis is "dementia," an actual loss of previous intellectual abili-ties for some biological reason (American Psychiatric Association, 1987).

Degrees of Retardation

Most of us recognize and are familiar with mildly retarded people—for example, some individuals with Down's syndrome may be seen working in the com-munity. More severely retarded people, on the other hand, usually live in special homes and institutions. Four categories of retardation are recognized: mild, moderate, severe, and profound. Each category is defined by a specific IQ range (Baumeister, 1987). In **mild mental retardation,** the category with the largest number of individuals, IQ scores range from 50 to 70. Mildly retarded children often aren't recognized until they've done poorly in elementary school and have been referred for testing.

In **moderate mental retardation**, IQ scores range from 35 to 49. This group makes up about 12 percent of the retarded population. **Severe mental retardation** is defined by IQ scores ranging from 20 to 34, and indi-viduals with **profound mental retardation** have scores below 20.

When dealing with mentally retarded children in school, we encounter different labels. The special edu-cation category of **educable mentally retarded** corre-sponds roughly with mild mental retardation. In many states, the term "learning disabilities" is applied to conditions in which the difficulty seems to be in a spe-cific area of learning rather than in intelligence per se (Baumeister, 1987). The special education category **trainable mentally retarded** corresponds to moderate and severe mental retardation.

The special education terminology refers to pro-grams for the retarded, not strictly to IQ levels. Educa-ble mentally retarded children are taught fundamental academic skills they'll need to function independently as adults. Most trainable mentally retarded children, on the other hand, are considered unlikely to progress beyond the second-grade level in academics. Their curriculum emphasizes vocational, self-help, and social skills.

Causes of Retardation

What agents or conditions are responsible for these different levels of mental retardation? Sometimes, the problem is genetic or chromosomal. Down's syndrome (a disease caused by a chromosomal abnormality) is one of the most common inherited conditions that causes mental retardation. At other times, when a child is born retarded, the condition may have been caused by a disease, such as syphilis, or a drug, such

There are several controversial issues involved in testing children for intel-ligence, including the possibility of built-in cultural bias and the problem of "teaching to the test." We discuss the latter issue more fully as well as the testing instruments commonly used in schools today in Knowledge in Action: School-Age Children. Here, we discuss the more theoretical issue of "nature

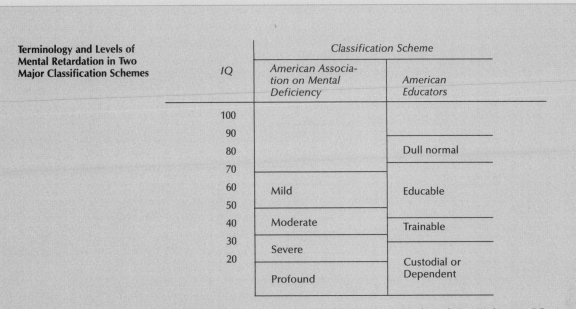

Terminology and Levels of Mental Retardation in Two Major Classification Schemes	IQ	Classification Scheme	
		American Association on Mental Deficiency	American Educators
	100		
	90		
	80		Dull normal
	70		
	60	Mild	Educable
	50		
	40	Moderate	Trainable
	30		
	20	Severe	Custodial or Dependent
		Profound	

SOURCES: Grossman, H. (Ed.). (1983). Classification in mental retardation. *Washington, DC: American Association on Mental Deficiency.*
Smith, R. (1971). An introduction to mental retardation. *New York: McGraw-Hill.*

as alcohol. Mental retardation can be caused during childhood by injury, such as a blow to the head in an auto accident, or by disease, such as meningitis or encephalitis. Children can also become mentally retarded from ingesting toxic substances like lead.

Sometimes, children are mentally retarded because they've been neglected by their parents and haven't received enough cognitive stimulation. As we've mentioned in several other contexts, mental development is correlated with parental responsiveness and involvement and with the availability of play materials in the home (Yarrow, Rubenstein, & Pederson, 1971; Ainsworth & Bell, 1973; White & Watts, 1973; Bradley, Caldwell, & Rock, 1988). A fairly high percentage of mild retardation is associated with deprived environments, which tend to occur more frequently in the homes of economically disadvantaged families. Lower socioeconomic status is also associated with greater environmental hazards, poor medical care, and malnutrition, all of which can contribute to impaired mental functioning as well (Brockman & Ricciuti, 1971; Winick, 1976).

Different environments and backgrounds can also produce different approaches to problem solving, which then can lead to different performances on intelligence tests. Children with these different approaches may score lower on IQ tests when they don't actually have any mental impairment (Baumeister, 1987; Miller-Jones, 1989). Because socioeconomic status is correlated with race, a large percentage of individuals judged to be mildly mentally retarded are from racial minorities (Grossman, 1983). It seems clear that some of these judgments may be made on the basis of *different* mental functioning rather than impaired mental functioning.

This possibility was at the heart of a California Federal District Court decision that banned the use of IQ scores as a basis for placing children in special education classes (Larry P. V. Riles, 1974). The judge declared intelligence tests to be **culturally biased**—constructed and evaluated in such a way that they reflect the specific approach to problem solving found in the dominant, white, middle-class culture. As mentioned elsewhere in this chapter, IQ tests are likely to come under fire increasingly in the 1990s as their limitations become more apparent.

versus nurture." This theoretical issue addresses the question of whether children come into the world with their intellectual abilities established or whether their intelligence is something that grows and develops, or languishes and withers, with their experiences in the world. We also address the issue of cultural bias.

Intelligence: Fixed at Birth or Influenced by Environment?

We've all heard people refer to someone's IQ as a fixed number, even if the person hasn't had an IQ test in years. Is IQ stable over long periods of time, even over a whole lifetime? Does performance on an IQ test indicate a potential for intellectual functioning that remains constant? This has been the traditional view of intelligence. According to this view, intelligence is determined primarily by genetics. A child who receives a score of 90 on an IQ test at age 7 should receive a score of 90 again at 10, regardless of whether the child's environment has changed.

Obviously, experience influences whether a child will get any single item correct on an intelligence test, since children learn new words, acquire more information, and develop more sophisticated ways of thinking as they get older. But according to the genetic view of intelligence, a child's *capacity* to learn is unchangeable. A child may pass more items at age 10 than at age 7 because she's had more experiences, but a child who inherited more intelligence would be expected to learn more from experience in those three years than a child who inherited less. Her IQ at 10 would still be the same in relation to her peers as it was when she was 7.

The genetic view of intelligence has been challenged and fiercely debated for many years. What are the contributions of nature and nurture to intelligence? Can the two ever be separated? To get some answers to these questions, many researchers have compared the IQs of people who are related to each other biologically but have been raised in different environments. Some of those studies are considered next.

STUDIES OF IQ AND KINSHIP. In one classic type of study, researchers compared identical twins who had been brought up in different environments (Newman, Freeman, & Holzinger, 1937; Shields, 1962). Since identical twins have the same genetic make-up, this kind of study was thought to reveal whether intelligence is determined more by genetic inheritance or by environmental conditions. The results have been interpreted to mean that genetic inheritance is the stronger determinant. Identical twins reared apart, for example, have been found to be closer in intelligence than fraternal twins reared together.

But these results have been challenged. Critics point out that adopted children aren't assigned to new families at random. If parents give up a twin, they usually place the baby with a relative or a family similar to their own in important ways, such as socioeconomic level. Agencies, too, try to place babies in the kind of home their biological parents would have given them. Even though they're reared apart, then, these twins might have been raised in very similar environments (Kamin, 1974; Schwartz & Schwartz, 1974). Identical twin studies may not really assess the effects of different environments and so don't resolve the original question.

A variation of this kind of study involves comparing the intelligence of adopted children to the intelligence of both their biological and their adoptive parents. In one study, babies of mothers with IQs in the 80s who were placed in good foster homes before they were 6 months old were found to have IQs of about 110 (Skodak & Skeels, 1949). The researchers claimed that the differences between the IQs of the mothers and those of the babies indicate that environment plays an important role in determining intelligence.

FIGURE 14-7
Will the mental abilities of these children be closer to those of their biological parents or their adoptive parents? Although researchers have been eager to study adopted children, the results of their studies are complicated by the presence of other factors, especially in the case of cross-cultural adoptions. Children from Southeast Asia, for example, may score lower on IQ tests than American-born children because of communication difficulties, cultural differences, or the effects of trauma on their cognitive abilities.

This study has also been criticized. For one thing, children don't inherit their parents' characteristics to the same extent that their parents have them. Instead, they differ from their parents in the direction of the mean (average) of the population. For example, if a parent has a very high IQ, the child's IQ is expected to be somewhat less high, and if the parent has a very low IQ, the child's IQ is expected to be somewhat less low. This statistical phenomenon is referred to as **regression toward the mean.** In the study just described, part of the difference in IQ between the children and their biological parents could be explained by this phenomenon, which is genetic in origin (Jensen, 1973).

Another criticism of this study is that the children were selected for adoption on the basis of their good health. In addition, there was a probationary period during which the adoptive parents could reject any child they thought was intellectually impaired. The children actually adopted may have been the ones who were most capable intellectually to begin with. Again, their higher IQs may have been a result of genetic factors rather than, or in addition to, improved environmental conditions.

Most of the kinship studies have proved inadequate in settling the nature-nurture controversy. Separating the effects of genetics from the effects of the environment has proved harder than anyone dreamed it would be when twin studies were first undertaken.

STUDIES OF CHANGED ENVIRONMENTAL CONDITIONS. Other researchers have taken a somewhat different approach to the nature-nurture question, one that involves altering children's environment intentionally to see how intelligence is affected. We saw in Chapter 5 that some research has been done in which stimulation was added to babies' environments to see if it would speed up their physical

FIGURE 14-8
Despite this sentimentalized depiction of children in an orphanage from earlier times, the reality was that such children suffered from lack of intellectual stimulation and from inadequate emotional attachment. Both conditions are associated with impaired mental functioning. The children in this "homeless little girls' dormitory" may never have achieved their fullest intellectual potential.

development. When they were given colorful objects to look at, they were found to begin reaching and grasping earlier than normal (White, 1971). Similarly, research has been done to determine if adding stimulation to the environment affects children's intelligence.

In a classic study of this kind, two young girls living in an orphanage were transferred by chance to a home for retarded children when they were about 18 months old (Skeels, 1966). There they were cared for by the older girls on the ward. The girls took great interest in the babies and showered them with attention they hadn't received at the crowded, unstimulating orphanage. After a few months, the two children, who had previously been thought to be retarded, showed amazing alertness.

As a result of this development, a research study was undertaken in which thirteen 18-month-old children were transferred from the ward to the home for retarded children. A control group remained in the orphanage. After two years, the children who had been transferred showed an average increase in IQ of about 28 points, and the children who remained behind showed a decline of about the same amount. Because the transferred children no longer showed signs of being retarded, eleven of them were adopted.

A follow-up study of the two groups was done when they had reached adulthood. All thirteen of those who had been transferred were self-supporting adults, and many held good jobs. Most had received a high school education. Those who had remained in the orphanage didn't fare nearly as well. Several were still in institutions, and those who weren't held unskilled jobs. Most had completed only a few years of school. Data from this study provide some evidence that the environment can affect intellectual functioning.

Of course, not even the strongest advocates of the genetic position deny that intelligence is affected by environmental factors. The controversy is over the relative importance of the two domains and whether their effects can be

FIGURE 14-9
Although middle-class white children as a group score higher on IQ tests than other groups, these results don't mean that other groups are less intelligent. If intelligence tests measured the cognitive skills acquired in the course of growing up in a traditional Native American community, this Navaho boy would probably score higher than his white middle-class counterparts.

separated at all. Many experts think that nature and nurture interact in complex ways to affect development and that it is almost impossible to untangle the effects of one from the other. Still, disagreement about the relative effects of nature versus nurture flourishes today, and one of the reasons for the continuing controversy is that different groups have different tested IQs, a topic we turn to text.

GROUP DIFFERENCES IN TESTED INTELLIGENCE. Different groups tend to have different IQs, and these differences are associated with race and with social class, which is defined by income, education, and occupation. Middle-class children have higher IQs as a group than poor children, and black children have IQs that average about 15 points lower than those of white children (Jensen, 1969). (Although some of Jensen's conclusions have been found highly problematic, as mentioned earlier in this book, these data have been judged to be valid.) People have asked the same question about group IQs as they have about individual IQs—are differences due to genetic inheritance or environmental factors?

Research has cast doubt on genetic explanations of group differences in IQ (Scarr & Weinberg, 1978; Weinberg, 1989). In two studies of adoption, one involving white adolescents, the other involving black children adopted into white homes, the results suggest that differences are not genetically based. Black children raised in white middle-class families have an average IQ of 110, about 15 points higher than the IQs of black children raised by their own parents. The average IQ score of both black and white adopted children (110) was higher than the average IQ of their biological parents, which was estimated on the basis of their educational level to be about 100. But adopted children didn't score as high as the biological children of adoptive parents (116.7) or as the adoptive parents themselves (119). The researchers concluded that individual differences within a group from similar environments, such as middle-class white children, may be largely genetic in origin, and that group differences are due largely to differences in environment.

CULTURAL BIAS IN INTELLIGENCE TESTS. What is it about the environment that affects how groups score on IQ tests? Since the 1960s, many people have suggested that standard intelligence tests reflect the values and interests of white middle-class culture so strongly that they contain an inherent bias against individuals from other backgrounds. The subjects covered, the experiences assumed by the questions, the format of the test, the notion of sitting down and taking a test, and the testing situation itself, all imply an approach to problem solving and a view of intelligence that aren't necessarily shared by other cultures. In fact, some people are now suggesting that there are several different kinds of intelligence and that current IQ tests measure only one of them. Gardner (1983), for example, has proposed that intelligence can be linguistic, logical-mathematical, spatial, musical, bodily-kinesthetic, or personal in nature and that different people can have varying amounts of each kind.

Differences in measured intelligence, then, can result from differences in culture. Tests standardized on one cultural group are likely to yield biased results when used with other groups. Experts believe IQ tests might not indicate children's total mental capacity or the level at which they're truly capable of functioning if they are members of minority groups (Miller-Jones, 1989). (Some attempts to design nondiscriminatory tests have been made, and we discuss these in Knowledge in Action: School-Age Children.) Since cultural diversity is increasing in the United States, intelligence testing is likely to remain a hotly debated issue in education into the 1990s.

ACHIEVEMENT MOTIVATION

"I know he can do better, and that's why I've asked you to come in," the sixth-grade teacher explained to Gregory's parents. "An F in math doesn't reflect his real ability at all. As you know, his IQ is very high. Gregory's problem is motivation."

"We're aware there's a problem," Gregory's father replied. "It's been getting worse for a few years now, since about third grade. He has a lot of interests—playing the drums, skateboarding, collecting baseball cards—but he doesn't seem to care about books or school very much. We just don't know how to motivate him to hit the books."

Conversations like this are difficult for parents and teachers alike. The complex phenomenon of motivation may be harder to define and understand than intelligence, but it's just as important to a child's ultimate success or failure in school. Gregory, for example, had a high IQ, indicating that he had the ability to get above-average grades in math. But for some reason, he wasn't directing his abilities toward the goal of mastering the mathematics required for his grade. Gregory lacked **achievement motivation**, a term used to refer to factors other than ability that influence the tasks a child engages in and the effort the child applies to the tasks.

FIGURE 14-10
Children who are motivated to learn make the teacher's job easier and the classroom more fun. These fourth graders are both interested in what's going on, although one is a little more confident at the moment. Children with low achievement motivation for schoolwork tend to spend their classroom time daydreaming or disturbing other children.

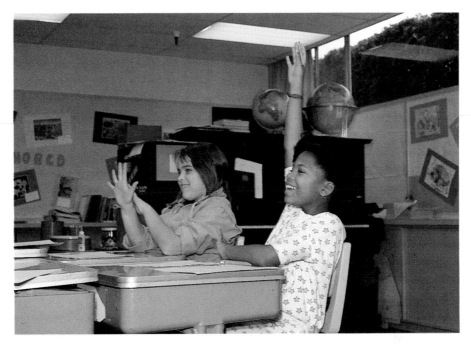

Testing Achievement Motivation

If the school counselors wanted to measure Gregory's achievement motivation directly, they would have used an assessment instrument in which the person being tested is asked to create stories about pictures. A picture might show two men, identified as "inventors," working on a machine in a shop, for example; or a young boy and a violin; or a boy sitting at a desk with an open book in front of him (McClelland et al., 1976, p. 375). The person looks at the pictures and then answers the following questions about each one (McClelland et al., 1976, p. 98):

1. What is happening? Who are the people?
2. What were the circumstances leading up to the situation in the picture?
3. What are the characters thinking? What do they want?
4. What will happen? What will be done?

Subjects are told that this is a test of creativity and that there are no right or wrong answers.

The tester judges the stories in terms of achievement goals—concern about success in competition with a standard of excellence. Subjects who refer to achievement goals frequently receive high achievement motivation ratings. Subjects who rarely refer to such goals receive low ratings.

Factors Influencing Achievement Motivation

HISTORY OF SUCCESS OR FAILURE. As you might expect, several different factors contribute to achievement motivation. One is the child's history of past achievement in the subject in question. If a child consistently has difficulty

History of success or failure

Child's schoolwork has been individualized enough to enable her to experience reasonable success.

Perception of competence and locus of control

Child believes she succeeds or fails through her own efforts.

Fear of negative judgements

Child wants to avoid poor grades, retention in same grade, low opinion of peers.

Achievement motivation

Parental values

Education is considered important at home; reading and intellectual pursuits are encouraged; and books, ideas, and discussion are valued.

FIGURE 14-11
Factors influencing achievement motivation. In the case described here, all the factors support high achievement motivation. If conditions are different—for example, if reading, schoolwork, and academic success are not especially important to a child's family—the child is less likely to be motivated to achieve in school.

understanding math, for example, and earns only mediocre grades, the child's motivation in math is likely to decrease. This is one reason why teachers need to individualize schoolwork so that all children experience success, given reasonable effort, no matter what their level of ability.

PERCEPTION OF COMPETENCE AND LOCUS OF CONTROL. Another factor in achievement motivation is the child's perception of her own competence, her subjective view of her abilities. Some children perceive themselves to be highly competent, and others with the same achievement record perceive themselves to be not as competent (Phillips, 1988). This self-perception plays an independent role in determining motivation. Some high-ability children have an "illusion of incompetence"—they think they can't do something when they actually can (Langer, 1979). Because of this, they aren't as persistent on academic tasks as they might be, and their achievement suffers.

Why do some children have this mistaken perception of themselves? One reason seems to reflect children's assumptions about what causes things to happen in the world. After an exam, for example, children can attribute their performance to (1) themselves ("I'm smart"; "I tried hard"; "I didn't study hard enough"); (2) others ("The teacher likes me"; "The teacher doesn't explain things very well"); (3) the situation ("The room is too noisy to study"); or (4) luck ("Some people do okay, other's don't. That's just the way it is"). People who think that outcomes can be attributed to their own efforts and abilities are considered to have an **internal locus of control**; that is, they locate control within themselves. People who think things happen because of factors outside of themselves are considered to have an **external locus of control**; that is, they locate control outside themselves (Rotter, 1954, 1966).

Locus of control affects how children change their expectation about themselves after a success or a failure. Children with an internal locus of control adjust their expectation of future successes and their view of their own competence on the basis of how much effort they put into a situation. If they study hard and still do poorly on a test, they're likely to conclude that they're not very good at something. If they don't study hard and do poorly, their view of their own competence isn't lowered. They might say, "I'll study harder and do better next time."

On the other hand, children with an external locus of control adjust their behavior erratically after a success or a failure. They don't make any systematic judgments about it based on how difficult the test was or how much effort they put into studying. For these children, a failure might do more to damage their sense of competence than is warranted by the situation. Children with an internal locus of control are likely to have higher achievement motivation, provided they meet with some success. Like the infants who discover they're able to make things happen in the world by their own efforts, they believe they have some control over their lives. They develop an "I can do it" attitude toward new activities and challenges.

Among the children who have an internal locus of control, however, boys and girls tend to have different attitudes toward success and failure. Boys as a group are likely to attribute success to ability and failure to lack of effort. Girls, on the other hand, tend to attribute success to effort and failure to lack of ability. As a result, girls are likely to respond to failure by decreasing their efforts and their perception of their own competence. Boys who fail believe that if they increase their efforts, they will succeed; girls think they lack the ability to succeed (Dweck, 1978).

FEAR OF NEGATIVE JUDGMENTS. With their growing social cognition, including the ability to think about what others are thinking, school-age children become more aware of themselves and of what others think of them. They usually become more concerned about failure and negative judgments by others during this time. Children may be motivated to achieve in school by their desire to avoid negative judgments by adults—such as bad grades. (If they don't care about negative judgments, they may have low achievement motivation.)

Because they're more conscious of others' opinions than they were when they were younger, school-age children can be quite vulnerable to judgments. They may work hard to receive positive feedback, but negative feedback can pose a severe threat to their perception of their own competence (Dweck & Elliot, 1983). Because of this vulnerability, some schools don't give grades during the first few years of elementary school, although they do evaluate the children and have conferences with parents.

PARENTAL VALUES. Values also play a part in achievement motivation. When parents view education as important and engage in intellectual activities at home, such as reading books, children often behave similarly, demonstrating high achievement and achievement motivation (Bradley, Caldwell, & Rock,

FIGURE 14-13
School children are quick to recognize and comment on other children's abilities, and fear of negative judgments is an important element in achievement motivation. This boy will want to do well in school if academic success is valued by his peer group, as it usually is among school children.

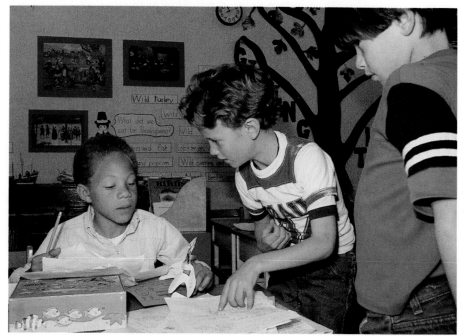

1988). When parents value other, nonacademic activities more highly, children are likely to value education and academic achievement less.

As you can see, many factors interact in complex ways to influence achievement motivation. What do adults do—and what should they do—to affect children's desire to succeed?

The Socialization of Achievement Motivation

THE ROLE OF PARENTS. We mentioned previously that children's perception of their own competence and their sense of internal or external control over success and failure were important factors in achievement motivation. Where do these assumptions come from? How do children come to have these beliefs about themselves? The answer is, they learn them during the process of socialization. Parents' beliefs about their child are a potent factor in the formation of the child's self-image, and the parents' view of the child's intellectual abilities strongly influences the child's perception of her own competence. In fact, in one study, third graders' views of their academic competence were related more to their parents' beliefs about their abilities than to their actual record of achievement in the early elementary grades (Phillips, 1987).

Apparently, different parents judge similar levels of performance differently. Some see minor errors as evidence of lower competence, and others dismiss them as relatively insignificant. Parental attitudes and behavior also influence how children view tasks. The same task may be viewed by some children as easy and by other children with the same ability as hard (Parsons, Adler, & Kaczala, 1982).

These perceptions of self and tasks can, in turn, influence children's initiative and persistence (Phillips, 1984). They can be particularly powerful when

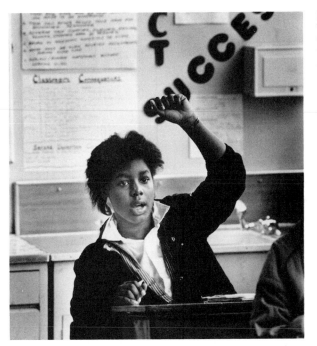

FIGURE 14-14
When families and schools tell students, especially girls, to "expect success," it can make a surprising difference in their achievement. The important confidence-building message is, "We know you can do it."

children initially meet with a little failure at a task. Children who perceive themselves to be competent and who judge tasks to be relatively easy are more likely to keep on trying when something turns out to be more difficult than they expected. Children with the opposite perceptions and beliefs may give up without really trying. Many children who persist will probably eventually succeed, and their original perceptions will be confirmed. Children who give up, in contrast, fail at the task, and their original perceptions are confirmed too. Over time, children who consistently avoid challenging tasks become less competent in reality, because they withdraw themselves from situations and experiences in which they could learn.

THE CASE OF GIRLS AND MATH ACHIEVEMENT. An important example of the difference between actual and perceived competence is in the area of mathematics achievement in girls. Girls consistently perceive their academic competence to be lower than boys' in math, even though their records of achievement in elementary school equal or surpass those of boys (Frieze et al., 1978; Dweck, Goetz, & Strauss, 1980; Dweck & Licht, 1980). Girls' perception that they're less competent than they actually are could be due to different judgments about task difficulty. They could view math as being harder than boys do, for example, which would make their expectation of success lower, despite equal ability. Or girls could be socialized differently about math, perhaps by parental beliefs that girls aren't as good at math as boys or that mathematical ability isn't as important for girls as it is for boys.

Recent research has revealed that first-grade girls don't consider their performance in math an important ingredient in determining their academic self-image, and boys do (Entwisle et al., 1988). In other words, girls don't base their developing academic self-image on math ability, even when that ability is high. Girls base their self-image on school conduct and reading achievement; boys base theirs on achievement in math and reading.

Other research has shown that mothers stress achievement in math for boys but not for girls (Baker & Entwisle, 1986), which could account for the different importance boys and girls give to it. Because first graders probably wouldn't realize that their mothers' attitudes were a result of sex-role stereotyping, girls might interpret the lower expectations for their math achievement personally. In other words, they may believe their parents think they're not competent in math. Lower perception of math ability can lead to lower achievement motivation, as explained previously, and ultimately it can lead to lower achievement

FIGURE 14-15
An interested, enthusiastic teacher conveys much more to a child than the content of a lesson. Inspirational adults, such as this craft teacher who has been working with children for 50 years, can make a lasting difference in children's lives.

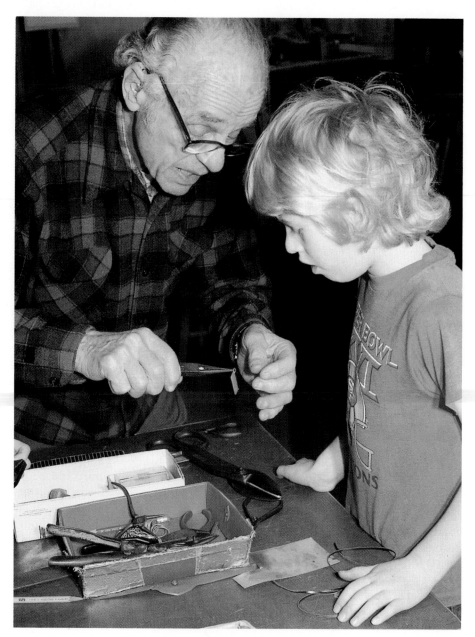

because of avoidance of situations in which they could use and practice math skills.

THE ROLE OF TEACHERS. Teachers respond to boys and girls differently too. When boys fail, teachers tend to attribute their poor performance to their lack of neatness, failure to follow directions, and other nonintellectual aspects of their work. When girls fail, teachers tend to attribute it to their intelligence or ability. One researcher found that teachers attributed boys' failure to motivation problems eight times more often than they did girls' failure (Dweck, 1978). Teachers are giving boys the message, "You can do anything, if you'll just try." They're telling girls, "Well, you can't be good in everything."

OTHER ADULT BEHAVIORS AFFECTING ACHIEVEMENT MOTIVATION. Adults contribute to children's achievement and achievement motivation in other ways as well. High-achieving children often have parents who are demanding and critical, who evaluate their performance, and who apply some pressure. They also offer praise, get emotionally involved in their children's performance, and provide facilitative help (help that makes a task easier for the child to do or understand) rather than intrusive help (help that takes away from the child's sense of accomplishment and competence) (Rosen & D'Andrade, 1975).

Parental pressure and demands are only effective, however, when the expectations are reasonable and the child perceives himself to be competent. When the child doesn't believe himself to be competent, or when parental expectations are unrealistic, or when the parent's help is dominating and intrusive, the child's achievement and achievement motivation can be low (Dweck & Elliot, 1983).

Innumerable other factors can contribute to a child's achievement and achievement motivation in school. There may be a particularly inspiring teacher one year, someone whom children admire and wish to please and imitate. On the other hand, there may be a teacher who in some way discourages children and lowers their desire to achieve. Problems or changes at home, events in the child's life outside of school, and difficulties in relationships with other children all can have an effect on the child's performance in school. When a child isn't doing well in school despite average or above-average intelligence, it may take some careful detective work to uncover the source of the problem. But given the importance of success in school, it's worth the effort of parents, teachers, and children alike to improve achievement motivation.

OVERVIEW

School is the defining experience of middle childhood; going to school is what children do. Here, in the elementary years, they gain basic skills in reading, writing, and math, and they begin to learn about science, music, art, geography, social studies, and the environment. Their new abilities to understand, remember, and acquire knowledge are a function of their steadily developing cognitive skills. Without these skills, they wouldn't be able to organize information, study for tests, or respond to the demands of the elementary school curriculum. And since success in school is such an important factor in children's lives, teachers and parents need to encourage and support their budding intellectual abilities in every way they can.

CHAPTER REVIEW

- Metacognition—the ability to think about thinking—develops during the school-age years. Children start to be able to mobilize their thoughts, target a problem, and apply these thoughts to a solution. They can play with thoughts and tell and understand jokes.
- The development of metacognitive abilites allows children to monitor their understanding of what they hear or read. Studies have shown that young school-age children show some awareness when they don't understand material, but most children can't articulate the problem until they're 10 or 11 years old.
- Because younger children are particularly vulnerable to ambiguous or unclear materials, teachers have to be sensitive to the clarity of their presentations. They can also help children feel comfortable about expressing their confusion when they don't understand instructions.
- As children mature, they develop increasingly sophisticated mental strategies that help them study. Younger children don't have the metacognitive skills to use memory efficiently. The ability to remember is related to knowledge, experience, and concepts that one can use to organize what one has read or learned.
- The emergence of metacognitive abilities makes it possible for children to develop the study skills critical to success in school, but teachers need to help by teaching these skills directly.

INTELLIGENCE TESTS

- The IQ test is used to determine a child's mental age in relation to chronological age, which in turn helps educators measure a child's intellectual abilities.
- A person is considered mentally retarded who has lower than average intellectual functioning and delayed development in the social and self-help skills needed to function in daily life. Most children with mild mental retardation (IQ between 50 and 70) aren't diagnosed until they perform poorly in school. As a result of Public Law 94–142, many children who are mildly and moderately retarded are educated in regular classrooms—a practice known as mainstreaming.
- The major controversy involved in intelligence testing is whether intelligence is determined genetically or influenced by a child's experiences and environment. Despite many studies, researchers have been unable to arrive at an irrefutable conclusion. What can be said is that heredity plays an important role in determining intelligence and environmental factors influence, both positively and negatively, what nature has given the child.
- Different groups test differently on IQ tests; experts believe these differences are due largely to differences in environment.
- Another problem with IQ tests is their cultural bias. It has been suggested that IQ tests are slanted toward the cultural framework of the white middle class and that their results with other groups are unfairly biased. As cultural diversity in the United States increases, new standards and definitions of intelligence will probably come into use.

ACHIEVEMENT MOTIVATION

- Achievement motivation is an important element in a child's success in school.
- Several factors influence achievement motivation. When children have experienced success, their achievement motivation is more likely to remain high. When they feel their successes are due to their own efforts—that is, when they have an internal rather than an external locus of control—they continue to be motivated to study and achieve. Fear of negative judgments, such as bad grades, can be a powerful motivator. Finally, parental values—the importance parents place on education, high grades, and intellectual activities like reading—are a powerful stimulus to achievement.
- The assumptions and ideas related to achievement motivation are learned during the socialization process. Children's perceptions of their own intelligence and competence are powerfully influenced by their parents ideas about them. When parents show that they believe their children to be competent and easily able to succeed at most tasks, these children tend to have higher achievement motivation.
- Young girls often believe they're not competent at math, even though their math achievement equals or sur-

passes that of boys. Parents and teachers may convey ideas and feelings to girls that contribute to their distorted perceptions.

• Children tend to be motivated to achieve when their parents have high expectations for success and apply subtle, reasonable pressure. They're motivated by other factors as well, including particularly inspiring teachers.

KEY TERMS

concrete operational thinking
metacognition
social cognition
metalinguistic awareness
norms
mental age

chronological age
intelligence quotient (IQ)
mainstreaming
mild mental retardation
moderate mental retardation
severe mental retardation

profound mental retardation
educable mentally retarded
trainable mentally retarded

cultural bias
regression toward the mean
achievement motivation
internal locus of control
external locus of control

SUGGESTIONS FOR FURTHER READING

Brody, E. B., & Brody, N. (Eds.). (1976). *Intelligence: Nature, determinants, and consequences.* New York: Academic Press.

This book includes a thorough discussion of the Arthur Jensen issue. It also provides considerable historical context pertaining to IQ testing.

Gardner, H. (1983). *Frames of mind: The theory of multiple intelligence.* New York: Basic Books.

In this book, Gardner makes the case for different kinds of intelligences and for different distributions of these among individuals. Provides an intriguing view of intelligence written by a recipient of one of the McArthur Foundation "genius" awards.

Gloeckler, T., & Simpson, C. (1988). *Exceptional students in regular classrooms.* Mountain View, CA: Mayfield.

A practical text and resource guide to the basic competencies a teacher in the regular classroom requires for instructing students with basic needs.

Sigel, I. E. (1985). *Parental belief systems.* Hillsdale, NJ: Erlbaum.

This book contains several interesting chapters on the relationship between different parental beliefs and children's behavior.

Sternberg, R. J. (1985). *Beyond IQ: A triarchic theory of human intelligence.* New York: Cambridge University Press.

This book makes a major contribution to the continuing discussion about the nature of IQ.

chapter 15

LANGUAGE DEVELOPMENT IN SCHOOL-AGE CHILDREN

"Dad, what does 'ano-,' 'ano-,' let's see . . .'ano-NY-mous' mean?" called 9-year-old Alex from his room.

"How do you spell it?" his dad responded.

"A-n-o-n-y-m-o-u-s," he answered.

"Anonymous. It means without a name, someone whose name you don't know."

A few minutes later, Alex called out again, "Dad, what does 'cat-a-clysm' mean?"

"A disaster."

"Dad, what about 'in-gen-i-ous'?"

"Here, I'll help you find it in the dictionary."

Alex's dad had made his way to Alex's room with dictionary in hand. As they flipped through pages together to find the "I" section, Alex's dad asked, "What are you reading, anyway?"

"Oh, it's The Voyages of Doctor Doolittle, *by Hugh Lofting. I got it out of the library. It's got a lot of big words in it. I used to skip over words I didn't know, but I'm starting to want to know what they all mean."*

Within just a few years, Alex has progressed from a beginning reader to quite an accomplished one. When he first started reading, he sounded out words and recognized them once he said them out loud. Now he chooses more difficult books, so he often comes across words he doesn't know or hasn't heard pronounced. This is one way he increases his vocabulary.

Alex is even more skilled at oral language than he is at reading. He understands and uses many more words than he did a few years ago, and he speaks in longer sentences. Although he hasn't yet mastered every aspect of oral language, he does have the language to formulate and express fairly complicated ideas about the important things in his life. He can also think about and

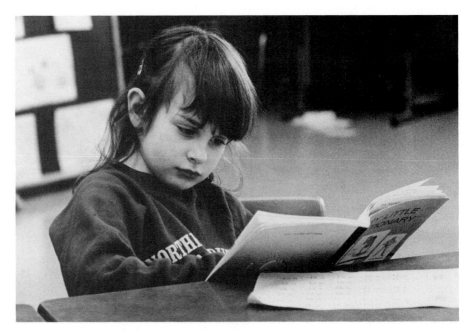

manipulate language in ways that were previously impossible for him. With this ability, he understands and tells jokes and riddles, one of the language hallmarks of the school-age years.

In this chapter, we describe the advances school-age children make in oral language—using and understanding speech—and in written language—reading and writing. We also discuss some other aspects of language development, such as how children learn a second language and how they learn to read. Looking at writing development, we pay special attention to children's early spelling strategies; we complete our discussion of language development by considering the development of "visual literacy"—children's ability to understand the meanings conveyed in film.

ORAL LANGUAGE

Most school-age children speak their language with apparent ease and fluidity, and they delight in the twists of language that make jokes funny. Despite their basic oral competence, however, children this age still have a thing or two to master. For example, they're confused by some complex sentence constructions. In this section, we turn first to a discussion of these typical stumbling blocks and then take a closer look at jokes and riddles.

Understanding Syntax

We saw in chapter 11 that preschool children are confused about some words (like "promise") because they assume they're used the same way as other words (like "tell"). In a similar way, school-age children are confused by certain seemingly parallel usages. The critical study of this problem was done by Carol Chomsky (1969). She seated children at a table with a blindfolded doll and asked them, "Is this doll easy to see or hard to see?" If the child answered that the doll was hard to see, Chomsky asked the child to make her easy to see. If the child answered that the doll was easy to see, Chomsky asked the child to make the doll hard to see. Children who answered that the doll was hard to see thought they were being asked if it was hard or easy for *the doll* to see, not if it was hard for *them* to see the doll.

Consider the responses of Lisa, aged 6 years, 5 months (Chomsky, 1969, p. 30):

> Is this doll easy to see or hard to see?
> Hard to see.
> Will you make her easy to see?
> If I can get this untied.
> Will you explain why she was hard to see?
> (To doll) Because you had a blindfold over your eyes.
> And what did you do?
> I took it off.

Children who understood the question, on the other hand, responded like Ann, aged 8 years, 7 months (Chomsky, 1969, p. 31):

> This is Chatty Cathy. Is she easy to see or hard to see?
> Easy.
> Would you make her hard to see?
> So you can't see her at all?
> OK.
> (Places doll under table.)
> Tell what you did.
> I put her under the table.

Lisa's confusion in the earlier example apparently resulted from her attempt to use the same strategy she might use with a sentence like "John is eager to see." In this sentence, it's John who will do the seeing.

FIGURE 15-2
Many school-age children still don't understand certain English language usages that adults take for granted. In Carol Chomsky's experiment, a $6\frac{1}{2}$-year-old responded to the request to "make the doll easy to see" by removing the doll's blindfold.

School-age children also confuse the words "ask" and "tell." Consider the example of Samuel, aged 8 years, 5 months (Chomsky, 1969, p. 57):

> Ask Ellen what to feed the doll.
> Feed her hamburgers.
> All right now, tell Ellen what to feed her.
> Again?
> M-hm.
> Tomato.
> Now I want you to ask Ellen something. I want you to ask her what to feed the doll.
> Feed her this thing, whatever it's called.
> All right. Now listen very carefully, because I don't want you to tell her anything this time. I want you to ask her what to feed the doll. Can you do that?
> Let's see, I don't get it.
> OK, just go ahead, and ask her what to feed the doll.
> Feed her eggs.

Samuel interpreted "tell" correctly, but he interpreted "ask" the same way. In Chomsky's examples, even 9- and 10-year-olds were confused by the words "ask" and "tell."

Part of younger children's problem with these constructions is that they still may be relying heavily on context to understand language. They tend to ignore syntax and respond in terms of pragmatic considerations instead—that is, in terms of whether their responses make sense in the situation (Warden, 1986). Sometimes their responses to "ask" and "tell" requests depend on whether they themselves know the answer to the question (Tanz, 1983). If they know the answer, they tend to "tell" rather than "ask." If they don't know the answer, they're more likely to "ask" than to "tell." Sometimes 5- and 6-year-olds seem to understand how these words are used and sometimes they don't, depending on whether they know the answer or not.

Jokes and Riddles

Anyone planning to spend time with school-age children should be prepared to listen to endless jokes and riddles. What is it about middle childhood that makes these language games so popular?

Jokes and riddles are based on ambiguity in the way words are used. It can be ambiguity about how words are pronounced (referred to as **phonologically based ambiguity**), about what words mean (**lexically based ambiguity**), or about how sentences are interpreted (**syntactically based ambiguity**). A child who can't yet think about language at these various levels and who can't make the sophisticated mental comparisons characteristic of Piaget's concrete operational stage won't be able to understand jokes and riddles (McGhee, 1971, 1979).

The ability to pay attention to the form of the language—to the structures used to convey meaning—instead of to the meaning itself is called *metalinguistic awareness.* (We saw in Chapter 14 that the prefix *meta* means "above" or "beyond," so *metalinguistic* literally means, "above language.") Children who can tell jokes and riddles have this awareness. They play games with the form of language, trying to get the listener headed down one meaning track instead of another. The punchline reveals the trick meaning:

"Why did the farmer name his hog Ink?"
"Because he kept running out of the pen."

This joke is based on lexically based ambiguity: The word *pen* can mean either a writing tool or an enclosed area for animals. Children who tell jokes like this understand that words can have more than one meaning. They exploit this knowledge about language to trick the listener.

The following joke uses phonologically based ambiguity—ambiguity about the sound and pronunciation of words:

"Knock knock."
"Who's there?"
"Duane."
"Duane who?"
"Duane the tub . . . I'm dwowning."

Knock-knock jokes are structured to make the listener expect that a person — in this case, "Duane"—is knocking on the door. But "Duane" is a phonological distortion of "drain." The distortion is deliberate, of course, to create an ambiguous situation. In the punchline, the listener finds out that "Duane" actually should have been interpreted as "drain."

In the next joke, it's the structure of the sentence itself—the syntax—that the child exploits:

"Do you know how long cows should be milked?"
"How long?"
"As long as short ones, of course."

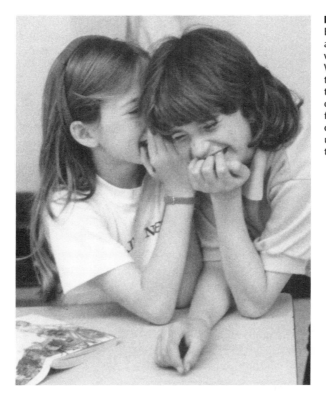

FIGURE 15-3
By third grade, children appreciate puns, plays on words, riddles, and jokes. Word play not only tickles their imagination but gives them a way to handle disconcerting thoughts and feelings—which is why off-color jokes have such an undying popularity among this age group.

In the first question, the word *long* can be interpreted as an adjective modifying cows or as an adverb indicating how long the cows are to be milked. The sentence is ambiguous syntactically, although common sense suggests that we should interpret "long" as an adverb. (The length of a cow is probably not an issue in milking.) The listener interprets "long" as an adverb, only to find out that it's being used as an adjective.

A young child who doesn't understand the two possible "deep" structures of the first sentence is likely to respond to the punchline with, "But how long or short a cow is doesn't matter." A child who *does* understand the ambiguity of the sentence's syntax might say, "Oh, that's funny. I thought you meant how long the cows should be milked, not how the long cows should be milked." The truth value, or meaning, is put aside in appreciation of how language can be manipulated to play tricks and amuse.

Children's ability to understand the different levels of ambiguity emerges at different times. Children start to understand phonological ambiguity first ("duane the tub"), at age 6 or 7. They understand lexical ambiguity next ("pen"), with appreciation increasing for several years as more and more words are learned. They grasp syntactic ambiguity last, usually not until about 11 or 12 years of age (Shultz & Pilon, 1973). This makes sense when we realize that children don't fully understand complex syntactic structures until the age of 9 or 10.

Not understanding ambiguity doesn't prevent younger children from trying to tell jokes, however. Preschoolers master the sentence form of jokes but not their content. Here's an attempt at joke telling by a 5-year-old:

> "Why did the radiator leave the room?"
> "I don't know. Why did the radiator leave the room?"
> "Because he was tired of sitting in it!" (followed by
> much laughter on the part of the joke teller)

No ambiguity is created in this joke, and none is resolved in the punchline. The child knows that when you tell a joke you ask a question, wait for a response (usually, "I don't know"), and then tell the punchline (make an explanatory statement). This kind of practice with the sentence structure and turn-taking aspects of joke telling is very common among older 4-year-olds and 5-year-olds. By the time they get to elementary school, they know how to structure and present jokes to other people. What they still have to figure out during the school-age years is exactly what makes jokes funny.

Learning a Second Language

If you visited a school in almost any large American city, you would find children whose native tongue is a language other than English. And you would find a tremendous variety of native tongues—Spanish, Chinese, Vietnamese, Tagalog, and many others. The population of American public schools is changing once again, as it's changed in the past. And once again, children are being asked to learn English to succeed in the American educational system and, presumably, in the mainstream of American life. How are all these children taught English?

FIGURE 15-4
Because the United States is experiencing a tremendous wave of immigration, mainly from countries in Asia and Latin America, there are currently many non-English-speaking students in American schools. Educators are divided on whether the immersion method or the bilingual approach is the more effective way to teach English to these students. Like other new arrivals, this Chinese boy has to figure out what his teacher explains to him in English as well as what his classmates say to him in various American dialects.

TWO APPROACHES TO TEACHING A SECOND LANGUAGE. There are two main approaches to teaching children English (or any second language) in school. In one method, called Teaching English as a Second Language (TESL), children are taught in English-only classrooms. This approach is known as **immersion** in the new language. The school usually doesn't provide instruction in any subjects in languages other than English. TESL programs are often found in schools with multilingual populations, perhaps eight or ten different first languages. In most cases, it wouldn't be practical or even possible to teach in all those languages.

The second approach is to establish a bilingual program. Children are given instruction in the new language, but they're taught classroom subjects (math, reading, social studies, and so on) in their native language until they become proficient in the second language. These "transition" bilingual programs prepare children to enter classrooms where only the second language is used. Bilingual programs recognize that it's difficult for children to learn a subject when they don't understand the language in which it's taught. This approach helps prevent those children from falling behind while they're learning the new language.

As you might expect, there's controversy over which is the better approach to teaching English in American schools. Some people think that having the native language available makes it harder for children to learn English—they have less need and motivation to become proficient in it. These people also point to schools as the avenue by which millions of immigrants learned English in the past and became assimilated into American life. They think immersion programs like TESL are the best methods of teaching a second language.

Others think that children should be able to maintain their native language (and culture) on an equal level with their new language, and they favor the bilingual approach. They think a bilingual or multilingual culture offers greater variety and depth to a society, prevents cultural arrogance, and helps children from diverse backgrounds maintain their cultural integrity and self-esteem. Proponents of this view think there should be more than one "official" language in the United States.

These differences of opinion are likely to increase in the years ahead as the make-up of the American people continues to change and as schools come to serve an increasing number of non–English-speaking children. But aside from the political and cultural aspects of this debate, what are the educational merits of the different approaches to teaching a second language? How do people actually learn a second language?

HOW IS A SECOND LANGUAGE ACQUIRED? We know that children learn new languages very readily, but it's not obvious how they do it. Three theories have been proposed to account for the process of learning a new language (McNamara, 1976, p. 46):

1. The child acquires the second language in exactly the same way an infant acquires it as a first language. In other words, learning a second language is **identical in process** as learning the same language as a first language.
2. The child uses the structures from her first language to form structures in the second language. This process assumes that there is **interference** between the first and second languages, since different languages have different ways of saying things (different grammars).
3. The child formulates **unique grammatical structures**, using neither the structures of her first language nor the typical developmental structures of the new language.

To study the acquisition of a second language, a researcher has to find people who have mastered a first language and are beginning to learn a second. The researcher also has to be familiar with the syntax of both languages and understand the typical sequence of development that children go through in learning each language as a first language. For example, if you recall from Chapter 11, English-speaking children's first questions ("Where it is?") and negative statements ("No go out") are constructed differently from those of older speakers. These first utterances undergo several predictable changes before the standard patterns appear.

The researcher compares the developmental patterns of the person learning the second language with the typical developmental patterns of native speakers of each of the two languages. Let's say, for the sake of discussion, that the speaker's native language is French and the language being acquired is English. If the patterns match those of a child learning English as a first language, the evidence supports the identical process model. If the patterns match patterns and structures in French, then the evidence supports the interference model.

Most research has supported the identical process model of second language learning. For example, in one study, two Norwegian children learning English as a second language formed questions with "Wh" words the same way children learning English as a first language do, even though this wasn't how they formed questions in their native Norwegian (Raven, 1974). They said, "What she is doing?" just as English-speaking toddlers do, rather than "What is she doing?"

Even when children have mastered a language whose structure could be applied to English, they don't use what they already know. This is also true when children's first language doesn't resemble English—they don't apply the structures of their own language but pass through the same stages as a child learning English as a first language. Not until children are age 10 or 12 and have well-developed metalinguistic and cognitive abilities do they begin to apply the structures of their native language when learning a second language.

THE SOCIAL CONTEXT OF SECOND LANGUAGE LEARNING. Evidence from studies of second language learning indicates that the immersion approach is the preferable one. It appears that people learn a second language most quickly when they spend a lot of time communicating with native speakers in a natural way. One implication of this finding is that children learning a new language should get involved with children who know the language. This, of course, is easier said than done. Not knowing the language can create barriers for children in play situations, but these barriers are not insurmountable. One researcher asked children who were learning a new language how they managed to "count themselves in" (Fillmore, 1976, cited in McLaughlin, 1978, pp. 108–110). Following are some of their strategies:

- Join a group and act as if you understand what's going on, even if you don't. (a social strategy)

FIGURE 15-5
When interest is high, language differences don't stand in children's way. In fact, some children don't even realize that a new playmate doesn't speak the same language they do. The easiest way to learn a new language is by using it everyday in comfortable interactions with native speakers.

- Assume that people's statements are directly relevant to the situation at hand or to what they or you are experiencing. Metastrategy: Guess! (a cognitive strategy)
- Give the impression—with a few well-chosen words—that you can speak the language (For example, say "Look" or "Wait a minute"). (a social strategy)
- Give the impression that you understand, and start talking. (a cognitive strategy)
- Look for recurring structures in the formulas you know. (a cognitive strategy)
- Work on the big things first, save the details for later (a cognitive strategy)

The process these children described is remarkably similar to the one children go through when they learn a first language. They use situations to figure out meanings, and then they use meanings to figure out the language. People who speak the language—friends in the case of children learning a second language, parents in the case of infants acquiring a first language—help them by trying to understand what they're saying. The skilled speakers also simplify their own statements and use gestures and facial expressions to communicate their meanings.

OTHER FACTORS AFFECTING THE ACQUISITION OF A SECOND LANGUAGE. The immersion method works well in natural situations, and it also works in some classroom situations. The method has been successful in Canadian schools, for example, when English-speaking students are placed in French-speaking classrooms. The native English speakers are able to keep up with their schoolwork while learning the second language (Lambert, Just, & Segalowitz, 1970). But in American classrooms, non–English-speaking children often don't do very well if they're not given help in learning English (Pflaum, 1986).

Why the different outcomes in these two situations? There are several possible reasons. First, the children in the French immersion programs were middle-class children who had good adult models of bilingualism, enriched preschool backgrounds, and parents who wanted them to learn French. Their native language, English, was not considered less prestigious in Canadian society than the language they were learning. In other words, their acquisition of a second language was strongly supported in many other areas of their lives.

In contrast, many of the non–English-speaking children in American schools come from lower socioeconomic-status families who haven't been able to provide preschool experiences. These children's lower achievement could be caused as much by their lack of early school-like experiences as by their language-immersion experience. Furthermore, in the United States, many people find that their native tongue is considered less prestigious than English. Being forced to learn a new language that's considered superior to their own can involve an assault on children's self-esteem, which, in turn, can lower learning ability in general. Finally, non–English-speaking children in the United States often have few adult bilingual models to copy or look up to for encouragement or inspiration (Pflaum, 1986).

The solutions to some of these problems obviously go beyond the choice of a method for teaching English in schools. Some combination of immersion and bilingual methods may be the best approach to helping non–English-speaking children get their bearings in American classrooms. But the best support for learning English as a second language would be provided by larger changes in American society, such as improvements in the economic well-being of more segments of society and greater acceptance of the value of other cultures.

American Dialects

Children whose first language isn't English aren't the only ones who have trouble understanding and making themselves understood in American class-rooms. Different dialects of English are spoken by children as well. **Dialects** are variations within a language. They may be different in pronunciation, in syntax, or in the meaning given to some words. Everyone speaks a dialect, of course—the majority dialect is just one of several variations within a language.

The most common—or the most recognized—dialect in the United States is one associated with ethnicity (as opposed to geographical region or some other distinguishing factor). It's known as Black English, but it's not, of course, spoken by everyone who is black. The grammar of Black English and standard English are quite similar—they're forms of the same language, after all—but there are some differences. In Black English, for example, the verbs *come* and *say* aren't always marked for past tense. A person might use, "He say," rather than, "He said." Auxiliary verbs may also be dropped, resulting in, "What you mean?" rather than "What do you mean?" And "s" may be left off pos-sessives, resulting in sentences like, "This is Susan sweater."

There are also phonological (pronunciation) differences between standard English and various dialects, and these can make it hard for teachers to under-stand children's speech. In addition, some spelling errors can result from these pronunciation differences (Kligman & Cronnell, 1974). For example, if a child says "nuffin" instead of "nothing," she's not likely to include a "g" at the end of the word. A child who says "pack" instead of "park" will probably spell it "pak." A child who pronounces "idea" as "idear" is likely to spell it with an "r" at the end. These are just a few examples of the many dialect-related pronunciation differences that can affect children's spelling (Goodman et al., 1987). Of course, many words in English aren't spelled the way they sound anyway, which makes all children prone to spelling errors when they first learn to write, as we see in the next section.

Some of the same social and political issues involved in the teaching of English as a second language apply to the teaching of the standard English dialect to children who speak other dialects, particularly Black English. Both Black English and standard English are legitimate languages with their own rules and complexities. As a language, one is neither better nor worse than the other. But different dialects do have different social currency. Standard English is the accepted language of schools, businesses, and government in the United States. Children who know standard English will have more choices and options than childen who don't know it. If children can acquire standard English in a way that doesn't threaten their positive feelings about their own dialect, it's to their advantage to do so. This issue, like the teaching of English as a second language, is likely to remain controversial for some years to come.

WRITTEN LANGUAGE: LITERACY DEVELOPMENT

In first grade, Will kept a "story journal." This was a book in which he could write stories and draw pictures to illustrate them, or draw pictures to illustrate stories the teacher told the class. Will often asked his teacher to spell words for him because he didn't know how to write them. Sometimes she wrote down in his book what he said. Other times she pronounced the words slowly, emphasizing the sounds within them, and helped Will think about which letters might be used to code them. Often, these two approaches showed up in the same writing sample. Following are some of the entries from his journal:

November 14. Tatterhood. This is the castle room where the big Christmas tree is and this is one of the trolls.

January 9. Sno Wit and Ros Rd (Snow White and Rose Red). This is the hows in sprigtim (This is the house in springtime). The first vines from the red rose are starting to bloom.

March 4. The Emperor's New Clothes. This is the emperor sitting in his bedroom. And this is the prim ministr looking at the cloth that the crooks are not reale makeng (And this is the prime minister looking at the cloth that the crooks are not really making).

In second grade, Will kept another journal. This one was a log of personal entries—a kind of diary. By now, Will had had a lot of experience sounding out words, although he knew this didn't always produce correct spellings. He also had learned to read in first grade, and his interest in reading for fun gave him the opportunity to see how many words are spelled.

FIGURE 15-6
Keeping a journal of stories and pictures is an appropriate literacy activity for first graders. These girls are gaining important reading and writing skills and solidifying their understanding of the connection between oral and written language.

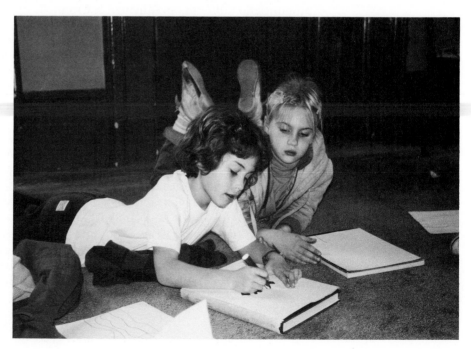

But Will didn't really worry about spelling, because he knew he could correct it later if he wanted to publish something for the class library. He just wanted to get his thoughts down. His journal was for himself and no one else, unless he wanted to show it to someone. The following are some entries he was willing to share:

October 3. Tomareoe I em going to Morgan's huos. After I go to Morgan's huos then the nex day Ryan will cyom ovr. I kant wat.

December 15. Last Toosdy my tooth fell owt. I got a korter fore it. Yestrdy we wedt ies skating. I liek ies skating.

March 26. I got a crikit. It is a fymale. I hop it has babies.

March 29. Yestrday my criket askapt. It was in the bathroom right wen I cam in. I coght it wen I saw it. I em glad it was in the bathroom at the same time I was.

It looked like Will's writing had deteriorated from his first-grade level, but that was because he was more on his own now. His phonetic spelling is a good reminder of how many unusual spellings there are in English. By third grade, Will's spelling had improved a bit:

September 15. The day before scool started I came back from High Lake. It is a tarifck plaes to go on vacation. I plaed pewe golf. I colekted rocks. I plaed shufllboard. I liked it alott.

October 25. Fore Halloween I am going to be a ninja. Marcus is going trick or treting with me. I cant wate.

April 20. I had a grate Eastre! I woke up and saw a big Eastre basket. I had a milk chocklat bunny, a chickin filled with marshmelo and other candy.

By fourth grade, Will's spelling was becoming much more standard, and his ideas about writing had changed quite a lot too:

November 5. It was Thursday September 17, 3987. The battle raged on. "We got some reinforcements, but still it looks bad" (said Capitan Feragon). "Boss, they are launching an attack on the base." "I wonder why the aliens want to fight. I sent a squad of 5 to get some energy." They were having better luck than we were . . .

May 23. I was walking down the path to my secret club, then I tripped on a big rock. I was so mad I kicked it 2 feet away from me and under it fownd a tresure map and a golden medaliun. I ran home. When I got there I was almost completely out of breth. I ran upstairs like who knows what! I quickly unrolled the map and looked for a name on the map. The name was Sir Fransis Fake. "What a name!" I said . . .

By now, Will had learned many words from all the literacy activities he engaged in both in and out of school. Although quite a few spellings still eluded him, his continuing exposure to books and other written material in the years ahead would help him master the intricacies of written English.

Reading and writing are intimately connected. The improvement in Will's writing from first to fourth grade is due in large part to the reading he's done. The books and stories his parents and teachers read to him also gave him important literacy experiences. Reading is considered the most critical skill children acquire in the early school years.

As you might expect with anything considered so important, there is debate over the best way to teach reading. In this section, we discuss some of the thinking on reading instruction, summing up what is currently known about this topic. We then discuss the development of writing, with special attention to children's unusual spelling strategies.

Learning to Read

Learning to read is a complex process, one that involves the integrated use of many different skills. In Chapter 11, we discussed some of the preliminary components of reading that are often acquired by preschoolers. These included the understanding that reading involves getting meaning from print, the knowledge that letters of the alphabet represent phonemes (single speech sounds), and the ability to recognize letters of the alphabet. Many children, but not all of them, bring these understandings to their first-grade reading instruction. How do they get from this level of emergent literacy to a level we would call "beginning reader"? How do they learn to read?

TWO APPROACHES TO TEACHING READING. Some teachers typically teach reading using a **skills approach**. They focus on teaching "word attack" skills that children can use to "get to meaning." Once children can sound out or recognize printed words, they're able to read and understand the text. Other teachers use a **whole language approach** to teaching reading. They focus on the meaning of a text and rely on children's thinking ability to abstract and arrive at word attack skills.

FIGURE 15-7
Hearing a story read in a listening/reading corner is a whole language activity that gives children the chance to associate spoken language with print. This first grader's reading skills will improve as he follows along with the text in a book.

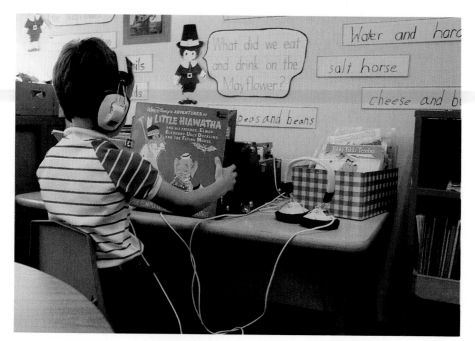

Before the whole language view became popular in recent years, the "great debate" about teaching reading in American schools centered on two different skills approaches. One, called the **phonics approach**, is a synthetic (meaning "building" or "putting together") approach that emphasizes knowledge of letter-sound correspondences. Children start with letters and combine them to build words. The second, called the **"look-say" approach**, is an analytic approach that starts with whole words and expects that children will eventually begin to think about them in terms of their parts—letters and sounds.

THE BASIS OF THE WHOLE LANGUAGE APPROACH. The difference between both of the skills approaches and the whole language approach is that the whole language approach emphasizes language at a level higher than that of individual words. It also focuses on cueing systems other than the visual-graphic (letter-sound knowledge). According to this view, children use three cueing systems when they read. For one, they predict the parts of speech—nouns, verbs, and so—that are likely to come next on the basis of their knowledge of oral language. Only certain kinds of words will fit grammatically at various points in a sentence. These cues about syntax are known as **syntactic cues**. For another, they predict words that will make sense in the context of what they're reading. They will realize that a man flew off in a plane, for example, not in a plant. Cues about context are known as **semantic cues**.

Finally, readers use visual-graphic information—letter-sound correspondences—but not as the only, or even the most important, source of cues about the passage they're reading. This is why advocates of the whole language approach believe that word attack and word recognition skills should not be the only or the primary focus in beginning reading programs (Newman, 1985).

In this view, skills won't get readers very far if they don't have an extensive oral vocabulary and if they don't make predictions about the sense of the passage. Emphasizing isolated skills (such as letter names or sight words learned from drills, lists, and workbooks) can even lead children to develop misconceptions about reading. They might think reading is a matter of "word calling" or "sounding out" without checking whether the word makes sense. Children who read this way can't possibly understand what they read. They won't even be able to sound out a lot of words, since letter-sound correspondence isn't very uniform in English (as we saw in Will's journal). It's only with the help of context and a good oral vocabulary that children learn to read such words as "laugh," "knee," "water," or "cow" (Goodman & Goodman, 1977; Smith, 1983; Newman, 1985).

EVIDENCE FOR THE SUPERIORITY OF A COMPREHENSIVE APPROACH. Although the word attack approach to reading has its merits, it tends to focus too narrowly on isolated decoding skills. The whole language approach, incorporating phonics skills, is a more comprehensive way to teach reading in elementary school. It's also the favored approach to helping children with severe reading problems (see Research Focus—Dyslexia: When Children Can't Read). The debate over the best way to teach reading is likely to continue, but at this point, we can make the following assertions with reasonable certainty:

1. Children whose parents read them storybooks during the preschool years do well at reading when they get to school. Parental storybook reading—a

RESEARCH FOCUS

Dyslexia: When Children Can't Read

"I thought I must have been absent the day the other kids learned how to read."

So spoke a child whose inability to read caused him embarrassment and confusion before he was finally diagnosed as dyslexic. His reaction is typical of children (and adults) who have trouble doing what they see others doing so easily—getting meaning from print. Although they appear normal in every other way, these people are unable to learn to read (or have extreme difficulty learning to read). *Dyslexia* is a generic term that simply refers to this difficulty in individuals who don't have any other condition (such as mental retardation) that would account for the problem. Dyslexia is not uncommon, but it's difficult to say exactly how many children suffer from it because poor reading can be caused by so many other factors.

WHAT CAUSES DYSLEXIA?

Over the years, many hypotheses have been proposed to explain dyslexia. Neuropsychiatrist Samuel Torry Orton suggested that it was caused by vision problems. He had noticed that dyslexics often see letters and words as their mirror images—for example, "b" for "d" or "was" for "saw." He also observed that dyslexics often reversed letters and words in their writing. (As you recall, letter reversals are normal in children's writing during the emergent literacy stage.) Other experts identified visual-motor or motor problems as the cause of dyslexia (Metzger & Werner, 1984; Regcher & Kaplan, 1988). They hypothesized that improper visual tracking or scanning or some other visual problems were the culprits.

Current research is pointing not to visual deficits but to language processing as the primary problem in dyslexia. Researchers have found that children with dyslexia often have trouble segmenting words phonemically, discriminating among words, and remembering words on the basis of their phonological (sound) characteristics. These children have much more difficulty using letter sounds to decode words than normal readers do. They also have more difficulty distinguishing between grammatical and ungrammatical sentences, understanding sentences read to them, and naming letters, words, and colors (Vellutino, 1987).

HOW CAN DYSLEXICS BE HELPED?

In the past, many remedial treatments were based on the visual-motor theories of dyslexia and involved visual and perceptual training techniques (Metzger & Werner, 1984). Not surprisingly, given current research, these early techniques were not very successful.

Today, the focus is much more on direct tutoring of reading skills. Even though dyslexics are particularly weak in phonics, experts don't recommend stressing this area alone (Vellutino, 1987). Instead, they recommend that remedial reading programs take a holistic approach and emphasize all the cueing systems used in reading—syntactic, semantic, and visual-graphic. As we've seen, learning to read involves much more than just knowing letter-sound correspondences and being able to segment words phonemically. It also involves developing vocabulary, learning words in meaningful contexts, becoming familiar with print conventions, having access to writing materials, and so on. Dyslexic children need plentiful opportunities both to develop oral language skills and to learn more specific reading skills. With direct tutoring and extra effort, they *can* learn to read.

whole language activity—is the best predictor of reading achievement in elementary school, perhaps because it contributes so much to language and vocabulary development (Hayes & Ahrens, 1988; Whitehurst et al., 1988).

2. Children who know the names of letters in kindergarten have a high level of reading achievement in first grade. But teaching the names of letters through drills doesn't increase children's reading skill. Apparently, the letter name knowledge observed during kindergarten in children who later achieve well in first grade correlates with other knowledge necessary for reading acquisition but doesn't by itself lead to high achievement in reading.

3. It's possible for children to learn the names of letters in context. For example, when children see print in books, ask about words on traffic signs or in stores, and try to write their names on pictures, adults can name letters and also make explicit how they function to represent sounds in words: "That says 'ssstttooppp,' s-t-o-p."

4. Good readers almost always have good phonics skills, but this doesn't mean that good phonics skills came first. Children learn a lot of phonics from

FIGURE 15-8
By giving a cooking lesson in her daughter's classroom, this Hispanic woman is providing the children with opportunities to learn word meanings in context. In this case, teaching may be working both ways—she may be learning some English words from them.

their reading, although they do have to have some rudimentary phonics skills, such as knowing initial consonants or the long sound of the vowels, to get started in independent reading.

5. Good readers always integrate phonics skills with predictions about sense, strategies for self-correction, and knowledge of word meanings. Phonics skills are just one of the skills required to read.

6. If phonics skills are taught in conjunction with other reading tactics, they're best taught in context and for a fairly limited time period of perhaps a year or two. For example, a teacher might ask the children to spell the words needed for a class story and record them on a chart, or the class might make a list of all the "ch" words in a storybook.

7. Children's reading ability improves the more they read books. Teachers should encourage them to use whatever phonics skills they have by reading books. Predictable books (books with rhyming or repeating words), already familiar to children from the teacher's reading them, can enable children with minimal phonics skills to read.

8. Good reading instruction doesn't emphasize one set of reading skills to the exclusion of others. Teachers need to offer a balanced program of opportunities for children to learn all the skills—to use all the syntactic, semantic, and visual-graphic cues—that are involved in reading. They should make sure children have plenty of time to put all their skills to use in reading connected text in books.

Learning to Write

Like reading, writing begins during the preschool years. As described in Chapter 11, preschoolers delight in scribble-writing, and they expend great efforts on creating shopping lists, stories, and letters to grandma. Many of them

FIGURE 15-9
Third graders have sufficient literacy skills to do a library project. They can read well enough to research a topic, and they can write well enough to put together a report. But it always makes life easier to do a joint project with a buddy.

understand that writing is a pencil-and-paper version of spoken language. They also start to understand some print conventions, such as that print is read from left to right and from top to bottom. As much as they learn between the ages of 3 and 6, however, the development of writing only begins in that period. The ability to express ideas and thoughts in writing continues to develop throughout the elementary school years and beyond.

THE LETTER-NAME SPELLING STRATEGY. One of the first ideas that is often solidified in first grade, if not earlier, is that spoken words are represented on paper by mapping their sounds to alphabet letters. This insight (again, as described in Chapter 11) assumes the ability to think about speech at the phonemic level— the level of individual speech sounds, as opposed to the level of syllables or words. Once children know the names of letters and have phonemic awareness, they can begin to create words using a **letter-name spelling strategy.** Because the names of letters include at least one sound that the letter makes— if you say the letter A, you hear the long A sound—children can begin to spell words using their knowledge of letter names.

Words spelled using this simple strategy are pretty unusual looking, of course. We saw some examples of it in Will's journal—words like "wat" ("wait"), "ovr," "wen," and "hop" ("hope"). Children's early spellings are invented, created according to their own rules or perhaps we should say, their own best guess.

Sometimes the letter-name strategy leads to an especially unusual spelling. For example, a child might write "chicken" as HIKN. At first glance, you might assume the child was just sloppy and forgot the "c" at the beginning of the word. But actually, the child figured this spelling out carefully by going through the letters until she came to one that contained the "ch" sound—the letter "h." Examples of typical spellings based on a letter-name strategy are given in Table 15.

SPELLING WORDS WITH SHORT VOWELS. Other unusual spellings are the result of even more amazing detective work. For example, children have a problem when they hear a sound in a word that doesn't have a letter name match. This is the case for all the short vowels; a, e, i, o, and u contain their long sound rather than their short one. To handle these situations, children often analyze the sound of these short vowels to see which long vowels they most closely resemble (Read, 1975).

To explain this, we have to digress for a moment with a discussion of phonetic features. Any sound we make can be described in terms of a set of phonetic features. For example, a sound in which air is stopped as it passes through the throat or mouth is described as a closed sound, and one in which air is not stopped is described as an open sound. Consonants are closed sounds, and vowels are open sounds. When air is stopped, it can be stopped in the back of the throat (g, k), behind the teeth (l, s, t), or with the lips (m, n, p). Vowels, too, can be described in terms of where in the mouth they are articulated.

Like the distinctive features of written alphabet letters (described in Chapter 11), the phonetic features of sounds overlap. Even though sounds differ in one or more feature—which is why we can perceive them as different sounds—they also share some features. When children are trying to decide how to represent a short vowel, they simply search the phonetic features of the long vowels until they get to the letter whose name "says" that sound. The letter they come up with is often an incorrect one that shares phonetic features with the right one.

For example, a child might write "then" as THIN. The short e in "then" has some phonetic features in common with both long i and long e. It shares a similar shape of the vocal track—the position of the tongue in relation to the roof of the mouth—with long i. It shares place of articulation—the specific spot in the vocal track where the sound is formed—with long e. Apparently, young children experience shape of the vocal track as a more dominant feature than place of articulation. This is why they first represent short e with i. To

TABLE 15-1
Examples of Children's Invented Spellings

Words Created Using a Letter-Name Strategy	Words Created by Substituting the Nearest Tense Vowel for a Lax Vowel	Words Created by Focusing on the Affrication in T and D Followed by R
Kit (kite)	Fes (fish)	Chran (train)
Da (day)	Pan (pen)	Chra (tray)
Mi (my)	Mas (mess)	Chri (try)
Kat (Kate)	Git (got)	Griv (drive)
Tabl (table)	Biks (box)	Gri (dry)
Hare (cherry)		
Hrh (church)		
Lade (lady)		
Babe (baby)		
Fas (face)		
Tigr (tiger)		

see for yourself, form the short e and long i in your mouth, and observe the similarities and differences. More examples of word spelling based on this strategy are included in Table 15–1.

SPELLING WORDS WITH OTHER PHONETIC FEATURES. Another phonetic feature sometimes trips up children. Some sounds are **affricated**—spoken with a release of air. The sound associated with the letters "ch" and the soft sound of the letter "g" are examples of affricated sounds. Some letters are affricated in some contexts but not in others. The letters "d" and "t" fall into this category. They're usually not affricated, as in "dog" and "toy," for example, but when they're followed by "r," as in "drain" and "train," they are affricated.

Our language writes these sounds as "d" and "t" regardless of whether they're affricated or not. But children notice the affrication of "d" and "t" when they're followed by "r" and think they aren't sounds that should be represented by the letters "d" and "t." They focus on the affrication as the dominant feature and associate the sounds with other affricated sounds. Consequently, to represent an affricated "d" they choose "g," and to represent an affricated "t" they choose "ch." The result is "train" written as CHRAN and "trouble" written as DRBL. More examples are included in Table 15–1.

Invented spellings look terribly bizarre to naive adults, who sometimes worry that the child is afflicted with some dreadful auditory or visual discrimination problem. The only problems, of course, are that the child has a very keen ear for detecting similar phonetic features and that he doesn't yet know all the sounds that each letter can represent. Children also have no knowledge of markers, such as silent e and double vowels, which signal that the preceding vowel is to be pronounced in its long version (kite, eat).

As children see more and more words spelled in the standard way, in books, on signs, and so on, they gradually learn which phonetic features are attended to for the sake of spelling and which ones are ignored. They also learn the whole set of sounds each letter of the alphabet can represent and the "tricks of the trade" in spelling English words, such as the function of silent e. Like Will, they progress from strict phonetic transcription of sounds they hear in words to more sophisticated conventional spelling over the course of middle childhood (Treiman, 1985).

LEARNING THE LANGUAGE OF FILM: BECOMING VISUALLY LITERATE

A movie is in progress. A middle-aged woman is sitting in a rocking chair, staring out into space. She seems to be deep in thought. The image on the screen becomes hazy and then fades. The film cuts away to an image of a baby playing on the grass. The scene is shot at a distance and the lighting is dim. We can't see exactly what the baby is doing. We get the idea, however, that this image represents what the woman is thinking and that she's probably remembering something from her past.

Understanding Film Conventions

A young child would find it impossible to understand what this scene means. Film conveys meaning through its own conventions, just as speech and print do. The language of film is made up of visual effects, such as different camera angles, fades, cuts, zooms, close-ups, pans, and so on, as well as sound effects and music. We learn to understand film as a result of both general cognitive development and experience with filmed images. In our society, dominated as it is by the visual image—on TV, in movies, and in videos—visual literacy is becoming an important kind of language development.

As we saw in Chapter 12, young children can't distinguish reality from fiction on TV. When they're under 3 years of age, they attribute equal reality to everything on TV. Then, at 3 to 4 years, they become skeptical and start to think that everything on TV is fictional. They believe that real events, such as those reported in news programs, are pretend. By age 5 or 6, they're starting to have a fairly accurate idea of which television events are based on reality— those that can and do happen—and which would be improbable or impossible in the real world. Between the ages of 7 and 10, children sort out whether things that appear to be real on TV are staged events, such as historical dramas or commercials, or live events, such as the news or documentaries (Gardner & Brown, 1984, p. 47).

Features of Fictionalized versus Real-Life Events on Film

Children learn to distinguish reality from fiction on TV partly by becoming familiar with some of the technical devices and formal features typically associated with each kind of event. Staged events, for example, use a variety of interesting camera angles, close-ups, zooms, and dissolves. There are controlled variations in lighting, changes in pace, and a contrived sound track. Sound effects and music are used to build suspense and fill transition moments. If we saw a film depicting scenes from the life of a United States Senator that contained these elements, we would probably perceive it to be a fictionalized account.

Presentations of live events usually don't have any of these features. They have a less rehearsed, more natural feeling to them. People talk in a more realistic way, with greater discontinuity in their speech; devices like flashbacks and fades are missing (Huston et al., 1985). If we saw a film depicting scenes from the life of a Senator that had these characteristics, we would probably judge it to be a documentary. It takes a fair degree of sophistication and experience to discriminate between staged and live events—something we often forget, until we hear a child ask, "Is this really happening?"

Children have trouble making another discrimination on TV as well—the one between programs and commercials. It's hard for them to perceive or

FIGURE 15-10
Interpreting visual images on a computer screen is rapidly becoming an important literacy skill. Today's elementary schools must meet the challenge of preparing children for life and work in a computerized world.

understand the features that indicate a change in time and place, either within a program or between the program and the ad. For example, in Batman cartoons, a twirling bat is used to mark the end of one scene and the beginning of the next (Wright & Huston, 1985). At 5 or 6 years, children don't understand what markers like this mean, and they don't realize the scene has changed. During middle childhood, children develop an accurate understanding of scene changes in TV shows, and they learn how to distinguish between program content and commercials.

Pictures and other visual images are currently used in our society as much as, if not more than, words to convey meaning. Children have to learn to "read" these images just as they learn to read print if they are to become educated, informed, and competent members of society.

OVERVIEW

Children enter first grade with a firm grasp of oral language and, in many cases, some important understandings about written language as well. Over the course of the next several years, they typically master all the basics of grammar and syntax and become fluent readers and competent writers. Thanks to their developing metalinguistic awareness, they delight in jokes, riddles, and games with words and language—the hallmark of the school-age years. By the time children leave elementary school, their language development is virtually complete. In the years ahead, their remaining tasks will include expanding their vocabulary, tackling increasingly sophisticated books, and refining their writing skills.

CHAPTER REVIEW

ORAL LANGUAGE

- Young school-age children have mastered the rudiments of language, but they're still confused by certain words and usages, such as "ask" and "tell." They often rely less on syntax than on whether they know an answer or think a particular answer makes sense. Even at 9 and 10 years, children still confuse some words.
- School-age children love jokes and riddles because they've just begun to understand the ambiguous use of words, the heart of verbal humor. The ambiguity can be based on similar-sounding words, words with similar meanings, or sentences that can be understood in different ways. Understandings of these different types of ambiguity develop at different ages.
- The ability to notice deep linguistic structures rather than the meaning of words is known as metalinguistic awareness. Preschool children learn the form of jokes, but they don't have the metalinguistic understanding to know what makes jokes funny.
- American public schools have traditionally been filled with children of different backgrounds who learned to speak English in the classroom. Today, we are again experiencing a rise in diversity in school populations.
- The two main approaches to teaching English to non-native speakers are Teaching English as a Second Language (TESL) and bilingual programs. The TESL program is based on immersion of the students in the new language. In the bilingual approach, children are taught English, but they learn classroom subjects in their native language until they become somewhat proficient in English. There is debate over which of these approaches is preferable.
- There are three theories about how children learn a second language: they learn it the same way native speakers learn it as toddlers (the identical process theory); they use structures from their own native tongue (the interference theory); or they devise new grammatical structures as they learn (the unique grammatical structure theory) Most research supports the identical process model of learning a second language.
- Children learn a second language most quickly when they spend time playing and communicating with other

children who speak the language. There is a definite socioemotional component that influences children's attitudes toward learning a second language.

- Dialects are variations in pronunciation, syntax, or word meanings within a language. The most common dialect in the United States is Black English, which differs from standard English in several ways. Teachers need to help children learn the most accepted dialect at the same time that they convey respect for the children's first dialect.

WRITTEN LANGUAGE: LITERACY DEVELOPMENT

- Reading and writing are intimately connected. Reading is considered the most important skill children learn in the early school years.
- There are two main approaches to teaching reading: the skills approach, which is actually two different approaches—the phonics approach and the look-say approach—and the whole language approach.
- The whole language approach, which relies on several cueing systems rather than focusing on isolated skills, is currently a popular method of teaching reading. It suggests that children must have an extensive oral vocabulary before they can learn to read and that they have to make predictions about the sense of the passage they're reading.
- When children first learn to write, they use a letter-name spelling strategy, relying on letters to "say" their names. Early writing looks unusual but can be deciphered phonetically. Invented spellings give way to conventional ones during the school years.

LEARNING THE LANGUAGE OF FILM: BECOMING VISUALLY LITERATE

- Like speech and writing, film conveys meaning through its own system of symbols, a repertoire of visual and auditory effects. Children have to learn the language of film to understand this medium.
- At first, children have trouble sorting out what is and is not real on TV. They also have difficulty recognizing that a program has ended and a commercial has taken its place. Since visual images are becoming increasingly pervasive in our society, children must learn to interpret them if they're to be educated citizens.

KEY TERMS

phonologically based ambiguity	immersion	skills approach	semantic cues
lexically based ambiguity	identical process theory	whole language approach	dyslexia
syntactically based ambiguity	interference theory	phonics approach	letter-name spelling strategy
metalinguistic awareness	unique grammatical structure theory	"look-say" approach	affricated
	dialect	syntactic cues	

SUGGESTIONS FOR FURTHER READING

Bissex, G. (1980). *GNYS AT WRK: A child learns to write and read.* Cambridge, MA: Harvard University Press.
This book presents a case study of the author's son from age 5 to age 9. It chronicles his writing and reading development. Very interesting reading!

Geller, L. G. (1985). *Word play and language learning for children.* Urbana, IL: National Council of Teachers of English.
This book provides a thorough discussion of children's use of jokes and riddles.

Goodman, K. S., Smith, E. B., Meredith, R., & Goodman, Y. (1987). *Language and thinking in school: A whole-language curriculum.* (3rd ed.). New York: Richard C. Owen.
This undergraduate text provides useful information about the theoretical basis of the whole language approach to the teaching of reading and writing. It also provides useful guidance for teachers who want to implement a whole language program.

McLaughlin, B. (1984). *Second-language acquisition in childhood.* (Vol. 1). Hillsdale, NJ: Lawrence Erlbaum.
This book provides a good overview of second-language acquisition. Chapters cover different second-language acquisition situations, such as simultaneous acquisition of two languages and successive acquisition of two languages.

Read, C. (1975) *Children's categorization of speech sounds in English.* Urbana, IL: National Council of Teachers of English.
This is the classic source in which young children's inventive spellings are analyzed. Provides vital information for understanding this child behavior.

chapter 16

SOCIAL AND EMOTIONAL DEVELOPMENT IN SCHOOL-AGE CHILDREN

A group of fourth graders were huddled together at one end of a table in the lunchroom, talking in hushed tones. They looked for all the world like conspirators hatching a plot— which is just exactly what they were doing.

"Look, we've got to have enough time to get the streamers tacked into the wall, the balloons blown up and hung from the windows, the cupcakes on her desk, and 'Happy birthday, Mrs. Townsend' written on the blackboard," said Paul. "That'll take maybe ten minutes. But how do we get her out of the classroom for that long?" He looked around the circle of intent faces. "Any ideas?"

"How about if we get Mr. Steinberg to call her on the intercom to come to the office to get a message?" suggested Amy.

"No, that won't work," Paul responded. "She always sends one of us to the office to get messages."

"I know!" said David. "We'll have someone fake getting hurt on the playground and have to go to the nurse's office. Then the nurse can call Mrs. Townsend to come see if it's okay for the kid to come back to class. Then on the way back to the classroom, the kid could faint, and Mrs. Townsend would . . ."

"That doesn't make any sense," interrupted Gina. "The nurse always decides if you can come back to the classroom. Teachers don't decide that. And anyway, Mrs. Townsend would realize something was funny if the nurse asked her to come down."

"Let's tell her we met her husband out front with their baby and he wants her to come out because he can't make the baby stop crying!" exclaimed Leroy.

"She'd never fall for that!" Paul scoffed. "That's ridiculous!"

"Then you think of something!" retorted Leroy. And they all fell silent for a few minutes . . . waiting for the next idea to surface.

It's not easy to figure out how to give someone a surprise birthday party. The remarkable thing is that these fourth graders were able to think about it at all—to invent ruses and then imagine how Mrs. Townsend might react to them. Younger children would be completely incapable of thinking this way. The ability to put oneself in someone else's place and anticipate what that person is likely to think, feel, or do—known as **social role-taking** ability—is one of the hallmarks of the social and emotional development of the school-age child.

In this chapter, we discuss the growth of this new awareness, which gives school-age children so much more social sophistication than they had just a few years earlier. They're also developing better social skills and becoming much more interested in friendship and acceptance by the group. Unfortunately, some children aren't successful at making friends or interacting with a group, and their experience of rejection is a matter of serious concern. Children's popularity, or lack of it, is the second topic covered in this chapter, along with some strategies for teaching unpopular children how to get themselves included in the group.

We also examine the development of moral reasoning in school-age children, and we describe three different theories of how their moral reasoning advances. Finally, we look at cognitive and personality differences between boys and girls, and we consider why these sex differences exist. Social and emotional development is broad and complex during the school years, and this chapter suggests some of the richness of children's experience.

SOCIAL ROLE-TAKING ABILITY

We could see the ability to understand the feelings, thoughts, and intentions of another in Paul, Gina, and the other fourth graders who were trying to plan a surprise birthday party for their teacher. The social role-taking ability they demonstrated is just one part of **social cognition**—the child's growing understanding of a broad range of social and interpersonal events. This understanding gradually increases during middle childhood, the period from 6 to 10 years of age (Shantz, 1975).

Social role-taking ability involves judging what cognitive and emotional processes other people are going through. It leads children to a greater understanding of others as well as of themselves, since they can now think of themselves from the point of view of others. This ability consists of several different, but interacting, components—understanding emotions, understanding intentions, and understanding thinking. In this section, we consider how children develop in relation to each of these dimensions.

Understanding Other People's Emotions

Children make great advances in understanding emotions during middle childhood. We've seen that as infants, they were able to discriminate emotions by reading people's happy or angry faces, and between 2 and 3 years, they began to label and talk about emotions. Between ages 4 and 7, children start to be able to match appropriate emotional responses to specific situations

(Barden et al., 1980; Borke, 1971). But at this age they still lack sophisticated understandings about emotions. They don't know, for example, that two different emotions can be felt simultaneously about the same situation. They also don't understand that a situation can elicit different emotions from different people. These are some of the understandings they acquire during the school-age period.

UNDERSTANDING SIMULTANEOUS EMOTIONS. Experiences of emotions can be simple and straightforward, or they can be complex and difficult. Consider this situation:

The Golden Eagles soccer team coach was awarding his players their plaques at the end-of-season pizza party. He was surrounded by noisy, excited 7- and 8-year-olds. After he handed out the last plaque, he uncovered a large trophy still to be awarded. The two best players on the team fixed their eyes on the trophy eagerly. "The trophy this year," announced the coach, "is for team spirit. It goes to the player who did the most for the whole team. He was always enthusiastic at practices and games, and he gave tremendous support to all the other players—Jasper!"

"Jasper! Why does he get the trophy?" wailed the team star.

"Yeah—he didn't score any goals," cried his rival, as parents exchanged exasperated looks and applauded loudly to drown out their voices.

Jasper jumped up to receive his trophy with a broad smile on his face. Later, when his parents asked him how he felt at that moment, he said, "I felt happy that I got it."

"But didn't you feel mad when Max said that you didn't deserve it, that the trophy should go to the player who made the most goals?"

"No, not really."

That night, Jasper's parents discussed his good-natured approach to life. "He takes things so well," his dad said. "I would have been furious if my teammates said I didn't deserve the trophy. But not Jasper. He just felt happy that he'd gotten it."

When Jasper's dad placed himself in his son's situation, he readily admitted that he would feel "mixed emotions"—happy about winning the trophy but mad about the comments made by the others when it was awarded. But Jasper didn't seem to experience conflicting emotions. He felt happy about winning the trophy, and that was it. This is typical of children's "all or none" reactions. They seem to feel all sad, all happy, or all angry, but not more than one of these emotions at the same time. An adult, in contrast, might feel more than one emotion about the same event—happiness and sadness about a child's going away to school, for example, or anger and sadness about a fire that was set deliberately.

Two researchers have developed a model for thinking about how children progress in their ability to experience and talk about simultaneous emotions (Harter & Buddin, 1987). They proposed the notions of **targets**—the object, person, or situation at which an emotion is directed—and of **valence**—the positive or negative nature of the emotion. They hypothesized that it might be easier for children to experience two positive emotions directed toward the same target simultaneously than a positive and a negative emotion toward the same target.

The study they did confirmed this hypothesis. They found that children aged 4 to 6 weren't able to put feelings together simultaneously at all. Some-

FIGURE 16-1
The thrill of a merry-go-round gives two boys unmixed joy. Children's emotional experiences are direct and intense, partly because they don't have the internal buffer adults have. As they become more sophisticated emotionally, children learn to distinguish different feelings more clearly and to handle their emotions in a greater variety of ways.

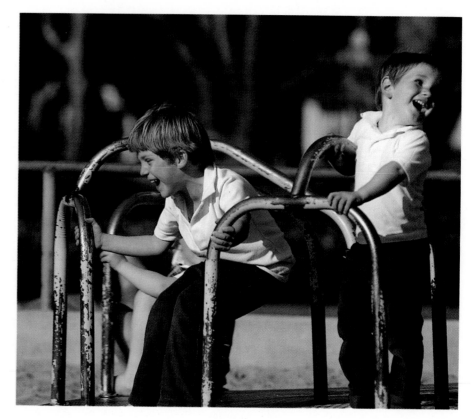

times they denied that two feelings could be experienced at the same time, or they sequenced two feelings ("First I'd feel excited; then I'd feel happy."). These children do have concepts for separate emotions, but they can't differentiate and integrate them at the same time. They sequence them instead.

Children aged 6 to 8 acknowledged that they experienced two emotions at the same time, but they included only same-valence emotions directed toward the same target ("I felt happy and excited about getting an A on my spelling test."). But they had difficulty feeling two different positive emotions about two different targets ("I felt happy about my new board games and very excited about the tickets to the baseball game.")

Children aged 8 to 9 said they could experience two same-valence emotions directed toward different targets at the same time ("I'd feel happy about the spelling test and excited about the class picnic"), but they couldn't imagine being able to feel two different-valence emotions—one positive, one negative—at the same time. One child said, "I couldn't feel happy and frightened at the same time; I would have to be two people at once!" (Harper & Buddin, 1987, pp. 392–393).

Ten-year-olds said they experienced two different-valence emotions at the same time, but only when they were directed at two different targets ("I was scared in the theatre watching the movie, but I was happy that I had popcorn to eat."). Their range of emotions was larger than ever, but they couldn't bring a positive and a negative emotion to a single target at the same time ("The movie made me feel happy and scared.").

Not until they were 11 or 12 years old did children say they could feel opposite emotions toward the same target at the same time ("I was happy that I was going to overnight camp, but I was scared about staying in a new place.").

This study shows that children become more sophisticated about how they understand and experience their emotions as they develop. The study also suggests that out of a mass of undifferentiated positive and negative emotions, children gradually distinguish and form concepts of different, distinct feelings. An older child or adult might have distinguished and named a variety of feelings evoked by the situation Jasper found himself in—pride, pleasure, excitement, embarrassment, anger, humiliation. Jasper mentioned only that he felt "happy." As he develops, his understanding of his emotions will become more refined and sophisticated.

UNDERSTANDING SITUATIONS. An important part of understanding how other people are feeling involves understanding situations and the feelings they typically evoke in people. Not being invited to a friend's party would make most people feel hurt, for example, and winning a prize in a contest would make most people feel excited. But other situations are more equivocal (ambiguous) than these—some people might feel good about them, others might feel bad.

Young children often don't recognize that some situations are more equivocal than others. One group of researchers set out to discover how children of different ages thought people would feel about a variety of situations (Gnepp, McKee, & Domanic, 1987). Would they realize that some situations are quite clear-cut but that others aren't so clear? The researchers presented kindergartners and first, second, and third graders with a series of equivocal situations (for example,"child gets an egg salad sandwich for lunch" or "child is approached by a small dog while playing") and unequivocal situations (for example, "all the lights go off when child is playing alone" or "child drops and breaks favorite toy") (Gnepp, McKee, & Domanic, 1987, p. 116).

The children were asked to tell how a "story child" (a hypothetical child) would feel about the situation. After stating an emotion they believed the story child would feel, children were asked to explain why they thought the child would feel that way. The researchers wondered if children would respond to an equivocal situation by attributing a wider range of emotional reactions to the child pictured in the situation than they would for unequivocal situations. This would indicate that they realized that the equivocal situation is more likely to evoke different emotions from different people. They found that children did respond this way. They also found that older children recognized equivocal situations more clearly than younger ones, suggesting that as children get older, they develop more sophisticated knowledge about the emotions that different situations can elicit.

Children also gave different kinds of explanations for their choices of emotion for the equivocal situations than they did for the unequivocal ones. In the equivocal situations, children explained why the story child felt the way she did by referring to her supposed interpretation of the event ("She would be happy about an egg salad sandwich, because she knows that eggs are good for her."). This indicates that they realized that people's responses to a situation might vary, depending on how they viewed or interpreted the event.

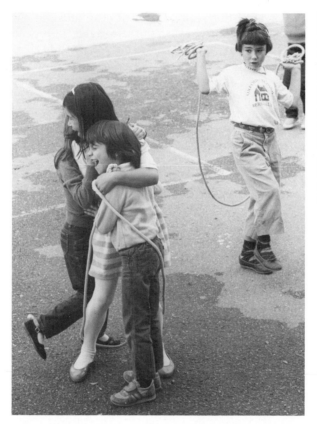

FIGURE 16-2
Playing alone while other children are playing together nearby is a situation that would make most children feel sad. But the girls having such a good time may not have any idea they're causing another child to feel excluded. If she asked to join them, they might say, "Sure." Only at about 10 or 11 years of age do children begin to understand how certain situations make other people feel.

UNDERSTANDING INDIVIDUAL DIFFERENCES. Of course, we can't know for sure how a person will feel about a particular situation, even an unequivocal one, unless we know the meaning of that situation to the person. For example, many children would feel anxious about failing a test, but if a child hadn't studied very hard, she might not be upset at all, knowing that she could do well the next time with a little effort.

As children develop, their understandings of all these factors become more refined. They realize that people can have mixed emotions, that some situations are more ambiguous than others, and that people may react differently than expected because of their individual histories and interpretations of events. In many ways, children become more "emotionally literate" as they move through middle childhood.

Understanding Other People's Intentions

"Mom, Kelly broke the lid of my treasure box!"

"I didn't mean to! I didn't know it was under the paper when I leaned on the table!"

"It's all cracked! You broke it, and I'm gonna break something of yours to pay you back!"

Parents and teachers are sometimes surprised when children don't recognize and respond differently when something happens accidentally. Children don't seem to notice or care how or why an event occurred—they care only about the event itself and its consequences. Adults, in contrast, understand that unfortunate events, such as breaking something or hurting someone, can occur under a variety of circumstances. They base their responses in part on the intentions of the person responsible for the event, on whether it was deliberate or accidental. Why don't children respond this way?

One problem for children is that the discrimination between "deliberate" and "accidental" is difficult for them to make. Most adults judge intentions by cues they get from people's facial expressions and verbalizations. An angry expression accompanied by a sarcastic statement would lead most adults to conclude that the speaker's intentions were hostile. A surprised or sad expression accompanied by the statement, "I'm sorry—I was only trying to help," would lead most adults to assume a prosocial intention.

Children younger than age 6 or 7 aren't very skillful at detecting intentions in situations where damage occurs. In one study, kindergartners and second and fourth graders were shown videotaped vignettes of a child destroying an object (Dodge, Murphy, & Buchsbaum, 1984), and the youngest children were confused about intentions. The vignettes showed hostile intent (the child destroyed something on purpose); prosocial intent (the child unintentionally destroyed something while trying to help another child); an accidental event (the child destroyed something without meaning to, such as by stepping backward and bumping into it); ambiguous intent (the child's intention wasn't stated and wasn't clear from the situation); and "merely present" (the child was blamed by another child).

In each vignette (except the ambiguous one), the actual intention of the child was conveyed by facial expressions and verbalizations to the child who

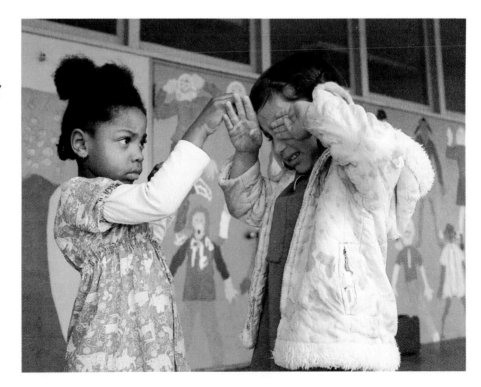

FIGURE 16-3
It's very hard for children to distinguish deliberate actions from accidental ones. If another child says, "I'm sorry" and tries to help, as this girl is doing, the hurt child is more likely to respond appropriately.

observed the tape. Researchers found that the younger the children were, the less able they were to identify or discriminate intention cues. Older children were much more skilled at perceiving prosocial, accidental, and merely present cues. Some intentions were easier for all the children to recognize and discriminate than others. All children did well in identifying hostile intentions, accurately identifying them 96 percent of the time. And all did poorly in understanding ambiguous situations, getting them right only 9 percent of the time. Overall, they accurately identified accidents 86 percent of the time and prosocial intentions 79 percent of the time.

This study emphasizes the necessity of helping young children understand situations that are even slightly ambiguous. Adults can point out people's expressions to children to encourage them to look for intention cues: "Look at how sad Kelly's face looks. She feels bad about breaking the lid of your box." They can also teach children to take the words "I'm sorry" as a cue that something was an accident and calls for a different response. In this case, though, adults need to be certain that the apology is genuine, rather than a response that the child has picked up as a way to "get off the hook."

If young children have a hard time understanding intention when it's clearly stated, they're completely in the dark when someone deliberately tries to mislead them. This means they're virtually defenseless against the claims of television advertising. Even sixth graders aren't very skillful at taking intentions into account when judging the information given about products in television commercials (Ross et al., 1981). They take the information at face value without allowing for the fact that the advertiser may be trying to deceive them. Even though children begin to be able to detect intention at about 6 years, and their abilities improve throughout the school years, detecting deception is very difficult even for 11- and 12-year-olds.

Understanding Other People's Thinking

Chairs were arranged in the middle of the classroom to make a train, and children were busy getting dressed up to go on a trip. Alice was behind the ticket counter selling tickets marked "New York," "New Jersey," "Maine," "Canada," and "Florida." As the first customer approached the ticket counter, Alice asked, "Where are you going?"

"To my grandma's house," replied Natalie.

Alice looked at the teacher as if to say, "What do I do now?" She knew she didn't have any tickets that said that. The teacher suggested she ask Natalie where her grandma lived.

"Where's she live?" Alice inquired.

"Next door to Mrs. McKinney," answered Natalie.

Alice again looked at the teacher in bewilderment.

"Ask what city her grandma lives in, or what state."

"What city does she live in?" Alice asked.

"I don't know," came the reply.

Finally, the teacher intervened. "Natalie, when you go on a trip to see your grandma, your mom tells me that you're going to New Jersey. Is that where you want to go on the train today?"

"Uh-huh."

"Give this lady one ticket to New Jersey," the teacher told Alice, who then searched through the pile of tickets to find an appropriate ticket.

FIGURE 16-4
"He may think I'll make this move, so I'll make a different one instead. . ." Some researchers assessed children's social role-taking ability by studying how they play strategy games. When they begin to think about what others may be thinking, they become capable of greater self-awareness and greater understanding of others.

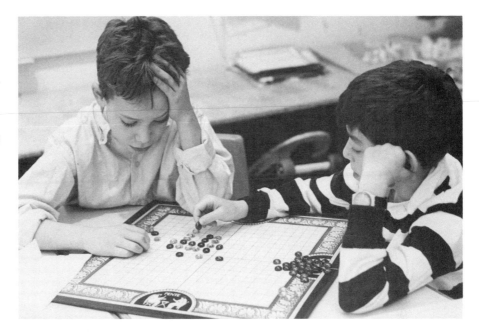

A third aspect of social role-taking ability, besides understanding other people's emotions and intentions, is understanding their thinking and what they know. The incident just described, which took place in a preschool classroom, illustrates how limited the 4- or 5-year-old's ability is in this area. Natalie couldn't understand what Alice didn't know, and Alice couldn't understand what Natalie didn't know. But during the school-age years, children develop the ability to think about other people's knowledge and thinking.

Children's ability to think about other people's thinking and their own thinking has been studied in a variety of ways. Some researchers have asked children to play strategy games, which by their very nature require children to think about the other person's thinking (see Research Focus—Studying Role-taking Ability with Strategy Games).

Other researchers have asked children to give directions for constructing a design to a second child whose view of the design is blocked (Krauss & Glucksberg, 1969). Still other researchers have presented dilemmas to children involving social role-taking ability and asked them to think about other people's thinking. A classic study involved a dilemma involving a girl named Holly (Selman, 1976):

> Holly is an 8-year-old girl who likes to climb trees. She is the best tree climber in the neighborhood. One day while climbing down from a tall tree, she falls off the bottom branch but does not hurt herself. Her father sees her fall. He is upset and asks her to promise not to climb trees any more. Holly promises.
>
> Later that day, Holly and her friends meet Shawn. Shawn's kitten is caught up in a tree and can't get down. Something has to be done right away, or the kitten may fall. Holly is the only one who climbs trees well enough to reach the kitten and get down, but she remembers her promise to her father.

After hearing the dilemma, children are asked several questions, including, "What does Holly think her father will do if he finds out she climbed the tree?"

RESEARCH FOCUS

Studying Role-taking Ability with Strategy Games

Playing a strategy game with a 6-year-old is on about the same level as listening to a 6-year-old's jokes. Children this age enjoy the form of the game or the verbal pun, and they want to try it because they see how it amuses other people, but the content eludes them. In the case of games, they just don't have the ability to understand that two different points of view are involved.

To study the development of children's role-taking ability, Rheta DeVries (1970) observed how children of different ages played a common strategy game. She asked them to guess in which hand an adult had concealed a penny, and she also asked them to try to conceal the penny from the adult themselves. Skilled players of this game base their guessing and concealing on what they think the other player will think they're thinking. "She hid it in the right hand the last time," a player might think. "She probably thinks I'll choose the left hand this time. But I won't. I'll choose the right hand again because she'll hide it there, thinking I'll choose the left." This sophisticated kind of thinking is rare in children younger than age 6 or 7.

DeVries distinguished five stages in the development of role-taking ability as measured in this game. In the first two stages, children don't even understand that the game involves uncertainty. They search for the penny in the same hand every time. When they hide

the penny, they may extend the hand in which it's concealed or tell the adult, "pick this hand." They don't understand that the game involves two roles, the concealer and the guesser.

In Stage 3 (ages 4 and 5), children realize that the game is competitive. When they hide the penny, they're delighted when the guesser picks the wrong hand. But apparently they don't realize that the guesser is thinking about their strategy—they hide the penny in a predictable pattern, first in one hand, then in the other. They assume the adult is also using this strategy when hiding the penny, and they guess alternating hands.

By Stage 4 (ages 5 and 6), children use an unpredictable pattern when hiding the penny. They're clearly thinking about what their opponents are thinking, and they're trying to outwit them. But when they guess, they revert to the predictable, alternating strategy. They apparently don't realize that the other player can think about their thinking in the same way they can think about the other player's.

Finally, in Stage 5, children use an unpredictable strategy for both hiding and guessing. They're thinking about their opponent's thinking, and they know their opponent is thinking about their thinking. Children don't attain this sophisticated understanding until they're about 6 or 7 years old.

On the basis of this type of study, Selman and his colleagues concluded that children's ability to think about other people's thinking evolves through five stages:

Stage 0 (ages 4 to 6)—**egocentric role taking.** At the beginning of this stage, children are unaware of differences in points of view. They think there's only one point of view, the one held by them—and by everyone else. A child at this stage typically answers the question about Holly's father by saying, "He will feel happy because he likes kittens." By the end of this stage, children begin to realize that people's views can differ.

Stage 1 (ages 6 to 8)—**social-information role taking.** The child understands that people interpret situations differently but thinks the source of these different views is different information. The child doesn't realize that people can have different views about the same information. The child isn't really taking the role of another person except in the limited sense of thinking about what the other person doesn't know. "If he didn't know why she climbed the tree, he would be angry," the child says about Holly's father. "But if Holly told him why she did it, he would realize that she had a good reason." The child doesn't realize that even if he knew why Holly climbed the tree, her father might still be angry—because of his view of the situation.

Stage 2 (ages 9 and 10)—**self-reflective role taking.** Children know that people think about their thoughts and feelings. They can think about their own thinking or about another person's thinking about them, but they can't consider both people's thinking simultaneously. They may say that Holly's father won't be angry: "Holly knows that her father will understand why she climbed the tree, so she knows that he won't want to punish her at all." Or they may say that Holly's father *will* be angry because he knows that she understands his concern about her climbing trees.

Stage 3 (ages 10 to 12)—**mutual role taking.** Children can now consider their point of view and another point of view simultaneously, as a disinterested third party. The child can speculate about what people are thinking about other people's thoughts. "Let's see," the child might say about Holly, "Holly wanted to get the kitten because she liked kittens, but she knew that she wasn't supposed to climb trees. Holly's father knew that Holly had been told not to climb trees, but he couldn't have known beforehand about this situation. He'd probably punish her anyway, just to enforce his rule."

Stage 4 (ages 12 to 15 and older)—**social and conventional system role taking.** The child appreciates the view of the "generalized other"—the social system—and uses it to help understand the view of a particular person. The perspective of the social group is now taken into account. "Holly's father would probably get angry and punish her," the child might say, "because that's what fathers must do if they want their children to obey." If the child has moved beyond a conventional view of morality (see the discussion of Kohlberg later in this chapter), the child might say, "You'd really have to know Holly's father to know if he would get angry. Some fathers would get angry; others wouldn't."

All the studies of children's social role-taking ability showed that older children are better able than younger children to think about what other people think, know, or understand. But even adults sometimes get confused in social situations, projecting their own thoughts and feelings onto others. It's easy to see that children need help when it comes to understanding the inner thought processes of other people. The gradual development of social role-taking ability is a measure both of their growing emotional and cognitive maturity and of the help and support they receive from the adults in their lives.

Social Role-taking Ability and Social Behavior

You might expect that as children develop higher levels of social role-taking ability, their social behavior will improve. After all, they will be capable of more sophisticated interpretations of other people's behavior as well as more appropriate responses to it. Some studies have shown this to be true (Buckley, Siegel, & Ness, 1979), but others haven't (Eisenberg-Berg, 1979; Strayer, 1980), perhaps because of inadequate measuring tools or flaws in the studies.

There really isn't any reason for a relationship between awareness and actions to exist, however. A child's ability to understand emotions, detect intentions, and think about what another person is thinking doesn't automatically lead to good social behavior. The ability to see the world through another's eyes may lead a child to act on the other's behalf, "but this ability may also be used to one's own advantage at another's expense" (Smith et al., 1983, p. 121).

Children's motivations and values—their ideas of what a "good person" would do and their motivation to live up to those standards—play a part in determining how they will use their awareness. (See the discussion of moral development later in this chapter.) Although their understanding improves during middle childhood, whether they become more prosocial depends on factors other than social role-taking ability.

SOCIAL SKILLS AND POPULARITY

How children actually behave in social situations depends on a number of factors, including their developing understanding and awareness about others, their motivations and values, their temperamental predispositions, the socialization techniques their parents have used, and many others. By the time children are in elementary school, they usually have a social "style" that characterizes how they act with their peers, who become increasingly important during this period. Middle childhood is a time of friendships and wide-ranging peer interactions that offer opportunities for affection, learning, and just plain fun.

But some children don't have the experience of friendship during these years. Some children are unpopular, disliked by others, for a variety of reasons. This situation shouldn't be taken lightly. Not having friends in childhood is associated with poor achievement in school (Roff, Sells, & Golden, 1972; Green, Beck, & Forehand, 1980), a higher likelihood of dropping out of school (Ullman, 1971), juvenile delinquency (Roff, Sells, & Golden, 1972), and bad conduct discharges from the military (Roff, 1961). It's obviously very important to find out what makes a child unpopular and try to remedy this situation.

FIGURE 16-5
A sociogram can be constructed from children's responses to questions about which classmates they like the best or want to sit near. Researchers can then determine which children are popular—those whose names come up most often—and which children may need some help with their social skills.

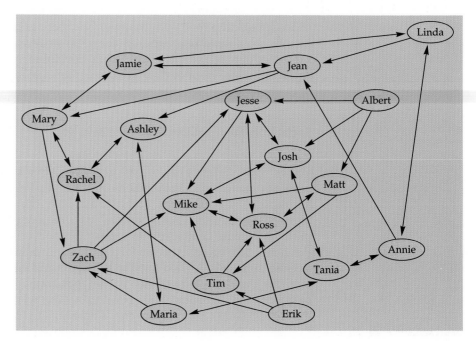

Popularity, or social status, is measured by sociometric techniques such as interviews and questionnaires. Usually, children are asked to name or list the classmates they like the most and the least. From their answers, researchers can determine which children are liked by many children (these children have **popular status**), which ones are disliked by many children (**unpopular status**), which ones are neither liked nor disliked by many children (**neglected status**), and which ones are both liked and disliked by other children (**controversial status**) (Asher & Dodge, 1986). Researchers have used a variety of observations and experiments to try to see how children get their status.

Popularity and Social Behavior

FRIENDLINESS. Popular children tend to be friendly, outgoing, agreeable, cooperative, enthusiastic, and helpful (Hartup, 1983). Unpopular or rejected children may also be outgoing and initiate a lot of social interactions, but their overtures tend to be aggressive and disruptive. For example, a preschool child may snatch a toy, run a short distance away, look back at the victim, and smile. The child may be making a bid to play, but the outcome of such harrassing tactics is usually rejection.

FIGURE 16-6
Researchers have found that one of the most successful group entry strategies is mimicking the peer group. Although the girl on the right doesn't have a partner right now, she's demonstrating that she understands the group activity and would be able to fit in if the opportunity arose. Since she doesn't appear aggressive or disruptive, her chances of being included may be quite good.

GROUP ENTRY STRATEGIES. In addition to being friendly in appropriate ways, popular children approach the entry of an ongoing play group in different ways than unpopular children do. The age-old problem of getting included in play has been the subject of a variety of studies. In one study, researchers organized second and third graders into "host" children, who were engaged in play with the researcher, and "entry" children, who were asked to enter the play (Putallaz & Gottman, 1981). The sociometric status of all the children had been determined previously.

Unpopular children tried to enter the group by asking more questions than popular children did, by talking more about themselves, and by disagreeing more. Popular children, in contrast, didn't behave in ways that interrupted the ongoing play or drew attention to themselves. Another difference was that when popular children disagreed with another child about something, they tended to state a general rule and provide an alternative action the playmate could take. "You're not supposed to pick a card from that pile," they might say, "You're supposed to draw from his hand." Unpopular children tended to state their objections in personal ways, such as "No!" or "Don't do that!", and they suggested no alternative.

A study of kindergartners turned up similar findings (Dodge et al., 1983). These researchers categorized children's peer-group entry strategies as follows: wait and hover; attention getting (but not aversive); group-oriented statements; questions; self-referent statements; and disruption (aversive).

They found that group-oriented statements were used more by popular children than by rejected or neglected children. Disruptive tactics, on the other hand, were used more—in fact, ten times more—by rejected children. Waiting and hovering was the tactic of choice for neglected children. Although entry into the group was fairly difficult for all children—that is, it typically required several bids—the tactics used by popular children were the most successful, and popular children were allowed to join the group more frequently than rejected or neglected children.

In studies with older children, the same researchers identified other successful strategies, which they labeled "mimicking the peer group" (Dodge et al., 1983) and "nonverbal synchrony with the group's activity," or gradually merging with the group (Dodge et al., 1987). The most successful sequence of tactics consisted of waiting and hovering, mimicking the peer group, and making group-oriented statements. Perhaps waiting and hovering gives the child time to size up the situation. Mimicking the group's behavior may signal to the group that the child would be able to join in the play. And making group-oriented statements may let them know that the child would not take over the play situation, which would be disruptive.

OTHER FACTORS ASSOCIATED WITH POPULARITY. In addition to the social skills and behaviors described above, birth order seems to play a part in a child's popularity (Miller & Maruyama, 1976; Sells & Roff, 1964). Firstborns tend to be less popular than their younger siblings, perhaps because younger siblings usually want to be included in their older siblings' play. Through experience, they gain the skills needed to adapt to other children's play.

Surprisingly, the commonness of a child's name is another factor associated with popularity (McDavid & Harari, 1966). No one knows why this is true. Maybe parents who give their children more unusual names are less social in some ways than parents who give their children common names. In this case, it might be the absence of some social skills that makes the child less popular— not the unusual name itself.

Physical attractiveness is also correlated with popularity (Lerner & Lerner, 1977; Cavior & Dokecki, 1973), and no one knows exactly why this is true either. Perhaps attractive children begin to draw more people into social inter-

RESEARCH FOCUS

Coaching Children in Social Skills

To improve unpopular children's social status, some adults have tried coaching them in social skills. In one training study, third and fourth graders were taught four different social skills: participation—getting involved and paying attention; cooperation—taking turns and sharing; communication—talking and listening; and validation—looking at the other person, giving support, and so on (Oden & Asher, 1977).

Seven steps were followed in instructing the child (Oden & Asher, 1977, p. 499):

1. The coach proposed the social skill and said it was an important skill that made playing fun.
2. The coach asked the child for some examples of the skill.
3. If the child gave an example, the coach repeated it. If the child couldn't think of any, the coach provided some examples.
4. The coach asked for an example of the opposite behavior.
5. The coach asked the child to evaluate the effect of the skill and its opposite.
6. The coach asked the child to try the skill while playing.
7. The coach said she would talk to the child after a play session to see if the ideas had worked.

In the following example of a coaching session, numbers are added in brackets to identify each of the steps (Oden and Asher, p. 500):

COACH: Okay, I have some ideas about what makes a game fun to play with another person. There are a couple of things that are important to do. [1] You should *cooperate* with the other person. Do you know what cooperation is? Can you tell me in your own words? [2]

CHILD: Ahh . . . sharing.

COACH: Yes, sharing. [3] Okay, let's say you and I are playing the game you played last time. What was it again?

CHILD: Drawing a picture.

COACH: Okay, tell me then, what would be an example of sharing when playing the picture-drawing game? [3]

CHILD: I'd let you use some pens too.

COACH: Right. You would share the pens with me. That's an example of cooperation. Now let's say you and I are doing the picture-drawing game. Can you also give me an example of what would *not* be cooperating? [4]

CHILD: Taking all the pens.

COACH: Would taking all the pens make the game fun to play? [5]

CHILD: No!

COACH: So you wouldn't take all the pens. Instead, you'd *cooperate* by *sharing* them with me. Can you think of some more examples of cooperation? (The coach waited for a response.) Okay, about taking turns . . . Let's say you and I . . . (etc.) Okay, I'd like you to try out some of these ideas when you play (name of new game) [6], and after you play I'll talk to you again for a minute or so and you can tell me if these things seem to be good ideas for having fun at a game with someone. [7]

The benefits of coaching have been demonstrated, but the limitations of this method for classroom use are also apparent, as mentioned in this chapter.

---

action in infancy by virtue of their "cuteness." Greater social experience would give them more practice in reading social cues and coordinating their behavior with that of others. Positive social responses might lead them to smile more and make more friendly gestures, which are also associated with greater popularity. Attractive children would have a long history of positive interactions by the time they entered school.

Strategies for Changing Children's Social Status

Since social skills are one important ingredient in children's social status, attempts have been made to teach social skills as a way of improving children's status. A successful training technique involves the use of **coaching** during individual sessions with an adult coach. An example of a training study, in which coaches taught skills such as cooperating, sharing, and taking turns, is described in Research Focus—Coaching Children in Social Skills. Other communication skills that adults have taught children include asking positive questions, offering useful suggestions, and offering supportive statements (Ladd, 1981).

In studies of this kind, children who were coached became significantly more popular with their peers. Coaching is clearly an effective way to improve the social status of disliked and rejected children. But such extensive individual training is a luxury beyond the capacity of most school systems, and usually it falls to the classroom teacher to try to help these children. Activities that require cooperation may help facilitate peer relations (Johnson & Johnson, 1974, 1978), and pairing unpopular children with popular children for activities can improve the unpopular children's status, at least temporarily (Chennault, 1967).

But children whose behavior is inappropriate and disruptive and who are rejected by their peers need more help than this. (For a discussion of the long-term correlates of early antisocial behavior, see Special Education Focus—Does Early Antisocial Behavior Fade Away?). Teachers may want to try adapting coaching techniques to classroom use. They can help less popular children in social situations in class by suggesting positive ways for them to interact. They can also give them feedback about the effects of their behavior on others. Instruction like this can be helpful in one way or another to all the children, even the most popular ones.

MORAL DEVELOPMENT

FIGURE 16-7
"Which child is naughtier?" 5-year-olds judged the two cases by how many cups were broken; 10-year-olds judged them by the boys' intentions. By questioning children of different ages about their beliefs, Piaget arrived at a timetable of moral development. He suggested that an important shift in moral reasoning occurs at 11 or 12, when children begin to think less in terms of God-given absolutes and more in terms of agreement and reciprocity among equals.

People used to assume that very young children could be taught to know "right" from "wrong" and that that was all there was to it. Now we know that moral development is a complex process that involves both cognitive and emotional growth. Several different researchers and theorists have proposed ways of thinking about children's moral development; we discuss three of them here.

Piaget's Study of Moral Reasoning

"WHICH CHILD IS NAUGHTIER?" To investigate children's moral reasoning, Piaget presented them with a pair of stories and asked them which child was "naughtier" (Piaget, 1965 p. 122):

A. A little boy who is called John is in his room. He is called to dinner. He goes into the dining room. But behind the door there was a chair, and on the chair there was a tray with twelve cups on it. John couldn't have known that there was all this behind the door. He goes in, the door knocks against the tray, bang go the twelve cups, and they all get broken!

B. Once there was a little boy whose name was Henry. One day when his mother was out he tried to get some jam out of the cupboard. He climbed up onto a chair and stretched out his arm. But the jam was too high up and he couldn't reach it and have any. But while he was trying to get it he knocked over a cup. The cup fell and broke.

Most adults wouldn't blame John for breaking the 12 cups. After all, he was called to dinner, and he didn't know the cups were behind the door. Henry, on the other hand, was doing something he wasn't supposed to be doing. Even though he broke only one cup, his intentions weren't very good.

Piaget found that children under 6 years of age judged John to be naughtier because he broke more cups. They based their judgment on the amount of damage done, not on the boys' intentions. By middle childhood, however, children were beginning to take intentions into account and to base their judgments on them. These children thought Henry was naughtier.

CHILDREN'S MORAL JUDGMENTS ABOUT LYING AND STEALING. Young children use similar criteria to judge lying. They judge the seriousness of a lie not by whether the child who told it intended to deceive but by how much the lie varies from the truth. A 6-year-old said one person was worse because what he said "could never happen." A character who said he saw a dog as big as a cow was judged worse by a 7-year-old because "there's no such thing." By the age of 10, chil-

FIGURE 16-8
Even very young children know it's wrong to "borrow" toys from school or the store. This child is well aware that shoplifting is a crime but does so anyway for reasons unknown to us.

SPECIAL EDUCATION FOCUS

Does Early Antisocial Behavior Fade Away?

Do children who are disruptive, aggressive, or destructive gradually become as cooperative and productive as their classmates? Unfortunately, no. Research indicates that early aggression and antisocial behavior are very good predictors of later social problems. These include juvenile delinquency (Roff, 1961; Farrington & West, 1971; Venezia, 1971; Loeber, 1982), lowered adult achievement, and marital instability (Caspi, Bem, & Elder, 1987). Apparently, it's the rare child who "outgrows" severe behavioral problems without some kind of help.

In one longitudinal study, researchers identified early classroom behaviors that were associated with later delinquency and school misconduct. These behaviors included the following (Spivack, Marcus, & Swift, 1986, p. 128):

- Annoying social behavior, such as poking and excessive talking and noisemaking in the classroom

- A tendency to rush into things without listening, reflecting impatience and a need to move ahead constantly without looking back or learning from experience

- Negative and defiant behavior toward the teacher

- Self-centered verbalization, such as interruptions, irrelevant remarks, and unexamined personal thoughts

These early behaviors seem to set in motion maladaptive social interactions that continue to snowball. Children without the social skills to get off to a good start in interactions with other children are rejected and excluded. Being left out deprives them of the experience and practice they need to develop the social skills they lack (Lieberman, 1977; Krantz, 1982; Dodge, Murphy, & Buchsbaum, 1984).

Some experts suggest that children whose behavior is extremely antisocial in the early grades may have been "temperamentally difficult" from early infancy. But we saw in our discussion of attachment in Chapter

8 that temperament alone isn't a very good predictor of later difficulties. Trouble usually develops only when the parents of a "difficult" child can't adapt to the child. This problem of the "match" between child temperament and parenting style may be at the root of some patterns of maladaptive classroom behavior (Spivack, Marcus, & Swift, 1986).

The first line of defense against the development of severe antisocial tendencies in children, then, is to facilitate attachment between infants and their parents. For children who miss out on this preventive step and arrive at preschool as aggressive and antisocial young children, therapeutic nursery schools can help. When antisocial children get to elementary school without having received any treatment, it's up to their teachers to help them break out of a vicious cycle. Teachers can try coaching children in social skills, as described in this chapter (Oden & Asher, 1977; Ladd, 1981). They can also try teaching the children social-cognitive problem solving (Spivack & Shure, 1982). This involves helping children think of other ways to behave in conflict situations and thinking through the consequences of different actions.

Teachers with an antisocial child in the classroom experience tremendous stress coping with the child's behavior, and they need to be able to talk to someone knowledgeable about this situation. Extremely skillful management of the child is necessary for an extended period of time. Appropriate treatment involves firmness without hostility, consistency without rigidity, and support for developing social and cognitive skills that will help the child learn to regulate his own behavior (Spivack, Marcus, & Swift, 1986, p.130). Unfortunately, few teachers have the time, energy, or training necessary to change the behavior of severely antisocial children. They need additional resources in the school and community to help problem children in any real way. As difficult as it is to provide for this kind of treatment, it's crucial to the child's future development. Early antisocial behavior doesn't simply fade away; it often simply gets worse.

---

dren judged the severity of a lie not in terms of its truth value but in terms of intention to deceive.

Perception of stealing follows a similiar pattern. Younger children judge the seriousness of stealing by the amount stolen, not by its purpose. When Piaget presented them with the case of a boy who stole a roll to give to a hungry friend and a girl who stole a ribbon for herself, 6-year-olds said the boy's theft was worse "because rolls cost more." But a 9-year-old said, "The little girl was worse. The little girl took the ribbon for herself. The little boy took the roll, but to give it to his friend who had no dinner" (Piaget, 1965).

THE SHIFT IN MORAL REASONING. Piaget found that between ages 5 and 10, children's reasoning moves from objective judgments—based on physical results

The antisocial child is a constant source of tension and disruption in the classroom. He may turn every situation into an occasion for malicious behavior. Often, outside help is needed to help the child learn better ways of interacting.

or damage—to subjective judgments—based on intentions and other psychological considerations (Piaget, 1965; Lickona, 1976). He referred to objective judgments as **moral realism.** The shift away from moral realism could be due to several factors. As we've seen, young children can't detect intentions very well. They often mistake accidents for hostile acts. It could be that they *are* considering intentions in making their moral judgments, but they're not very good at distinguishing deliberate acts from unintentional ones. In the case of John and Henry, they might not have recognized that John didn't mean to break the cups.

There may also be a cognitive-language aspect to the shift in moral reasoning. Young children may be able to identify false assertions that are unintentional (such as when a person is told something untrue and passes it on, believing that it's true), yet they still consider them lies (Wimmer, Gruber, & Perner, 1984). To these children, "lying" means making assertions that aren't true. As children get older, their ability to detect intentions may not improve as much as their understanding that "lying" includes *both* making a false statement *and* intending to deceive.

The socialization processes that parents and teachers have used may also influence children's development in moral reasoning. Children need to learn that intentions do make a difference in whether something is right or wrong, but very often their own intentions aren't valued. It's the rare child who hasn't protested, "I didn't mean to do it!" and yet still been punished. One parent explained his reaction to a situation like this by saying, "I know he didn't mean to do it, but he needs to learn to be careful anyway." Children may learn to be careful, but they may also learn to disregard other people's intentions the same way theirs have been ignored.

Piaget (1965) also studied children's moral reasoning by questioning children about the rules of games. He wanted to find out where children thought rules came from—were they made up by people, or were they "givens"? The ability to realize that rules of games are made by people presumably changes children's views about authority and the factors that they consider when deciding if an action is "right" or "wrong."

Kohlberg's Study of Moral Reasoning

Lawrence Kohlberg's work on moral reasoning is based on the work of Piaget, but it goes further. Piaget felt that children are capable of mature moral reasoning by the age of 11 or 12 when they routinely take intentions into account. In contrast, Kohlberg attempted to differentiate additional stages of moral development during adulthood, when, he believed, higher levels of moral reasoning could be reached.

THE CASE OF HEINZ. Kohlberg approached moral reasoning in terms of people's relationship to society's rules, as Piaget did when he questioned children about their understanding of rules of games. And like Piaget, Kohlberg posed moral dilemmas to people to gain insight into their reasoning. One dilemma he used is that of Heinz, a man who was faced with the choice of stealing medicine or letting his wife die (Kohlberg, 1969, p. 379):

> In Europe, a woman was near death from cancer. One drug might save her, a form of radium that a druggist in the same town had recently discovered. The druggist was charging $2,000, ten times what the drug cost him to make. The sick woman's husband, Heinz, went to everyone he knew to borrow the money, but he could only get together about half of what it cost. He told the druggist that his wife was dying and asked him to sell it cheaper or let him pay later. But the druggist said no. The husband got desperate and broke into the man's store to steal the drug for his wife. Should the man have done that? Why?

KOHLBERG'S LEVELS OF MORAL DEVELOPMENT. On the basis of responses to situations like this, Kohlberg identified three levels of moral development, with two stages at each level (see Table 16–1). At Level I, which he labeled *preconventional*, people make moral decisions on the basis of self-interest, either to avoid punishment or to gain rewards. Both of the following responses to the Heinz dilemma are considered Level I responses (Kohlberg, 1969, p. 381):

> Pro: If you let your wife die, you will get in trouble. You'll be blamed for not spending the money to save her and there'll be an investigation of you and the druggist for your wife's death.

> Con: You shouldn't steal the drug because you'll be caught and sent to jail if you do. If you do get away, your conscience would bother you thinking how the police would catch up with you at any minute.

At Level II, the *conventional* level, people have chosen to conform to the standards expected of them by society. They're guided by a concern for the general good and a desire to maintain social order. At Level III, labeled *postconventional*, people define their values in terms of principles, whether philosophical, religious, or personal in some other way. They're guided by concerns that transcend the maintenance of social order.

Kohlberg's levels and stages are hierarchical—a person moves forward through them one by one, and no stage can be skipped. Research hasn't consistently supported this claim (Rest, 1983; Hoffman, 1984). There's also some philosophical debate about whether a "universal principle of justice" really exists, as Kohlberg claims. Carol Gilligan, for example, has argued that Kohlberg ignored the social context of moral behavior. According to Gilligan, women are socialized *not* to base decisions on personal, self-chosen principles but to consider the consequences of moral decisions for others (Gilligan, 1977; 1982). Other critics have argued that Kohlberg's scheme reflects Western culture with its stress on the individual versus the group (Hogan, 1975; Wallach & Wallach, 1983).

FIGURE 16-9
In Kohlberg's scheme, people who have attained the highest level of moral reasoning define their values in terms of deeply felt moral convictions, even when they conflict with existing laws. Such people may act on their beliefs with civil disobedience or protests, as these opponents of offshore oil drilling are doing. The woman in the lead is obviously serving as a model for her admiring daughter.

TABLE 16-1 Kohlberg's Moral Stages

	Content of Stage		
Level and Stage	What Is Right	Reasons for Doing Right	Social Perspective of Stage
Level I—Preconventional Stage 1—Heteronomous morality	To avoid breaking rules backed by punishment, obedience for its own sake, and avoiding physical damage to persons and property.	Avoidance of punishment, and the superior power of authorities.	*Egocentric point of view.* Doesn't consider the interests of others or recognize that they differ from the actor's; doesn't relate two points of view. Actions are considered physically rather than in terms of psychological interests of others. Confusion of authority's perspective with one's own.
Stage 2—Individualism, instrumental purpose, and exchange	Following rules only when it is to someone's immediate interest; acting to meet one's own interests and needs and letting others do the same. Right is also what's fair, what's an equal exchange, a deal, an agreement.	To serve one's own needs or interests in a world where you have to recognize that other people have their interests, too.	*Concrete individualistic perspective.* Aware that everybody has his own interest to pursue and these conflict, so that right is relative (in the concrete individualistic sense).
Level II—Conventional Stage 3—Mutual interpersonal expectations, relationships, and interpersonal conformity	Living up to what is expected by people close to you or what people generally expect of people in your role as son, brother, friend, etc. "Being good" is important and means having good motives, showing concern about others. It also means keeping mutual relationships, such as trust, loyalty, respect, and gratitude.	The need to be a good person in your own eyes and those of others. Your caring for others. Belief in the Golden Rule. Desire to maintain rules and authority that support stereotypical good behavior.	*Perspective of the individual in relationships with other individuals.* Aware of shared feelings, agreements, and expectations which take primacy over individual interests. Relates points of view through the concrete Golden Rule, putting yourself in the other guy's shoes. Does not yet consider generalized system perspective.
Stage 4—Social system and conscience	Fulfilling the actual duties to which you have agreed. Laws are to be upheld except in extreme cases where they conflict with other fixed social duties. Right is also contributing to society, the group, or institution.	To keep the institution going as a whole, to avoid the breakdown in the system "if everyone did it," or the imperative of conscience to meet one's defined obligations. (Easily confused with Stage 3 belief in rules and authority.)	*Differentiates societal point of view from interpersonal agreement or motive.* Takes the point of view of the system that defines roles and rules. Considers individual relations in terms of place in the system.

Younger children (under age 10) are incapable of reasoning at Kohlberg's highest level, but they gain this ability as they get older. Children between 10 and 12 years old may be in Stage 2, 3, or 4, but they're rarely in Stage 5. Not until adolescence are children able to reason at the highest stages. But this doesn't mean that all adolescents—or all adults, for that matter—will reach the highest stages. The stage a person actually reaches depends on several factors, including exposure to moral dilemma situations and to the values of others. Such exposure can challenge people to reexamine and think through their moral beliefs.

TABLE 16-1 (continued)

Level and Stage	What Is Right	Reasons for Doing Right	Social Perspective of Stage
Level III—Postconventional, or principled Stage 5—Social contract or utility and individual rights	Being aware that people hold a variety of values and opinions, that most values and rules are relative to your group. These relative rules should usually be upheld, however, in the interest of impartiality and because they are the social contract. Some nonrelative values and rights like *life* and *liberty*, however, must be upheld in any society and regardless of majority opinion.	A sense of obligation to law because of one's social contract to make and abide by laws for the welfare of all and for the protection of all people's rights. A feeling of contractual commitment, freely entered upon, to family, friendship, trust, and work obligations. Concern that laws and duties be based on rational calculation of overall utility, "the greatest good for the greatest number."	*Prior-to-society perspective.* Perspective of a rational individual aware of values and rights prior to social attachments and contracts. Integrates perspectives by formal mechanisms of agreement, contract, objective impartiality, and due process. Considers moral and legal points of view, recognizes that they sometimes conflict and finds it difficult to integrate them.
Stage 6—Universal ethical principles	Following self-chosen ethical principles. Particular laws or social agreements are usually valid because they rest on such principles. When laws violate these principles, one acts in accordance with the principle. Principles are universal principles of justice: the equality of human rights and respect for the dignity of human beings as individual persons.	The belief as a rational person in the validity of universal moral principles, and a sense of personal commitment to them.	*Perspective of a moral point of view* from which social arrangements derive. Perspective is that of any rational individual recognizing the nature of morality or the fact that persons are ends in themselves and must be treated as such.

SOURCE: Kohlberg, L. (1976). Moral stages and moralization. In T. Lickona (Ed.), Moral development and behavior: Theory, research, and social issues (pp. 34–35). New York: Holt, Rinehart & Winston. Reprinted with permission.

Damon's Study of Moral Reasoning

The investigation of moral reasoning by a third researcher, William Damon, is also important to our study of children's moral development. Damon (1980) identified two components of social or moral reasoning, both of which relate to children in very meaningful ways. One is what he calls a "positive justice" component, which involves how children understand justice or fairness. Anyone who's heard children complain, "It's not fair!" knows that justice is a major issue for them. The other is an authority component, involving the questions of who has the right to lead others and why a person should obey—another concern children understand.

CHILDREN'S IDEAS ABOUT JUSTICE. To draw positive justice judgments from children, Damon posed such dilemmas as how to distribute the proceeds from a school fair for which children made crafts. The child was asked to decide which children should receive more of the money, given that one child worked hard, one was well behaved, one was poor, and so on. The child also had to justify the decision about distribution.

Damon based his ideas about levels of moral development on responses to dilemmas like this. He found that very young children (4- to 5-year-olds) make positive justice decisions and choices based on what they wish to be true—"I should get it because I want to have it." At the next level (5- to 6-year-olds), children still base decisions on desires, but they add a superficial justification—"We should get the most because we're the girls." Somewhat older children (7- to 8-year-olds) start to make decisions based on strict equality— "Everyone should get the same"—and equality is seen as preventing complaining and fighting.

When children are age 9 or 10, they start to talk about merit and deserving. They also refer to reciprocity—people should be paid back in kind for doing good or bad things. By age 10 or 11, a moral relativity develops out of the realization that different people can have different but equally valid claims to justice. Children lean heavily toward people with special needs, such as the poor, and they try to work out compromises between competing claims. Finally, by age 12 or 13, children reach a level at which they can coordinate a variety of claims and demands. Their decisions reflect their belief that all people should be given their due, although this doesn't always mean equal treatment.

CHILDREN'S IDEAS ABOUT AUTHORITY. To investigate the authority component of moral reasoning, Damon posed dilemmas that involved questions of leadership, power, and obedience. For example, he described a situation in which a child was required by his mother to clean his room before he could go on a picnic with friends. Damon asked children to explain why the mother had a right to make this demand and why the child should or shouldn't obey.

Children's responses again reflected a predictable pattern of development in reasoning ability. At the lowest level, children said the child should obey his mother simply because she was his mother. At a somewhat higher level, children referred to an authority figure's social or physical power ("the teacher can make you stay after school"). Still later, they started to legitimize authority by reference to talents or abilities that made the authority a superior person in their eyes.

As they get older, children start to justify authority on the basis of training or experience; they see an authority figure as better able to lead, and they see obedience as based on respect for this leadership ability. Finally, at the highest level, people legitimize authority on the basis of a particular person's special abilities or talents in a particular situation. They believe that a person might be a good leader in one situation but not in another. Authority is seen as a shared relation between parties, adopted temporarily by a leader for the good of all. Obedience is seen as a cooperative effort in a particular situation, not a general response to a superior person.

Overall, Damon's studies showed that children's thinking about justice and authority becomes more complex and less egocentric as they grow up. Among other things, these changes influence the characteristics that teachers must have, for example, if children are to feel respect for them, and the extent to which children can be helped to appreciate the value of the differing contributions that classmates make to a project.

Moral Reasoning and Behavior

Many people have been interested in these studies of moral reasoning as a way of understanding children's behavior. We've all seen children behave in appallingly selfish or unkind ways, and we know that most of them try out lying and cheating. Do these behaviors decrease as children's moral reasoning ability grows? Unfortunately, researchers have spent so much time sorting out and defining levels of moral reasoning that the question of the relationship between moral development and social behavior has been neglected (Shantz, 1975). The studies we do have indicate a consistent relationship between level of moral reasoning and behavior, although not a perfect one (Hoffman, 1984).

First graders, for example, were assessed for level of moral reasoning using Damon's positive justice classifications and then observed in their classrooms (Enright & Sutterfield, 1980). Researchers noted the number of times a peer approached a child, the number of interactions with positive outcomes, and the number of incidents that involved derogatory comments. They found that children with higher scores in moral reasoning also had more successful interactions and were approached more often by other children. Because Damon's scale involves the ability to think of others, it's understandable that children at higher levels were able to interact better and were sought out by peers.

Popular children also seem to be able to judge intentions more accurately and take other children's needs into account (Dodge, Murphy, & Buchsbaum, 1984). When provoked by another child, they're more likely to ask the child to explain the provocation rather than to respond aggressively. They withhold judgment before labeling the child "bad" or "mean."

Behavior is influenced by more things than moral reasoning ability, of course, as we've seen. Children are pulled in different directions by a host of conflicting forces. Even as adults we have to admit that our behavior often falls short of what we consider the "right" thing to do. But when we fail, we feel guilty or we experience cognitive dissonance—a conflict between what we think of ourselves and what we've done. Therefore, our behavior is probably consistently pulled toward higher moral levels by our ideas of the right thing to do.

SEX DIFFERENCES AND SEX-ROLE DEVELOPMENT

Margo burst into the house in tears after school one day, and her mother rushed into the room to see what was wrong.

"The boys say I can't play football with them any more," Margo sobbed. "They say they don't want to hang around with anyone who plays with Barbie dolls. Just because today I wanted to play Barbies at lunchtime with Becky and Sarah, they went off without me after school. When I caught up with them, they said if I was going to play girl things, I couldn't play with them. It's not fair! I can run faster and throw a football farther than almost any of them! It's just not fair!"

FIGURE 16-10
Very few physical, cognitive, or personality differences exist between boys and girls in middle childhood. Coed sports can help children break through the stereotyped view of girls as less competent physically than boys.

Margo has run headlong into sex-role stereotyping, the notion that people have to be confined to certain activities depending on whether they're male or female. We encounter these ideas every day in our society, but is there any basis for them in fact? Are there important differences in behavior between males and females? And if so, are they cultural or biological, learned or innate?

Every culture makes assumptions about the activities, abilities, social positions, and other characteristics that are appropriate for women and men. These learned characteristics together comprise **sex roles** in that culture (Angrist, 1969; Block, 1973). But there appears to be a biological basis for the differences in behavior, too. Here, we look first at differences in cognitive ability and personality between boys and girls. Then we discuss sex-role development—how and why girls and boys develop different patterns of behavior.

Sex Differences

Sex differences are average differences between boys and girls or between men and women. If we determined the average weight and height for men and women, for example, we would find that the means differ: Men are taller and heavier, on average, than women. This doesn't mean that we can't find a woman who is taller and heavier than a given man, because some women will be above average and some men will be below average. What it means is that the averages for the sexes line up this way. In addition to sex differences in physical characteristics, there are sex differences in cognitive abilities and personality. We note these below, along with some cautions about their interpretation.

COGNITIVE ABILITIES. There are no significant differences between girls and boys in overall IQ or on tasks requiring reasoning, logic, or verbal creativity. But some cognitive differences do exist, and these become accentuated in adolescence and adulthood. Girls have slightly better verbal skills during infancy and toddlerhood and again after adolescence begins. Boys take the lead in mathematics and spatial abilities, but again, not until adulthood. There is no general pattern of superiority: Girls are better at verbal analytical tasks, and boys are better at mathematical and spatial tasks. Since most of these differences emerge in adulthood, girls and boys in middle childhood show very few differences in cognitive abilities (see Table 16-2 for a summary of these differences and similarities).

PERSONALITY CHARACTERISTICS. Contrary to popular opinion, girls are not more sociable, nurturant, timid, fearful, or anxious than boys, nor are they less persistent on tasks or less achievement oriented than boys. Girls think just as well of themselves as boys do, although boys and girls (and men and women) apparently think well of themselves for different reasons.

Girls *are* less aggressive than boys. When they're in groups, they're less active than boys, although this wasn't true in infancy. When they're alone, girls and boys are equally active. Girls seem to have a lower expectation of success than boys, especially on novel intellectual tasks. And they feel less in

TABLE 16-2 Differences and Similarities between Boys and Girls in Cognitive Abilities

Differences	Similarities
1. Girls have better verbal abilities between birth and age 3 and after the age of 11 or 12. They vocalize more and talk earlier. During middle childhood, boys and girls have similar verbal abilities. 2. Boys are better in mathematical tasks but not until adolescence. 3. Boys have better spatial abilities, but again, the differences do not emerge decisively until adolescence. 4. Girls have fewer problems than boys with reading. 5. Girls get better grades in school than boys of all ages. 6. Boys do better than girls on analytic tasks involving mathematical or spatial abilities. 7. Girls do better than boys on verbal analytic tasks such as making different words from a set of letters.	1. Boys and girls do equally well in reasoning and logic as measured by tasks resembling those used by Piaget. 2. Boys and girls do equally well on tasks involving nonverbal creativity. 3. Boys and girls have the same group IQs. *SOURCES: Bee, H. (1978). Overview: Sex differences. In H. Bee (Ed.), Social issues in developmental psychology. New York: Harper & Row; Brooks-Gunn, J., (1979). Matthews, W. S. (1979). He and she: How children develop their sex-role identity. Englewood Cliffs, NJ: Prentice-Hall; Maccoby, E. E., & Jacklin, C. N. (1974). The psychology of sex differences. Stanford, CA: Stanford University Press; Tavris, C., & Offir, C. (1977). The longest war: Sex differences in perspective. New York: Harcourt Brace Jovanovich.*

control of what happens to them (see Table 16-3 for a summary of differences and similarities in personality).

INTERPRETING SEX-DIFFERENCE DATA. A few words of caution are in order about interpreting data that reveal cognitive and personality differences between boys and girls. First, studies that demonstrate sex differences are more likely to be published than studies that don't, because differences are considered more newsworthy. Problems of sampling and generalizability may make the published data even more distorted. If you recall from Chapter 2, researchers

TABLE 16-3 Differences and Similarities between Boys and Girls in Personality

Differences	*Similarities*
1. Boys are more aggressive than girls of all ages.	1. Boys and girls appear to be equally sensitive to people and social stimuli. For example, as infants they attend equally to faces and objects. (Studies yield mixed results on this issue, but consistent differences have not been found.)
2. Boys cry somewhat more than girls between the ages of 1 and 6, especially when frustrated, as when they are separated from their mothers.	
3. Boys show more anger and upset behavior than girls between the ages of 1 and 6, but it's uncertain whether they differ when they are older.	2. Boys and girls show the same degree of empathy or altruistic behavior, such as helping someone in distress.
4. Girls between 1 and 6 comply with demands from adults more readily than boys, but boys appear to be more susceptible to peer pressure, even in adulthood.	3. The data on the nurturant behavior of boys and girls in the United States reveal no differences. A review of cross-cultural studies does indicate that girls are more nurturant than boys. When communities are analyzed separately, however, there were often no differences; when there were, it was sometimes found that boys were more helpful than girls (in Okinawa, for example). One reason cross-cultural data in general show that girls are more often assigned responsibility for younger siblings than boys. Studies of communities in the United States, in which girls are not assigned this task, indicate that boys and girls do not differ in nurturant behavior.
5. Boys appear to be more peer oriented than girls at all ages and spend more time with groups of peers than girls do. Girls tend to spend their time with one or two best friends.	
6. Girls *report* more fear and anxiety than boys do, and teachers *report* that girls are more timid and anxious than boys.	
7. Boys between the ages of 1 and 12 may be more active than girls, but the data is inconclusive. When boys are alone, they seem no more active than girls, but when they're with a group of boys, they're apparently more active. During infancy, girls and boys have the same level of activity.	4. Girls and boys appear to be equally fearful, timid, and anxious when actual *behavior* is observed. However, if you recall, girls report more feelings of fear and anxiety.
8. Boys are judged to be tougher and more dominant between the ages of 1 and 12. In adulthood men appear to be more dominant than women, but in some situations the reverse may be true.	5. Girls and boys tend to be equally motivated to achieve in neutral situations. Boys seem to be aroused to achieve by competition to a greater extent than girls.
9. Girls have lower expectancies for success than boys, but the differences are not consistently apparent until adolescence and adulthood.	6. Girls and boys seem to be equal in self-esteem during childhood, but they seem to feel positively about themselves for different reasons. Girls and women seem to think positively about themselves for their social skills, but boys and men seem to think positively of themselves for more individual traits such as ambition or dominance.
	7. Girls and boys are equally persistent in most tasks.

SOURCES: Bee, H. (1978). Overview: Sex differences. In H. Bee (Ed.), *Social issues in developmental psychology*. New York: Harper & Row; Brooks-Gunn, J. & Matthews, W. S. (1979). *He and she: How children develop their sex-role identity*. Englewood Cliffs, NJ: Prentice-Hall; Maccoby, E. E., & Jacklin, C. N. (1974).*The psychology of sex differences*. Stanford, CA: Stanford University Press; Tavris, C., & Offir, C. (1977). *The longest war: Sex differences in perspective*. New York: Harcourt Brace Jovanovich; Ruble, D. N. (1984). *Sex-role development*. In M. H. Bornstein & M. E. Lamb (Eds.), *Developmental psychology: An advanced text*. Hillsdale, NJ: Lawrence Erlbaum.

have to be extremely careful about getting representative samples of children in their studies, and they have to make sure their results are generalizable to the rest of the population.

They also have to make clear what age children they're talking about when they find sex differences. As mentioned previously, some differences appear during toddlerhood, disappear during middle childhood, and reappear in adolescence and adulthood. If researchers report sex-related characteristics without specifying the age of the children exhibiting these characteristics, sex differences might appear to be more pervasive than they really are. A difference found between 3-year-olds might also be construed to exist between 8-year-olds.

Definitions create other problems. If we define sociability as making friends or seeking out the company of others, then we can conclude that boys are more sociable (Baumrind & Block, 1967; Whiting and Edwards, 1973). But if we define sociability as depicting people in drawings or enjoying the company of a few best friends rather than a large group of peers, then we can conclude that girls are more sociable (Goodenough, 1957; Waldrop, cited in Maccoby & Jacklin, 1974). The specific definition a researcher chooses can determine what differences the study demonstrates. And if we compare studies that have used different definitions, we find that the differences cancel out each other. On the basis of the studies just cited, for example, we can't really say whether boys or girls are more sociable.

A serious problem in interpreting the results of sex differences studies is that group differences for boys and girls are typically very small. This means that many individual boys and girls don't fit neatly into group patterns. For example, the average performance for girls in math falls below the average performance for boys. But some girls are well above average in math and thus perform better than most boys. Similarly, some boys are well above average in verbal ability and perform better than most girls. Many boys and girls are both above and below average in different skills for their gender group. The danger in talking about small differences—and these differences are very small—is that we start to assume that individual boys and girls will closely match the overall pattern for their gender group. These assumptions are what produce **sex-role stereotypes.**

Explaining Sex Differences

Boys and girls are more similar than they are different, especially in middle childhood. But the small differences that do exist have been well documented. The question is: Are these differences inborn, or are they learned through experience?

BIOLOGY AND SEX DIFFERENCES. Both spatial ability and aggression are more dominant in males than in females, and as a result, they are often explained in terms of biology. Some people have hypothesized, for example, that spatial ability may be a sex-linked recessive trait. If you recall from Chapter 3, girls (with their XX chromosomes) inherit an X chromosome from each parent, and boys (with XY chromosomes) inherit their one X chromosome from their mother. If the gene for spatial ability is carried on the X chromosome and is recessive, it could be overridden in girls by a dominant gene inherited from their father.

Because boys receive only one X chromosome, any recessive gene carried on it can be expressed. (This model is illustrated in Table 16-4) Thus, boys would have a better chance of inheriting good spatial abilities.

To explain aggression, researchers have pointed to the male sex hormone testosterone as a possible factor. During the sixth week of gestation, the testes begin to produce male sex hormones known as androgens. These hormones trigger the physical development of the male genitals. If the hormones aren't released, the fetus won't develop male genitals even though it has the typical XY male chromosome. Androgens may also act on the hypothalamus in the brain during puberty, triggering the emergence of male sexual behavior (Levine, 1966; Phoenix, Goy, & Resko, 1978).

Evidence for a link between male sex hormones and aggression comes from several sources. Animal studies have shown that female monkeys given testosterone before they were born engage in more aggressive play than untreated females (Young, Goy, & Phoenix, 1964). Female animals given testosterone in infancy engage in more fighting (Edwards, 1969; Joslyn, 1971).

In humans, prenatal accidents sometimes result in masculinized females, individuals with XX chromosomes but with male genitals. Even when these children's genitalia are corrected surgically, their mothers reported that they continued to display masculine behavior. They enjoyed outdoor play, thought of themselves as "tomboys," and didn't like to play with dolls (Erhardt & Baker, 1974). Since the male genitals would have produced testosterone during prenatal development, these girls would have had higher levels of the hormone in their bodies. Additionally, testosterone levels in boys have been found to be related to their aggressive behavior and attitudes (Olweus et al., 1980), and some evidence exists for a relationship between high testosterone levels and criminal behavior in males (Parke & Slaby, 1983).

TABLE 16-4
Possible Patterns for Spatial Genes in Males and Females

FEMALES		
Chromosomes		*Consequences*
X^1	X^2	
s	s	good spatial ability
s	S	carrier for good spatial ability but performs poorly
S	s	carrier for good spatial ability but performs poorly
S	S	poor spatial ability

This model predicts that one out of four females will inherit good spatial ability

MALES		
Chromosomes		*Consequences*
X	Y	
s	—	good spatial ability
S	—	poor spatial ability

This model predicts that one out of two males will inherit good spatial ability

SOURCE: From the longest war: Sex differences in perspective by Carol Tavris and Carole Offir, © 1977 by Harcourt Brace Jovanovich, Inc. Reprinted by permission of the publisher.

This evidence is suggestive, but it isn't conclusive. The strongest evidence comes from animal studies, and these can be an unreliable standard when it comes to humans. Hormones may not have the same powerful effect in humans that they have in animals, as we saw in the attachment and bonding studies described in Chapter 8. In the studies of masculinized girls, we must take into account the fact that their parents knew of their condition. They may have tolerated more aggressive behavior in these girls, thinking it appropriate because of their developmental histories. Their behavior may have been more a result of how they were socialized than of their biological development.

All in all, we can't really know for sure to what extent aggression, spatial abilities, or any other aspect of sex-role behavior is determined by biology. The alternative explanation for sex differences is socialization.

SOCIALIZATION AND SEX DIFFERENCES. If sex differences aren't innate—and the evidence is shaky, as we've shown—then they must be learned during the socialization process. This learning is explained differently by different theories. Social learning theory explanations call on the principles of reinforcement, punishment, and modeling. Cognitive explanations refer to the child's growing cognitive abilities and the concepts of gender identity and gender constancy (see Research Focus—The Development of Gender Identity).

Whatever theory we believe, we can easily see that boys and girls are treated differently. Research has supported these everyday observations. Fathers play more with their sons than they do with their daughters (Lamb, 1977; Weinraub & Frankel, 1977), and they play with them in more physical ways. Boys and girls own different kinds of toys, as mentioned in Chapter 8. Toddler boys are punished more than girls, and they misbehave more as well (Minton, Kagan, & Levine, 1971). Toddler boys play alone at home more than girls (Smith & Doglish, 1977). In the early elementary grades, teachers expect boys to be more active and unruly than girls (Minuchin & Shapiro, 1983). At home, elementary school-age boys are given more freedom from parental supervision than girls (Newson & Newson, 1978).

How can being treated differently lead to different behavior? First, more experience with rough-and-tumble play could make boys more familiar and comfortable with the kinds of behavior used in physical aggression. Second, boys' toys are oriented more toward war and fighting than girls' toys, and boys' toys support aggressive play. When children use aggressive toys, they're more likely to be aggressive with each other (Berkowitz & Le Page, 1967). Third, since toddler boys play alone more at home, their behavior may come under less scrutiny than girls. There are more opportunities for girls' behavior to be shaped into more socialized forms.

At school, teachers' expectations of boys may account for the fact that they praise boys more, give them more help, accept their comments more readily, and permit them to dominate classroom discussions (Sadaker & Sadaker, 1985). Teachers may feel that girls are already better behaved and need less praise and help. They may also think they're better able to wait for their turn and listen to others.

Direct reinforcement and punishment are supported by what children see modeled around them in real life, as summed up in the following excerpt (Huston, 1983, pp. 420–421):

RESEARCH FOCUS

The Development of Gender Identity

"When I'm growed up, I'll have a baby too," said 3-year-old Jacob, patting his mother's stomach. She looked at him blankly for a few moments before responding.

"No, Jacob," she finally said. "You're a boy."

"I know," he answered.

"Well . . . boys don't have babies," his mother went on slowly. "Men can be daddies, but only women can be mommies."

"I know. But when I grow up to be a woman, I'll have a baby."

Jacob's mother needn't be alarmed. Jacob knows he's a boy, but he doesn't know he'll always be a boy, and this is typical of children's understanding at this age. By age 2½ most children have **gender identity,** meaning they label themselves correctly as a boy or a girl (Slaby & Frey, 1975), but they don't yet have **gender constancy,** which is the understanding that they will always be the sex they are now. Cut your hair, change your clothes, act a little differently, and you can change your sex, too, according to a 3-year-old. The solid understanding that these criteria aren't what determine gender is not attained by most children until the age of 6 or 7 (Huston, 1983).

Lawrence Kohlberg, whose work on moral development is discussed in this chapter, based a theory of sex-role development on cognitive changes that occur as children get older. Because children think they can change gender up until the school years, they don't pay close attention to adult modeling of sex-typed behavior during the preschool years, and they don't model it systematically themselves. But as gender constancy emerges at about age 7, children begin to act increasingly like adults who are the same sex they are. They tend to conform rigidly to their ideas of appropriate behavior for their sex during middle childhood. Later, as they start to observe exceptions to the general rule that men and women behave differently and begin to be able to think about what might be (in adolescence), they moderate their views (Huston, 1983).

Parents and teachers who have made an effort to teach children that "boys and girls can do all the same things" may despair as they see school-age children adopting narrowly stereotyped roles and behaviors. Unless adults can somehow change the world in such a way that males and females don't model sex-typed behavior, children's advancing cognitive abilities will propel them inevitably to make these sex-typed distinctions. But just as inevitably, exceptions and even

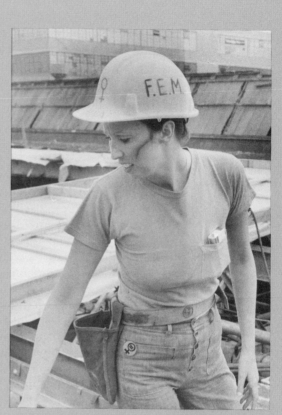

Nonstereotypical models, such as female construction workers and male elementary school teachers, open up the whole range of possible human experiences to children.

more advanced thinking will gradually make their mark, and this is where adults can make a difference. By exposing children to nonstereotypical sex-role behavior, they provide models and images that broaden perspectives. Children realize that they can accomplish things as human beings, not just as males or females. As their cognitive abilities continue to advance in adolescence, children are able to attain a greater degree of flexibility in their views of human potential.

The average child sees women cooking, cleaning, and sewing; working in "female" jobs such as clerical, secretarial, sales, teaching, nursing; choosing to dance, sew, or play bridge for recreation; and achieving in artistic or literary areas more often than in science and engineering. That same child sees men mowing the lawn, washing the car, or doing household repairs; working in "male" occupations; choosing team sports, fishing, and nights with "the boys" for recreation; and achieving in math, science, and technical areas more often than in poetry or art.

In school, the teachers of young children are women; the teachers of older students and the administrators with power are usually men. Peers and siblings pursue sex-stereotyped activities, games, and interests more often than they engage in cross-sex activity.

The mass media provide even more opportunities for children to observe sex-typed behavior. Virtually every study of the content of television shows has found that females are under-represented and that roles and behavior are stereotyped (Huston, 1983). Toy commercials are some of the worst offenders. Not only do they show boys and girls playing with completely different toys, but the ads themselves are made differently: "high levels of inanimate action, frequent changes to new scenes, rapid cuts, sound effects, and loud lively music typify boys' ads. Moderate levels of action, few scene changes, fades, dissolves, and soft tinkly music typify girls' ads (Leary, Huston, & Wright, 1983, p. 1).

Children's books also provide sex-stereotyped versions of life. A recent study analyzed the male and female characters and images in books that had received Caldecott awards and honors, given for excellence in children's books. Although the number of male characters in books published between 1981 and 1985 had dropped from the number found in the 1976 to 1981 books (Dougherty & Engel, 1986), the numbers still didn't match the equal proportions found in 1951 to 1955 books. And in books that kindergarten and primary-grade teachers read to children in the classroom, the main character is male over 70 percent of the time (Smith, Greenlaw, & Scott, 1987).

Females are typically presented as more dependent than males, as revealed in a study of themes in over 100 recently published fiction books (White, 1986). Females are more likely to receive help, and males are more likely to give it: "The girls and women in children's fiction do seem to reflect the cultural stereotype of the helpless female, the perennial damsel in distress in need of male protection" (White, 1986, p. 255).

Children can hardly help but get the message: Males and females act differently, are treated differently, and have different kinds of lives to live. And, in our society, males are dominant. Any biological differences that do exist are exaggerated by the subtle and not-so-subtle messages that bombard children from their earliest days of life.

FIGURE 16-11
Mom's encouragement sends a powerful message to this little girl about getting her nails done. In our society, girls learn at an early age that appearance and behavior are important concerns for them. Girls are praised for being pretty, nice, or good, while boys are approved for being strong, competent, or smart. Socialization seems to account for most of the behavior differences we see between the sexes.

OVERVIEW

Children acquire important social understandings during the school years, largely as a result of their growing ability to put themselves in someone else's shoes. This social role-taking ability allows them to become aware of other people's thoughts, feelings, and intentions, which in turn contributes to their developing moral sense. At the same time, school-age children are becoming more self-aware and more concerned about what others think of them. Friends become increasingly important, as children seek ways to define themselves in relation to others. Whether that self-image is positive or negative, the pattern of social interaction established during the school years often endures and becomes part of the individual's adaptation to life.

CHAPTER REVIEW

SOCIAL ROLE-TAKING ABILITY

- During the school years, children's social role-taking ability—the ability to judge what others are thinking and feeling—improves dramatically. This ability, just one aspect of social cognition, gives them greater personal insight and better understanding of others.
- Social role-taking ability has three components: understanding other people's emotions, understanding other people's intentions, and understanding other people's thinking.
- As they mature, children begin to understand how ambiguous and complex emotional responses can be. Young children typically have "all or none" emotional reactions. Later, they become able to make subtler distinctions between emotions and to be aware when they're experiencing conflicting emotions at the same time.

- They also come to realize that the same situation can evoke different emotional responses in different people and that people may react differently because of personal histories and interpretations.
- Toward the end of middle childhood, children begin to discriminate between "accidental" and "deliberate" intentions, and they learn they should respond accordingly. Even older children have difficulty detecting intentions when they're being deliberately deceived.
- School-age children gradually become able to realize that other people can have points of view and opinions other than they do. Children need help from adults to understand the inner thought processes of others.
- The development of social role-taking skills isn't necessarily associated with improved social behavior.

SOCIAL SKILLS AND POPULARITY

- Popular children tend to be friendly and outgoing in positive ways. Their strategies for entering an ongoing play situation are noticeably different from those of unpopular children.
- Birth order, commonness of first name, and physical appearance have all been correlated with children's popularity.
- Children's social status is important because unpopular children tend to have lower self-esteem, achieve less in school, and have more problems later in life. Coaching a child in social skills and adapting coaching techniques to classroom use can be effective methods of changing a child's social status.
- Children who are antisocial, disruptive, and destructive in elementary school need help to change their patterns of interaction before their behavior gets worse.

MORAL DEVELOPMENT

- Moral development is a complex process that involves both cognitive and emotional growth.
- Young children judge the seriousness of stealing by the amount stolen and the seriousness of lying by how much the lie varies from the truth. They don't take intentions or other factors into account
- Piaget found that between ages 5 and 10, children shift from objective judgments, based on physical results,

to subjective judgments, based on intentions and other psychological considerations. He felt that by age 11 or 12, children have shifted away from moral realism and have become capable of mature moral reasoning.

- Piaget suggested that children's understanding of the rules of games reflects their evolving sense of how "right" and "wrong" are established.
- Kohlberg suggested that the growth of moral reasoning is reflected in three levels of moral development. Children don't reach the highest level until adolescence, but not all adolescents (nor all adults) reach this level. Research hasn't consistently supported Kohlberg's claims.

- Damon identified two important components of moral reasoning, which he called positive justice—how children understand fairness—and authority—how children understand why a person should obey. Children think about justice and authority in much more complex and less egocentric ways as they get older.
- A relationship does exist between moral development and social behavior, but even as adults, our behavior may not always meet our moral standards.

SEX DIFFERENCES AND SEX-ROLE DEVELOPMENT

- Sex roles are the cultural assumptions about abilities, activities, social positions, and other characteristics appropriate to men and women. Sex differences are average differences between the sexes in physical characteristics, cognitive abilities, and personality.
- There are no significant differences between girls and boys in intelligence or reasoning ability. Some cognitive differences and some personality differences do exist, but differences are small and there is no overall pattern of superiority.
- The danger in focusing on small differences between boys and girls is that all children will be expected to fit into sex-role stereotypes.

- Researchers have investigated two characteristics of boys—their greater aggressiveness and their better spatial abilities—to see if they could link them to genetic or hormonal factors. But research has been unable to demonstrate the role played by biology in these characteristics.
- Boys and girls are treated differently by parents and teachers and represented differently in books and television programs. In their daily life, children observe women and men performing tasks traditionally associated with one sex or the other. Socialization probably accounts for most of the sex-typed behavior we see in children.

KEY TERMS

social role-taking ability
social cognition
targets
valence
egocentric role taking
social-information role
   taking

self-reflective role taking
mutual role taking
social and conventional
   system role taking
popular status
unpopular status
neglected status

controversial status
coaching
moral realism
sex roles
sex differences
sex-role stereotypes
gender identity
gender constancy

SUGGESTIONS FOR FURTHER READING

Archer, J., & Lloyd, B. (1982). *Sex and gender.* New York: Cambridge University Press.

    A very thorough treatment of the sex and gender issue, including chapters on physical sex differences, aggression and power, socialization, and possible changes in sex roles in the future.

Bornstein, M. H., and Lamb, M. E. (Eds.) (1988). *Developmental psychology: An advanced textbook* (2d ed.). Hillsdale, NJ: Lawrence Erlbaum.

    This book has good chapters on moral development and sex role development. Written at a higher level than the Grusec and Lytton book, which follows.

Coles, R. (1986). *The moral life of children.* Boston: Atlantic Monthly Press.

    This book, written by the noted psychiatrist, contains many examples of moral thinking evident in children.

Grusec, J. E., & Lytton, H. (1988). *Social development.* New York: Springer-Verlag.

    This book contains thorough chapters on moral development and sex role development. For the student who wants a readable yet extensive briefing on these topics.

SCHOOL-AGE CHILDREN

"Will you read Jackie's magazine to me tonight, Mama?" asked Daisy one night at bed-time. She was poring over the latest issue of National Geographic World.

"What about your new library book?" asked her mother, Suzanne. "I thought you wanted to read the latest Berenstain Bears book."

"But I want to know what all these pictures are. This one looks like someone in a space suit, but it's underwater, and this one looks like an octopus turning the water black."

"Sure, let's see what they're all about," Suzanne replied. She was used to her daughter being a dreamy child who spent hours drawing, pretending, and playing fantasy games. Now, half-way through first grade, Daisy was surprising her every day with her sophisticated new questions and interests. In the recent past, she had wanted to know why the moon was out during the day, what the difference was between digital clocks and regular clocks, whether it was possible to touch a rainbow, how the microwave oven cooked food, whether she lived in New York or the United States or both, how to write her friends' names in cursive, and what countless words spelled. She brought home crystals she had made in science class, practiced making up her own mazes and dot-to-dot pictures, and sent her parents to the encyclopedia to answer her questions on more than one occasion.

"What is going on?" thought Suzanne as Daisy settled into her lap clutching the magazine. "Reading about octopuses is not my idea of a bedtime story!" But as she observed her daughter's curiosity and intent interest in the article, she became caught up in it herself—and in the exciting, seemingly sudden, transformation in Daisy's intellectual interests.

At age $6\frac{1}{2}$, Daisy is in the process of becoming "rational." This dramatic cognitive change makes it possible for children to begin to learn and understand things in a completely new way. The elementary school curriculum assumes that children have reached this level of rationality, and children who haven't yet reached it are likely to have a difficult time with some of their school work.

The cognitive basis of the elementary school curriculum is one of the topics we address in Knowledge in Action: School-Age Children. We also discuss the growing problem of after-school child care for children whose parents work. Thousands upon thousands of "latchkey" children now go home to an empty house after school and take care of themselves until their parents get home. Families and communities have tried a variety of approaches to this situation, which is bound to become increasingly pressing in the 1990s. As in other knowledge-in-action sections, we also consider how children are assessed at this age, and we conclude with a discussion of living with the school-age child.

COGNITIVE DEMANDS OF THE ELEMENTARY SCHOOL CURRICULUM

It's during middle childhood that "formal" schooling begins. The term *formal* doesn't mean organized or thoughtful—education for infants, toddlers, and preschoolers is organized and thoughtful. But education at these lower levels isn't legally mandated—required by law—nor is it characterized by direct instruction. It's in these two senses that elementary schooling is "formal."

The fact that formal schooling begins at about age 6 or 7 isn't a coincidence. Throughout this book, we've discussed many developmental trends in children's cognitive abilities. Almost without exception—whether we're looking at insight into the notions of conservation, seriation, and classification; the ability to distinguish between reality and fastasy; or the understanding of such concepts as "alive" and "dead"; the awareness of what another person might be thinking; or the ability to honor the principles of conversation—the age of 7 for many children marks a significant shift toward reason and logic.

Every part of the elementary school curriculum—math, social studies, science, reading, writing, music—requires an understanding of the concepts of space, time, number, and classification. Basic cognitive skills are necessary for reading a map; understanding the relationship among city, state, country, and continent; realizing how a category, such as mammal, and a specific case, such as cow, are related; telling time; diagramming a sentence; and playing a musical instrument, to name just a few.

If children haven't reached the level of concrete operational thinking by the time they're in first grade, they can have difficulty coping with the curriculum, especially if it's taught in an abstract or didactic (teacher-directed) way. And many schools do still teach this way, even though research indicates that hands-on experience and discussion are better ways for children to learn. Math and science, for example, are often taught without the benefit of manipulatives or experiments. When children aren't able to see, to experience, to derive knowledge for themselves, they usually don't understand, even if they have concrete operational thinking.

Since this cognitive shift occurs for most children by about 7, it makes sense for schools to have a reasonably flexible first-grade curriculum, one that accommodates all the children. Schools can adopt a hands-on approach for first-grade learning activities that will support deep understanding. And parents can take trips to libraries and museums and use other community resources to help fill in gaps in their children's experiences.

FIGURE 1
School-age children have the cognitive skills to learn how to play an instrument and to read music. Perhaps even more important, they can understand that their playing will steadily improve if they practice regularly. When children are interested, as these second graders are, they may be ready for lessons.

AFTER-SCHOOL CARE FOR SCHOOL-AGE CHILDREN

"I'm home, Elliott!" Martha called out as she shoved open the front door with her attaché case in one hand and a bag of groceries in the other. But instead of the greeting she expected, she heard alarmed voices in the next room.

"Your mom's home!"

"Oh no!"

Walking into the family room, Martha saw a strange sight. Elliott, her 10-year-old son, was squeezing out a dripping towel, and Norm, his 11-year-old friend from next door, was mopping up water from the floor. The aquarium was half empty, and the gold-fish were darting back and forth at the far end of the tank.

"What happened?" Martha asked.

"Well, see, Norm had this idea . . . "

"But it was you who threw the marble that hit the aquarium . . . "

"But it was your idea to play bombardier . . . "

"You were throwing marbles?" Martha asked.

"Yeah. We each had a pile of them and we were seeing . . . "

"You were throwing marbles in the house?"

"Yeah. We were seeing how hard we could throw them, and one of them hit the fish tank."

"Is there glass in the fish tank?"

"No, I don't think so . . . well, just a little. See, it's just this little hole. The water stopped coming out after it got below the hole . . ."

Martha took off her coat and looked more closely at the damage.

"Well, let's get the fish out of there. I'm afraid you guys are going to have to buy a new aquarium. And Norm, I'm going to think about whether you can come over again after school when I'm not here."

"Okay."

"Whatever made you play a game like that? You know you're not supposed to throw anything in the house."

"Well, Mom, we're not supposed to throw balls in the house. You never said not to throw marbles in the house."

"Use your head, Elliott. Was this a good idea?"

"But I didn't know before that a marble could break an aquarium."

"Still, never throw anything in the house," Martha answered. "Now let's clean all of this up."

In her mind, Martha was wondering how many more times she would come home to a new, unexpected disaster. It seemed as if she couldn't keep ahead of her son's inventiveness. She knew he needed more supervision, and she desperately wished she could be at home after school or that there was some place for him to go. But so far, their community offered nothing in the way of after-school recreation or care programs. Martha resolved to put some more effort into finding or creating a solution to her family's after-school problem.

Even at age 10 or 11, children don't have the judgment and experience to know what the consequences of all their actions may be. Yet many school-age children are left alone after school until their parents get home from work. What to do about this period of two to three hours every day is a matter of tremendous concern for parents, teachers, and communities.

The Need for After-School Care

The gap between the time children finish school and the time working parents get home from their jobs is a consequence of the school schedule, which usually runs from about 8 A.M. to about 3 P.M. This schedule has been shaped by several forces, including the historical need for rural children to help with farm chores, the need for children to have a day that's not so long they get exhausted, the need for teachers to have planning and paper-grading time, and the need for schools to control their operating costs.

This isn't the first time that after-school care has been a problem. The theme of the 1943 American Association of School Administrators convention was "door key" children—children who wore a house key around their necks because they went home after school to an empty house. These were children whose mothers worked in defense-related jobs and whose fathers were away in the war (Stroman & Duff, 1982). By 1947, there had been a return to prewar "normalcy"—less than one mother in five was still working outside the home.

Today, however, child care patterns are being shaped not by a specific historical event but by long-term economic and social trends. No one expects the patterns of previous years, in which mothers were at home when children got out of school, to reappear. In 1986 more than three out of five mothers were working outside the home (Bailey, 1986). By 1990, nearly four out of five moth-

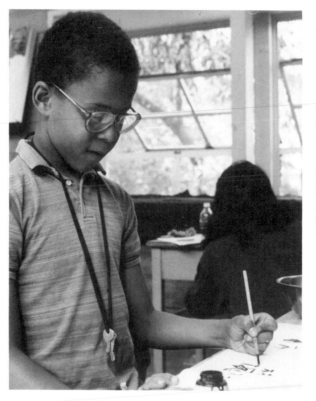

FIGURE 2
As the number of two-career and single-parent families increases, so does the number of children who let themselves into their homes after school with their own keys. What they do with their unsupervised time depends to a large degree on the child-rearing techniques their parents have used. A child with a variety of hobbies, interests, and skills, such as this boy practicing Japanese lettering, may have better ideas to draw on when faced with unfilled hours.

ers of school-age children were in the work force. Many of their children are "latchkey" children, who again are wearing keys around their necks to let themselves into their homes after school.

The Effects of Being a Latchkey Child

What are the consequences of being a latchkey child? Surprisingly few studies have been done to investigate this question, and the research that is available provides somewhat mixed findings. Several studies have found that urban children in first through sixth grades who were left alone after school feel afraid and lonely (Long & Long, 1982; Zill, 1983). They're afraid of noises, the dark, and intruders, and they report that they're bored.

Studies of suburban and rural children, on the other hand, haven't found the same patterns, although these studies didn't include children younger than fourth grade (Rodman, Pratto, & Nelson, 1985; Galambos & Garbarino, 1983). (In fact, some states have laws against leaving children alone who are under a certain age, usually 9 or 10.) These children might not have felt afraid because they were older or because their environments were relatively safer.

One study turned up an important relationship between child-rearing practices and susceptibility to peer pressure on the part of children—in this case, fifth, sixth, eighth, and ninth graders—who were left unsupervised after school (Steinberg, 1986). The study made use of three broad categories of child-rearing techniques and styles identified in earlier research by Diana Baumrind and labeled **permissive, authoritarian,** and **authoritative** (Baumrind, 1967). (For a

RESEARCH FOCUS

How Can Parents Raise Competent Children?

Most parents would probably agree that their goal is to raise children who will someday be competent, independent, and able to succeed on their own in the world. But how to achieve this goal is a question on which there's considerably less agreement (which is surprising when you consider how long people have been in the child-rearing business.) Some parents believe they should be kind and understanding and make few demands. Others belive they should be tough, stern, and aloof. Still others think they should demonstrate firm expectations but be willing to explain their stands. Is there an approach to parenting that leads more reliably than other approaches to competent and self-sufficient children? If so, what is it?

Psychologist Diana Baumrind investigated many parent-child relationships (1972) and identified three broad patterns or styles of parenting, which she labeled **authoritarian, authoritative,** and **permissive.** Parents identified as authoritarian have set expectations for children's conduct which often come from absolute standards, such as religious teachings. These parents demand obedience from their children, and they use forceful means to get it. Children aren't permitted to question rules and regulations, nor do parents attempt to explain them. Authoritarian parents might be described as rigid.

Parents identified as authoritative also have firm expectations, but they explain rules and discuss situations with their children. These parents acknowledge the child's interests and point of view but don't hesitate to enforce adult standards when the child and adult views are in conflict. They use both force—power—and reason to ensure that the child complies with adult expectations. Their expectations, however, aren't established according to absolute standards set by some higher authority.

Parents identified as permissive accept the child's behavior and wishes. They don't expect the child to conform to adult standards. When there is a difference of opinion between adult and child, the adult attempts to reason with the child but doesn't use power to force the child to comply.

In her study, Baumrind found that the most competent children were raised by authoritative parents. These children were both more responsible and more independent than children raised by either authoritarian or permissive parents. Baumrind emphasized that authoritative parenting isn't merely a compromise position between two extremes. As she put it, authoritative parents "reflect a synthesis and balancing of strongly opposing forces of tradition and innovation, divergence and convergence, accommodation and assimilation, cooperation and autonomous expression, tolerance and principled intractability" (1972, p. 257). This kind of flexible parenting, characterized by firm standards and the use of reason, seems to provide children with the kind of discipline and socialization that serves them well as they grow into adults.

discussion of Baumrind's work, see Research Focus—Styles of Parenting.) Researchers found that the authoritative style of parenting was associated with less susceptibility to peer pressure. In other words, parents who have brought their children up by reasoning with them and using induction, by listening and compromising, when appropriate, while at the same time setting limits, have children who are less likely to get into trouble when they're on their own after school. Parents who are either dictatorial (the authoritarian style) or lax about discipline (the permissive style) have children who are more likely to get into trouble.

The more removed from supervision the children in this study were, the more important was their child-rearing history. Some parents check on their children after school by telephone and know exactly where they'll be, even though the children are unsupervised. This parental knowledge is known as **distal supervision**. When even distal supervision was lacking, the effects of authoritative parenting showed up the most in different children's after-school choices and behaviors. Authoritative parenting has been shown to be the most effective style for helping children to internalize their parents' norms and standards for behavior, so it's not surprising that it would help children resist peer pressure.

Aside from these studies, there has been little research on the effects of being a latchkey child, either in the short or the long term. Future research

FIGURE 3
After-school programs provide a safe place for children to play, snack, and socialize. Activities typically include drawing and painting, playing games or sports, watching television or movies, and relaxing with friends.

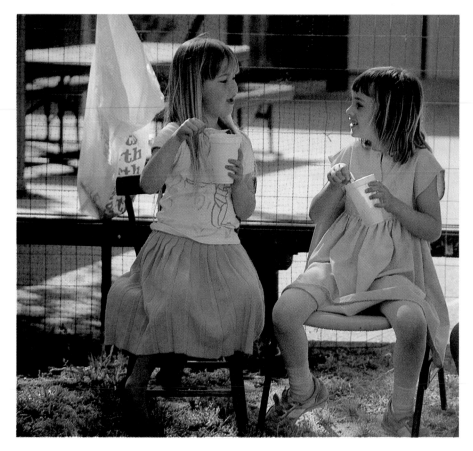

will have to tell us whether latchkey children are gaining important skills, developing feelings of responsibility and self-reliance, and using their time constructively or whether they're wasting time, feeling neglected, afraid, and resentful, and becoming more open to exploring undesirable activities.

After-School Programs and Services

What can parents, schools, and communities do to improve the child care situation for school-age children? Some communities have developed after-school programs in the public schools. In many schools in the Boston area, for example, after-school programs use school building space. The programs are funded by tuition payments, governed by parent boards, and operated with professional staff. In other communities, children go to a day care or child care center for an after-school program, sometimes by bus. In still other communities, there are various kinds of recreational programs to keep children active and supervised after school.

Hotline services are another approach to helping children cope with after-school time. Children can call to report problems, to get help with homework, or just to talk. A service called "PhoneFriend" is an example of a successful hotline set up for school-age children (Guerney & Moore, 1983). Run by the State College of Pennsylvania, it operates between 2:30 and 5:30 P.M. on weekdays. Volunteers are trained in listening and action skills, and they can instruct children in areas such as first aid, power failures, lost items, problems with pets, and general problem solving. Almost 50 percent of the calls are from children who are lonely, bored, or want to talk; about 8 percent are from children who are scared or worried. For a content analysis of the calls and the transcript of one call, see Box 1.

A program operated by the Reston Children's Center in Fairfax, Virginia, demonstrates another creative solution to the after-school child care problem. Known as the "Senior Satellite Program," it's designed for the oldest children associated with the center, the 11- to 13-year-olds. This program is based at the center, but it allows children to spend their time outside the center. Children check in after school, and then they might spend some time in the center, at home, or with friends. The center develops contracts between children and their parents that specify how after-school time is to be spent (McKnight & Shelsby, 1984).

Working parents want and need some form of care and activity programs for their school-age children. They fear that their children might be hurt in accidents, fires, or sports; that they might be accosted by strangers or burglars; or that they'll forget to lock doors. They also worry that their children spend too much time watching televison and wasting time. Finally, they worry that they'll be influenced by their peers to fight, drink, steal, misbehave, or try drugs (Farel, 1984). After-school child care—direct care for younger children and distal supervision for older children—is certain to be a critical issue in the 1990s as an increasing number of parents join the work force and are unable to be at home when school gets out.

ASSESSMENT OF THE SCHOOL-AGE CHILD

In Chapter 14, we discussed intelligence tests for school-age children, along with some of the issues associated with their use. Here, we discuss some of the specific assessment instruments that are commonly used with children this age.

Intelligence Tests

Children can be given intelligence tests either individually or in groups. Individual testing is more expensive and time-consuming because the tests are administered by skilled testors, usually psychologists. When children are tested in groups, the testor need not have special training.

Probably the best-known individually administered intelligence test is the **Stanford-Binet Intelligence Scale**. Developed at Stanford University as a modification of the orignal Binet and Simon test, this test is designed to be used with both preschool and school-age children. The test contains subtests for each age level, and these consist of items relating to such abilities as logical reasoning, perceptual-motor coordination, and language.

Another common, individually administered test is the **Wechsler Intelligence Scale for Children—Revised**, referred to as the **WISC-R** (Wechsler, 1974). This test, used with children between the ages of 6 and 16, is divided into verbal and performance sections, and each of these sections has six subtests. The subtests have different sections for children of different ages. A

BOX 1
Content of Calls to an After-School Hotline

Content of Calls	N	Calls Reported (%)
Immediate hang-ups; short silence or saying a few words and then hanging up before the worker can interact	300	23.7
Lonely/bored	304	24.0
Wants to talk	298	23.5
Scared/worried	104	8.2
Curious about PhoneFriend	68	5.4
Joke/story	46	3.6
Getting along with others, including siblings and schoolmates	34	2.7
Human sexuality, dating, pregnancy	33	2.6
Household maintenance (plumbing, etc.)	28	2.2
Use of phone	20	1.6
Cuts, scrapes, other minor medical	18	1.4
Housework/pets	13	1.0

Total calls reported: 1,266
Average calls per week: 40

Transcript of a specific call:

CHILD: My brother is not home from school yet and he's supposed to be here.

WORKER: It gets you all worried when he's not home on time.

CHILD: Yeah, he's supposed to be home at 4:00 and it's 4:30 now.

WORKER: And you can't figure it out . . . What is your first name?

CHILD: Susan.

WORKER: And how old are you, Susan?

CHILD: 9 years old.

WORKER: What have you done other times when he was late?

CHILD: He was never late before. My mother tells him to come right home.

WORKER: So it's hard to figure out what could be going on today.

CHILD: Yeah . . . Maybe the bus is late.

WORKER: He goes by bus? It could be late . . . what school does he go to? (Child responds.) And you go to a different school and get home earlier? Are you supposed to stay in the house until he gets home?

CHILD: Yes. And I want to go out now.

WORKER: So you sure wish he would get in.

CHILD: Yeah. Maybe he forgot something and had to go back or missed the bus.

WORKER: You keep wondering what might have happened.

CHILD: Yeah. I guess I'll watch some cartoons until he gets here.

WORKER: You think you've found a way to help yourself wait for him.

CHILD: Yeah. I like to watch (explains a little about the anticipated cartoons).

WORKER: O.K. You seem like you're feeling O.K. about doing that and you're hoping he'll come in soon. (Child answers affirmatively.) If he doesn't come in by the time your show is over, call me back if you like and we can talk about it some more. What time does your mom get home?

CHILD: 5:30.

WORKER: You can call then around 5:00 if you're still worried. Thank you for calling PhoneFriend.
(At 4:45 the child called back to say her brother was home. Bus was late.)

SOURCE: Guerney, L., & Moore, L. (1986). PhoneFriend: A prevention-oriented service for latchkey children. Children Today, 12(4), 8–9.

child receives three scores on this test, including a verbal IQ, a performance IQ, and a full-scale IQ, which is based on the first two scores.

The verbal part of the WISC-R tests children on information, comprehension, arithmetic, vocabulary, digit span, and the ability to distinguish similarities; the performance part tests them on picture completion, picture arrangement, block design, object assembly, coding, and the ability to work mazes. For an example of the kind of questions that appear on the WISC-R, see Box 2.

Probably the most commonly used group intelligence test is the **Otis-Lennon Mental Ability Test** (Otis & Lennon, 1967). When taking this test, children are given test booklets and answer cards or sheets to fill in. If younger children are taking the test, the testor explains each question orally. With older children, the testor gives general directions orally, and then the children go through the booklet on their own. The Otis-Lennon Test measures verbal, numerical, and reasoning abilities.

Achievement Tests

Unlike intelligence tests, which measure general abilities, achievement tests measure knowledge, information, and skills in specific areas such as math, science, or reading. They're usually administered to determine whether an individual child, or a group of children, has attained a grade-appropriate level of knowledge and competence.

One well-known achievement test is the **Three R's Test** (Cole et al., 1982), which measures achievement in reading, language, and math. There is a test for each grade level, from kindergarten through eighth grade. First graders taking the test are asked to select a word from a list that matches a word in a box at the top of the list and to answer simple comprehension questions after reading several sentences. In math, they're asked to fill in missing numbers in a sequence (for example, 10, 11, ___, 13), determine how many objects there are in two sets of objects pictured, and do simple addition and subtraction problems.

Third graders are asked to read several paragraphs and answer comprehension questions, alphabetize lists of words, and show that they can use a table of contents. In language, they're asked about punctuation rules, spellings, and parts of speech (for example, "Which word in the following sentence is an action verb?"). They're also asked to show that they understand how groups of words are related, such as the words "winter," "spring," and "summer." Children should indicate that these words describe seasons, not weather, years, or temperatures. In math, third graders are questioned about coin values, place value, and skills in adding, subtracting, and multiplying.

If children are to receive high scores on achievement tests that ask questions like these, obviously they must be taught the material covered in the test. When schools become concerned about children's scores as a reflection of the quality of their teaching and administration, they may fall into the pattern of designing curricula to match the tests. We saw in Knowledge in Action: Preschool Children that many schools are raising their kindergarten entrance requirements to ensure themselves high test scores at the end of the year, and the same problem is apparent in the later elementary grades. This is one of the issues we examine next.

BOX 2
Paraphrased Wechsler-like
Questions

GENERAL INFORMATION

1. How many wings does a bird have?
2. How many nickels make a dime?
3. What is steam made of?
4. What is pepper?

GENERAL COMPREHENSION

1. What should you do if you see a man forget his hat when he leaves his seat in a restaurant?
2. Why do some people save sales receipts?
3. Why is copper often used in electrical wires?

ARITHMETIC

1. Sue had two pieces of candy and Joe gave her four more. How many pieces of candy did Sue have all together?
2. Three children divided 18 pennies equally among themselves. How many pennies did each child receive?
3. If two pencils cost 15¢, what will be the cost of a dozen pencils?

SIMILARITIES

1. In what way are a lion and a tiger alike?
2. In what way are a saw and a hammer alike?
3. In what way are an hour and a week alike?
4. In what way are a circle and a triangle alike?

VOCABULARY

This test consists simply of asking, "What is a _____?" or "What does _____ mean?" The words cover a wide range of difficulty or familiarity.

PERFORMANCE TESTS

In addition to verbal tasks of the kinds illustrated above, there are a number of performance tasks involving the use of blocks, cut-out figures, paper and pencil puzzles, and so on.

SOURCE: *Paraphrased questions printed by permission of The Psychological Corporation, 757 Third Avenue, New York, N.Y.*

Issues in Testing

CULTURAL BIAS. Before we look at the issue of "teaching to the test," let's return briefly to the issue of cultural bias in intelligence testing. We saw in Chapter 14 that differences in measured intelligence can result from cultural differences and that tests standardized on white middle-class children yield biased results when used with children from other groups (Miller-Jones, 1989). Some attempts have been made to design nondiscriminatory, "culture fair" tests. Two of these are the **Raven Progressive Matrices Test** (Raven & Lewis, 1974) and the **Cattell Culture-Fair Intelligence Test** (Cattel & Cattell, 1973). Both of these tests have nonverbal items that require the subject to detect and complete a visual pattern. Whether these tests are really culture fair is a question still under debate. Most experts agree, however, that performance on any type of test is influenced by prior experience and that some experiences are more prevalent in some cultural and social groups than in others (Cole, 1985).

Because of the concern over bias in testing, some states have passed laws prohibiting schools from grouping children for instruction on the basis of intelligence test scores. In addition, the Education for All Handicapped Children Act of 1975 as well as other laws require that tests be administered in the child's native language. To prevent the misinterpretation and mishandling of scores, teachers and schools need to be alert to language and culture as a possible source of bias when they evaluate intelligence and achievement tests.

TEACHING TO THE TEST. Standardized tests that measure high-level skills and complex problem-solving abilities are relatively difficult to devise. It's easier to write multiple-choice test items that measure knowledge of facts. When a

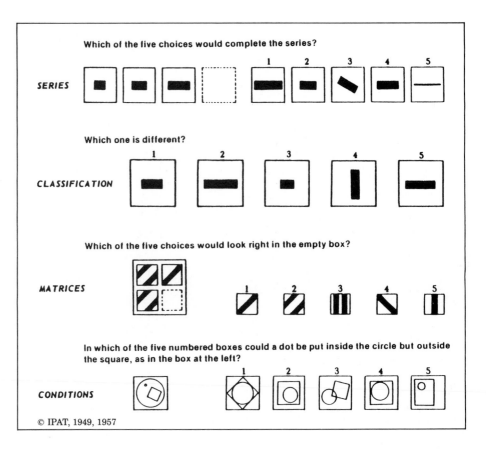

© IPAT, 1949, 1957

panel of psychologists analyzed the items on one standardized test, they judged 70 percent of questions to require memorization of facts, 15 percent to require comprehension, 12 percent to require analytical thinking, and 3 percent to require evaluations (Bowman & Peng, 1972). Most tests just don't test abilities such as drawing inferences, analyzing, or making judgments (Aiken, 1982).

Unfortunately, the level at which a subject is tested is likely to be the level at which it's taught. The result is that teaching often goes just as far as the test and no farther. As one observer has concluded, "Efficient tests tend to drive out less efficient tests, leaving many important abilities untested—and untaught" (Frederiksen, 1984). When test scores are valued as a measure of children's and teachers' success, the schools have their hands full just teaching the information typically found on the tests. They don't have time to explore more thoughtful activities, provide hands-on experiences, or teach at the level or pace required by individual children in the classroom. But experience has shown that these are the most effective approaches to teaching if meaningful learning is to take place. Like kindergarten entrance requirements, teaching to the test will be one of the controversial educational issues of the 1990s.

LIVING WITH THE SCHOOL-AGE CHILD

As in the previous stages of childhood, adults who live and work with school-age children have certain practical concerns, which we discuss next.

HEALTH FOCUS

Children and AIDS

Even very young children are falling victim to Acquired Immune Deficiency Syndrome, or AIDS. There is currently no cure for this disease, and it invariably leads to death. AIDS is caused by a virus that destroys the immune system and is transmitted through sexual contact or through contact with the blood of infected individuals. Although no cases are known to have occurred through any other kind of contact, the virus has been found in human saliva, which raises questions about transmittal through biting.

As of November 1988, 1230 cases of AIDS had been confirmed in children aged 12 and younger. The number of cases has grown rapidly; in November 1986, only 383 cases were confirmed (APA Task Force on Pediatric AIDS, 1989). Children contract AIDS in three main ways—prenatally, from their mothers (79 percent of all children's cases were contracted this way); from blood transfusions, as during surgery (13 percent); and from blood components used to treat blood coagulation disorders such as hemophilia (5 percent) (Siebert, 1987). Prenatal infection is expected to be the major source of children's cases in the future, since more women of child-bearing age are becoming infected from intravenous drug use or from sexual contact with infected intravenous drug users. Infection from blood supplies has decreased dramatically as blood screening tests have improved.

Concern arises when a child who is infected with the AIDS virus enrolls in day care, preschool, or school. Parents worry that their child will catch the virus from the infected child, and teachers worry that they too might become infected. All of the available evidence indicates that AIDS is not contracted through casual, everyday contact, and there have been no known cases of AIDS transmitted in schools or day care centers (Massachusettes Department of Public Health, 1985). On the basis of this fact, the Centers for Disease Control recommend that children with AIDS not be barred from school (Cooper, Pelton, & LeMay, 1988). This recommendation has also been endorsed by the U.S. Department of Education (Massachusetts Department of Public Health, 1985).

Under certain conditions, however, children with AIDS should not be placed in the regular day care, preschool, or elementary classroom. If the child has a tendency to bite, for example, or if there are open sores that can't be covered, the child shouldn't be in a regular classroom. AIDS-infected children under 3 years of age shouldn't be in group settings. At this age, children tend to drool and bite, and they aren't toilet trained (Cooper, Pelton, & LeMay, 1988). The departments of public health in most states have developed specific policies about school attendance by children with AIDS. School districts can obtain information from these departments or from state departments of education or day care licensing agencies.

Ensuring the Health of the School-Age Child

Middle childhood is a time of relatively robust energy and good health. Most children have been immunized against the childhood diseases that used to punctuate children's lives—mumps, measles, whooping cough, diphtheria, and polio. And because so many children attend day care and preschool, many of them have had chicken pox before they get to elementary school.

The main illnesses that school-age children have to contend with are virus-based colds accompanied by sore throat, cough, and fever; virus-based influenza; and bacterial-based strep throat with sore throat and fever. Children who are basically healthy and whose illnesses are properly tended with rest, fluids, and nutritious food usually don't have much trouble getting through colds and flu. Physicians usually control strep throat with antibiotics to keep it from turning into a more serious respiratory infection or rheumatic fever. An occasional child will get tonsillitis—tonsils that become abscessed and susceptible to repeated infections—and will have to have a tonsillectomy. One very serious problem on the rise among children is discussed in Health Focus—Children with AIDS.

Because children are usually so healthy at this age, adults can turn their attention to helping them develop healthy life-styles. Schools often teach the principles of good nutrition, and parents can talk about healthy foods with their children quite naturally when making lunches or snacks. Both schools and parents can help children develop skills in games and sports and learn to love physical activity. If children are overweight, adults can help them learn how to keep their weight under control, as discussed in Chapter 13. They can also teach them about the dangers of smoking, drinking, and taking drugs. But because of children's increased awareness of the world around them at this age and the different choices people make, probably the strongest and most valuable lesson adults can give them is the example of their own healthy life-style.

Ensuring the Safety of the School-Age Child

Another concern adults have is making sure school-age children are safe. Accidents are the leading cause of death at this age (Christopherson, 1989). Although children now have more knowledge and skills than they did as toddlers or preschoolers, they also have certain other internal and external pressures to contend with. For one, school-age children care very much about being accepted by peers. When they were younger, they may have been more interested in "doing what mom said." Now, they may be led into danger by their overwhelming desire to be part of the group.

Because they're more competent, school-age children also have more independence and autonomy from adult supervision. But this very independence means that they don't have the same access to adult judgment and planning

FIGURE 5
Healthy lunches still begin with milk, sandwiches, and fruit, much as they have for years. But today, parents have to contend with an avalanche of snack foods packaged for children's lunches, most of them full of sugar, salt and fat and with little or no nutritional value.

FIGURE 6
When children wear helmets, bicycle stunts like this are less likely to result in a serious head injury.

as they did when they were younger and more dependent (Zuckerman & Duby, 1985). And even 12-year-olds simply don't have the experience or judgment to cope with every situation that comes up. But adults can take some steps to keep children safe even when they can't be with them.

BICYCLE ACCIDENTS. Many children die every year in bicycle accidents, most of which (95 percent) involve a collision between a bike and a car. Of all children, those between the ages of 10 and 14 have the highest rate of bicycle fatalities, followed by those between the ages of 5 and 9. Boys are three-and-a-half times more likely to die in a bicycle accident than are girls (Friede et al., 1985).

Serious injuries and deaths almost always involve head injuries. The obvious conclusion is that if children wear well-fitted, specially designed helmets, they will be protected at least somewhat from this danger. Although no controlled studies have been done to determine exactly how effective helmets are in preventing head injuries, it seems probable that they do help (Friede et al., 1985). Less than 2 percent of elementary school children wear bicycle helmets (Weiss, 1986), probably in part because of their cost, which ranges from $30 to $70. But many parents consider this an inexpensive investment when measured against their child's safety and their own peace of mind.

Children can also be taught safe bicycle-riding procedures, such as riding with traffic rather than against it. Accidents in which children were riding toward oncoming traffic account for 5 percent of bicycle fatalities and 20 percent of nonfatal accidents (Friede et al., 1985). Additionally, bicycle accidents can be reduced when communities enforce traffic laws. In Minnesota, where some communities issue citations and require violators to attend a "bike violator's seminar," accidents have been reduced by between 30 and 100 percent (Friede et al., 1985). Communities can also make biking safer by establishing bike paths and building speed bumps, both of which are effective in reducing collisions between bicycles and cars.

SKATEBOARD ACCIDENTS. When skateboards were at the height of their popularity in the mid- to late 1970s, injuries ran as high as 140,000 per year, according to 1977 figures. Most of the injured children were between the ages of 10 and 14, but many were younger than 10 years as well (Greesher & Mofenson, 1985). As a result of safety campaigns and of reduced interest in skateboards, injuries fell to 87,000 in 1978 and to 14,700 in 1982.

When injuries were alarmingly high, the American Academy of Pediatrics issued guidelines for safe safeboarding. Their recommendations included the following (Greesher & Mofenson, 1985, pp. 135–136):

1. Children should use protective equipment—helmets, gloves, elbow and knee pads.
2. Skateboarding should be done on clean, smooth surfaces where there's no traffic.
3. Skateboard parks should be established.
4. Children should follow these safety rules:
   * one person to a skateboard
   * no stunts unless child is experienced
   * no hitching behind a car, truck, or bike
   * no skateboarding at night
   * no skateboarding on wet surfaces
   * no fast downhill racing
   * keep skateboards in good shape
   * learn proper falling techniques

Skateboarding remains extremely popular with some groups of school-age and older children, so adults should make sure they're aware of safe procedures.

PEDESTRIAN ACCIDENTS. A third kind of accident common among children is being hit by a car. About 2,000 children are killed each year by cars, and many more are injured (Guyer, Talbot, & Pless, 1985). Usually, the children involved in this kind of accident are between ages 5 and 9, are hit during daylight hours, and are struck when they dart out into the street (Rivara, Reay, & Bergman, 1989).

How to protect children from this kind of accident is a matter of some debate. Some experts think children should be taught safety rules and then allowed to negotiate streets by themselves. Others argue that even school-age children can't be taught to be careful enough. These experts say that 6- and 7-year-olds can't understand or follow rules necessary for crossing safely at intersections and that even 9-year-olds sometimes forget to look behind them before crossing a street (Rivara, Reay, & Bergman, 1989).

Adults probably should begin to teach children safe pedestrian rules early in the school years but not allow them to cross streets alone until they're 9 or 10 years old. Even at this age, however, children should be shown the safest way home from school and taught to cross busy streets where a crossing guard is available. Parents also need to lobby for appropriate speed limits on streets near their schools and homes.

EYE INJURIES. A final area in which adults can help keep children safer is protection of the eyes. The importance of good eyesight to everyday living makes the prevention of eye injuries especially important. Most eye injuries in children occur between the ages of 6 and 14 (Grin, Nelson, & Jeffers, 1987), many more of them in boys than in girls. The highest percentage of these injuries occur during a sports activity (16 percent), closely followed by incidents involving sticks or branches (9 percent) and BB guns (8 percent). They also occur when a child is struck in the eye by a thrown object, such as a rock or a snowball, or jabbed in the eye with a pen or pencil. In sports, the highest rate of injury occurs in baseball (when the child is hit in the eye with the ball while batting) and in tennis, followed by soccer, basketball, and hockey.

Most sports-related injuries can be prevented, according to the National Society to Prevent Blindness, if some safety guidelines are followed. They recommend that children wear safety helmets with face protectors for baseball, face masks for hockey, and eye guards for other sports. Children whose eyesight is already impaired should wear safety goggles for all sports and not participate in certain sports, such as boxing.

Eye injuries from air-powered guns (BB guns) could be reduced if children weren't allowed to use them, and seven states have laws prohibiting their use by individuals under age 18 (Grin, Nelson, & Jeffers, 1987). Many parents don't realize that these guns can cause serious and permanent eye damage. Adults can help prevent other injuries by teaching children how to keep their eyes and their friends' eyes safe—by not shaking bottles containing carbonated beverages (they could explode), by not throwing objects, by not playing with sticks and branches, and by using pens and pencils properly.

Supporting the School-Age Child's Play

WHAT DO THEY LIKE TO PLAY? Now that so much has been said about these first through sixth graders, we can ask what *they* might consider the most important question of all—what do they like to play? Playing is still an integral part of their lives, as it was when they were toddlers and preschoolers, although they've added many interests and activities. They enjoy active games and board games, jokes and riddles, and physical activities like bike riding and ball playing. They like sports, reading, movies, theater productions, television, concerts, and hobbies. Their newly emerging ability to classify makes collecting (stamps, coins, rocks, insects, baseball cards, bottle caps) an activity they can understand and enjoy.

School-age childen typically prefer playing with other children to playing alone. And they can usually play in harmony for long periods of time without adult guidance or intervention. When they're together, younger school-age childen are often given to bursts of giggling and silliness. When adults ask, "What's so funny?" they only laugh harder.

Younger school-age children still love pretend play, although they pretend much less than when they were preschoolers. They play school, go off on long fantasy adventures, and pretend with dolls, stuffed animals, and toy figures. Although toy manufacturers try to appeal to school-age children with bright plastic toys of every description, these children probably get more pleasure from making up games with a few objects they find in their toy boxes or around the house.

FIGURE 7
Practically unknown in the United States 20 years ago, soccer has gained widespread popularity in recent years. Because it's fast-moving, involves a variety of physical skills, and gives many children the opportunity to play, soccer is an excellent sport for school-age children.

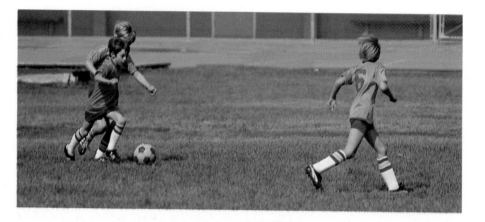

TOYS AND PLAYTHINGS. Because of their advancing physical and cognitive skills, school-age children enjoy toys and games that are beyond the abilities and understanding of younger children. Playthings that support a child's large motor skills might include a baseball bat, ball and glove, skis, a basketball and hoop, a soccer ball, roller skates, ice skates, a frisbee, a bicycle, a scooter, and a jump rope.

To support fine motor development, parents might provide marbles, jacks, yo-yos, model and craft kits, and drawing and construction material such as markers, paints, paper, scissors, scotch tape, and glue. Particularly appropriate for school-age children's level of cognitive development are cameras, calculators, microscopes, binoculars, magnets, and materials for hobbies. Because of their new understanding of the world and their intense interest in it, school-age children can be delightful companions on expeditions to natural history museums, hikes and camping trips, and almost any other outing of mutual interest.

GAMES, BOOKS, AND MAGAZINES. As we saw in Chapter 14, school-age children are able to play strategy games because they can think about what other people are thinking. They're now capable of winning against the very adults who taught them the games just a few years earlier. Games they enjoy include checkers, chess, Chinese checkers, Othello, Risk, Scrabble, MasterMind, Battleship, Stratego, Boggle, and FourSight—all games that involve "second guessing" an opponent.

Most children become completely fluent readers during middle childhood, although they still don't have the understanding or vocabulary of an adult. They enjoy selecting their own books and reading them independently. A children's librarian can help them or their parents if they want ideas about interesting or appropriate books to read. Many children's magazines are published too, and a listing of some of them is provided in Table 1.

Even though children are independent readers now, parents and teachers may want to check their book selections for sexist and racist content. Several organizations have developed guidelines for selecting nonstereotypical children's books, including the Council on Interracial Books for Children (1841 Broadway, New York, NY 10012). They recommend checking illustrations for

FIGURE 8
Hobbies and activities that require very controlled fine motor skills are within the range of school-age children's ability. Models of cars and planes may begin to decorate their bedrooms, and lucky parents and relatives may start to receive handmade gifts, such as this fifth grader's personalized jewelry creation.

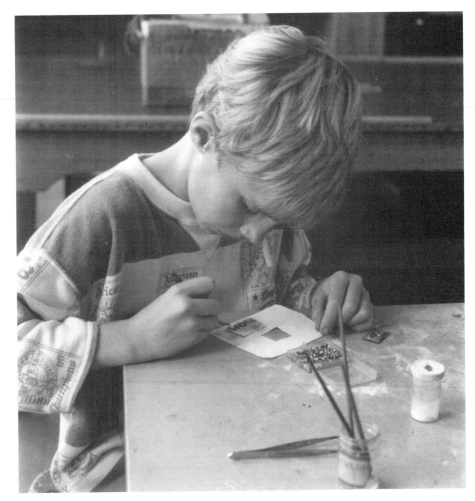

TABLE 1
Magazines for School-Age Children

Title	Ages	Content
Child Life	7–9	Health, safety, nutrition
Children's Digest	8–10	Health, safety, nutrition
Cobblestone	8–14	History
Creative Kids	6–14	Stories, poems, art, and music submitted by children
Cricket	6–12	Short stories, poems
Faces	8–14	History
Highlights for Children	2–12	Stories, poems, learning activities
Jack and Jill	6–8	Health, safety, nutrition
National Geographic World	8–13	General interest
Odyssey	8–14	Astronomy and space science
Owl	8–14	Environmental education
Penny Power	8–14	Consumer education
Ranger Rick	6–12	Nature study
Stone Soup	6–13	Stories, poems, and art submitted by children
Contact	8–14	Science and technology

SOURCE: Adapted from Children's Magazine List. *(1987). Glassboro, NJ: Glassboro State College, Educational Press Association of America.*

stereotyping, such as pictures of Native Americans wearing headdresses and loincloths and pictures of girls and women wearing only dresses. Content also can be checked for stereotyped roles, such as blacks portrayed only as laborers and women portrayed only as housewives.

However, since school-age children inevitably encounter sexist and racist attitudes in our society, it may be unrealistic to try to protect them from such images, whether in books, ads, movies, or on TV. The surer course may be to discuss the issues of racism and sexism openly with older children, explain their historical roots, and impart nonracist and nonsexist values both verbally and by example.

VIDEO GAMES. A whole new kind of activity opened up to school-age children in the 1980s with the advent of video games. Millions of parents brought these games home from the toy or electronics store and hooked them up to their TV sets, and many others allowed their children to play video games at the arcades that seemed to spring up overnight in communities all over the country. After watching their children play these games—eyes glued intently to the TV screen or body hunched over a game machine in a darkened, deafeningly noisy arcade—many parents wondered how positive an experience they were having.

Although long-term studies haven't been done, some experts believe that playing video games is a stressful, destructive activity that needs to be strictly controlled, if not eliminated. It involves children in a tense, indoor, nonphysical activity, sometimes for hours on end, usually with very little interaction with other children or adults. Some children get bored fairly quickly, but for others it's an addictive activity they can't control without adult help. The content of many video games is violent, and some of it is sexist and racist as well.

Once exposed to video games, however, many school-age children are interested in trying them, for the challenge of beating the game if nothing else. Some parents believe in strictly limiting the hours a child can play per day; others allow unlimited playing so the child will tire of it sooner. Some refuse to buy video games; others would rather have their child playing at home than spending time in the less desirable arcade environment. Whatever parents decide to do, they'll want to keep a close eye on both the content of the games and their child's behavior during and after playing.

OVERVIEW

School-age children are increasingly able to take care of themselves. They have rational understandings of how the world works; they can read, write, and express themselves; they're starting to get a grasp on social interactions; and they're physically strong and healthy. Yet they still have limitations and need responsible adult supervision in many situations.

This is why after-school care is important even for 11- and 12-year-olds. It also accounts for the high rate of accidents among school-age children. Adults who live and work with children this age have to find a balance between keeping them safe and allowing them the independence they need to continue maturing.

KNOWLEDGE IN ACTION REVIEW

COGNITIVE DEMANDS OF THE ELEMENTARY SCHOOL CURRICULUM

- The elementary school curriculum assumes that children have reached the level of concrete operational thinking. The shift toward rationality usually occurs at about age 7.
- Children who don't have these cognitive abilities will probably have a hard time with the first grade curriculum, which requires a comprehension of the concepts of space, time, number, and classification. Even concrete operational children need hands-on learning experiences to understand and remember what they're taught.

AFTER-SCHOOL CARE FOR SCHOOL-AGE CHILDREN

- As long-term economic trends propel more and more parents into the work force, after-school care for their school-age children becomes an important concern.
- Studies indicate that children who have been raised by parents using the authoritative style of parenting, as opposed to the authoritarian or permissive style, are better able to resist peer pressure when left unsupervised after school. The long-term effects of being a latchkey child are still unknown.
- Some schools and communities have after-school programs for school-age children, and other communities have hotlines for children at home alone after school.

ASSESSMENT OF THE SCHOOL-AGE CHILD

- The intelligence tests most commonly administered to school-age children are the Stanford-Binet Intelligence Scale, the Wechsler Intelligence Scale for Children—Revised (both individually administered tests), and the Otis-Lennon Mental Ability Test (a group administered test). The most commonly used achievement test is the Three R's Test
- Cultural bias is a matter of great concern in testing, and some states prohibit the use of intelligence test scores as a basis for grouping children for instruction. Attempts at devising nondiscriminatory tests have produced the Raven Progressive Matrices Test and the Cattell test.
- Another important issue is "teaching to the test." Some experts claim that the emphasis on tests and test scores has driven out flexible, individualized instruction and the teaching of complex problem-solving skills.

LIVING WITH THE SCHOOL-AGE CHILD

- School-age children tend to be healthy and active. Adults can help them develop and maintain healthy life-styles by teaching them about nutrition and encouraging them to participate in sports and other physical activities.
- AIDS is a problem of growing proportions among children, who most often contract it prenatally. Currently, the Centers for Disease Control recommend that children with AIDS attend school unless they have a tedency to bite, have open sores, or are under 3 years of age.
- Accidents are the leading cause of death among school-age children. Adults can enforce a variety of measures to keep children safe when they're riding bicycles or skateboards or crossing streets. Adults can also teach children not to endanger their eyes and can make sure their eyes are protected during sports.
- School-age children enjoy a variety of games, activities, and sports. They prefer playing with other children to playing alone. They're skilled readers and enjoy picking out their own books. Adults can support their reading with frequent visits to the library and with magazine subscriptions.
- Parents may want to watch their children's reading material for sexist and racist content. They'll probably also want to monitor their television viewing and the amount of time they spend playing video games.

KEY TERMS

permissive parenting
   style
authoritarian parenting
   style
authoritative parenting
   style
distal supervision

Stanford-Binet
   Intelligence Scale
Wechsler Intelligence
   Scale for Children—
   Revised (WISC-R)
Otis-Lennon Mental
   Ability Test

Three R's Test
Raven Progressive
   Matrices Test
Cattell Culture Fair
   Intelligence Test

SUGGESTIONS FOR FURTHER READING

Baroody, A. (1987). *Children's mathematical thinking.* New York: Teachers College Press.

This readable book discusses the development of mathematical concepts in children during the preschool and elementary school years. It also provides interesting discussions of the shift from "informal" mathematics to the formal mathematics required in school.

Klein, E. (Ed.). (1985). *Children and computers. New directions in child development.* San Francisco: Jossey-Bass.

Computers are being used in many elementary school classrooms. This book provides some data on the effects that computer use might have on children's problem-solving strategies, children's knowledge about change and motion, and their story editing. Interesting reading for computer enthusiasts.

Martin, A. (1988). Screening, early intervention, and remediation: Obscuring children's potential. *Harvard Educational Review, 58*(4), 488–501.

This account, written from an elementary teacher's perspective, points out some of the limits of testing. She contrasts both the information provided by formal evaluations with that provided by teacher observation and the recommendations made by outside specialists with those provided by teaching colleagues.

Shepard, L. A., & Smith, M. L. (1988). Escalating academic demand in kindergarten: Counterproductive policies. *Elementary School Journal, 89,* 135–145.

This article focuses primarily on the problems resulting from the use of formal tests to screen for, and make retention decisions about, kindergarten, but wider issues of test use are discussed as well. The effects of extensive test use, including "teaching to the test," are discussed.

MILESTONES IN SCHOOL-AGE DEVELOPMENT

AGE	PHYSICAL	COGNITIVE	LANGUAGE	SOCIAL-EMOTIONAL
6 yrs.	Has adult-sized brain Reaches about two-thirds of adult height Begins to lose baby teeth Moves a writing or drawing tool with the fingers while the side of the hand rests on the table top Can skip Can tie a bow	Begins to demonstrate concrete operational thinking Demonstrates conservation of number on Piaget's conservation tasks Can create series operationally rather than by trial and error	Might use a letter-name spelling strategy, thus creating many invented spellings Appreciates jokes and riddles based on phonological ambiguity Begins to distinguish between possible and impossible events on film	Feels one way only about a situation Has some difficulty detecting intentions accurately in situations where damage occurs Demonstrates Kohlberg's preconventional moral thinking
7 yrs.	Is able to make small, controlled marks with pencils or pens due to more refined finger dexterity Has longer face Continues to lose baby teeth	Begins to use some rehearsal strategies as an aid to memory Becomes much better able to play strategy games May demonstrate conservation of mass and length	Appreciates jokes and riddles based on lexical ambiguity Might have begun to read using a print-governed approach, but coordination of cueing systems might be imbalanced	May express two emotions about one situation, but these will be same valence Demonstrates Kohlberg's conventional thinking Understands gender constancy Uses unpredictable strategy when hiding and searching for an object
8 yrs.	Plays jacks and other games requiring considerable fine motor skill and good reaction time Jumps rope skillfully Throws and bats a ball more skillfully	Still has great difficulty judging if a passage is relevant to a specific theme May demonstrate conservation of area	Begins to sort out some of the more difficult syntactic difficulties, such as "ask" and "tell" Still has some difficulty differentiating between live and staged TV events Might be able to integrate all cueing systems smoothly reading Becomes more conventional speller	May express two same-valence emotions about different targets at the same time Understands that people may interpret situation differently but thinks this is due to different information Views justice in terms of strict equality—everybody should get the same
9 yrs.	Enjoys hobbies requiring high levels of fine motor skill (sewing, weaving, model building)	May demonstrate conservation of weight	Interprets "ask" and "tell" correctly	Can think about own thinking or another person's thinking but not both at the same time.
10 yrs.	May begin to menstruate	Begins to make better judgments about relevance of a text Begins to delete unimportant information when summarizing	Demonstrates high levels of ability to differentiate between live and staged TV programs	Begins to view justice in terms of merit and reciprocity—paying people back in kind Can take own view and view of another as if a disinterested third party
11 yrs.	May begin preadolescent growth spurt if female	May demonstrate conservation of volume	Begins to appreciate jokes and riddles based on syntactic ambiguity	Still has trouble detecting deception Spends more time with friends
12 yrs.	Has reached about 80 percent of adult height if male, 90 percent if female Has all permanent teeth except for two sets of molars Plays ball more skillfully due to improved reaction time Probably has begun to menstruate	Shows much greater skill in summarizing and outlining		May begin to demonstrate Kohlberg's postconventional moral thinking Begins to be able to coordinate different claims and demands about justice

part five

ADOLESCENTS

Sometime between the child's eleventh and fourteenth years of life, the course of development set so long ago takes a dramatic turn. Puberty brings the undeniable signs that childhood is coming to an end and a new way of life is soon going to begin. Leaving behind their immature bodies, their protected place within the family, their elementary school routines, children embark on the exciting adventure of adolescence. Although teenagers reach important new levels in cognition, language, moral reasoning, and other areas, their lives are dominated by development in two domains—the physical and the social-emotional. As they gain in emotional maturity and social sophistication, they build on earlier patterns of interaction and consolidate what they've learned as children—at home, at school, and in the community—to establish a firm sense of self-identity. Although they will continue to change and learn throughout their lives, in many ways their development will be complete by the time they leave adolescence.

chapter 17

PHYSICAL DEVELOPMENT IN ADOLESCENTS

"Hurry up in there, Kathy," shouts Charlie at 7:30 one school morning. "I need to use the bathroom too!"

But inside, Kathy hardly hears her older brother. With her face pressed up close to the mirror, she's dabbing acne lotion on a pimple and searching her skin for signs of new trouble spots. Moving back for a better look, she studies her face with dissatisfaction. Her skin looks blotchy, her nose is way too big, her eyebrows are too thin, and the shape of her face is a problem, at least according to one of the teen magazines she reads with her girlfriends.

Kathy moves to the full-length mirror to see how she looks in her new sweater. Her breasts started to develop a year ago, before she was 12, and they're about the same size as many of the other girls', but still they don't compare with what she sees in ads and on TV. She'd like them to be bigger, but not too big . . .

Kathy looks most critically at her legs. "Too pudgy," she thinks. "And too hairy! I wonder if I should start shaving them. And should I shave my underarms? I better ask Mom to get me a new deodorant, one that works for a change. Otherwise, I may die of embarrassment . . ."

"Kathy, I need to use the bathroom!" comes a shout through the door. "You're not the only one in this family, you know!"

"Oh, all right," Kathy mutters. Turning sideways to the mirror, she takes a last look, and then throws open the bathroom door. Ready or not, she has to face another day of seventh grade.

Adolescence starts for most children with a burst of physical development that signals the beginning of "childhood's end." The relatively peaceful years of middle childhood, when growth was slow and steady and changes came in manageable increments, are swept away on a flood of hormones. The child's

FIGURE 17-1
Something as simple as appearing in a bathing suit can be an excruciating experience for young adolescent girls, unsure of themselves and their bodies. In just a few years, they'll have completed their physical transformation into young women.

body grows in every direction, but not evenly. The nose, the feet, the arms, the hands—all may grow at different rates for a few years. The two sides of the body may even grow at different rates. The skin gets oily, the sweat glands become more active, and hair shows up on new parts of the body. Signs of actual sexual maturation—the growth and development of the sex organs—appear, but they appear at different times in different children, creating another source of anxiety for the self-conscious young person. For many, early adolescence is truly "the awkward age."

Other cultures mark the physical transition from childhood to adulthood with rites of passage—rituals and ceremonies that express in both tangible and symbolic ways the ending of one way of life and the beginning of another. Most American children don't have a community experience that affirms their sexual maturation, and the transition can be confusing, both for them and for the adults in their lives. But gradually, with the support and understanding of parents, teachers, and friends, they make it through the tumultuous years of puberty and emerge to find their children's bodies transformed into those of young adults.

Physical developments are only the first and most obvious of the many changes that children go through during adolescence, of course, and we discuss all of them in these last chapters of the book. In this chapter, we focus on the physical—exactly how the body changes in size and shape, how and why sexual maturation takes place, and what variations in the timing of development exist among different individuals.

We also see that body image—the *idea* of the body—is just as important to some teenagers as physical development itself. The diseases of anorexia and bulimia among girls and the growing use of anabolic steroids to build up muscles among boys are all related to ideas about what the body *ought* to look

FIGURE 17-2
Most of the rites of passage in our society are religious ones—confirmations, bar mitzvahs, and bat mitzvahs. Here, a Jewish girl reads the Torah with her rabbi to mark her coming of age and her entry into the religious community.

like. Finally, we discuss the growing motor coordination and strength of adolescents—and their need for more physical activity to develop healthy lifestyles.

PHYSICAL GROWTH

Before the onset of puberty, the point at which actual sexual reproduction becomes possible, tremendous physical changes take place. This period of growth and change is known as **pubescence**. Not since infancy has growth been so rapid. The increase in height and weight is so dramatic and so fast, in fact, that it's referred to as a **growth spurt**.

Increases in Height and Weight: The Pubescent Growth Spurt

Starting at about age 9 or 10, girls grow as much as 6 or 7 inches in two or three years. Boys start later, at about age 11 or 12, and grow as much as 8 or 9 inches (Tanner, 1978). Girls' growth rate reaches a peak at about 12 years and then starts to decline. Boys grow fastest at about 14 years. Figure 17-3 provides a graphic representation of the growth spurt in girls and boys. Most adolescents continue to grow after this big spurt, but not at such a rapid rate. For all practical purposes, adolescents have reached their full adult height by the time the two- or three-year period of pubescence ends.

THE HORMONAL BASIS FOR THE GROWTH SPURT. What triggers this sudden growth spurt? The whole process of growth and maturation is controlled by a complex interplay of hormones. Under the influence of a "biological clock," the hypo-

FIGURE 17-3
Relative growth rate from 1 to 18 years of age. The rate of growth declines throughout childhood, as this graph shows, until the growth spurt begins. The growth spurt peaks for girls at approximately 12 years of age, on the average, and for boys at approximately 14 years of age.

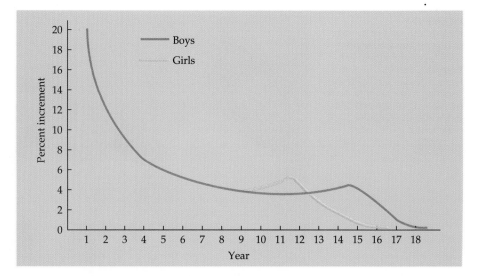

thalamus at the base of the brain signals the pituitary gland to send out hormones to the **gonads** (sex glands) as well as to other endocrine glands such as the thyroid and the adrenals. The "awakened" ovaries and testes begin to secrete the sex hormones estrogen and testosterone, respectively. These hormones in turn trigger the appearance of the secondary sex characteristics, which we describe below. Along with human growth hormone from the pituitary, they also produce rapid body growth.

BONE GROWTH. The great increases in height (shown graphically in Figure 17-4) are a result of bone growth, first in the legs and then in the trunk. The child's head doesn't grow very much at all during the adolescent growth spurt, since the brain had achieved almost its entire adult weight by the time the child was age 6. The ratio of head size to body size decreases, and body proportions become more and more like those of an adult (Figure 17-5).

FIGURE 17-4
Growth in height between 2 and 18 years of age. Where the slope of the line is steeper, growth is more rapid. Note that girls have reached their adult height by about 14 or 15 years of age. Boys continue to grow until about 18 years of age.

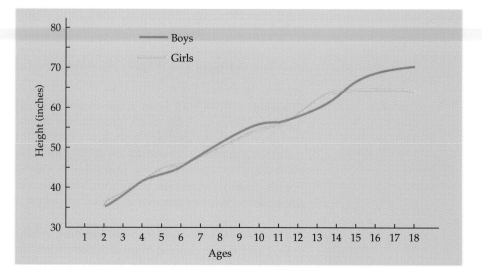

FIGURE 17-5
The adolescent growth spurt finally brings the child's body proportions into line with the adult's.

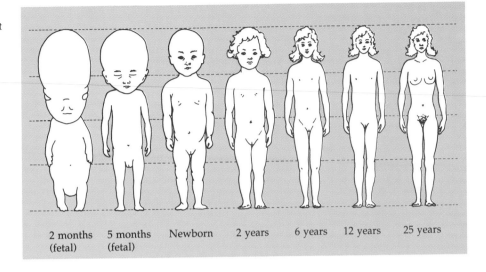

2 months (fetal)   5 months (fetal)   Newborn   2 years   6 years   12 years   25 years

At the same time that bones are lengthening, soft connective cartilege is ossifying (turning into bone) and the ends of bones are gradually hardening and closing. When the bone ends are completely closed, the skeleton is considered mature, and no further bone growth will occur. This is the process that is completed during adolescence. Once the tremendous increases in height have occurred, however, other skeletal changes take place. The child's chest and shoulders broaden, more in boys than in girls, and the girl's hips widen.

Not all body parts grow at the same time, as mentioned above. When children first shoot up in height, they're likely to be thin and gawky. Their hands and feet may grow a lot at first and seem to dangle at the ends of long, slender limbs. Children at this stage stumble over their own feet for physical reasons as well as emotional ones. The face elongates and the features may seem overly prominent. But gradually, muscle and fat cells catch up, the body and face round out, and everything comes back into proportion.

TISSUE GROWTH. Although both boys and girls add flesh during pubescence, girls add more fat and boys add more muscle (Figure 17-6). In girls, the layer of subcutaneous fat increases, giving their bodies the rounded, curving lines of women. In boys, some fat is lost during adolescence and the proportion of muscle to fat increases. Up to this point, boys and girls have been equally strong, but now boys become stronger than girls. They also have larger hearts and lungs, which gives them even more of an edge in physical strength, since a larger supply of oxygen in the blood means they can metabolize muscle wastes faster. Boys also have more opportunities for physical activities in our society, so their greater physical prowess is due to experience as well (Katchadourian, 1977).

Body Image

People are bombarded every day with images of the ideal body in our society, and children are acutely aware of these standards. Today's feminine ideal includes large breasts on an otherwise slender figure, a shape exaggerated to

FIGURE 17-6
Growth in weight between 2 and 18 years of age. Dramatic weight gains occur during the growth spurt, especially in boys. The average boy weighs 80 pounds at age 11 and 150 pounds at age 16—an increase of almost 100 percent.

the point of caricature in Barbie dolls and some cartoons and comic books. Even if girls realize these figures have impossible dimensions, they still compare their bodies to the slender silhouettes of models, actresses, and pop stars. Adequate self-esteem helps adolescents cope with their own bodies in relation to these unrealistic standards.

FIGURE 17-7
Even before her body has started to develop very much, the girl on the right has adopted a style of dress she perceives to be fashionably sexy. Despite their skepticism at the moment, her friends will probably be dressing in a similar way before too long.

Recent research suggests that concern about being overweight among adolescent girls is widespread (Moses, Mansour-Max, & Lifshitz, 1989). When concern becomes obsession, as it does in an increasing number of cases, the result can be an eating disorder. Anorexia nervosa and bulimia are two serious—in fact, life-threatening—afflictions that physicians are seeing and attempting to treat more and more often today. In anorexia, the better known of the two, victims begin with voluntary dieting, but they lose emotional and physical control of their eating habits and begin to starve themselves. If they don't receive treatment, they may starve themselves to death. For a detailed description of both anorexia and bulima and how they're treated, see Health Focus—Eating Disorders in Adolescence: Anorexia and Bulimia.

The ideal male physique in our society is broad-chested, slim-hipped, and muscular. Exaggerations of this form appear in children's pop culture too. By the time boys are age 14 or 15, many are eager to develop their new muscles, and they're willing to work out in gyms to do it. But others want even more muscle mass than occurs naturally, and a new "quick fix" is available in anabolic steroids. Use of these illegal and dangerous drugs has increased alarmingly among adolescent boys, trying to build their bodies up to massive size and improve their athletic performance. The practice and dangers of using steroids are detailed in Health Focus—Beauty's Only Skin Deep: The Dangers of Anabolic Steroids.

SEXUAL MATURATION

Of course, all the visible changes on the outside are accompanied by important changes on the inside. In addition to the growth hormone that triggers the growth of the skeleton, the pituitary also secretes hormones that "turn on" the ovaries and testes, as mentioned previously. The ovaries become ready to produce mature egg cells and to release them in monthly cycles, and the testes become ready to produce sperm (Katchadourian, 1977).

Primary and Secondary Sex Characteristics

The pituitary also releases hormones that control and regulate the production of hormones by the sex glands themselves. The ovaries produce estrogen, which stimulates the development of secondary sex characteristics in girls, including budding breasts, pubic hair, axillary (underarm) hair, larger sex organs, a slight growth of hair on the upper lip (in some girls), more rounded contours, and so on. The **secondary sex characteristics** aren't involved in reproduction, but they create a greater physical distinction between the sexes. The ovaries also release progesterone, which controls ovulation (release of an egg) and menstruation. The appearance of the **primary sex characteristics**—in girls, ovulation and menstruation—indicates that the reproductive organs have reached maturity.

Under the influence of hormones from the pituitary in boys, the testes start to produce testosterone, which triggers the appearance of male secondary sex characteristics, including the appearance of body, facial, and pubic hair; the growth of the sex organs; the lengthening of the vocal chords, which deepens the voice; and so on. The primary sex characteristics in boys are sperm pro-

HEALTH FOCUS

Eating Disorders in Adolescence: Anorexia and Bulimia

ANOREXIA

Anorexia nervosa has received a great deal of attention recently, but it's not a new disease. In the nineteenth century, it was identified as a female nervous disorder among adolescent girls in England and France, and papers reported cases of miraculous "fasting girls" who lived without taking any nourishment (Showalter, 1985). Many fasting girls seemed to be sacrificing themselves unselfishly, renouncing earthly appetites and taking care of others as they became steadily more insubstantial themselves. It's even been suggested that some female saints of earlier centuries were anorectics whose mystical experiences were actually delirious visions caused by starvation.

Today we view anorexia nervosa as a serious medical and psychiatric disorder that requires intensive treatment if the victim is to survive. A disease of intentional self-starvation, it afflicts about 1 out of every 200 girls between the ages of 12 and 18 (Crisp, Palmer, & Kalucy, 1976). Most anorectics are middle-class girls or women between the ages of 10 and 30; only about 4 to 6 percent of all anorectics are male (Halmi & Falk, 1979).

What Are the Symptoms?

Anorectics often begin as average or slightly above-average-weight girls who start dieting to lose weight and then never stop. They pursue thinness relentlessly, both by starving themselves and by burning a tremendous number of calories through physical exertion. At some point, they develop a distorted body image—while they're wasting away to nothing, they think they're still "fat." When their body fat drops below a certain level, they develop **amenorrhea**—their menstrual periods stop. Amenorrhea is often the first sign that something is wrong with a thin adolescent girl.

Once they're very thin, anorectics are weak and unable even to walk very far. When there's no more fat on the body and the muscles are wasted, the body turns to its own organs in its desperate search for protein. If the disorder is untreated, death can come from heart failure caused by chemical imbalance.

Although the anorectic denies herself food, she's obsessed by it. She may show a sudden interest in cooking and preparing food and spend hours poring over recipes. She may hide food or refuse to eat with her family. Even when she looks more like a skeleton than a living person, she's plagued by anxiety about becoming fat. Carefully counting out calories, she thinks of nothing but her diet.

The symptoms of anorexia may be summarized as follows (American Anorexia/Bulimia Association Newsletter, February, 1986):

- Weight loss of 20 to 25 percent of total body weight
- Amenorrhea
- Hyperactivity
- Continual extreme dieting
- Intense fear of weight gain
- Unusual behavior toward food

What Causes Anorexia?

Experts are divided about the causes of this disorder. The great emphasis on slimness in our society may spur on a dieting adolescent girl who believes she'll be more popular or socially accepted if she's thinner. The feminine ideal is now thinner, more tubular, and more boyish than it used to be, a trend we can see if we compare Playboy models and winners of Miss America pageants from today with those of 20 years ago (Love & Johnson, 1986).

Many experts have looked at the families of anorectics for common patterns of behavior. Often, anorectics come from model families where perfection is the only acceptable standard. One of the parents is often overly concerned about eating habits and interested in fad diets. Some studies have also found that anorectics, especially those who develop the disorder before puberty, were "problem eaters" in infancy or early childhood (Jacobs & Isaacs, 1986).

Although anorexia begins with dieting, people on diets don't just become trapped by anorexia. The disorder is caused not by dieting but by a distortion of body image, perhaps caused by an underlying emotional or psychological problem (Attel & Brooks-Gunn, 1989). One of the important psychological issues in anorexia is control. Taking charge of their eating habits, although in a self-destructive manner, may be a way anorectics exercise control over their families and their own lives.

How Is Anorexia Treated?
Some nineteenth-century physicians thought "control" was at the heart of anorexia, but they believed it was conscious control. They regarded girls who wouldn't eat as deceitful, self-centered attention-seekers, and they recommended neglect, ridicule, and buckets of cold water to cure them of their stubborn ways (Showalter, 1985).

Today, medical and psychiatric treatments are used to help anorectics, but treatment is difficult. Clinging to their own perceptions of reality, anorectics usually deny that they're ill. Often they can be made to eat only if they're hospitalized. Because of the complex interpersonal relations that seem to foster and maintain the disorder, the whole family usually has to enter therapy if the anorectic girl is to recover. If the family doesn't respond well to counseling, chances of a successful cure are lower. Even so, only about 25 percent of all anorectics can be considered cured (Zucker, 1986).

BULIMIA
Bulimia nervosa isn't as well known as anorexia because it was more recently identified as a separate disorder. It's also less visible than anorexia because bulimics may be of normal weight and size. Like anorectics, they have a distorted body image and an intense fear of becoming fat, but unlike anorectics, they have an uncontrollable urge to consume huge quantities of food at one sitting. After such a binge, they induce vomiting to prevent the food from being absorbed into their bodies. They also purge themselves by using laxatives and diuretics. Bulimics may binge 20 or 30 times a day, consuming over 6,000 calories in 24 hours (a normal person consumes about 2,500 calories per day) (Gregory, 1987, p. 28).

Eating habits like these place tremendous stress on the body, often resulting in kidney failure, loss of vital minerals, and infection. Tooth enamel erodes, and the teeth decay from constant contact with vomited stomach acids.

Bulimics tend to come from white, upper middle-class, high-achieving families, often with a high incidence of drug or alcohol abuse. At least 4 to 5 percent of high school girls are thought to suffer from the disorder (Pyle et al., 1983; Johnson et al., 1984; Van Thorne & Vogel, 1985). One study found that 13 per-

cent of college-age students showed signs of bulimia, many more of them female than male (Halmi & Falk, 1981). Many bulimics are girls who weigh in at the high end of the normal range.

What Are the Symptoms of Bulimia?
Bulimics are secretive about their habits. They may eat meals with their families or friends and then gag themselves in the bathroom without anyone realizing what they're doing. Because their weight is relatively normal, they can often keep their disorder a secret for years. Binges are usually solitary, however, and after they binge, bulimics often feel guilty or ashamed. To cope with these feelings, they may fast for a while, or they may binge again.

Although they have a distorted body image and think they should be thinner than they are, bulimics don't create their own reality to the extent that anorectics do. Bulimics have a relatively normal appearance; they know their eating habits are socially unacceptable and need to be concealed. Anorectics are out of touch with reality and believe their skeletal appearance is actually attractive.

Symptoms of bulimia may be summarized as follows (American Anorexia/Bulimia Association Newsletter, February, 1986):

- Uncontrollable urges to eat
- Cycles of binge eating and self-induced vomiting
- Excessive use of laxatives and diuretics
- Feelings of guilt and depression
- Menstrual irregularities, swollen glands
- Large fluctuations in weight
- Dental decay

What Causes Bulimia?
The sylphlike feminine ideal is again the focus when we look for a cause of bulimia. Girls who are trying to get or stay thin and who already have a poor self-image and underlying emotional problems may be susceptible to cycles in which they binge, fast, and purge. They may be trying to win the approval of others by being thin, at the same time that they crave the physical and oral satisfactions of eating. With bulimia, they can have both. Many bulimics come from families that value success and attractiveness above all else (Schwartz, Barrett, & Saba, 1985). Like anorectics, bulimics are trying to achieve perfection.

How Is It Treated?
Bulimia is even harder to treat than anorexia, partly because there are more physical complications. Treatment usually involves a combination of medical therapy, psychotherapy, and behavior modification techniques. Once the victim accepts treatment, she has to learn self-control strategies, new eating habits, and healthier ways of coping with the world. (Anyone concerned about anorexia or bulimia can get information and support from the American Anorexia/Bulimia Association, Inc., 133 Cedar Lane, Teaneck, NJ 07666.)

duction and ejaculation. Primary and secondary sex characteristics in both males and females are shown in Figure 17-8.

The Sequence of Development in Girls and Boys

The development of sexual characteristics proceeds in a definite sequence. For girls, it starts with the growth spurt at about age 9 or 10 and the first stages of breast development. Within the next year or two, the sex organs grow rapidly and the fastest rate of body growth occurs. Menstruation begins only after this peak of physical growth is reached, about two and a half years after the growth spurt begins. In the next two to four years, the breasts and hips continue to fill out to create the adult body shape.

In boys, the sequence begins with the growth of the testes and scrotum and the first appearance of pubic hair at about age 11 or 12. Only at this point does the growth spurt begin for boys, along with the rapid growth of the penis. In the next year or two, the voice starts to change, hair appears on the upper lip, and the sex organs grow rapidly. When ejaculation occurs, often during sleep, the boy has reached sexual maturity, but he doesn't reach the age of maximum growth until after this point, usually two to three years after the sequence begins. Later in adolescence, further changes complete development, and physical strength reaches its peak. The sequence of maturation for both girls and boys is summarized in Boxes 17-1 and 17-2.

FIGURE 17-8
The physical changes that occur at puberty result from a complex interaction of hormones released by both the pituitary gland and the sex glands. Body shape and size change, secondary sex characteristics appear, and both males and females become capable of reproduction.

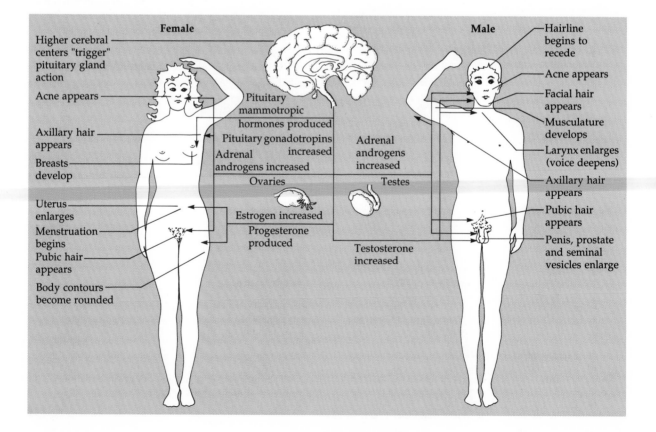

BOX 17-1
Sequence of Maturation in Girls

1. Adolescent growth spurt begins.
2. Down (nonpigmented) pubic hair makes its initial appearance.
3. Elevation of the breast (so-called bud stage of development) and rounding of hips begins.
4. The uterus and vagina, as well as labia and clitoris, increase in size.
5. Pubic hair grows rapidly and becomes slightly pigmented.
6. Breasts develop further; nipple pigmentation begins; areola increases in size. Axillary hair is becoming slightly pigmented.
7. Growth spurt reaches peak rate and then declines.
8. Menarche, or onset of menstruation, occurs (almost always *after* the peak rate of growth in height has occurred).
9. Pubic hair development is completed, followed by mature breast development and completion of axillary hair development.
10. Period of "adolescent sterility" ends, and girls become capable of conception (up to a year or so after menarche).

Other Effects of Increased Glandular Activity

With puberty comes another, less welcome, development—increased activity in the glands in the skin. The sweat glands, especially those in the armpits, start to produce substances with a pronounced odor. At the same time, oil-producing glands in the skin, especially the skin of the face, start to secrete more oil than the pores can handle. When pores become plugged, blackheads appear, and when blackheads become infected, pimples appear.

Acne isn't usually a serious medical problem, but adolescents are often so acutely conscious of their appearance already that any additional problem can be relatively traumatic. A variety of treatments for acne are available, both over the counter and by prescription, but sometimes the individual has to wait to get older before the skin completely clears up.

The activity of the endocrine glands also affects emotional stability. The mood swings and extreme sensitivity that some adolescents experience may have a physical basis apart from the individual's emotional life. These teenagers may have a tumultuous life until their bodies are back in balance, usually later in adolescence.

BOX 17-2
Sequence of Maturation in Boys

1. Testes and scrotum begin to increase in size.
2. Pubic hair begins to appear.
3. Adolescent growth spurt starts; the penis begins to enlarge.
4. Voice deepens as larynx grows.
5. Hair begins to appear under the arms and on the upper lip.
6. Sperm production increases, and nocturnal emission (ejaculation of semen during sleep) may occur.
7. Growth spurt reaches peak rate; pubic hair becomes pigmented.
8. Prostate gland enlarges.
9. Sperm production becomes sufficient for fertility; growth rate decreases.
10. Physical strength reaches a peak.

HEALTH FOCUS

Beauty's Only Skin Deep: The Dangers of Anabolic Steroids

The Fastest Man Alive

In 1988 the eyes of the world were on Canadian runner Ben Johnson when he won the gold medal in the 100-meter sprint in the Summer Olympics in Seoul, Korea. Johnson's astonishing finish time set a world record that seemed beyond human ability. The press proclaimed him "the fastest man alive."

But just two days later, media attention, this time unwelcome attention, again focused on the athlete, as he was stripped of his medal and sent home in disgrace. Blood tests revealed that he had been taking anabolic steroids, banned by the International Olympic Committee since 1975. It was also revealed that Johnson's coach, Charlie Francis, had himself been exposed to anabolic steroids during the 1972 Olympic Games in Munich and had used them the next year when he won the Canadian national championship in the 100 meter competition (Janofsky, 1989).

The Olympic Committee banned steroids because their use wasn't in keeping with the spirit of the Olympics, where athletic prowess is supposedly the result of personal effort and discipline. In more recent years, the actual physical dangers of using steroids have been documented, and sports officials and others have redoubled their efforts to keep them out of the hands of athletes. Unfortunately, steroids still seem to be more popular among adolescent boys in search of bulkier muscles, greater speed, and improved endurance.

What Are Anabolic Steroids?

Anabolic steroids are synthetic male hormones with some of the same effects as testosterone. During puberty, testosterone is partially responsible for the tremendous muscle and bone growth experienced by adolescent boys. It also affects the appearance of the primary and secondary sex characteristics, and it increases certain behavioral traits, such as aggressiveness. Anabolic steroids are manufactured to minimize the sexual effects and maximize the muscle-building effects of testosterone (*anabolic* means "building up"). They also increase aggressiveness, a trait that may translate into the extra "energy" athletes need to give their all during competitions (Committee on Sports Medicine, 1989). As Ben Johnson demonstrated to the world, anabolic steroids can be stunningly effective in improving athletic performance.

Why Are They Dangerous?

The problem with these synthetic hormones is that they have many negative physical side effects. They can lead to both benign and malignant tumors in the liver, increase the rate at which atherosclerosis (hardening of the arteries due to fat deposition) occurs, and result in toxic hepatitis. They also affect the reproductive system, causing reduced sperm production and atrophy of the testicles. Fluid retention, high blood pressure, high levels of cholesterol, and impaired immune system functioning can all result from their use (Committee on Sports Medicine, 1989). When women take steroids, they develop masculine characteristics, such as body and facial hair and a lowered voice. When children take them, they mature quickly and stop growing prematurely.

Anabolic steroids can also cause severe mood swings and violent behavior (Committee on Sports Medicine, 1989). Psychiatrists report that there has been an increase in violent crimes by people using

VARIATIONS IN THE TIMING OF PUBERTY

The sequence of development is basically the same for all adolescents, but the timing, as we've seen, can vary considerably. Girls as a group begin to mature two to three years earlier than boys as a group. Any sixth or seventh grade teacher can attest to the fact that most girls are taller than most boys. It takes the boys a few years to catch up to the girls in height and then a few more years to surpass them.

But aside from these group differences, individual boys and girls experience maturation at widely different times. For boys, it may begin as early as age $10\frac{1}{2}$ and end as late as age 16, although the average age of onset is 13 years. For girls, the growth spurt can start anytime between ages $8\frac{1}{2}$ and $10\frac{1}{2}$ (Tanner, 1981). Why do some children develop early, acquiring the bodies and sexual characteristics of adults by the time they're in sixth or seventh grade, while others develop late, remaining "children" into eighth, ninth, or even tenth grade? And what are the effects of these variations on the adolescents themselves, especially the very early and the very late bloomers?

anabolic steroids, including murder by people who seemed to undergo a complete personality change under the influence of the drug (Daniel, 1989). The judgment of legislators and the medical community has been that these compounds are too dangerous to be legal in our country.

How Can the Use of Steroids Be Stopped?
Physicians used to give athletes prescriptions for steroids, but when use of these drugs was banned, a thriving underground trade sprang up. Because so many other drug problems demanded attention in the 1980s, federal law-enforcement officials ignored the illicit steroid market until recently. But with more attention being focused on their dangers and their widespread use, laws have been stiffened and some attempts at enforcement have been made. As with other drug problems, however, supply responds to demand, and as long as demand is high—which it seems to be—the supply also will be high (Kahler, 1989).

Because of the nature of the problem, the American Academy of Pediatrics has alerted physicians to the dangers of these drugs and recommended procedures for counseling boys who come to them for the physical exams required for participation in school sports. Physicians hope that when young people realize the dangers of steroids early in their athletic careers, they'll avoid them altogether (Committee on Sports Medicine, 1989). Information and education, combined with more balanced attitudes toward the nature and definition of "masculinity," should slow the acceptance of steroids in the 1990s.

Body building the safe way is hard work, but it pays off in the long run. Anabolic steroids have too many damaging side effects to be worth the risk.

What Determines When Puberty Will Occur?

A variety of factors, including nutrition, general health, genetic inheritance, and metabolic rate, determines when puberty will begin for any specific person. As with other aspects of development, the earliest and latest limits for an individual may be established by heredity, but environmental factors may influence the timing within that range. For example, girls have to have a specific level of body fat in proportion to muscle tissue before they start getting their menstrual periods (Peterson, 1979). When girls use a tremendous number of calories every day in an activity like dancing or running, they may not reach this level of fat, and consequently they don't begin to menstruate. When fat deposition reaches the necessary level, menstruation begins or resumes.

Environmental factors are thought to be responsible for the earlier and earlier onset of puberty in the United States and other industrialized countries. In 1900, for example, the average age of menarche (onset of menstruation) for American girls was 14 years and 2 months. Today, it's 12 years (Peterson, 1979; Tanner, 1981). This change, known as the **secular growth trend**, is probably

FIGURE 17-9
Early-maturing girls may feel ambivalent about their bodies, especially if they aren't ready to deal with the social implications of their physical development. They may feel excited about growing up at the same time that they're reluctant to leave childhood behind so suddenly and so soon. Overall, early-maturing girls don't seem to fare as well in academic and social areas as their later-maturing counterparts.

FIGURE 17-10
Puberty may be delayed in female athletes who have very little fat on their bodies, such as this girl. If the body doesn't have enough fat to support a pregnancy, menstrual periods don't occur.

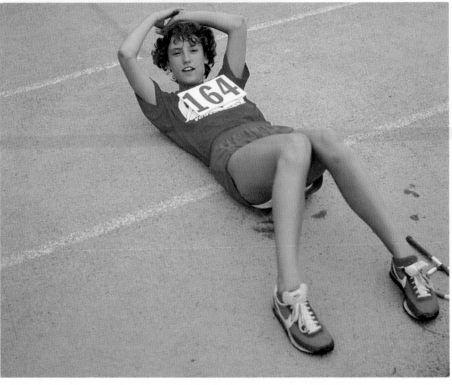

due to better nutrition and health care than in years past. Some people have wondered if the age at which puberty occurs could keep going down indefinitely and if we would eventually see pubescent toddlers or preschoolers. Luckily, as nutrition and health reach some optimum level, this downward movement is expected to stop. In other words, there are genetic and biological limits to the age at which individuals can become sexually mature, no matter how healthy the environment.

The onset of puberty obviously has important effects on the individual's self-concept. We turn now to a discussion of these effects and how they differ depending on the person's sex.

What Are the Effects of Early and Late Maturing?

> Are you there, God? It's me, Margaret. Gretchen, my friend, got her period. I'm so jealous, God. I hate myself for being so jealous, but I am. I wish you'd help me just a little. Nancy's sure she's going to get it soon, too. And if I'm the last I don't know what I'll do. Oh, please, God. I just want to be normal.

The suspense can be tortuous, as this excerpt from Judy Blume's popular book indicates (1970, p. 100). When other girls are developing breasts and getting their periods—or when other boys are growing beards and talking in deeper voices—the children who are showing no signs of development can feel, like Margaret, that they've been left behind, betrayed by their genes or some other unknown force. On the other hand, girls who look two or three years older than their sixth-grade classmates and boys who already need to shave at age 13 may feel at least as uncomfortable as children like Margaret. What are the immediate and long-term effects of early and late maturation?

EFFECTS OF EARLY AND LATE MATURING IN GIRLS. In one study, researchers found that girls who mature in the late elementary grades often feel out of place because they're taller than their peers and because their sexual development brings some unwanted reactions from boys (Simmons & Blyth, 1987). But the girls in this study who were late bloomers also reported negative feelings about themselves during early adolescence. In the long run, however, later maturation seemed to be advantageous for girls. The later-maturing girls reported more positive feelings about themselves in later adolescence than the early-maturing girls did.

It's not clear what causes these different outcomes. Perhaps early-maturing girls are under pressure for sexual relationships before they can cope with them emotionally, and this lowers their self-esteem. Or perhaps later-maturing girls, in the absence of attention from boys, develop more skills and abilities that serve them better in the long run. Whatever the reason, when compared with early-maturing girls, late-maturing girls tend to complete more years of schooling, be truant less often, and engage less often in troublesome behavior, such as smoking and drinking (Magnusson, Stattin, & Allen, 1985).

EFFECTS OF EARLY AND LATE MATURING IN BOYS. Boys' experiences are different, of course, but research findings about their reactions to early and late maturing differ from study to study. Some studies have found that early-maturing boys have an advantage over later-maturing boys. They're more social and popular with their peers; more athletic because of their larger size, better coordination, and greater strength; and more likely to be leaders in school activities (Jones, 1949; Gross & Duke, 1980; Simmons & Blyth, 1987). Their level of development matches that of girls the same age more closely than does that of most boys, so they're more attractive to girls. They're also likely to be interested in more sophisticated heterosexual relationships. All of these factors tend to give the early-maturing boy higher social status in early adolescence.

Other studies, however, suggest that earlier maturation may have some disadvantages in the long term. Early-maturing boys have been shown to have less self-control and to be more inclined than later-maturing boys to smoke, drink, and get into trouble with the law (Duncan et al., 1985; Sussman et al., 1985). Further research is needed that takes into account all the relevant variables (such as those discussed below) to help us fully understand the effects of early and late maturation.

THE IMPORTANCE OF OTHER FACTORS. Whatever the biological timing for an individual boy or girl, other factors influence how comfortable or uncomfortable the transition to adulthood actually is, including cultural expectations, intellectual ability, parental reaction, and individual perceptions (Tobin-Richards, Boxer, & Peterson, 1983; Hill et al., 1985; Peterson & Taylor, 1980). For example, a late-maturing girl with above-average intellectual ability might be able to maintain her self-esteem through academic successes, while a girl with more social interests might suffer more from late development. Or a child going into adolescence with a secure sense of self from earlier stages of development might not be as affected by late development as a more insecure child.

FIGURE 17-11
This 15-year-old high school football player, an early-maturing boy, enjoys more prestige and popularity than do later-maturing boys. But early maturation may be troublesome for him in the long run, just as it is for girls.

An early-maturing girl from a family and a culture that value traditional roles for women might fare better than an early-maturing girl whose family and culture expect high academic achievement and a nontraditional career. Even the physical attractiveness of the individual must be considered. Unattractive girls, who presumably base their positive feelings about themselves on other factors, suffer less loss of self-esteem during pubertal change than do attractive girls. The timing of puberty may be less important to them for this reason (Zakin, Blyth, & Simmons, 1984). Of course, sensitive parents and teachers who understand, support, and validate the experience of every individual help make puberty a manageable experience.

MOTOR DEVELOPMENT AND SKILLS

Olympic champions are sometimes as young as 14 or 15 years old and often no more than 26 or 28 years old. These statistics reflect the fact that the physical skills required for athletic events usually reach their peak during adolescence and early adulthood. The strength, stamina, and coordination that were growing in middle childhood continue to develop during the teenage years. Bones harden, becoming more dense due to the deposition of minerals, and muscles become stronger, as we've seen. The adolescent is capable of impressive physical feats.

However, current research shows that only about half of the adolescents in the United States participate in regular, vigorous, prolonged physical activity of the kind that most effectively conditions the cardiorespiratory system (Ross & Gilbert, 1985). Girls especially seem to become less active once they reach puberty, perhaps because they find themselves temporarily more awkward at sports they enjoyed in childhood, or because they're more self-conscious about

FIGURE 17-13
People have begun to take women's sports more seriously in recent years, leading to more attention and funding for organized sports for girls. Even though these girls have just had a disappointing loss, the experience of playing a team sport provides them with important opportunities for physical, social, and emotional growth.

their bodies and being in front of an audience, or because our culture deems sports less important for girls than for boys.

Good physical education programs can help both girls and boys to build physical fitness and body strength, as can sports such as basketball, soccer,

TABLE 17-1
Physical Activities of Adolescent Boys and Girls

Top 15 self-reported physical activities for boys and girls in grades 5 to 12 based on the portion of total physical activity time outside physical education class spent on the activities (Ross & Gilbert, 1985, p. 8)

Boys	Rank	Girls
bicycling	1	swimming
basketball	2	bicycling
football (tackle)	3	disco or popular dancing
baseball/softball	4	roller skating
swimming	5	walking quickly
weightlifting/training	6	baseball/softball
fishing	7	basketball
football (touch/flag)	8	calisthenics/exercise
hunting	9	jogging (distance running)
jogging (distance running)	10	gymnastics-free
soccer	11	volleyball
lacrosse	12	aerobic dance
king of the hill	13	tennis
roller skating	14	horseback riding
disco or popular dancing	15	cheerleading/pom-pom
wrestling	15	
karate/judo/martial arts	15	

FIGURE 17-14
When the whole family exercises together, parents keep in shape and children learn that fitness is a natural part of life.

volleyball, field hockey, and track. The trick is to educate and motivate young people to participate in these programs and sports. When they do engage in physical activities outside of school, teenage boys' top choices are bicycling, basketball, football, baseball, and swimming. Girls' top choices are swimming, bicycling, dancing, roller skating, and walking. The top 15 choices of both boys and girls are shown in Table 17-1.

Physical activity is important, not just for the body but for the mind as well. As many people know from experience, and as research confirms, physical fitness increases self-esteem and self-confidence (McGowan, Jarmon, and Peterson, 1974). Physical activities also provide adolescents with important opportunities for peer interaction.

Despite the benefits of physical activity, most people in our society lead a relatively sedentary life. Labor-saving devices eliminate the need for most physical exertion, television provides endless hours of passive entertainment, employment is usually indoors, and schools are often able to provide only basic academic education because of limits on their financial resources. In recent years, some people have begun to take physical fitness more seriously, but this trend needs to be expanded to more segments of the population, including adolescents. Experts suggest that the coordinated efforts of schools, community organizations, and parents are needed to encourage adolescents to adopt physically active life-styles.

OVERVIEW

Adolescence brings dramatic physical changes. Children now experience the fastest rate of growth since the earliest months of infancy, reaching their adult height, or close to it, within a few years. Girls' bodies become more rounded; boys' become more muscular. Even more dramatic than the growth spurt are the changes associated with sexual maturity, which is reached by both boys and girls in early adolescence. They emerge from the typically awkward transition period of puberty with adult bodies and the ability to conceive children. Now more than ever they need to adopt habits that lead to responsible, healthy life-styles.

CHAPTER REVIEW

PHYSICAL GROWTH

- During the period of growth and change known as pubescence, children experience a tremendous growth spurt. Girls grow 6 or 7 inches in two or three years; boys can grow 8 or 9 inches.
- Girls experience the growth spurt earlier than boys, beginning at about age 9 or 10. Boys start at about age 11 or 12. Some growing continues after this period, but adolescents are basically full grown when pubescence ends.
- Pubescence occurs as a result of complex hormonal activities initiated by the pituitary gland, which secretes both growth hormone and hormones that "awaken" the gonads. The ovaries begin to secrete estrogen, and the testes begin to secrete testosterone.
- Bones grow rapidly and bone ends harden, terminating growth. Body proportions become more and more adult. Girls' bodies increase in fat tissue, and boys add muscle.

- Teenagers are very concerned with how their bodies compare to cultural ideals. Girls who become obsessed with their bodies may develop anorexia or bulimia. These eating disorders are widespread and can be life threatening.
- Anorexia is characterized by self-starvation and a distorted body image. Bulimia is characterized by cyclic fasting and purging. Victims of both these disorders need intensive care, including hospitalization in many cases, to get well.
- Some teenage boys take anabolic steroids to build up their muscles and improve their athletic performance. These synthetic male hormones have many dangerous side effects, including atherosclerosis, atrophy of the testes, high blood pressure, high cholesterol, and impaired immune system functioning.

SEXUAL MATURATION

- Triggered by the pituitary, the sex glands secrete hormones that stimulate the development of the primary and the secondary sex characteristics. The primary sex characteristics are ovulation and menstruation in girls and sperm production and ejaculation in boys. The secondary sex characteristics are those physical traits that create a greater distinction between the sexes—in girls, these traits include breasts, pubic hair, fuller body proportions, and so on; in boys, these traits include facial hair, pubic hair, longer vocal chords, and so on.
- Development proceeds in a definite sequence. In girls, it begins with the growth spurt, followed by the appearance of pubic hair, the development of breasts, the growth of the sex organs, menarche (onset of menstruation), and a tapering off of growth.
- In boys, the sex organs increase in size, pubic hair appears, the growth spurt begins, the voice deepens, facial hair appears, sperm production begins, and the growth spurt tapers off.
- Maturation begins at different times for different people. For girls, it may begin as early as age $8\frac{1}{2}$, and for boys as early as age $10\frac{1}{2}$.

- The timing of maturation is determined by both genetic inheritance and environmental factors, including nutrition, health, and metabolic rate. Girls have to have a certain proportion of body fat before they start menstruating.
- Puberty has been occurring earlier and earlier in American children since the beginning of this century. The secular growth trend, as this change is known, is probably due to improved health and nutrition, but there are biological limits to how early puberty can occur.
- The timing of maturation can have powerful effects on children. Girls who develop late seem to have advantages in the long run over girls who develop early. Findings are mixed for boys, with some studies showing that early maturing is more advantageous and others showing that late maturing is preferable.
- Other factors, including individual, family, and cultural values and perceptions, affect how individual children react to the timing of sexual maturation.

MOTOR DEVELOPMENT AND SKILLS

- Many physical abilities reach their peak in adolescence and early adulthood. Bones and muscles mature, endurance improves, and strength increases. Adolescents are strong, fast, and long-winded.

- Many adolescents, especially girls, become less active at this time, just when their physical potential is at its height. Because of the benefits to be gained from a physically active life-style, adolescents need to be encouraged to participate in physical activities.

KEY TERMS

pubescence
growth spurt
gonads
amenorrhea

secondary sex
  characteristics
primary sex characteristics
secular growth trend

SUGGESTIONS FOR FURTHER READING

Cratty, B. J. (1986). *Perceptual and motor development in infants and children* (3rd ed.) Englewood Cliffs, NJ: Prentice-Hall.
  This is the classic book on physical and motor development in children. Well written and interesting.
Haywood, K. M. (1986). *Life span motor development.* Champaign, IL: Human Kinetics.
  A very readable book about several aspects of motor development, including the effects of practice and the extent to which body build is genetically determined.
Katchadourian, H. (1977). *The biology of adolescence.* New York: W. H. Freeman.
  A comprehensive discussion of the physical and physiological changes that occur during adolescence.

chapter 18

COGNITIVE DEVELOPMENT IN ADOLESCENTS

Thirteen-year-old Simon was concerned about the environment. He knew that toxic chemicals were filtering into ground water in some areas of the country and polluting lakes and streams. He'd read that pesticide residue was sometimes present in the fruits and vegetables sold in supermarkets. He'd even sent a contribution from his allowance to an organization that lobbied for stricter regulation of pesticides and toxic wastes.

So, when his science teacher told his class about the citywide science fair, he knew right away that he wanted to do an environmental project. And when he came home to find that his apartment building had been fumigated, he got the idea of doing a study on the effects of pesticides on cockroaches. Maybe the exterminators didn't need to use so much poison to kill the cockroaches, he thought. Maybe less poison would do it, and poison humans less in the process. Or maybe less poison would kill a crucial segment of the population—the reproducing females, for example, or the babies. Maybe some kinds of cockroaches were more susceptible to certain poisons than others. If he could find out any of those things, he might even be able to make a difference in how the exterminators used their chemicals.

Later that night he told his mom about his ideas. "I'd like to get a whole bunch of cockroaches down at the pet shop," he explained. "They sell them to people who feed bugs to their snakes and turtles. I know they have the big South American kind and at least two other kinds. Then I'll ask Mr. Garvin to help me get some of the pesticide exterminators use. I could use a different concentration of pesticide on each strain of cockroach to see how much you really need to kill them."

"Where are you planning to conduct this experiment, Simon?" asked his mom, who didn't like the idea either of cockroaches or of pesticides in her home.

"Oh, Mr. Garvin said we can do all our work at school in the lab," Simon responded. Then he went on, "I could even apply different concentrations of pesticides to cockroaches of different ages. If they laid eggs I could treat some of the eggs, and then I could treat some of the babies."

"Wait a minute," interrupted his mom. *"If you use different concentrations of pesticides on different strains of cockroaches at different points in their life cycle, how will you know which variable you're testing? Don't you have to be more methodical than that?"*

Simon thought about this for a while and finally said, *"Yeah, I see what you mean."* He sat down at the desk to try to work the problem out on paper. After some time he called out, *"Mom, I think I've got it!"*

"What's your idea?" she asked.

"Well, listen to this. I get the three different strains of roach. I keep them until they have babies. I keep some of the babies until they're 3 weeks old. That gives me three different groups—adults, babies, and juveniles—for each of the three different strains."

"Okay."

"Then I also have three different concentrations of pesticide. I'll divide each of the nine groups into three subgroups and treat each subgroup with a different pesticide. I'll end up with 27 different subgroups. Then when a pesticide works, I'll know exactly what roaches it worked on. Like a certain low concentration might work on South American babies but not on South American adults."

"Excellent thinking, Simon."

"And if you killed baby cockroaches, you'd wipe out a whole roach population, wouldn't you? People would just have to wait a little while before they saw results."

"Sounds good to me."

"Then exterminators could use less poison. I think I'll go write this all up as a project proposal. Wait till Mr. Garvin hears about it!"

Simon's redesign of his science project revealed some very sophisticated thinking. He didn't have any cockroaches or pesticides in hand, but he was able to think about what he would do with them if he did have them. Moving beyond concrete thought, he was juggling variables and contemplating possibilities about situations that existed only in his mind—a more advanced approach to problem solving. All the possible combinations of variables in his experiment are shown in Figure 18-1.

This more mature cognitive level is apparent in many aspects of adolescents' thinking, whether they're debating social or political issues, formulating

FIGURE 18-1

All the possible combinations of variables in Simon's experiment. A younger child would be unable to juggle all these possibilities.

X Q A	X R A	X S A
Y Q A	Y R A	Y S A
Z Q A	Z R A	Z S A
X Q B	X R B	X S B
Y Q B	Y R B	Y S B
Z Q B	Z R B	Z S B
X Q J	X R J	X S J
Y Q J	Y R J	Y S J
Z Q J	Z R J	Z S J

A, B, J = Adults, babies, and juveniles
X, Y, Z = Three strains of cockroach
Q, R, S = Three concentrations of pesticide

FIGURE 18-2
These 14- and 15-year-olds can think about abstract ideas like the one written on the blackboard behind them—how social change contributed to the evolution of nineteenth-century Victorian values into twentieth-century mores. Most younger children would have a difficult time making sense of such an idea.

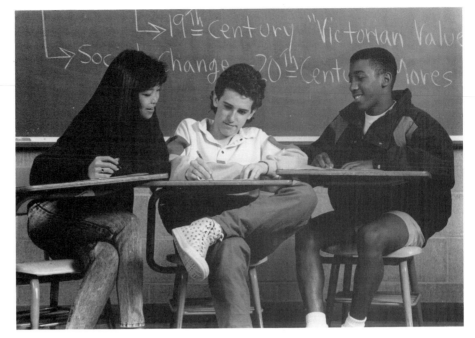

abstract ideas, using logic, understanding literature, or solving science problems. Perhaps the best way to characterize this new way of thinking is to say that adolescents are released from concrete interpretations of words and situations. They're able to imagine possibilities, build concepts, use metaphors, and construct hypotheses. Their thinking becomes both more rational and more imaginative.

In this chapter, we discuss these exciting developments in cognition, which move the adolescent toward adult understandings. Beginning with Piaget's conception of cognitive development during adolescence, known as formal operational thinking, we then move on to the challenges to the Piagetian tasks and interpretations that distinguish the information-processing view of cognitive development. Finally, we describe some of the other dimensions of adolescent thinking that are characteristic of this period, ranging from the ability to think in abstract terms to the tendency to think of oneself as the center of the whole world.

FORMAL OPERATIONAL THINKING

Simon's thinking advanced to a new level of complexity only recently. In fact, when he first told his mother about his idea for the project, he hadn't designed it in a way that would give him clear results. But when the problem was pointed out to him, he was able to alter his design. He had the ability to consider how multiple variables might interact at the same time.

A year or even a few months earlier, he probably wouldn't have been able to engage in this kind of thinking. He might have gone ahead with his first plan and concluded that baby cockroaches were more susceptible to pesticides without considering that they were from a particular strain or had received the highest dosage. Or he might have concluded that the combination of low age and high dosage leads to a high death rate.

This kind of observation-based thinking is an example of Piaget's *concrete operational* thinking rather than **formal operational thinking**. The child in the concrete operational stage can readily report on events he has witnessed, both in terms of exactly what happened and in terms of the conditions that prevailed when the events took place. But he fails to notice when variables are confounded—when they're operating together—and therefore draws an inaccurate conclusion about what caused the event. The inability to pinpoint exact causes from among a number of possibilities, by designing and carrying out a systematic procedure for eliminating some of the possibilities, is the major limitation of concrete operational thinking.

Formal operational thinking, on the other hand, is characterized by the ability to think in this systematic way. As one researcher has said, "the adolescent makes reality secondary to possibility. . . . he begins not by observing the empirical results, but by thinking of the possiblities inherent in the situation" (Ginsberg & Opper, 1988, pp. 200–201). Formal operational thinking, then, is abstract, governed by propositions and formal logic.

Tasks Used to Assess Formal Operational Thinking

As with the other levels of cognitive development, Piaget devised a number of tasks to test individuals for formal operational thinking. The goal of all these tasks is to isolate the cause of a phenomenon from among several possible factors.

THE PENDULUM TASK. One of the most famous experiments Piaget designed to test this level of thinking is the pendulum task (Inhelder & Piaget, 1958). The subject is asked to figure out what determines the period of the pendulum— the time it takes the pendulum to make one full swing. Four factors, or some combination of the four, could be at work: (1) the length of the string, (2) the

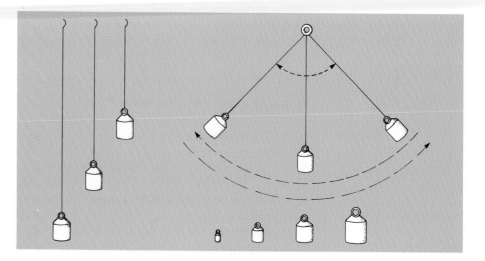

FIGURE 18-3
In the Piagetian pendulum task, the child has to think about four variables—the length of the string, the size of the weight, the height from which the weight is let go, and the force with which the weight is let go. Formal operational thinkers can test each variable systematically to arrive at an answer.

size of the weight hanging from the string, (3) the height from which the string and weight are let go, and (4) the force with which the string and weight are pushed when let go (Figure 18-3).

To determine which of the variables is responsible for the pendulum's period, the subject has to vary each one while holding the others constant. If he doesn't do this—if he shortens the string at the same time that he decreases the weight, for example—then he won't know which change is responsible for any change he might observe in the pendulum's period, or if the change is due to their combined effect.

Concrete operational thinkers change the variables in an unsystematic way and often change more than one at a time. They report the situation accurately ("a long string and a heavy weight versus a short string and a light weight"), and they report the action of the pendulum accurately ("it goes slower now"), but they don't think logically about causation ("the heavy weight and the long string make it go slower"). Formal operational thinkers realize they have to be more thorough: "It could be the length of the string or the size of the weight. I'm going to have to use the same weight while I change the length of the string or I won't know which one causes the pendulum's period to change." By excluding all the possibilities one at a time, they discover that the pendulum's period is determined by the length of the string alone.

THE COMBINATION OF CHEMICALS TASK. A second task involves combining liquids to produce a liquid of a certain color (Inhelder & Piaget, 1958). The child is shown four bottles of clear liquids, labeled 1, 2, 3, and 4, and some beakers. There is also a fifth bottle, labeled g, called an indicator bottle (Figure 18-4). The chemicals in the bottles are such that combining liquids 1 + 3 + g yields a yellow liquid. If some liquid from bottle 2 is added to liquid 1 + 3 + g, the yellow color remains. If liquid from bottle 4 is added to liquid 1 + 3 + g, the yellow color disappears and the liquid becomes clear.

When the experiment begins, two beakers contain liquid. One contains liquids 1 + 3 and the other contains liquid 2 only. The experimenter adds a

FIGURE 18-4
The combination of chemicals task requires that the child think about more than one liquid at a time and figure out a way to combine them to solve the problem.

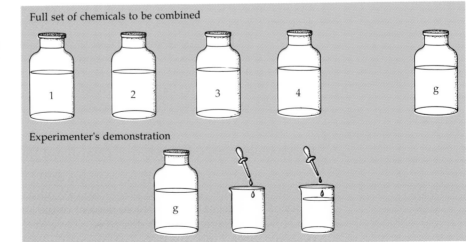

drop of liquid from g, the indicator bottle, to beaker 1, and the liquid turns yellow. When the experimenter adds a drop from g to beaker 2, its contents remain clear. The child is then invited to experiment with the liquids to find out which combinations create the yellow liquid.

Children in the concrete operational stage test the liquids in the bottles one by one, adding a drop of g to each beaker in turn to see if the liquid turns yellow. When none turns yellow, they believe that they've tried everything. If the experimenter suggests that they might try something additional, they combine liquids from two bottles and test them, but not in a systematic way. They might try 1 + 4 + g, for example, and then add 3 and then 2. They become confused when they're confronted with so many possibilities.

Children in the formal operational stage also begin by testing one liquid at a time, but when this fails they realize that they have to mix them. They combine the liquids systematically (1 + 2, 1 + 3, 1 + 4, and so on) and keep track of what they've done—until they discover the combination that turns yellow when g is added. Some children even go on to see if combinations of three different liquids from the bottles will turn yellow and to speculate about what the relationship of 4 is to g, since it turns the yellow color clear again.

PROBABILITY TASKS. A third type of task involves the ability to take probability into account. In one experiment, a collection of colored shapes is placed in a bag and an identical set of shapes is placed on a table in front of the child (Figure 18-5). The child is asked to predict which shape is most likely to be drawn from the bag. If the set includes five green squares, two yellow triangles, one red circle, and one orange rectangle, it is most probable that a green square will be drawn out of the bag. But as the drawing proceeds and the bag's contents are depleted, the probability of drawing the different shapes changes. If four green squares and one red circle have already been drawn, the odds are that the next draw will yield a yellow triangle rather than the orange rectangle or the last green square.

To play the probability game, children must consider not only what was in the bag at the start, which is represented by the shapes on the table, but what has been taken from the bag in each subsequent drawing. Concrete operational thinkers understand the first rule and predict that the experimenter will draw a green square. But they don't change their predictions systematically as the drawing proceeds. They aren't able to keep track of the changing quantity of objects in the bag or coordinate that information with their ideas about probability. Typically, they continue to predict that the experimenter will draw a green square. Formal operational thinkers, on the other hand, are able to keep track of the objects that have been drawn and change their predictions based on the changing probabilities (Brainerd, 1978).

Do All Adolescents Develop Formal Operational Thinking?

As many experienced high school teachers could tell you, formal operational thinking is absent in a large proportion of adolescents. Even among well-educated adolescents, only 30 to 40 percent of the students in American schools can solve the Piagetian tasks described above at the formal operational level (Keating, 1980; Linn, 1983). In fact, many adults can't solve the tasks at this

FIGURE 18-5
In probability problems, children have to take changing conditions into account in order to make likely predictions. Formal operational thinkers realize the odds change after each draw.

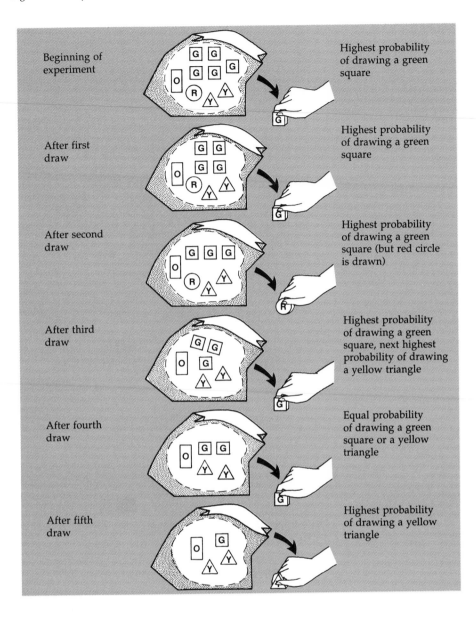

level and therefore aren't considered to have attained Piaget's highest cognitive stage (Neimark, 1981; Kuhn, 1984). These findings suggest that formal operational thinking is not a universal developmental milestone.

WHY DO THE DIFFERENCES EXIST? Why do some people develop formal operational ways of thinking while others don't? Some research suggests that variations in experience account for the differences. For example, when subjects who don't use formal operational thinking are tutored on the Piagetian tasks and similar problems, they are often then able to solve problems at this level (Siegler & Liebert, 1975; Stone and Day, 1980). Furthermore, people living in Western cultures are more likely to show formal operational thinking than

FIGURE 18-6
Because of their experience with scientific thinking and mathematical calculation in a high school chemistry lab, these students are likely to demonstrate formal operational thinking. People without scientific experience often don't reveal this kind of thinking, leading some experts to question its existence as a universally achieved cognitive stage.

people in non-Western cultures, suggesting that the Western scientific and technological approach to problem solving supports the development of this ability (Laboratory of Comparative Human Cognition, 1983).

Finally, differences exist even in scientifically oriented cultures, with more adolescent boys than girls showing formal operational thinking (Meehan, 1984). Since more boys than girls take science courses at the high school level, their greater experience with scientific and mathematical thinking could account for this difference.

IS FORMAL OPERATIONAL THINKING TASK SPECIFIC? The findings of differences between adolescent boys and girls led some researchers to speculate that the content of the Piagetian tasks, predominantly oriented as it is toward math and science, makes them more familiar, appealing, and interesting to some subjects than to others. They wondered if students who weren't math or science oriented would do better if they were given tasks with other content. They found that when they altered the tasks, girls who weren't interested in science did better than they did on the standard tasks (Peskin, 1980). These results suggest that formal operational thinking is not, as Piaget believed, an overall pattern of thinking that generalizes to all situations once it's achieved. Rather, it seems to be a task-specific way of approaching certain problems common not to all human beings older than 12 or 13 but only to individuals who have had experiences that helped them learn to think in a certain way.

FIGURE 18-7
Fewer girls than boys show formal operational thinking, but fewer girls also take math courses in high school. Girls who do take math are just as likely to use formal operational thinking as their male counterparts. If we're interested in seeing more people advance to this level of thinking, we have to put more effort into making math a valuable choice for girls.

AN INFORMATION-PROCESSING VIEW OF ADOLESCENT THINKING

Critics have taken exception to some of Piaget's assertions about formal operational thinking and some of the ways he tested it. The findings about its situation-specific nature just mentioned provide support for what is known as an **information-processing view** of cognition. Researchers who hold this view believe that cognitive advances are due not to changes in overall modes of thinking but to improvements in memory, attention, knowledge, and problem-solving strategies.

Thinking is considered to develop continuously, as memory, knowledge, and strategies accumulate (Siegler, 1976; 1986), rather than progressing through qualitatively different stages. The researchers claim that if formal operations were a general way of thinking, we would expect it to emerge in virtually all people, and we would expect individuals to apply it across all situations once they attained that level. Instead, it emerges in only some people, and those who have reached it seem to use it to solve certain kinds of problems but not others.

The Information-Processing Approach to the Piagetian Tasks

Researchers with an information-processing view of cognitive development have often analyzed solutions to the standard Piagetian tasks in terms of sets of rules. They also change how the tasks are presented, and they predict how subjects who use different rules will respond. We can illustrate this approach by looking at a study of Piaget's balance beam task conducted by Robert Siegler, the most active of these researchers.

In the standard balance beam task, children are asked to predict if a balance beam will balance under a variety of conditions (Inhelder & Piaget, 1958). In each trial of the task, the experimenter varies the weights on either side of the beam and the distances of the weights from the fulcrum (Figure 18-8). To predict accurately, the child has to consider and coordinate both weight and distance.

Piaget found that concrete operational children focus on the weights, not on the distances from the fulcrum. If each side of the balance beam had the same number of weights, the child predicted that the beam would balance, regardless of how far they were from the fulcrum. Adolescents considered both weights and distances and were able to predict more accurately when the balance beam would and would not be in equilibrium.

Siegler (1976, 1978) presented the same tasks, altering weights and distances on different trials. But he also proposed four different rules that he thought children would use to solve the problems, depending on their age. The rules are listed in Box 18-1, along with Siegler's predictions of which kinds of problems can be solved accurately using each of the rules. You can see that of the six different problem types (shown on the bottom left of the box), three

FIGURE 18-8
In the balance beam task, Piaget asked children to predict whether the beam would balance as he varied the weights on each side and the distance of the weights from the fulcrum. He found that formal operational thinkers realized they had to coordinate weight and distance to answer correctly.

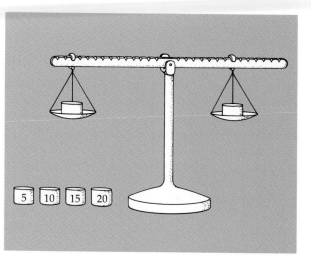

BOX 18-1 Siegler's Rules for Solving the Balance Beam Problem

Rule 1. Subjects using this rule consider only the weights and disregard the distances of the weights from the fulcrum. When the number of weights is equal, they predict that the scale will balance. If the number isn't equal, they predict that the scale won't balance.

Rule 2. Subjects using this rule also consider only weight, except when the weights on both sides are equal. When this is the case, they consider distances as well. If the distances are equal, they predict that the scale will balance; if they're not equal, they predict that it won't balance.

Rule 3. Subjects using this rule consider both weight and distance. If weights are equal and distances aren't, they base their decision on distances. If distances are equal and weights aren't, they base their decision on weights. But if both weights and distances are unequal, they can't make a judgment, and they just guess.

Rule 4. Subjects using this rule consider both weight and distance. They realize that multiplying the weights by the distance on each side and comparing the two products will tell them if the scale will balance.

	RULE			
Problem Type	I	II	III	IV
1. Equal weight-equal distance	100%	100%	100%	100%
2. Unequal weight-equal distance	100%	100%	100%	100%
3. Unequal distance-equal weight	0% should say "Balance"	100%	100%	100%
4. Conflict-weight (more weight on one side, more distance on the other, configuration arranged so side with more weight goes down)	100%	100%	33% (chance responding)	100%
5. Conflict-distance (similar to conflict-weight, but side with greater distance goes down)	0% should say "Right side down"	0% should say "Right side down"	33% (chance responding)	100%
6. Conflict-balance (like the above two problems, except the scale remains balanced)	0% should say "Right side down"	0% should say "Right side down"	33% (chance responding)	100%

can be solved using Rule 1, four can be solved using Rule 2, three can be solved accurately and three will be guessed using Rule 3, and all can be solved using Rule 4.

Siegler found that children of different ages consistently used different rules and thus were able to solve different problems. Children who were 5 years old, for example, used Rule 1 most often. The 9-year-olds used rules 2 and 3. Subjects between the ages of 13 and 17 used Rule 3 most of the time. Almost no one used Rule 4.

Implications of the Findings

Siegler's findings are not inconsistent with Piaget's. The difference is that Siegler gives a specific description of the rules needed to solve each of the problem types, whereas Piaget conceives of the ability to solve these problems as a reflection of an across-the-board, qualitative change in overall thinking. Siegler also assumes that children can be taught the rules they don't yet know and that this can improve their performance on tasks. In Piaget's conception, direct teaching isn't considered very effective in altering overall thinking patterns.

Siegler even found that providing feedback to children about the accuracy of their predictions caused some to move to a more advanced rule. This happened more frequently with older children than with younger ones, however. Younger children, 5-year-olds, for example, focused almost exclusively on the weights and didn't seem to notice the variations in distance. Even with feedback—seeing that their predictions turned out to be wrong—they didn't notice the second variable. Only when variation in distance was pointed out did they take this variable into account and improve their performance. Siegler (1983) claims that very specific feedback is needed if children are to figure out what's going wrong and how they can improve their predictions.

Piaget never disputed the fact that children could be trained to perform better on specific tasks. His claim was that the training wouldn't generalize to new tasks—that a new way of thinking, in general, can't be trained, at least not in the short run. One of the differences between concrete operational and formal operational thinking is the understanding that you have to identify all the relevant variables in a situation and vary each one systematically to determine its causative effect. Knowing that all the variables must be identified was itself a part of formal operational thinking, as Piaget conceived it.

What Piaget didn't consider enough, perhaps, is the extent to which a history of tutoring on variable identification and manipulation lays the groundwork for formal operational thinking. The information-processing researchers are helping to make explicit the kind of experiences that are probably required if formal operational thinking is to emerge. They're also showing teachers that helping children learn how to identify all possible dimensions of a situation can improve their ability to think.

OTHER DIMENSIONS OF ADOLESCENT THINKING

Nine-year-old Mark was in the habit of reading the funnies in the newspaper every day, but one morning he was distracted by a headline and a picture he didn't understand. After studying the article for a while, he said to his 16-year-old sister, "Janice, what does this mean—'Anti-Abortion Demonstrators Close Clinic'?"

Janice glanced at the headline. "It's about a group of people who don't think women should be allowed to have abortions."

"What's an abortion?"

"What's an abortion? Well, sometimes when a woman is pregnant, for one reason or another she doesn't want to have the baby. An abortion is a procedure that doctors can do that ends the pregnancy. They take the fetus out of her body a long time before it would have been born."

"Why are these people against it?"

"Some people think that life begins when the baby is conceived and that taking it out of the mother's womb is the same as killing it. Other people think the woman should have a choice about whether or not she has the baby."

"Oh." Mark seemed to be thinking about these notions, so after a while Janice said, "What do you think?"

"What do I think about what?" he replied.

"About abortion. Would you think it would be more important to protect the unborn baby or to allow the woman to have control over her body?"

"Well, I don't know, because I don't know anyone who's having a baby right now."

"Well, imagine that you know someone who's having a baby."

"Like who?"

"Well, imagine that Mom is pregnant again. Would you think it would be OK for her to do something so she wouldn't have the baby?"

"But she's not pregnant."

"Well, but you remember when she was pregnant with Molly. Would it have been okay for her not to have had Molly?"

"Well, I don't know, because she did have Molly. Molly's right there."

"Then suppose that it was another baby after Molly, another little brother or sister."

"Well . . . I guess that if there was another kid in our family, I wouldn't get as much attention, and maybe I wouldn't get as many toys for Christmas or my birthday, and I might even have to share my room. So I guess I wouldn't want her to have another baby."

"That's not exactly what it's all about, Mark!" Janice exploded. "It's not about whether you get more presents for Christmas! It's about figuring out when you think life begins. It's about whether aborting a baby is the same as killing a person. It's about whether a woman has the right to control her body or whether the government is going to tell her what she can do."

"Well, I don't know," Mark muttered. "I don't even understand what you're talking about. Let me read the funnies, will you?"

Although Mark is a fourth grader with above-average intelligence, he can't discuss an issue like abortion with his tenth-grade sister. He's not being thick-headed; he's just not able to think in these sophisticated terms. Janice, on the other hand, has no trouble thinking about this issue. And because she knows her brother is bright, she can't understand why he's having so much difficulty. Her thinking is fundamentally different from his, and in her conversation we can see several characteristics of adolescents' formal operational thinking that we haven't discussed above.

Hypothetical Thinking and Abstract Ideas

An outstanding feature of Janice's thought is that she can think in terms of hypothetical situations, generating problems and considering various ways of addressing them. She's able to "imagine" and "suppose" virtually any set of circumstances, no matter how unrealistic or unlikely. If she had gotten a little further in her conversation with Mark, she might even have asked him to try to imagine how he would feel if he had to have a baby he didn't want. There's no question but that Mark would have answered, "That's impossible! I'm a boy."

Although Mark has no problem "pretending"—he's been able to pretend play since he was a toddler—his imagination doesn't extend to experiences that are very different from his own. Mark also has some social role-taking ability (which we discussed in Chapter 16) and is quite capable of "putting himself in someone else's shoes." But again, the shoes have to be a fairly good fit to start out. Mark's moral development is what we would expect of a fourth grader as well. He believes in the golden rule and takes pride in being a loyal friend—characteristics of Kohlberg's conventional stage of moral development (also discussed in Chapter 16). What Mark can't do that Janice can is put all these cognitive abilities together and apply them to a hypothetical situation. In adolescence, children become capable of using and integrating all the achievements of the earlier cognitive stages in a systematic way.

Janice can also think in terms of abstract concepts, ideas about broad principles rather than particular instances. She can think about justice, fairness, rights, and ideas such as when life may be said to begin or in what ways abortion may be the same as or different from killing a person. Furthermore, she can see ideas about these concepts as points of view or opinions that different people have. She not only can articulate both sides of the abortion issue but would be able to argue either side in a formal debate using principles

FIGURE 18-9
Adolescents are capable of thinking about social and political issues in terms of justice and other broad moral principles. These teenagers at a rally protesting South Africa's policy of apartheid are demonstrating not only their capacity for abstract thought but their altruism and idealism.

of logical reasoning, no matter what her personal convictions. Mark would find it impossible to defend a position that was the opposite of his own.

Finally, Janice thinks about important moral, ethical, and political issues. As adolescents' cognitive abilities advance, their interest in complex social and philosophical problems increases. In the later high school years and beyond, they discuss and debate not just the questions of the day—Is nuclear power a viable source of energy? Is surrogate motherhood an acceptable alternative to adoption? What can be done to house the homeless?—but the timeless questions that people have been asking for thousands of years—Who or what is God? Why is there evil in the world? What is the meaning of life?

Of course, teenagers have endless mundane concerns as well and spend a great deal of time thinking and talking about them. But just as tutoring can elicit improved performances on the Piagetian tasks, careful teaching can help teenagers think more systematically about complex problems. Debating team coaches, for example, can teach adolescents how to use logical propositions and construct persuasive arguments, and English teachers can help students understand sophisticated forms of symbolic communication.

Adolescent Idealism

Because their thinking is so expansive, adolescents see what is and imagine for the first time what could be. Their thinking is typically **idealistic**, and more often than not they side with the underdog, whether that means ethnic or racial minorities, underprivileged groups, the homeless, the poor, or people

FIGURE 18-10
Youthful idealism is apparent when teenagers organize a car wash to raise money for a good cause, whether it's to benefit a local hospital or to assist disaster victims on the other side of the world.

fighting for freedom from oppressive governmental regimes. They may visualize a perfect world where all problems have been solved.

Unfortunately, in many cases the ideal world imagined by adolescents can't be achieved under real world conditions. In addition, adolescents rarely have a well thought out plan to remedy most of the problems they critique (Adelson, 1975). Adolescent idealism gradually wanes as young people become more experienced with the complexities of the real world. They often find that they have to settle for a somewhat better world rather than some abstract ideal world. As Winston Churchill once said, "Anyone who isn't a liberal at 20 has no heart; anyone who isn't a conservative at 40 has no head."

These characteristics of adolescent thinking indicate that it clearly has many more dimensions than are tested in the specific Piagetian tasks. Yet they are all aspects of what we think of as formal operational thinking. The common element is a new flexibility that allows the mind to soar above concrete indi-

FIGURE 18-11
Exuberance, inexperience, and self-centered thinking too often lead to risk-taking behavior among adolescents. These boys no doubt know what they're doing is dangerous, but they probably don't believe they could be hurt.

vidual experiences, to make previously unseen connections, to see the invisible as well as the visible. In fact, it's the kind of wide-ranging, creative thinking that allowed Piaget to devise a theory of universal human cognitive development that stands today, despite numerous successful challenges, as our main way of understanding the complex area of intellectual functioning.

Adolescent Egocentrism

Although teenagers don't have all the information, knowledge, or experience that adults have, their thinking "equipment" is basically complete. However, adolescent thinking does have one major limitation: It's often distorted by their **egocentrism**. They tend to focus too much on their own ideas as the only possible solutions to problems—a trait that can make their idealism rigid and unyielding. They may feel that they have the answers, if only others would listen and agree to their plan.

They also tend to believe that others are focused as much on them as they are on themselves, a notion partly responsible for the excruciating self-consciousness so typical of this age. Concern about hair, skin, teeth, body size, sexual development, clothing—all may seem excessive to the adult who can't perceive any of the defects causing the teenager so much despair. Because they're constantly viewing and thinking about themselves, adolescents believe that others are doing the same thing. They create and react to an **imaginary audience**, a source of continuous approval or disapproval (Elkind, 1976).

Another form of adolescent egocentricity is what has been called the **personal fable** (Elkind, 1978). Teenagers believe that they're special, that bad things happen only to others. They have the feeling that they're immune, exempt, even immortal. Personal fable beliefs may be behind some of the reckless, seemingly self-destructive behavior we see too often in adolescents. Although they know that drinking impairs the ability to drive, for example, they think accidents happen only to others. Although they know that sexual intercourse produces babies, they think only others get pregnant. As they move on into adulthood, people usually are successful at letting go of these beliefs and coming to a more rational agreement with the real world.

OVERVIEW

Important cognitive changes take place now, as the concrete, literal thinking of the school-age child gives way to the more imaginative and yet more rational thinking of the adolescent. This new way of thinking is characterized by the ability to manipulate ideas in the abstract, to imagine possibilities, and to understand symbols. Teenagers can use the scientific method to construct experiments; they can use logic to argue philosophical issues; and they can use metaphors to express their ideas. Because they imagine the world as it could be, they may challenge the status quo and even inspire social and political change. Although their experience doesn't yet match their intellect, adolescents possess the potential for mature, adult thought.

CHAPTER REVIEW

FORMAL OPERATIONAL THINKING

- Piaget investigated formal operational thinking with experiments that tested the subject's ability to isolate the cause of a phenomenon from among several possible factors.
- In his pendulum task, subjects had to figure out what determined the time it took the pendulum to make one full swing. They had to test each of four factors separately to discover that the length of the string was the only relevant factor. In the combination of chemicals task, they had to figure out how to combine chemicals to produce a liquid of a certain color.
- Piaget also used probability tasks to see if children could change their predictions as conditions in an experiment changed the probability of a certain outcome.
- Not all adolescents (or adults) attain formal operational thinking, suggesting that it's not a universal developmental milestone. Research indicates that variations in experience may explain why some people attain it and others don't. It appears more commonly in those who live in Western cultures than those who don't; in adolescent boys than girls; and in those who have had math and science training.
- Current thinking is that formal operational thinking is a task-specific way of thinking, characteristic of people who have had certain experiences.

AN INFORMATION-PROCESSING VIEW OF ADOLESCENT THINKING

- In the information-processing view of cognition, advances in thinking are due to improvements in memory, attention, knowledge, and problem-solving strategies.
- Proponents of this view have analyzed various Piagetian tasks in terms of rules that subjects might follow to arrive at their solutions. They have found that teaching rules to children, especially older children, can improve their performance, as can giving them feedback about their mistakes.
- This view isn't in conflict with Piaget's view, but it focuses more on the specific experiences that can improve children's performance and help them achieve formal operational thinking.

OTHER DIMENSIONS OF ADOLESCENT THINKING

- Adolescents become capable of thinking in hypothetical terms and imagining all the possibilities inherent in a situation. They put together all the achievements of earlier cognitive stages in a systematic way.
- Adolescents also become able to think about abstract concepts, to argue different points of view, even if they don't agree with them, and to explore sophisticated political, moral, and philosophical ideas.
- Good teaching can help teenagers think logically about important issues and appreciate the richness available to them in their cultural heritage.
- Adolescents often imagine a better world than the one we live in, and their thinking is often idealistic. As they gain more experience of the complexity of the situations they critique, they typically lose some of their idealism.
- The one major limitation of adolescent thinking is its egocentrism. Adolescents often think that the world revolves around them, that everyone is looking at and thinking about them, and that they are exempt from the hazards and misfortunes of life. They tend to drop these ideas as they gain more experience of the world.

KEY TERMS

formal operational
  thinking
information-processing
  view of intellectual
  development

idealism
egocentrism
imaginary audience
personal fable

SUGGESTIONS FOR FURTHER READING

Ginsburg, H. P., & Opper, S. (1988). *Piaget's theory of intellectual development* (3rd ed.) Englewood Cliffs, NJ: Prentice-Hall.

This book provides a very readable overview of Piaget's theory, including formal operational thinking.

Kimmel, D. C., & Weiner, I. B. (1985). *Adolescence: A developmental transition.* Hillsdale, NJ: Lawrence Erlbaum.

This book contains a chapter on cognitive development and intelligence in adolescence. It is written from a Piagetian perspective.

Siegler, R. S. (1983). Information processing approaches to development. In W. Kessen (Ed.), *Handbook of child psychology: Vol. 1. History, theory, and methods* (4th ed., pp. 129–211). New York: Wiley.

This chapter provides a discussion of a theory of intellectual development and functioning that competes with Piaget's. Not easy reading.

Siegel, I. E., Brodzinsky, D. M., & Golinkoff, R. M. (Eds.). (1981). *New directions in Piagetian theory and practice.* Hillsdale, NJ: Lawrence Erlbaum.

Several chapters in this volume concern cognitive development and functioning during the adolescent years.

c h a p t e r 19

LANGUAGE DEVELOPMENT IN ADOLESCENTS

"Mom, we're home! We're back early because Eric was scared by a frisky dog who knocked down a little boy as he was playing ball in the park. I told Eric the dog was just a big puppy, not really a mean dog who was going to hurt him, but he wouldn't listen. What a scaredy cat! If you're thinking of sending me to the park with him again, just forget it."

"I'm not a scaredy cat! See, Mom, there was this great big dog. A man had him on a leash, but then he let him go. He ran all over the place and jumped up and down. A little boy was in the park, and he was playing ball. Then the dog ran over and jumped on him. He fell down, and then he started to cry. I didn't want to get knocked down too, so I made Brad bring me home. It was a big, mean dog!"

Brad, aged 15, and Eric, aged 8, tell the same story to their mother, but they tell it in two very different ways. Eric uses more sentences, and he uses shorter ones. It takes him six separate sentences to describe what happened, each one adding another small detail about the incident with the dog that he had witnessed. Brad, on the other hand, uses just one sentence to relate all of the critical details of the incident. His ability to be concise illustrates one of the major ways in which the language of older children differs from that of younger children. In fact, adolescent language is characterized by a new efficiency and coherence of expression.

Although language acquisition is basically complete by the beginning of adolescence, important refinements are made during this period. These include greater precision in speaking, greater sophistication in writing, and better understanding in reading. Most of these advances reflect improving cognitive abilities, but some changes—the adoption of a distinctive slang and an increased potential for difficult communication with adults—are tied more to social and emotional developments. In this chapter we discuss all these characteristics of adolescent language.

ORAL LANGUAGE DEVELOPMENT

As we saw in the case of Eric and Brad, younger children use many sentences to say what older children might say in just one or two (Muma, 1986). When younger children make longer utterances, it's usually because they're combining several simple sentences with the conjunction *and*. Older children use grammatical devices to subordinate some information to other information. This ability allows the older child to communicate relationships among information more precisely and to speak more efficiently (Loban, 1975).

The Cognitive Basis for Language Advances

Older children's greater sophistication in speaking—their ability to create complex sentences that contain many clauses—is made possible by advances in intellectual functioning. To use clauses, they must be able to relate the elements of a message to each other. For example, they have to decide which elements are primary, or superordinate, and which are secondary, or subordinate.

This type of thinking involves creating classes and categories and determining the relationships among a variety of elements. We saw in Chapter 10 that class inclusion understandings and skills appear fairly late in cognitive development. Younger children can't create superordinate and subordinate relationships in their thinking, so naturally they can't encode such relationships in their language. They simply make many short statements without

FIGURE 19-1
The diagram of a simple sentence couldn't be more straightforward. The diagram of a complex sentence reveals the many complex relationships expressed by a more advanced thinker and speaker.

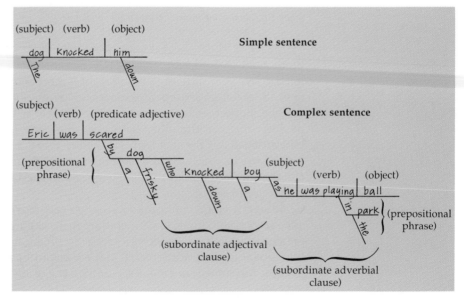

observing any hierarchical organizing principles. The diagramming of a simple and a complex sentence is shown in Figure 19–1.

Escape from Literal Interpretation

Older children's cognitive advances appear not only in their speech but in their understanding of others' speech. Now they begin to make sense of figurative uses of language. School-age children are notorious for interpreting what they hear literally, whether they do it from inexperience or from an irresistible urge to act silly. Tell an 8-year-old to "cut it out" and he's likely to respond, "Let me go get my scissors." Between ages 5 or 6 and 9, children sort out the meanings of many figures of speech (Geller, 1985). By the age of 11 or 12, children no longer focus on the literal meanings of metaphors and begin to be able to appreciate language on a whole new level.

This new ability enables older children and adolescents to understand language devices, such as parables and proverbs. One researcher who was studying language development found that children responded differently to proverbs depending on their ages (Saltz, 1979, p. 511). Here are a few of the proverbs he asked them to interpret:

Proverb 1. Never go into deep water until you can swim.

Age	Response
5	"Because you'll drown if you don't know how to swim."
7	"Cause you'll drown."
9	"Learn how to swim first."
10	"Wait till you're older."
11	"Only do what you know you can do."

Proverb 2. People in glass houses shouldn't throw stones.

Age	Response
5	"Because it breaks the glass."
7	"You know people don't live in glass houses. I don't see no glass houses."
9	"If you buy a glass house, expect to have a broken window."
11	"If you hurt people, you may get hurt yourself."

Proverb 3. When the cat's away, the mice will play.

Age	Response
4½	"Cause the mouse scares the cat."
6	"When the cat goes, the mice stay."
7	"Because the cat would eat the mice so they play when the cat is gone."
10	"When parents are away, children will wreck the house."

We see that by the time children are 10 or 11 years old, they begin to escape from literal interpretations of language. As discussed in Chapter 18, this trend is just one aspect of the overall cognitive change that occurs in early adolescence as concrete operational thinking gives way to formal operational thinking. By early adolescence they can fully understand parables, fables, proverbs, and similar forms (Elkind, 1976). The realization that words can have symbolic meaning beyond their reference to physical objects opens up the world of adult literature to the adolescent reader.

Increases in Vocabulary and Refinements in Word Use

Children's vocabularies increase throughout the school years and adolescence. (Adults, too, add words to their vocabulary, as long as they have experiences that introduce new words.) Children continue to refine their understandings of word meanings as well, the more they're exposed to them in context. We saw in Chapter 11 that children's use of the words *glass* and *cup* evolves for many years after the words enter the child's lexicon.

Adolescents' appreciation of nonliteral meanings also allows them to understand words on multiple levels, which younger children can't do. Children's dictionaries typically give only one or two meanings for a word, but adult dictionaries sometimes give more than half a dozen, including the figurative ones. For example, the following entries are from the Macmillan *Very First Dictionary* (1983):

cotton   Cotton is a kind of cloth.

nail   A nail is a thin piece of metal. A nail is also the hard part on the ends of your fingers and toes.

In contrast, Webster's *New World Dictionary* (1983) lists the following definitions for these two words:

cotton
The soft, white seed hairs filling the seed pods of various shrubby plants . . . of the mallow family . . . ;
The crop of such plants.
Thread or cloth made of cotton.
A downy, cottonlike substance growing on other plants.
To become drawn to; take a liking to.
To become aware of a situation.
To try to ingratiate oneself, or make friends with.

nail
The thin, horny substance growing out at the ends of the fingers and toes of man, monkeys, etc.
A tapered piece of metal, commonly pointed and having a flattened head, driven with a hammer, and used for holding pieces as of wood together.
To fix (eyes, attention, etc.) steadily on an object.
To catch, capture, seize, or intercept.
To hit squarely.
To settle definitely; make sure.

When asked to define words, adolescents respond differently than younger children do. Their definitions are more abstract, and they often include the superordinate category to which the object belongs. An adolescent might define a chair, for example, as a piece of furniture on which people sit. A younger child would indicate that a chair is for sitting but wouldn't mention the class of things—furniture—to which it belongs (Wehren, DeLisi, & Arnold, 1981).

We saw in Chapter 11 that context is crucial for young childrens' understanding of word meanings. Research has shown that older children and adolescents are better able than younger children to learn word meanings from formal definitions, such as those found in a dictionary (Dickinson, 1984).

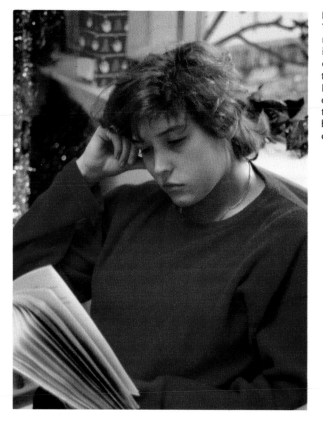

FIGURE 19-2
Younger children are taught new words and word meanings in school, but adolescents and adults increase their vocabulary by reading. If this 18-year-old regularly chooses a good book over television, she'll probably become a literate, well educated adult.

Adolescents can also derive meanings from observing how words are used in the books they read (Werner & Kaplan, 1952). However, research indicates that even adolescents need to read elaborate texts—texts in which new words are encountered many times in different contexts—if they are to learn accurate and complete meanings of the words they read (Herman et al., 1987).

Adapting Language to Different Situations

We're all aware that different social contexts require different ways of acting and talking, and young children are aware of this too. Even 4-year-olds will vary their language registers, depending on the person to whom they're speaking. If they're speaking to an infant, for example, they'll use the high pitch characteristic of Baby Talk. Elementary school children are able to adapt their language to specific people and situations, such as giving a presentation to their class or talking to Grandma on the telephone.

By adolescence, individuals are very adept at varying their way of talking. They talk one way when they're out with a peer group, another way when they're with their parents, and still another way when they're talking to teachers at school. Teenagers become very skilled at observing and mimicking different ways of speaking and by age 14 or 15 can use these skills to create parodies—ridiculous imitations—of others (Geller, 1985). These sophisticated comedic abilties are well beyond the reach of younger children.

BOX 19-1
Comparison of the writings of
a 6-year-old and a 13-year-old

WHEN THE EASTER BUNNY CAME BY JOANNA ESTRADA, AGE 6

Once upon a time there was a little Easter Bunny. He had to hide the eggs for the kids. And so he did. And then it all went that one day the other egg hatched. He looked and looked for the chicks to help him. And then it happened. Easter Day came, and he still hadn't found the chicks.

He said, "Where did those little chicks go? I need them, I need them, I need them. Help me, help me, help me," said the Bunny.

"Because the chicks have to try and help find the kids, because there is a lake at the end and they can't walk. They are crawling, and someone may take them away. Those little kids need help and I'm going to help them, no matter what it takes."

And he did.

Well, he found them finally. Nothing could stop him. He said, "Chicks." And the chicks helped him find the kids.

It was so nice when the Easter Bunny came. Everything was loving and caring and sharing. Birds were whistling, "Tweet, tweet, tweet, tweet, wh-wh-wh-wh, tweet, tweet, tweet, tweet." And bunny rabbits were hopping up and down, up and down, up and down. And the frogs were jumping in the ponds, and the swans they just sat there and looked at the people. But the biggest swan, she did float and swim, slowly, slowly.

Whenever the little duck was swimming in the pond, the Easter Bunny said, "The duck is drowning in the water." So the Easter Bunny jumped in and saved the little duck. And the little duck started shaking and shaking and shaked almost everything away, because the Easter Bunny could have been ruined with water.

And they loved life. And they loved life. And they loved life. And everyone kept on saying, "Love life, love life, love life." And then the love life really came true. And so, everything became such fun !

From Stone Soup. *(March/April 1988). 17(4), 16–17. Copyright © 1988 by the Children's Art Foundation, 915 Cedar Street, Santa Cruz, CA 95060.*

WRITTEN LANGUAGE DEVELOPMENT

What Adolescents Can Write

Just as their greater use of subordinate clauses makes adolescents' spoken language more precise and efficient than that of younger children, their grasp of more complex sentence and paragraph structure makes their writing more sophisticated. We can see the difference between the writing of a 6-year-old and that of a 13-year-old in the stories presented in Box 19-1.

TWO STORIES: THE DIFFERENCE BETWEEN AGES 6 AND 13. The 6-year-old writes about the Easter Bunny in simple, repetitive sentences and an occasional compound sentence. She juxtaposes ideas—presents them in a series—rather than relating them to each other in complex ways. After she makes the statement that the Easter Bunny "had to hide the eggs for the kids," she feels that she also has to say, "And so he did." Even though she has written an exceptionally well-organized and long story for a 6-year-old, it reveals the linear, literal thinking of the young child.

The 13-year-old, on the other hand, has written an evocative, tightly organized story that gains much of its sophistication from the way it's put together. The title reveals the single focus of the story—the house her grandparents lived in when she was younger. If we think about this piece in terms of class inclusion, we see that everything in the story relates to this topic: the house and yard, the activities that went on in them, and what they meant to her.

BOX 19-1 (continued)

GRANDMA AND GRANDPA'S HOUSE BY MARA LEICHTMAN, AGE 13

Three years ago, my grandparents got divorced. Although I've learned to accept their new spouses and the changes in their lives, what I miss the most is the house in which they used to live. That house holds all the happy memories for me when they were together.

The backyard, with its lake, was my favorite place. My grandma, sister, and I used to take walks along the shore there. My father once even took us for a canoe ride along that lake, and later we went fishing and swimming in it.

I remember another time we picked crabapples from the tree that grew next to the swingset behind the house. My mother and grandmother turned those bitter apples into the most delicious applesauce I had ever eaten. We also ate tomatoes, carrots, and cucumbers from Grandma's vegetable garden. Marigolds and rose bushes surrounded that garden, adding even more color to the red, orange, and green rainbow blooming there.

The yard was filled with many sounds. The birds chirped happily as they ate from the birdfeeders Grandma always kept full. I can still hear my grandpa's voice echoing throughout the yard as he figured out the next answer to his crossword puzzle. There was also the bell Grandma rang to chase the geese away.

The inside of the house was as special as the outside. Every Friday night when we would eat there, my grandma would light the sabbath candles, and then my grandpa would say *kiddush*.* My sister, brother, and I would often sleep at Grandma and Grandpa's house. Being the oldest, I got to sleep in a room that once was my aunt's. Standing opposite the bed was the glass case that enclosed her favorite childhood doll. As I fell asleep, I liked to imagine what she had been like when she was my age. I also liked washing my hands with the different soaps in her bathroom which was filled with glass birds and colorful paintings.

Every night, my grandpa would read the paper or watch TV while my grandma would hustle in the kitchen. I would read, finding myself pleasantly distracted by the aromas of that night's meat and vegetables filling the air. After dinner, while my grandma sewed, she would share with me the sad stories of her life in Poland. Memories of those days were captured in the paintings and wall-hangings she had made.

Some evenings, my sister and I would play Barbies. We used the dollhouse made by Grandpa and furnished by Grandma. My favorite miniature piece was the white china cat with brown ears and a striped tail. Later, my brother, sister, and I would play games from the "secret closet" under the staircase.

Strangers now live in that house. All the things I remember so well, including my grandpa's books and my grandma's paperweight collection, have been moved to different and separate places. Yet, the house itself still stands as a memorial of the days when my grandparents lived happily together.

*a Jewish ceremony for sanctifying the sabbath by reciting a blessing over a cup of wine or over bread.
From Stone Soup. (November/December 1988). 17(2), 9–11.

The writer also begins her paragraphs with topic sentences that introduce and include the ideas she's elaborating on in each paragraph. For example, when she begins a paragraph, "The yard was filled with many sounds," she goes on to enumerate those sounds: the birds, her grandfather's voice, the bell her grandmother used to chase the geese. When she wants to move from the yard to the house, she finds a way of stepping back and explaining what her next topic, her next category of descriptions, will be: "The inside of the house was as special as the outside."

This writer also uses complex sentence structure that allows her to relate ideas to each other in efficient ways. By using superordinate and subordinate clauses, she weaves many ideas into single sentences. For example, she writes, "Being the oldest, I got to sleep in a room that once was my aunt's," and "I

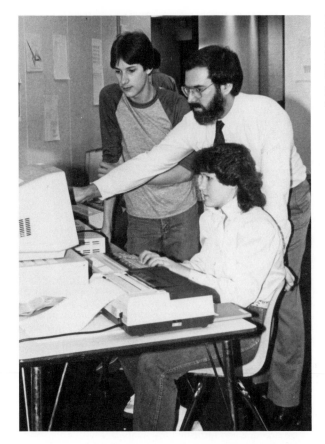

FIGURE 19-3
Student newspapers give students practice in expressing their thoughts and polishing their writing skills. These sophomores are working out a newspaper layout on a computer.

also liked washing my hands with the different soaps in her bathroom which was filled with glass birds and colorful paintings." A younger child would need many more sentences to express these ideas—"There was a bathroom with glass birds and paintings. It was my aunt's bathroom a long time ago. It had a lot of different soaps. I liked washing my hands with them. I got to use it because I was the oldest."

Many other characteristics mark this story as the work of a sophisticated thinker. Perhaps the most noticeable is her ability to relate various time periods to each other in a coherent way. She distinguishes the distant past ("the sad stories of her life in Poland"), the less distant past ("the house holds all the happy memories for me when they were together"), the recent past ("three years ago, my grandparents got divorced"), and the present and future ("strangers now live in that house . . . yet the house itself still stands as a memorial of the days when my grandparents lived happily together."). All in all, we can see that a very thoughtful and literate mind is at work in constructing this story.

THE IMPORTANCE OF INSTRUCTION AND PRACTICE. Not all adolescents write as well as the author of "My Grandma and Grandpa's House," of course, nor does writing ability improve naturally or spontaneously as thinking ability advances. Children and adolescents must have instruction and practice to learn how to apply their more mature thinking skills to their writing. Studies of American

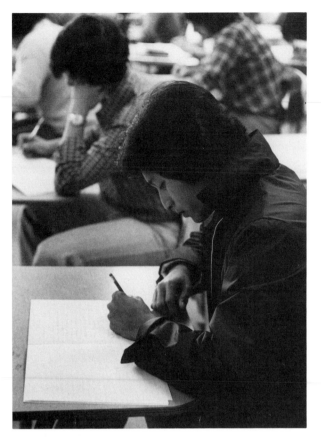

FIGURE 19-4
Many high schools don't provide direct instruction in writing even though the correct and coherent use of written language is an asset both in school and throughout life. This young man will benefit from the ability to express himself clearly whether he's filling out a college form, applying for a job, or writing a letter to his girlfriend.

students' writing indicate that they often fail to get the practice in this skill that they need. For an analysis of contemporary student writing, see Research Focus—How Well Do American Students Write?

What Adolescents Can Understand

As they get older, children and adolescents become increasingly capable of interpreting and remembering written texts. The development of these critical study skills has wide-ranging implications for academic achievement. We saw in Chapter 14 that children in the upper elementary grades are beginning to be able to make distinctions between more and less important parts of a text. In one study described in that chapter, third, fifth, seventh, and twelfth graders were asked to rate parts of texts in terms of relevance to a theme (Brown & Smiley, 1977). The third graders were unable to identify relevant or irrelevant material; fifth graders could identify only the most relevant material; seventh graders could judge both the most relevant and the most irrelevant material; and the twelfth graders alone were able to distinguish among totally irrelevant, somewhat irrelevant, somewhat relevant, and very relevant material.

Abilities such as this are crucial to learning. Effective studying requires that students identify the most important material and spend more time on it. Young children typically use extra study time in nonstrategic ways—they reread everything rather than work on the most important parts. They gain less from

RESEARCH FOCUS

How Well Do American Students Write?

Because of concern over declining American test scores and academic achievement, Congress mandated a study in 1984 known as The National Assessment of Student Progress. As part of the study, the writing ability of 55,000 fourth, eighth, and eleventh graders was examined and evaluated (Applebee, Langer, & Mullis, 1986).

Students taking the test wrote responses to questions that were designed to elicit three different kinds of writing—informative (reporting and analyzing), persuasive (convincing others and refuting an opposing argument), and imaginative. Each writing sample was evaluated by adults who taught writing. Samples were scored as unsatisfactory, minimal, adequate, or elaborated. The focus was on composition skills, such as the development of an argument and coherence, so spelling and other mechanical errors were disregarded.

The following samples from the study illustrate the kind of performances that were judged minimal and adequate:

Informative Writing: Analytical
Task: Describe a favorite type of music and explain why it is liked.

Minimal rating:
I'm having some problems over friends and a ex-boyfriend and when I listen to pop it helps me figure out my problems. I don't like slow songs with all music. My favorite pop singer is Linoll Richard my favorite groups is "Airstepp". "Truly" and "Just Once" is my favorite songs (p. 22).

Adequate rating:
My favorite kind of music is soft, easy rock because it is soothing and relaxing. I don't like the hard rock kind, it give me a headache. Soft rock has a nice beat, but it doesn't annoy you like hard rock. It's easy to sing along with, too, because you can understand what they're saying.

Persuasive Writing: Refuting an Opposing Position
Task: Give reasons why the class should be allowed to visit a local radio station despite the manager's concerns.

Minimal rating:
Dear Mr. Station Manager:

Me and my class would really like to visit your studio. We are all concerned about it. We were hoping you could change your mind. We would love to go and see all the equipment.

Thank
You.

Sincerely,   (p. 32)

Adequate rating:

Dear Mr. Brown:

Our class has suggested to have a field trip to your studio. We have been studying about radios and radio waves. We would like to be shown these methods on how they are done. We have decided to pay our own way to go there. We also made a solem promise to be quiet. We are going to break down in groups and each group will go one at a time. Please think this over and I am grateful that you shall put some thought into this.

Our class have solved your problem and I hope you will put some thought into this. I myself would like to go in and discover the radio programs. Some of our students have their future as a radio programer. Thank you for you consideration.

Sincley,

(pp. 33–36)

Tables 1 through 5 show the percentage of students at each grade level who received minimal and adequate ratings on each kind of writing task. At all grade levels, fewer than 5 percent of the writing samples received the highest rating.

These results indicate that consistent and major changes in writing ability do occur between grades 4 and 8, as concrete operational thinking evolves into formal operational thinking between the ages of 9 and 13. But the improvement in writing is noticeable only at the minimal performance level, indicating that much of it is due solely to the children's cognitive advances. If they were being given adequate practice and instruction, we would expect to see their writing becoming increasingly skillful in all areas as they advanced from elementary to junior high to high school.

This study makes it clear that American students have serious problems with writing. According to the authors (Applebee, Langer, & Mullis, 1986), most students are unable to "produce evidence, reason logically, and make a well-developed point" (p. 24). They also falter on creative writing, a problem that was apparent on tasks that "required them to project themselves imaginatively into a scene and to provide a lively and interesting description of what was going on around them" (p. 42). The study recommended that writing receiving more emphasis in the school curriculum, that it be integrated into many courses across the curriculum, and that ways of teaching writing be studied and improved. Until some changes are made, we can expect schools to continue turning out students whose writing doesn't match their intellectual potential.

TABLE 1 Informative Writing—Reporting. Percentage of Students at or Above the Minimal and Adequate Levels of Task Accomplishment

Writing Task	Grade 4		Grade 8		Grade 11	
	% Minimal or Better	% Adequate or Better	% Minimal or Better	% Adequate or Better	% Minimal or Better	% Adequate or Better
From Personal Experience						
Pets	73.2	2.1	89.1	18.9	—	—
Job Application	—	—	—	—	81.2	64.9
From Given Information						
Plants	85.4	41.2	—	—	—	—
Appleby House	68.2	24.1	86.8	52.4	86.5	59.4
XYZ Company	46.3	34.4	85.5	67.2	—	—
Dali	41.7	2.9	72.2	17.4	81.8	31.7

TABLE 2 Informative Writing—Analytic. Percentage of Students at or Above the Minimal and Adequate Levels of Task Accomplishment

	Grade 4		Grade 8		Grade 11	
	% Minimal or Better	% Adequate or Better	% Minimal or Better	% Adequate or Better	% Minimal or Better	% Adequate or Better
From Personal Information						
Favorite Music	52.9	1.9	80.3	8.3	80.9	7.0
From Given Information						
Food on the Frontier	40.3	1.9	81.0	18.3	85.2	24.6

TABLE 3 Persuasive Writing—Convincing Others. Percentage of Students at or Above the Minimal and Adequate Levels of Task Accomplishment

	Grade 4		Grade 8		Grade 11	
	% Minimal or Better	% Adequate or Better	% Minimal or Better	% Adequate or Better	% Minimal or Better	% Adequate or Better
School Rule	61.7	4.1	83.5	14.6	90.1	21.7
Dissecting Frogs	—	—	84.8	17.9	—	—
Swimming Pool	53.3	4.5	66.7	12.0	75.9	19.4
Split Sessions	—	—	34.4	9.0	59.8	15.1
Spaceship	66.8	23.5	—	—	—	—
Space Program	—	—	—	—	82.0	28.0

(continued on page 622)

RESEARCH FOCUS (continued)

TABLE 4 Persuasive Writing—Refuting an Opposing Position. Percentage of Students at or Above the Minimal and Adequate Levels of Task Accomplishment

	Grade 4		Grade 8		Grade 11	
	% Minimal or Better	% Adequate or Better	% Minimal or Better	% Adequate or Better	% Minimal or Better	% Adequate or Better
Recreation Opportunity	—	—	47.3	14.3	71.1	24.6
Radio Station	46.6	16.2	71.0	33.5	—	—
Aunt May	48.6	25.2	—	—	—	—
Uncle	—	—	—	—	73.6	24.1
Bike Lane	—	—	—	—	66.0	26.9

TABLE 5 Imaginative Writing. Percentage of Students at or Above the Minimal and Adequate Levels of Task Accomplishment

	Grade 4		Grade 8		Grade 11	
	% Minimal or Better	% Adequate or Better	% Minimal or Better	% Adequate or Better	% Minimal or Better	% Adequate or Better
Hole in the Box	39.4	3.2	62.3	18.1	66.0	17.9
Flashlight	66.9	8.9	88.4	30.8	90.4	36.2
Ghost Story	81.4	8.2	88.9	37.5	88.3	48.3

Tables 1 through 5 from Applebee, A. N., Langer, J. A., and Mullis, I.V.S. (1986). The writing report card: Writing achievement in American schools. Princeton, NJ: Educational Testing Service. (p. 17, 23, 28, 33, 39)

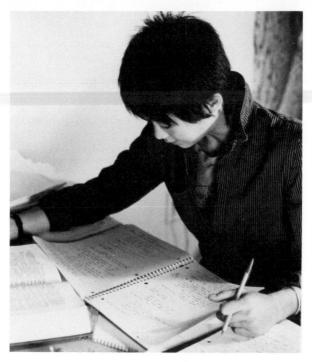

FIGURE 19-5
The heavy homework load of high school and the even heavier demands of college require extremely sophisticated study skills. This young woman appears to have worked out some effective strategies, such as studying with her textbook and notebook together and taking notes on both.

extra study time than older students do, unless they're helped to focus on what may be important (Brown & Smiley, 1978).

The most skilled studiers go beyond "deletion" strategies—removing unimportant information from the focus of their attention—to "invention" strategies —creating new superordinate categories under which to organize and condense material. In one study, very few fifth graders used invention strategies, and only about one-third of the tenth graders used them (Brown & Day, 1983). Those who used invention and other sophisticated summarizing strategies explained their methods with statements like those shown in Table 19-1.

Like sophisticated writing, effective study skills are a reflection of advancing cognitive abilities. Before a person can use invention strategies, for example, such as organizing material under superordinate headings, she has to understand the principles of class inclusion and be able to manipulate ideas mentally. But as with writing, study skills don't emerge on their own. Instruction and practice apparently play major roles in their development. For this reason, effective educational programs should include direct instruction in study skills at the elementary, junior high, and high school levels.

TABLE 19-1
Examples of Summarizing Strategies as Explained by Skilled Studiers

Strategy	Example
Deletions	"The details are dropped for a summary of this type. You need the generalizations, not the details." (trivia)
	"This essay wastes two sentences. Both state the simple fact that desert animals are nocturnal due to the heat. You can omit one." (redundancy)
Superordination	"One thing I've done is drop the kinds of plants. Instead of writing daisies, poppies, marigolds and lilies, all I've written is 'annual plants', again leaving out details and talking about generalization."
Topic sentence selection	"This sentence contains the essential point of the paragraph, it states the process by which plant life is maintained. It has to be included in any summary."
Topic sentence invention	"The paragraph is about the cycle of the annual plants that produce seeds, wait until rainfall, bloom, produce seeds again, etc. Although it doesn't say so explicitly, all you need is to state this cycle then you can drop the rest."
Combining across paragraphs	"In the first two paragraphs the only really essential information is the facts about the heat and the lack of water in the desert. I'll combine the first two paragraphs into only two sentences—that contains all the information that I need. One sentence is simple, the other is a compound sentence."
	"On the third and fourth paragraphs, information is given about plant life. The third is about annual flowers and the fourth is about the cactus, a flower particular to the desert. Now, a lot of information is given there. The details can be dropped. And the two paragraphs can be combined to one single paragraph since they both deal with plant life."

From Brown, A. L., and Day, J. D. (1983). Macrorules for summarizing texts: The development of expertise. Journal of Verbal Learning and Verbal Behavior, 22, *p. 9. Reprinted with permission of the publisher.*

COMMUNICATING WITH ADOLESCENTS

Even though they share a language with the rest of American society, adolescents are often hard to understand, and sometimes even harder to reach with words. When they're with each other, they may use their own form of communication, and when they're with adults, they may appear to be deaf. These two dimensions of adolescent communication are a reflection of social and emotional development rather than cognitive development.

Teenagers Talking to Each Other

Friday afternoon . . . several ninth graders mill around outside of school, talking about a history exam and making plans for the weekend . . .
    "That test was totally harsh!"
    "I was fully bummed!"
    "Mr. Harris is some serious uncool!"
    "What's up with tonight? Wanna go see that new movie? I hear it's excellent."
    "Yeah, it's supposed to be hot!"
    "Jerry saw it. He said it was totally awesome!"
    "I hope it's cool with my folks."
    "Catch you later!"
    "I'm outa here!"

Teenagers often have a special way of talking to each other, a **teen slang** that adults sometimes find hard to penetrate. Today's teenagers aren't the first young people to coin their own terms, of course. Every generation of adolescents uses different terms to describe life-styles and behavior patterns, to express approval and disapproval, to define what's "in" and what's "out."

In the fifties and early sixties, for example, we might have heard people talking about "the beat generation" or about "hoods" or "squares." They would have used words like "cool," "hip," "neat," and "groovy." In the late sixties we would have heard of "hippies," "heads," and "freaks." People on drugs were "high" or "stoned," and people who didn't take drugs were "straight." In the seventies people might have been characterized as "nerds," "dorks," or "preppies," and in the early eighties, an event might be "grody to the max"

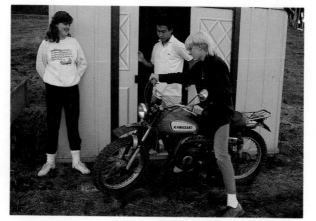

FIGURE 19-6
Fashionable slang is the coin of the realm for teenagers; they use it to send messages about personal sophistication and social awareness everywhere they go. These teenagers understand each other perfectly, even if their parents think their language is incomprehensible, at least compared to the slang from *their* youth.

or "totally tubular." The late eighties found things to be "wiggin'," "harsh," "intense," "awesome," "radical," "buff," or "fine."

Using the latest teen slang serves two purposes: it marks adolescents as belonging to a particular peer group, and it sets them apart both from younger children and from adults. As we see in Chapter 20, adolescents come to define themselves largely in terms of their friends, peers, cliques, and crowds. They become more independent of their parents and seek a sense of identity through interpersonal relationships with other teenagers.

In contemporary American society, adolescents share a distinctive youth subculture, with its own music, clothes, culture heroes, and vocabulary. They participate in similar patterns of behavior, agree implicitly on a hierarchical status system by which they judge other teenagers, and share a well-understood system of communication. When teenagers adopt the distinctive slang terms and usages popular with their peers, they're trying out a way of belonging, of defining themselves, of working toward a sense of identity they can carry into adulthood. In the years ahead, their speech will once again become "normalized," although people of every age use some of the slang terms that are popular in contemporary culture.

Adults Talking to Teenagers

Communication between teenagers and adults can be stressful at times, not just because of vocabulary differences. The difficult and important social and emotional changes that adolescents are going through can make them sensitive, volatile, rebellious, or resentful of adult authority. Their parents and teachers may see them as moody, sullen, rude, or withdrawn. And for their part, teenagers may see adults as overbearing, pompous, insensitive, nagging, or hostile. But no matter how thorny teenagers' personalities become, and no matter how obtuse adults may seem to be when interacting with them, adolescents still need and want the mature guidance and concerned support of their parents and teachers. How can adults maintain honest communication and positive relationships with teenagers?

Many experts have observed the various ways that adults interact with children and adolescents and commented on what seems to work and what doesn't. One psychologist has identified what he calls the "typical twelve" counterproductive responses parents make to their children's statements. They

FIGURE 19-7
Exasperation and irritation characterize many teen-adult interactions. "You don't understand" seems to be the message the teenager on the left is sending to her mother. Positive communication, on the other hand, allows adolescents to share their thoughts and accept the guidance they need from caring adults. The boy on the right has found a sympathetic friend in one of his high school teachers.

FIGURE 19-8
If parents have maintained a friendly, supportive relationship with their children for the first 12 years or so, they can usually expect to have basically sound interactions during adolescence as well.

include ordering, threatening, preaching, advising, giving logical arguments, blaming, disagreeing, agreeing, ridiculing, analyzing, sympathizing, probing, and humoring (Gordon, 1975, pp. 41–45). All of these responses, according to this writer, tend to make children and adolescents stop talking. As a constructive alternative, he recommends the communication technique known as **active listening**—sending back and affirming the child's own message rather than conveying a parental message ("You sound angry about flunking your exam," rather than "Well, study harder and you'll do better"). This technique can smooth some adult-teenager interactions.

The best communication during adolescence, however, is a function of good relationships, and truly sound relationships with children begin back in early infancy with a strong, secure attachment between parent and child. The baby communicates by gazing, smiling, sobering, and crying; the sensitive parent responds in ways that answer the baby's true needs. In childhood, good relationships grow when parents use verbal methods of socialization, explaining their expectations and their actions. In adolescence, the effectiveness of earlier interpersonal patterns becomes visible. When parents have used intrusive, harshly critical, or guilt-inducing forms of communication, adolescents are more likely to be troubled, isolated, and low in self-esteem (West, 1981). But when communication has been open and supportive, adolescence can be a time of continuing positive interactions. And when adolescents move on into adulthood, open communication can provide the basis for a lifelong friendship between parents and their grown children.

OVERVIEW

Children have mastered the basics of their language by the time they complete elementary school, but important refinements are made during adolescence. Many of these refinements are a result of cognitive advances, as when the ability to classify information translates into the use of superordinate and subordinate clauses in oral and written language. But intellectual advances don't guarantee improvements in writing, and schools have to provide instruction and practice if adolescents are to reach their full potential in language development.

CHAPTER REVIEW

ORAL LANGUAGE DEVELOPMENT

- Adolescents speak more efficiently and coherently than younger children, mainly because they use grammatical devices to subordinate some information to other information.
- Their ability to create complex sentences with superordinate and subordinate clauses is due to cognitive advances that allow them to create classes, categorize information, and determine relationships among elements.
- Older children and adolescents begin to understand figurative uses of language and symbolic language devices like proverbs and parables.
- Adolescents continue to increase their vocabularies, and they begin to appreciate the nonliteral meanings of words they know. They begin to define words in terms of superordinate categories rather than just concrete characteristics.
- Teenagers become skilled at varying their use of language and even creating parodies of others.

WRITTEN LANGUAGE DEVELOPMENT

- Adolescents' improved cognitive skills are also reflected in their written language. Many are capable of writing well-organized essays and stories with complex linguistic constructions and figurative language.
- In general, however, American students are not good writers and need much more instruction and practice if their writing is to match their intellectual potential.
- Students also need instruction in study skills to help them direct their cognitive abilties into effective learning techniques.

COMMUNICATING WITH ADOLESCENTS

- Teenagers usually adopt a slang way of talking that marks them as part of the youth culture and as belonging to a particular peer group. When they get older, they drop many of these terms.
- Communication is often a problem between teenagers and their parents and teachers. Communication techniques like active listening can smooth some of the difficulties, but the best communication comes from positive relationships. Sensitive parents who have relied on verbal methods of communication and discipline have the best foundation for continuing good communication with their adolescent children.

KEY TERMS

active listening
teen slang

SUGGESTIONS FOR FURTHER READING

Applebee, A. N., Langer, J. A., & Mullis, V. S. (1986). *The writing report card: Writing achievement in American schools.* Princeton, NJ: Educational Testing Services. This small volume describes the methods used to assess the writing ability of young Americans and presents the findings. Provides many writing samples to illustrate the categories that were used in the assessment.

Garner, R. (1987). *Metacognition and reading comprehension.* Norwood, NJ: Ablex. An interesting book written for teachers who want to apply what is known about metacognition to helping children read better.

c h a p t e r 20

SOCIAL AND EMOTIONAL DEVELOPMENT IN ADOLESCENTS

"Eileen, I finally got through to you!" exclaims the voice over the telephone. "Your line's been busy for almost two hours! Who were you talking to?"

"Hi, Denise!" answers Eileen, recognizing her sister's voice. "I wasn't talking to anyone. It was your nephew talking to his friends."

"For two hours?"

"That's nothing. One time I found him using both our lines at the same time. He was talking to two different girls, one phone on each ear."

"Well, at least he's popular."

"I don't know. I gather they were asking him about some other guy. He's trying to figure out how to make them like him."

"So what do you tell him?"

"You know—the same thing Mom and Dad told us—'Be yourself and people will like you.'"

"And does he say the same thing we said to Mom and Dad?"

"Of course—'How do I do that? I don't know what it means to be myself. I don't know who I am!' Then his sister says, 'I know who you are. You're Shawn Arthur Ballard, that's who you are.' And he groans and says, 'No one understands,' and stomps off to his room."

"Just the way we did."

"Yeah. But at least he's still talking to us, even if he thinks we don't understand him. Remember when we couldn't imagine that Mom and Dad were ever young? At least, as young as we were?"

"Or how they'd ever managed to have children?"

"Yes. Well, I'm afraid that's how Shawn sees Tom and me now."

"The more things change, the more they stay the same."

"Apparently."

With his long telephone conversations, his desire for acceptance, and his uncertainty about himself, Shawn is by no means an unusual 15-year-old. In fact, his concerns are typical of adolescence. Along with the physical changes and cognitive advances of this period comes a revolution in social and emotional development. Restless at home, adolescents begin to pursue relationships with friends and peers with increasing interest. They discover the complexities and satisfactions of deep emotional involvement beyond the family, and they explore the mysteries of sex and love. At the heart of their exploration is the search for self, for a unique identity, with which they will approach the adult world.

In this chapter, we discuss the twin quests for independence and intimacy that characterize adolescent social and emotional development. We look at relationships with peers and with parents as well as teenagers' sexual behavior and their thinking about sex. Finally, we address the problems that arise for some teenagers when the transition to adulthood is too overwhelming—drug and alcohol dependency, dropping out of school, juvenile delinquency, and suicide—and we consider how adults can help these individuals get their lives back on track.

ADOLESCENT SOCIAL BEHAVIOR: THE QUEST FOR INDEPENDENCE

Relationships with Peers

We saw that friends and peers become steadily more important to the child throughout the school-age years. By the time they're in fifth or sixth grade, many children are playing games or sports with their friends after school and occasionally on weekends. A typical 10-year-old's social event might be a roller-skating party followed by a trip to a pizza parlor, all supervised by adults.

FIGURE 20-2
Younger adolescents usually form same-sex cliques; groups of older adolescents are often mixed. This boy feels comfortable being with some female friends at a mall, and they feel comfortable including him. When they're a year or two older, these teenagers will spend more time in male-female couples.

With the arrival of adolescence, the child's social life changes radically. Friendships, intimate relationships, and group activities become all-important features of the child's life. The boy who was content to spend Friday night watching TV with his parents now wants only to be at the school basketball game or local movie theater where his friends are "hanging out." If his gang is meeting at the shopping mall on Saturday afternoon, he *has* to be there. And when he gets home from the latest social event, he heads straight for the phone to call up one of the friends he just left.

Teenagers often go around in a **clique**—a group of friends with similiar interests and backgrounds—or a **crowd**—a larger group, often a collection of cliques. They may form a clique based on their academic or social status or on their participation in a sport or a special activity, such as cheerleading, computer "hacking," skateboarding, or working part-time together after school. Or they may just live in the same neighborhood, be in the same classes at school, and share the tastes of the youth subculture in movies, music, clothes, and romances. Less desirably, cliques may form around antisocial or illegal activities, such as drinking or taking drugs.

Why this sudden, all-consuming interest in friends and peers? Adolescents are in a state of transition. Their rapid physical growth at puberty, the maturation of their sexual organs, and their experience of surging sexual interest and energy, known as **libido**, all tell them that the end of childhood is quickly approaching. They're awakened to the possibilities of adult life; they begin to think ahead to what it will be like to live as adults in the larger society. They wonder what kind of people they are and what they will become. They ask themselves a new question: Who am I?

THE ROLE OF PEERS IN THE SEARCH FOR IDENTITY. Facing this challenge, teenagers sense that they must separate themselves from their parents and their past lives as children if they are to become independent people. Struggling to differentiate and define themselves, they seek the support of people like themselves—their peers (Youniss & Smoller, 1985; Steinberg & Silverberg, 1986). With peers, they can practice adult roles, share problems, and learn to adjust to other people.

Sometimes parents worry that their teenage children have merged so fully with their peer group that instead of establishing a sense of individual identity, they've lost it completely. They look alike, dress alike, talk alike, and go everywhere and do everything together. The influence of peers is greater in early adolescence than it is later (Hill & Holmbeck, 1986), perhaps because when teenagers first become more independent of their parents, they don't yet have a clear sense of identity. The price of emotional autonomy from parents may be a type of emotional dependence on peers (Steinberg & Silverberg, 1986). A few years later, when actual autonomy begins to develop, adolescents begin to be able to conform less to their peer group.

Teenagers tend to prefer peers who resemble themselves and who have similar backgrounds and values. They tend not to like peers with very different values, backgrounds, and personality characteristics (Cavior & Dokecki, 1973). Groups and cliques may try to differentiate themselves from other groups by adopting subtle and not-so-subtle variations in clothes, postures, and behaviors. In a large school, for example, a teenager would probably be able to point out the "preppies," the "jocks," the "brains," the "stoners," the "nerds," and so on. And probably everyone in those groups would agree.

ERIKSON ON IDENTITY AND ROLES. Erik Erikson, whose theory of child development we discussed in Chapter 2, thought that adolescent cliques and their stereotyping of themselves and their "enemies" were defenses against what he called "role confusion" on the part of teenagers. "To keep themselves together they temporarily overidentify, to the point of apparent complete loss of iden-

FIGURE 20-3
Most teenagers choose friends with backgrounds and interests similar to their own, making peer groups fairly homogeneous. But there are always individuals willing to look beyond the surface to find interesting friends among other groups, as these two have done.

FIGURE 20-4
Gertrude Stein tells the story of an angry man who dragged his father along the ground through his orchard until at last the old man cried, "Stop! Stop! I did not drag my father beyond this tree!" Although many teen behaviors are designed to shock, parents need only recall their own youthful tastes and temperaments to put hairstyles like this in perspective.

tity, with the heroes of cliques and crowds" (Erikson, 1963, p. 262). This idea is part of Erikson's larger theory of psychosocial development.

According to Erikson, at adolescence, the individual enters the fifth of the eight developmental stages of life. The crisis of adolescence involves establishing a sense of identity. Adolescents are striving to "be somebody." They're looking for a place among peers, a role to play, a sense of who they are. All these things are as yet unknown to them, and it will take many years—for some, well into adulthood—before they resolve these puzzles satisfactorily.

Adolescents are also beginning to search for a vocation or a life's work to which they can commit themselves. During the school-age years, they gained the basic skills required for success in our society. Now they have to perfect them and learn how to put them to use. Their tasks include improving their abilities to communicate and interact effectively; gaining competence in academic subjects, sports, and other activities; and setting a general course for the years following high school.

When individuals meet these challenges, they achieve a positive sense of self that Erikson terms **ego identity**. If they fail to resolve the crises of adolescence, they experience **role confusion**—a lack of focus about who they are and what roles they should and can play. They may hold on to more childish

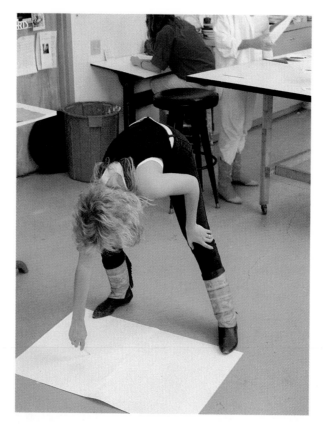

FIGURE 20-5
Some adolescents are attracted to the role of artist—the creative individual, living outside the bounds of conventional society. This girl may have the talent to pursue a career in art, or she may try out other roles before settling into her adult identity.

ways, accepting the values and life goals their parents set for them, or they may drift aimlessly, unable to commit themselves to anything substantial. Some teenagers who experience role confusion adopt a **negative identity,** defining themselves by their disdain for the larger culture. Self-doubt leading to role confusion can create self-destructive tendencies, resulting in psychological problems and juvenile delinquency for some teenagers.

Researcher James Marcia (1980) formulated ideas similar to Erikson's about the development of identity by interviewing young people about their values and career choices. On the basis of these interviews, he constructed four categories of identity status, each reflecting a different degree of identity development. He labeled the categories **identity achievement** (identity crisis is past and commitments have been made); **identity moratorium** (identity crisis is in progress and the search for commitments continues); **identity foreclosure** (commitments are made, but they come from authority figures, not self-search); and **identity diffusion** (no specific commitment is made and no active search is going on, due to unresolved identity crisis or absence of crisis).

Putting the search for identity on hold for a period of time—Marcia's "moratorium"—allows adolescents and young adults to try on a number of different roles and identities before they "find themselves." Their experimentation may go on for many years, well into their working life or college career, as they search for a way to be true to themselves and yet serve a useful social function. In a way, prolonging the resolution of the identity crisis is a constructive response to the great variety of options available in our society.

Defining the Self

We've seen that adolescents use the peer group to help them answer the question, Who am I? But what are the elements that go into the concept of self, the sense of identity? People define themselves by many experiences—successes and failures, social encounters with peers and adults, performance in terms of some ideal or standard. One researcher has identified four different kinds of experiences in terms of which people may measure and judge themselves (Coopersmith, 1967):

- Power—the ability to influence and control others
- Significance—the acceptance, attention, and affection of others
- Virtue—the adherence to ethical and moral standards
- Competence—success at meeting achievement demands

This researcher believes that teenagers measure their self-worth primarily in terms of competence (how well they do in school) and significance (how well liked they are). Another researcher suggests that male and female adolescents consider different kinds of experiences important when they're defining themselves (Pomerantz, 1979). Males are more likely to define themselves by their performance and achievements; females are more likely to define themselves in terms of their social interactions.

The specific terms in which adolescents judge their self-worth are likely to vary depending on their cultural and family background. With today's changing expectations and options for women, for example, we would expect fewer adolescent girls to define themselves solely in terms of their skill in social interactions. At the same time, we may see growing respect for the ability to mix intimacy and identity, as changes in cultural ideals lead us away from an aggressive, dominance-oriented approach to people and the world.

Relationships with Parents

Adolescence can be a trying time for parents (Conger & Petersen, 1984), but they have a great role to play in their children's quest for independence. Contrary to what some people think, most teenagers do *not* want to sever their relationships with their parents or leave their family behind. Rather, they want their parents to be expansive and flexible enough to accept all their experiments and mistakes without rejecting them as people. Although they value their peers' opinions on many social and personal matters, teenagers want and need their parents' advice on the important issues of their lives (Brittain, 1963).

STRESSES OF ADOLESCENCE FOR PARENTS. The difficult task of parents of teenagers is to begin letting go of their children. Established patterns of interaction are breaking down and new ones are evolving. Challenged by their children, parents often have to re-examine and adjust their feelings, expectations, and child-rearing methods. When a teenager wants more freedom and independence, parents have to make important judgments about whether situations are safe and whether their child is trustworthy and competent.

Teenagers may also try their parents' patience with their everyday behavior. They may be irritable, moody, or overly critical of the parents they previously

FIGURE 20-6
A strong parent-child relationship is important for adolescents just as it is for younger children. Parents of teenagers have to know how to be supportive without stifling their children's developing sense of autonomy. This runner feels close enough to his dad to share his feelings and his victory with him after a race.

idolized. Often, they take out their insecurities and frustrations on their parents precisely because they see the home as a safer place to express themselves than the peer group. But increasingly, teenagers are away from home—in the evening, during meals, sometimes for a whole weekend. This absence evokes many feelings in parents, ranging from worry and anger to envy or nostalgia (Csikszentmihalyi & Larson, 1984).

Many parents of teenagers are changing and maturing in new ways themselves, and others are going through a divorce or struggling with single parenthood. The changes their children are going through put additional stress on their ability to cope. And as they see that their children's dependence on them is coming to an end, they realize that they, too, are approaching a new stage of life. Their adolescent's growth toward autonomy and adulthood sets in motion a major transformation in their lives.

HOW PARENTS CAN SUPPORT AUTONOMY. Although adolescence is a time of change, it doesn't have to be a time of major conflict. Through their methods of discipline, the models they provide, the values they support, and the autonomy they allow, parents can help their children grow and can smooth their transition to adulthood. Their attitude toward the quest for autonomy is especially important. Some parents hinder their teenagers' development by refusing to allow them greater independence, perhaps because they feel that any errors of judgment their children make will reflect badly on them (Saltzman, 1973).

Other parents adopt a completely laissez-faire attitude toward adolescence and fail to provide enough guidance and support.

Studies have shown that parents' child-rearing methods have a strong impact on how independent and socially competent their teenagers become. In Knowledge in Action: School-Age Children, we discussed the three different general parenting styles—authoritarian, authoritative, and permissive—that one researcher has identified (Baumrind, 1971). As mentioned there, children with the highest levels of social competence tend to come from families characterized by the authoritative style (Table 20-1).

An earlier study suggested the same thing—teenagers who rate highest in autonomy and independence tend to come from authoritative families, where parents listen to their children's opinions and explain the rules they make (Elder, 1963). Adolescents with the lowest levels of self-confidence and independence tend to have authoritarian, or autocratic, parents who don't explain their rules.

Researchers conclude that parents provide their children with the best foundation for eventually becoming strong, independent adults by giving rational explanations for what they do and allowing the children to express their own views. These methods also lay the groundwork for positive family relationships throughout adolescence. When parents have occasion to exercise power, adolescents who have been raised in a democratic environment react more positively than those raised by authoritarian or permissive parents (Kelly & Goodwin, 1983).

When adolescents are troubled or delinquent, they often come from families with low levels of emotional expressiveness, little positive communication, and a lack of help or support for family members (Leflore, 1988). Parents whose verbal interactions consist mainly of guilt inducement, harsh criticism, or intrusive questions and commands are fostering low self-esteem, negative attitudes, and poor social competence in their children (West, 1981). Family members who can listen to each other without prejudice, on the other hand, and who can respond in a way that acknowledges the other's point of view experience fewer conflicts (Bell & Bell, 1983). These families are comfortable with the differences and disagreements that naturally result when separate individuals live together.

TABLE 20-1
Parenting Style and Social Competence

Parenting Style	Characteristics	Adolescent Social Behavior
Authoritarian	Punitive, restrictive, controlling	Ineffective social interaction; inactive
Authoritative	Encourages independence; warm and nurturing; control with explanation; adolescent expresses views	Social competence and responsibility
Laissez-faire (permissive)	Lack of involvement; nonpunitive; few demands; adolescent has a lot of freedom	Immature; poor self-restraint; poor leadership

Adapted from: Baumrind, D. (1971). Current patterns of parental authority. Developmental Psychology Monographs, 4 (1, pt. 2).

FIGURE 20-7
Falling in love is practically the defining experience of adolescence. The intense emotions these adolescents feel may lead them into a sexual relationship, and if they're like many of their peers, they may not use adequate contraceptive protection.

SEXUAL BEHAVIOR: THE QUEST FOR INTIMACY

The second great transformation of adolescence—besides the awakening to the peer group and to social life beyond the family—is the awakening to sexuality. As adolescents experience their own burgeoning sexuality, they begin to define themselves as sexual beings and to seek sexual relationships with others. Over the course of the next few years, most of them experience romantic love for the first time and explore a variety of sexual behaviors.

Intimate, romantic involvements are important events in adolescent emotional development, whether they're platonic or sexual. The love, trust, and honesty of intimate relationships help teenagers evaluate themselves positively. But many of these relationships, especially in later adolescence, do become sexual ones. The 12-year-old's first "crush" is a prelude to the older teenager's first love affair and the adult's more mature love relationships.

In too many cases, however, early love relationships and sexual experiences also lead to teenage pregnancies. Helping adolescents develop healthy, responsible sex lives—whether through birth control or abstinence—is an important task for parents and educators. What are teenagers' experiences of sex and love? Where do they get the information they need about sex? And what are the consequences of ignorance and misinformation? These are some of the questions we address in this section.

Teenage Sexual Practices

Most teenagers feel the stirrings of sexuality long before they have an outlet for their desires. The first sexual practice many regularly engage in is masturbation. One of the most widespread but least talked-about sexual behaviors, it serves the function of relieving sexual tension without the complications of an emotional relationship with another person. Although masturbation has no negative effects and in fact can help adolescents learn about sexual functioning, in our culture it's considered shameful by many people, including many teenagers (Coles & Stokes, 1985). Research reports indicate that about 50 percent of all boys and about 30 percent of all girls masturbate and that this behavior often begins prior to adolescence (Sorenson, 1972; Coles and Stokes, 1985).

Teenagers also report other sexual practices, such as kissing, petting, genital touching, and intercourse. We know that they're sexually active at an earlier age than ever before, although statistics vary. A 1984 study of adolescent boys found that three-quarters of them had had intercourse, most of them by the time they were age 14 (Cohen & Rose, 1984). Another survey reported that half of the teenage boys questioned had had intercourse by age 13 and two-thirds of the girls had had intercourse by age 15 (Coles & Stokes, 1985). A 1988 survey of college students showed that 82 percent of the men and 74 percent of the women were sexually active. Age of first experience for men in this group was 16 and for women, 17 (Murstein, 1989). This early sexual activity is reflected in statistics: 30,000 babies are born each year to girls under the age of 15 (Stark, 1986). One out of ten teenage girls becomes pregnant every year, and about half of these girls have babies.

ADOLESCENT SEXUAL BEHAVIOR AS A RELFECTION OF SOCIAL TRENDS. Teenagers' greater and earlier sexual activity today, compared with that of earlier generations (Committee on Adolescence, 1989), reflects the overall trend toward more sexual freedom and openness in our society. Premarital sex is widespread and accepted, unmarried couples live together openly, and some live-in couples choose to have babies without getting married.

As we enter the last decade of the twentieth century, however, sexual attitudes seem to be changing again. The 1988 survey of college students mentioned above showed a drop in sexual behavior for both women and men between 1979 and 1986, with age at first sexual experience rising (although the figures still indicated that the majority of older adolescents are sexually active) (Murstein, 1989). Under the two influences of a more conservative general outlook in society and the increased threat of sexually transmitted diseases, including the deadly AIDS, we may be seeing more caution toward sexual experimentation and a greater emphasis on stability and commitment in relationships.

TRANSMISSION OF CULTURAL MESSAGES ABOUT SEX TO ADOLESCENTS. How do these social trends and attitudes filter down to teenagers? And where do they get their information about sex? Many adolescents read adult magazines, including *Seventeen, Cosmopolitan,* and *Playboy.* Most of them listen to rock music on MTV, radio, records, and tapes. A survey conducted a few years ago indicated that teenagers watch about two hours of music videos a day (Sun & Lull, 1986). The content of 75 percent of the videos that are based on a theme is sexual in nature (Sherman & Dominick, 1986). And almost all of them watch television, at a rate of about 23 hours per week. Much of adult programming has content dealing with sexual relationships. The American Association of Pediatricians

FIGURE 20-8
We don't have to look very hard to see where these girls get their information about clothes, behavior, and sex. But we can certainly expect magazines to send some responsible message about sex in this age of sexually transmitted diseases and AIDS.

has called for more restraint by the television industry (Committee on Communication, 1989).

Although the sexual content of the messages teenagers receive from all these media is extremely high, it's often unrealistic and misleading. For example, television often suggests that couples are about to have sexual intercourse, but it never shows them discussing their method of birth control. Adults may understand the omission, but teenagers are likely to get the message that birth control is unnecessary.

As we might expect, almost all reports on contraceptives indicate that their use is low among teenagers (Nicholas et al., 1989). One study found that only 34 percent of boys under age 15 used contraceptives during intercourse, with somewhat higher rates for 15- to 17-year-olds (49 percent) and for those 18 and older (59 percent) (Zelnick & Kanter, 1980). The types of birth control typically used by young people—withdrawal and rhythm (watching the calendar for fertile and nonfertile days)—are the least effective methods (Murstein et al., 1989).

Furthermore, teenage boys report that the prospect of using a condom or of a girl's inserting a diaphragm before sex is a "turn off." The idea that girls might carry condoms and spermicidal foam is even more unsettling to them. Such girls wouldn't be seen as taking responsibility for their own sexuality; they would simply be labeled "sluts." The conclusion one Planned Parenthood educator drew from talking to teenagers was that "when boys and girls go out on a date, boys should have sex and girls shouldn't" (Charlotte Schramm, personal communication, July 1989).

In the future, we may see an increase in the use of contraceptives or other changes in sexual behavior in response to the threat of AIDS and other sexually transmissible diseases. However, studies to date don't indicate a very high level of knowledge among teenagers about how AIDS is transmitted (Nicholas et al., 1989).

Teenage Thinking about Sex

Although adolescents are vitally interested in sex and engage in various sexual activities, it seems to take them a long time to assimiliate all the facts. Even when they've learned something, they often don't believe it or act on their knowledge. Teenage girls often believe they won't get pregnant because it's the wrong time of the month, they're too young or sex is too infrequent, they think they must have intercourse many times before they can become pregnant, or the male told them he was sterile (Shaw, Zelnick, & Kantor, 1975). They may think they can prevent conception by having intercourse in a certain position, taking a bath afterwards, or counting on the male to withdraw before he ejaculates.

There may also be a sense of personal immunity or exemption—the "personal fable" discussed in Chapter 18. Studies indicate that girls wait over a year after becoming sexually active to obtain contraceptives (Kreutner, 1981). One teenage mother said (Marek, 1989, p.61):

> I gotta tell you. I never used birth control. I mean, now I do, but before, well, I just never thought I would get pregnant. I was like, that can't happen to me. I thought that only happened to the bad girls across town. Who do drugs and stuff. But I didn't do none of that, so I thought I was safe. You know, like when you think it just can't happen to you. To other people yes, but not to you.

For some girls, pregnancy can occur as a result of a generally passive attitude toward what happens to them and their bodies. One observer noted, "perhaps having a baby is less a question of ignorance or choice than one of inevitability. Once a girl is sexually active, it is not *having* a baby that requires choice and conscious action, but *not* having one" (Marek, 1989, p. 62). (For a closer look at the consequences of teenage pregnancies for both babies and parents, see Health Focus—The Consequences of Teenage Pregnancies.)

The best solution to the problem of teenage pregnancies, of course, is prevention through education, and we discuss the important subject of sex education in Knowledge in Action: Adolescents.

FIGURE 20-9
A realistic understanding of the consequences of teen pregnancy can be seen in the faces of these girls at a sweet sixteen party. Their friend will have a harder time finishing school, achieving financial security, and providing for her child than she would if she hadn't gotten pregnant as a teenager.

HEALTH FOCUS

The Consequences of Teenage Pregnancy

Most teenagers aren't ready to be parents. Although they're capable of producing babies, they haven't yet completed their own cognitive, emotional, social, or even physical development. They don't know who they are or what they may accomplish in life. Parenthood forces them to turn away from these pressing concerns and redirect their time, attention, and energy onto the helpless being they've brought into existence. Usually, everyone suffers.

What are the social and medical consequences of adolescent parenthood for the teenagers themselves and for their babies? First, teenage mothers often drop out of school, thereby radically shifting the course of their lives, at least temporarily (Garcia & Rosenfeld, 1977; Hofferth, 1987). With the arrival of the baby, they must assume an emotional and economic responsibility for which they're unprepared. The most stable situation probably occurs for those who are able to continue living with their parents and return to school at the earliest opportunity.

Teenage parents who marry have higher rates of divorce and suicide and are four times as likely to be poor as couples under age 25 without children (Children's Defense Fund, cited in Stark, 1986, p. 34). They're also more likely to require economic assistance and to be an economic burden to society. The Center for Population Options in Washington, D.C., reported that teenage childbearing in 1985 cost the United States $16.65 billion (Stark, 1986, p 34).

Pregnancy and childbirth are also costly to the teenage mother's health. She has a greater risk of anemia and toxemia in pregnancy, prolonged labor, and other complications of birth. Some of these problems are related to poor nutrition and poor prenatal care. Whether she's trying to hide or deny her pregnancy, doesn't know the importance of eating well during

pregnancy, or doesn't have the financial means to get nutritious food, the pregnant teenager often fails to provide herself and her unborn child with the nutrients required for good health.

Babies born to teenage mothers suffer, too. The infant mortality rate is higher among these babies, as is the likelihood of low birth weight and prematurity. They have a greater risk of poor perceptual abilities and motor coordination and of neurological impairments such as blindness, deafness, and mental retardation, which are associated with low birth weight (Schinke, Gilchrist, & Small, 1979). There is also an increased risk of some genetic and chromosomal disorders, such as Down's syndrome, among babies of teenage mothers.

The good news is that teenage mothers who manage to complete their education, control future pregnancies, and enter stable marriages "recover" from their early child-bearing experience (Furstenberg, Brooks-Gunn, & Morgan, 1987). And many of the medical and physical risks to mothers and babies can be reduced with good prenatal and postnatal care. In a special program developed at the University of Colorado Medical School, an obstetric clinic was established for young pregnant women, and follow-up care was provided after delivery. In the group receiving this care, most of the medical risks were greatly reduced (Perkins et al., 1978). If care like this could be made available to more women, more of their babies would get a better start in life. But nothing supports the healthy development of children like parents who are ready, willing, and able to care for them. Prevention of teenage pregnancy is still the best way to ensure healthy environments for children when they enter the world.

PROBLEMS IN ADOLESCENCE

Although adolescence doesn't have to be a time of trouble or conflict, problems of one kind or another often do arise. Some problems seem to stem from teenagers' increasing independence, their curiosity and interest in new experiences, their inclination to take risks, and their tendency not to consider the point of view of others or the consequences of their actions. Other problems seem to result more from pre-existing psychological problems, poor self-concept, inadequate ways of handling anger and aggression, and alienation from family and society, coupled with the stresses of adolescence. Changes in their family situations can have an impact too. (See Research Focus—Children and Divorce.)

Many teenagers experiment with drugs or alcohol, for example, but those with underlying emotional problems are much more likely to become addicts or alcoholics than those with basically healthy adjustments to life (Joshi & Scott, 1988; Marston et al., 1988). Serious adolescent problems aren't just personal or family matters—they affect the very fabric of our society. In this section, we discuss several issues currently reaching crisis proportions, including drug and alcohol dependency, dropping out of school, juvenile delinquency, and adolescent suicide.

Drug and Alcohol Abuse

Like sexual behavior, the use of drugs and alcohol among teenagers reflects adult behavior in the larger society. The use of drugs in the United States has skyrocketed in the last 25 years, moving from the "drug daze" of the late 1960s and 1970s to the multimillion-dollar international criminal business of today. Law enforcement agencies seem unable to stop the flow of drugs even to elementary school children in some areas, and many communities focus instead on educating young people about the dangers of addiction. (We discuss the most effective type of drug education program in Knowledge in Action: Adolescents.)

TOBACCO. Even though the damaging effects of smoking are well known, tobacco is one of the most commonly used drugs in our society (see Table 20-2). Teenage smokers (and drinkers) are often hoping to look more attractive or sophisticated by imitating these so-called adult behaviors. Adolescents are also highly influenced by their peers in the use of alcohol and cigarettes, more so as they get older (Sarvela & McClendon, 1983).

TABLE 20-2 Drug Use Among High School Seniors 1975–1982

Substance	Ever Used[1] (Percent): Class of—								Daily Users[2] (Percent): Class of—							
	'75	'76	'77	'78	'79	'80	'81	'82	'75	'76	'77	'78	'79	'80	'81	'82
Marijuana	47	53	56	59	60	60	60	59	6	8	9	10.7	10.3	9.1	7	6.3
Inhalants	NA	10	11	12	13	12	12	13	NA	0.0	0.0	0.1	0.0	0.1	0.1	0.1
Amyl and butyl nitrites[3]	NA	NA	NA	NA	11	11	10	10	NA	NA	NA	NA	0.0	0.1	0.1	0.0
Hallucinogens	16	15	14	14	14	13	13	13	0.1	0.1	0.1	0.1	0.1	0.1	0.1	0.1
LSD	11	11	10	10	10	9	10	10	0.0	0.0	0.0	0.0	0.0	0.0	0.1	0.0
PCP[3]	NA	NA	NA	NA	13	10	8	6	NA	NA	NA	NA	0.1	0.1	0.1	0.1
Cocaine	9	10	11	13	15	16	17	16	0.1	0.1	0.1	0.1	0.2	0.2	0.3	0.2
Heroin	2	2	2	2	1	1	1	1	0.1	0.0	0.0	0.0	0.0	0.0	0.0	0.0
Other opiates	9	10	10	10	10	10	10	10	0.1	0.1	0.2	0.1	0.0	0.1	0.1	0.1
Stimulants	22	23	23	23	24	26	32	36	0.5	0.4	0.5	0.5	0.6	0.7	1.2	1.1
Sedatives	18	18	17	16	15	15	16	15	0.3	0.2	0.2	0.2	0.1	0.2	0.2	0.2
Barbiturates	17	16	16	14	12	11	11	10	0.1	0.1	0.2	0.1	0.0	0.1	0.1	0.1
Methaqualone	8	8	9	8	8	10	11	11	0.0	0.0	0.0	0.0	0.0	0.1	0.1	0.1
Tranquilizers	17	17	18	17	16	15	15	14	0.1	0.2	0.3	0.1	0.1	0.1	0.1	0.1
Alcohol	90	92	93	93	93	93	93	93	5.7	5.6	6.1	5.7	6.9	6.0	6.0	5.7
Cigarettes	74	75	76	75	74	71	71	70	26.9	28.8	28.8	27.5	25.4	21.3	20.3	21.1

[1]*Ever used: used one or more times.*
[2]*Daily users: used 20 or more times in the month before survey.*
[3]*Separate questions about the use of PCP and amyl and butyl nitrites were not asked until 1979.*
NOTE: These numbers were gathered in annual nationwide surveys conducted for the National Institute on Drug Abuse by the University of Michigan Institute for Social Research. The eight surveys involved more than 100,000 high school seniors from public and private schools. NA indicates data not available.
SOURCE: National Institute on Drug Abuse.
(From National Institute on Drug Abuse: Student drug use, attitudes, and beliefs: National trends, 1975–1982. DHHS Publication No. (ADM) 83–1260, Washington, DC, U.S. Government Printing Office, 1982; with permission.)

RESEARCH FOCUS

Children and Divorce

For adults, divorce means the end of a marriage. For children, it means the end of everyday life as they know it. The disruption and stress of divorce are experienced profoundly by children, at least temporarily. And it's an experience with which more and more children are becoming familiar. In the United States, about half of all marriages now end in divorce, and about half of all children are expected to live in a household with just one parent during some portion of their childhood (Grusec & Lytton, 1988). The rate of divorce in the United States is the highest of any country in the world (Weitzman & Adair, 1988). How do children react to divorce, and what can parents do to protect them from long-term negative effects?

GENERAL EFFECTS OF DIVORCE
Divorce is extremely stressful for all family members. The only situations in which this isn't true are those in which there was a great deal of conflict between the parents before the divorce. In these situations, the divorce can actually be a relief. But divorce always involves the separation of the child from one parent, and this separation requires a major adjustment.

In addition to this adjustment, the child might move, might have to get used to a lower standard of living, and might need to adapt to a mother's beginning to work full time. Young children often have to enter and adjust to day care. Because divorce is highly traumatic for the parents, most children also experience disruptions in parenting behavior (Emery, Hetherington, & Dilalla, 1984; Grusec and Lytton, 1988).

STAGES OF REACTION TO DIVORCE
Children's adjustment to divorce goes on for some time, often two to three years. Their reactions a few years later are usually quite different from what they were in the beginning.

Three stages of adjustment have been identified by researchers Weitzman and Adair (1988). In the first, known as the *acute stage,* there is considerable trauma and disruption. This is the time when one parent leaves, when the child and one parent might move, and when parents are likely to be the most irritable, depressed, or anxious. Children typically show the most troubled behavior during the two-year acute stage. They might be aggressive, or they might regress, such as when an older child reverts to bedwetting. If the child is in school, there might be a decline in grades. Not all children react in these ways, of course; some children's academic achievement actually improves after a divorce.

The second stage is labeled the *transitional stage.* Changes still occur during this stage, but the child's life is much more predictable now, as is the behavior of the parents. The biggest adjustment the child might have to make is to the parent's new relationships with other adults or to a stepparent (Weitzman & Adair, 1988). The third stage is the *postdivorce stage.* By this time, everyone is accustomed to the dissolution of the previous family, and a sense of stability has emerged.

HOW DO CHILDREN OF DIFFERENT AGES REACT TO DIVORCE?
Not surprisingly, children's reactions to divorce vary depending on their age. Preschoolers typically show the most regression in their behavior and seem the most fearful about their own welfare. They may become concerned about being abandoned and over-

---

Adults who have quit smoking, or who have tried to break the nicotine habit and failed, are dismayed when they see young people take up smoking. Again, the "personal fable" seems to be at work. Adolescents believe themselves to be exempt from the effects of smoking, which they place far in the future. They also tend to believe they can easily quit whenever they wish.

The facts are that shortness of breath and damage to lung cells are associated with smoking right from the start, that the nicotine addiction is a strong one and can be almost impossible for some individuals to break, and that smoking during pregnancy is known to affect the fetus in many undesirable ways. In 1988, U.S. Surgeon General Everett Koop stated that nicotine addiction is so strong that if tobacco were illegal, we would see a cigarette-related crime rate comparable to that associated with cocaine.

Several smoking education programs are available for use in secondary schools (Bailey, 1985). The American Lung Association of Maryland has developed a program that uses worksheets, role playing, and suggested humorous responses, referred to as "smart answers," to teach young adolescents how to react to routine separations. They also tend to blame themselves for the divorce more than older children do (Grusec & Lytton, 1988).

Young school-age children tend to have more overt, direct reactions than preschoolers. They may cry, or they may express feelings of rejection. They may feel and express more anger and less fear than preschoolers. These children usually feel less responsible for the divorce than preschoolers do, but they're more aware of issues of loyalty to one or the other parent. Even so, they usually don't side with one parent against the other. Older school-age children also react angrily to a divorce, often blaming one parent and siding with the other to resolve the loyalty issue (Grusec & Lytton, 1988).

Adolescents are buffered somewhat from the effects of divorce because they're already distancing themselves from their parents in the normal course of developing autonomy. Divorce does make adolescents feel anxious, though, especially about their own likelihood of success in marriage. They sometimes deal with issues of loyalty by rejecting both parents. In any case, they rarely align themselves with either parent (Grusec & Lytton, 1988). Perhaps they can understand the complexities of the situation better than the 9- or 10-year old, who often does choose one parent over the other.

HOW CAN ADULTS EASE THE EFFECTS OF DIVORCE ON CHILDREN?

Children's adjustment to divorce, especially in the long run, has a lot to do with the amount of conflict between parents both before and after the divorce. If parents can keep conflict in check and work together in parenting, the child's long-term adjustment is greatly facilitated (Weitzman & Adair, 1988).

Children also do better if they are able to have consistent contact with the noncustodial parent (the parent who doesn't live with the child) (Grusec & Lytton, 1988). It doesn't seem to matter whether both parents have actual custody (*joint custody*) or whether one parent has custody and the other has visitation rights. The important predictors of long-term outcome are contact with the noncustodial parent and absence of parent conflict and anxiety (Kline et al, 1989). The family's financial situation and the degree of communication within the family, especially about the divorce itself, have also been found to affect the child's adjustment (Grusec & Lytton, 1988).

WHAT IS THE OUTCOME FOR CHILDREN OF DIVORCE?

Divorce alone is not a crucial factor in children's ultimate adjustment to life. More important is the amount of conflict the child sees and expriences in the family. Children from intact families with high levels of conflict fare worse than children from divorced families with low levels of conflict (Brown, 1980). It's not so much specific events or circumstances that shape the child's development, but *family process variables*—how the family functions.

Preschool and young school-age children react most negatively to divorce, probably because of their greater vulnerability and dependence on their parents. Regardless of age, many children make a good long-term adjustment to divorce. Stability isn't achieved, however, until at least two to three years after the initial breakup of the family.

resist peer pressure to try cigarettes. The American Heart Association has developed a student-run program that turns cigarette advertising upside-down by depicting smokers as unglamorous and addicted rather than happy and attractive. Students wearing antismoking buttons and soliciting pledges not to smoke reverse the usual direction of peer pressure.

ALCOHOL. Alcohol is the drug most frequently used by young people (see Table 20–2). The overwhelming majority of high school students in the United States have tried alcohol, and 20 to 30 percent are estimated to have a serious drinking problem (Turner, 1984). Alcohol is an anesthetic, and people under its influence can't function at normal levels. It depresses the central nervous system, interferes with intellectual processes, and impairs perception, sensorimotor coordination, and thinking speed. The greatest risk associated with drinking is automobile accidents. More accidents are caused by drunk drivers than by any other single factor, and male drivers in their late teens are the worst offenders.

FIGURE 20-10
These young teenage girls are about to do what over 90 percent of their peers do at one time or another—experiment with alcohol. It may make them sick this time, but they'll probably drink again on many occasions before they reach the legal drinking age.

As with other problem behaviors, out-of-control drinking and teenage alcoholism occur more commonly among individuals who had problems long before they ever had a drink. They tend to have negative attitudes toward school, low grades, and poor relationships with their parents (Barnes, 1984). Social competence, facilitated by skillful parents, seems to have a lot to do with preventing problem drinking, as well as other problem behaviors (Joshi & Scott, 1988).

MARIJUANA. Although other drugs, including LSD, cocaine, PCP, and amphetamines, are used by teenagers, marijuana is probably the most widely used psychoactive (mind-altering) drug among adolescents. In 1984, 34 percent of high school seniors reported that they smoked marijuana, some of them starting as early as sixth grade (Erickson, 1984). Other studies show that 40 percent of high school students use marijuana regularly (AMA Council on Scientific Affairs, 1981). They smoke it for various reasons, including the following (Dusek, 1977):

- Curiosity—they want to see if it alters consciousness, and how.
- Social pressure—they want to be seen as daring and sophisticated, or they don't want to be left out ("Everyone's doing it").
- Imitation of adult models—they see parents or other adults smoking it, or they see it modeled as a glamorous activity in movies.
- Escape from anxieties and problems—they find it reduces stress and emotional discomfort.

Classified as a hallucinogen, marijuana is a drug that affects the brain in ways we still don't fully understand. In low doses, it usually creates a pleasant feeling of euphoria and relaxation, a heightening of some sensory experiences, and a slowed-down sense of time. Although no acute medical effects of moderate use of marijuana have ever been clearly demonstrated, it does interfere with several physiological processes, including sexual performance, memory, thinking, and motor coordination (Archer & Lopata, 1979; Kulberg, 1986). The current trend of adding other substances to marijuana, such as "angel dust," embalming fluid, and other toxic chemicals, obviously increases the hazards associated with its use.

Because marijuana lowers inhibitions, reduces the ability of the user to feel stress, and induces a worry-free state of mind, teenagers may be drawn to it for "help" with their everyday problems and anxieties (Joshi & Scott, 1988). Unfortunately, marijuana doesn't solve any problems or make them go away— it simply puts a screen between them and the user. The danger of this drug, especially during adolescence, is that users may never get around to facing or resolving the critical issues of life that everyone encounters. They smoke marijuana instead of developing new or more mature ways of handling emotional and social difficulties.

Marijuana use can dramatically alter school performance, according to psychiatrist Arthur Kornhaber, who outlines the following chain of behaviors in users of this drug (Jones & Lovinger, 1985, pp. 214–215):

1. Decrease in concentration and attention span; increase in fantasy, day dreaming, and withdrawal.
2. Decrease in personal hygiene, physical exercise, and logical thinking processes.

FIGURE 20-11
A teenager who takes drugs alone has gone beyond experimentation and is using them to deal with personal problems. Loneliness or a painful home life may have driven this boy to the park to smoke marijuana.

3. Increase in school absence, cutting classes, and problem behavior.
4. Search for a peer group with similar problems.

Adults should be alert to the signs and symptoms of drug dependency among teenagers. If their grades go down or they suddenly become withdrawn or emotionally distant, on the one hand, or rebellious or unusually irritable, on the other, it may be a sign of trouble. Similarly, if they lose interest in activities or hobbies they used to enjoy or they suddenly change their group of friends, parents and teachers may want to look more closely at the possibility that their lives are starting to center around drugs. Individual and family counseling and drug treatment programs are some of the approaches favored for these problems.

COCAINE AND CRACK. The most dangerous drug in wide use among adolescents today is cocaine. As with drugs in general, use of cocaine increased dramatically throughout the late 1970s and early 1980s (Kulberg, 1986; Miller, 1987). In the decade between 1979 and 1989, cocaine use tripled among high school students, a figure that underestimates the actual use of the drug because many teenage cocaine users aren't in school (Shannon et al., 1989). Among adolescents still in school, however, there was a slight decline in cocaine use by 1986 (Bennett, 1987).

Cocaine is a powerful stimulant that produces a feeling of euphoria lasting 10 to 20 minutes. Like amphetamines (or "speed"), cocaine causes users to become talkative and argumentative, often in the belief they they're unusually clever or insightful. Because it overstimulates the central nervous system, cocaine can cause tremors or convulsions, vomiting, respiratory collapse, and heart failure. Long-term use is associated with anxiety and depression (Kulberg, 1986).

In addition to the direct effects of cocaine on the primary user, unborn babies suffer many deleterious effects when their mothers use cocaine, as described in Chapter 3. Among other effects, there is an increase in stillbirths (infants born dead) and an increase in malformations of the heart and skull (Mofenson & Caraccio, 1987).

Crack is an intensified form of cocaine with faster, stronger, and more damaging effects. Because it's cheap, highly addictive, and readily available in cities, suburbs, and many small towns, it has become one of today's most dangerous drugs. Crack is largely responsible for the increasing violence on many city streets. Creative solutions are needed in the 1990s to stop this tide of life-destroying drugs. "Just Say No" approaches to drug control will be effective in deterring recreational drug use among young people who have no major emotional or social problems. More complex interventions are necessary to stop drug use among other populations of youth (Meyer, 1989).

Dropping Out of School

Sometimes the pressures of school seem so intense that teenagers believe they would be better off dropping out. This is almost never true: Without skills or education, high school dropouts are likely to face a lifetime of social and economic hardship. Yet 22 percent of all adolescents in the United States fail to complete high school (Jones, 1977). At least half of them are estimated to be of average or above-average intelligence. Why do they drop out?

The most common reason for dropping out of school is teenage pregnancy, although schools no longer require a pregnant girl to withdraw. In most other cases, dropping out of school probably appears to be the best choice at the time. Many dropouts are from underprivileged and minority groups, and they may have trouble coping with stresses in their daily lives as well as in school.

Many other dropouts are from middle- and upper-class backgrounds, and their choice may have more to do with their family situation. Affluent underachievers, for example, may be indirectly rebelling against the pressure put on them by their parents to succeed (Gallatin, 1975). All dropouts are under some kind of stress that makes it difficult for them to continue on the normal path to adulthood in our society. Schools and other community groups are working hard to solve this problem.

Delinquency

Criminal activities enacted by juveniles—defined as persons under 16 years in some states, under 18 years in others—are a serious problem in our society. About 1.5 million juveniles were arrested in 1986 for such crimes as vandalism and drug abuse, and close to 1 million were arrested for serious crimes such as rape, robbery, and murder (Patterson, De Baryshe, & Ramsey, 1989). Many delinquent acts are committed by groups or gangs (Empey, 1975), often spontaneously and when the teenagers have been drinking or taking drugs.

WHO BECOMES A JUVENILE DELINQUENT? Contrary to popular belief, juvenile delinquency isn't confined to lower socioeconomic groups, although these cases are more likely to be recorded by legal authorities and reported in the press (Empey, 1975). When the teenagers themselves report their activities, no dif-

FIGURE 20-12
A variety of social and economic conditions can contribute to juvenile delinquency, but child-rearing techniques are a consistently related factor in delinquent behavior. These boys may have parents who are uninvolved or not present in their lives, or they may have abusive, alcoholic, or drug-addicted parents. In any case, they probably have never had the attention or love of an adult long enough to develop much sense of self-worth.

TABLE 20-3
Family Influences and Character Development

Family Relationships	Character
Rejecting, inconsistent, no rules	Amoral (impulsive, egocentric)
Lenient, unthinking, inconsistent approval	Expedient (concerned about others for personal gain; behaves to obtain rewards or avoid punishment)
Consistent, autocratic, authoritarian	Conforming (follows rules and accepts roles)
Consistent, loving, democratic, lenient; rational discipline	Rational and altruistic (perceptive and concerned with the well-being of others)

SOURCE: Peck, R. F., & Havighurst, R. J. (1960) *The psychology of character development.* New York: Wiley.

ferences show up in the average number of delinquent acts committed by lower-, middle-, and upper-class high school students (Kratcoski & Kratcoski, 1975).

Juvenile delinquency *is* associated with certain child-rearing techniques and patterns of family relationships, regardless of socioeconomic status. Consistent relationships have been found between juvenile delinquency and "harsh and inconsistent discipline, little positive parental involvement with the child, and poor monitoring and supervision of the child's activities" (Patterson, DeBaryshe, & Ramsey, 1989). One classic study found significant relationships between family interactions and character development (Peck & Havighurst, 1960). This study considered both the consistency of parental rules and expectations and the general style of child-rearing and rule enforcement. The researchers found that positive character development, described as "rational-altruistic," is associated with consistently democratic and loving family relationships. Amoral and expedient character development are both associated with rejecting, inconsistent, and permissive family relationships. These findings are summarized in Table 20–3.

Although this study found the highest association between delinquency and very permissive parents, other studies have found parents of delinquents to be overly strict and rigid (Dusek, 1977). In either case, families of delinquents are often characterized by rejecting and unaffectionate behavior, poor communication, and low parental aspirations for the child.

HOW CAN JUVENILE DELINQUENCY BE TREATED? Experts currently believe that the best approach to juvenile delinquency is to prevent it before it occurs—that is, to intervene with children before they reach adolescence. Teachers and other adults can and should identify at-risk children early in elementary school so that preventive steps can be taken. Programs that teach parents better ways of managing and interacting with their children can be effective in side-tracking families who seem to be headed for trouble (Kazdin, 1987). And the children themselves can be given direct help with academic work and social skills (Patterson, DeBaryshe, & Ramsey, 1989). The earlier help can be provided, the better the chances are of redirecting a troubled child into a productive life. As with so many other aspects of child rearing, the best solution to this very complex and difficult problem is better parenting when the child is very young.

FIGURE 20-13
Life is stressful by definition; how people handle stress is the crucial factor in psychological well-being. Adolescents are particularly vulnerable because they don't yet have an adequate repertoire of coping mechanisms. This boy may not know of any healthy ways to help himself through change, pain, or loss.

Suicide

Of all problem behaviors of adolescence, teenage suicide is the one that most troubles adults. "He had his whole life ahead of him," they often comment. "If only he could have known that no matter how bad he felt at the moment, his feelings would change in time." But some of the characteristics of adolescent thinking and behaving (discussed in this chapter and in Chapter 18 on cognitive development in adolescence) prevent the teenager from realizing that his feelings *will* change in time. As mentioned earlier, adolescents often don't think ahead to consider what all the possibilities of the future may be. If they're severely depressed or anxious, if they feel worthless or helpless, they may see suicide as the only escape from despair.

At the same time, suicidal teenagers are attempting to express and communicate their need for help. Unsuccessful suicide attempts peak during adolescence, running as high as 200 attempts per year for every suicide. In adults, the ratio of attempts to success is about 10 to 1 (Marks, 1980). A troubled teenager may make several suicide attempts before succeeding or reaching some other resolution to his problems. On the other hand, some adolescent suicides are impulsive and spontaneous.

TABLE 20-4
Suicide Rates by Country in 1970 and Changes by 1980

	Total Population		Youth (Aged 15–24)	
	1970	% Change by 1980	1970	% Change by 1980
Australia	12.4	−11.2	8.6	+30.2
Austria	24.4	+6.2	16.5	+9.1
Bulgaria	11.9	+14.3	6.9	+34.8
Canada	11.3	+23.9	10.2	+50.0
Chile	6.0	−18.3	10.1	−31.7
Denmark	21.5	+47.0	8.5	+42.4
Finland	21.3	+20.7	14.7	+60.5
France	15.4	+26.0	7.0	+52.9
Germany (West)	21.3	−1.9	13.4	−6.7
Greece	3.2	+3.1	1.5	+20.0
Guatemala	3.2	−62.5	5.5	−50.9
Hong Kong	13.6	−0.7	7.7	+1.3
Hungary	34.8	+29.0	18.9	+5.8
Israel	5.8	+3.4	3.7	+64.9
Italy	5.8	+25.9	2.9	+34.5
Japan	15.2	+15.8	13.0	−3.8
Netherlands	8.1	+24.7	4.0	+50.0
New Zealand	9.6	+12.5	8.0	+73.7
Norway	8.4	+47.6	3.7	+224.3
Portugal	7.5	−1.3	4.5	+2.2
Singapore	8.9	+25.8	7.8	+32.1
Spain	4.2	+4.8	1.4	+92.9
Sweden	22.3	−13.0	13.3	−13.5
Switzerland	18.6	+38.2	13.0	+80.0
Thailand	4.2	+76.2	7.2	+77.8
UK: England & Wales	8.0	+10.0	6.0	+6.7
UK: Scotland	7.6	+31.6	5.8	+65.5
USA	11.5	+2.6	8.8	+39.8
Venezuela	6.8	−23.5	14.5	−28.3

*Suicide rates (per 100,000 per year) in 1970 and changes by 1980 for the total population and for those aged 15–24
NOTE: Rates are per 100,000 per year.
SOURCE: From Lester, D. Youth Suicide: A cross-cultural perspective. Adolescence, 23(92), 1988, p. 956.

Suicide is the third leading cause of death (following accidents and homicides) among 15- to 24-year-old males and the fourth leading cause (following accidents, cancer, and homicides) among 15- to 24-year-old females (Zuckerman & Dubey, 1985; Spirito et al., 1989). Suicide rates for the total population have increased in many countries over the past few decades, but the rates have generally increased more within the adolescent population than among other age groups (Lester, 1988). (The suicide rates for several specific countries are shown in Table 20-4.) Why have teenagers turned increasingly to such drastic and self-destructive measures?

WHAT UNDERLIES ADOLESCENT SUICIDE? Some experts have suggested that teenage suicide is related to the young person's social support system and to the degree of alienation from society he feels—the extent to which he finds or fails to find a useful place for himself in the social structure (Wynne, 1979). Supporting this claim is the work of nineteenth-century sociologist Emil Durkheim, who found suicide rates higher among Protestants than Catholics, among

FIGURE 20-14
Nothing to do, nowhere to go—a sense of meaninglessness can settle quickly on teenagers who drop out of school and can't get a job. Suicide is a danger for individuals with underlying problems who lack meaningful connections to others.

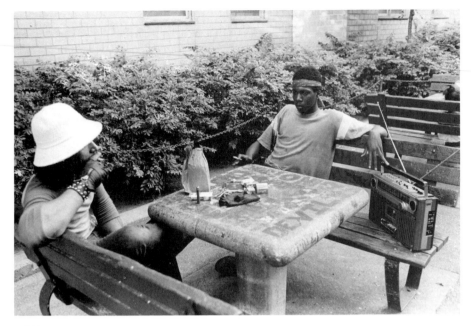

those who lived in cities than those who lived in the country, among those who worked in professions than those who labored with their hands, and among those with ample means than those who were poor. According to this expert, these data indicate the following (Wynne, 1979, p. 4):

> . . . people [are] shielded from suicidal impulses because of the communal intensity of their religion, the stability of life patterns, the predictability of their aspirations, the intensity and complexity of their social commitments, the focus of their responsibilities, and the tangibility of their work products. . . . These forces [place] human beings in complex but predictable patterns of human relations that [move] toward identifiable goals.

In other words, if people have strong ties to their family and community, stable patterns of life and work, and a perception that they and what they do are needed by others, they are unlikely to kill themselves. "The most 'pressured' status," says this expert, "is that of being left without apparent and immediate responsibilities to help others" (Wynne, 1979, p. 4).

It's not difficult to see that for many adolescents in our society, the conditions that "shield" people from suicidal impulses are missing. Relationships with parents can be difficult, ties with friends tenuous, connections to the community fragile, and life patterns disrupted by moving or divorce. Most of all, meaningful work is hard for adolescents to come by, either at home, at school, or in the larger society. As jobs become more specialized and complex, they require an ever-increasing period of preparation and education. Adolescents may have a very hard time seeing how they'll fit in or how their contribution will matter. If they have underlying psychological problems, which older adolescent suicide victims often do, suicide may seem to be the only course open to them (Trautman and Shaffer, 1989).

All young people face similar problems fitting into the larger society, of course, and most find a place for themselves. What specific characteristics distinguish suicidal youths? Very often, they have a history of emotional disorders, substance abuse, or chronic illness. They may also have a history of aggressiveness, impulsiveness, or feelings of hopelessness. Adolescents who have grown up in families with parents who themselves have drug and alcohol problems, psychiatric difficulties, or suicidal tendencies are at risk for suicide as well (Blumenthal & Kupfer, 1988).

Some researchers have also found poor problem-solving skills and a tendency to cope with stress by avoiding problems among adolescents who have made suicide attempts (Spirito et al., 1989). Adolescents are at higher risk for suicide under certain circumstances: if they've had a humiliating experience or suffered a loss of self-esteem, if they have a serious illness, if a family member has died, or if their parents have recently divorced (Blumenthal & Kupfer, 1988).

HOW CAN SUICIDAL ADOLESCENTS BE HELPED? Suicide prevention has to occur at many levels. Adults who live and work with youths should be aware of the risk factors associated with suicide that are described in this section. They can also be alert to the signs indicating that a young person may be heading for a suicide attempt. These signs include withdrawal from social relationships, becoming less involved in activities previously enjoyed, and onset of academic problems. Although most teenagers are moody on occasion, suicidal teenagers often cut themselves off completely. They may give away personal possessions

FIGURE 20-15
Although everyone has moments of loneliness and low self-esteem, most people pull through and learn something from their experience. This girl may be able to cope with feelings of depression by relying on an effective personal and social support system, including friends she can talk to, parents who know how to listen, school, community, or religious counseling services, and her own underlying sense of personal worth.

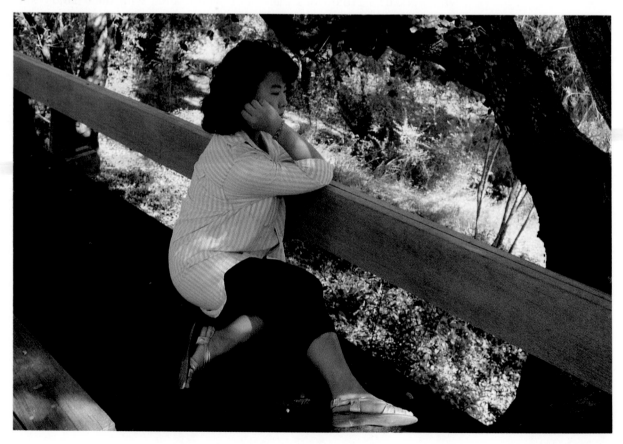

or make comments about suicidal intentions, which parents and teachers shouldn't take lightly.

On another level, the resources to help suicidal adolescents have to exist in the community. Treatments include psychotherapy, family counseling, placement in hospitals or treatment centers, and other professional services. Some communities have suicide hotlines and "teen lines," where individuals can talk to workers trained in listening and providing emergency counseling and referrals. All these services can help suicidal adolescents receive the long-term help they want and deserve in getting their lives back on track.

Finally, we have to take a hard look at the social and personal problems that feed despair—poverty, homelessness, alcoholism and drug abuse, unemployment, and mental illness. If social conditions were improved and troubled parents given support, a drop in adolescent suicide rates would probably follow. We also have to gain more understanding of the influence of parenting on teenagers' attitudes and actions. Parents who give their teenagers support despite the inevitable conflicts, and who demonstrate understanding at the same time that they continue to exert appropriate influence, seem to provide the environment that fosters the development of healthy coping skills in their adolescents (Powers, Hauser, & Kilner, 1989). Young people with a repertoire of problem-solving strategies and a confident, optimistic outlook are generally able to handle the ups and downs they inevitably encounter as they leave childhood behind and approach adult life.

OVERVIEW

Even though they're physically mature, adolescents still need to grow and develop socially and emotionally. Perhaps the main task of adolescence is to discover and establish a sense of identity that will serve the individual in adulthood. Adolescents seek to define themselves by separating from their parents and identifying—or overidentifying—with others their own age. Thus, the context of the family is replaced, or supplemented, by the context of the peer group. In previous eras, adolescents went out into the world on their own, ready or not. Today, the period of prolonged economic dependency within the family gives them the opportunity to explore possibilities without financial pressures, to practice adult relationships, to experiment with different life styles, and to grow.

CHAPTER REVIEW

ADOLESCENT SOCIAL BEHAVIOR: THE QUEST FOR INDEPENDENCE

- Friends and peers become increasingly important to teenagers. They spend more and more time with peers in a clique or a crowd.
- Teenagers rely on peers to help them become emotionally independent from their families and discover a clear sense of identity. They often seem to merge completely with their peer group for a time before they become autonomous. They prefer peers who are like themselves.
- According to Erikson, the task of adolescence is to establish a sense of ego identity and to overcome role confusion, a lack of focus about themselves and their roles. Their temporary overidentification with a clique and their use of stereotyping are defenses against role confusion.
- The prime ingredients of teenagers' sense of self-worth may be how well they do in school and how well liked they are. Some research has indicated that males define themselves more in terms of achievements and females define themselves more in terms of social skills, but

research in this area of rapidly changing values and expectations needs to be kept up to date.

- Adolescents continue to want their parents' involvement in their lives, especially when it comes to important issues and decisions.
- Parents can experience their children's teenage years as stressful, especially if they're going through changes of their own, such as a divorce or a change in career.
- Parents can support their teenagers' healthy social and emotional development by their child-rearing methods. The most competent and independent teenagers come from authoritative, democratic families in which parents give rational explanations for their actions and listen to their children's point of view. The authoritarian style of parenting is associated with low social competence in adolescents, and the permissive style is associated with immaturity. Families with poor communication and negative interactions foster low self-esteem and poor social skills in adolescents.

SEXUAL BEHAVIOR: THE QUEST FOR INTIMACY

- The first sexual behavior many teenagers engage in is masturbation. About half of all boys and about 30 percent of all girls masturbate.
- Teenagers are becoming sexually active at an earlier age than ever before. Many have had sexual intercourse by the time they're age 14 or 15.
- Adolescent sexual behavior reflects the trend toward greater sexual freedom that has dominated American society for the past 25 years, but more conservative values may become prevalent again in response to the threat of AIDS.
- Adolescents are often unrealistic in their thinking about sex and don't use contraceptives until well after they become sexually active. They think pregnancy can't happen to them.
- Teenage mothers and their babies are at greater risk for medical problems than adult mothers and their babies, and their economic and social circumstances are likely to be more precarious. Adequate prenatal and postnatal care can reduce many of the medical and physical risks associated with teenage motherhood.

PROBLEMS IN ADOLESCENCE

- Many teenagers try drugs and alcohol, but only some—those with underlying psychological problems or ineffective ways of dealing with problems—are likely to become addicts or alcoholics.
- The widespread use of drugs and alcohol among adolescents reflects the acceptance and availabilty of these substances in the larger society.
- Many teenagers smoke cigarettes, although the rates have dropped in recent years. Alcohol is the drug most frequently used by teenagers. Driving under the influence of alcohol is a serious problem among adolescents, especially adolescent boys.
- Marijuana is the most widely used psychoactive drug among adolescents. This drug interferes with several physiological processes and can lead young people to avoid problems rather than trying to solve them. The outward signs of drug dependency can include falling grades, emotional withdrawal, and a change in habits, interests, or friends.
- Cocaine is a dangerous central nervous system stimulant gaining in popularity among young people. Crack, an intensified form of cocaine, is responsible for the high rates of addiction among youths today and for much of the violence on city streets.
- About 22 percent of all adolescents drop out of school, many of them of average or above-average intelligence. The most common reason for dropping out of school is teenage pregnancy. Dropouts come from all socioeconomic classes.
- Juvenile delinquency is not associated with any particular socioeconomic class, but it is associated with certain kinds of child-rearing methods. Parents who use harsh and inconsistent discipline, who are either overly strict or overly permissive, and who communicate poorly are more likely to have delinquent children. The best treatment for juvenile delinquency is intervention while the child is still young. Parents can learn better ways of interacting with their children, and children can be helped with their academic and social skills to avoid delinquent behavior.
- Suicide is the third leading cause of death among adolescent boys and the fourth leading cause among adolescent girls. It has been suggested that suicide is related to an inability to find a meaningful, responsible place to fit into society. Characteristics associated with teenage suicide are a history of emotional problems, substance abuse, or chronic illness; a family history of substance abuse or psychiatric problems; and a recent experience that was emotionally traumatic.
- Suicidal adolescents have to be treated on several lev-

els. Adults should be alert to the signs that teenagers are considering suicide; these signs include withdrawal, giving away their possessions, and comments about suicide. Community resources have to be available for treatment. Larger social problems also need to be addressed to eliminate the conditions that lead to despair. Perhaps most important, parents and other adults need to help children and adolescents learn healthy coping skills with which to meet the inevitable ups and downs of adult life.

KEY TERMS

libido	identity achievement	acute stage of adjustment to divorce	postdivorce stage of adjustment
ego identity	identity moratorium	transitional stage of adjustment to divorce	joint custody
role confusion	identity foreclosure		family process variables
negative identity	identity diffusion		

SUGGESTIONS FOR FURTHER READING

Bennett, W. J. (1987). *What works? Schools without drugs.* Pueblo, CO: U.S. Government Printing Office.

This government booklet was written by Bennett while he was the U.S. Secretary of Education. It details drug use among the young, describes illicit substances, and makes recommendations for ways that families, schools, and communities can help to solve the drug problem. The lists of resources at the end of the book are especially helpful.

Green, R. (1987). *The "Sissy-Boy Syndrome" and the development of homosexuality.* New Haven, CT: Yale University Press.

This book reports on a longitudinal study of 66 boys who as young children cross-dressed, said they wanted to be girls, and expressed interest in being mothers. Data were available at follow-up 15 years later on 44 of the original 66 boys. Very interesting reading about the complexities of the development of sexual orientation.

Hayes, C. (Ed.). (1987). *Risking the future: Adolescent sexuality, pregnancy, and child-bearing.* (Vol. I). Washington, DC: National Academy Press.

This report, sponsored by the National Research Council, provides essential information on sexuality and reproduction among teenagers.

Jones, E. F. (1986). *Teenage pregnancy in industrialized countries.* New Haven, CT: Yale University Press.

This book, containing cross-cultural data from 36 countries, sheds light on why the teenage pregnancy rate is so high in the United States compared with countries similar to ours. The study itself was sponsored by the Alan Guttmacher Institute.

Waterman, A. S. (Ed.). (1985). Identity in adolescence: Processes and contents. *New Directions in Child Development, No. 30.* San Francisco: Jossey-Bass.

This edited book contains an interesting collection of chapters on identity for the student who wants to know more.

ADOLESCENTS

"I'm home from school, Dad, and I'm not going back!" shouted Alison as she stormed through the front door and hurled her books into a chair.

"What happened?" asked her dad. "Did something go wrong?"

"Yes, everything!" Alison replied. "I hate it! It's awful. I never knew where I was supposed to be all day long. I just kept being pushed up and down these long halls by these big kids—and I mean big! I must be the smallest person in the whole school!"

"So you had a hard time finding your classrooms?"

"Yes! I had this stupid little schedule I was supposed to read, and I only had three minutes between classes, and some of my classes are way the heck down in some other part of the school."

"That sounds really hard."

"A different teacher every hour. And they all gave me homework!"

"Already?"

"But the worst thing was, I hardly knew anyone. The only kids from Garfield in my home room are Jeannie and Joanne. I didn't even see my best friends until lunch time!"

"What a day!"

"Yeah. I sure hope tomorrow's better."

The first day at a new school is difficult at best. But when it's an entirely new kind of school, the confusion and discomfort can be overwhelming, at least temporarily. The transition to adolescence is usually marked by this kind of change in the school experience, along with a certain amount of accompanying stress for many children. As time goes on, the shock wears off, and the new experience becomes routine.

Education for the adolescent is the first topic we discuss here. Included in the discussion are two special areas of increasing importance in junior high and high schools today: sex education and education about drug use. We then look at the assessment of achievement and intelligence during adolescence, focusing briefly on the all-important "SAT score." Finally, we discuss issues in living with the adolescent—how to help them stay healthy, how to ensure their safety, and how to support their recreational activities and their choices for healthy life-styles.

EDUCATING THE ADOLESCENT

The Transition to Junior High

One of the reasons Alison had such a hard first day in junior high was that she was coming from an elementary school where she had spent the last six years in relative tranquility. Most elementary schools are fairly small, and they often serve just a few specific neighborhoods. Children spend an entire year in the same classroom, with the same classmates and the same teacher.

At the end of fifth or sixth grade, students typically switch to a junior high or middle school for two, three, or four years before entering a senior high school. Here, the organization is quite different from what children have expe-

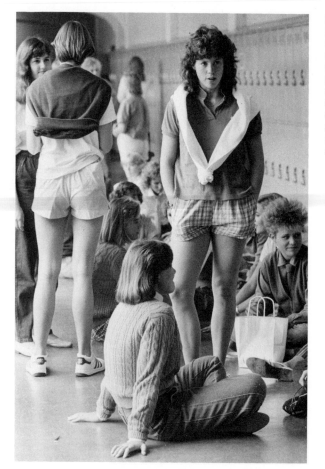

FIGURE 1
Junior high and high school routines are radically different from those of elementary school. These ninth graders have to take responsibility for knowing their schedules, getting to class on time, keeping track of assignments, and—last but not least—maintaining a social life.

rienced so far. Junior high and high schools can be enormous compared to elementary schools, often serving an entire city or several consolidated rural school districts. For the first time since kindergarten, children have to meet a whole new set of classmates and adapt to a demanding new schedule.

In most junior high and high schools, subjects are departmentalized—taught by different teachers—and students move from room to room throughout the day. Study periods are also scheduled during the day, and students are expected to allocate their study time as needed to cope with the demands of all their classes. More responsibility for deciding how and what to study falls on the individual.

Other decisions have to be made, too. In many schools, students are required to take certain core subjects but are free to choose other classes from a group of electives. The number of electives typically increases in senior high school, as different students decide on different career paths for life after high school.

At the same time, some decisions are made for the student. Ability grouping, a practice sometimes referred to as **tracking,** also becomes commonplace during junior high school. Students who excel academically are offered advanced math, science, or English, and students who are less advanced are offered basic math or science. Of course, many students may have had experience with ability groups within their classroom in elementary school. But being in

FIGURE 2
The term *tracking* usually brings to mind images of students in high school auto mechanics classes, but this girl has been tracked into an advanced chemistry class and is headed for college. The disadvantage of tracking is that it tends to place limits on the intellectual growth of the general high school population.

classes where everyone is basically at the same level in academic skills is usually a new experience for students in junior high school.

Sometimes tracking is carried even further, and whole schools are organized around academic or vocational pursuits. Vocational schools offer basic academic subjects along with classes that train students for specific jobs. Academic schools, on the other hand, offer a wide range of courses in math, the sciences, and the humanities in preparation for college, but they give no specific job training.

Problems in Junior High and High School Organization

The kinds of changes involved in moving from elementary to junior high or middle school often engender a variety of social and emotional difficulties as described here (Jackson & Hornbeck, 1989, p. 833):

> For most young adolescents, the shift from elementary to junior high or middle school means moving from a small neighborhood school and the stability of one classroom to a larger, more impersonal institution, typically at a greater distance from home. In the new setting, teachers and classmates will generally change as many as six or seven times a day, creating real obstacles to students in establishing stable peer groups and close relationships and support from caring and reliable adults. The change is abrupt and discordant for the student, particularly in terms of the impersonality and anonymity of the environment. At a time when intimacy needs remain strong, these changes are likely to present difficulties for many youth.

Other problems arise too. Tracking, for example, informs students in a very direct way how they compare academically with their peers. At a time of personal sensitivity, being placed in low tracks can be especially damaging to self-esteem and achievement motivation. Tracking can also cut short the basic, liberal education a student receives, limiting career options later in school and in life (Oakes, 1985).

Concern about tracking in recent years has led to the recommendation that a basic, liberal education be provided to all high school students, regardless of academic track (Bennett, 1987). Such an education keeps more educational and career doors open to a greater number of students, for longer periods of time, and gives them more choices later in life. This recommendation recognizes the importance of a well-educated populace, no matter what the career choice, as well as the reality that many people will change careers three or four times during their lifetime. Neither of these goals is served by narrow job training.

SPECIAL AREAS OF ADOLESCENT EDUCATION

Many people expect schools these days to go beyond their basic academic mission. They want schools to provide adolescents with information and guidance on important personal and social issues such as sexuality, reproduction, and drug use, and many schools are doing so. Some school districts are even starting education programs during the elementary years, in part because of the urgency of the problems, especially teenage pregnancy, AIDS, and drug abuse.

Sex Education

As we saw in Chapter 20, a great deal of teenage sexual activity is based on half-truths and dangerous misconceptions. Teenagers obviously need and deserve to know about their own sexuality. How can we make sure they get the information that will help them develop healthy sex lives?

PARENTS AND SEX EDUCATION. Many people believe that the prime responsibility for teaching children about sex belongs to parents. Studies have reported that parents do want to participate in their teenagers' sex education (Roberts & Gagnon, 1978) and that teenagers want to talk to their parents about sex (Sorensen, 1972; General Mills, 1979). But these desires and intentions often don't carry over into actual communication about sex. Discussions tend to be infrequent and characterized by confusion and a lack of clarity. Parents often think they've communicated more than they have, and teenagers aren't willing to tell their parents what their own experiences have been. Because of these problems, professionals in the health, medical, and educational fields have assumed some of the responsibility for providing sex education to teenagers.

SEX EDUCATION IN THE SCHOOLS. Sex education is currently taught in about three-fourths of the junior high and senior high schools in the country, although many courses provide minimal information over a very brief period of time (Grant & Demetriou, 1988). Quite a few schools give ten hours of instruction or less (Hayes, 1987)—not a very well considered course of study.

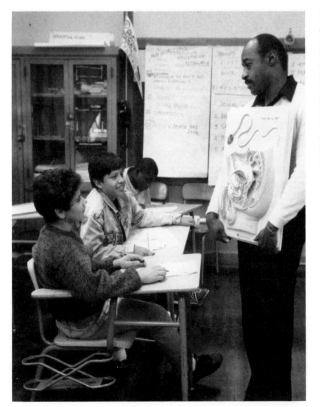

FIGURE 3
A male teacher makes sex education more comfortable for boys than it would be otherwise, but it's still cause for considerable giggling. Providing sex education in the schools is a controversial issue in some communities, even though it's not associated with increased sexual activity or teenage pregnancies.

FIGURE 4
Since biological urges are undeniable, some communities have developed sex education programs designed to help adolescents think through the consequences of their sexual behaviors. With more information, adolescents like this pair can make responsible decisions about their sexual relationship.

Why this lack of attention to sex education in the schools? Traditionally, of course, sex education has been a controversial issue. The unspoken assumption in many cases is that the more knowledge and information teenagers have about sex, the more likely they are to engage in it. However, we have no evidence that increasing adolescents' knowledge about sex increases their sexual involvement (Dawson, 1986; Marsiglio & Mott, 1986). What studies do show is that lack of knowledge leads to less contraceptive use and more pregnancies. It seems that adolescents who have a solid base of information about their bodies, birth control, and sex and its consequences are better equipped to make responsible decisions about sexual behavior. Several programs have been designed to provide this information.

SEX EDUCATION PROGRAMS. Effective sex education programs have to take into account the confusion and denial that characterize adolescent thinking about sex. One program, entitled "Postponing Sexual Involvement," has been developed at the Emory University/Grady Memorial Hospital in Atlanta, Georgia, for adolescents aged 13 to 15. Going beyond biological information, it addresses relationships, societal pressures, and assertive responses that adolescents can use in peer pressure situations (Reece, 1984). Aimed at reducing teenage pregnancy by curbing sexual activity, the program is now being used in Atlanta public schools.

A second program, based on cognitive and behavioral principles, consists of four parts (Schinke, Gilchrist, & Small, 1979):

- Providing access to relevant, accurate, and complete information on reproductive biology, contraceptive methods, options for resolving pregnancy, and normal sexual development in adolescence
- Encouraging accurate perception, comprehension, and storage of the information through small-group study, hypothetical situations, quizzes, and rewards
- Encouraging the use of information in decision making by relating facts to personal attitudes, beliefs, and values and by translating facts into personal statements. At this point in the program,

  adolescents must evaluate the consequences of taking knowledge-based action. Since such action usually involves other people, each self-statement includes their anticipated responses. For example, a young man might verbalize the following thoughts: "*Fact.* Unprotected intercourse frequently results in pregnancy. That means: If Ann and I have sex without birth control, she might get pregnant. Since neither of us wants her to get pregnant, we had better start using birth control. She doesn't like the pill, so I guess we better talk about using something else." (p. 86)

- Helping students implement decisions and practice for real situations by using small-group discussions, modeling, role play, feedback, and verbal instruction.

This program is particularly strong because it encourages students to think about information, about what they can do in specific situations, and about the consequences of their actions. It provides effective sex education because it acknowledges the important part sexual activity plays in human development and relates abstract knowledge to the individual's personal experience.

Other sex education programs have been developed in response to the threat of AIDS (discussed further later in this chapter). The key to these programs is accurate information about how AIDS is transmitted and how individuals can protect themselves and learn safe sexual practices. Several guides have been written to assist communities in devising AIDS prevention programs, including *Guidelines for Effective School Health Education to Prevent the Spread of AIDS* (Centers for Disease Control, 1988) and *Steps to Help Your School Set Up an AIDS Education Program* (National Coalition of Advocates for Students). This tragic disease may be the force that motivates school districts throughout the country to develop or continue adequate sex education programs in all junior high and high schools.

Drug Education

Another problem reaching epidemic proportions in our society is drug abuse, especially among young people, as discussed in Chapter 20. Many experts believe that the best approach to this problem is prevention through education (Newcomb & Bentler, 1989). Their thinking is that teenagers who don't try drugs can't become dependent on them. What are the best ways to educate young people about drugs?

Drug education programs fall into two general categories—indirect approaches and direct approaches. Indirect approaches involve building students' self-esteem, improving their academic skills, and increasing their recreational

BOX 1
A Plan for Achieving Schools Without Drugs

PARENTS:

1. Teach standards of right and wrong, and demonstrate these standards through personal example.

2. Help children to resist peer pressure to use drugs by supervising their activities, knowing who their friends are, and talking with them about their interests and problems.

3. Be knowledgeable about drugs and signs of drug use. When symptoms are observed, respond promptly.

SCHOOLS:

4. Determine the extent and character of drug use and establish a means of monitoring that use regularly.

5. Establish clear and specific rules regarding drug use that include strong corrective actions.

6. Enforce established policies against drug use fairly and consistently. Implement security measures to eliminate drugs on school premises and at school functions.

7. Implement a comprehensive drug prevention curriculum for kindergarten through grade 12, teaching that drug use is wrong and harmful and supporting and strengthening resistance to drugs.

8. Reach out to the community for support and assistance in making the school's antidrug policy and program work. Develop collaborative arrangements in which school personnel, parents, school boards, law enforcement officers, treatment organizations, and private groups can work together to provide necessary resources.

STUDENTS:

9. Learn about the effects of drug use, the reasons why drugs are harmful, and ways to resist pressures to try drugs.

10. Use an understanding of the danger posed by drugs to help other students avoid them. Encourage other students to resist drugs, persuade those using drugs to seek help, and report those selling drugs to parents and the school principal.

COMMUNITIES:

11. Help schools fight drugs by providing them with the expertise and financial resources of community groups and agencies.

12. Involve local law enforcement agencies in all aspects of drug prevention: assessment, enforcement, and education. The police and courts should have well-established and mutually supportive relationships with the schools.

SOURCE: From Bennett, W. J. (1987). What works: Schools without drugs. *Washington, DC: U.S. Department of Education.*

opportunities. Direct approaches involve providing knowledge about the adverse effects of drugs and teaching tactics that help students resist peer pressure to use drugs in various social situations (Tobler, 1986). The U.S. Department of Education (1986) has developed a "Plan for Achieving Schools without Drugs," calling for action on the part of parents, schools, students, and communities. This plan is shown in Box 1.

To date, most drug education programs haven't been very effective at preventing young people from using drugs. The most successful programs have been those that focus on strategies for resisting peer pressure. Among the population of teenagers at risk for drug abuse and other problem behaviors, alternative programs that provide greater opportunities for leisure and physical activities have been the most effective. Programs that rely on scare tactics or knowledge alone haven't been useful, perhaps because teenagers generally see themselves as invulnerable (Newcomb & Bentler, 1989). The most effective drug programs for the 1990s will probably be those that provide the facilities and resources adolescents need to make responsible, healthy choices about their lives.

ASSESSING THE ADOLESCENT

FIGURE 5
Too often, a negative approach is taken to a problem that requires a positive solution. Realistic drug programs provide constructive alternative activities for adolescents. These teenagers would be more likely to say no to drugs if they were offered recreational programs, organized sports, friendly adults to talk to, or places to socialize instead.

A generation or two ago, people would have been mystified if you talked about "SAT scores" and their importance to many high school students. Today, these and other test scores are momentous factors in millions of young people's lives, influencing where they go to college and what course their lives will take. Like the other assessment instruments we've discussed throughout this book, achievement and IQ tests used with adolescents measure knowledge and levels of intellectual functioning. Another type of test used at this age evaluates interest and ability in various vocations.

Achievement Tests

Achievement tests are used to measure high school students' accomplishments in various areas of study. The three most commonly used achievement tests are the **School and College Ability Tests** (SCAT), developed by Educational Testing Service (ETS) (1979); the **Scholastic Aptitude Tests** (SAT), developed by the College Entrance Examination Board; and the **American College Testing Program** (ACT), developed by the American College Testing Program (1984).

All the tests include verbal and quantitative (math) parts, although some tests emphasize one more than the other. The SAT and the SCAT, for example, contain just two parts, one verbal and one mathematical. The ACT, on the other hand, has four parts—English usage, mathematics usage, social sciences reading, and natural sciences reading. The ACT emphasizes reading and other language abilities more than the SAT and the SCAT do.

The SAT and the ACT are currently the tests most commonly used for college admissions. Both are correlated with college grades, but neither is as good a predictor of college grades as high school grades are. As additional information, however, these test scores improve the prediction of college grades by about 10 percent over high school grades alone (Aiken, 1985). Most colleges consider a number of factors in their admissions decisions, giving rank in high school class the most weight. Higher test scores would improve a particular student's eligibility, and lower test scores would lower it. But a high test score would probably not greatly improve a student's chances for admission if the student had a very low class ranking in high school.

Intelligence Tests and Interest Tests

Unlike achievement tests, intelligence tests aren't necessarily tied closely to skills developed by schooling. They presumably provide a picture of "capacity to learn" rather than achievement, although, as discussed in earlier chapters, considerable debate exists about what abilities IQ tests actually do measure.

The intelligence test used most widely with adolescents and adults is the **Wechsler Adult Intelligence Scale—Revised** (Wechsler, 1981). It includes 14 subtests covering a variety of verbal and performance abilities. Subjects are asked to answer arithmetic problems, give word definitions, complete pictures, make block designs, and assemble objects. The test's 14 scores are taken from these subtests.

Another type of test has been developed to help adolescents—and adults—sort out their inclinations and aptitudes for various fields and vocations. One widely used interest and vocational preference test is the **Kuder General Interest Survey, Form E** (Kuder, 1975). It measures interest in ten areas—outdoor, mechanical, computational, scientific, persuasive, artistic, literary, musical, social service, and clerical.

Another well known interest test is the **Strong-Campbell Interest Inventory** (Strong & Campbell, 1981), which includes seven parts. Subjects are asked questions such as how they would feel about participating in various occupations, how well they like certain subjects in school, how much they like certain kinds of people, and what they like to do for recreation. Either of these tests, when used in conjunction with other measures such as achievement in specific areas, can help individuals make decisions about career directions.

FIGURE 6
Standardized achievement tests create a real problem for high school students who have learning disabilities and therefore need more time to come up with answers. Tutoring can help on an individual level; less reliance on test scores for college admissions will help on a broader scale.

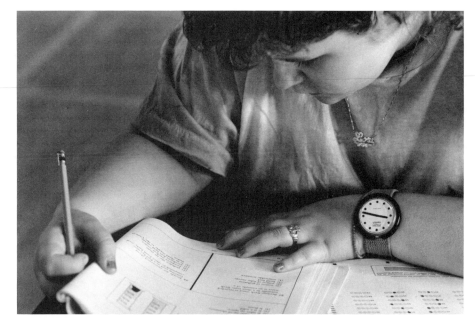

LIVING WITH THE ADOLESCENT

When there's an adolescent in the family, challenges abound, ranging from the trivial (careless borrowing of deodorants and shampoos, for example) to the tragic (teenage pregnancy, drug and alcohol abuse, and adolescent suicide). Many of these issues have already been discussed in various contexts in previous chapters. Here, we focus on three somewhat different concerns—health, safety, and recreation.

Keeping the Adolescent Healthy

Like middle childhood, adolescence is a time of relatively good health, both in terms of viral and bacterial illnesses and in terms of major diseases like cancer and hypertension. In many ways, adolescence and young adulthood are the "prime" of life. But there are risks to health during adolescence. One is suicide, which we discussed in Chapter 20. Another is **sexually transmitted diseases (STDs),** including AIDS.

THE NATURE AND INCIDENCE OF SEXUALLY TRANSMITTED DISEASES. STDs are contagious diseases caused by bacterial and viral organisms that live in the reproductive tract and organs. Contact with an infected person, through intercourse, for example, exposes an individual to these infections. Common STDs include the bacterial diseases gonorrhea and syphilis and the viral diseases cytomegalovirus and herpes.

When promiscuous populations (such as prostitutes) are excluded from the statistics, teenagers have the highest rates of the common STDs (Millstein, 1989). Few cases of AIDS have been found among adolescents, but the number has been increasing. Unfortunately, one-fifth of the AIDS cases reported in the United States have occurred in individuals between the ages of 20 and 29.

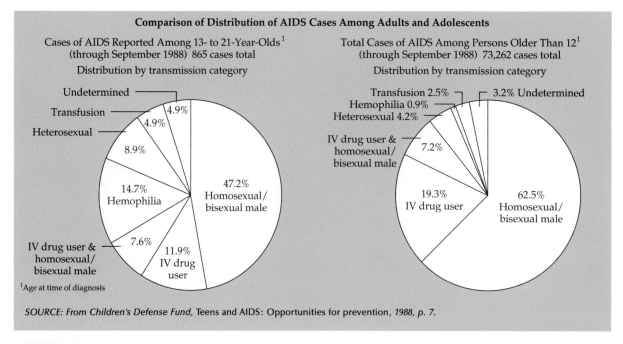

Comparison of Distribution of AIDS Cases Among Adults and Adolescents

Cases of AIDS Reported Among 13- to 21-Year-Olds[1]
(through September 1988) 865 cases total
Distribution by transmission category

Undetermined — 4.9%
Transfusion — 4.9%
Heterosexual — 8.9%
14.7% Hemophilia
47.2% Homosexual/bisexual male
IV drug user & homosexual/bisexual male — 7.6%
11.9% IV drug user

[1]Age at time of diagnosis

Total Cases of AIDS Among Persons Older Than 12[1]
(through September 1988) 73,262 cases total
Distribution by transmission category

Transfusion 2.5%
Hemophilia 0.9%
Heterosexual 4.2%
3.2% Undetermined
IV drug user & homosexual/bisexual male — 7.2%
19.3% IV drug user
62.5% Homosexual/bisexual male

SOURCE: From *Children's Defense Fund,* Teens and AIDS: Opportunities for prevention, *1988, p. 7.*

FIGURE 7
A smaller percentage of persons with AIDS under 21 years of age are homosexual or bisexual than is true of the total population. Blood transfusions and hemophilia account for many cases of AIDS among teenagers. A group not represented in these graphics is children under 12, the fastest-growing population of persons with AIDS. Infants can be infected by mothers who are IV drug users or sexual partners of IV drug users.

Since the incubation period for this disease is so long, many of these people were probably infected during adolescence (Brooks-Gunn & Furstenberg, 1989). Correspondingly, many cases of AIDS that were contracted during the teen years of today's adolescents will undoubtedly come to light. (See Figure 7 for information about routes of infection for the AIDS virus among adolescents as compared with adults.)

PREVENTING SEXUALLY TRANSMITTED DISEASES. The high rates of STDs among adolescents is hardly surprising when we consider the increase in adolescent sexual activity that has occurred over the past 20 years. Teenagers also have a relatively high number of sexual partners, both because of the short-term nature of many teenage love relationships and because of an increase in "casual sex"—sex outside a love relationship. All these factors—early onset of sexually active behavior, high number of sexual partners, and unprotected intercourse (without a condom)—put individuals at risk for STDs (Brooks-Gunn, Boyer, & Hein, 1988; Peterson & Marin, 1988).

As mentioned earlier in this chapter, our best defenses against the spread of STDs among the teenage population are twofold: (1) effective sex education efforts and (2) programs that provide adolescents with the social skills they need to resist sexual activity at an early age and to follow safe procedures if and when they decide to engage in sexual activity (Children's Defense Fund, 1988; Peterson & Marin, 1988).

Keeping the Adolescent Safe

Not surprisingly, accidents are the leading cause of death during the adolescent years. Fatal accidents most often involve automobiles, motorcycles, bicycles, and sports, especially swimming. Alcohol is often implicated in many of these accidents, particularly those involving automobiles (Zuckerman & Duby, 1985).

ACCIDENTS AND ADOLESCENT RISK-TAKING BEHAVIOR. Some experts suggest that the risk-taking behavior so common during adolescence is responsible for the high number of accidental deaths among teenagers (Zuckerman & Duby, 1985; Irwin, 1989). Risk-taking behavior, of course, is related to the typical adolescent feeling of invulnerability, the sense that bad things happen only to others.

Because teens often take even more risks if they're trying to impress their friends and be accepted in their peer group (Irwin, 1989), intervention programs for adolescents often focus on helping them resist peer pressure. For example, some programs train young people in using specific verbal replies to peer pressure (McAlister, Perry, & Maccoby, 1979). Other programs try to bolster self-esteem, based on the assumption that individuals who feel secure about themselves won't feel they have to prove their worth to others. Involving adolescents in organized—and thus supervised—sports and other constructive activities can also help reduce dangerous risk-taking behavior (Zuckerman & Duby, 1985).

Finally, many high schools have started programs encouraging students not to drink and drive. Alcohol-free graduation parties and proms reduce the

FIGURE 8
Believing themselves exempt from injury and death, these teenage boys dare their friends to join them on the slippery rocks beneath a waterfall. Everyone has such false beliefs to some extent, but adolescents are much more likely to act on them. More realistic approaches to life are fostered in many communities by such programs as Students Against Drunk Driving.

likelihood that party-goers will have auto accidents. All these efforts need the active support of parents, school, and community to succeed.

VIOLENCE AND ACCIDENTAL DEATHS. In recent years, homicide has become the second most frequent cause of death among 15- to 24-year-olds. Black males are at special risk for death from homicide. In fact, they're six times more likely to be victims of homicide than are nonblack males the same age (Spivak, Prothrow-Stith, & Hausman, 1988). In 1983 the U.S. Department of Health and Human Services considered this problem so severe that it set a goal of reducing teenage homicides by the year 1990 (U.S. Public Health Service, 1983).

Among teenagers, death by violence is related to the generally dismal urban environment in which many young people live. Violence, both within their families and on the streets, is a fact of life, learned early and carried on into adolescence and adulthood. The increased number of guns on the streets, bought with money from drug sales, has intensified the problem in recent years. Simple disagreements now are likely to end in a gun battle and possibly in a violent death.

A long-term solution to this problem isn't simple. It requires putting massive efforts into changing the social and economic conditions in our cities, defusing adolescents' anger by improving the quality of their lives, and giving people hope for a decent future by creating educational, recreational, and employment opportunities. Although the problems are daunting, we can begin to reclaim the lives of urban youths by making these improvements a national priority.

Leisure Activities during Adolescence

HOW DO TEENAGERS SPEND THEIR TIME? The interests and activities of teenagers change over the course of adolescence. Since they have more freedom to spend time away from home, for example, older adolescents watch less television than children or younger adolescents. In fact, television viewing peaks during early adolescence at four hours a day (Liebert, 1986). Amount of time spent reading for fun also changes. According to the 1984 National Assessment of Educational Progress (NAEP) survey, 52 percent of 9-year-olds read for fun on a daily basis; 35 percent of 13-year-olds reported reading as a leisure activity; and only 33 percent of 17-year-olds said they read daily for fun (Neuman, 1988).

This same survey elicited information about other "media activities." As shown in Table 1, most adolescents spend more time watching TV than reading, and many also spend more time listening to music than reading. In later adolescence, listening to music often surpasses watching TV as a preferred leisure activity. Playing video games is also popular, although interest in this activity drops dramatically by 17 years of age.

As discussed in Chapter 20, teenagers also like to spend their time being with friends, talking to friends on the phone, and playing sports (Neuman, 1988). Table 2 shows that time spent with friends increases considerably between 9 and 17 years of age. We can also see that the increased time 13-year-olds spend participating in sports comes out of the general play time reported by 9-year-olds, since both groups report about the same amount of time in front

TABLE 1
Media Activities Most Often Engaged in During Leisure Time for Three Groups as Reported on NAEP

Media Activity	Hispanic	Black	White
9-year-olds			
Watch TV	25%	30%	29%
Read a book	5%	9%	10%
Play video games	9%	9%	7%
Listen to music	7%	6%	9%
Read a newspaper	1%	0%	1%
13-year-olds			
Watch TV	25%	33%	24%
Read a book	3%	7%	6%
Play video games	6%	5%	2%
Listen to music	17%	11%	14%
Read a newspaper	2%	1%	1%
17-year-olds			
Watch TV	15%	17%	12%
Read a book	3%	9%	4%
Play video games	1%	0%	0%
Listen to music	18%	16%	21%
Read a newspaper	2%	2%	1%

SOURCE: From Neuman, S. B. (1988). The displacement effect: Assessing the relation between television viewing and reading performance. Reading Research Quarterly, 23(4), 434.

TABLE 2
Leisure Activities Most Often Engaged in During Leisure Time for Three Groups as Reported on NAEP

Leisure Activity	Hispanic	Black	White
9-year-olds			
Watch TV	25%	30%	29%
Call a friend	1%	3%	2%
Be with friends	8%	9%	13%
Play sports	9%	8%	9%
Eat snacks	2%	1%	2%
Play	5%	1%	1%
13-year-olds			
Watch TV	25%	33%	24%
Call a friend	6%	8%	7%
Be with friends	11%	8%	14%
Play sports	11%	12%	14%
Eat snacks	0%	1%	1%
17-year-olds			
Watch TV	15%	17%	12%
Call a friend	9%	12%	7%
Be with friends	17%	13%	21%
Play sports	17%	13%	12%
Eat snacks	1%	2%	1%

SOURCE: From Neuman, S. B. (1988). The displacement effect: Assessing the relation between television viewing and reading performance. Reading Research Quarterly, 23(4), 435.

of the TV. But 17-year-olds report a dramatic reduction in time spent watching TV, suggesting that their time participating in sports and socializing with friends comes from previous television-viewing time. Another view of adolescent leisure activities is given in Figure 9.

HOW CAN ADULTS SUPPORT POSITIVE LEISURE ACTIVITIES FOR TEENAGERS? Given how teenagers spend their time, it's clear that their development is strongly affected by the quality of sports programs and facilities, television programming, music,

FIGURE 9
Although adolescents spend
a great deal of their time in
leisure activities, they don't
devote much of their leisure
time to reading. Spending
just a little of their TV-watch-
ing time with a good book
would be likely to increase
their achievement both in
and out of school.

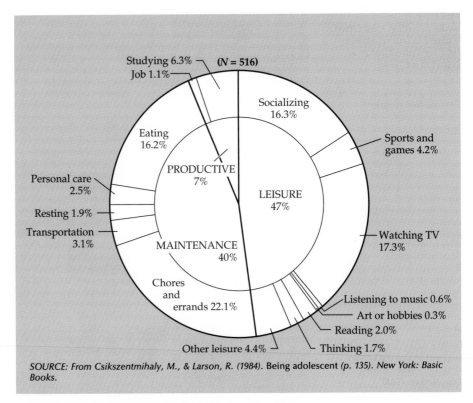

SOURCE: From Csikszentmihaly, M., & Larson, R. (1984). *Being adolescent* (p. 135). New York: Basic Books.

and libraries. Communities have to make a concerted effort to make sure these facilities and programs are appropriate for young people. They can also support positive social development by providing places where teenagers can get together and have fun—a resource sorely lacking in most communities.

The low level of recreational reading reported by today's teenagers is a worrisome statistic, since independent reading, both in and out of school, is related to level of achievement. Furthermore, some of the books that adolescents favor when they *do* read are a source of dismay to adults. Making connections between popular teenage books and more complex literature is one way teachers may be able to encourage more reading of better-quality books (see Box 2). Adolescents who read more do better in school and become better educated; those who don't read miss out on their own rich heritage. Studies show that many younger children spend only 4 to 5 minutes a day reading at home, compared with 130 minutes watching television (U.S. Department of Education, 1986).

Concern over children's interest in reading was behind the development of *Reading Rainbow*, a public television program designed for elementary age children. In some areas of the country commercial television stations have created their own programs to support reading. In the Boston area, for example, two programs ("It's a Likely Story" and "Long Ago and Far Away") were launched in 1988. The assumption is that an early start in recreational reading will help build a lifelong love of reading. Perhaps the current generation of children, who have been exposed to these programs, will enjoy reading more as adults. But an early interest in reading might be sustained better if specific television programs were developed for the adolescent audience.

BOX 2
Adolescent Literature: Starting Where the Learners Are?

A question of continual controversy concerns secondary school English and adolescent literature: Are they compatible? Traditionally, the content of high school English has been the classics, from *Beowulf* to James Joyce, including a heavy dose of Shakespeare and the romantic poets, with lengthy excerpts from the works of Nathaniel Hawthorne, O'Henry, Edgar Allen Poe, and perhaps even Jack Kerouac. Whatever the specifics, the content is selected as representing some dimension of significant, written expression by adults for adults. The levels of abstraction are high and the plots are complex, complete with subtle interplays of recurring themes and dramatic irony. In short, all aspects of writer's license are explored, most of all the use of symbolic communication. The complexities of the human condition in the hands of skillful craftspersons and wordsmiths such as Jane Austen or Herman Melville are viewed as the foundation for secondary school courses in literature.

But what of the adolescents themselves? What are they reading if left to their own choice? Perhaps a few can be found browsing through Elizabeth Barrett Browning or *Twelfth Night,* but most are reading works of a totally different genre. Adolescent literature is just that: novels written with a deliberate appeal to teenagers. The plots are less complex by design. Good recent examples include Zindel's *My Darling, My Hamburger,* Klein's *Mom, the Wolfman and Me,* and Childress's *A Hero Ain't Nothing but a Sandwich.* The main characters clearly represent a variety of unambiguous values. Generally brief and to the point, the novel has a message that is clear from beginning to end. In a sense these writings are very similar in construction to daytime TV soap operas. If we borrow from our own framework in this volume, an analysis of the main themes would place most adolescent literature at a level at which appearance, peer group pressure, and conventionality are dominant values.

So the paradox. Teenagers avidly devour their own literature—the romantic mysteries and the Harlequin romances (which, recently, are only modernized versions of the Hardy Boys, Nancy Drew, and the "fabulous" Maxwell Brothers). Yet these works cannot be considered uplifting. They do little to deepen a person's understanding of life, and they can hardly be the means of increasing the majesty and mystery of humanity. In developmental terms there is almost too much of a match between adolescent literature and the adolescent. The literature mirrors almost exactly the point where most teenagers are developmentally. Yet, on the other hand, teenagers are clearly not ready to delve into the likes of Dostoevski's *Crime and Punishment.* That is, the traditional material is often too great a mismatch, as we have noted.

Solutions to such a dilemma are hard to come by, but it is clear that the need for them is great. Classic works of literature and adolescents are, to quote from a great work, "like ships passing in the night"—only in this case, there is not even a hail in the night before darkness descends again. A developmental solution would require substantial research and trial, but we can, at least, outline a possible direction here. Starting where the learner is would require teaching adolescents how to analyze their own literature, as a beginning. To write off their own literature with a grand gesture of disgust is clearly not the way to proceed. After analysis could come the gradual introduction of works representing slightly greater levels of complexity. Comparative examination could then become the first step on the path to more complex readings, where the works no longer represent where the teenager is now but, rather, what the teenager is in the process of becoming.

From Sprinthall, N. A., & Collins, W. A. (1984). Adolescent Psychology (pp. 116–117). Reading, MA: Addison-Wesley.

WHAT IF TEENAGERS WORK? Many teenagers spend part of their out-of-school time working. The number of teenagers who work has been increasing steadily for the past 25 years. In fact, at least one-third of all high school students have part-time jobs (Charner & Fraser, 1988), and in some communities, well over half of all seniors in high school work at least 16 hours per week. Adolescents work for a variety of reasons, such as to earn spending money, to buy cars, to gain work experience, to help out with family expenses, or to save for a college education (Berryman & Schneider, 1982; Wirtz, 1987).

When teenagers hold part-time jobs, they have less time available for the leisure and recreational activities their peers are enjoying, including the activ-

FIGURE 10
Part-time jobs have both advantages and disadvantages for adolescents. This Navaho girl may gain a sense of competence and responsibility from working at a service station, along with the more obvious monetary rewards, but she may also miss out on important school and recreational activities while she's on the job. Working more than 20 hours a week seems to be counterproductive for teenagers.

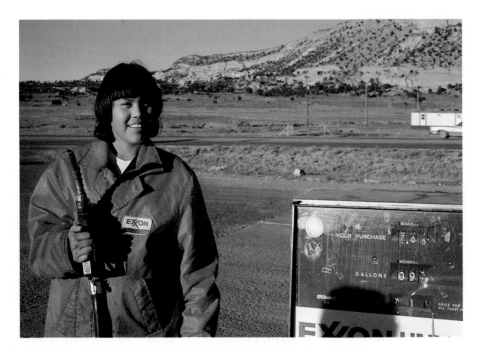

ities sponsored by their school. When they spend excessive time working— more than 20 hours a week—their academic achievement often suffers as well (Charner & Fraser, 1988). Although part-time work can have benefits for teenagers, including a greater sense of responsibility and improved work habits and skills, too much time spent working can reduce adolescents' opportunities to develop recreational interests and academic abilities. Adults need to help adolescents achieve a balance among work, school, and leisure activities that will serve them well as they move on into their adult lives.

FIGURE 11
High school graduation marks the end of a known way of life for many adolescents and the beginning of a new, unknown one. The qualities they take with them into adulthood depend on innumerable factors, ranging from inborn traits to ideas and values they've acquired over the years. Parents, grandparents, teachers, counselors—all played important roles in shaping them from infancy onward. Now, whether the older generation thinks their job is done or not, these young adults are eager to be off on their own.

OVERVIEW

Teenagers spend more and more time away from home, both at school and in leisure activities. The role of adults is increasingly to support their growing autonomy by providing the conditions for positive experiences and healthy choices. In school, this means giving teenagers the information they need about sex and drugs, and giving it in ways that are useful to them. It also means helping them make the transition to junior high and high school and later the even more challenging transition to college or work. In leisure activities, it means having resources available for young people that will give them a truly viable alternative to dangerous or unhealthy choices—resources like sports facilities and programs, teen social centers, supervised recreational programs, individualized guidance and counseling, and, most important of all, responsible adults who are involved in their lives and who care about what they make of themselves.

KNOWLEDGE IN ACTION REVIEW

EDUCATING THE ADOLESCENT

- The organization of junior high or middle school is usually quite different from that of elementary school; subjects are departmentalized, students move from room to room throughout the day, and more responsibility falls on the individual.
- Junior high schools often practice ability grouping, or tracking, based on judgments about what path—college or vocation—different students are likely to take after school. Tracking is considered detrimental to the goals of creating a well-educated general populace and keeping a variety of career opportunities open to students.

SPECIAL AREAS OF ADOLESCENT EDUCATION

- Although parents want to be involved in their children's sex education, the responsibility has fallen increasingly to the schools. Many school districts neglect this important area, perhaps because they believe that the more teenagers know about sex, the more likely they will be to engage in it. Actually, the more information teenagers have about sex, the less likely they are to become pregnant or contract a sexually transmitted disease, including AIDS.
- Effective sex education programs have to take into account the denial and confusion that characterize adolescent thinking about sex. The most successful programs combine verbal instruction—information about reproduction and relationships—with role playing and other behavioral techniques that help teenagers think through consequences and practice assertive responses.
- The most effective drug education programs are those that combine information about the dangers of drugs with greater opportunities for alternative recreational activities.

ASSESSING THE ADOLESCENT

- Achievement tests commonly used to assess adolescents' knowledge include the SCAT, the SAT, and the ACT. Colleges use students' scores on these tests to help determine admissions, but the single most important factor in college admissions is rank in high school class.
- The most commonly used intelligence test for adolescents is the Wechsler Intelligence Scale—Revised, and the best known interest tests are the Kuder General Interest Survey, Form E, and the Strong-Campbell Interest Inventory. Interest tests help individuals make decisions about career directions.

LIVING WITH THE ADOLESCENT

- Physically, adolescents are in the prime of life, but they do face certain health risks, including suicide and sexually transmitted diseases (STDs).
- The most common STDs are gonorrhea, syphilis, cytomegalovirus, and herpes. Less common, but on the rise, is AIDS. Teenagers are at risk for these diseases because of the early onset of their sexually active behavior, their high number of sexual partners, and their high incidence of intercourse without condoms.
- Concern about STDs and AIDS has led to more interest in comprehensive sex education programs in schools and communities.
- Accidents are the leading cause of death among adolescents, in part because of their tendency to take risks based on their feelings of invulnerability. Safety programs aimed at teenagers often focus on raising self-esteem, teaching ways to resist peer pressure, providing sports and other constructive activities, and reversing social pressure to drink alcohol.
- Homicide is the second leading cause of death among people aged 15 to 24 and is particularly prevalent among black male adolescents in urban areas. Protecting these youths from violent death by improving living conditions and opportunities for education and employment should be made a national priority.
- Teenagers spend less time at home as they get older, and their preferred leisure activities change. Reading for fun declines throughout adolescence, as do watching TV and playing video games. The older they get, the more time teenagers spend with their friends.
- Constructive leisure activities for teenagers are supported by sports programs and facilities, quality television programming, good libraries, and community centers where teenagers can gather and socialize.
- At least one-third of all high school students have part-time jobs. Although working provides some benefits to adolescents, excessive working deprives them of the social and recreational opportunities their peers enjoy.

KEY TERMS

tracking
School and College
   Ability Tests
Scholastic Aptitude Tests

American College Testing
   Program
sexually transmitted
   diseases (STDs)

Kuder General Interest
   Survey, Form E
Strong-Campbell Interest
   Inventory

SUGGESTIONS FOR FURTHER READING

Goodlad, J. (1984). *A place called school: Prospects for the future*. New York: McGraw-Hill.
   This book contains a wealth of information about American schools (including secondary schools) and suggestions for changes to improve them.

Hayes, C. D. (Ed.). (1987). *Risking the future: Adolescent sexuality, pregnancy, and childbearing* (Vol. 1). Washington, DC: National Academy Press.
   Provides detailed information about this problem.

Oakes, J. (1985). *Keeping track*. New Haven, CT: Yale University Press.
   A very readable discussion of the educational practice of grouping students of similar achievement or ability levels together for instruction.

MILESTONES IN ADOLESCENT DEVELOPMENT

AGE	PHYSICAL	COGNITIVE	LANGUAGE	SOCIAL-EMOTIONAL
13 yrs.	Has reached and passed peak of growth spurt if female Has probably reached puberty (begun menstruation) if female	May demonstrate formal operational thinking	Speaks in longer sentences, uses principles of subordination Understands metaphors, multiple levels of meaning Increases vocabulary	Still has weak sense of individual identity, is easily influenced by peer group Spends more time with friends May begin sexual relationships, especially if male
14 yrs.	Is reaching peak of growth spurt if male Is gaining muscle cells if male, fat cells if female May develop anorexia or bulimia, expecially if female Is getting deeper voice if male Has probably reached maximum height if female	Continues to gain metacognitive abilities and improve study skills	Improves reading comprehension abilities and study skills Writes longer, more complex sentences	Seeks increasing emotional autonomy from parents
15 yrs.	Has probably reached puberty (begun sperm production) if male May reach fastest reaction time	Views world idealistically	Can adapt language to different contexts Uses teen slang	Seeks intimate friendships and relationships May have had sexual intercourse
16 yrs.	Has probably reached maximum height if male May reach peak performance level in some sports	Is egocentric, believes in imaginary audience and personal fable	May fail to develop writing ability if not instructed	Is actively involved in search for personal identity Is likely to be sexually active May use alcohol and cigarettes May have dropped out of school
17 yrs.	Is still gaining muscle strength if male	May take SAT or ACT test as part of college admissions process	With instruction and practice, adolescents' metacognitive abilities and study skills continue to improve	May have part-time job May make decisions that bear on later occupational choices May be preparing to leave home, separate from parents

Credits (continued from the copyright page)

Photo Credits

GLOSSARY

accommodation   With respect to the human eye, refers to the ability of the lens to adjust to objects at different distances. With respect to Piaget's theory, refers to the process of change in mental structures.

achievement motivation   Motivation directed toward accomplishing a goal according to a standard.

achievement tests   Tests designed to reflect mastery of instructional programs geared for specific grade levels.

active listening   A communication technique advocated by Thomas Gordon in his Parent Effectiveness Program.

acuity   The resolving power of the eye—its ability to see closely spaced, thin lines versus widely spaced, broad lines, for example.

acute stage of adjustment to divorce   The initial two years following a divorce, during which children are likely to show the most disruption in their behavior.

affrication   A feature of speech that is characterized by the slow release of air.

amenorrhea   Absence of menstruation that can occur for a number of reasons, including a severe reduction in body fat due to anorexia nervosa or extremely high levels of physical activity.

American College Testing Program   The publisher of the ACT test, which is used extensively as part of college application packages.

amniocentesis   Analysis of amniotic fluid to determine the presence of various chromosomal and chemical abnormalities in the fetus.

anoxia   Oxygen deprivation.

anxious/ambivalent attachment   A pattern of mother-child relationship marked by a mixture of approach and withdrawal behavior on the part of the child upon reunion with the mother after separation.

anxious/avoidant attachment   A pattern of mother-child relationship marked by avoidance of the mother by the child during play and upon reunion after separation.

Apgar scale   An assessment instrument used to assess infants' physiological functioning at birth.

apnea   A period during which breathing stops.

assimilation   A process basic to Piaget's theory of intellectual development that involves the taking in of new information by current mental structures.

attachment   The emotional tie between infants and their caregivers, usually their parents.

authoritarian parenting style   Parenting behavior marked by high levels of adult control and references to absolute authority as a result of parental status or religious doctrine.

authoritative parenting style   Parenting behavior marked by firm parental control accompanied by reasoning about the basis for expectations.

aversive stimulus   A stimulus that someone finds repulsive and tries to avoid.

axons   The part of a nerve cell that carries impulses away from its own cell toward another.

babbling Early vocalization consisting of consonant-vowel combinations.

Babinski reflex A reflex present in young infants characterized by fanning of the toes when the outer edge of the sole is stroked.

baseline data The data collected in a research study before a treatment is introduced to assess natural or typical conditions.

beginning reader The initial stage of conventional reading in which cueing systems are not smoothly balanced.

behavior modification A specific behavioral technique that utilizes reinforcement systematically to change behavior.

behavioral states The varying patterns of sleep and wakefulness found in infants.

behaviorism A theoretical orientation that emphasizes external influences on behavior and direct observation of behavior in research.

biased sampling Subjects included in a study who are not representative of the population of interest as a whole.

bilirubin A by-product of red blood cell destruction that is excreted from the body.

binocular vision The ability to use both eyes in a coordinated fashion when looking at objects.

blind study A study in which the researchers have no knowledge about which subjects have certain characteristics of interest.

bonding Refers to the initial emotional tie that some researchers and theorists believe mothers have toward their newborn infants.

book babble A type of expressive jargon that has the intonation patterns of reading versus conversation.

brain stem evoked response A test used to detect an infant's ability to hear. It uses electrodes to measure brain reaction to sound.

Brazelton Neonatal Behavioral Assessment Scale An assessment designed to measure young infants' reflexive and adaptive behavior.

cardinality rule/cardinality principle Knowing that the last item counted in a group also represents the numerosity of the group.

Cattell Culture Fair Intelligence Test A nonverbal test devised to eliminate cultural bias presumed to be inherent in standard intelligence tests.

center of gravity The point in the body around which the weight is distributed evenly.

centering According to Piaget, the tendency of preschool children to focus on one dimension of a relationship at a time instead of coordinating two dimensions.

cephalocaudal trend The pattern of physical and motor development that proceeds from the head to the tail.

chicken pox A common childhood disease caused by a virus and characterized by itchy skin lesions.

child-directed educational approach Educational programs in which children's interests and choices are taken into account.

childhood animism The tendency of young children to consider inanimate objects as being alive.

childhood realism The tendency of young children to consider thoughts as objects with material substance.

chorionic villus sampling A biopsy procedure in which tissue from the chorion is extracted for analysis to determine the presence or absence of chromosomal abnormalities in the fetus.

chromosomes The strands of DNA inside the nucleus of the cell that contain the genes.

chronological age Age measured from the birthdate.

class inclusion The concept of hierarchical classes necessary to understand complex classification schemes.

classical conditioning The pairing of a stimulus with another stimulus that reliably produces a response, such that the second stimulus itself begins to elicit the response.

clique A closely knit peer group based on specific interests such as music, sports, or physical appearance.

closed method Refers to observational studies in which specific data-collection techniques are used to enable researchers to collect more reliable data.

coaching Instructional technique in which skills are taught directly, practiced, and then refined in relation to feedback from a coach.

cohort A group of subjects who share the same history of experience.

cohort effects Differences among age groups that are due to historical events rather than to developmental differences.

colostrum The substance excreted from the breast before the milk begins to flow.

compensation A specific kind of reasoning about spatial rearrangement of objects of mass in which the child logically multiplies one dimension (e.g., height) with another (e.g., width) to account for differences in appearance from a standard.

concepts Ideas about general sets of characteristics that apply across many individual cases.

concrete operational thinking Thinking characterized by logic about events observed.

conditioned response The response elicited by the conditioned stimulus that was originally elicited by the unconditioned stimulus.

conditioned stimulus The stimulus paired with the unconditioned stimulus in classical conditioning, such that it elicits the response initially elicited by the unconditioned stimulus.

conservation The ability to realize that changes in spatial arrangement of objects or liquids, for example, do not change their number or amount.

consolability The ease with which an upset baby can be quieted.

context bound A characteristic of early language comprehension in which word meaning is heavily dependent on clues in the situation.

control group A subject group in an experimental research study that is excluded from the treatment but is like the treatment group in every other way.

controversial sociometric status Status in which a child receives many like and dislike elections by peers who are asked to list children who fall within these two categories.

conversational babble A type of expressive jargon that has the intonational patterns of conversation.

coordination errors A type of error made by young children when they count objects, such that their verbal tags aren't coordinated with the objects they are counting.

correlational study A study in which variables of interest are studied in naturally occurring groups of subjects instead of subjects who have been randomly assigned to treatment groups.

counting all A combining procedure used by young children when they must determine the sum of two groups. Children count all of the objects across the two groups as if they all belong to one group.

counting on A counting procedure used to combine two groups of objects. Children start with one group, without counting the objects, and then count up to the sum of the two groups by pointing to the objects in the second group.

Crib-O-Gram A procedure used to measure auditory response directly by assessing brain waves.

critical period The specific time frame during which specific behaviors are thought by some to develop.

cross-sectional design A research design that uses groups of subjects of different ages to determine differences due to development.

cross-sectional/short-term longitudinal design A research design that combines the study of different age groups and the same age groups over a period of time to determine developmental differences.

crowning During the birthing process, the first showing of the infant's head outside the birth canal.

culturally biased tests Tests that contain a predominance of items that are more consistent with the experiences of some cultural groups than with others.

decentration The trend in cognitive development that allows children to see things from points of view other than their own. In pretend play, decentration is shown when children remove themselves from the center of the action.

decontextualization The trend in pretend play that involves object substitution.

deferred imitation Imitation separated in time from the observance of the behavior.

dendrites Nerve fibers that carry impulses to the cell.

dependent variable The behavior observed by a researcher to see if changes occur as a result of changes made in the independent variable.

dialect Slight variations within a language.

distal supervision A characteristic of school-age child care programs in which children call or check in but are allowed to leave the program premises to engage in activities or go home.

distinctive features The variations in lines which can be combined in a number of ways to create different alphabet letters.

dominant gene A gene that always expresses its trait.

Down's syndrome A collection of physical and mental difficulties caused by the inheritance of an extra twenty-first chromosome.

drive reduction Refers to satiation of sex, hunger, and thirst, for example.

ductus arteriosus Route of fetal blood circulation that circumvents the lungs.

dyad A pair, as in mother and child.

dyslexia Extreme difficulty learning to read, which is most often caused by problems with language processing.

early reader A child who learns to read before entering kindergarten, without the benefit of specific instruction in reading.

ectopic pregnancy A pregnancy in which the embryo develops outside the womb, most typically in the fallopian tube.

educable mentally retarded Retardation within a very moderate range such that the person can learn academic skills to a certain level with the help of special education.

ego A term used by Freud and Erikson to refer to that part of personality that is reality oriented and seeks to satisfy the id in ways that are not punished.

ego identity Refers to concept of self formulated during adolescence.

egocentric role taking The description used by Selman to refer to an individual's assumption that different views of the same situation are due to differences in information about the situation.

egocentrism A notion central to Piaget's theory of intellectual development, which refers to the young child's difficulty in thinking about things from another's point of view.

embryoblast The part of the ball of cells, forming soon after fertilization, that will become the embryo itself.

emergent literacy Refers to the forms of written language behavior that precede conventional forms. For example, young children read their storybooks using picture-governed, rather than print-governed, strategies.

empathy The ability to understand how others feel.

empirical Related to data or experience rather than to theory.

encopresis Inability to control bowel function, often due to distension of musculature of the anus.

endogenous smile Grimace of face resembling a smile that is caused by internal factors.

enuresis Failure to control the bladder at night.

environmental print Print found on such things as road signs, store fronts, and food containers.

epigenic Refers to development in which structures change in form rather than simply increasing in size.

equilibration A Piagetian notion that the individual tries to keep assimilation and accommodation in balance.

ethology The study of animal behavior.

Eustachian tube Small tube that connects the middle ear to the throat.

exhortation Verbal appeals for prosocial behavior.

experimental study A research study in which subjects are randomly assigned to treatment groups.

expressive jargon A type of talk in which nonsense words are used with realistic-sounding intonation patterns.

external locus of control Refers to individuals who believe chance or fate rather than their own actions has the major effect on events in their life.

external validity Refers to the extent to which conclusions drawn in one study can be generalized to individuals not included in the study.

extinction In behavioral theory, refers to the reduction of a behavior due to lack of response to it.

failure-to-thrive Terminology that refers to infants who fail to grow normally.

fallopian tubes Tubes that connect the ovaries to the uterus and through which the egg passes and in which fertilization takes place.

family process variables Characteristics of families having to do with relationships rather than demographics.

fontanelles Soft spots on the top of a baby's head that will close as the skull grows and fuses.

formal operational thinking Piaget's highest level of intellectual development in which deductive, if-then reasoning becomes possible.

fraternal twins Twins who aren't identical genetically because they originated from two different eggs.

gag reflex Involuntary movement elicited when the back of the throat is pushed by something.

gender constancy The realization that sex does not change with alterations in hairstyle or clothing.

gender identity The categorization of oneself as a boy or a girl.

genes The basic units of inheritance in all living things.

germ cells Cells involved in reproduction—sperm in the male and ova in the female.

gestation Prenatal development.

glial cells Cells surrounding nerve cells in the brain that serve a supportive, nutritive function, such as the production of myelin.

glycogen The form in which starch is stored in the body before being converted to sugar and metabolized.

gonads Sex organs that create sperm and ova.

grasping reflex The involuntary movement resulting in the curling of toes or fingers when the sole of the foot or the palm of the hand is stroked or pressed.

growth spurt A rapid increase in growth such as that which occurs during pubescence.

habituation The decrement in response that follows repeated presentation of a stimulus.

head lice Small parasites that infect the head and cause itching.

hidden or invisible displacement A technique for hiding an object during the administration of the Piagetian object permanence task in which the object hidden is first placed inside a container.

hierarchical inclusion The embedding of subordinate classes within superordinate classes within a classification framework.

High-Risk Registry An interview technique for identifying infants at risk for hearing loss.

holophrase A word-word utterance that carries the meaning of a whole statement.

hyaline membrane disease A condition in which the lungs do not work properly due to the absence of surfactant—common among infants born prematurely.

hyperbilirubinemia A condition in which too much bilirubin is present in the bloodstream.

hypothermia A condition in which the body temperature dips below normal.

id The term coined by Freud to refer to that part of personality driven by inherited and unconscious instincts.

idealism Thinking touched little by knowledge of practical limitations.

identical process theory Refers to a theory of second language acquisition in which it is assumed the child learns the second language in the same way a child would for whom it is a first language.

identical twins Twins resulting from division of the same zygote.

identification A term from Freudian theory that refers to the aligning of behavior and values with another person, usually a child with an adult.

identity, identity argument The justification given for

a judgment of conservation that mentions that nothing has been added or taken away from the original amount or number.

identity achievement The end result of the searching and decision-making process that begins in adolescence and continues into young adulthood through which individuals select a vocation, decide how they fit into a peer group, and choose what kind of person they want to be.

identity confusion Mixed feelings in the absence of firm decisions about where one fits into society in terms of a vocation, peer group, and so on.

identity foreclosure A premature ending of the search for identity by making decisions without first exploring and thinking through many different options.

identity moratorium A temporary stopping of the search for identity, sometimes due to the desire to avoid going through the conflicts associated with making major decisions.

idiopathic growth retardation Growth retardation that is caused by hormonal problems rather than other disease or lesions.

imaginary audience Elkind's description of adolescent egocentrism in which adolescents imagine that everyone looks at and thinks about them as much as they look at and think about themselves.

imitation The copying of another's behavior.

immersion An approach to second language learning in which the learner is placed in close contact with native speakers and is expected to pick up the language without special instruction.

immunoglobulins Proteins that are responsible for the body's resistance to specific diseases.

independent reader Someone who has become skillful in coordinating the various cues used in reading.

independent variable The variable in an experimental study that is changed to see if it has an effect on other variables.

induction Used by Hoffman to refer to a particular socialization procedure in which the child is helped to see the effects of his behavior on others.

inflection Changes in the endings of words to indicate singular or plural or tense.

information-processing view of intellectual development A view that contrasts with Piaget's and that stresses increases in memory and rules learned from experience rather than qualitative differences captured by the notion of stages.

informed consent Consent given for participation in a research study after receiving detailed information about the study's procedures and possible detrimental effects.

instinct According to Freud, the mental representation of body states and needs.

instrumental aggression Aggressive acts committed for the purpose of obtaining some reward.

instrumental conditioning Conditioning that results from the use of rewards and punishments following a behavior.

integration of play Complex combining of themes in pretend play.

intelligence quotient A score computed by considering a person's chronological age in relation to his or her mental age as determined on an intelligence test.

interference theory Refers to a theory of second language acquisition in which the child is assumed to use knowledge of his or her first language when learning a second language.

internal locus of control Refers to an individual's view that his or her own actions are what affect life's events.

internal validity Refers to characteristics of the design of a research study that determine whether the researcher can infer correlation or causation, for example.

intrinsic motivation Motivation that comes from within the person rather than from external rewards.

intrinsic reinforcement Reinforcement that comes from the individual's own pleasure following a behavior rather than from praise or tokens provided by others.

intuitive Behavior based on what seems or feels right rather than on well thought-out logic.

irreversibility The inability of young children to play back an action in their heads to recreate an original position of objects, for example.

joint custody A legal agreement that stipulates a child spend time living with both parents.

kernicterus Staining of the brain with bilirubin.

Kuder General Interest Survey, Form E An instrument used to measure an individual's aptitude for various occupations.

lanugo The covering of hair typical on newborn infants.

lateralization of the brain The specialization of functions on one side of the brain over the other.

letter-name spelling strategy Exploitation of the sound information found within letter names to create unconventional spellings.

lexically based ambiguity Language ambiguity caused by double meanings for some words and by words that are pronounced the same even though they are spelled differently.

libido Another name for sex drive.

locomotor skills Motor skills that involve movement using the legs and feet.

longitudinal design A research design used in developmental research in which the same group of children is studied over a period of time.

"look-say" method of teaching reading A teaching method that relies primarily on the teaching of sight words rather than decoding skills.

mainstreaming The placement of children with special needs in classrooms with children who are not disabled.

malocclusion Misalignment of the teeth that often is corrected by wearing braces.

marked-time climbing The procedure of climbing in which both feet are placed on each step before one foot is placed on the next step.

maturation Physical changes attributed to genetic control.

meninges The lining surrounding the spinal cord and brain.

mental age The child's level of functioning as measured by an IQ test.

metacognition Thinking that is about thinking.

metacognitive Having to do with the ability to think about thinking.

metalinguistic awareness A specific aspect of metacogniton that refers to awareness of the structure and form of language.

mild mental retardation A measured IQ between 50 and 70.

mock letters Marks used by young children to write. These marks contain features of conventional letters, but in combinations other than those that define actual alphabet letters.

modeling Term used by social learning theorists to refer to demonstrations of behavior that can be observed and repeated by others.

moderate mental retardation Measured IQ within the range of 34 to 50.

molded A characteristic of an infant's head that results from the skull being squeezed together as it passes through the birth canal.

moral realism The term used by Piaget to refer to the young child's tendency to confuse physical damage and intention in making moral judgments.

Moro reflex Movement caused by a sudden dropping back of the head or by loud noises.

morpheme The smallest unit of meaning in a language.

morphological rules Rules that govern how words can be changed to alter their meaning. Changes in verb tenses, for example, are morphological changes.

multifactorial causation Multiple causes rather than a single cause.

multischeme combinations Complex pretend play in which a variety of actions pertaining to a play theme are combined.

mutual role-taking Term used by Selman to refer to the ability to stand back and think about your own thinking and another's thinking, all at the same time.

myelin The fatty substance that coats the outer surface of neurons and makes impulses travel efficiently.

myelination The process whereby the fatty sheath is formed on the outside of neurons.

nature-nurture controversy The debate about whether genetic inheritance or environment exerts the most influence over development.

negative identity Description applied to individuals who have chosen to align themselves with characteristics held in disdain by the larger culture.

negative reinforcement Something withdrawn from the environment following a behavior, which has the effect of increasing the frequency of that behavior in the future.

negatively correlated The relationship between two variables when an increase in one results in a decrease in the other.

neglected status A sociometric rating in which a child receives few like or dislike nominations from peers.

neonate An infant under one month of age.

neonatal period The period from birth up to one month after birth.

Neurological Examination of the Full-Term Newborn Infant Assessment instrument developed by Pretchel to determine the neurological integrity of the newborn.

neurological ripening Refers to maturation of the nervous system controlled by genes.

neurons The type of cells found in the brain.

non-custodial parent The parent the child does not live with following a divorce.

norm Age-related expectations for behavior that are established by determining when half of the children of a given age can perform the behavior.

object permanence Refers to knowing that objects out of sight still exist.

observational learning Learning by watching others.

open observation methods Methods in which little is decided beforehand and the observer tries to note all that occurs.

operant conditioning Changes in behavior brought about by the responses that follow specific behaviors.

operational A description of Piaget's third level of intellectual thinking in which logic—thinking processes—overrule perception.

orthography A writing system for representing an oral language.

ossification The process of mineral deposition in bones.

Otis-Lennon Mental Ability Test A group intelligence test.

otitis-media Infection of the middle ear.

overextend What children do with words when they apply them outside the boundaries of accepted meaning.

overgeneralize The application of a rule of language, or of a word meaning, beyond the accepted range.

palmar grasp Reflex in which the fingers fold inward toward the palm of the hand when the palm is stroked or pushed.

partitioning error A counting error that results from

failure to distinguish objects that already have been counted from those still needing to be counted.

perinatal Referring to the time period immediately after birth.

period of the embryo The time period from implantation to the eighth prenatal week.

period of the fetus The time period from the eighth prenatal week to birth.

permissive parenting Parenting behavior marked by few expectations for and little control of child behavior.

personal fable The belief of adolescents that bad things happen to other people, not to them.

phoneme The smallest unit of sound in a language.

phonemic awareness The child's conscious awareness of the individual sounds within words.

phonics approach to reading Teaching technique that stresses decoding skills versus sight words or prediction strategies.

phonologically based ambiguity Language ambiguity based on how things sound.

phototherapy A procedure used to reduce bilirubin in the blood of newborn infants.

pincer grasp Grasp formed by juxtaposing the thumb and forefinger.

popular status Sociometric rating in which a child receives many like nominations from peers.

positive correlation Two variables that are related, such that when one increases, the other increases or when one decreases, the other decreases.

positive reinforcement Something that is added to the environment after a behavior is exhibited, which results in an increase in the behavior.

post-divorce stage of adjustment This is the final of three stages of response to a divorce in which new patterns of family living have been established in the family.

preadolescent growth spurt Rapid increase in growth, particularly in height, that occurs just prior to puberty.

predictable text Text that has a high level of rhyming words or repeated phrases, which make it easy to remember.

prehesion Grasping with hands.

prelinguistic Refers to vocal behavior prior to the stage when real words are used.

premature babies Babies born before the typical period of gestation has passed. Typically, babies born before the thirty-eighth week.

prenatal Prior to birth.

prenatal development Development that occurs prior to birth.

preoperational thinking Piaget's second level of intellectual development, during which thinking is dominated by perception rather than logic.

preprogrammed Refers to neurological structures that are thought to be innate.

pretense Pretend.

pretesting Data collection on variables of interest prior to a treatment.

primary rewards Things that satisfy primary drives, such as hunger or sex.

primary sex characteristics Bodily changes that are vital to preparing for reproduction versus the accompanying changes such as growth of pubic and facial hair.

productive speech Refers to the language the person says or produces versus the language a person can understand.

profound mental retardation Extreme deficits in mental ability—measured IQ below 35.

projective space An aspect of space having to do with the point of view or the vantage point from which something is seen.

prosocial Positive social behavior such as helping and sharing.

protowords Short strings of consonant-vowel combinations that sound like words.

proximodistal trend The development of muscular control that proceeds from the center of the body to the extremities, such as the hands.

pseudoimitation Repetition of a behavior that is already in the child's repertoire.

pubescence The period prior to puberty—sexual maturity—marked by rapid growth and other physical changes.

punishment In operant theory, any response that has the effect of reducing a behavior.

Raven Progressive Matrices Test One of the intelligence tests designed to be culture-fair.

reaction time The time it takes for the individual to process an event and make some response, such as swinging a bat at a pitched ball.

readiness Usually means a certain level of development assumed to be achieved by maturation of the nervous system.

reading readiness An outdated term that was once used to refer to levels of development thought necessary before children could learn about written language.

receptive speech The language a person can understand.

recessive Refers to a specific kind of gene whose trait is not expressed unless it is paired with a second gene of the same type.

reflexes Involuntary movements elicited by specific stimuli.

regression toward the mean A statistical term that means extremes or exceptions tend not to be maintained.

reinforcement Any response to a behavior that has the effect of increasing the behavior.

reliability The extent to which data collected at one time or by one researcher would agree with data collected at another time or by another researcher.

representational thinking The ability to think using symbols rather than having to think through sensorimotor actions.

representative sample A sample that includes people with the range of characteristics needed to generalize the study's results to the general population.

research bias The influence on a study's results that comes from the researcher's views, not from the data.

response costs Refers to punishment using the removal of rewards.

retrolental fibroplasia blindness Blindness often found in severely premature infants who have been given oxygen for long periods of time.

reversals Letters written in mirror image or upside-down, which are frequently characteristic of the writing of preschool and young elementary-age children.

reversibility The characteristic of thinking that allows one to replay an action in his or her mind.

risk factor Some characteristic of a group that increases its members' chances of having developmental problems.

role confusion A problem adolescents can encounter as they develop their identity. Characterized by an inability to commit to an occupational choice, for example.

rooming-in The arrangement made in hospital maternity wards for newborns to stay in the mother's room for long periods instead of remaining in the infant nursery.

rooting reflex The movement involving turning of the head and searching with the mouth, following stroking of the cheek.

scheme Term used by Piaget to refer to an organized pattern of behavior.

School and College Ability Tests The publisher of the SAT tests, which are frequently used as part of the application package for college admissions.

scribble writing Wavy lines or tight bunches of lines that capture the linear nature of print but lack specific alphabet letters.

secondary rewards Something that is present when a primary reinforcer satisfies a primary need, such that in time it, too, becomes a reinforcer.

secondary sex characteristics Physical changes that are not directly related to reproductive capacity.

secular growth trend The trend toward increases in height with each succeeding generation.

secure attachment The pattern of behaviors thought to characterize the optimal relationship between adult and child.

self-reflective role-taking Selman's description of his Stage 2 in which children can think about their own

thoughts or another's thoughts, but not simultaneously.

semantic cues used in reading Reliance on the meaning of words to predict and monitor one's reading.

sensorimotor period Piaget's first period of intellectual development, which lasts from birth up to about 24 months of age.

separation distress Upset state resulting when an infant's primary caregiver leaves.

seriation The ability to place items in order according to size.

severe mental retardation A term used in educational circles to refer to profound retardation.

sex differences Differences in personality, cognition, and social behavior that have been found to be related to gender.

sex-linked inheritance Inherited characteristics due to genes carried on the X or Y chromosome.

sex-role stereotypes Specific social behavior and statuses assigned and assumed on the basis of gender.

sex roles Sets of social and occupational behaviors commonly found more often in members of one sex than in members of the opposite sex.

sexually transmitted diseases (STDs) Diseases transmitted through sexual intercourse or other sexual behavior.

shaping The technique of using rewards to gradually develop a desired behavior.

shared meaning An understanding between toddlers about the social game they're playing.

single-scheme combinations A type of pretend play in which the child confines actions to a single idea, such as feeding a baby.

skills approach to the teaching of reading Any of the approaches that focus on identifying words specifically versus relying on context or language to predict.

small-for-date baby A baby who is full term but who, for nutritional or other reasons, hasn't attained a normal birth weight.

social and conventional system of role-taking The highest level in Selman's scheme, which is characterized by the ability to think about another's view in terms of the view held by others in the social system.

social cognition Thinking about social phenomena.

social games Repetitive actions involving two children or an adult and child.

social information role-taking Selman's stage in which children realize that they see a situation differently than someone else, but assume the different views are due to differing information.

social learning theory A branch of behavioral theory that stresses observational learning.

social referencing The use of adult facial expressions by infants to make judgments about the safety of new situations or people.

social role-taking ability The ability to think about what another person is thinking or to understand what another person is feeling.

social smile Smile elicited by social stimuli.

socialization The processes by which children learn to behave according to social expectations and standards.

sociodramatic play A type of pretend play involving several children who adopt different roles.

somatic cells All cells in the body except those involved in reproduction.

sphincters Circular muscles that control the opening of the bladder and anus, for example.

Stanford-Binet Intelligence Scale One of the most frequently used, individually administered, standard intelligence tests for children.

stranger anxiety Distress shown by infants, beginning around 6 months of age, toward unfamiliar adults.

Strong-Campbell Interest Inventory A measurement tool that is commonly used to determine an individual's likes and dislikes as they might relate to different occupations.

sucking reflex The expression-suction motion that is elicited in an infant when the roof of the mouth is stroked or pressed.

superego The part of the personality thought by Freud to serve as the conscience to control impulses of the id.

suprasegmental features of language Features having to do with intonation and stress.

surfactant Substance in the lungs that prevents collapse after a breath is exhaled, the absence of which creates problems in premature infants.

syllabic hypothesis A hypothesis entertained by young children when they write words by using one mark for every "beat," or syllable, contained within a word.

symbolic representation Thinking by manipulating ideas or images in one's head.

syntactic cues used in reading Cues that come from the reader's knowledge of the grammar of his or her language.

syntactically based ambiguity Language ambiguity derived from the different ways a sentence can be interpreted.

syntax Refers to the basic rules in a language that govern the grammatical organization of sentences.

tags Term used to refer to number words used in counting.

target The term used to indicate the thing, person, or situation that elicits a feeling from an individual.

task facilitation plan A technique for reducing temptation in which children are taught to focus on a task.

teacher-directed education An approach in which children are given little leeway to make decisions or follow their interests.

teen slang Language coined by adolescents to set their culture apart from adult culture.

telegraphic speech A characteristic of toddler speech that refers to the presence of only those words necessary for getting the message across.

temperament Basic pattern of behaving characterized by things such as activity level, irritability level, and degree of inhibition and thought to be determined primarily by inheritance.

temptation inhibition plan A technique for reducing temptation in which the child is taught to think about something else.

teratogens Chemicals or other agents, such as irradiation, that cause defects in the developing fetus.

theme Refers to the content of a play episode—what the playing is about.

theory Sets of hypotheses used to explain phenomena.

Three R's Test An achievement test used with elementary school children.

time out A form of punishment in which the individual is removed from situations in which rewards prevail.

tonic neck reflex A reflex exhibited in infants in which the leg and arm on the side of the body the head faces are extended, while the leg and arm on the other side are flexed.

tonus Muscle tension.

tracking An educational term that refers to the practice of placing students of similar achievement and ability levels together for instruction.

trainable mentally retarded A description used by educators to refer to moderately retarded individuals.

transitional stage of adjustment to divorce The middle period between the first adjustment to the divorce and a later period of settling into new patterns of family relationships.

trophoblast That part of the developing mass of cells formed from the zygote that will become the tissues that support a developing fetus.

ultrasound Sound waves moving so fast that they can't be heard. The sound waves that are transformed into images to visualize a baby in utero.

unconditioned response A response that naturally follows a specific stimulus.

unconditioned stimulus A stimulus that naturally leads to a given response.

underextend What children do when they don't apply a word as broadly as the word's meaning actually allows.

unique grammatical structures theory A theory of second language acquisition in which it is assumed that the learner doesn't apply knowledge from his first language and doesn't approach it the way a first language learner would either.

unpopular status A sociometric category for individuals who receive many dislike nominations from peers—they are rejected by peers.

valence Used by researchers who study emotions to refer to positive or negative emotions.

validity The extent to which instruments measure what they are intended to measure.

variable Something that is changed or changes to take on a different value or form.

variance A difference between groups.

varicella vaccine A vaccine developed to prevent the viral infection known as chicken pox.

vernix caseosa The greasy white covering common on newborns that lubricates their skin and protects them from infection.

Wechsler Intelligence Scale for Children A well-known intelligence test.

whole language approach to the teaching of reading An approach that stresses the use of context and language knowledge more than decoding strategies that focus on individual words.

zygote The cell that results when an ovum is fertilized by a sperm.

REFERENCES

Acredolo, L. P. (1978). Development of spatial orientation in infancy. *Developmental Psychology, 14*, 224–234.

Adelson, J. (1975). The development of ideology in adolescence. In S. E. Dragastin & G. H. Elder (Eds.), *Adolescence in the life cycle*. Washington, DC: Hemisphere.

Aiken, L. R. (1982). Writing multiple-choice items to measure higher-order educational objectives. *Educational and Psychological Measurement, 42*, 803–806.

——. (1985). Review of ACT Assessment Program. In J. V. Mitchell (Ed.), *The ninth mental measurement yearbook*. Lincoln, NB: University of Nebraska Press.

Ainsworth, M., & Wittig, B. (1969). Attachment and exploratory behavior of one-year-olds in a strange situation. In B. Foss (Ed.), *Determinants of infant behavior* (Vol. 4). New York: Barnes & Noble.

Ainsworth, M. D. S., & Bell, S. M. (1973). Mother-infant interaction and the development of competence. In K. Connolly & J. Bruner (Eds.), *The growth of competence*. New York: Academic Press.

Ainsworth, M. D. S., Blehar, M. D., Waters, E., & Wall, S. (1978). *Patterns of attachment*. Hillsdale, NJ: Lawrence Erlbaum.

Aleksandrowicz, M. K., & Aleksandrowicz, D. R. (1974). Obstetrical pain-relieving drugs as predictors of infant behavior variability. *Child Development, 45*, 935–958.

Als, H. (1977). The newborn communicates. *Journal of Communication, 27*(2), 66–73.

AMA Council on Scientific Affairs. (1981). Marijuana: Its health hazards and therapeutic potentials. *Journal of the American Medical Association, 246*, 1823–1877.

American College Testing Program. (1984). *Counselor's handbook*. Iowa City, IA: American College Testing Program.

American Psychiatric Association. (1987). Diagnostics and Statistical Manual of Mental Disorders. (3rd ed. revised). Washington, D.C.

Ames, L. B. (1937). The sequential patterning of prone progression in the human infant. *Genetic Psychology Monographs, 19*, 409–460.

Anderson, A. B., Teale, W. H., & Estrada, E. (1980). Low income children's preschool literacy experience: Some naturalistic observations. *The Quarterly Newsletter of the Laboratory of Comparative Human Cognition, 2*, 59–65.

Anderson, D. R., Field, D. E., Collins, P. A., Lorch, E. P., and Nathan, J. C. (1985). Estimates of young children's time with television: A methodological comparison of parent reports with time-lapse video home observation. *Child Development, 56*, 1345–1357.

Angrist, S. S. (1969). The study of sex roles. *Journal of Social Issues, 25*, 215–232.

Anisfeld, E. (1982). The onset of social smiling in preterm and full-term infants from two ethnic backgrounds. *Infant Behavior and Development, 5*, 387–395.

APA Task Force on Pediatric AIDS. (1989). Pediatric AIDS and human immunodeficiency virus infection: Psychological issues. *American Psychologist, 44*(2), 258–264.

Apgar, V. (1953). Proposal for a new method of evaluating the newborn infant. *Anesthesia and Analgesia, 52,* 260–267.

Appel, M., & Campos, J. J. (1977). Binocular disparity as a discriminable stimulus parameter for young infants. *Journal of Experimental Child Psychology, 23,* 47–56.

Applebee, A. N., Langer, J. A., & Mullis, V. S. (1986). *The writing report card: Writing achievement in American schools.* Princeton, NJ: Educational Testing Service.

Archer, J., & Lopata, A. (1979). Marijuana revisited. *Personnel and Guidance Journal, 51,* 244–250.

Ariagno, R. L. (1984). Evaluation and management of infantile apnea. *Pediatric Annals, 13* (3), 210–211.

Aro, H., & Taipale, V. (1987). The impact of timing of puberty on psychosomatic symptoms among fourteen-to-sixteen-year-old Finnish girls. *Child Development, 58*(1), 261–268.

Asher, S. R., & Dodge, K. A. (1986). Identifying children who are rejected by their peers. *Developmental Psychology, 22*(4), 444–449.

Astington, J. W., Harris, P. L., & Olson, D. (Eds.). (1988). *Developing theories of mind.* New York: Cambridge University Press.

Attel, I., & Brooks-Gunn, J. (1988). Development of eating problems in adolescent girls: A longitudinal study. *Developmental Psychology, 25*(1), 70–79.

Bailey, S. M. (Ed.). (1986). When school is out and nobody's home. *Research Report* (Wellesley College Center for Research on Women, Wellesley, MA), 5(2), 1.

Bailey, W. J. (1985). Ten smoking education programs for schools. *Journal of School Health, 55*(1), 33–34.

Baillargeon, R. (1987). Letter to the Editor. *Cognition, 26,* 189–190.

Baillargeon, R., Spelke, E. S., & Wasserman, S. (1985). Object permanence in five-month-old infants. *Cognition, 20,* 191–208.

Baker, D. P., & Entwisle, D. R. (1986). The influence of mothers on the academic expectations of young children: A longitudinal study of how gender differences arise. *Social Forces, 65,* 670–694.

Bandura, A. (1973). *Aggression: A social learning analysis.* Englewood Cliffs, NJ: Prentice-Hall.

———. (1977). *Social learning theory.* Englewood Cliffs, NJ: Prentice-Hall.

Bandura, A., & Mischell, W. (1965). Modifications of self-imposed delay of reward through exposure to live and symbolic models. *Journal of Personality and Psychology, 2,* 698–705.

Bandura, A., & Walters, R. (1963). *Social learning and personality development.* New York: Holt, Reinhart & Winston.

Banks, M.S. (1980). The development of early infancy. *Child Development, 51,* 646–666.

Banks, M. S., & Salapatek, P. (1983). Infant visual perception. In P. Mussen (Ed.), *Handbook of child psychology: Vol. 2. Infancy and developmental psychobiology* (4th ed., pp. 435–571). New York: Wiley.

Barcus, E. F., & McLaughlin, L. (1978). *Food advertising on children's television: An analysis of appeals and nutritional content.* Newtonville, MA: Action of Children's Television.

Barden, R. C., Zelko, F. A., Duncan, S. W., & Masters, J. C. (1980). Children's consensual knowledge about the experiential determinants of emotion. *Journal of Personality and Social Psychology, 39,* 968–976.

Barnes, F., & Hassid, P. (1985, Fall). Bradley/Lamaze. *Childbirth Educator,* Special Issue, 40–47.

Barnes, G. M. (1984). Adolescent alcohol abuse and other problem behaviors: Their relationships and common parental influences. *Journal of Youth Adolescence, 13*(4), 329–348.

Baroody, A. (1987). *Children's mathematical thinking.* New York: Teachers College Press.

Bates, E. (1979). *The emergence of symbols.* New York: Academic Press.

Baumeister, A. A. (1987). Mental retardation. *American Psychologist, 42*(8), 796–800.

Baumrind, D. (1971). Current patterns of parental authority. *Developmental Psychology Monographs, 4*(1), 72.

———. (1972). *Socialization and instrumental competence in young children.* In W. W. Hartup (Ed.), *The young child: Reviews of research* (Vol. 2, pp. 202–274). Washington, DC: The National Association for the Education of Young Children.

Baumrind, D., & Block, A. E. (1967). Socialization and practices associated with dimensions of competence in preschool boys and girls. *Child Development, 38,* 291–329.

Bayley, N. (1969). *Bayley scales of infant development: Manual.* New York: The Psychological Corporation.

Beaty, J. J. (1986). *Observing the development of the young child.* Columbus, OH: Merrill.

Bee, H. (1978). Overview: Sex differences. In H. Bee (Ed.), *Social issues in developmental psychology* (2nd ed.). New York: Harper & Row.

Bell, D. C., & Bell, L. G. (1983). Parental validation and support in the development of adolescent daughters. In H. D. Grotevant and C. R. Cooper (Eds.), *Adolescent development in the family.* San Francisco: Jossey-Bass.

Bell, R. D., Pincus, J. K., Swenson, N. M., Sanford, W. C., Pfeufer, R., & Cane, B. (1973). *Our bodies, ourselves.* New York: Simon & Schuster.

Bell, T. W. (1971). Stimulus control of parent or caretaker behavior by offspring. *Developmental Psychology, 4,* 63–72.

Belmont, J. M., & Butterfield, E. C. (1971). Learning strategies as determinants of memory deficiencies. *Cognitive Psychology, 2*, 411–420.

Belsky, J. (1984) The determinants of parenting: A process model. *Child Development, 55*, 83–96.

———. (1988). The effects of infant day care, reconsidered. *Early Childhood Research Quarterly, 3* (3), 235–272.

Belsky, J., & Rovine, M. (1988). Nonmaternal care in the first year of life and infant-parent attachment security. *Child Development, 59*, 157–176.

Beltramini, A. V., & Hertzig, M. E. (1983). Sleep and bedtime behavior in preschool-aged children. *Pediatrics, 71*(2), 153–158.

Bennett, W. J. (1987a). *James Madison High School*. Pueblo, CO: U. S. Government Printing Office.

Bennett, W. J. (1987b). *What works? Schools without drugs*. Pueblo, CO: U. S. Government Printing Office.

Berger, M. J., & Goldstein, D. P. (1980). Impaired reproductive performance in DES-exposed women. *Obstetrics and Gynecology, 55*, 25–27.

Berkowitz, L., & LePage, A. (1967). Weapons as aggression—eliciting stimuli. *Journal of Personality and Social Psychology, 1*, 202–207.

Berkowitz, R. L., Agras, W. St., Korner, A. F., Kraemer, H. C., & Zeanah, C. H. (1985). Physical activity and adiposity: A longitudinal study from birth to childhood. *Journal of Pediatrics, 106*(5), 734–738.

Berryman, C., & Schneider, D. (1982). *Patterns of work experience among high school students: Educational implications*. Paper presented at the Annual Meeting of the National Council for the Social Studies, Boston, MA.

Bertenthal, B. J., & Campos, J. J. (1987). New directions in the study of early experience. *Child Development, 58*(3), 560–567.

Bever, R. G., Mehler, J. H., & Vallian, V. (1974). Linguistic capacity of very young children. In T. G. Bever and W. Weksel (Eds.), *The acquisition of structure*. New York: Holt, Rinehart & Winston.

Bever, T. G. (1970). The cognitive basis for linguistic structures. In J. R. Hayes (Ed.), *Cognition and the development of language*. New York: Wiley.

Binet, A., & Simon, T. (1905). Methodes nouvelles pour le diagnostic du niveau intellectual des anormous [New methods for diagnosing children's intellectual development]. *L'Année Psychologique, 11*, 191–244.

Bissex, G. (1980). *GYNS at work: A child learns to write and read*. Cambridge, MA: Harvard University Press.

Blass, E. M., Ganchrow, J. R., & Steiner, J. E. (1984). Classical conditioning in newborn humans 2–48 hours of age. *Infant Behavior and Development, 7*, 223–235.

Blehar, M. C. (1974). Anxious attachment and defensive reactions associated with day care. *Child Development, 45*, 683–692.

Block, J. H. (1973). Conceptions of sex role: Some cross-cultural and longitudinal perspectives. *American Psychologist, 28*, 512–576.

Bloom, B. S. (1984). Changing infant mortality: The need to spend more while getting less. *Pediatrics, 73*(6), 862–865.

Bloom, L., Lightbown, P., & Hood, L. (1975). Imitation in language development. *Monographs of the Society for Research in Child Development, 40* (Serial No. 160).

Blume, J. (1970). *Are you there God? It's me, Margaret* (p. 100). New York: Bradbury Press.

Blumenthal, S. J., & Kupfer, D. J. (1988). Overview of early detection and treatment strategies for suicidal behavior in young people. *Journal of Youth and Adolescence, 17*(1), 1–17.

Bodner, B., Benjamin, A., McLean, F. H., & Usher, R. H. (1986). Has use of cesarean section reduced the risks of delivery in the preterm breech presentation? *American Journal of Obstetrics and Gynecology, 154*(2), 244–249.

Bonica, J. J. (1967). *Principles and practices of obstetric analgesia and anesthesia*. (Vol. 1). Philadelphia: Davis.

Borke, H. (1971). Interpersonal perception of young children: Egocentrism or empathy? *Developmental Psychology, 5*, 263–269.

Bornstein, M., & Sigman, M. (1986). Continuity in mental development from infancy. *Child Development, 57*(2), 251–274.

Bower, T. G. R. (1974). *Development in infancy*. San Francisco: W. H. Freeman.

———. (1977). *A primer of infant development*. San Francisco: W. H. Freeman.

Bowlby, J. (1969a). *Attachment*. New York: Basic Books.

———. (1969b). *Attachment and loss: Vol. 1, Attachment*. London: Hogarth.

Bowman, C. M., & Peng, S. S. (1972). *A preliminary investigation of recent advanced psychology tests in the GRE program—an application of a cognitive classification system*. Unpublished ETS report, Princeton, NJ.

Brackbill, Y., Kane, J., Manniello, R. L., & Abramson, D.(1974). Obstetric premedication and infant outcome. *American Journal of Obstetrics and Gynecology, 118*, 377–384.

Bradley, L., & Bryant, P. (1983). Categorizing sounds and learning to read: A causal connection. *Nature, 301*, 491–521.

Bradley, R. H., Caldwell, B. M., & Rock, S. L. (1988). Home environment and school performance: A ten-year follow-up and examination of three models of environmental action. *Child Development, 59*(1), 852–867.

Brainerd, C. J. (1978). *Piaget's theory of intelligence*. Englewood Cliffs, NJ: Prentice-Hall.

Branigan, G., & Stokes, W. (1976). Introduction: A sketch of language development. *Journal of Education, 158*, 4–11.

Brazelton, T. B. (1961). Psychophysiologic reactions in the neonate. *The Journal of Pediatrics, 58,* 513–518.

_____. (1969). *Infants and mothers.* New York: Delacorte/Seymour Lawrence.

_____. (1970). Effects of prenatal drugs on the behavior of the neonate. *American Journal of Psychiatry, 126,* 95–100.

_____. (1973a). *Neonatal assessment scale.* Philadelphia: J. B. Lippincott.

_____. (1973b). *Neonatal behavioral assessment scale.* London: Heinemann.

Brazy, J. E. (1988). Effects of crying on cerebral blood volume and cytochrome aa3. *Journal of Pediatrics, 112*(3), 457–461.

Brehm, S. S. (1981). Oppositional behavior in children: A reactance theory approach. In S. S. Brehm, S. M. Kassin, & F. X. Gibbons (Eds.), *Developmental social psychology theory* (pp. 96–121). New York: Oxford University Press.

Brennan, W. M., Ames, E. W., & Moore, R. W. (1966). Age differences in infants' attention to patterns of different complexities. *Science, 151,* 354–356.

Brenner, J., & Mueller, E. (1982). Shared meaning in boy toddlers' peer relations. *Child Development, 53*(2), 380–391.

Bretherton, I. (1984). Representing the social world in symbolic play: Reality and fantasy. In I. Bretherton (Ed.), *Symbolic play* (pp. 3–41). New York: Academic Press.

Bretherton, I., Fritz, J., Zahn-Waxler, C., & Ridgeway, D. (1986). Learning to talk about emotions: A functionalist perspective. *Child Development, 57,* 529–548.

Brittain, C. (1963). Adolescent choice and parent-peer cross-pressures. *American Sociological Review, 28,* 385–391.

Brockman, L. M., Ricciuti, H. N. (1971). Severe protein-calorie malnutrition and cognitive development in infancy and early childhood. *Developmental Psychology, 4,* 312–319.

Bronson, W. (1981). *Toddlers' behaviors with agemates: Issues of interaction, cognition and affect.* Norwood, NJ: Ablex.

Brook, C. G. B., Huntley, R. M. C., & Slack, J. (1975). Influences of heredity and environments in determination of skinfold thickness in children. *British Medical Journal, 2,* 719–721.

Brookhart, J., & Hock, E. (1976). The effects of experimental context and experiential background on infants' behavior toward their mothers and a stranger. *Child Development, 47,* 333–340.

Brooks-Gunn, J., Boyer, C. B., & Hein, K. (1988). Preventing HIV infection and AIDS in children and adolescents: Behavioral research and intervention strategies. *American Psychologist, 43*(11), 958–964.

Brooks-Gunn, J., & Furstenberg, F. F. (1989). Adolescent sexual behavior. *American Psychologist, 4*(2), 249–257.

Brown, A. L., & Day, J. D. (1983). Macrorules for summarizing texts: The development of expertise. *Journal of Verbal Learning and Verbal Behavior, 22,* 1–14.

Brown, A. L., & Smiley, S. S. (1977). Rating the importance of structural units of prose passages: A problem of metacognitive development. *Child Development, 48,* 1–8; 1088–1096.

_____. (1978). The development of strategies for studying texts. *Child Development, 49,* 1076–1088.

Brown, J. V., & Bateman, R. (1978). Relationships of human others with their infants during the first year of life: Effects of prematurity. In R. W. Bell & W. P. Smotherman (Eds.), *Maternal influences and early behavior.* Holliswood, NY: Spectrum.

Brown, R. (1973). *A first language.* Cambridge, MA: Harvard University Press.

Brown, R., & Fraser, C. (1964). The acquisition of syntax. In U. Bellugi & R. Brown (Eds.), The Acquisition of Language. *Monographs of the Society for Research in Child Development, 29,* 43–79.

Brown, R., & Hanlon, C. (1970). Derivational complexity and order of acquisition in child speech. In J. R. Hayes (Ed.), *Cognition and the development of language.* New York: Wiley.

Brown, R. H. (1980). Marital discord and divorce. In S. B. Friedman & R. A. Hockelman (Eds.), *Behavioral pediatrics: Psychosocial aspects of child health care* (pp. 255–258). New York: McGraw-Hill.

Brown, W. A. (1979). *Psychological care during pregnancy and the postpartum period.* New York: Raven.

Brownell, K. D., Kelman, J. H., & Stunkard, A. J. (1983). Treatment of obese children with and without their mothers. Changes in weight and blood pressure. *Pediatrics, 71,* 515–523.

Bruce, B., & Michaels, S. (1988, October). *Different ways of talking, doing, and learning science—in that order: A preliminary exploration.* Paper presented at the 13th Annual Boston University Conference on Language Development, Boston, MA.

Brunell, P. A., Novelli, V. M., Lipton, S. V., & Pollock, B. (1988). Combined vaccine against measles, mumps, rubella, and varicella. *Pediatrics, 81*(6), 779–789.

Bruner, J. S. (1975a). From communication to language—A psychological perspective. *Cognition, 3,* 255–287.

_____. (1975b). The ontogenesis of speech acts. *Journal of Child Language, 2,* 1–19.

Bryan, J. H., & Schwartz, T. (1971). Effects of film material upon children's behavior. *Psychological Bulletin, 75,* 50–59.

Bryan, J. H., & Walbek, N. H. (1970a). Preaching and practicing generosity: Children's actions and reactions. *Child Development, 41,* 329–353.

_____. (1970b). The impact of words and deeds concerning altruism upon children. *Child Development, 41,* 747–757.

Buckley, N., Siegel, L. S., & Ness, S. (1979). Egocentrism, empathy, and altruistic behavior in young children. *Developmental Psychology, 15*, 329–330.

Bumpers, D. (1984). Securing the blessings of liberty for posterity: Preventive health care for children. *American Psychologist, 39*(8), 896–900.

Butarescu, G. F. (1978). *Perinatal nursing: Vol. 1. Reproductive health.* New York: Wiley.

Butler, R. A. (1953). Discrimination learning by rhesus monkeys to visual exploration motivation. *Journal of Comparative Physiological Psychology, 46*, 95–98.

Caesareans up. (1987, November 3). *San Jose Mercury News*, pp. 1, 16A.

Caldwell, B. M. (1970). *Preschool inventory.* Princeton, NJ: Educational Testing Service.

Calwell, J. (1984). A baby-safe home: What you can do to keep your toddler from getting hurt. *The Boston Globe*, p. 6.

Calvert, S. L., & Wright, J. C. (1982). *Relation of age, sex, and SES to children's patterns of home television viewing.* Paper presented at the Biennial Meeting of the Southwestern Society for Research in Human Development, Galveston, TX.

Campbell, A. V. (1984). Ethical issues in prenatal diagnosis. *British Medical Journal, 288*, 1633–1634.

Campos, J. J., Barret, K. C., Lamb, M. E., Goldsmith, H. H., & Stenberg, C. (1983). Socioemotional Development. In Paul H. Mussen (Ed.), *Handbook of child psychology* (4th ed). New York: Wiley.

Campos, J. J., Hiatt, S., Ramsay, D., Henderson, C., & Svejda, M. (1978). The emergence of fear on the visual cliff. In M. Lewis & L. Rosenblum (Eds.), *The development of affect*, (pp. 149–182). New York: Plenum Press.

Cannon, C. (1989, February 12). Children: A growing concern in Congress. *San Jose Mercury News*, p. 14.

Carlson, V., Barnett, D., Cicchetti, D., & Braunwald, K. (1989). Disorganized/disoriented attachment relationships in maltreated infants. *Developmental Psychology, 25*(4), 525–531.

Carlsson, S. G., Fagerberg, H., Horneman, G., Hwange, C. P., Larsson, K., Rodgab, M., Schaller, J., Danielsson, B., & Gundewall, C. (1978). Effects of amount of contact between mother and child on the mother's nursing behavior. *Developmental Psychology, 11*, 143–150.

Carter, A. (1975). The transformation of sensorimotor morphemes into words: A case study of the development of "more" and "mine." *Journal of Child Language, 2*, 233–250.

Cashore, W. J., & Stern, L. (1982). Neonatal hyperbilirubinemia. *Pediatric Clinics of North America, 29*(5), 1191–1203.

Caspi, A., Bem, D. J., & Elder, G. H. (1987). Moving against the world: Life-course patterns of explosive children. *Developmental Psychology, 23*(2), 308–313.

Cattell, R. B., & Cattell, A. K. S. (1973). *Culture-Fair Intelligence Test.* Champaign, IL: Institute for Personality and Ability Testing.

Cavior, N., & Dokecki, P. R. (1973). Physical attractiveness, perceived attitude similarity, and academic achievement as contributors to interpersonal attractiveness among adolescents. *Developmental Psychology, 9*, 44–54.

Cazden, C. (1972). Suggestions from studies of early language acquisition. In C. Cazden (Ed.), *Language in early childhood education.* Washington, DC: National Association for the Education of Young Children.

———. (1987, October). *The dangerous myths of decontextualization and autonomous texts.* Paper presented at the Twelfth Annual Boston University Conference on Language Development, Boston. (11)

Centers for Disease Control. (1988, January 29). Guidelines for effective school health education to prevent the spread of AIDS. *Morbidity and Mortality Weekly Report 37* (Suppl. S-2).

Cernoch, J., & Porter, R. H. (1985). Recognition of maternal axillary odors by infants. *Child Development, 56*(6), 1593–1598.

Chaffee, S. H., & Mcleod, J. M. (1972). Adolescent television use in the family context. In G. A. Comstock & E. A. Rubinstein (Eds.), *Television and social behavior: III, television and adolescent aggressiveness.* Washington, DC: U. S. Government Printing Office.

Chall, J. S., & Snow, C. E. (1988). School influences on the reading development of low-income children. *The Harvard Education Letter, 4*(1), 1–4.

Charner, I., & Fraser, B. (1988). *Youth and work: What we know, what we don't know, what we need to know.* Washington, DC: Institute for Educational Leadership.

Chayen, S. (1978). An assessment of the hazards of amniocentesis. *British Journal of Obstetrics and Gynecology, 85*, 2–5.

Chennault, M. (1967). Improving the social acceptance of unpopular educable mentally retarded pupils in special classes. *American Journal of Mental Deficiency, 72*, 455–458.

Children's Defense Fund. (1987). *A children's defense budget.* Washington, DC: The Children's Defense Fund.

Children's Defense Fund. (1988). *Teens and AIDS: Opportunities for prevention.* Washington, DC: Children's Defense Fund.

Chomsky, C. (1969). *The acquisition of syntax in children from 5 to 10.* Cambridge, MA: MIT Press.

Chomsky, N. (1959). A review of *Verbal behavior*, by B. F. Skinner. *Language, 35*, 26–58.

———. (1965). *Aspects of the theory of syntax.* Cambridge, MA: MIT Press.

Christophersen, E. R. (1989). Injury control. *American Psychologist, 44*(2), 237–241.

Clark, E. (1978). Non-linguistic strategies and the acquisition of word meaning. In L. Bloom (Ed.), *Readings in language development*. New York: Wiley.

Clark, M., Hager, M., & Gosnell, M. (1986, May). A breakthrough against CF? *Newsweek*, p. 69.

Clarke, C. A. (1968). The prevention of rhesus babies. *Scientific American, 219*,46–65.

Clarke-Stewart, A., & Fein, G. (1983). Early childhood programs. In M. M. Haith and J. J. Campos (Eds.), P. H. Mussen (Series Ed.), *Handbook of child psychology: Vol. 2 Infancy and developmental psychobiology*. New York: Wiley.

Clarke-Stewart, K. A., Vanderstoep, L. P., & Killian, G. A. (1979). Analysis and relocation of mother-child relations at two years of age. *Child Development, 50*, 777–793.

Clay, M. (1976). *The early detection of reading difficulties: A diagnostic survey*. Auckland, New Zealand: Heinemann.

———. (1987). *Writing begins at home*. Portsmouth, NH: Heinemann Educational Books.

Cline, V. B., Croft, R. G., & Courrier, S. (1972). The desensitization of children to television violence. *Proceedings of the American Psychological Association, 80*, 99–100.

Clyman, R. B., Emde, R. N., Kempe, J. E., & Harmon, R. J. (1986). Social referencing and social looking among twelve-month-old infants. In T. B. Brazelton & M. W. Yogeman (Eds.), *Affective development in infancy* (pp. 75–94). Norwood, NJ Ablex.

Cohen, B. H., Lilienfeld, A. M., & Huang, P. C. (Eds.). (1978). *Genetics issues in public health and medicine*. Springfield, IL: Charles C. Thomas.

Cohen, D. D., & Rose, R. D. (1984). Male adolescent birth control behaviors: The importance of developmental factors and sex differences. *Journal of Youth and Adolescence, 13*(3), 329–352.

Cohen, D. H., & Stern, V. (1983). *Observing and recording the behavior of young children*. New York: Teachers College Press.

Cohen, F. L. (1984). *Clinical genetics in nursing practice*. Philadelphia: Lippincott.

Cohen, L., & Gelber, E. (1975). Infant visual memory. In L. B. Cohen & P. Salapatek (Eds.), *Infant perception: From sensation to cognition* (Vol. 1). New York: Academic Press.

Cohen, L. B., & Strauss, M. S. (1979). Concept acquisition in the human infant. *Child Development, 50*,419–424.

Cohen, S. E., & Parmelee, A. H. (1983). Prediction of five-year Stanford-Binet scores in preterm infants. *Child Development, 54*, 1242–1253.

———. (1988). Antecedents of school problems in children born prematurely. *Journal of Pediatric Psychology, 13*(4), 493–508.

Cole, M. (1985). Mind as a cultural achievement: Implications for IQ testing. In E. Eisner (Ed.), *Learning and teaching the ways of knowing*. Chicago: National Society for the Study of Education.

Cole, N. S., Trent, E. R., Wadell, D. C., Thorndike, R. L., & Hogan, E. (1982). *The 3-R's Test*. Chicago, IL: Riverside Publishing.

Coles, R., & Stokes, G. (1985). *Sex and the American teenager*. New York: Harper & Row.

Collias, N. E. (1956). The analysis of socialization in sheep and goats. *Ecology, 37*, 228–239.

Collis, G. M. (1977). Visual co-orientation and maternal speech. In H. R. Schaffer (Ed.), *Studies in mother-infant interaction*. London: Academic Press.

Collis, G. M., & Schaffer, H. R. (1975). Synchronization of visual attention in mother-infant pairs. *Journal of Child Psychology and Psychiatry, 16*, 315–320.

Committee on Adolescence. (1989). Care of adolescent parents and their children. *Pediatrics, 83*(1), 138–140.

Committee on Sports Medicine. (1989). Anabolic steroids and the adolescent athlete. *Pediatrics, 83*(1), 127–128.

Comstock, G., Chafee, S., Katzman, N., McCombs, M., & Roberts, D. (1978). *Television and human behavior*. New York: Columbia University Press.

Conger, J. J., & Petersen, A. C. (1984). *Adolescence and youth*. New York: Harper & Row.

Connell, J. P., & Goldsmith, H. H. (1982). A structural modeling approach to the study of attachment and strange situation behaviors. In R. J. Emde & R. J. Harmon (Eds.), *The development of attachment and affiliative systems*. New York: Plenum.

Conway, E., & Brackbill, Y. (1970). Delivery medication and infant outcome: An empirical study. *Monographs of the Society for Research in Child Development, 35*, 24–34.

Cooper, E. R., Pelton, S. I., & LeMay, M. (1988). Acquired immunodeficiency syndrome: A new population of children at risk. *Pediatric Clinics of North America, 35*(6), 1365–1387.

Coopersmith, S. (1967). *The antecedents of self-esteem*. San Francisco: W. H. Freeman.

Crall, J. J. (1986). Promotion of oral health and prevention of common pediatric dental problems. *Pediatric Clinics of North America, 33*(4), 887–898.

Cratty, B. J. (1986). *Perceptual and motor development in infants and children*. Englewood Cliffs, NJ: Prentice-Hall.

Crikelair, G. F., & Dhaliwal, A. S. (1976). The cause and prevention of electrical burns of the mouth in children. *Plastic and Reconstructive Surgery, 58*, 206–209.

Crisp, A. H. Palmer, R. L., & Kalucy, R. S. (1976). How common is anorexia nervosa? A prevalence study. *British Journal of Psychiatry, 27*, 1030–1035.

Crnic, K. A., Ragozin, A. S., Greenberg, M. T., Robinson, M. M., & Basham, R. B. (1983). Social interaction and developmental competence of preterm and full-term infants during the first year of life. *Child Development, 54*, 1199–1210.

Crockenberg, S.B. (1981). Infant irritability, mother responsiveness and social support influences on the security of infant-mother attachment. *Child Development, 52,* 856–865.

_____. (1985). Toddlers' reactions to maternal anger. *Merrill-Palmer Quarterly, 31*(4), 361–373.

Cruttenden, A. (1970). A phonetic study of babbling. *British Journal of Disorders in Communication, 5,* 110–118.

Csikszentmihalyi, M., & Larson, R. (1984). *Being adolescent.* New York: Basic Books.

Damon, W. (1980). Patterns of change in children's social reasoning: A two-year longitudinal study. *Child Development, 51,* 1010–1017.

Daniel, J. (1989, March 14). Fatal attraction: Steroids—The athlete's drug. *The Tab,* pp. 40–41.

Dargassies, S. (1966). Neurological maturation of the premature infant of 28 to 41 weeks' gestation age. In F. Faulkner (Ed.), *Human development.* London: W. B. Saunders.

Darwin, C. (1859). *The origin of species.* London: Murray.

Dawe, H. C. (1934). An analysis of two hundred quarrels of preschool children. *Child Development, 5,* 139–157.

Dawson, D. A. (1986). The effects of sex education on adolescent behavior. *Family Planning Perspectives, 18,* 162.

Day, B. (1988). What's happening in early childhood programs across the United States. In C. Warger (Ed.), *Public school early childhood programs: A resource guide.* Alexandria, VA: Association for Supervision and Curriculum Development.

Delisle, J. (1979). Things my child likes to do. In R. S. Renzulli, S. M. Reis, & L. H. Smith (Eds.), *The revolving door identification model.* Mansfield Center, CT: Creative Learning Press.

DeLoache, J. S., Cassidy, D. J., & Brown, A. L. (1985). Precursors of mnemonic strategies in very young children. *Child Development, 56*(1), 125–137.

DeLoache, J. S., Sugarman, S., & Brown, A. L. (1985). The development of error correction strategies in young children's manipulative play. *Child Development, 56*(4), 928–939.

Delpit, L. D. (1988). The silent dialogue. *Harvard Education Review, 58*(3), 280–298.

Demetras, M. J., Post, K. N., & Snow, C. E. (1986). Feedback to first language learners: The role of repetitions and clarification questions. *Journal of Child Language, 13,* 275–292.

Denham, S. (1986). Social cognition, prosocial behavior, and emotions in preschoolers: Contextual validation. *Child Development, 57,* 194–201.

Dennis, W. (1960). Causes of retardation among institutional children: Iran. *Journal of Genetic Psychology, 96,* 47–59.

Desmond, M. M., Franklin, R. R., Vallbona, C., Hilt, R. H., Plumb, R., Arnold, H., & Watts, J. (1963). The clinical behavior of the newly born I. *Journal of Pediatrics, 12,* 307–325.

Desor, J. A., Maller, O., & Andrews, K. (1975). Ingestive responses of human newborns to salty, sour, and bitter stimuli. *Journal of Comparative and Physiological Psychology, 89,* 966–970.

deVilliers, J., & deVilliers, P. (1973). Development of the use of word order in comprehension. *Journal of Psycholinguistic Research, 2,* 331–341.

DeVries, R. (1970). The development of role-taking as reflected by behavior of bright, average, and retarded children in a social guessing game. *Child Development, 41,* 759–770.

Diagnostic and statistical manual of mental disorders (3rd. ed.)—revised. (1987). Washington, DC: *American Psychiatric Association.*

Dickinsin, D., & Snow, C. (1987, May). *Oral language correlates of reading behavior.* Paper presented at the Thirty-Second Annual Meeting of the International Reading Association, Anaheim, CA.

Dickinson, D. K. (1984). First impressions: children's knowledge of words gained from a single exposure. *Applied Psycholinguistics, 5,* 359–373.

Dietz, W. H. (1986). Prevention of childhood obesity. *Pediatric Clinics of North America, 33*(4), 823–833.

Dietz, W. H., & Gortmaker, S. L. (1984). Factors within the physical environment associated with childhood obesity. *American Journal of Clinical Nutrition, 39,* 619–624.

Dobbing, J. (1984). Infant nutrition and later achievement. *Nutrition Reviews, 42*(1), 1–7.

_____. (Ed.). (1987). Early nutrition and later achievement. London: Academic Press.

Dodge, K., Murphy, R. R., & Buchsbaum, K. (1984). The assessment of intention-cue detection skills in children: Implications for developmental psychopathology. *Child Development, 55,* 163–173.

Dodge, K. A., Schlundt, D. C., Schocken, I., & Delugach, J. D. (1983). Social competence and children's sociometric status: The role of peer group entry strategies. *Merrill-Palmer Quarterly, 29*(3), 309–336.

Dodge, K. A., Petit, G. S., McCloskey, C. L., & Brown, M. M. (1987). *Social competence in children. Monographs of the Society for Research in Child Development, 51*(2, Serial No. 213).

Doleys, D. M., & Dolce, J. J. (1982). Toilet training and enuresis. *Pediatric Clinics of North America, 29*(2), 297–312.

Domonick, J. R., & Greenburg, B. S. (1972). Attitude toward violence: The interaction of television exposure, family attitudes, and social class. In G. A. Comstock & E. A. Rubinstein (Eds.), *Television and social behavior: Vol. 3. Television and adolescent aggression.* Washington, DC: U. S. Government Printing Office.

Donaldson, M. (1978). *Children's minds.* New York: Norton.

Dorfman, S. F. (1983). Deaths from ectopic pregnancy, United States, 1979–1980. *Obstetrics and Gynecology, 62*(3), 334–338.

Dornbusch, S. M., Carlsmith, J. M., Gross, R. T., Martin, J. A., Jennings, D., Rosenberg, A., & Duke, P. (1981). Sexual development, age and dating: A comparison of biological and social influences upon one set of behaviors. *Child Development, 52*(1), 179–185.

Dougherty, W. H., & Engel, R. E. (1986). An 80s look at sex equality in Caldecott winners and honor books. *The Reading Teacher, 40*(4), 394–398.

Downs, M. P. (1978, Fall). That a child may hear. *Deafness Research Foundation Receiver.*

Doyle, A. (1975). Infant development in day care. *Developmental Psychology, 11*, 655–656.

Drabman, R. S., & Thomas, M. H. (1974). Does media violence increase children's toleration of real-life aggression? *Developmental Psychology, 10*, 3–13.

Drillien, C. M., Thomson, A. J. M., & Burgayne, K. (1980). Low birthweight children at early school age: A longitudinal study. *Developmental Medicine and Child Neurology, 22*, 26–47.

Drucker, J. (1975). Toddler play: Some comments on its functions in the developmental process. *Psychoanalysis and Contemporary Science, 4*, 479–527.

Duncan, P. D., Ritter, P. L., Dornbusch, S. M., Gross, R. T., & Carlsmith, J. M. (1985). The effects of pubertal timing on body image, school behavior, and deviance. *Journal of Youth and Adolescence, 14*, 227–235.

Dunn, J., & Kendrick, C. (1982). *Siblings.* Cambridge, MA: Harvard University Press.

Durkin, D. (1966). *Children who read early.* New York: Teachers College Press.

Dusek, J. B. (1977). *Adolescent development and behavior.* Chicago: Science Research Associates.

Dweck, C. S. (1978). Achievement. In M. E. Lamb (Ed.), *Social and personality development* (pp. 114–130). New York: Holt, Rinehart & Winston.

Dweck, C. S., & Elliot, E. S. (1983). Achievement motivation. In Paul H. Mussen (Series Ed.), *Handbook of child psychology* (4th ed.). E. Mavis Hetherington (Ed.), *Vol. 4: Socialization, personality, and social development* (pp. 643–692). New York: Wiley.

Dweck, C. S., Goetz, T. E., & Strauss, N. L. (1980). Sex differences in learned helplessness: IV. An experimental and naturalistic study of failure generalization and its mediators. *Journal of Personality and Social Psychology, 38*, 441–452.

Dweck, C. S., & Licht, B. G. (1980). Learned helplessness and intellectual achievement. In J. Garber and M. Seligman (Eds.), *Human helplessness: Theory and applications.* New York: Academic Press.

Early Childhood Education Commission (1986). *Take a giant step: Final report of the early childhood commission.* New York: Office of the Mayor.

Eckerman, C., Whatley, J., & Kutz, S. (1975). Growth of social play with peers during the second year of life. *Developmental Psychology, 11*, 42–49.

Educational Testing Service. (1979). *School and college ability tests II and III.* Monterey, CA: CTB/McGraw-Hill.

Edwards, D. A. (1969). Early androgen stimulation and aggressive behavior in male and female mice. *Physiology and Behavior, 4*, 333–338.

Egan, M. C. (1977). Federal nutrition support programs for children. *Pediatric Clinics of North America, 24*, 229–239.

Egeland, B., & Farber, E. A. (1984). Infant-mother attachment: Factors related to its development and changes over time. *Child Development, 55*, 753–771.

Eilers, R., Wilson, W., & Moore, J. (1977). Developmental changes in speech discrimination. *Journal of Speech and Hearing Research, 20*, 766–780.

Eimas, P. D. (1974). Auditory and linguistic processing of cues for place of articulation by infants. *Perception and Psychophysics, 16*, 513–521.

Eimas, P. D., Sikqueland, D. R., Jusczyk, P., & Vigorito, J. (1971). Speech perception in infants. *Science, 171*, 303–306.

Eisenberg-Berg, N. (1979). Development of children's prosocial judgment. *Developmental Psychology, 15*, 128–137.

Elardo, R., Bradley, R., & Caldwell, B. M. (1975). The relation of infants' home environments to mental test performance from six to thirty-six months: A longitudinal analysis. *Child Development, 46*, 71–76.

Elbers, L., & Ton, J. (1985). Playpen monologues: The interplay of words and babbles in the first-words period. *Journal of Child Language, 12*, 551–565.

Elder, G. H. (1963). Parental power legitimation and its effects on the adolescent. *Sociometry, 26*, 50–65.

Elkind, D. (1976). *Child development and education: A piagetian perspective.* New York: Oxford University Press.

———. (1978). *The child's reality: Three developmental views.* Hillsdale, NJ: Lawrence Erlbaum.

Elliot, R., & Vasta, R. (1970). The modeling of sharing: Effects associated with vicarious reinforcement, symbolization, age and generalization. *Journal of Experimental Child Psychology, 10*, 8–15.

Ellis, G. T., & Sekyra, F. (1972). The effect of aggressive cartoons on the behavior of first grade children. *Journal of Psychology, 81*, 37–43.

Elstner, C. L., Carey, J. C., Livingston, G., Moeschler, J., & Lubinsky, M. (1984). Further delineation of the 10p deletion syndrome. *Pediatrics, 73*(5), 670–675.

Emde, R. N., & Gaensbauer, T. (1981). Some emerging models of emotion in human infancy. In K. Immelmann, G. W. Barlow, L. Petrinovich, & M. Main (Eds.), *Behavioral development: The Bielefeld Interdisciplinary project* (pp. 568–588). New York: Cambridge University Press.

Emde, R. N., Gaensbauer, T. J., & Harmon, R. J. (1976). Emotional expression in infancy: A behavioral study. *Psychological Issues, A Monograph Series, 10,*(7,37). New York: International Press.

Emery, R. E., Hetherington, E. M., & Dilalla, L. F. (1984). Divorce, children, and social policy. In H. W. Stevenson & A. E. Siegel (Eds.), *Child development research and social policy* (Vol. 1, pp. 189–266). Chicago: University of Chicago Press.

Empey, L. T. (1975). Delinquency theory and research. In R. Grinder (Ed.), *Studies in adolescence* (pp. 475–490). New York: Macmillan.

Enright, R. D., & Sutterfield, S. J. (1980). An ecological validation of social cognitive development. *Child Development, 51,* 156–161.

Entwisle, D. R., Alexander, K. L., Pallas, A. M., & Cadigan, D. (1988). The emergent academic self-image of first graders: Its response to social structure. *Child Development, 58,*(5), 1190–1206.

Epstein, L. H., Wing, R. R., & Valoski, A. (1985). Childhood obesity. *Pediatric Clinics of North America, 32*(2), 363–379.

Erhardt, A. A., & Baker, S. W. (1974). Fetal androgens, human central nervous system differentiation, and behavior sex differences. In R. C. Friedman, R. M. Richart, and R. L. Vandewiele (Eds.), *Sex differences in behavior.* New York: Wiley.

Erickson, E. H. (1963). *Childhood and society.* New York: Norton.

Erickson, J. (1984). Drug use: The family connection. *Family Learning, 1*(1), 100.

Erikson, P. S., Gennser, G., Lofgran, O., & Nilsson, K. (1983). Acute effects of maternal smoking on fetal breathing and movements. *Obstetrics and Gynecology, 61*(3), 367–372.

Fantz, R. L. (1963). Pattern vision in newborn infants. *Science, 140,* 296–297.

Fantz, R. L., Ordy, J. M., & Udelf, M. S. (1962). Maturation of patterns of vision in infants during the first six months. *Journal of Comparative and Physiological Psychology, 55,* 907–917.

Farel, A. M. (1984). Planning after-school activities for young adolescents: Parents' preferences and needs. *Children Today, 13*(2), 28–31.

Farrington, D. P., & West, D. J. (1971). A comparison between early delinquents and young aggressives. *British Journal of Criminology, 11,* 341–358.

Farrior, E. S., & Ruwe, C. H. (1987). Women, Infants, and Children Program prenatal participation and dietary intakes. *Nutrition Research, 7,* 451–459.

Federman, E. J., & Yang, R. K. (1976). A critique of obstetrical pain-relieving drugs as predictors of infant behavior variability. *Child Development, 47,* 294–296.

Fein, G. (1975). A transformational analysis of pretending. *Developmental Psychology, 11*(3), 291–296.

———. (1981). Pretend play in childhood: An integrative review. *Child Development, 52,* 1095–1118.

———. (1984). The self-building potential of make-believe play, or "I got a fish, all by myself." In T. D. Yawkey & A. D. Pellegrini (Eds.), *Child's play: Developmental and applied* (pp. 125–142). Hillsdale, NJ: Lawrence Erlbaum.

Fein, G., Johnson, D., Kosson, N., Stork, L., & Wasserman, L. (1975). Sex stereotypes and preferences in the toy choices of 20-month-old boys and girls. *Developmental Psychology, 11* (4), 527–528.

Fein, G., & Rivkin, M. (Eds.). (1986). *The young child at play: Reviews of research* (Vol. 4). Washington, DC: National Association for the Education of Young Children.

Feinman, S., & Lewis, M. (1983). Social referencing at ten months: A second-order effect on infants' responses to strangers. *Child Development, 54* (4), 878–887.

Fenson, L. (1984). Developmental trends for action and speech in pretend play. In I. Bretherton (Ed.), *Symbolic play,* (pp. 249–270). New York: Academic Press.

Fenson, L., & Ramsay, D. S. (1980). Decentration and integration of the child's play in the second year. *Child Development, 51,* 171–178.

Ferguson, C. (1977). Baby talk as a simplified register. In C. Snow & C. Ferguson (Eds.), *Talking to children.* Cambridge, England: Cambridge University Press.

Fernald, A. (1984). The perceptual and affective salience of mothers' speech to infants. In L. Feagans, C. Garvey, & R. Golinkoff (Eds.), *The origins and growth of communication.* Norwood, NJ: Ablex.

———. (1985). Four-month-old infants prefer to listen to motherese. *Infant Behavior and Development, 8,* 181–195.

Ferreiro, E. (1986). The interplay between information and assimilation in beginning literacy. In W. Teale and E. Sulzby (Eds.), *Emergent literacy.* Norwood, NJ: Ablex.

Ferreiro, E., & Teberosky, A. (1979) *Literacy before schooling.* Portsmouth, NH: Heinemann Educational Books.

Ferris, T. (1988). *Coming of age in the Milky Way.* New York: Morrow.

Field, T., Dempsey, J., & Shuman, H. H. (1983). Five-year follow-up of preterm respiratory distress syndrome and post-term postmaturity syndrome infants. In T. Field & A. Sostek (Eds.), *Infants born at risk: Physiological, perceptual, and cognitive processes* (pp. 317–335). New York: Grune & Stratton.

Finkelstein, N. W., & Ramey, C. T. (1977). Learning to control the environment in infancy. *Child Development, 48,* 608–619.

Fisher, L., Harris, V. G., & VanGuren, J. (1980). Assessment of a pilot child playground injury prevention project in New York State. *American Journal of Public Health, 70,* 1000–1007.

Flavell, J. H., Beach, D. H., & Chinsky, J. M. (1966).

Spontaneous verbal rehearsal in memory tasks as a function of age. *Child Development, 37,* 283–299.

Flavell, J. H., Everett, B. A., Croft, K., & Flavell, E. (1981). Young children's knowledge about visual perception: Further evidence of Level 1-Level 2 distinctions. *Developmental Psychology, 17,* 99–103.

Flavell, J. H., Green, F. L., & Flavell, E. R. (1986). Development of knowledge about the appearance-reality distinction. *Monographs of the Society for Research in Child Development, 51*(1, Serial No. 212).

Flavell, J. H., Shipstead, S. G., & Croft, K. (1978). Young children's knowledge about visual perception: Hiding objects from others. *Child Development, 49,* 1208–1211.

Flavell, J. H., Speer, J. R., Green, F. L., & Augrest, D. L. (1981). The development of comprehension monitoring and knowledge about comprehension. *Monographs of the Society for Research in Child Development 46:* (Serial No. 192).

Foch, T. T., & McClearn, G. E. (1980). Genetics, body weight and obesity. In A. J. Stunkard (Ed.), *Obesity.* Philadelphia: Saunders.

Fraiberg, S. (1974). Billy: Psychological intervention for a failure-to-thrive infant. In M. D. Klaus & M. A. Trause (Eds.), *Maternal attachment and mothering disorders* (pp. 13–19). Sausalito, CA: Johnson & Johnson.

———. (1975). Intervention in infancy: A program for blind infants. In B. Z. Friedlander, G. M. Steritt, & G. E. Kirk (Eds.), *Exceptional infant* (Vol. 1). New York: Brunner/Mazel.

Fraser, C., Bellugi, U., & Brown, R. (1963). Control of grammar in imitation, comprehension, and production. *Journal of Verbal Learning and Verbal Behavior, 2,* 122–125.

Frasier, S. D. (1979). Growth disorders in children. *Pediatric Clinics of North America, 26,* 1–12.

Fredericks, B. C., & Kendrick, A. S. (1985). Health and safety—A special look at day care for sick children. *Child Care News, 12*(3), 4–5.

Frederiksen, N. (1984). The real test bias. *American Psychologist, 39*(3), 193–202.

Freidrich, L. K., & Stein, A. H. (1973). Aggressive and prosocial television programs and the natural behavior of preschool children. *Monographs of the Society for Research in Child Development, 38*(151).

Frenkel, L. D. (1986). Pertussis immunization. *Pediatric Annals, 15*(6), 452–454.

Freud, S. (1925). Instincts and their vicissitudes. In S. Freud, *Collected papers* (Vol. 4). London: Institutes for Psycho-analysis & Hogarth Press.

Friede, A. M., Carey, V., Azzara, M. A., Gallagher, S. S., & Guyer, B. (1985). The epidemiology of injuries to bicycle riders. *Pediatric Clinics of North America, 32*(1), 141–151.

Frieze, I. H., Fisher, J., Hanusa, G., McHugh, M. D., & Valle, V. A. (1978). Attributions of the causes of success and failure as internal and external barriers to achievement in women. In J. Sherman & F. Denmark (Eds.), *Psychology of women: Future directions of research.* New York: Psychological Dimensions.

Friman, P. C. (1986). A preventive context for enuresis. *Pediatric Clinics of North America, 33*(4), 871–885.

Frisch, J. L. (1977). Sex stereotypes in adult-infant play. *Child Development, 48,* 1671–1675.

Frodi, A. M., & Lamb, M. E. (1978). Fathers' and mothers' responses to the face and cries of normal and premature infants. *Developmental Psychology, 14* (5), 490–498.

Furrow, D., & Nelson, K. (1986). A further look at the motherese hypothesis: A reply to Gleitman, Newport, and Gleitman. *Journal of Child Language, 13,*163–176.

Furstenberg, F. F., Brooks-Gunn, J. I., & Morgan, S. P. (1987). *Adolescent mothers in later life.* New York: Cambridge University Press.

Fuson, K. (1982). An analyst of the counting-on solution procedure in addition. In T. P. Carpenter, J. M. Moser, & T. A. Romberg (Eds.), *Addition and subtraction: A cognitive perspective* (pp. 67–81). Hillsdale, NJ: Lawrence Erlbaum.

———. (1988). *Children's counting and concepts of number.* New York: Springer-Verlag.

Gaensbauer, T. J., & Harmon, R. J. (1982). Attachment behavior in abused/neglected and premature infants. In R. N. Emde & R. J. Harmon (Eds.), *The development of attachment and affiliative systems* (pp. 263–279). New York: Plenum Press.

Galambos, N. L., & Garbarino, J. (1983). Identifying the missing link in the study of latchkey children. *Children Today, 12*(4), 2–4.

Gallatin, J. E. (1975). *Adolescence and individuality.* New York: Harper & Row.

Galler, J. (1987). The interaction of nutrition and the environment in behavioral development. In J. Dobbing (Ed.), *Early nutrition and later achievement,* (pp. 125–207).

Garcia, C., & Rosenfeld, D. L. (1977). *Human fertility: The regulation of reproduction.* Philadelphia: F. A. Davis.

Gardner, H. (1983). *Frames of mind: The theory of multiple intelligences.* New York: Basic Books.

Gardner, H., & Brown, L. K. (1984). Symbolic capabilities and children's television. In J. P. Murray & G. S. Salomon (Eds.), *The future of children's television.* Boys Town, NB: Boys Town.

Garn, S. M. (1966). Body size and its implications. In L. W. Hoffman & M. L. Hoffman (Eds.), *Review of child development research* (Vol. 2). New York: Russell Sage Foundation.

Garn, S. M., & Clark, D. C. (1976). Trends in fatness and the origins of obesity. *Pediatrics, 57,* 443–456.

Garrett, W., & Robinson, D. E. (1970). *Ultrasound in clinical obstetrics.* Springfield, IL: Charles C. Thomas.

Garvey, C. (1977). *Play*. Cambridge, MA: Harvard University Press.

Gathercole, V. C. (1985). More and more and more about more. *Journal of Experimental Child Psychology, 40*, 73–104.

Gedda, L. (1961). *Twins in history and science*. Springfield, IL: Charles C. Thomas.

Geller, L. G. (1985). *Word play and language learning for children*. Urbana, IL: National Council of Teachers of English.

Gelman, R. (1982). Basic numerical abilities. In R. J. Sternberg (Ed.), *Advances in the psychology of intelligence* (Vol. 1, pp. 181–205). Hillsdale, NJ: Lawrence Erlbaum.

Gelman, R., & Gallistel, C. R. (1978). *The child's understanding of number*. Cambridge, MA: Harvard University Press.

Gelman, R., & Meck, E. (1983). Preschoolers' counting: Principles before skill. *Cognition, 13*, 343–359.

General Mills, Inc. (1979). *Family health in an era of stress: The General Mills American family report*. Minneapolis, MN: General Mills.

George, C., & Main, M. (1981). Social interactions of young abused children: Approach, avoidance, aggression. In E. M. Hetherington & R. D. Parke (Eds.), *Contemporary readings in child psychology* (2nd ed.). New York: McGraw-Hill.

Gerbner, G. (1972). Violence in television drama: Trends and symbolic function. In G. A. Comstock & E. A. Rubenstein (Eds.), *Television and social behavior: Vol. 1. Media content and control*. Washington, DC: U. S. Government Printing Office.

Gerbner, G., Gross, L., Signorelli, N., Morgan, M., & Jackson-Beeck, M. (1979). *Highlights of violence profile no. 10*. Unpublished manuscript, Annenberg School of Communication, University of Pennsylvania, Philadelphia, PA.

Gesell, A. (1954). The ontogenesis of infant behavior. In L. Carmichael (Ed.), *Manual of child psychology* (pp. 335–373). New York: Wiley.

Gesell, A., & Thompson, H. (1929). Learning and growth in identical infant twins: An experimental study of the method of co-twin control. *Genetic Psychology Monographs, 6*, 1–124.

Gibson, E. (1969). *Principles of perceptual learning and development*. Englewood Cliffs, NJ: Prentice-Hall.

Gibson, E. J., & Walk, R. (1960). The "visual cliff." *Scientific American, 202*, 64–72.

Gil, D. G. (1970). *Violence against children: Physical child abuse in the United States*. Cambridge, MA: Harvard University Press.

Gilligan, C. (1977). In a different voice: Women's conceptions of the self and of morality. *Harvard Educational Review, 47*, 481–517.

———. (1982). *In a different voice: Psychological theory and women's development*. Cambridge, MA: Harvard University Press.

Ginsburg, H. P., & Opper, S. (1988). *Piaget's theory of intellectual development* (3rd ed.). Englewood Cliffs, NJ: Prentice-Hall.

Glucksberg, S., Krauss, R. M., & Higgins, E. T. (1975). The development of referential communication skills. In F. D. Horowitz (Ed.), *Reviews of child development research* (Vol. 4). Chicago: University of Chicago Press.

Glueck, S., & Glueck, F. (1950). *Criminal careers*. New York: Knopf.

Gnepp, J., McKee, E., & Domanic, J. A. (1987). Children's use of situational information to infer emotion: Understanding emotionally equivocal situations. *Developmental Psychology, 22*(1), 114–123.

Goldberg, S. (1982). Some biological aspects of early parent-infant interaction. In S. Moore & C. Cooper (Eds.), *The young child: Reviews of research* (Vol. 3, pp. 35–36). Washington, DC: National Association for the Education of Young Children.

———. (1983). Parent-infant bonding: Another look. *Child Development, 54*(6), 1355–1382.

Goldin-Meadow, S., Seligman, M., & Gelman, R. (1976). Language in the two-year-old. *Cognition, 4*, 189–202.

Goldman, A. S., & Smith, C. W. (1973). Host resistance factors in human milk. *Journal of Pediatrics, 82*, 1082.

Golinkoff, R. M. (1986). 'I beg your pardon?': The preverbal negotiation of failed messages. *Journal of Child Language, 13*, 455–476.

Goodenough, E. (1957). Interest in persons as an aspect of sex differences in the early years. *Genetic Psychology Monographs, 55*, 287–323.

Goodman, K., & Goodman, Y. (1977). Learning about psycholinguistic processes by analyzing oral reading. *Harvard Educational Review, 47*, 317–333.

Goodman, K. S., Smith, E. G., Meredith, R., & Goodman, Y. M. (1987). *Language and thinking go to school* (3rd ed.). New York: Richard C. Owen.

Gopnik, A., & Astington, J. W. (1988). Children's understanding of representational change and its relation to the understanding of false belief and the appearance of reality distinction. *Child Development, 59*(1), 26–37.

Gopnik, A., & Graf, P. (1988). Knowing how you know: Young children's ability to identify and remember the sources of their beliefs. *Child Development, 59*(5), 1366–1371.

Gordon, T. (1975). *P.E.T.: Parent Effectiveness Training*. New York: New American Library.

Grant, L. M., & Demetriou, E. (1988). Adolescent sexuality. *Pediatric Clinics of North America, 35*(6), 1271–1289.

Grantham-McGregor, S., Schonfield, W., & Powell, C. (1987). Development of severely malnourished children who received psychosocial stimulation: Six-year follow-up. *Pediatrics, 79*, 247–254.

Granucci, P. (1986). *A case study of one child's literacy development from 24 to 36 months.* Unpublished doctoral dissertation, Boston University.

Green, A. H., Gaines, R. W., & Sandgrund, A. (1974). Child abuse: Pathological syndrome of family interaction. *American Journal of Psychiatry, 131,* 882–886.

Green, J. A., Gustafson, G. E., & West, M. J. (1980). Effects of infant development on mother-infant interactions. *Child Development, 51,*199–207.

Green, K. D., Beck, S. J., & Forehand, R. (1980). Validity of teacher nomination of child behavior problems. *Journal of Abnormal Child Psychology, 8*(3), 397–404.

Greenburg, M., Pelliteri, O., & Barton, J. (1957). Frequency of defects in infants whose mothers had rubella during pregnancy. *Journal of the American Medical Association, 165,* 675–678.

Greenough, W. T., Black, J. E., & Wallace, C. S. (1987). Experience and brain development. *Child Development, 58*(3), 539–559.

Greensher, J., & Mofenson, H. C. (1985). Injuries at play. *Pediatric Clinics of North America, 32*(1), 127–139.

Greenwood, S. G. (1979). Warning: Cigarette smoking is dangerous to reproductive health. *Family Planning Perspectives, 11*(3), 168–172.

Grin, T. R., Nelson, L. B., & Jeffers, J. B. (1987). Eye injuries in childhood. *Pediatrics, 80*(1), 13–17.

Gross, R. T., & Duke, P. M. (1980). The effect of early versus late physical maturation in adolescent behavior. *Pediatric Clinics of North America, 27,* 71–77.

Grossman, H. J. (Ed.). (1983). *Classification in mental retardation* (8th ed.). Washington, DC: American Association on Mental Deficiency.

Grubb, W. N., & Lazerson, M. (1982). *Broken promises.* New York: Basic Books.

Grusec, J., & Skubinski, S. (1970). Model nurturance, demand characteristics of the modeling experiment, and altruism. *Journal of Personality and Social Psychology, 14,* 352–359.

Grusec, J. E., & Lytton, H. (1988). *Social development.* New York: Springer-Verlag.

Guerney, L., & Moore, L. (1983). Phone Friend: A prevention-oriented service for latchkey children. *Children Today, 12*(4), 5–10.

Gustafson, G. E. (1984). Effects of the ability to locomote on infants' social and exploratory behaviors: An experimental study. *Developmental Psychology, 20*(3), 397–405.

Guttmacher, A. F. (1973). *Pregnancy, birth and family planning.* New York: New American Library.

Guyer, B., Talbot, A. M., & Pless, I. B. (1985). Pedestrian injuries to children and youth. *Pediatric Clinics of North America, 32*(1), 163–174.

Haaf, R. F., & Bell, R. Q. (1967). A facial dimension in visual discrimination by human infants. *Child Development, 38,* 893–899.

Hales, D. J., Lozoff, B., Sosa, R., & Kennel, J. H. (1977). Defining the limits of the maternal sensitive period. *Developmental Medicine and Child Neurology, 19,* 454–461.

Hall, C. S., & Lindzey, G. (1970). *Theories of personality* (2nd ed.) New York: Wiley.

Hallman, M., & Gluck, L. (1982). Respiratory distress syndrome—update 1982. *Pediatric Clinics of North America, 29*(5), 1057–1075.

Halmi, K. A., Casper, R. C., Eckert, E. D., Goldberg, S. C., & Davis, J. M. (1979). Unique features associated with age of onset of anorexia nervosa. *Psychiatric Research, 1,* 209–215.

Halmi, K. A., & Falk, J. R. (1981). Common psychological changes in anorexia nervosa. *International Journal of Eating Disorders, 1,* 16–27.

Harlow, H. F. (1958). The nature of love. *American Psychologist, 13,* 673–685.

Harris, D. B. (1963). *Children's drawing as measures of intellectual maturity.* New York: Harcourt Brace Jovanovich.

Harris, P. L. (1983). Infant cognition. In P. H. Mussen (Ed.), *Handbook of child psychology* (4th ed.): *Vol. 2. Infancy and developmental psychobiology.* New York: Wiley.

Harris, P., Kruithof, A., Terwogt, M. M., & Visser, P. (1981). Children's detection and awareness of textual anomaly. *Journal of Experimental Child Psychology, 31,* 212–230.

Harter, S. (1986). Cognitive-developmental processes in the integration of concepts about emotions and self. *Social Cognition, 4,* 119–151.

Harter, S., & Buddin, B. J. (1987). Children's understanding of the simultaneity of two emotions: A five-stage developmental acquisition sequence. *Developmental Psychology, 22*(3), 388–399.

Hartup, W. W. (1974). Aggression in childhood: Developmental perspectives. *American Psychologist, 29,* 336–341.

———. (1983). Peer relations. In P. H. Mussen (Ed.), *Handbook of child psychology* (4th ed.) (Vol. III). New York: Wiley.

Harvey, J. H. (1982). Overuse syndromes in young athletes. *Pediatric Clinics of North America, 29*(6), 1369–1381.

Haviland, J. (1982). Sex-related pragmatics in infants. *Journal of Communication, 27,* 80–84.

Hayes, C. D. (Ed.). (1987). *Risking the future: Adolescent sexuality, pregnancy, and childbearing* (Vol. 1). Washington, DC: National Academy Press.

Hayes, D. P., & Ahrens, M. G. (1988). Vocabulary simplification for children: A special case of "motherese?" *Journal of Child Language, 15,* 395–410.

Haynes, H., White, B. W., & Held, R. (1965). Visual accommodation in human infants. *Science, 148,* 528–530.

Heath, S. B. (1983). *Way with words: Language, life, and work in communities and classrooms.* New York: Cambridge University Press.

Held, R., & Hein, A. (1963). Movement-produced stimulation in the development of visually guided behavior. *Journal of Comparative and Physiological Psychology, 56,* 822–876.

Herbst, A. L. (1972). Vaginal and cervical abnormalities after exposure to stilbestrol in utero. *Obstetrics and Gynecology, 40,* 287–298.

Herbst, A. L., Scully, R. E., & Robboy, S. J. (1975). Problems in the examination of DES-exposed females. *Obstetrics and Gynecology, 46,* 353–355.

Herman, P. A., Anderson, R. C., Pearson, P. D., & Nagy, W. E. (1987). Incidental acquisition of word meanings from expositions with varied text features. *Reading Research Quarterly, 22*(3), 263–284.

Herrman, H. J., & Roberts, M. W. (1987). Preventive dental care: The role of the pediatrician. *Pediatrics, 80*(1), 107–110.

Hershenson, M. (1964). Visual discrimination in the human newborn. *Journal of Comparative Physiological Psychology, 58,* 270–276.

Hersher, L., Moore, A. U., & Richmond, R. B. (1958). Effects of modified maternal care in the sheep and goat. *Science, 128,* 1342–1343.

Hiatt, S., Campos, J., & Emde, R. M. (1979). Facial patterning and infant emotional expressions: Happiness, surprise, and fear. *Child Development, 50,* 1020–1035.

Hill, J. P., & Holmbeck, G. (1986). Attachment and autonomy during adolescence. In G. Whitehurst (Ed.), *Annals of child development* (Vol. 3). Greenwich, CT: Jai Press.

Hill, J. P., Holmbeck, G. N., Marlow, L., Green, T. M., & Lynch, M. E. (1985). Menarchal status and parent-child relations in families of seventh-grade girls. *Journal of Youth and Adolescence, 14,* 301–316.

Hirschman, R., & Katkin, E. S. (1974). Psychophysiological functioning, arousal, attention, and learning during the first year of life. In H. W. Reese (Ed.), *Advances in child development and behavior.* (Vol. 7). New York: Academic Press.

Hofferth, S. L. (1987). The effects of programs and policies on adolescent pregnancy and childbearing. In S. L. Hofferth and C. B. Hayes (Eds.), *Risking the future: Adolescent sexuality, pregnancy, and childbearing* (Vol. 2, pp. 207–263). Washington, DC: National Academy Press.

Hoffman, M. L. (1984). *Moral development.* In M. H. Bronstein & M. E. Lamb (Eds.), *Developmental psychology: An advanced textbook.* (pp. 279–324). Hillsdale, NJ: Lawrence Erlbaum.

———. (1988). Moral development. In M. H. Bornstein and M. E. Lamb (Eds.), *Developmental psychology: An advanced textbook* 2nd ed. Hillsdale, NJ: Lawrence Erlbaum.

Hogan, R. (1975). Theoretical egocentrism and the problem of compliance. *American Psychologist, 30,* 533–540.

Hogge, W. A., Schonberg, S. A., & Golbus, M. S. (1986). Chorionic villus sampling: Experience of the first 1000 cases. *American Journal of Obstetrics and Gynecology, 154*(6), 1249–1252.

Honig, A. S., & Lally, J. R. (1972). *Infant caregiving: A design for training.* New York: Media Projects.

Honzik, M. P. (1983). Measuring mental abilities in infancy: The value and limitations. In M. Lewis (Ed.), *Origins of intelligence in infancy and early childhood* (pp. 67–105). New York: Plenum.

Hunt, J. McV. (1965). Intrinsic motivation and its role in psychological development. *Nebraska Symposium on Motivation, 13,* 189–282.

Hunziker, U. A., & Barr, R. G. (1986). Increased carrying reduces infant crying: A randomized controlled trial. *Pediatrics, 77*(5), 641–647.

Huston, A. C., Wright, J. C., Kerkham, D., Seigle, J., Rice, M., Bremer, M. (1983). *Family environment and television use by preschool children.* Paper presented at the Biennial Meeting of the Society for Research in Child Development, Detroit, MI.

Huston, A. C., Wright, J. C., Leary, A., & Eakins, D. (1985). *Effects of cognitive development and early viewing on children's understanding of television form.* Paper presented at the Annual Meeting of the American Psychological Association, Los Angeles, CA.

Huttenlocher, J., & Presson, C. B. (1973). Mental rotation and the perspective problem. *Cognitive Psychology, 4,* 277–299.

Hymes, J. (1982). *Early childhood education. The year in review: A look at 1981.* Carmel, CA: Hacienda Press.

———. (1987). *Early childhood education. The year in review: A look at 1986.* Carmel, CA: Hacienda Press.

———. (1988). *Early childhood education. The year in review: A look at 1987.* Carmel, CA: Hacienda Press.

———. (1989). *Early childhood education, the year in review: A look at 1988.* Washington, DC: National Association for the Education of Young Children.

Ingalls, A. J., & Salerno, M. C. (1975). *Maternal and child health nursing.* St. Louis: C. V. Mosby.

Inhelder, B., & Piaget, J. (1958). *The growth of logical thinking from childhood to adolescence.* New York: Basic Books.

———. (1969). *The early growth of logic in the child.* (E. A. Lunzer & D. Papert, Trans.) New York: Norton.

Irwin, C. E. (1989). Risk-taking behaviors in the adolescent patient: Are they impulsive? *Pediatric Annals, 18*(2), 122–133.

It's boom time for children's literature. (1989, January 1). *The Boston Globe,* pp. A101, A106.

Itons-Peterson, M. J., & Reddel, M. (1984). What do people ask about the neonate? *Developmental Psychology, 20*(3), 358–359.

Izard, C. D., & Dougherty, L. (1982). Two complementary systems for measuring facial expressions in infants and children. In C. E. Izard (Ed.), *Measuring emotions in infants and children*. New York: Cambridge University Press.

Jackson, A. W., & Hornbeck, D. W. (1989). Educating young adolescents: Why we must restructure middle grade schools. *American Psychologist, 44*(5), 831–836.

Jacobs, B. W., & Isaacs, S. (1986). Pre-pubertal anorexia nervosa: A retrospective controlled study. *Journal of Child Psychiatry, 27,* 237–250.

Jacobson, J. L., Fein, G. G., Jacobson, S. W., & Schwartz, P. M. (1984). Factors and clusters for the Brazelton Scale: An investigation of the dimensions of neonatal behavior. *Developmental Psychology, 20*(3), 339–353.

Jacobson, J. L., & Willie, D. E. (1984). Influence of attachment and separation experience on separation distress at 18 months. *Developmental Psychology, 20*(3), 477–488.

Jacobvitz, D., & Sroufe, L. A. (1987). The early caregiver-child relationship and attention-deficit disorder with hyperactivity in kindergarten: A prospective study. *Child Development, 58*(6), 1488–1495.

Janofsky, M. (1989, March 6). Coach's drug use shaped philosophy. *The New York Times,* p. C7.

Jensen, A. (1969). How much can we boost IQ and scholastic achievement? *Harvard Educational Review, 39,* 1–123.

––––––. (1973). *Educability and group differences.* New York: Harper & Row.

––––––. (1974). Cumulative deficit: A testable hypothesis? *Developmental Psychology, 10,* 996–1019.

––––––. (1977). Cumulative deficit in IQ of blacks in the rural south. *Developmental Psychology, 13,* 184–191.

Jensen, R., & Moore, S. G. (1977). The effect of attribute statements on cooperativeness and competitiveness in school-aged boys. *Child Development, 48,* 305–307.

Johnson, C., Lewis, C., Love, S., Lewis, L., & Stucky, M. (1984). Incidence and correlates of bulimic behavior in a female high school population. *Journal of Youth and Adolescence, 15*(1), 15–26.

Johnson, D. W., & Johnson, R. T. (1974). Instructional structure: Cooperative, competitive and individualistic. *Reviews of Educational Research, 44,* 213–240.

Johnson, H. R., Mykre, S. A., Ruvalcaba, R. H. A., Thuline, H. C., & Kelley, V. C. (1970). Effects of testosterone on body image and behavior in Klinefelter's syndrome: A pilot study. *Developmental Medicine and Child Neurology, 12,* 454–460.

Johnson, K. (1988). *Teens and AIDS: Opportunities for prevention.* Washington, DC: Children's Defense Fund.

Johnston, J. R., & Slobin, D. I. (1979). The development of locative expressions in English, Italian, Serbo-Croatian, and Turkish. *Journal of Child Language, 16,* 532–547.

Jones, H. C., & Lovinger, P. W. (1985). *The marijuana question.* New York: Dodd, Mead.

Jones, H. F. (1949). Adolescence in our society. In Anniversary Papers of the Community Service Society of New York: *The family in a democratic society* (pp. 70–82). New York: Columbia University Press.

Jones, W. M. (1977). The impact on society of youths who drop out or who are undereducated. *Educational Leadership, 34,* 413–416.

Joos, S. K., Pollitt, E., Mueleer, W. H., & Albright, D. L. (1983). The Bacon Chow study: Maternal nutritional supplementation and infant behavioral development. *Child Development, 54,* 669–676.

Joshi, N. P., & Scott, M. (1988). Drug use, depression, and adolescents. *Pediatric Clinics of North America, 35*(6), 1349–1364.

Joslyn, W. D. (1971). Androgen-induced social dominance in infant female rhesus monkeys. *Journal of Child Psychology and Psychiatry, 84,* 35–44.

Juergen, H., Wimmer, H., & Perner, J. (1986). Ignorance versus false belief: A developmental lag in attribution of epistemic states. *Child Development, 57*(3), 567–582.

Kagan, J., Kearsley, R. B., & Zelazo, P. R. (1978). *Infancy: Its place in human development.* Cambridge, MA: Harvard University Press.

Kahler, K. S. (1989, February 26). The growing traffic in illegal steroids. *The Boston Sunday Globe,* p. 78.

Kamhi, A. G. (1986). The elusive first word: The importance of the naming insight for the development of referential speech. *Journal of Child Language, 13,* 155–161.

Kamii, C. (1982). *Number in preschool and kindergarten.* Washington, DC: National Association for the Education of Young Children.

––––––. (1985). *Young children reinvent arithmetic.* New York: Teachers College Press.

Kamin, L. J. (1974). *The Science and Politics of IQ.* Potomac, MD: Lawrence Erlbaum.

––––––. (1978). A positive interpretation of apparent "cumulative deficit." *Developmental Psychology, 14,* 195–196.

Kaplan, E. L., & Kaplan, G. A. (1970). The prelinguistic child. In J. Eliot (Ed.), *Human development and cognitive processes* (pp. 358–381). New York: Holt, Rinehart & Winston.

Kappas, A., Drummond, G. S., Manola, T., Petmezoki, S., & Valaes, T. (1988). Sn-protoporphyrin use in management of hyperbilirubinemia in term newborns with direct Coombs-Positive ABO incompatibility. *Pediatrics, 81*(4), 485–497.

Kataria, S., Swanson, M. S., & Trevathon, G. E. (1987). Persistence of sleep disturbances in preschool children. *Journal of Pediatrics, 110*(4), 642–646.

Katchadourian, H. A. (1977). *The biology of adolescence.* New York: W. H. Freeman.

Katz, L., & Hamilton, J. R. (1974). Fat absorption in infants of low birth weight less than 1,300 gm. *Journal of Pediatrics, 85,* 6081.

Kaye, K. (1982a). *The mental and social life of babies*. Chicago: The University of Chicago Press.

_____. (1982b). Organism, apprentice, and person. In E. Z. Tronick (Ed.), *Social interchange in infancy: Affect, cognition, and communication*. Baltimore: University Park Press.

Kaye, K., & Charney, R. (1980). How mothers maintain "dialogue" with two-year-olds. In D. Oldson (Ed.), *The social foundations of language and thought*. New York: Norton.

Kazdin, A. E. (1987). Treatment of antisocial behavior in children: Current status and future directions. *Psychological Bulletin, 102*, 187–203.

Keating, D. (1980). Thinking processes in adolescence. In J. Adelson (Ed.), *Handbook of adolescent psychology*. New York: Wiley.

Kelley, B., & Gilman, J. (1983). Follow-up of 373 children born after second trimester amniocentesis. *Pediatric Nursing, 9*(2), 95–97.

Kelly, C., & Goodwin, G. C. (1983). Adolescents' perception of three styles of parental control. *Adolescence, 18*(71), 567–571.

Kelly, D. H., & Shannon, D. C. (1982). Sudden infant death syndrome and near sudden death syndrome: A review of the literature, 1964–1982. *Pediatric Clinics of North America, 29*(5), 1241–1261.

Kempe, R. S., & Kempe, C. H. (1978). *Child abuse*. Cambridge, MA: Harvard University Press.

Kerkay, J., Zsako, S., & Kaplan, A. (1971). Immunoelectrophoretic serum patterns associated with mothers of children affected with the G_1-trisomy syndrome (Down's syndrome). *American Journal of Mental Deficiency, 75*, 729–732.

Kerkman, D., Wright, J. C., Huston, A. C., Rice, M., & Bremer, M. (1983). *Preschoolers who get cable TV: Family patterns, media orientations, and media use*. Paper presented at the Biennial Meeting of the Society for Research in Child Development, Detroit, MI.

Klaus, M. H., & Fannaroff, A. A. (1973). *Care of the high-risk neonate*. Philadelphia: W. B. Saunders.

Klaus, M. H., Jerazauld, R., Kreger, N. C., McAlpine, W., Steffa, M., & Kennell, J. H. (1972). Maternal attachment importance of the first post-partum days. *New England Journal of Medicine, 286*, 460–463.

Klaus, M. H., & Kennell, J. H. (1976). *Maternal-infant bonding*. St. Louis: Mosby.

Klein, R. P. (1985) Caregiving arrangements by employed women with children under 1 year of age. *Developmental Psychology, 21*, 403–406.

Kligman, D., & Cronnell, B. (1974). *Black English and spelling*. ERIC ED 108 234. Washington, DC: U. S. Government Printing Office.

Kline, M., Tschann, J. M., Johnston, J. R., & Wallerstein, J. S. (1989). Children's adjustment in joint and sole physical custody families. *Developmental Psychology, 25*(3), 430–436.

Klinnert, M. (1981). *The regulation of infant behavior by maternal facial expression*. Unpublished doctoral dissertation, University of Denver, Denver, CO.

Kogan, D. P., Oulton, M., Gray, J. H., Liston, R. M., Luther, E. R., Peddle, L. J., & Young, D. C. (1986). Amniotic fluid phosphatdylglycerol and phosphyatidylcholine phosphorus as predictors of fetal lung maturity. *American Journal of Obstetrics and Gynecology, 154*(2), 226–230.

Kohlberg, L. (1966). A cognitive developmental analysis of children's sex-role concepts and attitudes. In E. E. Maccoby (Ed.), *The development of sex differences* (p. 82). Stanford, CA: Stanford University Press.

_____. (1969). Stage and sequence: The cognitive developmental approach to socialization. In D. A. Goslin (Ed.), *Handbook of socialization theory and research* (pp. 347–480). Chicago: Rand McNally.

_____. (1976). Moral stages and moralization. In T. Lickona (Ed.), *Moral development and behavior: Theory, research, and social issues* (pp. 219–249). New York: Holt, Rinehart & Winston.

Konner, M. (1982). Biological aspects of the mother-infant bond. In R. N. Emde & R. J. Harmon (Eds.), *The development of attachment and affiliative systems* (pp. 137–159; 237–259). New York: Plenum Press.

Kopp, C.B., & Krakow, J. B. (1983). The developmentalist and the study of biological risk: A view of the past with an eye toward the future. *Child Development, 54*, 1086–1108.

Korner, A. (1971). Individual differences at birth: Duplications for early experience and later development. *American Journal of Orthopsychiatry, 41*, 608–610.

Korner, A., & Grobstein, R. (1966). Visual alertness as related to soothing in neonates: Implications for maternal stimulation and early deprivation. *Child Development, 37*, 867–876.

Korner, A., & Thoman, E. B. (1972). The relative efficacy of contact and vestibular-proprioceptive stimulation on soothing neonates. *Child Development, 43*, 443–453.

Krantz, M. (1982). Sociometric awareness, social participation, and perceived popularity in preschool children. *Child Development, 53*, 376–379.

Kratcoski, P. E., & Kratcoski, J. E. (1975). Changing patterns in the delinquent activities of boys and girls: A self-reported delinquency analysis. *Adolescence, 37*, 53–91.

Krauss, R. M., & Glucksberg, S. (1969). The development of communication: Competence as a function of age. *Child Development, 42*, 255–266.

Kreutner, A. K. (1981). Adolescent contraception. *Pediatric Clinics of North America, 28*(2), 455–473.

Kristiansson, B., & Fallstrom, S. P. (1987). Growth at the age of 4 years subsequent to early failure to thrive. *Child Abuse and Neglect, 11,* 35–40.

Kron, R. E., Stern, M., & Goddard, K. E. (1966). Newborn sucking behavior affected by obstetrics sedation. *Pediatrics, 37,* 1012–1016.

Krongrad, E., & O'Neill, L. (1986). Near miss sudden infant death syndrome episodes? A clinical and electrocardiographic correlation. *Pediatrics, 77*(6), 811–815.

Kuder, G. F. (1975). *General interest survey (form E) manual.* Chicago: Science Research Associates.

Kuhn, D. (1984). Cognitive development. In M. H. Bernstein & M. E. Lamb (Eds.), *Developmental psychology.* Hillsdale, NJ: Lawrence Erlbaum.

Kulberg, A. (1986). Substance abuse: Clinical identification and management. *Pediatrics Toxicology, 33*(2), 325–361.

Kunkel, D., & Watkins, B. A. (1985). Children and television. *Washington Report of the Society for Research in Child Development, 1*(4), 1–8.

Kupfer, F. (1982). *Before and after Zachariah.* New York: Delacorte.

Laboratory of Comparative Human Cognition. (1983). Culture and cognitive development. In P. Mussen (Ed.), *Handbook of child psychology: Vol. 1. History, theory, and methods.* New York: Wiley.

Ladd, G. E. (1981). Effectiveness of a social learning method for enhancing children's social interaction and peer acceptance. *Child Development, 52,* 171–178.

Lamb, M. E., (1977). The development of parental preference in the first two years of life. *Sex Roles, 3,* 495–497.

———. (1982). Parent-infant interaction, attachment, and socioemotional development in infancy. In R. M. Emde & R. J. Harmon (Eds.), *The development of attachment and affiliative systems* (pp. 195–211). New York: Plenum Press.

Lambert, W. E., Just, M. N., & Segalowitz, N. (1970). Some cognitive consequences of following the curricula of the early school grades in a foreign language. In J. A. Alatis (Ed.), *Twenty-first annual round table: Bilingualism and language contact.* Washington, DC: Georgetown University Press.

Landrigan, P. (1981, December). *Report of the 84th Ross Conference on Pediatric Research.*

Langer, E. J. (1979). The illusion of incompetence. In L. C. Perlmutter & R. A. Monty (Eds.), *Choice and perceived control* (pp. 301–313). Hillsdale, NJ: Lawrence Erlbaum.

Larry, P. v. Riles, 343 F. Supp. 1306 (N. D. Cal. 1972), aff'd. 502 F. 2d 963 (9th Cir. 1974).

Lasch, C. (1977). *Haven in a heartless land.* New York: Basic Books.

Lavine, L. (1977). Differentiation of letterlike forms in prereading children. *Developmental Psychology, 13*(2), 89–94.

Leahy, R. L. (1976). Development of preferences and processes of visual scanning in the human infant during the first 3 months of life. *Developmental Psychology, 12*(3), 250–254.

Leary, A., Huston, A. C., & Wright, J. C. (1983, April). *The influence of television production features with masculine and feminine connotations on children's comprehension and play.* Paper presented at the biennial meeting of the Society for Research in Child Development, Detroit, MI.

Lefkowitz, M. M. (1981). Smoking during pregnancy: Long-term effects on offspring. *Developmental Psychology, 17*(2), 192–194.

Leflore, L. (1988). Delinquent youths and family. *Adolescence, 23,* 629–647.

Leifer, A. D., Leiderman, P. H., Barnett, C. R., & Williams, J. A. (1972). Effects of mother-infant separation on maternal attachment behavior. *Child Development, 43,* 1203–1218.

Leifer, A. D., & Roberts, D. F. (1972). Children's responses to television violence. In J. P. Murray, E. A. Rubenstein, & G. A. Comstock (Eds.), *Television and social behavior: Vol. 2. Television and social learning.* Washington, DC: U. S. Government Printing Office.

Lemish, D., & Rice, M. L. (1986). Television as a talking picture book: A prop for language acquisition. *Journal of Child Language, 13,* 254–274.

Lenz, W. (1966). Malformations caused by drugs in pregnancy. *American Journal of Diseases of Children, 112,* 99–106.

Lepper, M. (1973). Dissonance, self-perception, and honesty in children. *Journal of Personality and Social Psychology, 13,* 495–507.

Lerner, R. M., & Lerner, J. V. (1977). Effects of age, sex, and physical attractiveness on child-peer relations, academic performance, and elementary school adjustment. *Developmental Psychology, 13,* 585–590.

Lester, D. (1988). Youth suicide: A cross-cultural perspective. *Adolescence, 23*(92), 955–966.

Levine, S. (1966). Sex differences in the brain. *Scientific American, 214,* 84–90.

Liben, L. S. (1977). Memory from a cognitive-developmental perspective: A theoretical and empirical review. In W. Overton & J. Gallagher (Eds.), *Knowledge and development* (Vol. 1). New York: Plenum Press.

Liberman, I., Shankweiler, D., Fischer, F. W., & Carter, B. (1974). Explicit syllable and phoneme segmentation in the young child. *Journal of Experimental Child Psychology, 18,* 201–212.

Lickona, T. (1976). Research on Piaget's theory of moral development. In T. Lickona (Ed.), *Moral development and behavior: Theory, research, and social issues* (pp. 219–240). New York: Holt, Rinehart & Winston.

Lieberman, A. F. (1977). Preschoolers' competence with a peer: Relations with attachment and peer experience. *Child Development, 48,* 1277–1287.

Liebert, R. M. (1986). Effects of television on children and adolescents. *Journal of Development and Behavioral Pediatrics, 7*(1): 43–48.

Liebert, R. M., & Baron, R. A. (1972). Some immediate effects of televised violence on children's behavior. *Developmental Psychology, 6,* 469–475.

Lilienfield, A. M. (1969). *Epidemiology of mongolism.* Baltimore: Johns Hopkins Press.

Linn, M. C. (1983). Content, context, and process in reasoning. *Journal of Early Adolescence, 3,* 63–82.

Lipsitt, L. P. (1977). Taste in human neonates: Its effect on sucking and heart rates. In J. M. Weiffenbach (Ed.), *Taste and development: The genesis of sweet preference.* Washington, DC: U.S. Government Printing Office.

Lipsitt, L. P., Engen, T., & Kaye, H. (1963). Developmental changes in the olfactory threshold of the neonate. *Child Development, 34,* 371–376.

Lipsitt, L. P., & Levy, N. (1959). Electrotactual threshold in the neonate. *Child Development, 30,* 547–554.

Little, B. B., Snell, L. M., Klein, V. R., & Gilstrap, L. C. (1989). Cocaine abuse during pregnancy: Maternal and fetal indications. *Obstetrics and Gynecology, 73*(2), 157–160.

Livesley, W. J., & Bromley, D. B. (1973). *Person perception in childhood and adolescence.* London: Wiley.

Loban, W. (1975). *Language development: Kindergarten through grade twelve.* Urbana, IL: National Council of Teachers of English.

Loeber, R. (1982). The stability of antisocial and delinquent child behavior: A review. *Child Development, 53,* 1431–1446.

Long, T. J., & Long, L. (1982). *Latchkey children: The child's view of self care. Resources in Education,* (ERIC Document Reproduction Service No. ED 211 119).

Lowrey, G. H. (1978). *Growth and development of children* (7th ed.). Chicago: Year Book.

Lubchenco, L. O., Delivoria-Papodopoulos, M., & Searle, D. (1972). Long-term follow-up studies of prematurely born infants II. Influences of birth weight and gestational age on sequelae. *Journal of Pediatrics, 80,* 509–512.

Lucy, J. F., & Dangman, B. (1984). A reexamination of the role of oxygen in retrolental fibroplasia. *Pediatrics, 73*(1), 82–95.

Lyle, J., & Hoffman, H. (1972). Children's use of television and other media. *Television in everyday life: Patterns of use.* Washington, DC: U. S. Government Printing Office.

Maccoby, E. E. (1980). *Social development: Psychological growth and the parent-child relationship.* New York: Harcourt Brace Jovanovich.

Maccoby, E. E., & Jacklin, C. N. (1974). *The psychology of sex differences.* Stanford, CA: Stanford University Press.

Macmillan. *Very First Dictionary.* (1983). New York: Macmillan.

MacNamara, J. (1976). First and second language learning: Same or different? *Journal of Education, 158,* 39–54.

Maddi, S. R. (1976). *Personality theories.* Homewood, IL: Dorsey.

Magnusson, D., Stattin, H., & Allen, V. L. (1985). Biological maturation and social development: A longitudinal study of some adjustment processes from mid-adolescence to adulthood. *Journal of Youth and Adolescence, 14,* 267–283.

Maier, S., Seligman, M., & Solomon, R. (1969). Pavlovian fear conditioning and learned helplessness. In B. A. Campbell & R. M. Church (Eds.), *Punishment and aversive behavior.* New York: Appleton-Century-Crofts.

Main, M. (1981). Avoidance in the service of attachment: A working paper. In K. L. Immelmenn, G. W. Barlow, L. Petrinovitch, & M. Main (Eds.), *Behavioral development.* Cambridge, England: Cambridge University Press.

Mann, L., & Boyce, S. (1982). Fundamental frequency and discourse structure. *Language & Speech, 25,* 341–383.

Marcia, J. E. (1980). Identity in adolescence. In J. Adelson (Ed.), *Handbook of adolescent psychology* (pp. 159–187). New York: Wiley.

Marek, E. (1989, April). The lives of teenage mothers. *Harper's Magazine,* pp. 59–64.

Marks, A. (1980). Adolescent suicide: Epidemiologic study of recent trends. In F. A. Oski & J. N. Stockman (Eds.), *1980 yearbook of pediatrics.* Chicago: Yearbook.

Marland, S. P. (1972). Education of the gifted and talented. *Report to the Congress of the United States by the United States Commissioner of Education and background papers submitted to the United States Office of Education.* Washington, DC: U. S. Government Printing Office.

Marsiglio, W., & Mott, F. L. (1986). The impact of sex education on sexual activity, contraceptive use and premarital pregnancy among American teenagers. *Family Planning Perspectives, 17,* 132.

Marston, A. R., Jacobs, D. F., Singer, R. D., Widaman, K. F., & Little, J. D. (1988). Adolescents who apparently are invulnerable to drug, alcohol, and nicotine use. *Adolescence, 23*(9), 593–598.

Martin, A. D., Simpson, J. L., Rosinky, B. J., & Elias, S. (1986). Chorionic villus sampling in continuous pregnancies. *American Journal of Obstetrics and Gynecology, 154*(6), 1353–1362.

Marwich, C., & Simmons, D. (1984). Medical news: Changing childhood disease patterns linked with daycare boom. *Journal of the American Medical Association, 251,* 1245–1251.

Marx, G. F. (1961). Placental transfer and drugs used in anesthesia. *Anesthesiology, 22,* 294.

Mason, J. (1980). When do children begin to read? An exploration of four-year-old children's letter and word reading competencies. *Reading Research Quarterly, 15,* 203–227.

Massachusetts Department of Public Health, Public Health Fact Sheet: AIDS. (1985, November).

Matas, L., Arend, R. A., & Sroufe, L. A. (1978). Continuity of adaptation in the second year: The relationship between quality of attachment and later competence. *Child Development, 49,* 547–556.

McAllister, A. L., Perry, C. & Maccoby, N. (1979). Adolescent smoking: Onset and prevention. *Pediatrics, 63*(4), 650–658.

McClelland, D. C., Atkinson, I. W., Clark, R. A., & Lowell, E. L. (1976). *The achievement motive.* New York: Halsted Press.

McCune-Nicolich, L. (1981). Toward symbolic functioning: Structure of early pretend games and potential parallels with language. *Child Development, 52,* 785–797.

McCune-Nicolich, L., & Fenson, L. (1984). Methodological issues in studying early pretend play. In T. Yowkey & T. Pellegrini (Eds.), *Child's play.* Hillsdale, NJ: Lawrence Erlbaum.

McDavid, J. W., & Harari, H. (1966). Stereotyping of names and popularity in grade-school children. *Child Development, 37,* 453–459.

McGhee, P. E. (1971). Cognitive development and children's comprehension of humor. *Child Development, 42,* 123–138.

_____. (1979). *Humor: Its origin and development.* San Francisco: W. H. Freeman.

McGowan, R. W., Jarmon, B. O., & Peterson, D. M. (1974). Effects of a competitive endurance training program on self-concept and peer approval. *Journal of Psychology, 86,* 57–60.

McHan, J. (1986). Imitation of aggression by Lebanese children. *The Journal of Social Psychology, 125*(5), 613–617.

McKnight, J., & Shelsby, B. (1984). Checking in: An alternative for latchkey kids. *Children Today, 13*(3), 23–25.

McLaughlin, B. (1978). *Second language acquisition in childhood.* New York: Wiley.

McLaughlin, E., & Crawford, J. D. (1985). Burns. *Pediatric Clinics of North America, 32,* 61–75.

McNeill, D. (1966). Developmental psycholinguistics. In F. Smith & G. A. Miller (Eds.), *The genesis of language: A psycholinguistic approach* (pp. 15–84). Cambridge, MA: MIT Press.

McNeill, D. (1966). Developmental psycholinguistics. In F. Smith & G. A. Miller (Eds.), *The genesis of language: A psycholinguistic approach.* Cambridge, MA: MIT Press.

Meehan, A. M. (1984). A meta-analysis of sex differences in formal operational thought. *Child Development, 55,* 1110–1124.

Mennuti, M. T., DiGaetano, A., McDonnell, A., Cohen, A. W., & Liston, R. M. (1983). Fetal-maternal bleeding associated with genetic amniocentesis: Read time versus static ultrasound. *Obstetrics and Gynecology, 62*(1), 26–30.

Menyuk, P. (1969). *Language and maturation.* Cambridge, MA: MIT Press.

_____. (1977). *Language and maturation.* Cambridge, MA: MIT Press.

Meredith, H. V. (1975). Relation between tobacco smoking of pregnant women and body size of progeny. *Human Biology, 47,* 451–472.

Merritt, A., & Valdes-Dapena, M. (1984). SIDS research update. *Pediatric Annals, 13*(3), 193–207.

Mestayan, G., & Varga, R. (1960). Chemical thermoregulation of full-term and premature newborn infants. *Journal of Pediatrics, 56,* 623–629.

Metzger, R. L., & Werner, D. B. (1984). Use of visual training for reading disabilities: A review. *Pediatrics, 73*(6), 824–829.

Meyer, R. E. (1989). Who can say no to illicit drug use? *Archives of General Psychiatry, 46*(2), 189–190.

Milberg, A. (1976). *Street games.* New York: McGraw-Hill.

Millar, W. S. (1974). Conditioning and learning in early infancy. In B. Foss (Ed.), *New perspectives in child development.* Harmondsworth, England: Penguin.

Miller, L. G., & Bizzell, R. P. (1983). Long-term effects of four preschool programs: 6th, 7th, and 8th grades. *Child Development, 54,* 725–741.

Miller, M. (1987, November 23). Drug use: Down but not in the ghetto. *Newsweek, 110,* 33.

Miller, M. A., & Brooten, D. A. (1977). *The childbearing family: A nursing perspective.* Boston: Little, Brown.

Miller, N., & Maruyama, G. (1976). Ordinal position and peer popularity. *Journal of Personality and Social Psychology, 33,* 123–131.

Miller, R. E., & Rosenstein, D. J. (1982). Children's dental health: Overview for the physician. *Pediatric Clinics of North America, 29*(3), 429–438.

Miller, S. & Garvey, D. (1984). In I. Bretherton (ED.), *Symbolic play.* New York: Academic Press.

Miller-Jones, D. (1989). Culture and testing. *American Psychologist, 44*(2), 360–366.

Millstein, S. G. (1989). Adolescent health. *American Psychologist, 44*(5), 837–842.

Mineka, S., Gunnar, M., & Champoux, M. (1986). Control and early socioemotional development: Infant Rhesus monkeys reared in controllable versus uncontrollable environments. *Child Development, 57,* 1241–1256.

Minton, C., Kagan, J., & Levine, J. A. (1971). Maternal control and obedience in the two-year-old. *Child Development, 42,* 1873–1894.

Minuchin, P. P., & Shapiro, E. K. (1983). The school as a context for social development. In P. H. Mussen (Ed.),

Handbook of child psychology (4th ed., Vol. 4). New York: Wiley.

Mischel, W. (1976). *Introduction to personality.* New York: Holt, Rinehart & Winston.

Mischel, W., & Baker, N. (1975). Cognitive transformation of reward objects through instructions. *Journal of Personality and Social Psychology, 31,* 254–261.

Mischel, W., & Ebbesen, E. (1970). Attention in delay of gratification. *Journal of Personality and Social Psychology, 16,* 329–337.

Mitchell, A. (1987). *Young children in public schools: Preliminary results from a national survey of public school districts and site visits in twelve states.* New York: Bank Street College Center for Children's Policy.

Moely, B. E. (1977). Organizational factors in the development of memory. In R. V. Kail & J. W. Hagen (Eds.), *Perspectives on the development of memory and cognition.* Hillsdale, NJ: Lawrence Erlbaum.

Mofenson, H. C., & Caraccio, T. R. (1987). *Pediatric Annals, 16*(1), 864–874.

Moffit, A. R. (1971). Consonant cue perception by twenty- to twenty-four-week-old infants. *Child Development, 42,* 717–731.

Mood, D., Johnson, J., & Shantz, C. U. (1974). *Affective and cognitive components of empathy in young children.* Paper presented at the Southwest Regional Meeting of the Society for Research in Child Development, Chapel Hill, N.C.

Morishima, H. O., Daniel, S. S., Finster, M., Poppers, P. J., & James, L. S. (1966). Transmission of mepivocaine hydrochloride (carbocaine) across the human placenta. *Anesthesiology, 27,* 147–154.

Morphett, M. V., & Washburne, C. (1931). When should children begin to read? *Elementary School Journal, 31,* 496–503.

Moses, N., Mansour-Max, B., & Lifshitz, F. (1989). Fear of obesity among adolescent girls. *Pediatrics, 83*(3), 393–398.

Moskowitz, B. A. (1978). The acquisition of language. *Scientific American, 239,* 92–108.

Mueller, E., Bleir, M., Krakow, J., Hegedus, K., & Cournoyer, P. (1977). The development of peer verbal interaction among two-year-old boys. *Child Development, 48,* 284–287.

Mueller, E., & Brenner, J. (1977). The origins of social skills and interaction among playgroup toddlers. *Child Development, 48,* 854–861.

Muir, D., & Field, J. (1979). Newborn infants orient to sounds. *Child Development, 50,* 431–436.

Muma, J. R. (1986). *Language acquisition: A functionalistic perspective.* Austin, TX: Pro-Ed.

Murphy, C. M., & Messer, D. J. (1977). Mothers, infants, and pointing: A study of gesture. In H. R. Schaffer (Ed.), *Studies in mother-infant interaction.* London: Academic Press.

Murray, A. D. (1988). Newborn auditory brain stem evoked response (ABRs): Prenatal and contemporary correlates. *Child Development, 59*(3), 571–588.

Murray, A., Dolby, R. M., Nation, R. L., & Thomas, D. B. (1981). Effects of epidural anesthesia on newborns and their mothers. *Child Development, 52,* 71–82.

Murray, J. P., & Lonnborg, B. (undated). *Children and television.* Boys Town, NB: The Boys Town Center.

Murstein, B. L., Chalpin, M. J., Heard, K. V., & Vyse, S. A. (1989). Sexual behavior, drugs, and relationship patterns on a college campus over thirteen years. *Adolescence, 24,* 125–139.

Musick, J. S., Clark, R., & Cohler, B. (1981). The Mothers' Project: A program for mentally ill mothers of young children. In B. Weissbourd & J. Musick, (Eds.), *Infants: Their social environments.* Washington, DC: National Association for the Education of Young Children.

Naeye, R. (1983). Maternal age, obstetric complications, and the outcome of pregnancy. *Obstetrics and Gynecology, 61*(2), 210–216.

Naeye, R. L., Blanc, W., & Paul, C. (1973). Effects of maternal nutrition on the human fetus. *Pediatrics, 52,* 494–503.

National Association for the Education of Young Children. (1986). Position statement on developmentally appropriate practice in programs for 4- and 5-year-olds. *Young Children, 41,* 20–29.

National March of Dimes. (1973).

Needham, J. (1959). *A history of embryology.* New York: Abelard-Schuman.

Nelson, K. (1973). Structure and strategy in learning to talk. *Monographs of the Society for Research in Child Development, 38.*

Nelson, K. E., & Nelson, K. (1978). Cognitive pendulums and the linguistic realization. In K. E. Nelson (Ed.), *Children's language* (Vol. 1). New York: Gardner Press.

Neuman, S. B. (1988). The displacement effect: Assessing the relation between television viewing and reading performance. *Reading Research Quarterly, 23*(4), 414–440.

Neumann, C. G. (1977). Obesity in pediatric practice: Obesity in the preschool and school-age child. *Pediatric Clinics of North America, 24,* 117–122.

Newcomb, M. D., & Bentler, P. M. (1989). Substance use and abuse among children and teenagers. *American Psychologist, 44*(2), 242–248.

Newman, H. H., Freeman, F. N., & Holzinger, K. J. (1937). *Twins: A study of heredity and environment.* Chicago: University of Chicago Press.

Newman, J. M. (1985). Insights from recent reading and writing research and their implications for developing whole language curriculum. In J. M. Newman (Ed.), *Whole language: Theory in use.* Portsmouth, NH: Heinemann Educational Books.

Newport, E. L., Gleitman, H. J., & Gleitman, L. R. (1977). Mother, I'd rather do it myself: Some effects and noneffects of maternal speech style. In C. E. Snow &

C. A. Ferguson (Eds.), *Talking to children: Language input and acquisition*. Cambridge, England: Cambridge University Press.

Newson, J., & Newson, E. (1978). *Seven years old in the home environment*. London: Penguin.

Nicholas, S. W., Sondheimer, D. L., Willoughby, A. D., Yaffe, S. J., & Katz, S. L. (1989). Human immunodeficiency virus infection in childhood, adolescence, and pregnancy: A status report and national research agenda. *Pediatrics, 83*(2), 293–308.

Nicolich, L. (1977). Beyond sensorimotor intelligence: Assessment of symbolic maturity through analysis of pretend play. *Merrill-Palmer Quarterly, 23*, 89–99.

Nielsen, G., Collins, S., Meisel, J., Lowry, M., Eng, M., & Johnson, D. (1975). An intervention program for atypical infants. In B. Z. Friedlander, G. M. Sterritt, & G. E. Kirk (Eds.), *Exceptional infant: Assessment and intervention.* (Vol. 3). New York: Brunner/Mazel.

Nielson Television Index. (1981). *Child and teenage television viewing (special release)*. New York: Nielson Television Index.

Niemark, E. D. (1981). Confounding with cognitive style factors: An artifact explanation for the apparent non-universal incidence of formal operations. In I. Sigel, D. Brodzinsky, & R. Golnikoff (Eds.), *New directions in Piagetian research and theory*. Hillsdale, NJ: Lawrence Erlbaum.

Ninio, A., & Bruner, J. (1978). The achievement and antecedents of labelling. *Journal of Child Language, 5*, 1–15.

Nissen, H. W. (1930). A study of exploratory behavior in the white rat by means of the obstruction method. *Journal of Genetic Psychology, 37*, 361–376.

Nurss, J. R., & McGauvran, M. E. (1986). Metropolitan Readiness Assessment Program (5th ed.). Orlando, FL: Harcourt Brace Jovanovich.

O'Driscoll, K., & Foley, M. (1983). Correlation of decrease in perinatal mortality and increase in cesarean section rates. *Obstetrics and Gynecology, 61*(1), 1–5.

Oakes, J. (1985). *Keeping track: How schools structure inequality*. New Haven, CT: Yale University Press.

Oden, S., & Asher, S. R. (1977). Coaching children in social skills for friendship making. *Child Development, 48*, 495–506.

Oliver, J. E., & Taylor, A. (1971). Five generations of ill-treated children in one family pedigree. *The British Journal of Psychiatry, 119*, 473–480.

Olson, R. (Ed.). (1986). The manipulation of children's eating preferences. *Nutrition Reviews, 44*(10), 327–328.

Olweus, D., Mattsson, A., Schalling, D., & Low, H. (1980). Testosterone, aggression, physical and personality dimensions in normal adolescent males. *Psychosomatic Medicine, 42*, 253–269.

Ornstein, P. A., & Naus, M. J. (1978). Rehearsal processes in children's memory. In P. A. Ornstein (Ed.), *Memory development in children*. Hillsdale, NJ: Lawrence Erlbaum.

Otis, A. S., & Lennon, R. T. (1967). *Otis-Lennon Mental Ability Test Primary Level I*. New York: Harcourt, Brace & World.

Pai, A. C. (1974). *Foundations of genetics*. New York: McGraw-Hill.

Paneth, N. (1986). Etiologic factors in cerebral palsy. *Pediatric Annals, 15*(3), 191–201.

Papousek, H. (1967). Experimental studies of appetitional behavior in human newborns and infants. In H. Stevenson, E. Hess & H. Rheingold (Eds.), *Early behavior: Comparative and developmental approaches*. New York: Wiley.

Papousek, H., & Bernstein, P. (1969). The functioning of conditioning stimulation in human neonates and infants. In A. Ambrose (Ed.,), *Stimulation in early infancy*. New York: Academic Press.

Parke, R. D., & Lewis, N. G. (1981). The family in context: A multilevel interactional analysis of child abuse. In R. W. Henderson (Ed.), *Parent-child interaction: Theory, research, and prospects* (pp. 169–204). New York: Academic Press.

Parke, R. D., & Slaby, R. G. (1983). The development of aggression. In P. H. Mussen (Ed.), *Handbook of child psychology* (Vol. 4). New York: Wiley.

Parke, R. D., & Suomi, S. J. (1980). Adult male-infant relationships: Human and nonprimate evidence. In K. L. Immelmann, G. Barlow, M. Main & L. Petrinovitch (Eds.), *Behavioral development: The Bielefeld interdisciplinary project*. New York: Cambridge University Press.

Parsons, J. E., Adler, T. F., & Kaczala, C. M. (1982). Socialization of achievement attitudes and beliefs: Parental influences. *Child Development, 53*(2), 310–321.

Parten, M. (1932). Social play among preschool children. *Journal of Abnormal and Social Psychology, 27*, 243–269.

Pastor, D. L. (1981). The quality of mother-infant attachment and its relationship to toddler's initial sociability with peers. *Developmental Psychology, 17*, 326–338.

Patterson, C. J. (1982). Self-control and self-regulation in childhood. In T. Field & A. Huston-Stein (Eds.), *Review of human development*. New York: Wiley.

Patterson, C., & Mischel, W. (1976). Effects of temptation-inhibiting and task-facilitating plans on self-control. *Journal of Personality and Social Psychology, 33*, 209–217.

Patterson, G. L., Litman, R. A., & Bricker, W. (1967). Assertive behavior in children: A step toward a theory of aggression. *Monographs of the Society for the Research in Child Development, 32*, 1–43.

Patterson, G. R., DeBaryshe, B. D., & Ramsey, E. (1989). A developmental perspective on antisocial behavior. *American Psychologist, 44*(2), 329–335.

Peck, J. T., McCaig, G., & Sapp, M. E. (1988). *Kindergarten policies: What is best for children?* Washington, DC: National Association for the Education of Young Children.

Peck, R. F., & Havinghurst, R. I. (1960). *The psychology of character development*. New York: Wiley.

Perkins, R. P., Nakashima, I. I., Mullin, M., Dubansky, L. S., & Chin, M. L. (1978). Intensive care in adolescent pregnancy. *Obstetrics and Gynecology, 52*(2), 179–188.

Perlstein, P. H., Hersh, C., Glueck, C. J., & Sutherland, J. M. (1974). Adaptation to cold in the first three days of life. *Pediatrics, 54*, 411.

Peskin, J. (1980). Female performance and Inhelder's and Piaget's tests of formal operations. *Genetic Psychology Monographs, 101*, 245–256.

Peterson, A. C. (1979). Can puberty come any earlier? *Psychology Today, 12*, 45.

Peterson, A. C., & Taylor, B. (1980). The biological approach to adolescence: Biological change and psychological adaptation. In J. Adelson (Ed.), *Handbook of adolescent psychology* (pp. 117–155). New York: Wiley.

Peterson, J. L., & Marin, G. (1988). Issues in the prevention of AIDS among black and hispanic men. *American Psychologist, 43*(11), 871–877.

Pettit, G. S., & Bates, J. E. (1984). Continuity of individual differences in the mother-infant relationship from six to thirteen months. *Child Development, 55*, 729–739.

Pflaum, S. W. (1986). *The development of language and literacy in young children* (3rd ed.). Columbus, OH: Charles E. Merrill.

Phillips, C. (1974). Neonatal heat loss in heated cribs versus mothers' arms. *Child and Family, 4*, 307–314.

Phillips, D. (1984). The illusion of incompetence among academically competent children. *Child Development, 55*, 2000–2016.

Phillips, D. A. (1987). Socialization of perceived academic competence among highly competent children. *Child Development, 58*, 1308–1320.

Phinney, J. S., Freshbach, N. D. & Farver, J. (1986). Preschool children's response to peer crying. *Early Childhood Research Quarterly, 1*(3), 189–206.

Phoenix, C. H., Goy, R. W., & Resko, J. A. (1978). Psychosexual differentiation as a function of androgenic stimulation. In H. Bee (Ed.), *Social issues in developmental psychology* (2nd ed.). New York: Harper & Row.

Piaget, J. (1954). *The construction of reality in the child* (M. Cook, Trans.). New York: Ballantine Books.

———. (1962). *Play, Dreams, and Imitation*. (Trans., C. Gattegno & F. M. Hodgson) New York: Norton.

———. (1963). *The origins of intelligence in children* (M. Cook, Trans.). New York: Norton. (Original work published 1936).

———. (1965). *The moral judgment of the child* (M. Gabain, Trans.). New York: Free Press. (Original work published 1932).

———. (1967). *The child's conception of space* (F. T. Langdon & J. L. Lunger, Trans.). New York: Norton.

———. (1969). *The child's conception of the world*. (J. Tomlinson & A. Tomlinson, Trans.). Totowa, NJ: Littlefield, Adams.

Piaget, J., & Inhelder, B. (1967). *The child's conception of space*. (F. J. Langdon & J. L. Lunger, Trans.). New York: Norton. (Original work published 1948.)

———. (1969). *The psychology of the child* (H. Weaver, Trans.) New York: Basic Books.

Ploman, L., & Persson, B. (1957). On the transfer of barbiturates to the human fetus and their accumulation in some of its vital organs. *Journal of Obstetrics and Gynaecology of the British Empire, 64*, 706–711.

Plummer, G. (1952). Anomalies occurring in children exposed in utero to the atomic bomb in Hiroshima. *Pediatrics, 10*, 687.

Pollitt, E., Garza, C., & Leibel, R. L. (1984). Nutrition and public policy. In H. W. Stevenson & A. E. Siegel (Eds.), *Child development research and social policy* (pp. 421–470). Chicago: University of Chicago Press.

Pomerantz, S. C. (1979). Sex differences in the relative importance of self-esteem, physical self-satisfaction, and identity in predicting adolescent satisfaction. *Journal of Youth and Adolescence, 8*, 51–61.

Power, T. G., & Parke, R. D. (1982). Play as a context for early learning. In L. M. Laosa and I. E. Sigel (Eds.), *Families as Learning Environments for Children* (pp. 147–178). New York: Plenum Press.

Powers, S. I., Hauser, S. T., & Kilner, L. A. (1989). Adolescent mental health. *American Psychologist, 44*(2), 200–208.

Prechtl, H. F. R. (1974). Behavioral states of the newborn infant (a review). *Brain Research, 76*, 1304–1311.

———. (1982). Assessment methods for the newborn infant, a critical evaluation. In P. Stratton (Ed.), *Psychobiology of the human newborn* (pp. 21–52). New York: Wiley.

Prechtl, H. F. R., & Beintema, D. J. (1964). *The neurological examination of the full-term newborn infant: Clinics in developmental medicine*, No. 12. London: Heinemann.

Prechtl, H. F. R., & O'Brien, M. J. (1982). Behavioral states of the full-term newborn: The emergence of a concept. In P. Stratton (Ed.), *Psychobiology of the human newborn* (pp. 53–73). New York: Wiley.

Putallaz, M., & Gottman, J. M. (1981). An interactional model of children's entry into peer groups. *Child Development, 52*, 986–994.

Pyle, R., Mitchell, J., Eckert, E., Halverson, P., Neumann, P., & Goff, G. (1983). The incidence of bulimia in freshman college students. *International Journal of Eating Disorders, 2*, 75–85.

Radke-Yarrow, M., Zahn-Waxler, C., & Chapman, M. (1983). Children's prosocial dispositions and behavior. In P. H. Mussen (Ed.), *Handbook of child psychology*, (Vol. 4, 4th ed.). New York: Wiley.

Raiti, S., Kaplan, S. L., Vliet, V., & Moore, W. V. (1987). Short-term treatment of short stature and subnormal growth rate with human growth hormone. *Journal of Pediatrics, 110*(3), 357–361.

Ramey, C. T., & Finkelstein, N. W. (1978). Contingent stimulation and infant competence. *Journal of Pediatric Psychology, 3*, 89-96.

Randt, R. D. (1985). Ball-catching proficiency among 4-, 6-, and 8-year-old girls. In J. E. Clark & J. H. Humprey (Eds.), *Motor development: Current selected research* (Vol. 1). Princeton, NJ: Princeton Book.

Rao, D. C., MacLean, C. J., Moreton, N. E., and Yee, S. (1975). Analysis of family resemblances, V: Height and weight in northeastern Brazil. *American Journal of Human Genetics, 25*, 509–520.

Rappaport, L., & Levine, M. (1986). The prevention of constipation and encopresis: A developmental model and approach. *Pediatric Clinics of North America, 33*(4), 859–869.

Raven, J. C., & Lewis, H. K. (1974). *Raven Progressive Matrices Test.* Cleveland, OH: *The Psychological Corporation.*

Raven, R. (1974). The development of Wh-questions in 1st and 2nd language learners. In J. C. Richards (Ed.), Thought and Language/Language and Reading. *Harvard Educational Review,* (Reprint Series No. 14), 150–179.

Read, C. (1975). *Children's categorization of speech sounds in English.* Urbana, IL: National Council of Teachers of English.

Reese, H. W., & Lipsitt, L. P. (1970). *Experimental child psychology.* New York: Academic Press.

Regcher, S. M., & Kaplan, S. B. (1988). Reading disability with motor problems. *Pediatrics, 82*(2), 204–210.

Reichelderfer, T. E., Overbach, A., & Greensher, J. (1979). Unsafe playgrounds. *Pediatrics, 64*, 962–963.

Renner, M. J., & Rosenzweig, M. R. (1987). *Enriched and impoverished environments: Effects on brain and behavior.* New York: Springer-Verlag.

Renzulli, J. S. (1978). What makes giftedness? Re-examining a definition. *Phi Delta Kappan, 60*, 180–184.

Renzulli, J. S., Reis, S. M., & Smith, L. H. (1981). *The revolving door identification model.* Mansfield Center, CT: Creative Learning Press.

Renzulli, J. S., & Smith, L. H. (1981). The early childhood checklist. In J. S. Renzulli, S. M. Reis, & L. H. Smith (Eds.), *The revolving door identification model.* Mansfield Center, CT: Creative Learning Press.

Rest, J. R. (1983). Morality. In P. H. Mussen (Ed.), *Handbook of child psychology: Vol. 3. Cognitive development.* New York: Wiley.

Rhodes, L. (1981). I can read! Predictable books as resources for reading and writing instruction. *The Reading Teacher, 34*, 511–518.

Rice, M. E., & Grusec, J. E. (1972). Saying and doing: Effects of observer performance. *Journal of Personality and Social Psychology, 32*, 584–593.

Richards, M. P., & Bernal, J. F. (1972). An observational study of mother-infant interactions. In N. B. Jones (Ed.), *Ethological studies of child behavior.* London: Cambridge University Press.

Ricks, M. H. (1985). The social transmission of parental behavior: Attachment across generations. In I. Bretherton & E. Waters (Eds.), Growing points of attachment theory and research. *Monographs of the Society for Research in Child Development, 50*(1–2).

Rivara, F. P., Reay, D. T., & Bergman, A. B. (1989). Analysis of fatal pedestrian injuries in King County, WA, and prospects of prevention. *Public Health Reports, 104*(3), 293–297.

Roberts, E. J., & Gagnon, J. (1978). *Family life and sexual learning: Vol. 1. Summary Report.* Cambridge, MA: Population Education.

Roberts, J. E., Sanyal, M. A., Burchinal, M. R., Collier, A. M., Ramey, C. T., & Henderson, F. W. (1986). Otitis media in early childhood and its relationship to later verbal and academic performance. *Pediatrics, 78*(3), 423–430.

Roberts, W., & Strayer, J. (1987). Parents' responses to the emotional distress of their children: Relations with children's competence. *Developmental Psychology, 23*(3), 415–422.

Robertson, L. S. (1985). Motor vehicles. *Pediatric Clinics of North America, 32*(1), 87–94.

Robinson, S. L. (1987). Kindergarten in America: Five major trends. *Phi Delta Kappan, 68*(7), 529–530.

Robson, K. S. (1967). The role of eye-to-eye contact in maternal-infant attachment. *Journal of Child Psychology and Psychiatry and Allied Disciplines, 8*, 13–25.

Rode, S. S., Chang, P. N., Fisch, P. O., & Sroufe, L. A. (1981). Attachment patterns of infants separated from birth. *Developmental Psychology, 17*, 188–191.

Rodman, H., Pratto, D. J., & Nelson, R. S. (1985). Child care arrangements and children's functioning: A comparison of self-care and adult-care children. *Developmental Psychology, 21*, 413–418.

Roedell, W. C., Slaby, R. C., & Robinson, H. B. (1977). *Social development in young children,* Belmont, CA: Wadsworth.

Roff, M. (1961). Childhood social interactions and young adult bad conduct. *Journal of Abnormal and Social Psychology, 63*, 333–337.

Roff, M., Sells, S. B., & Golden, M. M. (1972). *Social adjustment and personality development in children.* Minneapolis: University of Minnesota Press.

Rose, S. A., & Blank, M. (1974). The potency of context in children's cognition: An illustration through conservation. *Child Development, 45*, 499–502.

Rosen, B. C. & D'Andrade, R. (1975). The psychosocial origins of achievement motivation. In U. Bronfenbrenner and M. H. Mahoney (Eds.), *Influences on human development* (2nd ed.) (pp. 438–450). Hinsdale, IL: Dryden Press.

Rosenblatt, J. S. (1969). The basis of synchrony in the behavioral interaction between the mother and her offspring in the laboratory rat. In B. M. Foss (Ed.), *Determinants of infant behavior* (Vol. 3). London: Methuen.

Rosenblith, J. F., & Sims-Knight, J. E. (1985). *In the beginning: Development in the first two years.* Belmont, CA: Wadsworth.

Rosenkoetter, L. I. (1973). Resistance to temptation: Inhibitory and disinhibitory effects of models. *Developmental Psychology, 8*, 80–84.

Rosett, H. L., Weiner, L., Lee, A., Zuckerman, B., Dooling, E., & Oppenheimer, E. (1983). Patterns of alcohol consumption and fetal development. *Obstetrics and Gynecology, 61*(5), 539–546.

Ross, J. G., & Gilbert, G. G. (1985). The national children and youth fitness study: A summary of findings. *Journal of Physical Education, Recreation and Dance, 56*(1), 3–8; 45–50.

Ross, R., Wartella, E., & Lovelace, V. (1982). *A conceptual framework for describing children's television viewing patterns.* Paper presented at the Biennial Meeting of the Southwestern Society for the Research in Human Development, Galveston, TX.

Rossman, F. (1980). *Preschoolers' knowledge of the symbolic function of written language in storybooks.* Unpublished doctoral dissertation, Boston University.

Rotter, J. G., (1954). *Social learning and clinical psychology.* Englewood Cliffs, NJ: Prentice-Hall.

———. (1966). Generalized expectancies for internal versus external control of reinforcement. *Psychological Monographs, 80* (Whole No. 609).

Rotter, J. G., Liverant, B., & Crowne, D. P. (1961). The growth and extinction of expectancies in chance controlled and skilled tests. *Journal of Psychology, 52*, 161–177.

Rovee-Collier, C. K., & Lipsitt, L. P. (1982). Learning, adaptation and memory in the newborn. In P. Stratton (Ed.), *Psychobiology of the human newborn* (pp. 147–190). New York: Wiley.

Rovet, J., & Netley, C. (1983). The triple X chromosome syndrome in childhood: Recent empirical findings. *Child Development, 54*(4), 831–845.

Rubenstein, J., & Howes, C. (1976). The effects of peers on toddler interaction with mother and toys. *Child Development, 47*, 597–605.

Rubin, J. Z., Provenzano, F. J., & Lurcia, Z. (1974). The eyes of the beholder: Parents' views on sex of newborns. *American Journal of Orthopsychiatry, 44*, 512–519.

Rutter, M. (1981). Socioemotional consequences of day care for preschool children. *American Journal of Orthopsychiatry, 51*, 4–28.

Sachs, J., & Truswell, L. (1978). Comprehension of two-word constructions by children in the one-word stage. *Child Language, 5*, 17–24.

Sadaker, M., & Sadaker, D. (1985). Sexism in the schoolroom of the '80s. *Psychology Today, 19*(3), 54–56.

Salapatek, P. (1968). Visual scanning of geometric figures by the human newborn. *Journal of Comparative and Physiological Psychology, 66*, 247–258.

———. (1975). Pattern perception in early infancy. In L. B. Cohen and P. Salapatek (Eds.), *Infant perception: From sensation to cognition: Vol. 1. Basic visual processes.* New York: Academic Press.

Salapatek, P., & Kessen, W. (1966). Visual scanning of triangles by the human newborn. *Journal of Experimental Child Psychology, 3*, 155–167.

Saltus, R. (1987, July 20). Tests can foretell genetic destiny. *Boston Globe*, p. 47.

Saltz, R. (1979). Children's interpretation of proverbs. *Language Arts, 56*, 508–514.

Saltzman, L. (1973). Adolescence: Epoch or disease. *Adolescence, 8*, 247–256.

Sameroff, A. J. (1972). Learning and adaptation in infancy. In H. W. Reese (Ed.), *Advances in child development and behavior* (Vol. 7). New York: Academic Press.

Sarvela, P., & McClendon, E. J. (1983). Correlates of early adolescent peer and personal substance use in rural northern Michigan. *Journal of Youth and Adolescence, 12*(4), 319–332.

Saxe, G. B., Guberman, S. R., & Gerhart, M. (1987). Social processes in early number development. *Monographs of the Society for Research in Child Development, 52*(2, Serial No. 216).

Scaife, M., & Bruner, J. S. (1975). The capacity for joint visual attention in the infant. *Nature, 253*, 265–266.

Scarr, S., & Weinberg, R. A. (1978). Attitudes, interests and IQ. *Human Nature, 1*, 29–36.

Schaeffer, B., Eggleston, V. H., & Scott, J. L. (1974). Number development in young children. *Cognitive Psychology, 6*, 357–379.

Schaffer, H. R., & Emerson, P. E. (1964). The development of social attachments in infancy. *Monographs of the Society for Research in Child Development, 29* (Serial No. 94).

Schaie, K. W. (1965). A general model for the study of developmental problems. *Psychological Bulletin, 64*, 92–107.

Schickedanz, D. (1976). *Effects of an intervention in child-rearing on Uzgiris-Hunt scale performance.* Paper presented at the Annual Meeting of the New Hampshire Speech and Hearing Association, Portsmouth, NH.

Schickedanz, J. (1985). *More than the ABCs: The early stages of reading and writing.* Washington, DC: National Associaton for the Education of Young Children.

———. (1986). *More than the ABCs: The early stages of reading and writing.* Washington, DC: National Association for the Education of Young Children.

———. (1987). *Adam: A case study in writing development from one to six years of age.* Unpublished manuscript.

———. (in press). *Adam's righting revolutions.* Portsmouth, NH: Heinemann.

Schickedanz, J., & Sullivan, M. (1984). Mom, what does U-F-F spell? *Language Arts, 61,*(1) 7–17.

Schields, J. (1962). *Monozygotic twins.* London: Oxford University Press.

Schinke, S., Gilchrist, L., & Small, R. (1979). Preventing unwanted adolescent pregnancy: A cognitive behavioral approach. *American Journal of Orthopsychiatry, 49,* 81–88.

Schleifer, M. J. (1987). Toothbrush adaptations. *Exceptional Parents, 17*(5), 22–24.

Schlesinger, I. M. (1974). Relational concepts and underlying language. In R. Schiefelbusch & L. Lloyd (Eds.), *Language perception: Acquisition, retardation and intervention.* Baltimore: University Park Press.

Schneider, P. E., & Peterson, J. (1982). Oral habits: Considerations in management. *Pediatric Clinics of North America, 29*(3), 653–668.

Schneirla, T. C., Rosenblatt, J. S., & Tobach, E. (1963). Maternal behavior in the cat. In H. L. Rheingold (Ed.), *Maternal behaviour in mammals* (pp. 122–168). New York: Wiley.

Schramm, W., Lyle, J., & Parker, E. B. (1961). *Television in the lives of our children.* Stanford, CA: Stanford University Press.

Schultz, T. R., & Pilon, R. (1973). Development of the ability to detect linguistic ambiguity. *Child Development, 44,* 728–733.

Schwartz, M., & Schwartz, J. (1974). Evidence against a genetical component to performance on IQ tests. *Nature, 248,* 84–85.

Schwartz, P. (1983). Length of day-care attendance and attachment behavior in eighteen-month-old infants. *Child Development, 54,* 1073–1078.

Schwartz, R. C., Barrett, M. J., & Saba, G. (1985). Family therapy for bulimia. In D. M. Garner & P. Garfinkel (Eds.), *Handbook of psychotherapy for anorexia nervosa and bulimia.* New York: Guilford Press.

Schweinhart, I. J., Weikart, D. P., & Larner, M. B. (1986). Consequences of three preschool curriculum models through age 15. *Early Childhood Research Quarterly, 1,* 15–45.

Seeds, J. W., & Cefalo, R. C. (1983). Techniques of early sonographic diagnosis of bilateral cleft lip and palate. *Obstetrics and Gynecology, 62*(Suppl.3), 2S–7S.

Select Committee on Hunger, U. S. House of Representatives. (1988, October). *Strategies for expanding the special supplemental food program for women, infants, and children (WIC) participation: A survey of WIC directors.* Washington, DC: U. S. Government Printing Office.

Sells, S. B., & Roff, M. (1964). Peer acceptance—rejection and birth order. *Psychology in the Schools, 1,* 156–162.

Selman, R. (1976). Social-cognitive understanding: A guide to educational and clinical practice. In T. Lickona (Ed.), *Moral development and behavior: Theory, research, and social issues* (pp. 219–240). New York: Holt, Rinehart & Winston.

Shannon, M., Lacouture, P. G., Roa, J., & Woolf, A. (1989). Cocaine exposure among children seen at a pediatric hospital. *Pediatrics, 83*(3), 337–342.

Shantz, C. U. (1975). The development of social cognition. In E. M. Hetherington (Ed.), *Reviews of Child Development Research* (Vol. 5, pp. 257–323). Chicago: University of Chicago Press.

Shaw, F., Zelnick, M., & Kanter, J. F. (1975). Unprotected intercourse among unwed teenagers. *Family Planning Perspectives, 7,* 39.

Shearer, M. H. (1984). Revelations: A summary and analysis of NIH Consensus Development Conference on ultrasound imaging in pregnancy. *Birth, 11*(1), 23–30.

Sheldon, W. H., Hartle, E. M., & McDermott, E. (1949). *Varieties of delinquent youth.* New York: Harper & Row.

Shelton, P. G., Ferratti, G. H., & Dent, M. (1982). Maintaining oral health. *Pediatric Clinics of North America, 29*(3), 653–668.

Sherman, B. L., & Dominick, J. P. (1986, Winter). Violence and sex in music videos, TV, and rock n' roll. *Journal of Communication,* pp. 79–93.

Sherman, T. (1985). Categorization of skills in infants. *Child Development, 56,* 1561–1573.

Shields, J. (1962). *Monozygotic twins.* London: Oxford University Press.

Shirley, M. M. (1933). *The first two years: A study of twenty-five babies* (Vol. II). Minneapolis: University of Minnesota Press.

Showalter, E. (1985). *The female malady: Women, madness, and English culture, 1830–1980.* New York: Penguin Books.

Shultz, T. (1988). Right from the start: Report of the National Association of State Boards of Education. National Early Education Task Force. Alexandria, VA: NASBE.

Shultz, T. R., & Pilon, R. (1973). Development of the ability to detect linguistic ambiguity. *Child Development, 44,* 728–733.

Siebert, J. M. (1987). AIDS FACTS: A profile of the growing problem. *APA Division 37 Newsletter, 10*(1), 1;7.

Siegel, L. (1983). The prediction of possible learning disabilities in preterm and full-term children. In T. Field & A. Sostek (Eds.), *Infants born at risk: Physiological, perceptual, and cognitive processes* (pp. 295–315). New York: Grune & Stratton.

Siegel, M., Fuerst, H., & Guinee, V. (1971). Rubella epidemicity and embryopathy. *American Journal of Diseases of Children, 121,* 469–473.

Siegler, R. S. (1976). Three aspects of cognitive development. *Cognitive Psychology, 8,* 481–520.

———. (1978). The origins of scientific reasoning. In R. S. Siegler (Ed.), *Children's thinking: What develops?* Hillsdale, NJ: Lawrence Erlbaum.

———. (1983). Information processing approaches to development. In P. H. Mussen (Ed.), *Handbook of child psychology: Vol. 1. History, theory, and methods.* New York: Wiley.

———. (1986). *Children's thinking.* Englewood Cliffs, NJ: Prentice-Hall.

Siegler, R. S., & Liebert, R. M. (1975). Acquisition of formal scientific reasoning by 10- and 13-year-olds: Designing a factorial experiment. *Developmental Psychology, 11,* 401–402.

Silvio, K. (1984). SIDS and apnea monitoring: A parent's view. *Pediatric Annals,13*(3), 229–231.

Simmons, R. G., & Blyth, D. A. (1987). *Moving into adolescence: The impact of pubertal change in school context.* New York: A. de Gruyter.

Sinclair, J. C. (1975). The effect of the thermal environment on neonatal mortality and morbidity. In K. Adamson & H. A. Fox (Eds.), *Preventability of perinatal injury.* New York: A. R. Liss.

Singer, J. L., & Singer, D. G. (1981). Television-viewing and aggression: Play observations. In J. L. Singer & D. B. Singer (Eds.), *Television, imagination and aggression: A study of preschoolers.* Hillsdale, NJ: Lawrence Erlbaum.

Siqueland, E. R., & Lipsitt, L. P. (1966). Conditioned headturning in human newborns. *Journal of Experimental Child Psychology, 3,* 356–376.

Skeels, H. M. (1966). Adult status of children with contrasting early life experiences. *Monographs of the Society for Research in Child Development, 31* (Serial No. 105).

Skodak, M., & Skeels, H. M. (1949). A final follow-up study of one hundred adopted children. *Journal of Genetic Psychology, 75,* 86–125.

Slaby, R. G., & Froy, R. S. (1975). Development of gender constancy and selective attention to same-sex models. *Child Development, 46,* 849–856.

Slade, A. (1987). Quality of attachment and early symbolic play. *Developmental Psychology, 23*(1), 78–85.

Slater, A. M., & Findlay, J. M. (1975). Binocular fixation in the newborn baby. *Journal of Experimental Child Psychology, 20,* 248–273.

Slater, L., & Brewer, M. F. (1984). Home versus hospital phototherapy for term infants with hyperbilirubinemia. *Pediatrics, 73*(4), 515–519.

Slobin, D. I. (1982). Universal and particular in the acquisition of language. In E. Wanner & L. R. Gleitman (Eds.), *Language acquisition: The state of the art.* Cambridge, England: Cambridge University Press.

Smith, C., & Lloyd, B. (1978). Maternal behavior and perceived sex of infant: Revisited. *Child Development, 49,* 1263–1265.

Smith, C. L., Leinbach, M. D., Stewart, B. J., & Blackwell, J. M. (1983). Affective perspective-taking, exhortations, and children's prosocial behavior. In D. L. Bridgeman (Ed.), *The nature of prosocial development.* New York: Academic Press.

Smith, D. P. (1986). Common day-care diseases: Patterns and prevention. *Pediatric Nursing, 12*(3), 175–179.

Smith, F. (1983). *Essays into literacy.* Portsmouth, NH: Heinemann Educational Books.

Smith, J. (1984). Psychosocial aspects of infantile apnea and home monitoring. *Pediatric Annals, 13,* 219–224.

Smith, M. C. (1978). Cognizing the behavior stream: The recognition of intentional action. *Child Development, 49,* 736–743.

Smith, N. J., Greenlaw, M. J., & Scott, C. J. (1987). Making the literate environment equitable. *The Reading Teacher, 40*(4), 400–407.

Smith, P. K., & Doglish, L. (1977). Sex differences in parent and infant behavior in the home. *Child Development, 48,* 1250–1254.

Snyder, L., Schonfeld, M., & Offerman, E. (1945). The Rh factor and feeble-mindedness. *Journal of Heredity, 36,* 9–10.

Sorenson, R. C. (1973). *Adolescent sexuality in contemporary America.* New York: World.

Sparrow, S. S., Balla, D. A., & Cicchetti, D. V. (1984). *Vineland Adoptive Behavior Scales.* (A revision of the *Vineland Social Maturity Scale* by E. A. Doll.) Circle Pines, MN: American Guidance Service.

Spirito, A., Stark, L., Fristad, M., Hart, K., & Owens-Stively, J. (1989). Adolescent suicide attempters hospitalized on a pediatric unit. In S. Chess, A. Thomas, & M. E. Hertzig (Eds.), *Annual progress in child psychiatry and child development.* New York: Brunner/Mazel.

Spivack, G., & Shure, M. B. (1982). Cognition of social adjustment: Interpersonal cognitive problem-solving thinking. B. B. Lahey & A. E. Kazden (Eds.), *Advances in child psychology* (pp. 323–72). New York: Plenum Press.

Spivak, H., Prothrow-Stith, D., & Hausman, A. J. (1988). Dying is no accident. *Pediatric Clinics of North America, 35*(6), 1339–1347.

Spivack, R., Marcus, J., & Swift, M. (1986). Early classroom behaviors and later misconduct. *Developmental Psychology, 22*(11), 124–131.

Sroufe, L. A. (1981, October). *Infant caregiver attachment and patterns of adaptation in preschool: The roots of maladaptation and competence*. Paper presented at the Minnesota Symposium.

Sroufe, L. A. (1982). Attachment and the roots of competence. In H. E. Fitzgerald & T. H. Carr (Eds.), *Human development: Annual editions*. Guildford, CA: Dushkin.

———. (1983). Infant-caregiver attachment and patterns of adaptation in preschool: The roots of maladaptation and competence. In M. Perlmutter (Ed.), *Minnesota symposium in child psychology* (Vol. 16, pp. 41–81). Hillsdale, NJ: Lawrence Erlbaum.

Sroufe, L. A., Fox, N. E., & Pancake, V. R. (1983). Attachment and dependency in developmental perspective. *Child Development, 54*, 1615–1627.

Stark, E. (1986). Young, innocent, and pregnant. *Psychology Today, 20*(10), 28–35.

Staub, E. (1971). A child in distress: The influence of nurturance and modeling on children's attempts to help. *Developmental Psychology, 5*, 124–132.

———. (1975). *The development of prosocial behavior in children*. Morristown, NJ: General Learning Press.

———. (1979). *Positive social behavior and morality*. (Vol. 2). New York: Academic Press.

Stein, A. H. (1967). Imitation of resistance to temptation. *Child Development, 38*, 157–159.

Stein, L., Ozdamar, O., Kraus, N., & Paton, J. (1983). Follow-up of infants screened by auditory brain stem response in the neonatal intensive care unit. *Journal of Pediatrics, 103*(3), 447–453.

Steinberg, L. (1986). Latchkey children and susceptibility to peer pressure: An ecological analysis. *Developmental Psychology, 22*, 433–439.

Steinberg, L., & Silverberg, S. B. (1986). The vicissitudes of autonomy in early adolescence. *Child Development, 57*(4), 841–851.

Stenberg, C., Campos, J., & Emde, R. (1983). The facial expression of anger in seven-month-old infants. *Child Development, 54*, 178–184.

Stern, D. (1977). *The first relationship: Infant and mother*. Cambridge, MA: Harvard University Press.

Stern, G. (1973). *Principles of human genetics* (3rd ed.). San Francisco: W. H. Freeman.

Stern, W. (1912). *The psychological methods of testing intelligence* (G. M. Whipple, Trans.). Baltimore: Warwick & York.

Stoch, M. B., & Smythe, P. M. (1963). Does undernutrition during infancy inhibit brain growth and subsequent intellectual development? *Archives of Diseases in Childhood, 38*, 546.

Stone, C. A., & Day, M. C. (1980). Competence and performance models and the characterization of formal operational skills. *Human Development, 23*, 323–353.

Stoner, L. J. (1978). Selecting physical activities for the young child, with an understanding of bone growth and development. *Reviews of Research for Practitioners and Parents, 1*, 32–42.

Stratton, P. (1982). Rhythmic functions in the newborn. In P. Stratton (Ed.), *Psychobiology of the human newborn* (pp. 119–145). New York: Wiley.

Straus, M. A., Gelles, R., & Steinmetz, S. (1980). *Behind closed doors*. New York: Doubleday.

Strayer, F. F. (1980). Social ecology of the preschool peer group. In W. A. Collins (Ed.), *Development of cognition, affect, and social relations: Minnesota Symposium in Child Development* (Vol. 3). Hillsdale, NJ: Lawrence Erlbaum.

Streeter, L. (1976). Language perception of 2-month-old infants shows effects of both innate mechanisms and experience. *Nature, 259*, 39–41.

Streissguth, A. P. (1979). Fetal alcohol syndrome. *Women and Health, 4*, 223–238.

Streissguth, A. P., Barr, H. M., & Martin, D. C. (1983). Maternal alcohol use and neonatal habituation assessed with the Brazelton Scale. *Child Development, 54*, 1109–1118.

Streissguth, A. P., Barr, H. M., Sampson, P. D., Darby, B. L., & Martin, D. C. (1989). IQ at age 4 in relation to maternal alcohol use and smoking during pregnancy. *Developmental Psychology, 25*(1), 3–11.

Strohner, H., & Nelson, K. E. (1974). The young child's development of sentence comprehension: Influence of event probability, nonverbal context, syntactic form, and strategies. *Child Development, 45*, 567–576.

Stroman, S. H., & Duff, R. E. (1982). The latchkey child: Whose responsibility? *Childhood Education, 59*, 76–79.

Strong, E. K., & Campbell, D. P. (1981). *Manual for the Strong-Campbell interest inventory* (3rd ed.). Stanford, CA: Stanford University Press.

Sulzby, E. (1985). Children's emergent reading of favorite storybooks: A developmental study. *Reading Research Quarterly, 20*(4), 458–481.

Sun, S. W., & Lull, J. (1986, Winter). The adolescent audience for music videos and why they watch. *Journal of Communication*, pp. 115–125.

Sussman, E. J., Nottelmann, E. D., Inhoff-Germain, G. E., Dorn, L. D., Cutler, G. B., Jr., Loriaux, D. L., & Chrousos, G. P. (1985). The relation of development and social-emotional behavior in young adolescents. *Journal of Youth and Adolescence, 14*, 245–264.

Svejda, M. J., Pannabecker, B. J., & Emde, R. N. (1982). Parent-to-infant attachment: A critique of the early "bonding" model. In R. M. Emde & R. J. Harmon (Eds.), *The development of attachment and affiliative systems*. New York: Plenum Press.

Takahashi, M. (1986). Clinical overview of varicella vaccine. Development and early studies. *Pediatrics*, (Special Suppl.), 736–741.

Tanner, J. M. (1970). Physical growth. In P. H. Mussen (Ed.), *Carmichael's Manual of Child Psychology* (Vol. 1, 3rd 3d). New York: Wiley.

_____. (1978a). *Education and physical growth* (2nd ed.). New York: International Universities Press.

_____. (1978b). *Fetus into man: Physical growth from conception to maturity*. Cambridge, MA: Harvard University Press.

_____. (1981). Growth and maturation during adolescence. *Nutrition Review, 39*, 43–55.

Tanz, C. (1983). Asking children to ask: An experimental investigation of the pragmatics of relayed questions. *Journal of Child Language; 10*, 187–194.

Tarby, T. J., & Volpe, J. J. (1982). Intraventricular hemorrhage in the premature infant. *Pediatric Clinics of North America, 29*(5),1077–1104.

Taub, H. B., Goldstein, K. M., & Caputo, D. V. (1977). Indices of neonatal prematurity as discriminators of development in middle childhood. *Child Development, 48*, 797–805.

Tavris, C., & Offir, C. (1977). *The longest war: Sex differences in perspective*. New York: Harcourt Brace Jovanovich.

Taylor, I. (1981). Writing systems and reading. In G. E. Mackinnon & T. G. Waller (Eds.), *Reading research: Advances in theory and practice* (Vol. 2). New York: Academic Press.

Teale, W. (1986). Home background and young children's literacy development. In W. Teale & E. Sulzby (Eds.), *Emergent literacy*. Norwood, NJ: Ablex.

Teale, W., & Sulzby, E. (1986). Emergent literacy as a perspective for examining how young children become writers and readers. In W. Teale and E. Sulzby (Eds.), *Emergent literacy*. Norwood, NJ: Ablex.

Teele, D. W., Klein, J. O., & Rosner, B. A. (1984). Otitis media with effusion during the first three years of life and development of speech and language. *Pediatrics, 74*(2), 282–287.

Teitz, C. C. (1982). Sports medicine concerns in dance and gymnastics. *Pediatric Clinics of North America, 29*(6), 1399–1421.

Terman, L. M. (1916). *The measurement of intelligence*. Boston: Houghton Mifflin.

Thomas, A. T., & Chess, S. (1977). *Foundations of physiological psychology*. New York: Harper & Row.

Thompson, R. (1988). The effects of infant day care through the prism of attachment theory: A critical appraisal. *Early Childhood Research Quarterly, 3*(3), 273–282.

Thompson, R. F. (1967). *Foundations of physiological psychology*. New York: Harper & Row.

Tobin-Richards, M. H., Boxer, A. M., & Peterson, A. C. (1983). The psychological significance of pubertal change: Sex differences in perception of self during early adolescence. In J. Brooks-Gunn & A. Peterson (Eds.), *Girls at puberty: Biological and psychosocial perspectives* (pp. 127–154). New York: Plenum Press.

Tobler, N. S. (1986). Meta-analysis of 143 adolescent drug prevention programs: Quantitative outcome results of program participants compared to a control or comparison group. *Journal of Drug Issues, 16*, 537–568.

Tonkova-Yampolskaya, R. (1969). Development of speech imitation in infants during the first 2 years of life. In translation of *Soviet Psychology, 7*, 48–54.

Torrance, E. P. (1981). *Thinking creatively in action and movement*. Bensenville, IL: Scholastic Testing Service.

Trautman, P. D., & Shaffer, D. (1989). Pediatric management of suicidal behavior. *Pediatric Annals, 18*(2), 134–143.

Trehub, S. (1973). Infants' sensitivity to vowel and tonal contrasts. *Developmental Psychology, 9*, 91–96.

Trehub, S. E., & Rabinovitch, M. S. (1972). Auditory-linguistic sensitivity in early infancy. *Development Psychology, 6*, 74–77.

Treiman, R. (1985). Phonemic awareness and spelling: Children's judgments do not always agree with adults'. *Journal of Experimental Child Psychology, 39*, 182–201.

Trickett, P. K., & Kuczynski, L. (1986). Children's misbehavior and parental discipline strategies in abusive and nonabusive families. *Developmental Psychology, 8*, 240–260.

Troy, M., & Sroufe, L. A. (1987). Victimization among preschoolers: Role of attachment relationship history. *Journal of the American Academy of Child and Adolescent Psychiatry, 26*(2), 166–172.

Tunmer, W., & Nesdale, A. (1985). Phonemic segmentation skill and beginning reading. *Journal of Educational Psychology, 77*, 417–427.

Turner, R. R. (1984). How big is the drug problem? *Family Learning, 1*(3), 6–7.

U. S. Consumer Product Safety Commission. (1981). *A handbook for public playground safety: Vol 1. General guidelines for new and existing playgrounds*. Washington, DC: U. S. Government Printing Office.

U. S. Department of Education. (1986). *What works: Research about teaching and learning*. Washington, DC: U. S. Department of Education.

U. S. Department of Health and Human Services. (1980). *Promoting health/preventing disease: Objectives for the nation*. Washington, DC: U. S. Government Printing Office.

U. S. Public Health Service. (1983). Promoting Health/ Preventing Disease. Public Health Service implementation plans for attaining the objectives for the nation. *Public Health Reports* (Suppl), p. 3.

Ullman, L., & Krasner, L. (1969). *Psychological approach to abnormal behavior*. Englewood Cliffs, NJ: Prentice-Hall.

Ungerer, J. A., Zelazo, P. R., Kearsley, R. B., & O'Leary, K. (1981). Developmental changes in the representation of objects in symbolic play from 18–35 months of age. *Child Development, 52*, 186–195.

Uzgiris, I. C. (1973). Patterns of cognitive development in infancy. *The Merrill-Palmer Quarterly, 19*, 181–204.

Uzgiris, I., & Hunt, J. McV. (1975). *Assessment in infancy: Ordinal scales of psychological development*. Urbana, IL: University of Illinois Press.

Van Thorne, D., & Vogel, F. (1985). The presence of bulimia in high school females. *Adolescence, 20*, 45–51.

Vaughn, B., Engeland, B., Sroufe, L. A., & Waters, E. (1979). Individual differences in infant-mother attachment at twelve and eighteen months: Stability and change in families under stress. *Child Development, 50*, 971–975.

Vaughn, B., Gove, F. L., & Egeland, B. (1980). The relationship between out-of-home care and the quality of infant-mother attachment in an economically disadvantaged population. *Child Development, 51*, 971–975.

Vellutino, F. R. (1987). Dyslexia. *Scientific American, 256*(3), 34–41.

Venezia, P. A. (1971). Delinquency prediction: A critique and suggestion. *Journal of Research in Crime and Delinquency, 8*, 108–117.

Verhulst, F. C., Donkhorst, I. D. (1985). The prevalence of nocturnal enuresis: Do DSM III criteria need to be changed? A brief research report. *Journal of Child Psychology, 16*(6), 989–993.

Verhulst, F. C., Van Der Lee, J. H., Akkerhuis, G. E., Sanders-Woudstra, J. A. R., Timmer, F. C., & Donkhorst, I. D. (1985). The prevalence of nocturnal enuresis: Do DSM III criteria need to be changed? A brief research report. *Journal of Child Psychology, 26*(6), 989–993.

Vernon, P. E. (1979). *Intelligence: Heredity and environment*. San Francisco: W. H. Freeman.

Walden, T. A., & Ogden, T. A. (1988). The development of social referencing. *Child Development, 59*, 1230–1240.

Walker, B. A., and Mehr, M. M. (1983). Adolescent suicide—a family crisis: A model for effective intervention by family therapists. *Adolescence, 18*(70), 285–292.

Wallach, M. A., & Kogan, N. (1965). *Modes of thinking in young children*. New York: Holt, Rinehart & Winston.

Wallach, M. A., & Wallach, L. (1983). *Psychology's sanction for selfishness: The error of egoism in theory and therapy*. San Francisco: W. H. Freeman.

Walters, J. (1975). Birth defects and adolescent pregnancies. *Journal of Home Economics, 67*, 23–27.

Warden, D. (1986). Notes and discussion: How to tell if children can ask. *Journal of Child Language, 13*, 421–428.

Waters, E., & Deane, K. E. (1982). Infant-mother attachment: Theories, models, recent data, and some tasks for comparative developmental analysis. In L. W. Hoffman, R. Gandelman, & H. R. Schiffman (Eds.), *Parenting: Its causes and consequences*. Hillsdale, NJ: Lawrence Erlbaum.

Watson, M. W., & Fischer, K. W. (1977). A developmental sequence of agent use in late infancy. *Child Development, 48*, 483–494.

Webster's New World Dictionary. (1983). New York: World.

Wechsler, D. (1974). *Manual for the Wechsler intelligence scale for children—Revised*. New York: Psychological Corporation.

————. (1981). *Wechsler Adult Intelligence Scale—Revised*. New York: Psychological Corporation.

Wehren, A., DeLisi, R., & Arnold, M. (1981). The development of noun definitions. *Journal of Child Language, 8*, 165–175.

Weinberg, R. A. (1989). Intelligence and IQ. *American Psychologist, 44*(2), 98–104.

Weinraub, M., & Frankel, J. (1977). Sex differences in parent-infant interactions during free play, departure, and separation. *Child Development, 48*, 1240–1249.

Weiss, B. D. (1986). Bicycle helmet use by children. *Pediatrics, 77*(5), 677–679.

Weitzman, M., & Adair, R. (1988). Divorce and children. *Pediatric Clinics of North America, 35*(6), 1313–1323.

Wellman, H. M., & Estes, D. (1986). Early understanding of mental entities: A reexamination of childhood realism. *Child Development, 59*, 386–396.

Wennberg, R., Woodrum, D., & Hodson, A. (1973). The perinate. In D. Smith and E. Bierman (Eds.), *The biologic ages of man*. Philadelphia: W. B. Saunders.

Werner, E. (1983). Alternate caregivers for children: A perspective. *Children Today, 12*(5), 22–27.

Werner, H., & Kaplan, B. (1952). The acquisition of word meanings: A developmental study. *Monographs of the Society for Research in Child Development, 15*(1, Serial No. 51).

West, K. L. (1981). Assessment and treatment of disturbed adolescents and their families: A clinical research perspective. In M. Lasky (Ed.), *Major psychopathology and the family*. New York: Grune & Stratton.

White, B. L. (1971). *Human-infants: Experience and psychological development*. Englewood Cliffs, NJ: Prentice-Hall.

White, B. L., & Watts, J. C. (1973). *Experience and environment: Major influences on the development of the young child*. Englewood Cliffs, NJ: Prentice-Hall.

White, H. (1986). Damsels in distress: Dependency themes in fiction for children and adolescents. *Adolescence, 21*, 251–256.

White, R. W. (1959). Motivation reconsidered: The concept of competence. *Psychological Review, 66*, 297–333.

Whitehurst, G. F., Falco, F. L., Lonigan, C. J., Fischel, J. E., DeBaryshe, B. D., Valdez-Menchaca, M. C., & Caulfield, M. (1988). Accelerating language development through picture book reading. *Developmental Psychology, 24*(4), 552–559.

Whiting, B., & Edwards, C. P. (1973). A cross-cultural analysis of sex differences in the behavior of children aged three through eleven. *The Journal of Social Psychology, 91*, 171–188.

Whiting, H. T. (1969). *Acquiring ball skills: A psychological interpretation*. London: Prentice-Hall.

Wilcox, B. M. (1969). Visual preferences of human infants

for representation of the human face. *Journal of Experimental Child Psychology, 7*, 10–20.

Will, J. A., Self, P. A., & Datan, N. (1976). Maternal behavior and perceived sex of infant. *American Journal of Orthopsychiatry, 46*(1), 135–139.

Williams, A. L., Uren, E. C., & Bretherton, L. (1984). Respiratory viruses and sudden infant death. *British Medical Journal, 288*, 1491–1493.

Williams, G. (1989). Lead paint alert. *Practical Homeowner, 4*(5), 24–26.

Williams, H. (1983). *Perceptual and motor development.* Englewood Cliffs, N.J: Prentice-Hall.

Wimmer, H., Gruber, S., & Perner, J. (1984). Young children's conceptions of lying: Lexical realism—moral subjectivism. *Journal of Experimental Child Psychology, 37*, 1–30.

Winick, M. (1974). Childhood obesity. *Nutrition Today, 9*, 6–12.

———. (1976). *Malnutrition and brain development.* New York: Oxford University Press.

Winitz, H., & Irwin, O. (1958). Syllabic and phonetic structure of infants' early words. *Journal of Speech and Hearing Research, 1*, 250–256.

Wirth, T. E. (1985, August 1). Children's Television Act of 1985. *The Congressional Record, 131*(106).

Wirtz, P. (1987). *Intense employment while in high school.* Washington, DC: George Washington University Graduate Institute for Policy Education and Research Working Paper.

Wittgenstein, L. (1963). *Philosophical investigations.* Oxford: Blackwell.

Wolf, T. M., & Cheyne, J. A. (1972). Persistence of effects in live behavioral, televised behavioral, and live verbal models on resistance to temptation. *Child Development, 43*, 1429–1436.

Wolff, P. (1965). The development of attention in young infants. *Annals of the New York Academy of Sciences, 118*, 815–830.

———. (1966). The causes, controls, and organizations of behavior in the newborn. *Psychological Issues, 5*, 1–105.

———. (1969). The natural history of crying and other vocalizations in early infancy. In B. Foss (Ed.), *Determinants of infant behavior* (Vol. 4). London: Methuen.

Wolff, P. H. (1969). Observations of the early development of smiling. In B. M. Foss (Ed.), *Determinants of Infant Behavior* (Vol. II). London: Methuen.

Wright, H. F. (1960). Observational child study. In P. H. Mussen (Ed.), *Handbook of research methods in child development.* New York: Wiley.

Wright, J. C., & Huston, A. L. (1985). *Developmental changes in children's understanding of form and content.* Paper presented at the Biennial Meeting of the Society for Research in Child Development, Toronto, Canada.

Wynne, E. A. (1979). Facts about the character of young Americans. *Character, 1*, 1–7.

Yarrow, L. J., Rubenstein, J. L., & Pedersen, F. A. (1971, April). *Dimensions of early stimulation: Differential effects on infant development.* Paper presented at the Biennial Meeting of the Society for Research in Child Development, Minneapolis, MN.

———. (1971). *Infant and environment: Early cognitive and motivational development.* New York: Wiley.

———. (1975). *Infant and environment: Early cognitive and motivational development.* New York: Wiley.

Yarrow, L., Rubenstein, J., & Pederson, F. A. (1975). *Infant and Environment: Early Cognitive and Motivational Development.* New York: Wiley.

Yarrow, M. R., Scott, P. M., & Waxler, C. Z. (1973). Learning concern for others. *Developmental Psychology, 8*, 240–260.

Young, W. C., Goy, R. W., & Phoenix, C. H. (1964). Hormones and sexual behavior. *Science, 143*, 212–218.

Youniss, J., & Smoller, J. (1985). *Adolescents' relations with mothers, fathers, and friends.* Chicago: University of Chicago Press.

Zakin, D. F., Blyth, D. A., & Simmons, R. G. (1984). Physical attractiveness as a mediator of the impact of early pubertal changes for girls. *Journal of Youth and Adolescence, 13*, 439–450.

Zelnick, M., & Kantner, J. F. (1980). Sexual activity, contraceptive use and pregnancy among metropolitan-area teenagers: 1971–1979. *Family Planning Perspectives, 12*, 230.

Zeskind, P. S., & Ramey, C. T. (1978). Fetal malnutrition: An experimental study of its consequences on infant development in two caregiving environments. *Child Development, 49*, 1155–1162.

Zigler, E. (1985). Assessing Head Start at 20: An invited commentary. *American Journal of Orthopsychiatry, 55*(4), 603–609.

Zill, N. (1983). *American children: Happy, healthy and insecure.* New York: Doubleday/Anchor Press.

Zimmerman, D. R. (1973). *Rh: The intimate history of a disease and its conquest.* New York: Macmillan.

Zucker, P. (1986). Interview with our new president. *American Anorexia/Bulimia Association, Inc., Newsletter, 9*(2), 3–4.

Zuckerman, B. S., & Duby, J. C. (1985). Developmental approach to injury prevention. *Pediatric Clinics of North America, 32*(1), 17–29.

Zussman, R. (1980). Situational determinants of parental behavior. *Child Development, 51*, 792–800.

AUTHOR INDEX

NOTE: Dates in parentheses refer to multiple-author studies.

SUBJECT INDEX

NOTE: Page numbers in *italics* refer to illustrations separated from accompanying text.

preschool practices for, 415
in school-age children, 441–55
Physical education, 441–42
for adolescents, 586–87
importance of, 452–54
Physical fitness, for adolescents, 585–87
Physical perspective, 327, 338
Physical punishment, disadvantages of, 378–80, 388–89, *390*
Piagetian tasks
on conservation, 317–20, 321, 458–59
feedback and, 602
information-processing approach to, 600–602
for preschool assessment, 422
Piaget, Jean
on childhood animism/realism, 331–33, 334–35
cognitive theory of, 59–61
on formal operational stage, 593–98
on infant learning, 134
infant and toddler studies by, 176, 182–93
on moral reasoning, 522–23, 524–25
on physical perspective, 327
on preoperational vs. concrete operational thought, 319–20
on sensorimotor development, 176, 182–93
on seriation, 322, 323–24
Pincer grasp, 160
Pituitary gland
disorders of, 447
pubescence and, 572, 575, 578
PKU (phenylketonuria), 94, 95
"Plan for Achieving Schools Without Drugs," 666
Play
See also Pretend play
cognitive development and, 193–99
infant attachment, 245
of infants and toddlers, 289–90
learning through, *177*
of preschoolers, 431–34
of school-age children, 559–62
sex differences in, 537
sex-typing with, 254–55
time sampling study of, 27
Playgrounds, safety concerns for, 308–9
Poisoning, as mental retardation cause, 467
Poison prevention, 285, 286–87
Popularity
attachment history and, 251–52
moral reasoning and, 531
school-age children and, 518–22
Popular status, 519
Positively correlated variables, 23
Positive reinforcement, 56–57
for prosocial behavior, 397
Postconventional moral stage, 527, 529
Power-assertive exhortation, 383–84
Praise, socialization and, 383
Preadolescent growth spurt, 445–46
Prechtl neonatal assessment test, 139, 140, 141
Preconventional moral stage, 526–27, 528

Pregnancy
See also Prenatal development
ectopic, 77–78
new practices in, 68–69
prenatal assessment in, 103–8
teenage, 639, 641, 642, 649
Prehension
assessing, 274
development of, 160, 161–63
enabling, 266
grasping reflex, 124
Prelinguistic vocal behavior, 204–6
Prematurity, 82–83, 134–38
attachment and, 93, 242, 244
breastfeeding in, 119
child abuse and, 240
cocaine and, 97, *98*
long-term effects of, 136–38
physical problems with, 135–36
social smiling and, 234
teenage pregnancy and, 642
Prenatal assessment, 103–8
ethical and social issues in, 105–8
Prenatal development, 75–83
of hearing, 130
problems in, 93–101. *See also* Teratogens
Sudden Infant Death Syndrome and, 278
teenage pregnancy and, 642
Preoperational thinking, 60, 316, 319–20
classification and, 326
Preprogramming, for attachment, 226
Preschoolers
aggression in, 386–96
appearance vs. reality for, 335–37
arithmetic skills of, 328–31
assessing, 416–25, 420–23
classification by, 324–26
cognitive development in, 315–42.
See also specific cognitive areas
comprehension in, 350–55
conservation concepts of, 317–22
divorce reactions in, 644–45
dreams and, 331–34
eating patterns of, 427–28
education and care programs for, 407–8, 409–17
fine motor development in, 300–301
gifted, 418–19
grammar acquisition by, 346–50
gross motor development in, 302–12
health care concerns of, 426–30
language development in, 345–71.
See also specific language components
number concepts of, 315–16, 317–22, 328–31
physical development in, 297-313.
See also specific motor development
physical perspective in, 327
play activities for, 431–34
preoperational stage in, 60
prosocial behavior by, *384*, 385, 396–400
reaction time improvement in, 312
role-taking ability test with, 516
safety concerns with, 530–31

self-control in, 400–403
seriation tasks and, 322–24
sleep habits of, 428–29
social/emotional development in, 373–405
socialization of, 374, 375–85
summary of changes in, 295
theory of mind of, 331–40
thinking about thinking by, 331–40
TV watching by, 392
Preschools
adult-child ratios in, 416
aggression control in, 387–88
appropriate practices for, 414–15
differences in, 407–8
funding alternatives for, 411
prosocial behavior learning in, 396, 397
socialization in, *376*, 383
teacher- vs. child-directed programs, 407–8, 411, 413
Pretend play, 193–99
appearance/reality distinction and, 340
developmental stages of, 198, 199
peer interaction in, 251
by preschoolers, 433
by school-age children, 559
Pretend vs. real. *See* Appearance vs. reality
Pretense. *See* Pretend play
Pre-testing, 19
Primary rewards, in classical conditioning, 55
Primary sex characteristics, 575, 578, 579
Privileges, denial of
for aggression control, 389–90
appropriate use of, 380, 390
Probability tasks, 596
Problem solving
infant attachment and, 245
information-processing approach to, 600–602
in sensorimotor stage, 182–87
Productive speech, 204
Progesterone, production of, 575
Project Head Start, 410–11, 413
Projection, 49
Projective concept, writing and, 367
Prosocial behavior
defined, 396
development of, 246–48
modeling of, *384*
by preschoolers, *384*, 385, 396–400
social cognition and, 385, 459–60
Protowords, 105
Proverbs, age and response to, 613
Proximodistal development, 159
Pseudoimitation, 187–88, 192
Psychoanalytical theory, 47–53
on attachment, 225–26
research orientation and, 61
Psychological problems
negative identity and, 634
suicide and, 652–54
Psychosexual vs. psychosocial theory, 52
Puberty
impact of, 446, 567, 569–71

ethological, 226–28
language development and, 214–19
maturational, 45–47
of mind, 331–40
practical effects of, 41–45
psychoanalytical, 47–53
psychosexual vs. psychosocial, 52
of second language learning, 490–91
social learning, 57
subjective basis of, 62–63
Things My Child Likes to Do Checklist, 419
Thinking
See also Thinking about thinking
abstract, 603–5
concrete operational, 319–20, 593–98, 602
formal operational, 593–98, 602
hypothetical, 603–4
idealistic, 605–7
information-processing view of, 599–602
preoperational, 316, 319–20
representational, 193, 199
in sensorimotor stage, 186–87
Thinking about thinking
appearance vs. reality, 335–37
false beliefs and, 338
of others, 514–17
by preschoolers, 331–40
by school-age children, 459–61, 514–17
Thorndike, Edward, instrumental conditioning by, 55
Three R's Test, 552
Threshold Mothers' Project, 268
Throwing skills development, 306, 309, 310–11
Thumb sucking, 155
malocclusion and, 445
as primary circular reaction, 183
Time out, for aggression control, 377, 389–91
appropriate use of, 380, 389, 390–91
disadvantages of, 378–79
Time sampling, 27, 28
Tissue growth, in adolescents, 573
Tobacco abuse. See Cigarette smoking
Toddlerhood; Toddlers, 112
aggression in, 386
assessment instruments for, 272–74
ball playing by, 310
books for, 289
counting errors by, 328–29
dental care for, 155
education and care programs for, 259–69
feeding, 281–82
gross motor development in, 302, 303, 304, 306, 310
health care for, 277–84
language development in, 203–21, 206–11
locative expressions in, 351, 353
locomotor development in, 302, 303, 304, 306
nesting cup task and, 323
peer interaction by, 248–53
physical development in, 149–72
preoperational stage in, 60

pretend play by, 193–99
prosocial behavior of, 246–48
safety for, 284–87
separation distress in, 237
sex differences in, 537
social/emotional development in, 223–57
social interaction by, 213–14
toilet training. See Toilet training
toys for, 289
TV watching by, 392
Toe grasp, 122, 124
Toilet training, 282–84
behavioral theory and, 43, 53, 54, 55, 57
cognitive-interactionist theory and, 43–44, 58
maturational theory and, 42
motor development and, 169, 171
psychoanalytical theory and, 42–43, 47, 51
psychosocial theory and, 52
theories in practice on, 41–45
Tonic neck reflex, 122, 123–24
cerebral palsy and, 125
Tonsillitis, 555
Tonus, in neonates, 125
Tooth decay, 155. See also Dental care
Torrance Test of Thinking Creatively in Action and Movement, 419
Toys
for infants and toddlers, 287–89
locomotor development and, 165
for preschoolers, 431–33
for school-age children, 559, 560
sex differences in, 537
sex-typing with, 253, 254, 255
Verbal Interaction Stimulus Materials, 264
Tracking, 661–62
Trainable mentally retarded, 466
Traveling skills development (basketball), 442
Trophoblast, 77
Trust vs. mistrust, 52, 53
attachment and, 224–25, 237
Tuberculosis, in day care centers, 280
Turn taking, in toddler social games, 250–51
TV viewing
aggression and, 23, 24, 25, 37
reading and, 5–6
Twins, 74–75
IQ testing of, 468

Ultrasound, for prenatal assessment, 68, 103–4, 105
Unconditioned stimulus/response, 54
Underextended word meaning, 206–7
Understanding
awareness of, 460–62
of others' intentions, 512–14
of simultaneous emotions, 508–12
of situations, 511–12
Unique grammatical structures, in second language learning, 490
Unpopular status, 519
Uzgiris-Hunt Ordinal Scales, 274

Vaccination. See Immunization
Valence, simultaneous emotions and, 509–11
Validity, 21
external, 17
internal, 19
of preschool testing, 423
Valium, as teratogen, 100
Values
role of, 7, 8
social role-taking ability and, 517–18
Variables, in experimental studies, 23, 24
dependent vs. independent, 23, 25
positively vs. negatively correlated, 23
selection issues, 21–22
Variance, multifactorial causation and, 21
Varicella vaccine, 427
Verbal aggression, 386
Verbal instruction
on prosocial behavior, 397
on self-control, 401–2
socialization by, 382–84
in social learning theory, 57, 58
Vernix caseosa, 116
Video games, 562
adolescents and, 672, 673
Videos, sexual activity and, 639
Vineland Adaptive Behavior Scales, 466
Violence. See Aggression
Viral infections, in school-age children, 555
Vision, of neonates, 128–29
"Visual cliff" study, 170, 180, 181, 238
Visual-graphic information, in reading, 497
Visual literacy, 502–4
Visual matching, preschool test of, 420, 421
Visual perception, development of, 177–82
motor development and, 170
in neonates, 131–32
preferred faces and, 180
scanning behavior, 178–79
"visual cliff" study on, 170, 180, 181
Vocal behavior, prelinguistic, 204–6. See also Language development; Oral language development
Vocational preference tests, 668
Vocational tracking, liberal curriculum vs., 662

"Waiting-room" metaphor, for language learning, 217
Waking activity, in neonates, 146, 147
Walking, 158
delayed, implications of, 275
development of, 163–65, 302, 303, 306
toys and, 287
Wallach and Kogan Creative Battery, 419
Watson, John B., behaviorism and, 55–56

741